Equilibrium Problems and Applications

Mathematics in Science and Engineering

Equilibrium Problems and Applications

Gábor Kassay
Faculty of Mathematics and Computer Science
Babes-Bolyai University
Cluj-Napoca, Romania

Vicenţiu D. Rădulescu
Faculty of Applied Mathematics
AGH University of Science and Technology
Kraków, Poland
Institute of Mathematics "Simion Stoilow" of the Romanian Academy
Bucharest, Romania

Series Editor
Goong Chen

ACADEMIC PRESS
An imprint of Elsevier

Academic Press is an imprint of Elsevier
125 London Wall, London EC2Y 5AS, United Kingdom
525 B Street, Suite 1650, San Diego, CA 92101, United States
50 Hampshire Street, 5th Floor, Cambridge, MA 02139, United States
The Boulevard, Langford Lane, Kidlington, Oxford OX5 1GB, United Kingdom

Notices

Knowledge and best practice in this field are constantly changing. As new research and experience
broaden our understanding, changes in research methods, professional practices, or medical treatment
may become necessary.

Practitioners and researchers must always rely on their own experience and knowledge in evaluating and
using any information, methods, compounds, or experiments described herein. In using such information
or methods they should be mindful of their own safety and the safety of others, including parties for
whom they have a professional responsibility.

To the fullest extent of the law, neither the Publisher nor the authors, contributors, or editors, assume any
liability for any injury and/or damage to persons or property as a matter of products liability, negligence
or otherwise, or from any use or operation of any methods, products, instructions, or ideas contained in
the material herein.

Library of Congress Cataloging-in-Publication Data
A catalog record for this book is available from the Library of Congress

British Library Cataloguing-in-Publication Data
A catalogue record for this book is available from the British Library

ISBN: 978-0-12-811029-4

For information on all Academic Press publications
visit our website at https://www.elsevier.com/books-and-journals

Working together
to grow libraries in
developing countries

www.elsevier.com • www.bookaid.org

Publisher: Candice Janco
Acquisition Editor: J. Scott Bentley
Editorial Project Manager: Susan Ikeda
Production Project Manager: Joy Christel Neumarin Honest Thangiah
Designer: Alan Studholme

Typeset by VTeX

This book is dedicated to the memory of my beloved mother, Erzsébet Kassay (1932-1992).

Gábor Kassay

With Gratitude to my parents, Professor Dumitru Rădulescu (1914–1982) and Ana Rădulescu (1923–2011). They are loved beyond words and missed beyond measure...

Vicenţiu D. Rădulescu

Contents

3.   Mathematical Tools for Solving Equilibrium Problems

4.   Existence of Solutions of Equilibrium Problems

5.   Well-Posedness for the Equilibrium Problems

A. Ekeland Variational Principle

B. Minimization Problems and Fixed Point Theorems

C. Nonsmooth Clarke Theory and Generalized Derivatives

D. Elements of Szulkin Critical Point Theory

About the Authors

Gábor Kassay received his Ph.D. thesis at the Babes-Bolyai University in Cluj-Napoca, Romania, under the supervision of József Kolumbán in 1994. He is a Professor in Mathematics at the same University, with more than 75 published research papers, several books, and book-chapters in the larger area of nonlinear analysis, and more than 1500 citations. Gábor Kassay delivered many invited and plenary talks, was session organizer and guest of honor at prestigious international conferences. He has more than 35 coauthors and collaborators from all over the world. He is currently the supervisor of the Research Group of Analysis and Optimization accredited by the Faculty of Mathematics and Computer Science of the Babes-Bolyai University. Between 2002 and 2004 he was an associate professor of Eastern Mediterranean University in Famagusta, Cyprus.

Vicenţiu D. Rădulescu received his Ph.D. at the Université Pierre et Marie Curie (Paris 6) in 1995 under the supervision of Haim Brezis. In 2003 he defended his Habilitation Mémoire at the same university. Rădulescu is Professor at the AGH University of Science and Technology in Kraków, Professorial Fellow at the "Simion Stoilow" Mathematics Institute of the Romanian Academy, and Professor of Mathematics at the University of Craiova. He is the author of more than 300 research papers in nonlinear analysis and several books, including *Variational and Nonvariational Methods in Nonlinear Analysis and Boundary Value Problems* (Kluwer, 2003), *Singular Elliptic Problems: Bifurcation and Asymptotic Analysis* (Oxford University Press, 2008), *Problems in Real Analysis: Advanced Calculus on the Real Axis* (Springer, 2009), *Variational Principles in Mathematical Physics, Geometry and Economics: Qualitative Analysis of Nonlinear Equations and Unilateral Problems* (Cambridge University Press, 2010), *Nonlinear PDEs: Mathematical Models in Biology, Chemistry and Population Genetics* (Springer, 2012), *Partial Differential Equations with Variable Exponents: Variational Methods and Qualitative Analysis* (CRC Press, 2015), *Variational Methods for Nonlocal Fractional Problems* (Cambridge University Press, 2016). He was a Highly Cited Researcher (2014). He was elected to the Accademia Peloritana dei Pericolanti (2014) and the Accademia delle Scienze dell'Umbria (2017).

Preface

There may be no Nobel in mathematics, but that need not stop many mathematicians winning the Nobel Prize for Economics[1]. Indeed, many of the winners of this prize either were mathematicians or had conducted notable research using mathematical models. For instance, Leonid Kantorovich and Tjalling Koopmans received the Nobel Prize in Economic Sciences "for their contributions to the theory of optimum allocation of resources". Both Kantorovich and Koopmans acknowledged that George B. Dantzig deserved to share their Nobel Prize for *linear programming*. Economists who conducted research in *nonlinear programming* also have won the Nobel prize, notably Ragnar Frisch (1969). The 1994 Sveriges Riksbank Prize in Economic Sciences in Memory of Alfred Nobel was awarded to John Forbes Nash Jr.,[2] John Harsanyi, and Reinhard Selten "for their pioneering analysis of equilibria in the theory of non-cooperative games". Many such examples can be provided but we refer only to Lloyd Shapley who won the Nobel Prize for Economic Sciences in 2012 "for the theory of stable allocations and the practice of market design". Lloyd Shapley described himself in an Associated Press interview: "I consider myself a mathematician and the award is for economics. I never, never in my life took a course in economics."

This monograph is intended to fill a gap in an interdisciplinary field at the interplay between applied mathematics, optimization, equilibria, and economic mathematics. Our analysis deeply relies on concrete models in the real world. Models play crucial roles in applied mathematics and economics, from identifying nonstandard behavior of mathematical models in economy to forecasting how economics will evolve. Yet major changes are afoot in equilibrium theory, triggered by global economic problems and the higher and higher impact of big data sets.

This volume is an attempt to study in a rigorous manner qualitative problems arising in applied sciences. More precisely, this monograph looks at modeling in these fields through three lenses. The first is that of *Nash equilibrium and management*, which are fundamental issues in experimental economics. The second is through the *variational analysis of equilibrium problems*, which has been challenged by the events of the macro-economy. The third looks at the *optimality and stability* of the models of economic analysis at the interface with powerful and efficient mathematical theories.

This monograph is a systematic exposition of the authors' research on general equilibrium models arising in optimization, economics, and applied sciences. It is intended to serve both as a graduate text on aspects of general equilibrium theory and as an introduction, for economists and mathematicians working in mathematical economics, to current research in a frontier area of general equilibrium theory. This book presents a systematic approach to problems in economic equilibrium based on fixed-point arguments and rigorous variational analysis methods. It describes the highest-level research on the classical theme, fixed points and economic equilibria, in the theory of mathematical economics, and also presents basic results in this area, especially in the general equilibrium theory and noncooperative game theory. Convexity theory and topology have been the central tools for the rigorous axiomatic treatment of economic theory since the 1950s. In this book, the notion of convexity is used to describe ideas within a mixture of alternative choices, a moderate view among extremes, and especially to ensure the existence of equilibrium depending on such stable actions as a fixed point for a mathematical model of society.

In this monograph we aim to show how a special mathematical method (a tool for thinking) can be utilized for constructing or developing part of an economic theory. The arguments also contain distinguishable developments of the main theme in the homology theory for general topological spaces, in the model theory and mathematical logic, and in the methodology and philosophy of social sciences.

Many of the theorems contained in this book are technical extensions of fixed-point arguments, variational analysis methods, and tools for economic equilibrium results. The main concern of this volume is not only to show abundant ways to apply such extensions, but also to list the minimal logical, analytic, or algebraic requirements for the construction of a solid economic equilibrium theory. Accordingly, we use in this monograph many highly abstract settings (e.g., fixed-point arguments based on algebraic settings, actions without continuity conditions or convexity assumptions, or spaces without linear structures) while basing our arguments on topics that are quite usual. Among others, the concept of convex combination, approximate and iterative methods, and arguments based on mathematical logic form the distinguishing features of this book's mathematical arguments.

A central role in this monograph is played by the study of some fundamental aspects related to the *Nash equilibrium*. This concept started to develop from the early insights of Émile Borel[3] and John von Neumann.[4] A couple of decades later, at the beginning of the 1950s, those insights were developed and generalized by John F. Nash Jr. His name, quite appropriately, became attached to the equilibrium state characterized by the condition that all possible unilateral actions of any actor in that state lead to states that are no better for the deviator than the original one. The fundamental result of Nash was that all games—(with constant-sum or nonconstant sum) with a finite number of players each endowed with a finite set of strategies and any kind of goal function (egoistic, altruistic, egalitarian) have an equilibrium in pure or mixed (probabilistic) strategies. In game theory, a Nash equilibrium is an array of strategies, one for each player, such that no player can obtain a higher payoff by switching to a different strategy while the strategies of all other players are held fixed. As pointed out in [161], "if Chrysler, Ford, and GM choose production levels for pickup trucks, a commodity whose market price depends on aggregate production, an equilibrium is an array of production levels, one for each firm, such that none can raise its profits by making a different choice". As pointed out in [1, p. 495], "in game theory, the single most important tool has proven to be Nash equilibrium".

This volume can serve as a graduate-level textbook on mathematical economics as well as an advanced monograph for students and researchers who are concerned about rigorous mathematical treatment in the social sciences.

Our vision throughout this volume is closely inspired by the following prophetic words of John F. Nash Jr., in an interview given in Oslo on May 18, 2015, the day before the Abel Prize ceremony:

"I had achieved my proof of the equilibrium theorem for game theory using the Brouwer fixed-point theorem, while von Neumann and Morgenstern used other things in their book. But when I got to von Neumann, and I was at the blackboard, he asked: "Did you use the fixed-point theorem?" "Yes," I said. "I used Brouwer's fixed-point theorem."

I had already, for some time, realized that there was a proof version using Kakutani's fixed-point theorem, which is convenient in applications in economics since the mapping is not required to be quite continuous. It has certain continuity properties, so-called generalized continuity properties, and there is a fixed-point theorem in that case as well. I did not realize that Kakutani proved that after being inspired by von Neumann, who was using a fixed-point theorem approach to an economic problem with interacting parties in an economy (however, he was not using it in game theory)".

Gábor Kassay and Vicenţiu D. Rădulescu
Cluj-Napoca and Craiova
May 11, 2018

NOTES

1. The Sveriges Riksbank Prize in Economic Sciences in Memory of Alfred Nobel was established in 1968 by the Bank of Sweden, and it was first awarded in 1969, more than 60 years after the distribution of the first Nobel Prizes. Although not technically a Nobel Prize, the Prize in Economic Sciences is identified with the award; its winners are announced with the Nobel Prize recipients, and it is presented at the Nobel Prize Award Ceremony. It is conferred by the Royal Swedish Academy of Sciences in Stockholm.

2. John Forbes Nash Jr. (1928-2015) was an American mathematician who made fundamental contributions to game theory, differential geometry, and the study of partial differential equations. In 1978 he was awarded the John von Neumann Prize for his discovery of the Nash Equilibria. His other influential work in mathematics included the Nash-Moser inverse function theorem, the Nash-De Giorgi theorem (a solution to David Hilbert's 19th problem), and the Nash embedding theorems. In 1999 he received a Leroy P. Steele Prize from the American Mathematical Society and in 2015 he was one of the two recipients of the Abel Prize, the other one being Louis Nirenberg. On May 23, 2015, on their way back home after spending one week in Oslo on the occasion of the Abel prize ceremony, John and Alicia Nash were killed in a taxi accident on the New Jersey Turnpike.

3. Émile Borel (1871-1956) was a French mathematician. Borel is known for his founding work in the areas of measure theory and probability. In 1922, he founded Paris Institute of Statistics, the oldest French school for statistics.

4. John von Neumann (1903-1957) was a Hungarian-American mathematician, physicist, computer scientist, and polymath. Von Neumann was generally regarded as the foremost mathematician of his time and said to be "the last representative of the great mathematicians". Economist Paul Samuelson judged John von Neumann "a genius (if that 18th century word still has a meaning)—a man so smart he saw through himself." With his pivotal work on quantum theory, the atomic bomb, and the computer, von Neumann likely exerted a greater influence on the modern world than any other mathematician of the 20th century.

Acknowledgments

Both authors thank Radu Precup for his constant interest and for kindly accepting to include some of his contributions to this subject in Chapter 8 of this book.

Gábor Kassay acknowledges the long and fruitful collaboration with Monica Bianchi and Rita Pini. Their joint papers constitute the basis of several chapters of this monograph. He thanks J.B.G. Frenk for their scientific collaboration started in early nineties which led to several results included in this book. Gábor Kassay is indebted to József Kolumbán, his former teacher and supervisor: their joint papers and interesting discussions on equilibrium problems opened the author's interest toward this topic. He also acknowledges the support by a grant of Romanian Ministry of Research and Innovation, CNCS-UEFISCDI, project PN-III-P4-ID-PCE-2016-0190, within PNCDI III.

Vicenţiu D. Rădulescu is grateful to Boualem Alleche for the multiple facets of their scientific collaboration during the last decade. A part of this monograph is inspired by our joint papers on equilibria and inequality problems. Rădulescu is indebted to Dušan D. Repovš for his meaningful remarks and comments about the subject covered in this book. He also thanks Souhail Chebbi for his continuous interest on this topic and for inviting this author to talk on equilibria and optimization issues at the conferences organized at the King Saud University in Riyadh in November 2015 and April 2018. Vicenţiu D. Rădulescu acknowledges the warm hospitality and the stimulating environment provided by the AGH University of Science and Technology in Krákow in November 2017 during the preparation of part of the current monograph. He thanks Petru Cojuhari, Witold Majdak and Jerzy Stochel for interesting discussions and support. The research of V.D. Rădulescu was supported by the Slovenian Research Agency grants P1-0292, J1-8131, J1-7025, N1-0064, and N1-0083. He also acknowledges the support through a grant of the Romanian Ministry of Research and Innovation, CNCS-UEFISCDI, project PN-III-P4-ID-PCE-2016-0130, within PNCDI III.

We are grateful to Goong Chen, Series Editor, for his efficient, enthusiastic and professional support. Our special thanks go also to Graham Nisbet, Senior Acquisitions Editor, and to Susan Ikeda, Editorial Project Manager, for the excellent quality of their work.

Gábor Kassay and Vicenţiu D. Rădulescu
May 11, 2018

Chapter 1

Preliminaries and Basic Mathematical Tools

Contents

Mathematics is the most beautiful and most powerful creation of the human spirit.

Stefan Banach (1892–1945)

Chapter points

- Some basic topological notions are introduced, as continuity and semicontinuity for single and set-valued mappings.
- Some basic algebraic notions are introduced, as convexity, convexly quasi-convexity (which generalizes both the convexity of set-valued mappings and the quasi-convexity of real single-valued mappings), and concavely quasi-convexity (which generalizes both the concavity of set-valued mappings and the quasi-convexity of real single-valued mappings).
- We provide a proof for Brouwer's fixed point theorem by Sperner's and KKM lemmata.

1.1 ELEMENTS OF FUNCTIONAL ANALYSIS

Let $\mathbb{R} =]-\infty, +\infty[$ denote the set of real numbers and $\overline{\mathbb{R}} = [-\infty, +\infty] = \mathbb{R} \cup \{-\infty, +\infty\}$. We will also use the following notation: $\mathbb{R}_+ = [0, +\infty[$, $\mathbb{R}_+^* =]0, +\infty[$, $\mathbb{R}_- = -\mathbb{R}_+$ and $\mathbb{R}_-^* = -\mathbb{R}_+^*$.

Equilibrium Problems and Applications. https://doi.org/10.1016/B978-0-12-811029-4.00009-2

1

We assume that the set $\overline{\mathbb{R}}$ is endowed with the topology extended from the usual topology of $\mathbb{R}$, and with the usual operations involving $+\infty$ and $-\infty$. For a subset A of a Hausdorff topological space X, we denote by cl A, the closure of A and by int A, the interior of A.

A subset K of a topological space is called compact if every open cover of K includes a finite subcover. That is, every family of open sets $\{V_i : i \in I\}$ satisfying $K \subset \cup_{i \in I} V_i$ admits a finite subfamily $V_{i_1}, \ldots, V_{i_n}$ such that $K \subset \cup_{k=1}^{n} V_{i_k}$. A topological space X is called compact space if X is a compact set. A family of subsets has the finite intersection property if every finite subfamily has a nonempty intersection.

Let us recall the following characterization of compact spaces.

Proposition 1.1. *A topological space is compact if and only if every family of closed subsets with the finite intersection property has a nonempty intersection.*

A subset L of a real vector space X is called linear subspace if $\alpha L + \beta L \subset L$ for all $\alpha, \beta \in \mathbb{R}$. The subset M of X is called affine if $\alpha M + (1 - \alpha)M \subset M$ for all $\alpha \in \mathbb{R}$. The linear hull of the set $S \subset X$ is defined by

$$lin(S) := \cap\{L : S \subset L \text{ and } L \text{ a linear subspace}\}$$

$$= \cup_{k=1}^{\infty} \left\{ \sum_{i=1}^{k} \alpha_i S : \alpha_i \in \mathbb{R} \right\},$$

while its affine hull by

$$aff(S) := \cap\{M : S \subset M \text{ and } M \text{ an affine set}\}$$

$$= \cup_{k=1}^{\infty} \left\{ \sum_{i=1}^{k} \alpha_i S : \alpha_i \in \mathbb{R} \text{ and } \sum_{i=1}^{k} \alpha_i = 1 \right\}.$$

For each nonempty affine set M there exists a unique linear subspace L_M satisfying $M = L_M + x$ for any given $x \in M$ (cf. [152]).

A subset K of a vector space is called cone if $\alpha K \subset K$, for all $\alpha \geq 0$. The conical hull of a subset S of a vector space is given by

$$cone(S) := \cap\{K : S \subset K \text{ and } K \text{ a cone}\}$$

$$= \cup_{k=1}^{\infty} \left\{ \sum_{i=1}^{k} \alpha_i S : \alpha_i \geq 0 \right\}. \tag{1.1}$$

By a set-valued mapping $F : X \rightrightarrows Y$, we mean a mapping F from a set X to the collection of nonempty subsets of a set Y. A mapping $f : X \to Y$ and the set-valued mapping $F : X \rightrightarrows Y$ defined by $F(x) := \{f(x)\}$ for every $x \in X$, will be identified and both will be called a single-valued mapping. That is, a single-valued mapping is a "classical" mapping or a set-valued mapping with singleton values. By a real set-valued mapping, we mean a set-valued mapping with values in $\mathbb{R}$. A real single-valued mapping is a single-valued mapping with values in $\mathbb{R}$. When $\overline{\mathbb{R}}$ is used instead of $\mathbb{R}$, we talk about extended real single-valued or extended real set-valued mappings.

For a subset S of a real vector space, conv$S$ will denote the convex hull of S.

If X denotes a real normed vector space, we denote by X^* the dual space of X and by $\langle \cdot, \cdot \rangle$ the duality pairing between X^* and X. The normal cone of $C \subset X$ at $x \in C$ is defined by

$$N_C(x) := \{x^* \in X^* : \langle x^*, y - x \rangle \leq 0, \ \forall y \in C\}.$$

1.1.1 Continuity of Functions

Let X and Y be Hausdorff topological spaces. A function f is said to be continuous at $x_0 \in X$ if for every open subset V of Y, $f^{-1}(V) = \{x \in X : f(x) \in V\}$ is a neighborhood of x_0. The function $f : X \to Y$ is continuous on a subset S of X if it is continuous at every point of S.

1.1.2 Semicontinuity of Extended Real-Valued Functions

In the investigation about solving equilibrium problems, the notions of semicontinuity and hemicontinuity on a subset play an important role. Various results on the existence of solutions of equilibrium problems have been obtained without the semicontinuity and the hemicontinuity of the bifunction on the whole domain, but just on the set of coerciveness.

Let X be a Hausdorff topological space. An extended real-valued function $f : X \to \overline{\mathbb{R}}$ is said to be *lower semicontinuous* at $x_0 \in X$ if for every $\epsilon > 0$, there exists an open neighborhood U of x_0 such that

$$f(x) \geq f(x_0) - \epsilon \quad \forall x \in U.$$

A function $f : X \to \overline{\mathbb{R}}$ is said to be *upper semicontinuous* at x_0 if $-f$ is lower semicontinuous at x_0.

We have considered extended real-valued functions in the above definitions because such functions are more general and convenient in our study. As pointed out by Rockafellar and Wets [155], considering such definitions for extended real-valued functions is also convenient for many purposes of the variational analysis.

A function $f : X \to \overline{\mathbb{R}}$ is said to be lower (resp., upper) semicontinuous on a subset S of X if it is lower (resp., upper) semicontinuous at every point of S. Obviously, if f is lower (resp., upper) semicontinuous on a subset S of X, then the restriction $f_{|S} : S \to \overline{\mathbb{R}}$ of f on S is lower (resp., upper) semicontinuous on S. The converse does not hold true in general.

Proposition 1.2. *Let X be Hausdorff topological space, $f : X \to \overline{\mathbb{R}}$ a function and let S be a subset of X. If the restriction $f_{|U}$ of f on an open subset U*

containing S is upper (resp., lower) semicontinuous on S, then any extension of $f_{|U}$ to the whole space X is upper (resp., lower) semicontinuous on S.

Proposition 1.3. *Let X be a Hausdorff topological space, $f : X \to \overline{\mathbb{R}}$ a function and S a subset of X. Then,*

1. *The following conditions are equivalent*
    (a) *f is lower semicontinuous on S;*
    (b) *for every $a \in \mathbb{R}$,*

$$cl\,(\{x \in X \mid f\,(x) \le a\}) \cap S = \{x \in S \mid f\,(x) \le a\};$$

  (c) *for every $a \in \mathbb{R}$,*

$$int\,(\{x \in X \mid f\,(x) > a\}) \cap S = \{x \in S \mid f\,(x) > a\};$$

In particular, if f is lower semicontinuous on S, then the trace on S of any lower level set of f is closed in S and the trace on S of any strict upper level set of f is open in S.

2. *The following conditions are equivalent*
    (a) *f is upper semicontinuous on S;*
    (b) *for every $a \in \mathbb{R}$,*

$$cl\,(\{x \in X \mid f\,(x) \ge a\}) \cap S = \{x \in S \mid f\,(x) \ge a\};$$

  (c) *for every $a \in \mathbb{R}$,*

$$int\,(\{x \in X \mid f\,(x) < a\}) \cap S = \{x \in S \mid f\,(x) < a\}.$$

In particular, if f is upper semicontinuous on S, then the trace on S of any upper level set of f is closed in S and the trace on S of any strict lower level set of f is open in S.

If X is a metric space (or more generally, a Fréchet-Urysohn space), then f is upper (resp., lower) semicontinuous at $x \in X$ if and only if for every sequence $(x_n)_n$ in X converging to x, we have

$$f\,(x) \ge \limsup_{n \to +\infty} f\,(x_n) \quad (\text{resp.,} \ \ f\,(x) \le \liminf_{n \to +\infty} f\,(x_n)),$$

where $\limsup_{n \to +\infty} f\,(x_n) = \inf_n \sup_{k \ge n} f\,(x_k)$ and $\liminf_{n \to +\infty} f\,(x_n) = \sup_n \inf_{k \ge n} f\,(x_k)$.

1.1.3 Hemicontinuity of Extended Real-Valued Functions

Let X be a normed vector space. An extended real-valued function $f : X \to \overline{\mathbb{R}}$ is said to be *hemicontinuous* at $x_0 \in X$ if the real-valued function $\phi : \mathbb{R} \to \overline{\mathbb{R}}$ defined by $\phi(\varepsilon) = f(x_0 + \varepsilon h)$ is continuous at the origin for every $h \in X$.

A hemicontinuous function at x_0 needs not be continuous at x_0. For example, the function $f : \mathbb{R}^2 \to \mathbb{R}$ defined by

$$f(x_1, x_2) = \begin{cases} \dfrac{x_2(x_1^2 + x_2^2)}{x_1} & \text{if } x_1 \neq 0 \\ 0 & \text{if } x_1 = 0 \end{cases}$$

is hemicontinuous and Gâteaux differentiable at $x = (x_1, x_2) = (0, 0)$, but not continuous.

1.2 KKM LEMMA AND THE BROUWER'S FIXED POINT THEOREM

The equivalent statements of Knaster,[1] Kuratowski,[2] and Mazurkiewicz[3] (KKM lemma) and Brouwer's[4] fixed point theorem represent two of the most important existence principles in mathematics. They are also equivalent to numerous, apparently completely different, cornerstone theorems of nonlinear analysis (see, for instance, [174], Chapter 77). In the sequel we provide a proof of the KKM lemma by using Sperner's[5] lemma a combinatorial analogue of Brouwer's fixed point theorem, which is equivalent to it. Then, Brouwer's fixed point theorem will be deduced by KKM lemma (see [175]).

1.2.1 The Sperner's Lemma

Let X be a real vector space. By an N-*simplex* with $N \geq 1$ we understand a set $S = \text{conv}\{u_0, ..., u_N\}$, where the vectors $u_0, ..., u_N \in X$ are affine independent, i.e., the vectors $u_1 - u_0, ..., u_N - u_0$ are linear independent. By a k-*face* of S we understand the convex hull of $k + 1$ distinct vertices of S, where $k = 0, 1, ..., N$.

By a *triangulation* of S we mean a finite collection $S_1, ..., S_J$ of N-simplices S_j such that:

(i) $S = \cup_{j=1}^{J} S_j$;

(ii) if $j \neq k$, then $S_j \cap S_k = \emptyset$ or $S_j \cap S_k$ is a common k-face, where $k = 0, ..., N - 1$.

A standard example of triangulation of S is the so-called *barycentric subdivision* described as follows. The vector $b := \frac{1}{N+1} \sum_{j=0}^{N} u_j$ is called the *barycenter* of S. The barycentric subdivision of the 1-simplex $S = \text{conv}\{u_0, u_1\}$ is the collection of the following two simplices: $S_0 = \text{conv}\{b, u_0\}$ and $S_1 = \text{conv}\{b, u_1\}$, where b is the barycenter of S. By induction, the barycentric subdivision of an N-simplex with barycenter b is the collection of all N-simplices $\text{conv}\{b, v_1, ..., v_{N-1}\}$, where $v_1, ..., v_{N-1}$ are vertices of any $N - 1$-simplex obtained by a barycentric subdivision of an $N - 1$-face of S.

Let one of the numbers $0, 1, ..., N$ be associated with each vertex v of the simplices $\mathcal{S}_j$ introduced above, according to the following rule: if

$$v \in \text{conv}\{u_{i_0}, ..., u_{i_k}\}, \ k = 0, ..., N, \tag{1.2}$$

then compulsorily one of the numbers $i_0, ..., i_k$ should be associated with v. $\mathcal{S}_j$ is called a *Sperner simplex* if and only if all of its vertices carry different numbers, i.e., the vertices of $\mathcal{S}$ carry the numbers $0, ..., N$.

Lemma 1.1. (E. Sperner [163]) *For every triangulation satisfying the rule (1.2), the number of Sperner simplices is odd.*

Proof. First, let $N = 1$. Then, each $\mathcal{S}_j$ is a 1-simplex (namely, a segment). A 0-*face* (vertex) of $\mathcal{S}_j$ is called distinguished if and only if it carries the number 0. We have exactly the following two possibilities:

(i) $\mathcal{S}_j$ has precisely one distinguished $(N - 1)$-face (namely, $\mathcal{S}_j$ is a Sperner simplex).

(ii) $\mathcal{S}_j$ has precisely two or no distinguished $(N - 1)$-faces (namely, $\mathcal{S}_j$ is not a Sperner simplex).

But since the distinguished 0-faces occur twice in the interior and once on the boundary, the total number of distinguished 0-faces is odd. Hence, the number of Sperner simplices is odd.

Secondly, let $N = 2$. Then, $\mathcal{S}_j$ is a 2-simplex. A 1-face (segment) of $\mathcal{S}_j$ is called distinguished if and only if it carries the numbers 0, 1. Then, conditions (i) and (ii) from above are satisfied for $N = 2$. The distinguished 1-faces occur twice in the interior. By (1.2), the distinguished 1-faces on the boundary are subsets of $\text{conv}\{u_0, u_1\}$. It follows from the first step that the number of distinguished faces on $\text{conv}\{u_0, u_1\}$ is odd. Thus, the total number of distinguished 1-faces is odd, and hence the number of Sperner 1-simplices is also odd.

Lastly, we use induction. Let $N \geq 3$. Suppose that the lemma is true for $N - 1$. Then it is also true for N. This follows as above. In this connection, an $(N - 1)$-face of $\mathcal{S}_j$ is called distinguished if and only if its vertices carry the numbers $0, 1, ..., N - 1$. $\qquad \square$

1.2.2 KKM Lemma

Now we can prove the following result.

Lemma 1.2. (B. Knaster, C. Kuratowski, and S. Mazurkiewicz [109]) *Let $S = conv\{u_0, ..., u_N\}$ be an N-simplex in a finite dimensional normed space X, where $N = 0, 1, ...$ Suppose that we are given closed sets $C_0, ..., C_N$ in X such that*

$$conv\{u_{i_0}, ..., u_{i_k}\} \subseteq \cup_{m=0}^k C_{i_m}, \tag{1.3}$$

for all possible systems of indices $\{i_0, ..., i_k\}$ and all $k = 0, ..., N$. Then $\cap_{j=0}^N C_j \neq \emptyset$.

Proof. For $N = 0$, $\mathcal{S}$ consists of a single point, and the statement is trivial. Now, let $N \geq 1$.

First of all, consider a triangulation $\mathcal{S}_1, ..., \mathcal{S}_J$ of $\mathcal{S}$. Let v be any vertex of $\mathcal{S}_j$, $j = 1, ..., J$, where

$$v \in \operatorname{conv}\{u_{i_0}, ..., u_{i_k}\} \text{ for some } k = 0, ..., N. \tag{1.4}$$

By (1.3), there is a set C_k such that $v \in C_k$.

We associate the number k with the vertex k. It follows from Lemma 1.1 that there is a Sperner simplex $\mathcal{S}_j$ whose vertices carry the numbers $0, ..., N$. Hence, the vertices $v_0, ..., v_N$ of $\mathcal{S}_j$ satisfy the condition $v_k \in C_k$ for all $k = 0, ..., N$.

Now, consider a sequence of triangulation of the simplex $\mathcal{S}$ such that the diameters of the simplices of the triangulation go to zero. For example, one can choose a sequence of barycentric subdivisions of $\mathcal{S}$.

Following the reasoning above, there are points:

$$v_k^{(n)} \in C_k \text{ for all } k = 0, ..., N \text{ and } n = 1, 2, ..., \tag{1.5}$$

such that

$$\lim_{n \to \infty} \operatorname{diam} \operatorname{conv}\{v_0^{(n)}, ..., v_N^{(n)}\} = 0. \tag{1.6}$$

Since the simplex $\mathcal{S}$ is compact, there exists a subsequence, again denoted by $(v_k^{(n)})$, such that $v_1^{(n)} \to v$ as $n \to \infty$ and $v \in \mathcal{S}$.

By (1.6), $v_k^{(n)} \to v$ as $n \to \infty$ for all $k = 0, ..., N$.

Since the set C_k is closed, this implies that $v \in C_k$, for all $k = 0, ..., N$. $\qquad\square$

1.2.3 Brouwer's Fixed Point Theorem

A fixed point of a function $f : X \to X$ is a point $x \in X$ satisfying $f(x) = x$. One of the most famous fixed point theorems for continuous functions was proven by Brouwer and it has been used across numerous fields of mathematics. This property is stated in the following theorem.

Theorem 1.1. *Every continuous function f from a nonempty convex compact subset C of a finite dimensional normed space X to C itself has a fixed point.*

Proof. Let us observe first that every nonempty convex compact subset $C \subset X$ is homeomorphic to some N-simplex $\mathcal{S}$ in X with $N = 0, 1, ...$ (see, for instance, Zeidler [175], Section 1.13, Proposition 9). Thus, it is enough to prove that every continuous function $f : \mathcal{S} \to \mathcal{S}$ has a fixed point, where $\mathcal{S}$ is an N-simplex, with $N = 0, 1, ...$.

For $N = 0$, the statement is trivial and for $N = 1$, the proof is provided by the following simple argument. Let $f : [a, b] \to [a, b]$ be a continuous function and set $g(x) := f(x) - x$, for all $x \in [a, b]$. Since $f(a), f(b) \in [a, b]$, we get that $f(a) \geq a$ and $f(b) \leq b$. Hence $g(a) \geq 0$ and $g(b) \leq 0$, then apply the intermediate-value theorem to conclude that the continuous real function g has a zero, say $u \in [a, b]$, i.e., $g(u) = 0$. Hence $f(u) = u$.

Now, let $N = 2$. Then, $S = \text{conv}\{u_0, u_1, u_2\}$, i.e., S is a triangle. Each point u in S has the representation

$$u = \alpha_0(u)u_0 + \alpha_1(u)u_1 + \alpha_2(u)u_2, \tag{1.7}$$

where

$$0 \leq \alpha_0, \alpha_1, \alpha_2 \leq 1, \text{ and } \alpha_0 + \alpha_1 + \alpha_2 = 1. \tag{1.8}$$

With $u - u_0 = \alpha_1(u)(u_1 - u_0) + \alpha_2(u)(u_2 - u_0)$ and $\alpha_0(u) = 1 - \alpha_1(u) - \alpha_2(u)$, it follows from the linear independence of $u_1 - u_0$, $u_2 - u_0$, that the barycentric coordinates $\alpha_0(u)$, $\alpha_1(u)$ and $\alpha_2(u)$ of the point u are uniquely determined by u and depend continuously on u, by [175], Section 1.12, Proposition 5. We set

$$C_j := \{u \in S : \alpha_j(f(u)) \leq \alpha_j(u)\}$$

for $j = 0, 1, 2$.

Since $\alpha_j(\cdot)$ and f are continuous on S, the set C_j is closed. Furthermore, the crucial condition (1.3) of Lemma 1.2 is satisfied, i.e.,

$$\text{conv}\{u_{i_0}, ..., u_{i_k}\} \subseteq \cup_{m=0}^k C_{i_m}, \ k = 0, 1, 2. \tag{1.9}$$

In fact, if this is not true, then there exists a point $u \in \text{conv}\{u_{i_0}, ..., u_{i_k}\}$ such that $u \notin \cup_{m=0}^k C_{i_m}$, i.e.,

$$\alpha_{i_m}(f(u)) > \alpha_{i_m}(u), \text{ for all } m = 0, ..., k \text{ and some } k = 0, 1, 2. \tag{1.10}$$

This is a contradiction to (1.8).

Moreover, if we renumber the vertices, if necessary, condition (1.10) means that:

$$\alpha_j(f(u)) > \alpha_j(u) \text{ for all } j = 0, ..., k \text{ and some } k = 0, 1, 2. \tag{1.11}$$

In addition, since $u \in S$ and $f(u) \in S$, it follows from (1.8) that

$$\alpha_0(u) + \alpha_1(u) + \alpha_2(u) = 1, \ \alpha_0(f(u)) + \alpha_1(f(u)) + \alpha_2(f(u)) = 1. \tag{1.12}$$

For $k = 2$, relation (1.11) is impossible, by (1.12). If $k = 1$ or $k = 0$, then $u \in \text{conv}\{u_0, u_1\}$ or $u \in \text{conv}\{u_0\}$ and hence $\alpha_2(u) = 0$ or $\alpha_1(u) = \alpha_2(u) = 0$, respectively. Again, (1.11) contradicts (1.12).

Lemma 1.2 tells us now that there is a point $v \in S$ such that $v \in C_j$ for all $j = 0, 1, 2$. This implies $\alpha_j(f(v)) \leq \alpha_j(v)$ for all $j = 0, 1, 2$.

According to (1.12) with $u = v$, we get $\alpha_j(f(v)) = \alpha_j(v)$ for $j = 0, 1, 2$, and hence $f(v) = v$. Thus, v is the desired fixed point of f in the case where $N = 2$.

If $N \geq 3$, then use the same argument as for $N = 2$ above.   □

1.3   ELEMENTS OF SET-VALUED ANALYSIS

1.3.1   Semicontinuity of Set-Valued Mappings

We denote by $F : X \rightrightarrows Y$ a set-valued mapping from X to Y, where X and Y are topological spaces. The graph of F is the set

$$\text{grph}(F) = \{(x, y) \in X \times Y \mid y \in F(x)\}.$$

For a subset B of Y, we define

$$F^-(B) = \{x \in X \mid F(x) \cap B \neq \emptyset\}$$

the lower inverse set of B by F. We also define

$$F^+(B) = \{x \in X \mid F(x) \subset B\}$$

the upper inverse set of B by F. The upper inverse set of B by F is called sometimes the core of B. It is easily seen that for every subset B of Y, we have

$$F^+(B) = X \setminus F^-(Y \setminus B).$$

This characterization provides an important relation between lower and upper inverse sets.

A set-valued mapping $F : X \rightrightarrows Y$ is said to be upper semicontinuous at a point $x_0 \in X$ if it is continuous at $x_0 \in X$ as a function from X to the set of subsets of Y endowed with the upper Vietoris topology. That is, F is upper semicontinuous at $x_0 \in X$ if whenever V is an open subset of Y such that $F(x_0) \subset V$, the upper inverse set $F^+(V)$ of V by F is a neighborhood of x_0.

For a set-valued mapping $F : X \rightrightarrows Y$ with closed values, F is upper semicontinuous at $x_0 \in X$ if for all $x_n \in X$, $y_0 \in Y$, and $y_n \in Y$ with $\lim_{n \to \infty} x_n = x_0$ and $\lim_{n \to \infty} y_n = y_0$, it follows that $y_0 \in F(x_0)$.

By analogy, a set-valued mapping $F : X \rightrightarrows Y$ is said to be lower semicontinuous at a point $x_0 \in X$ if whenever V is an open subset of Y such that $F(x_0) \cap V \neq \emptyset$, the lower inverse set $F^-(V)$ of V by F is a neighborhood of x_0. It turns out that F is lower semicontinuous at $x_0 \in X$ if and only if F is continuous at $x_0 \in X$ as a function from X to the set of subsets of Y endowed with the lower Vietoris topology.

Equivalently, $F : X \rightrightarrows Y$ is lower semicontinuous at $x_0 \in X$ if and only if for all $x_n \in X$ with $x_n \to x_0$ and for every $y_0 \in F(x_0)$, there is a subsequence (x_{n_k}) of (x_n) and there exists $y_k \in F(x_{n_k})$ such that $y_k \to y_0$.

Within the literature we also can find the term "upper/lower hemicontinuos" for the above concepts.

A set-valued mapping $F : X \rightrightarrows Y$ is said to be continuous at a point $x_0 \in X$ if it is lower and upper semicontinuous at $x_0 \in X$.

The set-valued mapping F is said to be lower semicontinuous on X if it is lower semicontinuous at every point of X. The continuity and upper semicontinuity on the space X are defined in the same manner. Clearly, F is lower (resp., upper) semicontinuous on X if and only if the lower (resp., upper) inverse set of any open subset V of Y is open.

We say that a set-valued mapping $F : X \rightrightarrows Y$ is lower semicontinuous (resp., upper semicontinuous, resp., continuous) on a subset S of X if it is lower semicontinuous (resp., upper semicontinuous, resp., continuous) at every point of S.

The following result shows how easy is to construct lower (resp., upper) semicontinuous set-valued mappings on a subset without being lower semicontinuous on the whole space. It is easy to prove.

Proposition 1.4. *Let X and Y be two topological spaces, $F : X \rightrightarrows Y$ a set-valued mapping and let S be a subset of X. If the restriction $F_{|U} : U \rightrightarrows Y$ of F on an open subset U containing S is lower (resp., upper) semicontinuous, then any extension of $F_{|U}$ to the whole space X is lower (resp., upper) semicontinuous on S.*

For a subset S of X, we denote respectively by $\mathrm{cl}\,(S)$ and $\mathrm{int}\,(S)$, the closure and the interior of S with respect to X.

The following lemma provides us with a characterization of lower and upper semicontinuity of set-valued mappings on a subset.

Proposition 1.5. *Let X and Y be two topological spaces, $F : X \rightrightarrows Y$ a set-valued mapping and let S be a subset of X. Then, the following statements hold.*

1. *The following conditions are equivalent*
   (a) *F is lower semicontinuous on S;*
   (b) *for every open subset V of Y, we have*

$$F^- (V) \cap S = int\left(F^- (V)\right) \cap S;$$

   (c) *for every closed subset B of Y, we have*

$$F^+ (B) \cap S = cl\left(F^+ (B)\right) \cap S.$$

   In particular, if F is lower semicontinuous on S, then $F^- (V) \cap S$ is open in S for every open subset V of Y, and $F^+ (B) \cap S$ is closed in S for every closed subset B of Y.

2. *The following conditions are equivalent*
   (a) *F is upper semicontinuous on S;*
   (b) *for every open subset V of Y, we have*

$$F^+ (V) \cap S = int\left(F^+ (V)\right) \cap S;$$

(c) *for every closed subset B of Y, we have*

$$F^- (B) \cap S = cl \left(F^- (B) \right) \cap S.$$

In particular, if F is upper semicontinuous on S, then $F^+ (V) \cap S$ is open in S for every open subset V of Y, and $F^- (B) \cap S$ is closed in S for every closed subset B of Y.

Proof. Since the second statement is similar to the first one, we state only the case of a lower semicontinuous set-valued mapping.

Assume first that F is lower semicontinuous on S and let V be an open subset of Y. Then, for every $x \in F^- (V) \cap S$, $F^- (V)$ is a neighborhood of x which implies that $x \in$ int $\left(F^- (V) \right)$. Thus, (1a) $\Longrightarrow$ (1b).

To prove (1b) $\Longrightarrow$ (1c), let B be a closed subset of Y and put $V = Y \setminus B$ which is open. By the properties of lower and upper inverse sets, we have

$$\begin{aligned}
cl \left(F^+ (B) \right) \cap S &= \left(X \setminus \left(\text{int} \left(X \setminus F^+ (B) \right) \right) \right) \cap S \\
&= \left(X \setminus \left(\text{int} \left(F^- (V) \right) \right) \right) \cap S \\
&= S \setminus \left(\text{int} \left(F^- (V) \right) \cap S \right) \\
&= S \setminus \left(F^- (V) \cap S \right) \\
&= \left(X \setminus \left(F^- (V) \right) \right) \cap S \\
&= F^+ (B) \cap S.
\end{aligned}$$

To prove (1c)$\Longrightarrow$ (1a), let $x \in S$ and V be an open subset of Y such that $F (x) \cap V \neq \emptyset$. It follows that $x \in F^- (V)$ and then, $x \notin F^+ (B)$ where $B = Y \setminus V$. Since $F^+ (B) \cap S = cl \left(F^+ (B) \right) \cap S$, it follows that $x \notin cl \left(F^+ (B) \right)$ which implies that $x \in$ int $\left(X \setminus F^+ (B) \right) = $ int $\left(F^- (V) \right)$. Therefore $F^- (V)$ is a neighborhood of x. $\qquad\square$

It is worthwhile noticing that based on the notion of lower and upper limit of nets of subsets in the sense of Kuratowski-Painlevé convergence, the lower and upper semicontinuity of set-valued mappings can be also characterized by means of nets. Although, these characterizations are important in many studies, we will not follow this approach in our proofs, but make use of the techniques developed in Proposition 1.5, which are based only on lower and upper inverse sets.

1.3.2 Selections of Set-Valued Mappings

Let X and Y be topological spaces and assume that $F : X \rightrightarrows Y$ is a set-valued mapping. The *lower section* of F at $y \in Y$ is the lower inverse set of the singleton $\{y\}$ by F, namely

$$F^- (y) = \{x \in X |\ y \in F (x)\}.$$

Notice that a set-valued mapping with open graph has open lower sections and, in turn, if it has open lower sections then it is lower semicontinuous.

A fixed point of set-valued mapping $F : X \rightrightarrows X$ is a point $x \in X$ satisfying $x \in F(x)$. The set of fixed points of F is denoted by Fix (F).

The following result is known in the literature as the Kakutani[6] fixed point theorem and it generalizes the Brouwer fixed point theorem in a straightforward way. This result has found wide applicability in economic theory, in the theory of games and in competitive equilibrium.

Theorem 1.2. *For any given positive integer n, let X be a nonempty, closed, bounded and convex subset of $\mathbb{R}^n$. If F is a convex-valued self-correspondence on X that has a closed graph, then F has a fixed point, that is, there exists $x \in X$ such that $x \in F(x)$.*

The requirement of the closed graph property in the statement of Kakutani's fixed point theorem can be replaced with upper semicontinuity when F is closed-valued.

A selection of a set-valued mapping $F : X \rightrightarrows Y$ is a function $f : X \to Y$ such that $f(x) \in F(x)$ for all $x \in X$. The axiom of choice guarantees that set-valued mappings with nonempty values always admit selections, but they may have no additional useful properties. Michael [126] proved a series of theorems on the existence of continuous selections that assume the condition of lower semicontinuity of set-valued mappings. One of these results is stated in the following theorem.

Theorem 1.3. *Every lower semicontinuous set-valued mapping F from a metric space to $\mathbb{R}^n$ with nonempty convex values admits a continuous selection.*

Collecting the Brouwer fixed point theorem and the Michael selection theorem, we deduce the following fixed point result for lower semicontinuous set-valued mappings.

Corollary 1.1. *Every lower semicontinuous set-valued mapping F from a nonempty convex compact subset $C \subset \mathbb{R}^n$ to C itself with nonempty convex values has a fixed point.*

Notice that, unlike the famous Kakutani fixed point theorem in which the closedness of grph (F) is required, in Corollary 1.1 the lower semicontinuity of the set-valued map is needed. No relation exists between the two results as the following example shows.

Example 1.1. The set-valued mapping $F : [0, 3] \rightrightarrows [0, 3]$ defined by

$$F(x) := \begin{cases} \{1\} & \text{if } 0 \le x \le 1 \\ (1, 2) & \text{if } 1 < x < 2 \\ \{2\} & \text{if } 2 \le x \le 3 \end{cases}$$

is lower semicontinuous and the nonemptiness of Fix (F) is guaranteed by Corollary 1.1. Notice that Fix $(F) = [1, 2]$. Nevertheless the Kakutani fixed point theorem does not apply since grph (F) is not closed.

On the converse, the set-valued mapping $F : [0, 3] \rightrightarrows [0, 3]$ defined by

$$F(x) := \begin{cases} \{1\} & \text{if } 0 \le x < 1 \\ [1, 2] & \text{if } 1 \le x \le 2 \\ \{2\} & \text{if } 2 < x \le 3 \end{cases}$$

has closed graph and the nonemptiness of Fix (F) is guaranteed by the Kakutani fixed point theorem. Again, we have Fix $(F) = [1, 2]$. Since F is not lower semicontinuous, Corollary 1.1 cannot be applied.

1.3.3   Elements of Convex Analysis

The notions of convexity and concavity of set-valued mappings have been considered in the literature as a generalization of convexity and concavity of real single-valued mappings. However, these notions are not limited to real set-valued mappings and so, they are not really adapted and very general. Applied to real single-valued mappings, they are in fact too stronger than the convexity and concavity and produce a sort of "linearity on line segments".

We will use the following notions of convexity of functions and set-valued mappings defined on real topological Hausdorff vector spaces.

Let X be a real topological Hausdorff vector space and D a (non necessarily convex) subset of X.

1. A function $f : D \longrightarrow \mathbb{R}$ is said to be
   (a) convex on D if for every finite subset $\{x_1, \ldots, x_n\} \subset D$ and $\{\lambda_1, \ldots, \lambda_n\} \subset \mathbb{R}_+$ such that $\sum_{i=1}^n \lambda_i = 1$ and $\sum_{i=1}^n \lambda_i x_i \in D$, then

$$f \left(\sum_{i=1}^n \lambda_i x_i \right) \le \sum_{i=1}^n \lambda_i f(x_i);$$

   (b) concave on D if $-f$ is convex on D.
2. A set-valued mapping $F : D \rightrightarrows \mathbb{R}$ is said to be
   (a) convex on D if for every finite subset $\{x_1, \ldots, x_n\} \subset D$ and $\{\lambda_1, \ldots, \lambda_n\} \subset \mathbb{R}_+$ such that $\sum_{i=1}^n \lambda_i = 1$ and $\sum_{i=1}^n \lambda_i x_i \in D$, then

$$F \left(\sum_{i=1}^n \lambda_i x_i \right) \supset \sum_{i=1}^n \lambda_i F(x_i)$$

where the sum denotes here the usual Minkowski sum of sets;

(b) concave on D if instead of the last inclusion, the following holds

$$F\left(\sum_{i=1}^{n} \lambda_i x_i\right) \subset \sum_{i=1}^{n} \lambda_i F(x_i).$$

Note that the notion of convex set-valued mappings on the whole space X has been already considered in the literature. One can easily verify that a set-valued mapping $F : X \rightrightarrows \mathbb{R}$ is convex on X if and only if its graph is convex.

We say that a function $f : D \to \mathbb{R}$ is quasi-convex on D if for every finite subset $\{x_1, \dots, x_n\} \subset D$ and $\{\lambda_1, \dots, \lambda_n\} \subset \mathbb{R}_+$ such that $\sum_{i=1}^{n} \lambda_i = 1$ and $\sum_{i=1}^{n} \lambda_i x_i \in D$, then

$$f\left(\sum_{i=1}^{n} \lambda_i x_i\right) \leq \max_{i=1,\dots,n} f(x_i).$$

In what follows, let C be a convex subset of X. We first introduce the notion of convexly quasi-convexity for real set-valued mappings which generalizes both the convexity of set-valued mappings and the quasi-convexity of real single-valued mappings.

A set-valued mapping $F : C \rightrightarrows \mathbb{R}$ is said to be *convexly quasi-convex* on C if whenever $\{x_1, \dots, x_n\} \subset C$ and $\{\lambda_1, \dots, \lambda_n\} \subset \mathbb{R}_+$ such that $\sum_{i=1}^{n} \lambda_i = 1$, then for every $\{z_1, \dots, z_n\}$ with $z_i \in F(x_i)$ for every $i = 1, \dots, n$, there exists $z \in F\left(\sum_{i=1}^{n} \lambda_i x_i\right)$ such that

$$z \leq \max\{z_i : i = 1, \dots, n\}.$$

For $\lambda \in \mathbb{R}$, we set $[F \leq \lambda] := \{x \in C : F(x) \cap]-\infty, \lambda] \neq \emptyset\}$.

Proposition 1.6. *Let C be a nonempty and convex subset of a real topological Hausdorff vector space. A set-valued mapping $F : C \rightrightarrows \mathbb{R}$ is convexly quasi-convex on C if and only if the set $[F \leq \lambda]$ is convex, for every $\lambda \in \mathbb{R}$.*

Proof. Let $\lambda \in \mathbb{R}$. Let $\{x_1, \dots, x_n\} \subset [F \leq \lambda]$ and $\{\lambda_1, \dots, \lambda_n\} \subset \mathbb{R}_+$ be such that $\sum_{i=1}^{n} \lambda_i = 1$. For every $i = 1, \dots, n$, choose $z_i \in F(x_i) \cap]-\infty, \lambda]$. Since F is convexly quasi-convex, let $z \in F\left(\sum_{i=1}^{n} \lambda_i x_i\right)$ be such that

$$z \leq \max\{z_i : i = 1, \dots, n\}.$$

Then $z \leq \lambda$, and therefore $\sum_{i=1}^{n} \lambda_i x_i \in [F \leq \lambda]$.

Conversely, let $\{x_1, \dots, x_n\} \subset C$ and $\{\lambda_1, \dots, \lambda_n\} \subset \mathbb{R}_+$ be such that $\sum_{i=1}^{n} \lambda_i = 1$. Take $\{z_1, \dots, z_n\}$ with $z_i \in F(x_i)$, for every $i = 1, \dots, n$. Put $\lambda = \max\{z_i : i = 1, \dots, n\} \in \mathbb{R}$. We have $x_i \in [F \leq \lambda]$, for every $i = 1, \dots, n$. By convexity of $[F \leq \lambda]$, it follows that $\sum_{i=1}^{n} \lambda_i x_i \in [F \leq \lambda]$ which means that there exists $z \in F\left(\sum_{i=1}^{n} \lambda_i x_i\right)$ such that $z \leq \lambda$. We conclude that $z \leq \max\{z_i : i = 1, \dots, n\}$. $\qquad\square$

Now, we introduce the notion of concavely quasi-convexity for real set-valued mappings which generalizes both the concavity of set-valued mappings and the quasi-convexity of real single-valued mappings.

A set-valued mapping $F : C \rightrightarrows \mathbb{R}$ will be said *concavely quasi-convex* on C if whenever $\{x_1, \ldots, x_n\} \subset C$ and $\{\lambda_1, \ldots, \lambda_n\} \subset \mathbb{R}_+$ such that $\sum_{i=1}^n \lambda_i = 1$, then for every $z \in F\left(\sum_{i=1}^n \lambda_i x_i\right)$, there exist $\{z_1, \ldots, z_n\}$ with $z_i \in F(x_i)$ for every $i = 1, \ldots, n$ such that

$$z \leq \max\{z_i : i = 1, \ldots, n\}.$$

For $\lambda \in \mathbb{R}$, we set $[F \subseteq \lambda] := \{x \in C : F(x) \subset \,]-\infty, \lambda]\}$.

Proposition 1.7. *Let C be a nonempty and convex subset of a real topological Hausdorff vector space. If a set-valued mapping $F : C \rightrightarrows \mathbb{R}$ is concavely quasi-convex on C, then the set $[F \subseteq \lambda]$ is convex, for every $\lambda \in \mathbb{R}$.*

Proof. Let $\lambda \in \mathbb{R}$. Let $\{x_1, \ldots, x_n\} \subset [F \subseteq \lambda]$ and $\{\lambda_1, \ldots, \lambda_n\} \subset \mathbb{R}_+$ be such that $\sum_{i=1}^n \lambda_i = 1$. Take $z \in F\left(\sum_{i=1}^n \lambda_i x_i\right)$. Since F is concavely quasi-convex, let $z_i \in F(x_i)$ for every $i = 1, \ldots, n$ be such that

$$z \leq \max\{z_i : i = 1, \ldots, n\}.$$

Since $\max\{z_i : i = 1, \ldots, n\} \leq \lambda$ and z is arbitrary in $F\left(\sum_{i=1}^n \lambda_i x_i\right)$, then $\sum_{i=1}^n \lambda_i x_i \in [F \subseteq \lambda]$. $\qquad\square$

Note that, if f is a real single-valued mapping, then $[f \leq \lambda] = [f \subseteq \lambda]$, for every $\lambda \in \mathbb{R}$. We have the following result.

Proposition 1.8. *Let C be a nonempty and convex subset of a real topological Hausdorff vector space. For a real single-valued mapping $f : C \to \mathbb{R}$, the following conditions are equivalent*

1. *f is quasi-convex on C,*
2. *f is convexly quasi-convex on C,*
3. *f is concavely quasi-convex on C.*

Example 1.2. Consider a quasi-convex function $f : \mathbb{R} \to \mathbb{R}$ which is not convex, and let $F : \mathbb{R} \rightrightarrows \mathbb{R}$ be the set-valued mapping defined by $F(x) := \{f(x)\}$, for every $x \in \mathbb{R}$. As mentioned before, f is identified to F in our purpose. By Proposition 1.8, F is convexly quasi-convex and concavely quasi-convex single-valued mapping, but it is neither convex nor concave in the sense of set-valued mapping.

We introduce in what follows a suitable notion of denseness. Let X be a real topological Hausdorff vector space. For $x, y \in X$, we denote the closed line segment in X with the endpoints x and y by

$$[x, y] = \{\lambda x + (1 - \lambda) y \mid \lambda \in [0, 1]\}.$$

Let V be a convex subset of X. A subset U of V is said to be self-segment-dense set in V if

1. $V \subset \mathrm{cl}\,(U)$;
2. for every $x, y \in U$, $[x, y] \subset \mathrm{cl}\,([x, y] \cap U)$.

The importance of the notion of self-segment-dense set has been highlighted in [115] and especially for dimensions greater than one. The following result (see [115, Lemma 3.1]) has been also obtained and it is important in the sequel. It is valid in the settings of Hausdorff locally convex topological vector spaces since the origin has a local base of convex, balanced, and absorbent sets.

Lemma 1.3. *Let X be a Hausdorff locally convex topological vector space, V a convex set of X and let $U \subset V$ a self-segment-dense set in V. Then, for all finite subset $\{x_1, \ldots, x_n\} \subset U$, we have*

$$cl\,(conv\,\{x_1, \ldots x_n\} \cap U) = conv\,\{x_1, \ldots x_n\}.$$

NOTES

1. Bronislaw Knaster (1893–1980) was a Polish mathematician; from 1939 a university professor in Lwow and from 1945 in Wroclaw. He is known for his work in point-set topology and in particular for his discoveries in 1922 of the hereditarily indecomposable continuum or pseudo-arc and of the Knaster continuum, or buckethandle continuum. Together with his teacher Hugo Steinhaus and his colleague Stefan Banach, he also developed the last diminisher procedure for fair cake cutting.
2. Kazimierz Kuratowski (1896–1980) was a Polish mathematician and logician. He was one of the leading representatives of the Warsaw School of Mathematics.
3. Stefan Mazurkiewicz (1888–1945) was a Polish mathematician who worked in mathematical analysis, topology, and probability. He was a student of Waclaw Sierpinski and a member of the Polish Academy of Learning (PAU). His students included Karol Borsuk, Bronislaw Knaster, Kazimierz Kuratowski, Stanislaw Saks, and Antoni Zygmund. For a time Mazurkiewicz was a professor at the University of Paris; however, he spent most of his career as a professor at the University of Warsaw.
4. L.E.J. Brouwer (1881–1966) was a Dutch mathematician and philosopher, who worked in topology, set theory, measure theory, and complex analysis. He was the founder of the mathematical philosophy of intuitionism. Brouwer was an Invited Speaker of the ICM in 1908 at Rome and in 1912 at Cambridge, UK.
5. Emanuel Sperner (1905–1980) was a German mathematician, best known for two theorems. He was a student at Carolinum in Nysa and then Hamburg University where his advisor was Wilhelm Blaschke. He was appointed Professor in Königsberg in 1934, and subsequently held posts in a number of universities until 1974.
6. Shizuo Kakutani (1911–2004) was a Japanese mathematician who contributed to many subfields, from functional analysis to stochastic processes and topological groups. He received two awards of the Japan Academy, the Imperial Prize, and the Academy Prize. Kakutani was a Plenary Speaker of the ICM in 1950 in Cambridge, Massachusetts.

Chapter 2

An Overview on Equilibrium Problems

Contents

> *If I were again beginning my studies, I would follow the advice of Plato and start with mathematics.*
>
> Galileo Galilei (1564–1642)

Chapter points

- The chapter is devoted to an overview of the equilibrium problem and some of its versions.
- There are discussed several classes of inequality and equilibrium problems and their relationship.
- The content of this chapter is at the interplay between equilibria, optimization, and nonlinear analysis.

2.1 THE EQUILIBRIUM PROBLEM AND ITS VARIANTS

In 1972, Ky Fan[1] [74] established the existence of solutions for an inequality which, along the years, has shown to be a cornerstone result of nonlinear analysis. Let us reproduce this result in its dual form:

Equilibrium Problems and Applications. https://doi.org/10.1016/B978-0-12-811029-4.00010-9
17

Theorem 2.1. *Let X be a Hausdorff topological vector space and K a nonempty compact convex subset of X. Suppose that* $f : K \times K \to \mathbb{R}$ *satisfies the following conditions:*

1. $f(x, x) \geq 0$ *for all* $x \in K$;
2. *For each* $x \in K$, $f(x, .)$ *is quasi-convex;*
3. *For each* $y \in K$, $f(., y)$ *is upper semicontinuous.*

Then there exists $x^* \in K$ *such that* $f(x^*, y) \geq 0 \ \forall y \in K$.

The problem itself was called *minimax inequality* by Ky Fan, but nowadays it is widely known within the literature as *equilibrium problem*. It plays a very important role in many fields, such as variational inequalities, game theory, mathematical economics, optimization theory, and fixed point theory. Although most of the authors claim that the term "equilibrium problem" was first coined by Blum and Oettli [42] in 1994, in fact it appeared two years earlier in the paper of Muu and Oettli [133], where three standard examples of (EP) have been considered: the optimization problems, the variational inequalities, and the fixed point problems. Further particular cases like saddle point (minimax) problems, Nash equilibria problems, convex differentiable optimization, and complementarity problems have been studied in the aforementioned article [42].

We formulate the (scalar) equilibrium problem (abbreviated (EP)), in a more general way, as follows. Let A and B be two nonempty sets and $f : A \times B \to \mathbb{R}$ a given function. The problem consists on finding an element $\bar{a} \in A$ such that

$$f(\bar{a}, b) \geq 0, \ \forall b \in B. \tag{2.1}$$

The element $\bar{a}$ satisfying (2.1) is called *equilibrium point* of f on $A \times B$.

(EP) has been extensively studied along the years (see, e.g., [12,22,82,92,93, 95,101] and the references therein).

Recently, the study of equilibrium problems has been extended from scalar to the vector case (see, for instance, [83] for a collection of articles focusing in this direction). To formulate this problem, let Y be a real topological vector space and C be a proper convex cone in Y with int$C \neq \emptyset$, where int$C$ denotes the topological interior of C. For a vector-valued function $f : A \times B \to Y$, the *weak vector equilibrium problem* (abbreviated (WVEP)) (see, for example, [83]) is to find $\bar{a} \in A$ such that

$$f(\bar{a}, b) \notin -\text{int}C \ \text{for all } b \in B, \tag{2.2}$$

and the *strong vector equilibrium problem* (abbreviated (SVEP)) (see, for example, [14,40]) is to find $\bar{a} \in A$ such that

$$f(\bar{a}, b) \notin -C \setminus \{0\} \ \text{for all } b \in B. \tag{2.3}$$

To obtain a more general problem which contains (WVEP) and/or (SVEP) as special cases, some authors considered set-valued maps (bifunctions) instead of (single-valued) vector bifunctions. Let $F : A \times B \rightrightarrows Y$. It is clear that in this way there are four possibilities to define a *set-valued equilibrium problem* (some authors also called *generalized vector equilibrium problem*, see, for instance, [15] and the references therein). Namely, the two weak versions are: find $\bar{a} \in A$ such that

$$F(\bar{a}, b) \subset Y \setminus (-\mathrm{int}C) \quad \text{for all } b \in B, \tag{2.4}$$

and

$$F(\bar{a}, b) \cap (Y \setminus (-\mathrm{int}C)) \neq \emptyset \quad \text{for all } b \in B, \tag{2.5}$$

while the two strong versions can be written as: find $\bar{a} \in A$ such that

$$F(\bar{a}, b) \subset Y \setminus (-C \setminus \{0\}) \quad \text{for all } b \in B, \tag{2.6}$$

and

$$F(\bar{a}, b) \cap (Y \setminus (-C \setminus \{0\})) \neq \emptyset \quad \text{for all } b \in B. \tag{2.7}$$

It is obvious that the above four variants of the set-valued equilibrium problems are related: namely, any solution of (2.4) is also a solution of (2.5), while any solution of (2.6) is also a solution of (2.7). Furthermore, the strong versions imply the corresponding weak versions: any solution of (2.6) is also a solution of (2.4), while any solution of (2.7) is also a solution of (2.5). Note that if F is single-valued, (2.4) and (2.5) collapse into (WVEP), while (2.6) and (2.7) collapse into (SVEP).

2.2 SOME IMPORTANT SPECIAL CASES OF EQUILIBRIUM PROBLEMS

In this section we focus on the most important particular cases of the equilibrium problem.

2.2.1 The Convex Minimization Problem

We start with a simple, but very important particular case of (EP). Let X be a topological vector space and $h : X \to \mathbb{R} \cup \{+\infty\}$ be a convex, lower semicontinuous and proper function. The convex minimization problem (CMP) is defined as:

$$\text{find } \bar{x} \in X \text{ such that } h(\bar{x}) \leq h(y) \text{ for all } y \in X. \tag{2.8}$$

If we take $A = B := \{x \in X : h(x) < +\infty\}$ and $f : A \times A \to \mathbb{R}$, $f(x, y) := h(y) - h(x)$ for all $x, y \in A$, then $\bar{x}$ is a solution of (CMP) if and only if $\bar{x}$ is a solution of (EP).

2.2.2 The Fixed Point Problem for Set-Valued Maps

Assume that X is a Hilbert space with inner product $\langle \cdot, \cdot \rangle$, and let $T : X \rightrightarrows X$ be an upper semicontinuous set-valued mapping such that $T(x)$ is a nonempty, convex, weakly compact subset of X for each $x \in X$. The fixed point problem (FPP) is defined as:

$$\text{find } \bar{x} \in X \text{ such that } \bar{x} \in T(\bar{x}). \tag{2.9}$$

If we take $f : X \times X \to \mathbb{R}$, $f(x, y) := \max_{u \in T(x)} \langle x - u, y - x \rangle$ for all $x, y \in X$, then $\bar{x}$ is a solution of (FPP) if and only if $\bar{x}$ is a solution of (EP).

Indeed, observe first that f is well defined, since for every $x, y \in X$ the function $u \mapsto \langle x - u, y - x \rangle$ is affine and continuous, hence weakly upper semicontinuous. Thus, the maximum exists on the weakly compact set $T(x)$ according to Weierstrass theorem. If $\bar{x}$ is a solution of (EP), denoting by $\bar{u}$ the corresponding maximum point, we have that $\langle \bar{x} - \bar{u}, y - \bar{x} \rangle \geq 0$ for all $y \in X$. Since X is the whole space, in particular $\bar{x}$ is an interior point of X, a standard argument shows that $\bar{x} = \bar{u}$, i.e., $\bar{x} \in T(\bar{x})$. Conversely, if $\bar{x}$ is a solution of (FPP), then for each $y \in X$, $0 = \langle \bar{x} - \bar{x}, y - \bar{x} \rangle \leq \max_{u \in T(\bar{x})} \langle \bar{x} - u, y - \bar{x} \rangle$, i.e., $\bar{x}$ is a solution of (EP).

2.2.3 The Complementarity Problem

Let X be a topological vector space, $K \subseteq X$ a closed convex cone and $K^* := \{x \in X^* : \langle x, y \rangle \geq 0 \text{ for all } y \in K\}$ its dual cone, where X^* is the topological dual space of X with $\langle \cdot, \cdot \rangle$ the duality pairing. Let $T : K \to X^*$ be an operator. The complementarity problem (CP) is defined as:

$$\text{find } \bar{x} \in K \text{ such that } T(\bar{x}) \in K^*, \quad \langle T(\bar{x}), \bar{x} \rangle = 0. \tag{2.10}$$

If we take $f : K \times K \to \mathbb{R}$, $f(x, y) := \langle T(x), y - x \rangle$ for all $x, y \in K$, then $\bar{x}$ is a solution of (CP) if and only if $\bar{x}$ is a solution of (EP).

Indeed, suppose that $\bar{x} \in K$ is a solution of (EP). By taking first $y = 2\bar{x} \in K$, then $y = 0 \in K$, we obtain that $\langle T(\bar{x}), \bar{x} \rangle = 0$. On the other hand, $0 \leq \langle T(\bar{x}), y - \bar{x} \rangle = \langle T(\bar{x}), y \rangle$, for all $y \in K$, hence $T(\bar{x}) \in K^*$, thus $\bar{x}$ is a solution of (CP). The reverse implication is trivial.

2.2.4 Nash Equilibrium of Noncooperative Games

Consider n-players called $1, 2, ..., n$ and assume that the set of pure strategies (also called actions) of player i is given by some nonempty set X_i for $i = 1, 2, ..., n$. Let $X := X_1 \times X_2 \times ... \times X_n$ and consider the functions $h_i : X \to \mathbb{R}$, $i = 1, 2, ..., n$ called the *payoff functions* of players $1, 2, ..., n$, respectively. The n-person noncooperative game consists on the following:

(i) player 1 chooses an element $x_1 \in X_1$, player 2 chooses an element $x_2 \in X_2$, ..., player n chooses an element $x_n \in X_n$, each independently on the others;

(ii) player 1 gains the amount $h_1(x_1, x_2, ..., x_n)$, player 2 gains the amount $h_2(x_1, x_2, ..., x_n)$, ..., player n gains the amount $h_n(x_1, x_2, ..., x_n)$.

The n-tuple $(\bar{x}_1, \bar{x}_2, ..., \bar{x}_n) \in X$ is called *Nash equilibrium point* of $h_1, h_2, ..., h_n$ on X if for all $i = 1, 2, ..., n$

$$h_i(\bar{x}_1, ..., \bar{x}_{i-1}, \bar{x}_i, \bar{x}_{i+1}, ..., \bar{x}_n) \geq h_i(\bar{x}_1, ..., \bar{x}_{i-1}, x_i, \bar{x}_{i+1}, ..., \bar{x}_n), \quad \forall x_i \in X_i. \tag{2.11}$$

In this way it is clear that $\bar{x}_i \in X_i$ is the optimal action (pure strategy) for player i ($i = 1, 2, ..., n$) if and only if $(\bar{x}_1, \bar{x}_2, ..., \bar{x}_n)$ is a Nash equilibrium point of $h_1, h_2, ..., h_n$. Let us see how can we relate the problem of finding a Nash equilibrium point to (EP).

Define $f : X \times X \to \mathbb{R}$ as follows: for arbitrary $x = (x_1, ..., x_n)$ and $y = (y_1, ..., y_n)$ in X, let

$$f(x, y) := \sum_{i=1}^{n} [h_i(x_1, ...x_{i-1}, x_i, x_{i+1}, ..., x_n) - h_i(x_1, ...x_{i-1}, y_i, x_{i+1}, ..., x_n)].$$

Then it is easy to see that $\bar{x} = (\bar{x}_1, ..., \bar{x}_n)$ is an equilibrium point of f if and only if it is a Nash equilibrium point for the functions $h_1, ..., h_n$. Indeed, if $\bar{x} = (\bar{x}_1, ..., \bar{x}_n)$ is an equilibrium point, then for arbitrarily fixed $j \in \{1, ..., n\}$ and $y_j \in X_j$ by substituting the element $y = (\bar{x}_1, ..., \bar{x}_{j-1}, y_j, \bar{x}_{j+1}, ..., \bar{x}_n)$ into the relation (2.1), we obtain

$$h_j(\bar{x}_1, ..., \bar{x}_{j-1}, \bar{x}_j, \bar{x}_{j+1}, ..., \bar{x}_n) \geq h_j(\bar{x}_1, ..., \bar{x}_{j-1}, y_j, \bar{x}_{j+1}, ..., \bar{x}_n),$$

i.e., $\bar{x}$ is a Nash equilibrium point of $h_1, ..., h_n$.

The reverse implication follows immediately by summing up the inequalities (2.11) for $i = 1, ..., n$.

2.2.5 The Saddle Point/Minimax Problem of Noncooperative Games

In this subsection we focus on another particular case of (EP), namely the saddle point problem related to a bifunction. We emphasize two domains where the saddle point (minimax) problem has a crucial role: *two person zero sum noncooperative games* and *duality in optimization*. Both are important in many applied fields of mathematics, we mention here only economics and engineering. The first is a special case of n-person noncooperative games discussed within the previous subsection. As it turns out, the optimal strategies of both players are related to the concept of saddle point of a given bifunction. Therefore, we start with defining this notion.

Let X, Y be two nonempty sets and $h : X \times Y \to \mathbb{R}$ be a given bifunction. The pair $(\bar{x}, \bar{y}) \in X \times Y$ is called a *saddle point of h on the set $X \times Y$* if

$$h(x, \bar{y}) \leq h(\bar{x}, \bar{y}) \leq h(\bar{x}, y), \quad \forall (x, y) \in X \times Y. \tag{2.12}$$

The next proposition provides a characterization of saddle points in terms of minmax and maxmin of h.

Suppose that for each $x \in X$ there exists $\min_{y \in Y} h(x, y)$, and for each $y \in Y$ there exists $\max_{x \in X} h(x, y)$. Then we have the following result.

Proposition 2.1. f admits a saddle point on $X \times Y$ if and only if there exist $\max_{x \in X} \min_{y \in Y} f(x, y)$ and $\min_{y \in Y} \max_{x \in X} f(x, y)$ and they are equal.

Proof. Suppose first that h admits a saddle point $(\bar{x}, \bar{y}) \in X \times Y$. Then by relation (2.12) one obtains

$$\min_{y \in Y} h(x, y) \leq h(x, \bar{y}) \leq h(\bar{x}, \bar{y}) = \min_{y \in Y} h(\bar{x}, y), \ \forall x \in X$$

and

$$\max_{x \in X} h(x, y) \geq h(\bar{x}, y) \geq h(\bar{x}, \bar{y}) = \max_{x \in X} h(x, \bar{y}), \ \forall y \in Y.$$

Therefore,

$$\min_{y \in Y} h(\bar{x}, y) = \max_{x \in X} \min_{y \in Y} h(x, y)$$

and

$$\max_{x \in X} h(x, \bar{y}) = \min_{y \in Y} \max_{x \in X} h(x, y),$$

and both equal to $h(\bar{x}, \bar{y})$. For the reverse implication take $\bar{x} \in X$ such that

$$\min_{y \in Y} h(\bar{x}, y) = \max_{x \in X} \min_{y \in Y} h(x, y)$$

and $\bar{y} \in Y$ such that

$$\max_{x \in X} h(x, \bar{y}) = \min_{y \in Y} \max_{x \in X} h(x, y).$$

Then by our assumption we obtain

$$\min_{y \in Y} h(\bar{x}, y) = \max_{x \in X} h(x, \bar{y}),$$

therefore, in the obvious relations

$$\min_{y \in Y} h(\bar{x}, y) \leq h(\bar{x}, \bar{y}) \leq \max_{x \in X} h(x, \bar{y})$$

one obtains equality in both sides. This completes the proof. $\square$

Remark 2.1. Observe that, for arbitrary nonempty sets X, Y and function $h : X \times Y \to \mathbb{R}$, the inequality

$$\sup_{x \in X} \inf_{y \in Y} h(x, y) \leq \inf_{y \in Y} \sup_{x \in X} h(x, y)$$

always holds. Therefore,

$$\max_{x \in X} \min_{y \in Y} h(x, y) \leq \min_{y \in Y} \max_{x \in X} h(x, y)$$

holds either, provided these two values exist.

One of the main issues in minimax theory is to find sufficient and/or necessary conditions for the sets X, Y and function h, which guarantee the reverse inequality. Such results are called *minimax theorems*.

As stressed at the beginning of this subsection, minimax theorems or, in particular, results on existence of a saddle point, are important in many applied fields of mathematics. One of them is the *noncooperative game theory* which will be discussed below. For more details, see [98].

(a) Two-Player Zero-Sum Games

To introduce a static two-player zero-sum (noncooperative) game and its relation to a minimax theorem we consider two players called 1 and 2 and assume that the set of pure strategies (also called actions) of player 1 is given by some nonempty set X, while the set of pure strategies of player 2 is given by a nonempty set Y. If player 1 chooses the pure strategy $x \in X$ and player 2 chooses the pure strategy $y \in Y$, then player 2 has to pay player 1 an amount $h(x, y)$ with $h : X \times Y \to R$ a given function. This function is called the payoff function of player 1. Since the gain of player 1 is the loss of player 2 (this is a so-called zero-sum game) the payoff function of player 2 is $-h$. Clearly player 1 likes to gain as much profit as possible. However, at the moment he does not know how to achieve this and so he first decides to compute a lower bound on his profit. He argues as follows: if he decides to choose action $x \in X$, then it follows that his profit is at least $\inf_{y \in Y} h(x, y)$, irrespective of the action of player 2. Therefore a lower bound on the profit for player 1 is given by

$$r_* := \sup_{x \in X} \inf_{y \in Y} h(x, y). \tag{2.13}$$

Similarly player 2 likes to minimize his losses but since he does not know how to achieve this he also decides to compute first an upper bound on his losses. To do so, player 2 argues as follows. If he decides to choose action $y \in Y$, it follows that he loses at most $\sup_{x \in X} h(x, y)$ and this is independent of the action of player 1. Therefore an upper bound on his losses is given by

$$r^* := \inf_{y \in Y} \sup_{x \in X} h(x, y). \tag{2.14}$$

Since the profit of player 1 is at least r_* and the losses of player 2 is at most r^* and the losses of player 2 are the profits of player 1, it follows directly that $r_* \leq r^*$. In general $r_* < r^*$, but under some properties on the pure strategy sets and payoff function one can show that $r_* = r^*$. If this equality holds and in relations (2.13) and (2.14) the suprema and infima are attained, an optimal strategy for both players is obvious. By the interpretation of r_* for player 1 and the interpretation of r^* for player 2 and $r^* = r_* := v$ both players will choose an action which achieves the value v and so player 1 will choose that action $x_0 \in X$ satisfying

$$\inf_{y \in Y} h(x_0, y) = \max_{x \in X} \inf_{y \in Y} h(x, y).$$

Moreover, player 2 will choose that strategy $y_0 \in Y$ satisfying

$$\sup_{x \in X} h(x, y_0) = \min_{y \in Y} \sup_{x \in X} h(x, y).$$

Another field, where the concept of saddle point plays an important role, is the so-called *duality in optimization*.

(b) Duality in Optimization

Let X be a nonempty subset of $\mathbb{R}^n$, $F : \mathbb{R}^n \to \mathbb{R}$ and $G : \mathbb{R}^n \to \mathbb{R}^m$ be given functions. For K a nonempty convex cone of $\mathbb{R}^m$, define the following optimization problem

$$v(P) := \inf\{F(x) : G(x) \in -K, x \in X\}. \tag{2.15}$$

This (general) problem has many important particular cases.

The optimization problem with inequality and equality constraints. Let $X := \mathbb{R}^n$, $K := \mathbb{R}_+^p \times \{0_{\mathbb{R}^{m-p}}\}$, where $1 \le p < m$, and $0_{\mathbb{R}^{m-p}}$ denotes the origin of the space $\mathbb{R}^{m-p}$. Then problem (2.15) reduces to the classical optimization problem with inequality and equality constraints

$$\inf\{F(x) : G_i(x) \le 0, i = 1, 2, \ldots, p, \; G_j(x) = 0, j = p + 1, \ldots, m\}.$$

The linear programming problem. Let

$$X := \mathbb{R}_+^n, \; K := \{0_{\mathbb{R}^m}\}, \; F(x) := c^T x, \; G(x) := Ax - b,$$

where A is a matrix with m rows and n columns (with all entries real numbers), $c \in \mathbb{R}^n$ and $b \in \mathbb{R}^m$ are given elements. Then (2.15) reduces to the following linear programming problem

$$\inf\{c^T x : Ax = b, x \ge 0\}.$$

The conical programming problem. Let $K \subseteq \mathbb{R}^n$ be a nonempty convex cone, let $X := b + L \subseteq \mathbb{R}^n$, where L is a linear subspace of $\mathbb{R}^n$, and let $F(x) := c^T x$, $G(x) := x$. Then we obtain the so-called *conical programming problem*

$$\inf\{c^T x : x \in b + L, x \in -K\}.$$

Denote by $\mathcal{F}$ the *feasible set* of problem (2.15), i.e., the set $\{x \in X : G(x) \in -K\}$. The problem

$$v(R) := \inf\{F_R(x) : x \in \mathcal{F}_R\}$$

is called a *relaxation* of the initial problem (2.15), if $\mathcal{F} \subseteq \mathcal{F}_R$ and $F_R(x) \leq F(x)$ for each $x \in \mathcal{F}$. It is obvious that $v(R) \leq v(P)$. Next we show a natural way to construct a relaxation of problem (2.15). Let $\lambda \in \mathbb{R}^m$, and consider the problem

$$\inf\{F(x) + \lambda^T G(x) : x \in X\}.$$

Clearly $\mathcal{F} \subseteq X$ and $F(x) + \lambda^T G(x) \leq F(x)$ for each $x \in \mathcal{F}$ if and only if $\lambda^T G(x) \leq 0$ for each $x \in \mathcal{F}$. Let $K^* := \{y \in \mathbb{R}^m : y^T x \geq 0, \forall x \in K\}$ be the *dual cone* of K. Now it is clear that $\lambda \in K^*$ implies $\lambda^T G(x) \leq 0$, for each $x \in \mathcal{F}$. Define the (Lagrangian) function $L : X \times K^* \to \mathbb{R}$ by $L(x, \lambda) := F(x) + \lambda^T G(x)$ and consider the problem

$$\theta(\lambda) := \inf\{L(x, \lambda) : x \in X\}. \tag{2.16}$$

Clearly $\theta(\lambda) \leq v(P)$ for each $\lambda \in K^*$, and therefore we also have

$$\sup_{\lambda \in K^*} \theta(\lambda) \leq v(P),$$

hence

$$\sup_{\lambda \in K^*} \inf_{x \in X} L(x, \lambda) \leq \inf_{x \in \mathcal{F}} F(x). \tag{2.17}$$

By this relation it follows that the optimal objective value $v(D)$ of the *dual problem*

$$v(D) := \sup\{\theta(\lambda) : \lambda \in K^*\}$$

approximates from below the optimal objective value $v(P)$ of the primal problem (2.15). Both from theoretical and practical point of view, an important issue is to establish sufficient conditions in order to have equality between the optimal objective values of the primal and dual problems. In this respect, observe that for each $x \in \mathcal{F}$ one has

$$\sup_{\lambda \in K^*} L(x, \lambda) = \sup_{\lambda \in K^*} (F(x) + \lambda^T G(x)) = F(x).$$

Therefore,

$$\inf_{x \in \mathcal{F}} F(x) = \inf_{x \in \mathcal{F}} \sup_{\lambda \in K^*} L(x, \lambda) = \inf_{x \in X} \sup_{\lambda \in K^*} L(x, \lambda).$$

Indeed, if $x \in X \setminus \mathcal{F}$, then $G(x) \notin -K$. By the *bipolar theorem* ([152]) we have $K = K^{**}$, hence it follows that there exists $\lambda^* \in K^*$ such that $\lambda^{*T} G(x) > 0$.

Since $t\lambda^* \in K$ for each $t > 0$, then

$$\sup_{\lambda \in K^*} L(x, \lambda) = \infty, \ \forall x \in X \setminus \mathcal{F}.$$

Combining the latter with relation (2.17) and taking into account that the "supinf" is always less or equal then the "infsup", one obtains

$$v(D) = \sup_{\lambda \in K^*} \inf_{x \in X} L(x, \lambda) \leq \inf_{x \in X} \sup_{\lambda \in K^*} L(x, \lambda) = v(P).$$

Hence we obtain that $v(D) = v(P)$, if a saddle point $(\bar{x}, \bar{\lambda})$ of the Lagrangian L exists. This situation is called *perfect duality*. In this case $\bar{x}$ is the optimal solution of the primal, while $\bar{\lambda}$ is the optimal solution of the dual problem.

2.2.6 Variational Inequalities

Let E be a real topological vector space and E^* be the dual space of E. Let $K \subseteq E$ be a nonempty convex set and $T : K \to E^*$ a given operator. As before, if $x \in E$ and $x^* \in E^*$, the *duality pairing* between these two elements will be denoted by $\langle x, x^* \rangle$. If $A = B := K$ and $f(x, y) := \langle T(x), y - x \rangle$, for each $x, y \in K$, then each solution of the equilibrium problem (EP) is a solution of the *variational inequality*

$$\langle T(x), y - x \rangle \geq 0, \ \forall y \in K, \tag{2.18}$$

and vice versa.

Variational inequalities have shown to be important mathematical models in the study of many real problems, in particular in network equilibrium models ranging from spatial price equilibrium problems and imperfect competitive oligopolistic market equilibrium problems to general financial or traffic equilibrium problems.

An important particular case of the variational inequality (2.18) is the following. Let $E := H$ be a real Hilbert space with inner product $\langle \ , \ \rangle$. It is well known that in this case the dual space E^* can be identified with H. Consider the bilinear and continuous function $a : H \times H \to \mathbb{R}$, the linear and continuous function $L : H \to \mathbb{R}$, and formulate the problem: find an element $\bar{x} \in K \subseteq H$ such that

$$a(\bar{x}, y - \bar{x}) \geq L(y - \bar{x}), \ \forall y \in K. \tag{2.19}$$

By the hypothesis, for each $x \in H$ the function $a(x, .) : H \to \mathbb{R}$ is linear and continuous. Therefore, by the Riesz representation theorem in Hilbert spaces (see, for instance, [157]) there exists a unique element $A(x) \in H$ such that $a(x, y) = \langle A(x), y \rangle$ for each $y \in H$. It is easy to see that $A : H \to H$ is a linear and continuous operator. Moreover, since L is also linear and continuous, again by the Riesz theorem, there exists a unique element $l \in H$ such that

$L(x) = \langle l, x \rangle$ for each $x \in H$. Now for $T(x) := A(x) - l$, problem (2.18) reduces to (2.19).

In optimization theory, those variational inequalities in which the operator T is a gradient map (i.e., the gradient of a certain differentiable function), are of special interest since their solutions are (in some cases) the *minimum points* of the function itself. Suppose that $X \subseteq \mathbb{R}^n$ is an open set, $K \subseteq X$ is a convex set and the function $F : X \to \mathbb{R}$ is differentiable on X. Then each minimum point of F on the set K is a solution of the variational inequality (2.18), with $T := \nabla F$. Indeed, let $\bar{x} \in K$ be a minimum point of F on K, and $y \in K$ be an arbitrary element. Then we have

$$F(\bar{x}) \leq F(\lambda y + (1 - \lambda)\bar{x}), \ \forall \lambda \in [0, 1].$$

Therefore,

$$\frac{1}{\lambda}(F(\bar{x} + \lambda(y - \bar{x})) - F(\bar{x})) \geq 0, \ \forall \lambda \in (0, 1].$$

Now letting $\lambda \to 0$ we obtain $\langle \nabla F(\bar{x}), y - \bar{x} \rangle \geq 0$, as claimed.

If we suppose further that F is a *convex function* on the convex set X, then we obtain the reverse implication as well, i.e., each solution of the variational inequality (2.18), with $T := \nabla F$, is a minimum point of F on the set K. Indeed, let $\bar{x} \in K$ be a solution of (2.18) and $y \in K$ be an arbitrary element. Then by convexity

$$Ff(\bar{x} + \lambda(y - \bar{x})) \leq (1 - \lambda)F(\bar{x}) + \lambda F(y), \ \forall \lambda \in [0, 1],$$

which yields

$$\frac{1}{\lambda}(F(\bar{x} + \lambda(y - \bar{x})) - F(\bar{x})) \leq F(y) - F(\bar{x}), \ \forall \lambda \in (0, 1].$$

By letting $\lambda \to 0$ one obtains from the latter that

$$\langle \nabla F(\bar{x}), y - \bar{x} \rangle \leq F(y) - F(\bar{x}),$$

which yields the desired implication.

2.2.7 Vector Minimization Problem

Let $C \subset \mathbb{R}^m$ be a closed convex cone, such that both C and its dual cone C^* have nonempty interior. Consider the partial order in $\mathbb{R}^m$ given by

$$x \preceq y \text{ if and only if } y - x \in C,$$
$$x \prec y \text{ if and only if } y - x \in \text{int}(C).$$

Let $F : S \to \mathbb{R}^m$ be a function, with S a nonempty set. The weak vector minimization problem (WVMP) is defined as:

$$\text{Find } \bar{x} \in S \text{ such that } F(x) \not\prec F(\bar{x}) \text{ for all } x \in S. \quad (2.20)$$

If we take $f : S \times S \to \mathbb{R}$, $f(x, y) := \max_{\|z\|=1, \, z \in C^*} \langle z, F(y) - F(x) \rangle$, then $\bar{x}$ is a solution of (WVMP) if and only if $\bar{x}$ is a solution of (EP) (cf. Iusem and Sosa [95]).

As observed, within all particular cases discussed above the sets A and B involved in the definition of (EP) are equal. In the next subsection we deal with a famous problem, particular case of (EP) as well, where these sets are not equal.

2.2.8 The Kirszbraun Problem

Let m and n be two positive integers and consider two systems of closed balls in $\mathbb{R}^n$: (B_i) and (B_i'), $i \in \{1, 2, ..., m\}$. Denote by $r(B_i)$ and $d(B_i, B_j)$ the radius of B_i and the distance between the centers of B_i and B_j, respectively. The following result is known in the literature as *Kirszbraun's theorem* (see [108]).

Theorem 2.2. *Suppose that*

(i) $\cap_{i=1}^m B_i \neq \emptyset$;
(ii) $r(B_i) = r(B_i')$, *for all* $i \in \{1, 2, ..., m\}$;
(iii) $d(B_i', B_j') \leq d(B_i, B_j)$, *for all* $i, j \in \{1, 2, ..., m\}$.

Then $\cap_{i=1}^m B_i' \neq \emptyset$.

To relate this result to (EP), let $A := \mathbb{R}^n$, $B := \{(x_i, y_i) : i \in \{1, 2, ..., m\}\} \subseteq \mathbb{R}^n \times \mathbb{R}^n$ such that

$$\|y_i - y_j\| \leq \|x_i - x_j\|, \ \forall i, j \in \{1, 2, ..., m\}. \quad (2.21)$$

Choose an arbitrary element $x \in \mathbb{R}^n$ and put

$$f(y, b_i) := \|x - x_i\|^2 - \|y - y_i\|^2 \quad (2.22)$$

for each $y \in \mathbb{R}^n$ and $b_i = (x_i, y_i) \in B$. Then $y \in \mathbb{R}^n$ is a solution of (EP) if and only if

$$\|y - y_i\| \leq \|x - x_i\|, \ \forall i \in \{1, 2, ..., m\}. \quad (2.23)$$

It is easy to see by Theorem 2.2, that the equilibrium problem given by the function f defined in (2.22) has a solution. Indeed, let $x \in \mathbb{R}^n$ be fixed and put $r_i := \|x - x_i\|$ for $i := 1, 2, ...m$. Take B_i the closed ball centered at x_i with radius r_i and B_i' the closed ball centered at y_i with radius r_i. Obviously, by (2.21), the assumptions of Theorem 2.2 are satisfied, hence there exists an element $y \in \mathbb{R}^n$ which satisfies (2.23).

Observe that, by compactness (i.e., the closed balls in $\mathbb{R}^n$ are compact sets), Theorem 2.2 of Kirszbraun remains valid for an arbitrary family of balls. More precisely, instead of the finite set $\{1, 2, ..., m\}$, one can take an arbitrary set I of indices. Using this observation, it is easy to derive the following result concerning the extensibility of an arbitrary nonexpansive function to the whole space. Let $D \subseteq \mathbb{R}^n$, $D \neq \mathbb{R}^n$ and $f : D \to \mathbb{R}^n$ a given *nonexpansive* function, i.e.,

$$\|f(x) - f(y)\| \leq \|x - y\|, \ \forall x, y \in D.$$

Then there exists a nonexpansive function $\bar{f} : \mathbb{R}^n \to \mathbb{R}^n$ such that $\bar{f}(x) = f(x)$, for each $x \in D$. Indeed, let $z \in \mathbb{R}^n \setminus D$ and take for each $x \in D$ the number $r_x := \|z - x\|$. Let B_x be the closed ball centered at x with radius r_x, and let B_x' be the closed ball centered at $f(x)$ with radius r_x. Then we obtain that the set $\cap_{x \in D} B_x'$ is nonempty. Now for $\bar{f}(z) \in \cap_{x \in D} B_x'$, the conclusion follows.

2.3 EQUILIBRIA AND INEQUALITY PROBLEMS WITH VARIATIONAL STRUCTURE

As mentioned in the previous sections, the equilibrium problem in the sense of Blum and Oettli [42] or inequality of Ky Fan-type, has been considered as an important and general framework for describing, in a common formulation, various problems arising in different areas of mathematics, including optimization problems, mathematical economic problems, and Nash equilibrium problems. Historically, this formulation has been first used as a pure mathematical object in the work by Ky Fan [74] on minimax inequality problems, which has been followed for a long time by several studies on equilibrium problems considered under different headings. It is worth mentioning that one of the interests of this common formulation, called simply the equilibrium problem, is that many techniques developed for a particular case may be extended, with suitable adaptations, to the equilibrium problem, and then they can be applied to other particular cases.

Although the equilibrium problem subsumes several kinds of problems, there are many models described by variational inequalities involving constraints that depend on the solution itself. In this direction, there are the quasi-variational inequalities considered early in the literature in connection with stochastic impulse control problems, where the constraint set is subject to modifications.

In the spirit to describe in a more again general framework most of problems arising in nonlinear analysis, it has been considered and adopted recently in the literature the notion of quasi-equilibrium problem, which appears as an equilibrium problem in which the constraint set is subject to modifications. The quasi-equilibrium problem is a unified formulation which encompasses many relevant problems such as quasi-variational inequalities, mixed quasi-variational like inequalities, and all the special cases of the equilibrium problem. The first existence results have been established and applied to different optimization problems including Nash equilibrium problems under constraints and quasi-variational inequalities for monotone operators.

Many problems related to the term "equilibrium" and arising from different areas of sciences can be mathematically modeled as special cases of the unified formulation called the equilibrium problem. Also, the equilibrium problem subsumes many mathematical special cases which are in relation with the term equilibrium such as Nash equilibrium problems and economic equilibrium problems. Then, one can naturally guess that this is the reason for which the term equilibrium problem has been chosen to name this unified formulation. It is now well-known that the last decades have witnessed an exceptional growth in theoretical advances on the equilibrium problem and its applications in concrete cases. Maybe, the simplicity of this formulation is the principal reason which has allowed all these advancements. We point out that the equilibrium problem has never been introduced in order to deal directly with other problems which are not described by the old existing concepts. If we assume that a problem is directly modeled as an equilibrium problem by using an inequality involving a bifunction, then nothing can impose that this inequality is a variational inequality. Unfortunately, this is not the task for which the concept of the equilibrium problem has been introduced, but to describe various existing concepts in a common way in order to deeply study them altogether.

At the interplay between mathematics and economics, broad applications include:

- optimization problems in relationship with equilibrium phenomena;
- static (or equilibrium) analysis in which the economic unit or economic system is modeled as not changing;
- dynamic analysis, which traces changes in an economic system over time.

2.3.1 Quasi-Hemivariational Inequalities

Let C be a nonempty, closed, and convex subset of a real Banach space E and let $\Phi : C \times C \longrightarrow \mathbb{R}$ be a bifunction satisfying $\Phi(x, x) = 0$, for every $x \in C$. Such a bifunction Φ is called an *equilibrium bifunction*.

Recall (see also relation (2.1)) that an *equilibrium problem* in the sense of Blum and Oettli [42] is a problem of the following form:

$$\text{find } x^* \in C \text{ such that } \Phi\left(x^*, y\right) \geq 0 \quad \forall y \in C, \tag{EP}$$

where its set of solutions is denoted by $SEP(C, \Phi)$.

Equilibrium problems also encompass quasi-hemivariational inequalities. Let E be a real Banach space which is continuously embedded in $L^p(\Omega; \mathbb{R}^n)$, for some $1 < p < +\infty$ and $n \geq 1$, where Ω is a bounded domain in $\mathbb{R}^m, m \geq 1$. Then a *quasi-hemivariational inequality* is a problem of the form:

$$\text{find } u \in E \text{ and } z \in A(u) \text{ such that}$$
$$\langle z, v \rangle + h(u) J^0(iu; iv) - \langle Fu, v \rangle \geq 0 \quad \forall v \in E,$$

where i is the canonical injection of E into $L^p(\Omega; \mathbb{R}^n)$, $A : E \rightrightarrows E^*$ is a nonlinear multi-valued mapping, $F : E \to E^*$ is a nonlinear operator, $J : L^p(\Omega; \mathbb{R}^n) \to \mathbb{R}$ is a locally Lipschitz functional and $h : E \to \mathbb{R}$ is a given nonnegative functional. We denote by E^* the dual space of E and by $\langle \cdot, \rangle$ the duality pairing between E^* and E.

Consider the following quasi-hemivariational inequality:

$$\text{find } u \in C \text{ and } z \in A(u) \text{ such that}$$
$$\langle z, v - u \rangle + h(u) J^0(iu; iv - iu) - \langle Fu, v - u \rangle \geq 0 \quad \forall v \in C, \quad \text{(QHVI)}$$

where its set of solutions is denoted by $\text{SQHVI}(C, A)$. Note that in the special case when C is the whole space E, the above two formulations of quasi-hemivariational inequalities are one and the same. A detailed analysis of quasi-hemivariational inequality problems will be developed in Chapter 10.

Studies about inequality problems captured special attention in the last decades where one of the most recent and general type of inequalities is the *hemivariational inequalities* introduced by P.D. Panagiotopoulos [137,138] as a variational formulation for several classes of mechanical problems with nonsmooth and nonconvex energy super-potentials. The theory of hemivariational inequalities has produced an abundance of important results both in pure and applied mathematics as well as in other domains such as mechanics and engineering sciences as it allowed mathematical formulations for new classes of interesting problems.

When h is equal to zero in the quasi-hemivariational inequality (QHVI) corresponding to convex super-potentials, we obtain the standard case of *variational inequalities*. The setting corresponding to h equal to 1 describes the hemivariational inequalities. These inequality problems appear as a generalization of variational inequalities, but they are much more general than these ones, in the sense that they are not equivalent to minimum problems but give rise to substationarity problems. The general case when h is nonconstant corresponds to *quasi-hemivariational inequalities*, which are studied in relationship with relevant models in mechanics and engineering.

2.3.2 Browder Variational Inclusions

Starting with Felix Browder's[2] pioneering contributions to variational inclusions [45], many authors have been interested in inclusions involving set-valued mappings. In recent years, the notion of "set-valued equilibrium problem" has been employed in [113,115] in connection with the so-called equilibrium problem or inequality of Ky Fan-type (see [42,74,133]), which has produced an abundance of results in various areas of mathematics.

Let C be a nonempty subset of a (suitable) Hausdorff topological space and $\Phi : C \times C \rightrightarrows \mathbb{R}$ a set-valued mapping. A *set-valued equilibrium problem* is a problem of the form

$$\text{find } x^* \in C \text{ such that } \Phi\left(x^*, y\right) \subset \mathbb{R}_+ \quad \forall y \in C. \qquad \text{(SVEP)}$$

It is worth to consider the following weaker set-valued equilibrium problem

$$\text{find } x^* \in C \text{ such that } \Phi\left(x^*, y\right) \cap \mathbb{R}_+ \neq \emptyset \quad \forall y \in C. \qquad \text{(SVEP(W))}$$

In connections with these problems, we recall that the "equilibrium problem" is a problem of the form

$$\text{find } x^* \in C \text{ such that } \varphi\left(x^*, y\right) \geq 0 \quad \forall y \in C \qquad \text{(EP)}$$

where $\varphi : C \times C \to \mathbb{R}$ is a bifunction.

Several problems arising in nonlinear analysis, such as variational inequality problems, optimization problems, inverse optimization problems, mathematical programming, complementarity problems, fixed point problems, and Nash equilibrium problems, are special cases of equilibrium problems. A central interest in the study of equilibrium problems is that they unify many problems in a common formulation.

Browder variational inclusions appear in the literature as a generalization of Browder-Hartman-Stampacchia variational inequalities. These inequality problems are presented as a weak type of multi-valued variational inequalities, since they involve set-valued mappings in their definition. Browder variational inclusions have many applications, incsluding applications to the surjectivity of set-valued mappings and to nonlinear elliptic boundary value problems. In recent studies, Browder variational inclusions have been reformulated by means of set-valued equilibrium problems and different results have been carried out.

Although set-valued equilibrium problems have already been considered in the literature, many authors have focused on the applications to Browder variational inclusions, or to other areas such as fixed point theory and economic equilibrium theory. When these results are applied to single-valued equilibrium problems, their assumptions become simple conditions of continuity and convexity. On the other hand, single-valued equilibrium problems have known in last decades several important and deep advancements.

A detailed analysis of Browder variational inclusions will be developed in Chapter 10.

2.3.3 Quasi-Variational Inequalities

The theory of quasi-variational inequalities has emerged as one of the most efficient fields of pure and applied nonlinear analysis. These inequality problems not only subsume the theories of variational inequalities and nonlinear partial differential inequations, but they provide a unified framework for studying general boundary value problems with complicated structure and involving possibly unilateral, boundary conditions. This field has developed on the basis of re-fined analytic tools in order to investigate a wide range of problems that arise in applied fields such as mechanics, economics, finance, optimization, optimal control, etc.

Let X and Y be reflexive Banach spaces such that X is compactly embed-ded into Y. Let $L : D(L) \subseteq X \to X^*$ be a linear, maximal monotone operator. Let $A : X \rightrightarrows X^*$ and $B : Y \rightrightarrows Y^*$ be multi-valued maps, let K be a nonempty, closed, and convex subset of K, let $\Phi : X \to \mathbb{R} \cup \{+\infty\}$ be a proper functional (that is, $\Phi \not\equiv +\infty$), and let $C : K \rightrightarrows K$ be a multi-valued map such that for any $z \in K$, $C(z)$ is a nonempty, closed, and convex subset of K, and let $f \in X^*$.

We formulate the following quasi-variational inequality: find $x \in C(x) \cap D(L) \cap D(\Phi)$ such that for some $a \in A(x)$ and $b \in B(ix)$, we have for all $z \in C(x) \cap D(L)$

$$\langle L(x) + a - f, z - x \rangle_X + \langle b, iz - ix \rangle_Y + \Phi(z) - \Phi(x) \geq 0. \tag{2.24}$$

This statement incorporates both elliptic and evolutionary inequality prob-lems. For instance, if the map A is single-valued with $D(A) = X$, $\phi = 0$, $B = 0$, and $L = 0$, then problem (2.24) reduces to the following quasi-variational in-equality introduced by A. Bensoussan and J.-L. Lions [29]: find $x \in C(x)$ such that

$$\langle A(x) - f, z - x \rangle \geq 0 \quad \text{for all } z \in C(x).$$

Additionally, if $C(x) = K$ for every $x \in K$, then problem (2.24) recovers the standard statement of variational inequality: find $x \in K$ such that

$$\langle A(x) - f, z - x \rangle \geq 0 \quad \text{for all } z \in K.$$

The statement of the quasi-variational inequality (2.24) covers evolutionary inequality problems due to the presence of the possibly unbounded operator L whose prototype is the time derivative $L(x) = x'$, with $X = L^p(0, T, V)$, with $1 < p < +\infty$, $T > 0$, and a reflexive Banach space V.

NOTES

1. Ky Fan (1914–2010) was a student of Maurice Fréchet and was also influenced by John von Neumann and Hermann Weyl. His work in fixed point theory, in addition to influencing nonlinear functional analysis, has found wide application in mathematical economics and game theory, potential theory, calculus of variations, and differential equations. In 1999, Fan and his wife donated one million US dollars to the American Mathematical Society, to set up the Ky and Yu-Fen Fan Endowment.

2. Felix Browder (1927–2016) was an American mathematician with pioneering contributions in nonlinear functional analysis. He received the National Medal of Science in 1999. He also served as president of the American Mathematical Society from 1999 to 2000.

Chapter 3

Mathematical Tools for Solving Equilibrium Problems

Contents

The object of pure physics is the unfolding of the laws of the intelligible world; the object of pure mathematics that of unfolding the laws of human intelligence.

James Joseph Sylvester (1814–1897)

Chapter points

- The two basic methods serving to show existence results for the equilibrium problems, KKM (fixed point) method and separation (Hahn-Banach) method are discussed.
- The equivalence of several fixed point results starting from Brouwer's theorem, including KKM and Schauder's fixed point theorem, is shown.
- The equivalence chain of several minimax results to the finite dimensional separation theorem is proved.

3.1 KKM THEORY AND RELATED BACKGROUND

Regarding the KKM method, we have seen in Chapter 1 how Brouwer's fixed point theorem (Theorem 1.1) can be proven by the KKM lemma (Lemma 1.2). An extension of the Brouwer's fixed point theorem to general (infinite dimensional) normed spaces has been provided by J. Schauder[1] and of KKM lemma for (infinite dimensional) Hausdorff topological vector spaces by Ky Fan.[2] In

Equilibrium Problems and Applications. https://doi.org/10.1016/B978-0-12-811029-4.00011-0

this section we show that all these results form an equivalent chain, including the first result on existence of (EP), known in the literature as Ky Fan's minimax inequality theorem, by reasoning as follows: we reproduce a general intersection theorem of KKM type whose proof is based on Brouwer's fixed point theorem (Theorem 3.1 below)[3] containing, in particular, Ky Fan's intersection theorem (Theorem 3.2 below). The latter serves to prove Ky Fan's minimax inequality theorem (Theorem 3.3 below), from which one can easily deduce the Schauder's fixed point theorem (Theorem 3.5 below). Then, as mentioned, we arrive back to Brouwer's fixed point theorem, the latter being a finite dimensional version of Schauder's fixed point theorem.

3.1.1 KKM and Generalized KKM Mappings

Let E and E' be two real Hausdorff topological vector spaces and X a subset of E. A set-valued mapping $F : X \rightrightarrows E$ is said to be a KKM mapping if for every finite subset $\{x_1, \ldots, x_n\}$ of X, we have

$$\operatorname{conv}\{x_1, \ldots x_n\} \subset \bigcup_{i=1}^{n} F(x_i).$$

A slightly more general concept was introduced by Kassay and Kolumbán [100] and, independently by Chang and Zhang [55]:

Definition 3.1. The mapping $F : X \to 2^{E'}$ is called *generalized KKM mapping*, if for any finite set $\{x_1, \ldots, x_n\} \subset X$, there exists a finite set $\{y_1, \ldots, y_n\} \subset E'$, such that for any subset $\{y_{i_1}, \ldots, y_{i_k}\} \subset \{y_1, \ldots, y_n\}$, we have

$$conv\{y_{i_1}, \ldots, y_{i_k}\} \subset \cup_{j=1}^{k} F(x_{i_j}). \tag{3.1}$$

It is clear that every KKM mapping is a generalized KKM mapping too. The converse of this implication is not true, as the following example shows.

Example 3.1. ([55]) Let $E = E' := \mathbb{R}$, $X := [-2, 2]$ and $F : X \to 2^E$ be defined by

$$F(x) := [-(1 + x^2/5), \ 1 + x^2/5].$$

Since $\cup_{x \in X} F(x) = [-9/5, 9/5]$, we have

$$x \notin F(x), \quad \forall x \in [-2, -9/5) \cup (9/5, 1].$$

This shows that F is not a KKM mapping. On the other hand, for any finite subset $\{x_1, \ldots, x_n\} \subset X$, take $\{y_1, \ldots, y_n\} \subset [-1, 1]$. Then for any $\{y_{i_1}, \ldots, y_{i_k}\} \subset \{y_1, \ldots, y_n\}$ we have

$$conv\{y_{i_1}, \ldots, y_{i_k}\} \subset [-1, 1] = \cap_{x \in X} F(x) \subset \cup_{j=1}^{k} F(x_{i_j}),$$

i.e., F is a generalized KKM mapping.

The importance of the concept of generalized KKM mapping consists on the following. While KKM property of a mapping is only a sufficient, but not a necessary condition for nonemptiness of the intersection, i.e., $\cap_{x \in X} F(x) \neq \emptyset$, the generalized KKM property will also be necessary (under some basic assumptions) for the latter. This will be clarified in the next subsection.

3.1.2   Intersection Theorems of KKM and Ky Fan Type

We start with the most general statement with respect to intersections.

Theorem 3.1. (See [100,55]) *Suppose that E is a real Hausdorff topological vector space, $X \subset E$ is nonempty, and $F : X \to 2^E$ is a mapping such that for each $x \in X$ the set $F(x)$ is finitely closed (i.e., for every finite dimensional subspace L of E, $F(x) \cap L$ is closed in the Euclidean topology in L). Then F is a generalized KKM mapping if and only if the family $\{F(x) : x \in I\}$ has the finite intersection property, i.e., for every finite subset $I \subset X$ the intersection of the subfamily $\{F(x) : x \in I\}$ is nonempty.*

Proof. Suppose first that for arbitrary finite set $I = \{x_1, ..., x_n\} \subset X$ one has

$$\cap_{i=1}^n F(x_i) \neq \emptyset.$$

Take $x_* \in \cap_{i=1}^n F(x_i)$ and put $y_i := x_*$, for each $i \in \{1, ..., n\}$. Then for every $\{y_{i_1}, ..., y_{i_k}\} \subset \{y_1, ..., y_n\}$ we have

$$conv\{y_{i_1}, ..., y_{i_k}\} = \{x_*\} \subset \cap_{i=1}^n F(x_i) \subset \cap_{j=1}^k F(x_{i_j}).$$

This implies that F is a generalized KKM mapping.

To show the reverse implication, let $F : X \to 2^E$ be a generalized KKM mapping. Supposing the contrary, there exists some finite set $\{x_1, ..., x_n\} \subset X$ such that $\cap_{i=1}^n F(x_i) = \emptyset$. By the assumption, there exists a set $\{y_1, ..., y_n\} \subset E$ such that for any $\{y_{i_1}, ..., y_{i_k}\} \subset \{y_1, ..., y_n\}$, relation (3.1) holds. In particular, we have

$$conv\{y_1, ..., y_n\} \subset \cup_{i=1}^n F(x_i).$$

Let $S := conv\{y_1, ..., y_n\}$ and $L := span\{y_1, ..., y_n\}$. Since for each $x \in X$, $F(x)$ is finitely closed, then the sets $F(x_i) \cap L$ are closed. Let d be the Euclidean metric on L. It is easy to verify that

$$d(x, F(x_i) \cap L) > 0 \quad \text{if and only if} \quad x \notin F(x_i) \cap L. \qquad (3.2)$$

Define now the function $g : S \to \mathbb{R}$ by

$$g(c) := \sum_{i=1}^n d(c, F(x_i) \cap L), \quad c \in S.$$

It follows by (3.2) and $\cap_{i=1}^n F(x_i) = \emptyset$ that for each $c \in S$, $g(c) > 0$. Let

$$h(c) := \sum_{i=1}^{n} \frac{1}{g(c)} d(c, F(x_i) \cap L) y_i.$$

Then h is a continuous function from S to S. By the Brouwer's fixed point theorem (Theorem 1.1), there exists an element $c_* \in S$ such that

$$c_* = h(c_*) = \sum_{i=1}^{n} \frac{1}{g(c_*)} d(c_*, F(x_i) \cap L) y_i. \tag{3.3}$$

Denote

$$I := \{ i \in \{1, ..., n\} : d(c_*, F(x_i) \cap L) > 0 \}. \tag{3.4}$$

Then for each $i \in I$, $c_* \notin F(x_i) \cap L$. Since $c_* \in L$, then $c_* \notin F(x_i)$ for each $i \in I$, or, in other words,

$$c_* \notin \cup_{i \in I} F(x_i). \tag{3.5}$$

By (3.3) and (3.4) we have

$$c_* = \sum_{i=1}^{n} \frac{1}{g(c_*)} d(c_*, F(x_i) \cap L) y_i \in conv\{y_i : i \in I\}.$$

Since F is a generalized KKM mapping, this leads to

$$c_* \in \cup_{i \in I} F(x_i),$$

which contradicts (3.5). This completes the proof. $\qquad\square$

Let us observe that by Theorem 3.1 one can easily deduce KKM lemma (Lemma 1.2) already discussed in Chapter 1 and proved by Sperner's lemma, recalled below.

Lemma 3.1. *(KKM lemma, see Lemma 1.2 in Chapter 1) Let $S = conv\{u_0, ..., u_N\}$ be an N-simplex in a finite dimensional normed space, where $N = 0, 1, ...$ Suppose that we are given closed sets $C_0, ..., C_N$ in X such that*

$$conv\{u_{i_0}, ..., u_{i_k}\} \subseteq \cup_{m=0}^{k} C_{i_m}, \tag{3.6}$$

for all possible systems of indices $\{i_0, ..., i_k\}$ and all $k = 0, ..., N$. Then $\cap_{j=0}^{N} C_j \neq \emptyset$.

Proof. Let $X =: \{u_0, ..., u_N\}$ and F given by $F(u_k) = C_k$ for all $k = 0, ..., N$. Then clearly F is a KKM mapping and the result follows by Theorem 3.1. $\quad\square$

Remark 3.1. It can be seen from the proof above that in KKM lemma the assumption of S to be a simplex is not essential, i.e., the lemma is valid for any finite set S.

The next result, known in the literature as Ky Fan's intersection theorem, is an immediate consequence of Lemma 3.1.

Theorem 3.2. (Ky Fan, 1961 [73]) *Let E be a real Hausdorff topological vector space, $X \subset E$ and for each $x \in X$, let $F(x)$ be a closed subset of E, such that*

(i) *there exists $\bar{x} \in X$, such that the set $F(\bar{x})$ is compact;*
(ii) *F is a KKM mapping.*

Then

$$\cap_{x \in X} F(x) \neq \emptyset.$$

Proof. Consider the family $G(x) := F(\bar{x}) \cap F(x)$ $(x \in X)$ in the compact space $F(\bar{x})$. Clearly, $\cap_{x \in X} G(x) = \cap_{x \in X} F(x)$, hence it is enough to check that $\cap_{x \in X} G(x) \neq \emptyset$. Using the characterization of compact spaces (Proposition 1.1), the latter amounts to show that the family $\{G(x) : x \in X\}$ has the finite intersection property, or, equivalently, the family $\{F(x) : x \in X\}$ has the finite intersection property. So let $\{x_0, ..., x_N\} \subset X$ and let Y be the finite dimensional subspace of X spanned by $\{x_0, ..., x_N\}$. Taking into account Remark 3.1 the sets $C_i := F(x_i) \cap \mathrm{conv}\{x_0, ..., x_N\}$ $(i = 0, ..., N)$ satisfy the assumptions of Lemma 3.1. Hence,

$$\emptyset \neq \cap_{i=0}^{N} C_i \subset \cap_{i=0}^{N} F(x_i). \qquad \square$$

3.1.3 The Rudiment for Solving Equilibrium Problems. Fixed Point Theorems

By means of Ky Fan's lemma (Theorem 3.2) one can prove the following existence result for (EP), also due to Ky Fan. This is known in the literature as *Ky Fan's minimax inequality theorem*. As far as we know, it is the first result concerning (EP).

Theorem 3.3. (Ky Fan, 1972 [74]) *Let A be a nonempty, convex, compact subset of a real Hausdorff topological vector space and let $f : A \times A \to \mathbb{R}$, such that*

$$\forall b \in A, \quad f(\cdot, b) : A \to \mathbb{R} \text{ is upper semicontinuous,} \qquad (3.7)$$

$$\forall a \in A, \quad f(a, \cdot) : A \to \mathbb{R} \text{ is quasi-convex} \qquad (3.8)$$

and

$$\forall a \in A, \quad f(a, a) \geq 0. \qquad (3.9)$$

Then there exists $\bar{a} \in A$ such that $f(\bar{a}, b) \geq 0$ for all $b \in A$, i.e., the equilibrium problem (EP) defined by f admits a solution.

Proof. For each $b \in A$, consider the set $F(b) := \{a \in A : f(a, b) \geq 0\}$. By (3.7), these sets are closed, and since A is compact, they are compact too. It is easy to see that the conclusion of the theorem is equivalent to

$$\cap_{b \in A} F(b) \neq \emptyset. \tag{3.10}$$

In order to prove relation (3.10), let $b_1, b_2, ..., b_n \in A$. We show that

$$conv\{b_i : i \in \{1, 2, ..., n\}\} \subset \cup_{i=1}^n F(b_i). \tag{3.11}$$

Indeed, suppose by contradiction that there exist $\lambda_1, \lambda_2, ..., \lambda_n \geq 0$, $\sum_{j=1}^n \lambda_j = 1$, such that

$$\sum_{j=1}^n \lambda_j b_j \notin \cup_{j=1}^n F(b_j).$$

By definition, the latter means

$$f(\sum_{j=1}^n \lambda_j b_j, b_i) < 0, \quad \forall i \in \{1, 2, ..., n\}.$$

By (3.8) (quasi-convexity), one obtains

$$f(\sum_{j=1}^n \lambda_j b_j, \sum_{j=1}^n \lambda_j b_j) < 0,$$

which contradicts (3.9). This shows that (3.11) holds. Now applying Theorem 3.2, we obtain (3.10), which completes the proof. $\quad\square$

In order to deduce Schauder's fixed point theorem, we first need the following result.

Theorem 3.4. *Let E be a normed space, $X \subset E$ be a compact convex set and $g, h : X \to E$ be continuous functions such that*

$$\|x - g(x)\| \geq \|x - h(x)\|, \quad \forall x \in X. \tag{3.12}$$

Then there exists an element $\bar{x} \in X$, such that

$$\|y - g(\bar{x})\| \geq \|\bar{x} - h(\bar{x})\|, \quad \forall y \in X.$$

Proof. Let $f : X \times X \to \mathbb{R}$ defined by $f(x, y) := \|y - g(x)\| - \|x - h(x)\|$. It is clear that this function satisfies the hypothesis of Theorem 3.3, thus there exists an element $\bar{x} \in X$ such that

$$\|\bar{x} - h(\bar{x})\| \leq \|y - g(\bar{x})\|, \quad \forall y \in X. \tag{3.13}$$

This completes the proof. $\qquad\qquad\qquad\qquad\qquad\qquad\qquad\qquad\qquad\square$

Observe, in case $g(X) \subset X$, we can put $y := g(\bar{x})$ in (3.13); in this way we obtain that $\bar{x}$ is a fixed point of f. Now it is immediate the well-known Schauder's fixed point theorem:

Theorem 3.5. (J. Schauder, 1930 [158]) *Let X be a convex compact subset of a real normed space and $h : X \to X$ a continuous function. Then h has a fixed point.*

3.2   SEPARATION AND RELATED RESULTS

As mentioned at the beginning of this chapter, another tool for proving existence results for the equilibrium problem (EP) is the separation of convex sets by hyperplanes. There are different kinds of separation, all of them represent the geometric form of the celebrated Hahn-Banach theorem. In what follows we use only separations in finite dimensional spaces, they may appear also in different forms as strong separation, or proper separation, for instance. We show that using a proper separation theorem in finite dimensional spaces allows us to prove existence results for (EP) in rather general framework (for instance, in topological vector spaces, or, even more, in just topological spaces).

We have seen in Chapter 2 that the minimax (saddle point) problem is a particular case of (EP). In this section we also show that known minimax results, some of them being cornerstones of noncooperative game theory, form an equivalent chain together with the strong separation theorem in finite dimensional spaces.

3.2.1   Finite Dimensional Separation of Convex Sets

Consider the following optimization problem, known as the problem of best approximation:

$$\vartheta(y) := \inf\{\|x - y\|^2 : x \in C\}, \tag{$P(y)$}$$

where $C \subset \mathbb{R}^n$ is a nonempty convex set and $y \in \mathbb{R}^n$.

Lemma 3.2. *If C is closed, then $(P(y))$ has a unique solution, called the metric projection of y to C, denoted by $P_C y$.*

Proof. Let $f(x) = \|x - y\|$ and $r > 0$ such that $D := \overline{B}(y, r) \cap C \neq \emptyset$, where $\overline{B}(y, r) = \{x \in \mathbb{R}^n : \|x - y\| \leq r\}$. Since D is compact and f is continuous on D, f admits a minimum point on D which clearly is a minimum point on C, too. Hence $(P(y))$ has a solution. For the uniqueness, suppose by contradiction that $x_1 \neq x_2$ are optimal solutions of $(P(y))$. We use the Parallelogram Law:

$$\|z_1 + z_2\|^2 + \|z_1 - z_2\|^2 = 2\|z_1\|^2 + 2\|z_2\|^2, \ \forall z_1, z_2 \in \mathbb{R}^n, \tag{3.14}$$

with $z_i = x_i - y$ $(i = 1, 2)$. Since C is convex, $\frac{1}{2}(x_1 + x_2) \in C$ and thus:

$$\left\|\frac{1}{2}(x_1 + x_2) - y\right\|^2 < \frac{1}{2}\|x_1 - y\|^2 + \frac{1}{2}\|x_2 - y\|^2 = \vartheta(y),$$

a contradiction. $\qquad\square$

A useful characterization of the metric projection is provided by the next result.

Lemma 3.3. *For every $y \in \mathbb{R}^n$ and $C \subset \mathbb{R}^n$ nonempty closed convex set, one has*

$$z = P_C y \Leftrightarrow z \in C \text{ and } (z - y)^T (x - z) \geq 0, \text{ for all } x \in C.$$

Furthermore, for all $x \in C$:

$$\|x - P_C y\|^2 + \|P_C y - y\|^2 \leq \|x - y\|^2.$$

Proof. To show the only if implication we observe that

$$0 \leq (z - y)^T (x - z) = -\|z - y\|^2 + (z - y)^T (x - y),$$

therefore, by the Cauchy-Schwartz inequality

$$0 \leq (z - y)^T (x - z) \leq -\|z - y\|^2 + \|z - y\|\|x - y\|, \tag{3.15}$$

for all $x \in C$.

Case 1. If $y \in C$, then taking $x = y$ in (3.15), we obtain that $0 \leq -\|z - y\|^2$, hence $\|z - y\|^2 = 0$. Since $y \in C$, it follows that $z = y = P_C y$.

Case 2. If $y \notin C$, then $\|z - y\| > 0$, hence by (3.15) $\|z - y\| \leq \|x - y\|$, for all $x \in C$. Therefore z is an optimal solution of $(P(y))$ and by uniqueness we get that $z = P_C y$.

To verify the if implication, it follows for $z = P_C y$ that $z \in C$, and since C is convex this shows

$$\|z - y\|^2 \leq \|\alpha x + (1 - \alpha)z - y\|^2 = \|z - y + \alpha(x - z)\|^2, \tag{3.16}$$

for all $x \in C$ and $0 < \alpha < 1$. Rewriting relation (3.16) we obtain for every $0 < \alpha < 1$ that

$$2(z - y)^T (x - z) + \alpha \|x - z\|^2 \geq 0, \tag{3.17}$$

and letting $\alpha \to 0$, the desired inequality follows. To show the triangle inequality, we observe using $\|z_1\|^2 - \|z_2\|^2 = \langle z_1 - z_2, z_1 + z_2 \rangle$, for every z_1, z_2 that

$$\|x - p_C(y)\|^2 - \|x - y\|^2 = \langle y - p_C(y), 2x - y - p_C(y) \rangle. \tag{3.18}$$

The last term equals $-\|y - p_C(y)\|^2 + 2\langle y - p_C(y), x - p_C(y) \rangle$ and applying now the first part yields the desired inequality. $\qquad \square$

An immediate consequence of the lemma above is the strong separation theorem (in finite dimensional spaces).

Theorem 3.6. *If $C \subset \mathbb{R}^n$ is a nonempty convex set and $y \notin cl(C)$, then there exists a nonzero vector $y_0 \in \mathbb{R}^n$ and $\epsilon > 0$ such that $y_0^T x \geq y_0^T y + \epsilon$, for all $x \in cl(C)$. In particular, the vector $y_0 := p_{cl(C)}(y) - y$ satisfies the inequality.*

Proof. By Lemma 3.3 we obtain for every $x \in cl(C)$ and the nonzero vector $y_0 := P_{cl(C)}(y) - y$ that $y_0^T x \geq y_0^T P_{cl(C)}(y)$. This shows

$$y_0^T x \geq \|y_0\|^2 + y_0^T y \tag{3.19}$$

and since $y_0 \neq 0$, the desired result follows. $\qquad \square$

Remark 3.2. The nonzero vector $y_0 \in cl(C) - y$ is called the normal vector of the separating hyperplane

$$H(\mathbf{a}, a) := \{x \in \mathbb{R}^n : \mathbf{a}^T x = a\},$$

with $\mathbf{a} = y_0$ and $a = y_0^T y + \frac{\epsilon}{2}$. Since $y_0 \neq 0$, we may take as a normal vector of the hyperplane the vector $y_0 \|y_0\|^{-1}$, and this vector has norm 1 and belongs to $cone(cl(C) - y)$.

The separation of Theorem 3.6 is called a strong separation between the set C and the vector y. One can also introduce strong separation between two convex sets.

The sets $C_1, C_2 \subset \mathbb{R}^n$ are called strongly separated if there exist some $y_0 \in \mathbb{R}^n$ such that

$$\inf_{x \in C_1} y_0^T x > \sup_{x \in C_2} y_0^T x.$$

An immediate consequence of Theorem 3.6 is given by the next result.

Theorem 3.7. *Consider the convex sets $C_1, C_2 \subset \mathbb{R}^n$ such that C_1 is compact, C_2 is closed and $C_1 \cap C_2 = \emptyset$. Then they can be strongly separated.*

Proof. The set $C := C_1 - C_2$ is closed and $0 \notin C$. The result follows by Theorem 3.6. □

The strong separation provided by Theorem 3.6 can be used to prove a "weaker" separation result valid under a weaker condition on the point y. To do this, let us first recall the concept of relative interior point.

Let $E := \{x \in \mathbb{R}^n : \|x\| < 1\}$ be the unit open ball. The vector $x \in \mathbb{R}^n$ is a relative interior point of the set $S \subset \mathbb{R}^n$ if $x \in aff(S)$ and there exists $\epsilon > 0$ such that

$$(x + \epsilon E) \cap aff(S) \subset S.$$

The relative interior of S is denoted by $ri(S)$ and is given by

$$ri(S) := \{x \in \mathbb{R}^n : x \text{ is a relative interior point of } S\}.$$

In order to prove the following separation theorem, we need the next two lemmas. For their proofs, see Frenk and Kassay [77].

Lemma 3.4. *If $C \subset \mathbb{R}^n$ is a nonempty convex set, then*

$$cl(ri(C)) = cl(C) \quad and \quad ri(C) = ri(cl(C)).$$

Lemma 3.5. *For every nonempty set $S \subset \mathbb{R}^n$ and $x_0 \in aff(S)$ one has*

$$aff(S) = x_0 + lin(S - x_0).$$

Theorem 3.8. *If $C \subset \mathbb{R}^n$ is a nonempty convex set and $y \notin ri(C)$, then there exists some nonzero vector y_0 belonging to the unique linear subspace $L_{aff(C)}$ such that $y_0^T x \geq y_0^T y$, for all $x \in C$. Moreover, for the vector y_0 there exists some $x_0 \in C$ such that $y_0^T x_0 > y_0^T y$.*

Proof. Consider for every $n \in \mathbb{N}$ the set $(y + n^{-1}E) \cap aff(cl(C))$, where $E := \{x \in \mathbb{R}^n : \|x\| < 1\}$. By Lemma 3.4 it follows that $y \notin ri(cl(C))$ and so there exists some vector y_n such that

$$y_n \notin cl(C) \quad and \quad y_n \in (y + n^{-1}E) \cap aff(cl(C)). \tag{3.20}$$

The set $cl(C)$ is a closed convex set and by relation (3.20) and Theorem 3.6 one can find some vector $y_n^* \in \mathbb{R}^n$ such that

$$\|y_n^*\| = 1, \quad y_n^* \in cone(cl(C) - y_n) \subset L_{aff(C)} \quad and \quad y_n^{*T} x \geq y_n^{*T} y_n, \tag{3.21}$$

for every $x \in cl(C)$.

Since $\|y_n^*\| = 1$, it follows that $\{y_n^* : n \in \mathbb{N}\}$ admits a convergent subsequence $\{y_n^* : n \in N_0\}$ with

$$\lim_{n \in N_0 \to \infty} y_n^* = y_0. \tag{3.22}$$

This implies by relations (3.20), (3.21) and (3.22) that

$$y_0^T x = \lim_{n \in N_0 \to \infty} y_n^{*T} x \geq \lim_{n \in N_0 \to \infty} y_n^{*T} y_n = y_0^T y, \tag{3.23}$$

for all $x \in cl(C)$ and

$$y_0 \in L_{aff(C)} \quad \text{and} \quad \|y_0\| = 1. \tag{3.24}$$

Suppose now that there does not exist some $x_0 \in C$, satisfying $y_0^T x_0 > y_0^T y$. By relation (3.23) this implies that

$$y_0^T (x - y) = 0,$$

for every $x \in C$. Since $y \in cl(C) \subset aff(C)$, using Lemma 3.5 we obtain

$$y_0^T z = 0$$

for every $z \in L_{aff(C)}$. Since by relation (3.24) the vector $y_0 \in L_{aff(C)}$, we obtain that $\|y_0\|^2 = 0$, contradicting $\|y_0\| = 1$. Hence it must follow that there exists some $x_0 \in C$ such that $y_0^T x_0 > y_0^T y$. $\qquad \square$

The separation of Theorem 3.8 is called a proper separation between the set C and the vector y. One can also introduce proper separation between two convex sets.

The sets $C_1, C_2 \subset \mathbb{R}^n$ are called properly separated if there exist some $y_0 \in \mathbb{R}^n$ such that

$$\inf_{x \in C_1} y_0^T x \geq \sup_{x \in C_2} y_0^T x$$

and

$$y_0^T x_1 > y_0^T x_2,$$

where $x_1 \in C_1$ and $x_2 \in C_2$.

An immediate consequence of Theorem 3.8 is given by the next result.

Theorem 3.9. *If the convex sets $C_1, C_2 \subset \mathbb{R}^n$ satisfy $ri(C_1) \cap ri(C_2) = \emptyset$, then they can be properly separated.*

Proof. We have the following relation:

$$ri(\alpha S_1 + \beta S_2) = \alpha ri(S_1) + \beta ri(S_2),$$

where $\alpha, \beta \in \mathbb{R}$ and $S_i \subset \mathbb{R}^n$, $i = 1, 2$ are convex sets. According to this, we obtain for $\alpha = 1$ and $\beta = -1$ that

$$ri(C_1 - C_2) = ri(C_1) - ri(C_2).$$

Then $ri(C_1) \cap ri(C_2) = \emptyset$ if and only if

$$0 \notin ri(C_1) - ri(C_2).$$

By Theorem 3.8 applying for $y = 0$ and the convex set $C_1 - C_2$, the result follows. □

3.2.2 Results Based on Separation

As announced at the beginning of this section, we present now some existence results on (EP) which uses separation tools in their proofs.

The result below is a particular case of a theorem due to Kassay and Kolumbán ([101]).

Theorem 3.10. *Let A be a nonempty, compact, convex subset of a certain topological vector space, let B be a nonempty convex subset of a certain vector space, and let $f : A \times B \to \mathbb{R}$ be a given function.*

Suppose that the following assertions are satisfied:

(i) *f is upper semicontinuous and concave in its first variable;*
(ii) *f is convex in its second variable;*
(iii) $\sup_{a \in A} f(a, b) \geq 0$, *for all $b \in B$.*

Then the equilibrium problem (EP) has a solution.

Remark 3.3. Condition (iii) in the previous theorem is satisfied if, for instance, $B \subseteq A$ and $f(a, a) \geq 0$ for each $a \in B$. This condition arises naturally in most of the particular cases presented above.

A similar, but more general existence result for the problem (EP) has been established by Kassay and Kolumbán also in [101], where instead of the convexity (concavity) assumptions on the function f, certain kind of generalized convexity (concavity) assumptions are supposed.

Theorem 3.11. *Let A be a compact topological space, let B be a nonempty set, and let $f : A \times B \to \mathbb{R}$ be a given function such that*

(i) *for each $b \in B$, the function $\varphi : A \to \mathbb{R}$ is usc;*
(ii) *for each $a_1, ..., a_m \in A$, $b_1, ..., b_k \in B$, $\lambda_1, ..., \lambda_m \geq 0$ with $\sum_{i=1}^{m} \lambda_i = 1$, the inequality*

$$\min_{1 \leq j \leq k} \sum_{i=1}^{m} \lambda_i f(a_i, b_j) \leq \sup_{a \in A} \min_{1 \leq j \leq k} f(a, b_j)$$

holds;

(iii) *For each $b_1, ..., b_k \in B$, $\mu_1, ..., \mu_k \geq 0$ with $\sum_{j=1}^{k} \mu_j = 1$, one has*

$$\sup_{a \in A} \sum_{j=1}^{k} \mu_j f(a, b_j) \geq 0.$$

Then the equilibrium problem (EP) admits a solution.

Proof. Suppose by contradiction that (EP) has no solution, i.e., for each $a \in A$ there exists $b \in B$ such that $f(a, b) < 0$, or equivalently, for each $a \in A$ there exists $b \in B$ and $c > 0$ such that $f(a, b) + c < 0$. Denote by $U_{b,c}$ the set $\{a \in A : f(a, b) + c < 0\}$ where $b \in B$ and $c > 0$. By (i) and our assumption, the family of these sets is an open covering of the compact set A. Therefore, one can select a finite subfamily which covers the same set A, i.e., there exist $b_1, ..., b_k \in B$ and $c_1, ..., c_k > 0$ such that

$$A = \cup_{j=1}^{k} U_{b_j, c_j}. \tag{3.25}$$

Let $c := \min\{c_1, ..., c_k\} > 0$ and define the vector-valued function $H : A \to \mathbb{R}^k$ by

$$H(a) := (f(a, b_1) + c, ..., f(a, b_k) + c).$$

We show that

$$\operatorname{conv} H(A) \cap \operatorname{int}(\mathbb{R}_+^k) = \emptyset, \tag{3.26}$$

where, as before, $\operatorname{conv} H(A)$ denotes the convex hull of the set $H(A)$ and $\operatorname{int}(\mathbb{R}_+^k)$ denotes the interior of the positive orthant $\mathbb{R}_+^k$. Indeed, supposing the contrary, there exist $a_1, ..., a_m \in A$ and $\lambda_1, ..., \lambda_m \geq 0$ with $\sum_{i=1}^{m} \lambda_i = 1$, such that

$$\sum_{i=1}^{m} \lambda_i H(a_i) \in \operatorname{int}(\mathbb{R}_+^k)$$

or, equivalently,

$$\sum_{i=1}^{m} \lambda_i (f(a_i, b_j) + c) > 0, \ \forall j \in \{1, ..., k\}. \tag{3.27}$$

By (ii), (3.27) implies

$$\sup_{a \in A} \min_{1 \leq j \leq k} f(a, b_j) > -c. \tag{3.28}$$

Now using (3.25), for each $a \in A$ there exists $j \in \{1, ..., k\}$ such that $f(a, b_j) + c_j < 0$. Thus, for each $a \in A$ we have

$$\min_{1 \leq j \leq k} f(a, b_j) < -c,$$

which contradicts (3.28). This shows that relation (3.26) is true. By the proper separation theorem in finite dimensional spaces (Theorem 3.8), the sets $\operatorname{conv} H(A)$ and $\operatorname{int}(\mathbb{R}^k_+)$ can be separated by a hyperplane, i.e., there exist $\mu_1, ..., \mu_k \geq 0$ such that $\sum_{j=1}^k \mu_j = 1$ and

$$\sum_{j=1}^k \mu_j (f(a, b_j) + c) \leq 0, \ \forall a \in A,$$

or, equivalently

$$\sum_{j=1}^k \mu_j f(a, b_j) \leq -c, \ \forall a \in A. \tag{3.29}$$

Observe, the latter relation contradicts assumption (iii) of the theorem. Thus the proof is complete. $\qquad\square$

3.2.3 Equivalent Chain of Minimax Theorems Based on Separation Tools

In this subsection we review known minimax results, some of them being the cornerstones of noncooperative game theory and show that these results are easy consequences of the first minimax result for a two person zero sum game with finite strategy sets published by von Neumann[4] in 1928 (see [168]).

According to [79], several well known minimax theorems form an equivalent chain and this chain includes the strong separation result in finite dimensional spaces between two disjoint closed convex sets of which one is compact (Theorem 3.7). The authors in [78] reduced the number of results in this equivalent chain and gave more transparent and simpler proofs. These results will be presented in the sequel.

Let X and Y be nonempty sets and $f : X \times Y \to \mathbb{R}$ a given function. Recall that a minimax result is a theorem which asserts that

$$\max_{x \in X} \min_{y \in Y} f(x, y) = \min_{y \in Y} \max_{x \in X} f(x, y). \tag{3.30}$$

In case min and/or max are not attained the min and/or max in the above expressions are replaced by inf and/or sup. The first minimax result was proved in a famous paper by von Neumann (cf. [168]) in 1928 for X and Y unit simplices in finite dimensional vector spaces and f affine in both variables. In this paper it was also shown why such a result is of importance in game theory. The minimax results needed in noncooperative game theory assumed that the sets X and Y represented sets of probability measures with finite support and the function f was taken to be affine in both variables. Later on, the condition on the function f was weakened and more general sets X and Y were considered. These results turned out to be useful also in optimization theory and were derived by means of short or long proofs using a version of the Hahn Banach theorem in either finite or infinite dimensional vector spaces. With the famous minimax result in game theory proved by von Neumann in 1928 (cf. [168]) as a starting point, we will show in this subsection that several of these so-called generalizations published in the literature can be derived from each other using only elementary observations. Before introducing this chain of equivalent minimax results we need the following notation. Let $\mathcal{F}(X)$ denote the set of probability measures on X with finite support. That is, if ϵ_x represents the one-point probability measure concentrated on X, this means by definition that $\lambda \in \mathcal{F}(X)$ if and only if there exists some finite set $\{x_1, ..., x_n\} \subseteq X$ and a sequence λ_i, $1 \leq i \leq n$ satisfying

$$\lambda = \sum_{i=1}^{n} \lambda_i \epsilon_{x_i}, \quad \sum_{i=1}^{n} \lambda_i = 1 \text{ and } \lambda_i > 0, 1 \leq i \leq n. \tag{3.31}$$

If the set X is given by $\{x_1, ..., x_n\}$ then it is clear that

$$\mathcal{F}(X) = \{\lambda : \lambda = \sum_{i=1}^{n} \lambda_i \epsilon_{x_i}, \sum_{i=1}^{n} \lambda_i = 1, \lambda_i \geq 0, 1 \leq i \leq n\}. \tag{3.32}$$

Moreover, the set $\mathcal{F}_2(X) \subseteq \mathcal{F}(X)$ denotes the set of two-point probability measures on X. This means that λ belongs to $\mathcal{F}_2(X)$ if and only if

$$\lambda = \lambda_1 \epsilon_{x_1} + (1 - \lambda_1) \epsilon_{x_2} \tag{3.33}$$

with x_i, $1 \leq i \leq 2$ different elements of X and $0 < \lambda_1 < 1$ arbitrarily chosen. Finally, for each $0 < \alpha < 1$ the set $\mathcal{F}_{2,\alpha}(X)$ represents the set of two point probability measures with $\lambda_1 = \alpha$ in relation (3.33). Also on the set Y similar spaces of probability measures with finite support are introduced. Within game theory any element of $\mathcal{F}(X)$, respectively $\mathcal{F}(Y)$ represents a so-called mixed strategy of player 1, respectively player 2 and to measure the payoff using those mixed strategies one needs to extend the so-called payoff function f to the Cartesian product of the sets $\mathcal{F}(X)$ and $\mathcal{F}(Y)$. The extension $f_e : \mathcal{F}(X) \times \mathcal{F}(Y) \to \mathbb{R}$ is defined by the expectation

$$f_e(\lambda, \mu) := \sum_{i=1}^{n} \sum_{j=1}^{m} \lambda_i \mu_j f(x_i, y_j) \tag{3.34}$$

with λ as in relation (3.31) and $\mu = \sum_{j=1}^{m} \mu_j \epsilon_{y_j}$. To start in a chronological order we first mention the famous bilinear minimax result in game theory for finite sets X and Y due to von Neumann and published in 1928 (cf. [168]).

Theorem 3.12. *If X and Y are finite sets then it follows that*

$$\max_{\lambda \in \mathcal{F}(X)} \min_{\mu \in \mathcal{F}(Y)} f_e(\lambda, \mu) = \min_{\mu \in \mathcal{F}(Y)} \max_{\lambda \in \mathcal{F}(X)} f_e(\lambda, \mu).$$

A generalization of Theorem 3.12 due to Wald [170] and published in 1945 is given by the next result. This result plays a fundamental role in the theory of statistical decision functions (cf. [171]). While in case of Theorem 3.12 the action sets of players 1 and 2 are finite, this condition is relaxed in Wald's theorem claiming that only one set should be finite.

Theorem 3.13. *If X is an arbitrary nonempty set and Y is a finite set then it follows that*

$$\sup_{\lambda \in \mathcal{F}(X)} \min_{\mu \in \mathcal{F}(Y)} f_e(\lambda, \mu) = \min_{\mu \in \mathcal{F}(Y)} \sup_{\lambda \in \mathcal{F}(X)} f_e(\lambda, \mu).$$

In order to prove Wald's theorem by von Neumann's theorem, we first need the following elementary lemma. For its proof, see, for instance, [79]. For every set Y let $\langle Y \rangle$ be the set of all finite subsets of Y.

Lemma 3.6. *If the set X is compact and the function $h : X \times Y \to \mathbb{R}$ is upper semicontinuous on X for every $y \in Y$ then $\max_{x \in X} \inf_{y \in Y} h(x, y)$ is well defined and*

$$\max_{x \in X} \inf_{y \in Y} h(x, y) = \inf_{Y_0 \in \langle Y \rangle} \max_{x \in X} \min_{y \in Y_0} h(x, y).$$

Since for every $\mu \in \mathcal{F}(Y)$ and $J \subseteq X$ it is easy to see that

$$\sup_{\lambda \in \mathcal{F}(J)} f_e(\lambda, \mu) = \sup_{x \in J} f_e(\epsilon_x, \mu) \tag{3.35}$$

we are now ready to derive Wald's minimax result from von Neumann's minimax result. Observe Wald (cf. [170]) uses in his paper von Neumann's minimax result and the Lebesgue dominated convergence theorem to derive his result.

Theorem 3.14. *von Neumann's minimax result $\Rightarrow$ Wald's minimax result.*

Proof. If $\alpha := \sup_{\lambda \in \mathcal{F}(X)} \min_{\mu \in \mathcal{F}(Y)} f_e(\lambda, \mu)$ then clearly

$$\alpha = \sup_{J \in \langle X \rangle} \max_{\lambda \in \mathcal{F}(J)} \min_{\mu \in \mathcal{F}(Y)} f_e(\lambda, \mu). \tag{3.36}$$

Since the set Y is finite we may apply von Neumann's minimax result in relation (3.36) and this implies in combination with relation (3.35) that

$$\alpha = \sup_{J \in \langle X \rangle} \min_{\mu \in \mathcal{F}(Y)} \max_{\lambda \in \mathcal{F}(J)} f_e(\lambda, \mu) \tag{3.37}$$

$$= \sup_{J \in \langle X \rangle} \min_{\mu \in \mathcal{F}(Y)} \max_{x \in J} f_e(\epsilon_x, \mu)$$

$$= - \inf_{J \in \langle X \rangle} \max_{\mu \in \mathcal{F}(Y)} \min_{x \in J} -f_e(\epsilon_x, \mu).$$

The finiteness of the set Y also implies that the set $\mathcal{F}(Y)$ is compact and the function $\mu \to f_e(\epsilon_x, \mu)$ is continuous on $\mathcal{F}(Y)$ for every $x \in X$. This shows in relation (3.37) that we may apply Lemma 3.6 with the set X replaced by $\mathcal{F}(Y)$, Y by X and $h(x, y)$ by $-f_e(\epsilon_x, \mu)$ and so it follows that

$$\alpha = \min_{\mu \in \mathcal{F}(Y)} \sup_{x \in X} f_e(\epsilon_x, \mu). \tag{3.38}$$

Finally by relation (3.35) with J replaced by X the desired result follows from relation (3.38). $\square$

Next we will reformulate Theorem 3.11 of Kassay and Kolumbán ([101]) given in the previous subsection. Let us denote by $\langle Y \rangle$ the set of all finite subsets of Y.

Definition 3.2. The function $f : X \times Y \to \mathbb{R}$ is called weakly concavelike on X if for every I belonging to $\langle Y \rangle$ it follows that

$$\sup_{\lambda \in \mathcal{F}(X)} \min_{y \in I} f_e(\lambda, \epsilon_y) \leq \sup_{x \in X} \min_{y \in I} f(x, y).$$

Since ϵ_x belongs to $\mathcal{F}(X)$ it is easy to see that f is weakly concavelike on X if and only if for every $I \in \langle Y \rangle$ it follows that

$$\sup_{\lambda \in \mathcal{F}(X)} \min_{y \in I} f_e(\lambda, \epsilon_y) = \sup_{x \in X} \min_{y \in I} f(x, y)$$

and this equality also has an obvious interpretation within game theory. The main result of Kassay and Kolumbán is given by the following theorem (cf. [101]).

Theorem 3.15. *If X is a compact subset of a topological space and the function $f : X \times Y \to \mathbb{R}$ is weakly concavelike on X and upper semicontinuous on X for every $y \in Y$ then it follows that*

$$\inf_{\mu \in \mathcal{F}(Y)} \max_{x \in X} f_e(\epsilon_x, \mu) = \max_{x \in X} \inf_{y \in Y} f_e(x, y).$$

At first sight this result might not be recognized as a minimax result. However, it is easy to verify for every $x \in X$ that

$$\inf_{y \in Y} f(x, y) = \inf_{\mu \in \mathcal{F}(Y)} f_e(\epsilon_x, \mu). \tag{3.39}$$

By relation (3.39) an equivalent formulation of Theorem 3.15 is now given by

$$\inf_{\mu \in \mathcal{F}(Y)} \max_{x \in X} f_e(\epsilon_x, \mu) = \max_{x \in X} \inf_{\mu \in \mathcal{F}(Y)} f_e(\epsilon_x, \mu)$$

and so the result of Kassay and Kolumbán is actually a minimax result.

We now give an elementary proof for Theorem 3.15 using Wald's minimax theorem.

Proof. Denote $\alpha := \inf_{\mu \in \mathcal{F}(Y)} \max_{x \in X} f_e(\epsilon_x, \mu)$, $\beta := \max_{x \in X} \inf_{\mu \in \mathcal{F}(Y)} f_e(\epsilon_x, \mu)$ and suppose by contradiction that $\alpha > \beta$. (The inequality $\beta \leq \alpha$ always holds.) Let γ so that $\alpha > \gamma > \beta$. Then by relation (3.39) and Lemma 3.6 we have

$$\gamma > \beta = \max_{x \in X} \inf_{y \in Y} f(x, y) = \inf_{Y_0 \in \langle Y \rangle} \max_{x \in X} \min_{y \in Y_0} f(x, y).$$

Therefore, there exists a finite subset $Y_0 \in \langle Y \rangle$ such that $\max_{x \in X} \min_{y \in Y_0} f(x, y) < \gamma$ and this implies by weak concavelikeness that

$$\sup_{\lambda \in \mathcal{F}(X)} \min_{y \in Y_0} f_e(\lambda, \epsilon_y) < \gamma. \tag{3.40}$$

Similarly to relation (3.39), it is easy to see that for every $\lambda \in \mathcal{F}(X)$ and every $\mu \in \mathcal{F}(Y)$ the relations

$$\inf_{\mu \in \mathcal{F}(Y_0)} f_e(\lambda, \mu) = \min_{y \in Y_0} f_e(\lambda, \epsilon_y)$$

and

$$\sup_{\lambda \in \mathcal{F}(X)} f_e(\lambda, \mu) = \max_{x \in X} f_e(\epsilon_x, \mu)$$

hold, and these together with (3.40) and Wald's theorem imply

$$\alpha > \gamma > \sup_{\lambda \in \mathcal{F}(X)} \inf_{\mu \in \mathcal{F}(Y_0)} f_e(\lambda, \mu) = \inf_{\mu \in \mathcal{F}(Y_0)} \sup_{\lambda \in \mathcal{F}(X)} f_e(\lambda, \mu)$$
$$\geq \inf_{\mu \in \mathcal{F}(Y)} \sup_{\lambda \in \mathcal{F}(X)} f_e(\lambda, \mu) = \inf_{\mu \in \mathcal{F}(Y)} \max_{x \in X} f_e(\epsilon_x, \mu) = \alpha,$$

a contradiction. This completes the proof. □

In 1952 Kneser (cf. [110]) proved in a two page note a very general minimax result useful in game theory. Its proof is ingenious and very elementary and uses only some simple computations and the well-known result that any upper semicontinuous function attains its maximum on a compact set.

Theorem 3.16. (Kneser, 1952) *If X is a nonempty convex, compact subset of a topological vector space and Y is a nonempty convex subset of a vector space and the function $f : X \times Y \to \mathbb{R}$ is affine in both variables and upper semicontinuous on X for every $y \in Y$ then it follows that*

$$\max_{x \in X} \inf_{y \in Y} f(x, y) = \inf_{y \in Y} \max_{x \in X} f(x, y). \tag{3.41}$$

One year later, in 1953, generalizing the proof and result of Kneser, Ky Fan (cf. [72]) published his celebrated minimax result. To show his result Ky Fan introduced the following class of functions which we call Ky Fan convex (Ky Fan concave) functions.

Definition 3.3. The function $f : X \times Y \to \mathbb{R}$ is called Ky Fan concave on X if for every $\lambda \in \mathcal{F}_2(X)$ there exists some $x_0 \in X$ satisfying

$$f_e(\lambda, \epsilon_y) \leq f(x_0, y)$$

for every $y \in Y$. The function $f : X \times Y \to \mathbb{R}$ is called Ky Fan convex on Y if for every $\mu \in \mathcal{F}_2(Y)$ there exists some $y_0 \in Y$ satisfying

$$f_e(\epsilon_x, \mu) \geq f(x, y_0)$$

for every $x \in X$. Finally, the function $f : X \times Y \to \mathbb{R}$ is called Ky Fan concave-convex on $X \times Y$ if f is Ky Fan concave on X and Ky Fan convex on Y.

By induction it is easy to show that one can replace in the above definition $\mathcal{F}_2(X)$ and $\mathcal{F}_2(Y)$ by $\mathcal{F}(X)$ and $\mathcal{F}(Y)$. Although rather technical, the above concept has a clear interpretation in game theory. It means that the payoff function f has the property that any arbitrary mixed strategy is dominated by a pure strategy. Eliminating the linear structure in Kneser's proof Ky Fan (cf. [72]) showed the following result.

Theorem 3.17. (Ky Fan, 1953) *If X is a compact subset of a topological space and the function $f : X \times Y \to \mathbb{R}$ is Ky Fan concave-convex on $X \times Y$ and upper semicontinuous on X for every $y \in Y$ then it follows that*

$$\max_{x \in X} \inf_{y \in Y} f(x, y) = \inf_{y \in Y} \max_{x \in X} f(x, y).$$

In what follows we show that Ky Fan's minimax theorem can easily be proved by Kassay-Kolumbán's result. Indeed, it is easy to see that every Ky Fan concave function on X is also weakly concavelike on X. By Theorem 3.15 and relation (3.39) it follows that

$$\max_{x \in X} \inf_{y \in Y} f(x, y) = \inf_{\mu \in \mathcal{F}(Y)} \max_{x \in X} f_e(\epsilon_x, \mu). \qquad (3.42)$$

Also, since f is Ky Fan convex on Y, for every $\mu \in \mathcal{F}(Y)$ there exists $y_0 \in Y$ such that $f_e(\epsilon_x, \mu) \geq f(x, y_0)$ for every $x \in X$. Thus,

$$\max_{x \in X} f_e(\epsilon_x, \mu) \geq \max_{x \in X} f(x, y_0) \geq \inf_{y \in Y} \max_{x \in X} f(x, y)$$

implying that

$$\inf_{\mu \in \mathcal{F}(Y)} \max_{x \in X} f_e(\epsilon_x, \mu) \geq \inf_{y \in Y} \max_{x \in X} f(x, y)$$

and this, together with (3.42) leads to

$$\max_{x \in X} \inf_{y \in Y} f(x, y) \geq \inf_{y \in Y} \max_{x \in X} f(x, y).$$

Since the reverse inequality always holds, we have equality in the last relation and the proof is complete.

We show now that the well-known strong separation result in convex analysis (see Theorem 3.7) can easily be proved by Kneser's minimax theorem. Next we recall Theorem 3.7 with a slight change in notations.

Theorem 3.18. *If $X \subseteq \mathbb{R}^n$ is a closed convex set and $Y \subseteq \mathbb{R}^n$ a compact convex set and the intersection of X and Y is empty then there exists some $s_0 \in \mathbb{R}^n$ satisfying*

$$\sup\{s_0^\top x : x \in X\} < \inf\{s_0^\top y : y \in Y\}.$$

Proof. Since $X \subseteq \mathbb{R}^n$ is a closed convex set and $Y \subseteq \mathbb{R}^n$ is a compact convex set we obtain that $H := X - Y$ is a closed convex set. It is now easy to see that the strong separation result as given in Theorem 3.18 holds if and only if there exists some $s_0 \in \mathbb{R}^n$ satisfying $\sigma_H(s_0) := \sup\{s_0^\top x : x \in H\} < 0$. To verify this we assume by contradiction that $\sigma_H(s) \geq 0$ for every $s \in \mathbb{R}^n$. This clearly implies $\sigma_H(s) \geq 0$ for every s belonging to the compact Euclidean unit ball E and applying Kneser's minimax result we obtain

$$\sup_{h \in H} \inf_{s \in E} s^\top h = \inf_{s \in E} \sup_{h \in H} s^\top h \geq 0. \qquad (3.43)$$

Since by assumption the intersection of X and Y is nonempty we obtain that 0 does not belong to $H := X - Y$ and this implies using H is closed that $\inf_{h \in H} \|h\| > 0$. By this observation we obtain for every $h \in H$ that $-h\|h\|^{-1}$ belongs to E and so for every $h \in H$ it follows that $\inf_{s \in E} s^{\top} h \leq -\|h\|$. This implies that

$$\sup_{h \in H} \inf_{s \in E} s^{\top} h \leq \sup_{h \in H} -\|h\| = -\inf_{h \in H} \|h\| < 0$$

and we obtain a contradiction with relation (3.43). Hence there must exist some $s_0 \in \mathbb{R}^n$ satisfying $\sigma_H(s_0) < 0$ and we are done. $\qquad\square$

Let Δ_n be the unit simplex in $\mathbb{R}^n$. Observe that without loss of generality one may suppose that the vector s_0 in Theorem 3.18 belongs to Δ_n. An easy consequence of Theorem 3.18 is the following result.

Lemma 3.7. *If $C \subseteq \mathbb{R}^n$ is a convex compact set, then it follows that*

$$\inf_{u \in C} \max_{\alpha \in \Delta_n} \alpha^{\top} u = \max_{\alpha \in \Delta_n} \inf_{u \in C} \alpha^{\top} u.$$

Proof. It is obvious that

$$\inf_{u \in C} \max_{\alpha \in \Delta_n} \alpha^{\top} u \geq \max_{\alpha \in \Delta_n} \inf_{u \in C} \alpha^{\top} u. \qquad (3.44)$$

To show that we actually have an equality in relation (3.44) we assume by contradiction that

$$\inf_{u \in C} \max_{\alpha \in \Delta_n} \alpha^{\top} u > \max_{\alpha \in \Delta_n} \inf_{u \in C} \alpha^{\top} u := \gamma. \qquad (3.45)$$

Let $\mathbf{e}$ be the vector $(1, \ldots, 1)$ in $\mathbb{R}^n$ and introduce the mapping $H : C \to \mathbb{R}^n$ given by $H(u) := u - \beta\mathbf{e}$ with β satisfying

$$\inf_{u \in C} \max_{\alpha \in \Delta_n} \alpha^{\top} u > \beta > \gamma. \qquad (3.46)$$

If we assume that $H(C) \cap \mathbb{R}^n_-$ is nonempty there exists some $u_0 \in C$ satisfying $u_0 - \beta\mathbf{e} \leq 0$. This implies $\max_{\alpha \in \Delta_n} \alpha^{\top} u_0 \leq \beta$ and we obtain a contradiction with relation (3.46). Therefore $H(C) \cap \mathbb{R}^n_-$ is empty. Since $H(C)$ is convex and compact and $\mathbb{R}^n_-$ is closed and convex, we may apply Theorem 3.18. Hence one can find some $\alpha_0 \in \Delta_n$ satisfying $\alpha_0^{\top} u - \beta \geq 0$ for every $u \in C$ and using also the definition of γ listed in relation (3.45) this implies that

$$\gamma \geq \inf_{u \in C} \alpha_0^{\top} u \geq \beta.$$

Hence we obtain a contradiction with relation (3.46) and the desired result is proved. $\qquad\square$

Finally we show that von Neumann's minimax theorem (Theorem 3.12) is an easy consequence of Lemma 3.7. In this way we close the equivalent chain of results considered in this note.

Proof of von Neumann's theorem by Lemma 3.7. Denote $m := card(X)$ and $n := card(Y)$. Introduce the mapping $L : \mathcal{F}(Y) \to \mathbb{R}^m$ given by

$$L(\mu) := (f_e(\epsilon_x, \mu))_{x \in X}.$$

It is easy to see that the range $L(\mathcal{F}(Y)) \subseteq \mathbb{R}^m$ is a convex compact set. Applying now Lemma 3.7 yields

$$\inf_{\mu \in \mathcal{F}(Y)} \max_{\lambda \in \mathcal{F}(X)} f_e(\lambda, \mu) = \inf_{u \in L(\mathcal{F}(Y))} \max_{\alpha \in \Delta_n} \alpha^\top u$$
$$= \max_{\alpha \in \Delta_n} \inf_{u \in L(\mathcal{F}(Y))} \alpha^\top u$$
$$= \max_{\lambda \in \mathcal{F}(X)} \inf_{\mu \in \mathcal{F}(Y)} f_e(\lambda, \mu),$$

which completes the proof. □

NOTES

1. Juliusz Pawel Schauder (1899–1943) was a Polish mathematician, known for his work in functional analysis, partial differential equations, and mathematical physics.
2. Ky Fan (1914–2010) was an American mathematician and Emeritus Professor of Mathematics at the University of California, Santa Barbara.
3. Theorem 3.1 was first published by Kassay and Kolumbán in 1990 [100] and one year later, independently by Chang and Zhang [55].
4. John von Neumann (1903–1957) was a Hungarian-American mathematician, physicist, computer scientist, and polymath. He made major contributions to a number of fields, including mathematics (foundations of mathematics, functional analysis, ergodic theory, representation theory, operator algebras, geometry, topology, and numerical analysis), physics (quantum mechanics, hydrodynamics, and quantum statistical mechanics), economics (game theory), computing (Von Neumann architecture, linear programming, self-replicating machines, stochastic computing), and statistics.

   Von Neumann was generally regarded as the foremost mathematician of his time and said to be "the last representative of the great mathematicians". He was a pioneer of the application of operator theory to quantum mechanics in the development of functional analysis, and a key figure in the development of game theory and the concepts of cellular automata, the universal constructor, and the digital computer. He published over 150 papers in his life: about 60 in pure mathematics, 20 in physics, and 60 in applied mathematics, the remainder being on special mathematical subjects or nonmathematical ones. His last work, an unfinished manuscript written while in the hospital, was later published in book form as The Computer and the Brain.

Chapter 4

Existence of Solutions of Equilibrium Problems

Contents

The study of mathematics, like the Nile, begins in minuteness but ends in magnificence.

Charles Caleb Colton (1780–1832)

Chapter points

- The results of this chapter are related to the existence of solutions for different kinds of vector and set-valued equilibrium problems.
- A special attention is given to the case when the equilibrium problem contains the sum of two bifunctions.
- The content of this chapter is based on recent results of the authors.

4.1 EXISTENCE OF SOLUTIONS OF VECTOR EQUILIBRIUM PROBLEMS

In Chapter 2 we already defined the weak and the strong vector equilibrium problems. Let us recall these problems for convenience. Let A and B be two

Equilibrium Problems and Applications. https://doi.org/10.1016/B978-0-12-811029-4.00012-2

57

nonempty sets, Y be a real topological vector space and C a proper convex cone of it with int$C \neq \emptyset$. For the vector-valued function $f : A \times B \to Y$, the *weak vector equilibrium problem* (abbreviated (WVEP)) is to find $\bar{a} \in A$ such that

$$f(\bar{a}, b) \notin -\text{int}C \quad \text{for all } b \in B, \tag{4.1}$$

while the *strong vector equilibrium problem* (abbreviated (SVEP)) is to find $\bar{a} \in A$ such that

$$f(\bar{a}, b) \notin -C \setminus \{0\} \quad \text{for all } b \in B. \tag{4.2}$$

In the next two subsections we discuss existence results together with some applications of these problems. We start with (SVEP).

4.1.1 The Strong Vector Equilibrium Problem

We begin with a general existence result on (SVEP) which has been established in [40] and can be seen as an extension of Theorem 3.11 presented in Chapter 3. Let us state our framework and recall some necessary concepts.

Given the topological vector space Y, consider the following partial order relation induced on Y by a convex pointed cone $C \subset Y$ with int $C \neq \emptyset$:

$$y_1 \leq_C y_2 \text{ if and only if } y_2 - y_1 \in C.$$

We recall that a cone is pointed if $C \cap (-C) = \{0\}$. The (positive) dual of the cone C is the set

$$C^* = \{y^* \in Y^* \mid y^*(c) \geq 0, \text{ for all } c \in C\},$$

while the quasi-interior of the cone C^* is the set

$$C^\sharp = \{y^* \in C^* | y^*(c) > 0, \text{ for all } c \in C \setminus \{0\}\}.$$

A nonempty convex subset V of C is called a base of C if

$$C = \{\lambda v : \lambda \geq 0, v \in V\} \text{ and } 0 \notin \text{cl } V.$$

If C is a nontrivial convex pointed cone of a Hausdorff locally convex space Y, then $C^\sharp \neq \emptyset$ if and only if C has a base.

The proof of the next result follows the idea of Theorem 3.11 adapted for the vector case. Instead of the finite dimensional separation theorem, we shall use its infinite dimensional counterpart: two nonempty disjoint convex subsets of a topological vector space can be separated by a closed hyperplane provided one of them has an interior point (see, for instance, [3]).

Let A and B be two nonempty sets, Y be a real topological vector space, C a proper convex cone of it and $f : A \times B \rightarrow Y$.

Theorem 4.1. *Suppose that f satisfies the following assumptions:*

(i) *if the system $\{U_b \mid b \in B\}$ covers A, then it contains a finite subcover, where*

$$U_b = \{a \in A \mid f(a, b) \in -C \backslash \{0\}\};$$

(ii) *for each $a_1, \ldots, a_m \in A$, $\lambda_1, \ldots, \lambda_m \geq 0$ with $\lambda_1 + \ldots + \lambda_m = 1$, $b_1, \ldots, b_n \in B$ there exists $u^* \in C^\sharp$ such that*

$$\min_{1 \leq j \leq n} \sum_{i=1}^{m} \lambda_i u^*\big(f(a_i, b_j)\big) \leq \sup_{a \in A} \min_{1 \leq j \leq n} u^*\big(f(a, b_j)\big);$$

(iii) *for each $b_1, \ldots, b_n \in B$, $z_1^*, \ldots, z_n^* \in C^*$ not all zero, it holds*

$$\sup_{a \in A} \sum_{j=1}^{n} z_j^*\big(f(a, b_j)\big) > 0.$$

Then, the strong vector equilibrium problem (SVEP) *admits a solution.*

Proof. Suppose by contradiction that (SVEP) admits no solution, i.e., for each $a \in A$ there exists $b(a) \in B$ such that

$$f(a, b(a)) \in -C \setminus \{0\}.$$

Since the family $\{U_{b(a)}\}_{a \in A}$, where

$$U_{b(a)} := \{a' \in A \mid f(a', b(a)) \in -C \setminus \{0\}\}, \tag{4.3}$$

covers the set A, then assumption (i) guarantees that there exist $b_1, \ldots, b_n \in B$ such that

$$A \subset \bigcup_{j=1}^{n} U_{b_j}. \tag{4.4}$$

We define the vector-valued function $F : A \rightarrow Y^n$ by

$$F(a) := \big(f(a, b_1), \ldots, f(a, b_n)\big),$$

and we have

$$\text{conv } F(A) \cap (C \setminus \{0\})^n = \emptyset, \tag{4.5}$$

where conv $F(A)$ denotes the convex hull of the set $F(A)$. To prove it, suppose by contradiction there exist $a_1, \ldots, a_m \in A$ and $\lambda_1, \ldots, \lambda_m \geq 0$ with

$\lambda_1 + \ldots + \lambda_m = 1$ such that

$$\sum_{i=1}^{m} \lambda_i F(a_i) \in (C \setminus \{0\})^n.$$

This is equivalent to

$$\sum_{i=1}^{m} \lambda_i f(a_i, b_j) \in C \setminus \{0\} \text{ for each } j \in \{1, \ldots, n\}. \tag{4.6}$$

Let $u^* \in C^\sharp$ be a functional for which assumption (ii) holds. Applying u^* to the above relation and taking the minimum over all $j \in \{1, \ldots, n\}$, we get

$$\min_{1 \leq j \leq n} \sum_{i=1}^{m} \lambda_i u^*\big(f(a_i, b_j)\big) > 0. \tag{4.7}$$

Thus, assumption (ii) and (4.7) imply

$$\sup_{a \in A} \min_{1 \leq j \leq n} u^*\big(f(a, b_j)\big) > 0. \tag{4.8}$$

Relation (4.4) guarantees that for each $a \in A$ there exists $j_0 = j_0(a) \in \{1, \ldots, n\}$ such that $a \in U_{b_{j_0}}$, i.e., $f(a, b_{j_0}) \in -C \setminus \{0\}$ for each $a \in A$. Applying $u^* \in C^\sharp$, we get

$$u^*\big(f(a, b_{j_0})\big) < 0 \text{ for all } a \in A.$$

Taking the minimum over $j \in \{1, \ldots, n\}$ and then the supremum over $a \in A$ in the previous relation, we obtain

$$\sup_{a \in A} \min_{1 \leq j \leq n} u^*\big(f(a, b_j)\big) \leq 0, \tag{4.9}$$

which is a contradiction to (4.8). Hence, condition (4.5) holds.

Therefore, the separation theorem implies that there exists a nonzero functional $z^* \in (Y^n)^*$ such that

$$z^*(u) \leq 0, \text{ for all } u \in \text{conv } F(A) \tag{4.10}$$

and

$$z^*(k) \geq 0, \text{ for all } k \in (C \setminus \{0\})^n. \tag{4.11}$$

Using the representation $z^* = (z_1^*, \ldots, z_n^*)$, we deduce $z_j^* \in C^*$ for all $j \in \{1, \ldots, n\}$ by a standard argument.

By (4.10) we have $z^*(F(a)) \leq 0$ for all $a \in A$, or equivalently,

$$\sum_{j=1}^{n} z_j^*(f(a, b_j)) \leq 0.$$

Since the above inequality holds for each $a \in A$ we obtain

$$\sup_{a \in A} \sum_{j=1}^{n} z_j^*\big(f(a, b_j)\big) \leq 0,$$

which is a contradiction to assumption (iii). □

Next we show that some continuity and generalized convexity properties of the bifunction f will guarantee the assumptions of Theorem 4.1. The next two continuity type concepts are generalizations of the upper semicontinuity of real-valued functions. (See [118] for other generalizations.)

Definition 4.1. A vector-valued function $F : A \to Z$ is said to be

(i) (see [118]) C-upper semicontinuous on A (C-usc in short) if for each $x \in A$ and any $c \in int\, C$, there exists an open neighborhood $U \subset A$ of x such that $F(u) \in F(x) + c - int\, C$ for all $u \in U$;

(ii) (see [40]) properly C-upper semicontinuous on A (properly C-usc in short) if for each $x \in A$ and any $c \in C \setminus \{0\}$, there exists an open neighborhood $U \subset A$ of x such that $F(u) \in F(x) + c - C \setminus \{0\}$ for all $u \in U$.

The function F is called (properly) C-lower semicontinuous if $-F$ is (properly) C-upper semicontinuous.

The next characterizations of upper semicontinuity has been given by T. Tanaka [166].

Lemma 4.1. *The following three statements are equivalent:*

(i) *F is C-upper semicontinuous on X;*

(ii) *for any $x \in X$, for any $k \in int\, C$, there exists a neighborhood $U \subset X$ of x such that $F(u) \in F(x) + k - int\, C$ for all $u \in U$;*

(iii) *for any $a \in Y$, the set $\{x \in X : F(x) - a \in -int\, C\}$ is open.*

Below we give a characterization of proper C-upper semicontinuity.

Proposition 4.1. *Let $F : A \to Z$. The following properties are equivalent:*

(i) *F is properly C-upper semicontinuous on A;*

(ii) *the set $F^{-1}(z - C \setminus \{0\})$ is open in A for each $z \in Z$.*

Proof. Let $z \in Z$. If $F^{-1}(z - C \setminus \{0\}) = \emptyset$, then (ii) holds. Assume that there exists $x_0 \in F^{-1}(z - C \setminus \{0\})$. Thus, we have $c := z - F(x_0) \in C \setminus \{0\}$. By the definition of properly C-usc, there exists an open neighborhood U of x_0 such that it holds

$$F(x) \in F(x_0) + c - C \setminus \{0\} = z - C \setminus \{0\}$$

for all $x \in U$. So, $F^{-1}(z - C \setminus \{0\})$ is an open subset of the space A.

For the reverse implication let $x_0 \in A$ and $c \in C \setminus \{0\}$. Since $x_0 \in F^{-1}(F(x_0) + c - C \setminus \{0\})$, which is an open set by condition (ii), there exists an open neighborhood U of x_0 such that

$$x \in F^{-1}(F(x_0) + c - C \setminus \{0\}) \text{ for all } x \in U,$$

and therefore F is properly C-usc at x_0. Since x_0 was arbitrarily taken, we deduce that F is properly C-usc on A. □

It is clear that every properly C-upper semicontinuous function is C-upper semicontinuous, but not vice versa. This can be easily seen if we take into account the characterization above. For example, set $A = Z$ and consider any cone $C \subset Z$ such that $C \setminus \{0\}$ is not an open set; then the identity function is not properly C-usc.

The next proposition provides sufficient conditions for assumption (i) of Theorem 4.1.

Proposition 4.2. *Suppose that A is a compact topological space and the function $f(\cdot, b) : A \to Z$ is properly C-usc on A for each $b \in B$. Then, the assumption (i) of Theorem 4.1 is satisfied.*

Proof. Let $U_b := \{a \in A \mid f(a, b) \in -C \setminus \{0\}\}$, for any $b \in B$. In what follows we show that the family of these sets is an open covering of A.

Take $a_0 \in U_b$ and consider $c' := -f(a_0, b) \in C \setminus \{0\}$. Since the function $f(\cdot, b)$ is properly C-usc at $a_0 \in A$, there exists a neighborhood $U \subset A$ of a_0 such that

$$f(u, b) \in f(a_0, b) + c' - C \setminus \{0\}$$
$$= f(a_0, b) - f(a_0, b) - C \setminus \{0\}$$
$$= -C \setminus \{0\}$$

for all $u \in U$. Hence, we get $f(u, b) \in -C \setminus \{0\}$ for all $u \in U$, which implies that U_b is an open set. Therefore, assumption (i) of Theorem 4.1 follows from the compactness of A. □

Next we need the following definition (see [40]).

Definition 4.2. A bifunction $f : A \times B \to Z$ is said to be

(i) C-subconcavelike in its first variable if for all $l \in int\,C$, $x_1, x_2 \in A$, $t \in [0, 1]$ there exists $x \in A$ such that

$$f(x, y) \geq_C tf(x_1, y) + (1 - t)f(x_2, y) - l \text{ for all } y \in B;$$

(ii) C-subconvexlike in its second variable if for all $l \in int\,C$, $y_1, y_2 \in B$ and $t \in [0, 1]$, there exists $y \in B$ such that

$$f(x, y) \leq_C tf(x, y_1) + (1 - t)f(x, y_2) + l \text{ for all } x \in A.$$

(iii) C-subconcavelike-subconvexlike on $A \times B$ if it is C-subconcavelike in its first variable and C-subconvexlike in its second variable.

Proposition 4.2 and the C-subconcavelikeness of a bifunction allow to achieve the following existence result as a corollary of Theorem 4.1.

Corollary 4.1. *Suppose A is a compact topological space, C a closed convex cone with a nonempty interior such that $C^{\sharp} \neq \emptyset$ and the bifunction f satisfies the conditions:*

(i) *$f(\cdot, b)$ is properly C-usc for all $b \in B$ and f is C-subconcavelike in its first variable;*

(ii) *for each $b_1, \ldots, b_n \in B$, $z_1^*, \ldots, z_n^* \in C^*$ not all zero it holds*

$$\sup_{a \in A} \sum_{j=1}^{n} z_j^*\big(f(a, b_j)\big) > 0.$$

Then, the vector equilibrium problem (SVEP) *admits a solution.*

Proof. It is enough to show that the C-subconcavelikeness of the function f in its first variable implies condition (ii) of Theorem 4.1. Take $a_1, \ldots, a_m \in A$, $b_1, \ldots, b_n \in B$, $\lambda_1, \ldots, \lambda_m \geq 0$ with $\lambda_1 + \ldots + \lambda_m = 1$ and $u^* \in C^{\sharp}$.

Thanks to the C-subconcavelikeness of f in its first variable, for each $l \in \operatorname{int} C$ there exists $\bar{a} \in A$ such that

$$\sum_{i=1}^{m} \lambda_i f(a_i, b_j) \leq_C f(\bar{a}, b_j) + l \text{ for each } j \in \{1, \ldots, n\}. \qquad (4.12)$$

Applying u^* to (4.12), we obtain

$$\sum_{i=1}^{m} \lambda_i u^* f(a_i, b_j) \leq u^*\big(f(\bar{a}, b_j)\big) + u^*(l) \text{ for each } j \in \{1, \ldots, n\}, \qquad (4.13)$$

and taking the minimum over j we get

$$\min_{1 \leq j \leq n} \sum_{i=1}^{m} \lambda_i u^*\big(f(a_i, b_j)\big) \leq \min_{1 \leq j \leq n} u^*\big(f(\bar{a}, b_j)\big) + u^*(l)$$

$$\leq \sup_{a \in A} \min_{1 \leq j \leq n} u^*\big(f(a, b_j)\big) + u^*(l).$$

Since this inequality holds for each $l \in \operatorname{int} C$, we obtain the assumption (ii) of Theorem 4.1 just taking $l \to 0$. $\qquad \square$

In the special case $Z = \mathbb{R}$ and $C = \mathbb{R}_+$, Corollary 4.1 collapses to the following result. (In this case for C-subconcavelike we simply write subconcavelike.)

Corollary 4.2. *Suppose A is a compact topological space and the bifunction f satisfies the conditions:*

(i) *$f(\cdot, b)$ is usc for all $b \in B$ and subconcavelike in its first variable;*

(ii) *for each $b_1, \ldots, b_n \in B$, $\mu_1, \ldots, \mu_n \geq 0$ it holds*

$$\sup_{a \in A} \sum_{j=1}^{n} \mu_j f(a, b_j) > 0.$$

Then, the scalar equilibrium problem (EP) admits a solution.

The next result follows from Theorem 4.1 via the above corollary.

Theorem 4.2. *Let A be a nonempty compact subset of a metrizable topological vector space E, C a closed convex cone with a nonempty interior and $e^* \in C^\sharp$. Suppose that $f : A \times B \to Z$ is C-subconcavelike-subconvexlike and the function $a \mapsto e^*(f(a, b))$ is upper semicontinuous on A for each fixed $b \in B$. Furthermore assume that*

$$\sup_{a \in A} e^*(f(a, b)) \geq 0, \ \forall b \in B.$$

Then, the strong vector equilibrium problem (SVEP) admits a solution.

Proof. We prove the theorem in two steps.

Step 1. Let $\tau \in C \setminus \{0\}$ and define the function $\psi : A \times B \to Z$ by $\psi(a, b) = f(a, b) + \tau$ for all $a \in A$ and $b \in B$. For the given $e^* \in C^\sharp$ we consider the real-valued function $e^* \circ \psi : A \times B \to \mathbb{R}$, which is defined as $(e^* \circ \psi)(a, b) = e^*(\psi(a, b))$ for all $a \in A$ and $b \in B$. We show that this function satisfies the assumptions of Corollary 4.2. Given any $\epsilon > 0$, there exists $l \in \text{int}\, C$ such that $e^*(l) = \epsilon$. Since f is C-subconcavelike in its first variable, for each $a_1, a_2 \in A$ and $t \in [0, 1]$ there exists $\bar{a} \in A$ such that

$$\psi(\bar{a}, b) \geq_C t\psi(a_1, b) + (1 - t)\psi(a_2, b) - l \text{ for all } b \in B.$$

Applying e^* to this inequality we obtain

$$e^*(\psi(\bar{a}, b)) \geq te^*(\psi(a_1, b)) + (1 - t)e^*(\psi(a_2, b)) - \epsilon \text{ for all } b \in B.$$

Thus, the function $e^* \circ \psi$ is subconcavelike in its first variable.

Take $b_1, \ldots, b_n \in B$, $\mu_1, \ldots, \mu_n \geq 0$ with $\mu_1 + \cdots + \mu_n = 1$. Since f is C-subconvexlike in its second variable, we have that for each $l' \in \text{int}\, C$ there exists an element $\bar{b} \in B$ such that

$$\psi(a, \bar{b}) \leq_C \sum_{j=1}^{n} \mu_j \psi(a, b_j) + l' \text{ for all } a \in A. \tag{4.14}$$

Applying the nonzero functional e^* to relation (4.14) we get

$$e^*(\psi(a, \bar{b})) \leq \sum_{j=1}^{n} \mu_j e^*(\psi(a, b_j)) + e^*(l') \text{ for all } a \in A. \tag{4.15}$$

By the assumptions and inequality (4.15), we deduce that

$$e^*(\tau) \leq \sup_{a \in A} e^*(f(a, \bar{b})) + e^*(\tau) \leq \sup_{a \in A} \sum_{j=1}^{n} \mu_j e^*(\psi(a, b_j)) + e^*(l').$$

Taking the limit as $l' \to 0$, we obtain

$$0 < e^*(\tau) \leq \sup_{a \in A} \sum_{j=1}^{n} \mu_j e^*(\psi(a, b_j)).$$

Hence, the assumptions of Corollary 4.2 are satisfied. Therefore, there exists a solution $\tilde{a} \in A$ of (EP), i.e.,

$$e^*(f(\tilde{a}, b)) + e^*(\tau) \geq 0 \text{ for all } b \in B.$$

Step 2. Applying Step 1 with e^*/n, we get that for all $n \in \mathbb{N}$ there exists a point $\tilde{a}_n \in A$ such that

$$e^*(f(\tilde{a}_n, b)) + \frac{1}{n}e^*(\tau) \geq 0 \text{ for all } b \in B \text{ and } n \in \mathbb{N}. \tag{4.16}$$

In this way we achieve a sequence $\{\tilde{a}_n\}$ of points of the compact set A. Since E is metrizable, compactness guarantees sequential compactness: thus, there exists a convergent subsequence of $\{\tilde{a}_n\}$ (also denoted by $\{\tilde{a}_n\}$ for the sake of simplicity), i.e., there is $\tilde{a} \in A$ such that $\tilde{a}_n \to \tilde{a}$ when $n \to \infty$. We show that $\tilde{a}$ solves (SVEP).

Since $a \mapsto e^*(f(a, b))$ is upper semicontinuous on A for any point $b \in B$, we have that it is upper semicontinuous at $\tilde{a}$, i.e., for any $\epsilon > 0$ there exists $n_0 \in \mathbb{N}$ such that

$$e^*(f(\tilde{a}_n, b)) < e^*(f(\tilde{a}, b)) + \epsilon \text{ for all } n \geq n_0.$$

Thanks to condition (4.16), we deduce

$$0 \leq e^*(f(\tilde{a}_n, b)) + (1/n)e^*(\tau) < e^*(f(\tilde{a}, b)) + (1/n)e^*(\tau) + \epsilon$$

for all $n \geq n_0$. Taking $n \to \infty$, we have

$$0 \leq e^*(f(\tilde{a}, b)) + \epsilon.$$

Since this inequality holds for any ϵ, we conclude that

$$0 \le e^*(f(\tilde{a}, b)).$$

Since this inequality holds for any $b \in B$, then $\tilde{a}$ is a solution of (SVEP). $\qquad\square$

When E is a normed space, according to Eberlein-Smulian theorem (see, for instance, [3]) weak compactness is equivalent to weak sequential compactness: therefore, the following stronger result can be achieved for the case of normed spaces, just arguing as in the previous proof.

Theorem 4.3. *Let A be a nonempty weakly compact subset of a normed space E, C a closed convex cone with a nonempty interior and $e^* \in C^\sharp$. Suppose that $f : A \times B \to Z$ is C-subconcavelike-subconvexlike and the function $a \mapsto e^*(f(a, b))$ is weakly upper semicontinuous on A for each fixed $b \in B$. Furthermore assume $\sup_{a \in A} e^*(f(a, b)) \ge 0$ for all $b \in B$. Then, the strong vector equilibrium problem (SVEP) admits a solution.*

Theorem 4.3 allows to get the following slight generalization of Theorem 3.2 of [84], in which convexlikeness is replaced by the weaker subconvexlikeness.

Corollary 4.3. *Let A be a nonempty weakly compact subset of a normed space E, C a closed convex cone with a nonempty interior and $e^* \in C^\sharp$. Suppose $f : A \times A \to Z$ is C-subconcavelike-subconvexlike and the function $a \mapsto e^*(f(a, b))$ is weakly upper semicontinuous on A for each fixed $b \in A$. Furthermore assume $f(a, a) \in C$ for all $a \in A$. Then, the strong vector equilibrium problem (SVEP) admits a solution.*

Proof. The thesis follows immediately from Theorem 4.3, just taking $A = B$ and noticing that $f(a, a) \in C$ for all $a \in A$ implies

$$\sup_{a \in A} e^*(f(a, b)) \ge e^*(f(b, b)) \ge 0 \text{ for all } b \in A. \qquad\square$$

Theorem 4.3 extends Theorem 3.2 of [84] also in two other ways: two different sets A and B are considered and the equilibrium condition $f(a, a) \in C$ is replaced by a weaker assumption involving appropriate suprema over A.

4.1.2 The Weak Vector Equilibrium Problems

In this subsection we provide existence results of (WVEP). Unless otherwise specified, we keep the notations used in the previous subsection. Recall the following well-known property, which is easy to prove.

Lemma 4.2. *If $z^* \in C^*$ is a nonzero functional, then $z^*(z) > 0$ for all $z \in$ int C.*

The proof of the next result follows the line given in Theorem 4.1.

Theorem 4.4. *Let A be a compact set and let $f : A \times B \to Z$ be a function such that*

(i) *for each $\bar{y} \in B$, the function $f(\cdot, \bar{y}) : A \to Z$ is C-usc on A;*

(ii) *for each $\bar{x}_1, \ldots, \bar{x}_m \in A$, $\lambda_1, \ldots, \lambda_m \geq 0$ with $\sum_{i=1}^{m} \lambda_i = 1$, $\bar{y}_1, \ldots, \bar{y}_n \in B$ there exists $u^* \in C^* \setminus \{0\}$ such that*

$$\min_{1 \leq j \leq n} \sum_{i=1}^{m} \lambda_i u^* \big(f(\bar{x}_i, \bar{y}_j) \big) \leq \sup_{\bar{x} \in A} \min_{1 \leq j \leq n} u^* \big(f(\bar{x}, \bar{y}_j) \big);$$

(iii) *for each $\bar{y}_1, \ldots, \bar{y}_n \in B$, $z_1^*, \ldots, z_n^* \in C^*$ not all zero one has*

$$\sup_{\bar{x} \in A} \sum_{j=1}^{n} z_j^* \big(f(\bar{x}, \bar{y}_j) \big) \geq 0.$$

Then the equilibrium problem (WVEP) *admits a solution.*

Proof. Suppose by contradiction that (WVEP) has no solution, i.e., for each $\bar{x} \in A$ there exists $\bar{y} \in B$ with the property $f(\bar{x}, \bar{y}) \in -\operatorname{int} C$. This means that for each $\bar{x} \in A$ there exists $\bar{y} \in B$ and $k \in \operatorname{int} C$ such that

$$f(\bar{x}, \bar{y}) + k \in -\operatorname{int} C.$$

Consider the sets

$$U_{\bar{y},k} := \{\bar{x} \in A \mid f(\bar{x}, \bar{y}) + k \in -\operatorname{int} C\},$$

where $\bar{y} \in B$ and $k \in \operatorname{int} C$. In what follows we show that the family of these sets forms an open covering of the compact set A.

Let $\bar{x}_0 \in U_{\bar{y},k}$ and $k \in \operatorname{int} C$. Since $\bar{x}_0 \in U_{\bar{y},k}$ we have that

$$f(\bar{x}_0, \bar{y}) + k \in -\operatorname{int} C \text{ that is, } -f(\bar{x}_0, \bar{y}) - k \in \operatorname{int} C.$$

Denote $k' := -f(\bar{x}_0, b) - k$, so $k' \in \operatorname{int} C$. Since the function $f(\cdot, \bar{y})$ is C-usc at $\bar{x}_0 \in A$, we obtain for k' that there exists a neighborhood $U_{\bar{x}_0} \subset E$ of $\bar{x}_0$ such that

$$\begin{aligned}
f(u, \bar{y}) &\in f(\bar{x}_0, \bar{y}) + k' - \operatorname{int} C \\
&= f(\bar{x}_0, \bar{y}) - f(\bar{x}_0, \bar{y}) - k - \operatorname{int} C \\
&= -k - \operatorname{int} C, \text{ for all } u \in U_{\bar{x}_0}.
\end{aligned}$$

Hence we have that $f(u, \bar{y}) + k \in -\operatorname{int} C$ for all $u \in U_{\bar{x}_0}$, which means that $U_{\bar{y},k}$ is an open set.

Since the family $\{U_{\bar{y},k}\}$ is an open covering of the compact set A, we can select a finite subfamily which covers the same set A, i.e., there exist $\bar{y}_1, \ldots, \bar{y}_n \in B$ and $k_1, \ldots, k_n \in \operatorname{int} C$ such that

$$A \subset \bigcup_{j=1}^{n} U_{\bar{y}_j, k_j}. \tag{4.17}$$

For these $k_1, \ldots, k_n \in \operatorname{int} C$, we have that there exist $V_1, \ldots, V_n$ balanced neighborhoods of the origin of Z such that $k_j + V_j \subset C$ for all $j \in \{1, \ldots, n\}$.

Define $V := V_1 \cap \cdots \cap V_n$, thus V is a balanced neighborhood of the origin of the space Z. Let $k_0 \in V \cap \operatorname{int} C$, so we have $-k_0 \in V$. Hence,

$$k_j - k_0 \in k_j + V \subset k_j + V_j \subset C, \quad \text{for all } j \in \{1, \ldots, n\},$$

which gives

$$k_j - k_0 \in C, \quad \text{for all } j \in \{1, \ldots, n\}. \tag{4.18}$$

Now define the vector-valued function $F : A \to Z^n$ by

$$F(\bar{x}) := \big(f(\bar{x}, \bar{y}_1) + k_0, \ldots, f(\bar{x}, \bar{y}_n) + k_0 \big).$$

Assert that

$$\operatorname{conv} F(A) \cap (\operatorname{int} C)^n = \emptyset, \tag{4.19}$$

where $\operatorname{conv} F(A)$ denotes the convex hull of the set $F(A)$. Supposing the contrary, there exist $\bar{x}_1, \ldots, \bar{x}_m \in A$ and $\lambda_1, \ldots, \lambda_m \geq 0$ with $\sum_{i=1}^{m} \lambda_i = 1$ such that $\sum_{i=1}^{m} \lambda_i F(\bar{x}_i) \in (\operatorname{int} C)^n$, or equivalently,

$$\sum_{i=1}^{m} \lambda_i [f(\bar{x}_i, \bar{y}_j) + k_0] \in \operatorname{int} C, \quad \text{for each } j \in \{1, \ldots, n\}, \quad \text{which gives}$$

$$\sum_{i=1}^{m} \lambda_i f(\bar{x}_i, \bar{y}_j) + k_0 \in \operatorname{int} C, \quad \text{for each } j \in \{1, \ldots, n\}. \tag{4.20}$$

Let $u^* \in C^*$ be a nonzero functional for which (ii) holds. Applying u^* to the relation above and taking into account Lemma 4.2 we obtain that

$$\sum_{i=1}^{m} \lambda_i u^* \big(f(\bar{x}_i, \bar{y}_j) \big) + u^*(k_0) > 0.$$

Passing to the minimum over j we have

$$\min_{1 \le j \le n} \sum_{i=1}^{m} \lambda_i u^* \left(f(\bar{x}_i, \bar{y}_j) \right) > -u^*(k_0), \qquad (4.21)$$

thus, assumption (ii) and relation (4.21) imply that

$$\sup_{a \in A} \min_{1 \le j \le n} u^* \left(f(a, b_j) \right) > -u^*(k_0). \qquad (4.22)$$

For each $\bar{x} \in A$, by relation (4.17) we have that there exists $j_0 \in \{1, \ldots, n\}$ such that $a \in U_{b_{j_0}, k_{j_0}}$, i.e., $f(a, b_{j_0}) + k_{j_0} \in -\operatorname{int} C$. This, together with (4.18) imply that

$$f(a, b_{j_0}) + k_0 \in -k_{j_0} + k_0 - \operatorname{int} C \subset -\operatorname{int} C.$$

By Lemma 4.2 and using the fact that $u^* \in C^*$ we obtain that

$$u^* \left(f(\bar{x}, \bar{y}_{j_0}) \right) + u^*(k_0) < 0.$$

Thus for each $a \in A$

$$\min_{1 \le j \le n} u^* \left(f(a, b_j) \right) < -u^*(k_0),$$

and passing to supremum over a we get a contradiction.

By the separation theorem of convex sets, we have that there exists $z^* \in (Z^n)^*$ a nonzero functional such that

$$z^*(u) \le 0, \quad \text{for all } u \in \operatorname{conv} F(A) \text{ and} \qquad (4.23)$$
$$z^*(c) \ge 0, \quad \text{for all } c \in (\operatorname{int} C)^n. \qquad (4.24)$$

Using the representation $z^* = (z_1^*, \ldots, z_n^*)$, by a standard argument we deduce that $z_j^* \in C^*$ for all $j \in \{1, \ldots, n\}$.

In particular, by (4.23), we have $z^*(u) \le 0$ for all $u \in F(A)$. This means that for any $\bar{x} \in A$, $z^*(F(\bar{x})) \le 0$, or equivalently,

$$\sum_{j=1}^{n} z_j^* \left(f(\bar{x}, \bar{y}_j) + k_0 \right) \le 0.$$

Taking into account the linearity of $z_j^* \in C^*$ for all $j \in \{1, \ldots, n\}$, Lemma 4.2 and the fact that not all z_j^* are zero we obtain

$$\sum_{j=1}^{n} z_j^* \left(f(\bar{x}, \bar{y}_j) \right) \le -\sum_{j=1}^{n} z_j^*(k_0) < 0.$$

Passing to supremum over $\bar{x} \in A$ in the upper relation we deduce that

$$\sup_{\bar{x} \in A} \sum_{j=1}^{n} z_j^* \big(f(\bar{x}, \bar{y}_j) \big) < 0,$$

which is a contradiction to assumption (iii). This completes the proof. $\square$

It is easy to check by induction that the concept of C-subconcavelikeness given in Definition 4.2 can be characterized as follows.

Proposition 4.3. *The function* $f : A \times B \to Z$ *is C-subconcavelike in its first variable if and only if for each $l \in \text{int}\, C$, $a_1, \ldots, a_m \in A$, $\lambda_1, \ldots, \lambda_m \geq 0$ with* $\sum_{i=1}^{m} \lambda_i = 1$ *there exists $\bar{a} \in A$ such that*

$$f(\bar{a}, b) \geq_C \sum_{i=1}^{m} \lambda_i f(a_i, b) - l, \text{ for all } b \in B.$$

Using Proposition 4.3 we obtain by Theorem 4.4 the following result.

Corollary 4.4. *Let A be a compact set and let $f : A \times B \to Z$ be a function such that*

(i) f *is C-usc and C-subconcavelike in its first variable;*

(ii) *for each $\bar{y}_1, \ldots, \bar{y}_n \in B$, $z_1^*, \ldots, z_n^* \in C^*$ not all zero one has*

$$\sup_{\bar{x} \in A} \sum_{j=1}^{n} z_j^* \big(f(\bar{x}, \bar{y}_j) \big) \geq 0.$$

Then the equilibrium problem (WVEP) *admits a solution.*

Proof. It is enough to show that assumption (ii) of Theorem 4.4 is satisfied. Let us prove that the C-subconcavelikeness of the function f implies assumption (ii) of the above theorem.

Fix $\bar{x}_1, \ldots, \bar{x}_m \in A$, $\bar{y}_1, \ldots, \bar{y}_n \in B$, $\lambda_1, \ldots, \lambda_m \geq 0$ with $\sum_{i=1}^{m} \lambda_i = 1$, and $u^* \in C^* \backslash \{0\}$.

By the C-subconcavelikeness of f in its first variable, for each $l \in \text{int}\, C$ there exists $\bar{a} \in A$ such that

$$\sum_{i=1}^{m} \lambda_i f(\bar{x}_i, \bar{y}_j) \leq_C f(\bar{a}, \bar{y}_j) + l, \text{ for each } j \in \{1, \ldots, n\}. \tag{4.25}$$

Applying u^*, relation (4.25) becomes

$$\sum_{i=1}^{m} \lambda_i u^* f(\overline{x}_i, \overline{y}_j) \leq u^* \left(f(\overline{\overline{x}}, \overline{y}_j) \right) + u^*(l), \quad \text{for each } j \in \{1, \ldots, n\}, \quad (4.26)$$

which, by passing to minimum over j yields

$$\min_{1 \leq j \leq n} \sum_{i=1}^{m} \lambda_i u^* \left(f(\overline{x}_i, \overline{y}_j) \right) \leq \min_{1 \leq j \leq n} u^* \left(f(\overline{\overline{x}}, \overline{y}_j) \right) + u^*(l)$$

$$\leq \sup_{\overline{x} \in A} \min_{1 \leq j \leq n} u^* \left(f(\overline{x}, \overline{y}_j) \right) + u^*(l).$$

Since this relation holds for each $l \in \text{int}\, C$ we obtain assumption (ii) of Theorem 4.4. Hence (WVEP) admits a solution. □

4.2 EXISTENCE OF SOLUTIONS OF SET-VALUED EQUILIBRIUM PROBLEMS

In this section, we obtain different results on the existence of solutions of set-valued equilibrium problems generalizing in a common way several old ones for both single-valued and set-valued equilibrium problems.

Set-valued equilibrium problems have been recently investigated in [6] under mild conditions of continuity, and also under the notion of self-segment-dense subset first introduced in [114]. We focus in this section only on continuity and convexity. We are aware of the rich development in last years of the field of equilibrium problems, which has taken different directions and involved several tools such as vector equilibrium problems.

We first present the strong and weak set-valued equilibrium problems. Next, we obtain three main results on the existence of solutions of strong and weak set-valued equilibrium problems, which generalize those for set-valued and single-valued equilibrium problems. Applications include Browder variational inclusions in the realm of real normed vector spaces. Results on the existence of solutions of Browder variational inclusions involving set-valued operators, with bounded in norm values and satisfying a condition related to the existence of a maximum rather than the weak* compactness, are presented. Results involving demicontinuous set-valued operators are also given.

4.2.1 The Strong and Weak Set-Valued Equilibrium Problem

Let C be a nonempty subset of a real topological Hausdorff vector space and $\Phi : C \times C \rightrightarrows \mathbb{R}$ be a set-valued mapping called *a set-valued bifunction*. Recall from Chapter 2 that the *strong set-valued equilibrium problem* is a problem of the form

$$\text{find } x^* \in C \text{ such that } \Phi\left(x^*, y\right) \subset \mathbb{R}_+ \quad \forall y \in C. \quad \text{(Ssvep)}$$

The *weak set-valued equilibrium problem* is a problem of the form

$$\text{find } x^* \in C \text{ such that } \Phi\left(x^*, y\right) \cap \mathbb{R}_+ \neq \emptyset \quad \forall y \in C. \tag{Wsvep}$$

In the special case where Φ is a single-valued mapping, the strong and the weak set-valued equilibrium problems are the same, and coincide with what is often called, an equilibrium problem in the sense of Blum, Muu, and Oettli or inequality of Ky Fan-type, due to their contribution to the field.

Example 4.1. Let C be a nonempty, closed, and convex subset of a real normed vector space X. Endowed with the weak topology, X is a real topological Hausdorff vector space. Let $F : C \rightrightarrows X^*$ be a set-valued operator. The problem

$$\text{find } x_0 \in C \text{ such that } \left\{\langle x_0^*, y - x_0\rangle : x_0^* \in F(x_0)\right\} \subset \mathbb{R}_+ \quad \text{for all } y \in C$$

is an example of a strong set-valued equilibrium problem in the real topological Hausdorff vector space X. The problem

$$\text{find } x_0 \in C \text{ such that } \left\{\langle x_0^*, y - x_0\rangle : x_0^* \in F(x_0)\right\} \cap \mathbb{R}_+ \neq \emptyset \quad \text{for all } y \in C$$

is an example of a weak set-valued equilibrium problem in the real topological Hausdorff vector space X.

In practice, examples are often taken in the settings of real normed vector spaces which are special cases of real topological Hausdorff vector spaces. The following example is an application of the strong set-valued equilibrium problems to fixed point theory.

Example 4.2. Let C be a nonempty, closed, and convex subset of a real normed vector space X and $F : C \rightrightarrows X^*$ be a set-valued operator. Solving the strong set-valued equilibrium problem

$$\text{find } x_0 \in C \text{ such that}$$
$$\text{dist}(y, F(x_0)) - \text{dist}(x_0, F(x_0))[0, +\infty[\subset \mathbb{R}_+ \quad \text{for all } y \in C$$

provides us with a tool to obtain a version of Kakutani fixed point theorem on the existence of fixed points of F.

The following example is an application of the weak set-valued equilibrium problems to economic equilibrium theory.

Example 4.3. Consider the simplex

$$M^n := \left\{ x := (x_1, \ldots, x_n) \in \mathbb{R}_+^n : \sum_{i=1}^n x_i = 1 \right\}$$

and a set-valued mapping $C : M^n \rightrightarrows \mathbb{R}^n$. According to Debreu-Gale-Nikaïdo theorem, under some conditions and if the Walras law holds which states that for every (x, y) in the graph of C we have $\langle y, x \rangle \geq 0$, then there exists $x_0 \in M^n$ such that

$$C(x_0) \cap \mathbb{R}^n_+ \neq \emptyset.$$

For every $x \in M^n$ and $y \in \mathbb{R}^n$, we set

$$\sigma(C(x), y) := \sup_{z \in C(x)} \langle z, y \rangle,$$

and we finally define the set-valued mapping $\Phi : M^n \times M^n \rightrightarrows \mathbb{R}$ by

$$\Phi(x, y) := \left]-\infty, \sigma(C(x), y)\right].$$

Solving the weak set-valued equilibrium problem

$$\text{find } x^* \in C \text{ such that } \Phi\left(x^*, y\right) \cap \mathbb{R}_+ \neq \emptyset \quad \forall y \in C,$$

provides us with a tool to obtain a version of Debreu-Gale-Nikaïdo-type theorem on the existence of $x_0 \in M^n$ such that

$$C(x_0) \cap \mathbb{R}^n_+ \neq \emptyset.$$

This result is a Debreu-Gale-Nikaïdo-type theorem, which extends the famous classical result in economic equilibrium theory by weakening the conditions on the collective Walras law. It has been obtained in [115, Theorem 5.1] under the weakened condition of assuming that the Walras law holds only on a self-segment-dense subset D of M^n.

4.2.2   Concepts of Continuity

The notions of convexity (concavity) and convexly quasi-convexity (concavely quasi-convexity) of set-valued mappings have been introduced in Chapter 1. Now we deal with continuity concepts of set-valued mappings. Lower and upper semicontinuity (defined also in Chapter 1) are the most known among them. However, these concepts applied to single-valued mappings, they produce the continuity, which is too strong in many applications.

As for convexity and concavity, the notions of lower and upper semicontinuity of set-valued mappings are not limited to extended real set-valued mappings and therefore, they may be too stronger than the lower and upper semicontinuity of extended real single-valued mappings. Here, we develop weaker notions of lower and upper semicontinuity for extended real set-valued mappings, which generalize both those for set-valued mappings and extended real single-valued mappings.

Let X be a Hausdorff topological space and $F : X \rightrightarrows \overline{\mathbb{R}}$ an extended real set-valued mapping. We first derive two definitions from lower semicontinuity of set-valued mappings.

We say that F is *l-lower semicontinuous* at $x \in X$ if for every $\lambda \in \mathbb{R}$ such that $F(x) \cap]\lambda, +\infty] \neq \emptyset$, there exists an open neighborhood U of x such that $F(x') \cap]\lambda, +\infty] \neq \emptyset$, for every $x' \in U$.

We observe that the notion of l-lower semicontinuous generalizes both lower semicontinuity of extended real single-valued mappings and that of lower semicontinuity of set-valued mappings.

We say that F is l-lower semicontinuous on a subset S of X if F is l-lower semicontinuous at every point of S.

Proposition 4.4. *Let X be a Hausdorff topological space, S a subset of X, and $F : X \rightrightarrows \overline{\mathbb{R}}$ a set-valued mapping. Then, F is l-lower semicontinuous on S if and only if for every $\lambda \in \mathbb{R}$, we have*

$$F^+ ([-\infty, \lambda]) \cap S = \mathrm{cl}\left(F^+ ([-\infty, \lambda])\right) \cap S.$$

Proof. Assume that F is l-lower semicontinuous on S and let $\lambda \in \mathbb{R}$. Let $x \in \mathrm{cl}\left(F^+ ([-\infty, \lambda])\right) \cap S$. If $x \notin F^+ ([-\infty, \lambda])$, then $F(x) \cap]\lambda, +\infty] \neq \emptyset$. Since $x \in S$, then there exists an open neighborhood U of x such that $F(x') \cap]\lambda, +\infty] \neq \emptyset$, for every $x' \in U$. It follows that $U \cap F^+ ([-\infty, \lambda]) = \emptyset$, which contradicts the fact that $x \in \mathrm{cl}\left(F^+ ([-\infty, \lambda])\right)$.

Conversely, let $x \in S$ and $\lambda \in \mathbb{R}$ be such that $F(x) \cap]\lambda, +\infty] \neq \emptyset$. Then $x \notin F^+ ([-\infty, \lambda])$ and therefore, $x \notin \mathrm{cl}\left(F^+ ([-\infty, \lambda])\right)$. Put $U = X \setminus \mathrm{cl}\left(F^+ ([-\infty, \lambda])\right)$, which is an open neighborhood of x. For every $x' \in U$, we have $x' \notin \mathrm{cl}\left(F^+ ([-\infty, \lambda])\right)$ and then, $x' \notin F^+ ([-\infty, \lambda])$. We conclude that $F(x') \cap]\lambda, +\infty] \neq \emptyset$, for every $x' \in U$. $\qquad\square$

Example 4.4. Consider the extended real set-valued mapping $F : \mathbb{R} \rightrightarrows \overline{\mathbb{R}}$ defined by

$$F(x) := \begin{cases} [0, +\infty], & \text{if } x = 0, \\ \left[\frac{1}{|x|}, +\infty\right], & \text{otherwise.} \end{cases}$$

Clearly, F is l-lower semicontinuous on $\mathbb{R}$. However, F is not lower semicontinuous at 0. Indeed, take $V =]a, b[, a, b \in \mathbb{R}_+$ and $a < b$. We have $F(0) \cap V \neq \emptyset$, but any open neighborhood of 0 contains a small enough point x such that $\frac{1}{|x|} > b$.

We say that F is *l-upper semicontinuous* at $x \in X$, if for every $\lambda \in \mathbb{R}$ such that $F(x) \cap [-\infty, \lambda[\neq \emptyset$, there exists an open neighborhood U of x such that $F(x') \cap [-\infty, \lambda[\neq \emptyset$, for every $x' \in U$.

Clearly, the notion of l-upper semicontinuous generalizes both upper semicontinuity of extended real single-valued mappings and lower semicontinuity of set-valued mappings. Also, an extended real set-valued mapping F is l-lower semicontinuous at $x \in X$ if and only if $-F$ is l-upper semicontinuous at x.

We say that F is l-upper semicontinuous on a subset S of X if F is l-upper semicontinuous at every point of S.

By a similar proof to that of Proposition 4.4, we obtain the following result for l-upper semicontinuous set-valued mappings.

Proposition 4.5. *Let X be a Hausdorff topological space, S a subset of X, and $F : X \rightrightarrows \overline{\mathbb{R}}$ a set-valued mapping. Then, F is l-upper semicontinuous on S if and only if for every $\lambda \in \mathbb{R}$, we have*

$$F^+ \left([\lambda, +\infty] \right) \cap S = \mathrm{cl} \left(F^+ \left([\lambda, +\infty] \right) \right) \cap S.$$

Example 4.5. Consider the extended real set-valued mapping $F : \mathbb{R} \rightrightarrows \overline{\mathbb{R}}$ defined by

$$F(x) := \begin{cases} [-\infty, 0], & \text{if } x = 0, \\ \left[\infty, -\frac{1}{|x|} \right], & \text{otherwise.} \end{cases}$$

Clearly F is l-upper semicontinuous on $\mathbb{R}$, but it is not lower semicontinuous at 0.

Now, we derive two other definitions from upper semicontinuity of set-valued mappings.

We say that F is *u-lower semicontinuous* at $x \in X$ if for every $\lambda \in \mathbb{R}$ such that $F(x) \subset]\lambda, +\infty]$, there exists an open neighborhood U of x such that $F(x') \subset]\lambda, +\infty]$, for every $x' \in U$.

We observe that the notion of u-lower semicontinuous generalizes both lower semicontinuity of extended real single-valued mappings and that of upper semicontinuity of set-valued mappings.

We say that F is u-lower semicontinuous on a subset S of X if F is u-lower semicontinuous at every point of S.

Proposition 4.6. *Let X be a Hausdorff topological space, S a subset of X, and $F : X \rightrightarrows \overline{\mathbb{R}}$ a set-valued mapping. Then, F is u-lower semicontinuous on S if and only if for every $\lambda \in \mathbb{R}$, we have*

$$F^- \left([-\infty, \lambda] \right) \cap S = \mathrm{cl} \left(F^- \left([-\infty, \lambda] \right) \right) \cap S.$$

Proof. Assume that F is u-lower semicontinuous on S and let $\lambda \in \mathbb{R}$. Let $x \in \mathrm{cl} \left(F^- \left([-\infty, \lambda] \right) \right) \cap S$. If $x \notin F^- \left([-\infty, \lambda] \right)$, then $F(x) \subset]\lambda, +\infty]$. Since $x \in S$, then there exists an open neighborhood U of x such that $F(x') \subset]\lambda, +\infty[$, for every $x' \in U$. It follows that $U \cap F^- \left([-\infty, \lambda] \right) = \emptyset$, which contradicts the fact that $x \in \mathrm{cl} \left(F^- \left([-\infty, \lambda] \right) \right)$.

Conversely, let $x \in S$ and $\lambda \in \mathbb{R}$ be such that $F(x) \subset]\lambda, +\infty]$. Then $x \notin F^- \left([-\infty, \lambda] \right)$ and therefore, $x \notin \mathrm{cl} \left(F^- \left([-\infty, \lambda] \right) \right)$. Put $U = X \setminus \mathrm{cl} \left(F^- \left([-\infty, \lambda] \right) \right)$, which is an open neighborhood of x. For every $x' \in U$, we have $x' \notin \mathrm{cl} \left(F^- \left([-\infty, \lambda] \right) \right)$ and then, $x' \notin F^- \left([-\infty, \lambda] \right)$. We conclude that $F(x') \subset]\lambda, +\infty]$, for every $x' \in U$. □

Example 4.6. Consider the extended real set-valued mapping $F : \mathbb{R} \rightrightarrows \overline{\mathbb{R}}$ defined by

$$F(x) := \begin{cases} \{0\}, & \text{if } x = 0, \\ \left[\frac{1}{|x|}, +\infty\right], & \text{otherwise.} \end{cases}$$

Clearly, F is u-lower semicontinuous on $\mathbb{R}$. However, F is not upper semicontinuous at 0. Indeed, take $V =]a, b[$, $a \in \mathbb{R}_-$ and $b \in \mathbb{R}_+$. We have $F(0) \subset V$, but any open neighborhood of 0 contains a small enough point x such that $\frac{1}{|x|} > b$.

We say that F is *u-upper semicontinuous* at $x \in X$ if for every $\lambda \in \mathbb{R}$ such that $F(x) \subset [-\infty, \lambda[$, there exists an open neighborhood U of x such that $F(x') \subset [-\infty, \lambda[$, for every $x' \in U$.

Clearly, the notion of u-upper semicontinuous generalizes both upper semicontinuity of extended real single-valued mappings and upper semicontinuity of set-valued mappings. Also, an extended real set-valued mapping F is u-lower semicontinuous at $x \in X$ if and only if $-F$ is u-upper semicontinuous at x.

We say that F is u-upper semicontinuous on a subset S of X if F is u-upper semicontinuous at every point of S.

By a similar proof to that of Proposition 4.6, we obtain the following result for u-upper semicontinuous set-valued mappings.

Proposition 4.7. *Let X be a Hausdorff topological space, S a subset of X, and $F : X \rightrightarrows \overline{\mathbb{R}}$ a set-valued mapping. Then, F is u-upper semicontinuous on S if and only if for every $\lambda \in \mathbb{R}$, we have*

$$F^-([\lambda, +\infty]) \cap S = \mathrm{cl}\left(F^-([\lambda, +\infty])\right) \cap S.$$

Example 4.7. Consider the extended real set-valued mapping $F : \mathbb{R} \rightrightarrows \overline{\mathbb{R}}$ defined by

$$F(x) := \begin{cases} \{0\}, & \text{if } x = 0, \\ \left[-\infty, -\frac{1}{|x|}\right], & \text{otherwise.} \end{cases}$$

Clearly, F is u-upper semicontinuous on $\mathbb{R}$, but it is not upper semicontinuous at 0.

As a summary, we have the following characterizations for extended real single-valued mappings.

Proposition 4.8. *Let X be a Hausdorff topological space and $x_0 \in X$. For an extended real single-valued mapping $f : X \to \overline{\mathbb{R}}$, the following conditions are equivalent:*

1. *f is lower semicontinuous at x_0,*
2. *f is l-lower semicontinuous at x_0,*
3. *f is u-lower semicontinuous at x_0.*

Proposition 4.9. *Let X be a Hausdorff topological space and $x_0 \in X$. For an extended real single-valued mapping $f : X \to \overline{\mathbb{R}}$, the following conditions are equivalent:*

1. f *is upper semicontinuous at* x_0,
2. f *is l-upper semicontinuous at* x_0,
3. f *is u-upper semicontinuous at* x_0.

4.2.3 Strong and Weak Set-Valued Equilibrium Problems: Existence of Solutions

In what follows, we deal with the existence of solutions of both strong set-valued equilibrium problems and weak set-valued equilibrium problems.

We first recall for convenience the notion of KKM mapping (given in Chapter 3) and the intersection lemma due to Ky Fan [73], (Theorem 3.2) which generalizes the Tychonoff fixed point theorem.

Let X be a real topological Hausdorff vector space and M a subset of X. A set-valued mapping $F : M \rightrightarrows X$ is said to be a KKM mapping if for every finite subset $\{x_1, \ldots, x_n\}$ of M, we have

$$\operatorname{conv}\{x_1, \ldots x_n\} \subset \bigcup_{i=1}^{n} F(x_i).$$

By Ky Fan's lemma [73], if

1. F is a KKM mapping,
2. $F(x)$ is closed for every $x \in M$, and
3. there exists $x_0 \in M$ such that $F(x_0)$ is compact,

then $\bigcap_{x \in M} F(x) \neq \emptyset$.

We define the following set-valued mappings $\Phi^+, \Phi^{++} : C \rightrightarrows C$ by

$$\Phi^+(y) := \{x \in C : \Phi(x, y) \cap \mathbb{R}_+ \neq \emptyset\} \quad \text{for all } y \in C,$$

and

$$\Phi^{++}(y) := \{x \in C : \Phi(x, y) \subset \mathbb{R}_+\} \quad \text{for all } y \in C.$$

We remark that $\Phi^{++}(y) \subset \Phi^+(y)$, for every $y \in C$ and

1. $x_0 \in C$ is a solution of the set-valued equilibrium problem (Wsvep) if and only if $x_0 \in \bigcap_{y \in C} \Phi^+(y)$,
2. $x_0 \in C$ is a solution of the set-valued equilibrium problem (Ssvep) if and only if $x_0 \in \bigcap_{y \in C} \Phi^{++}(y)$.

Set

$$\operatorname{cl} \Phi^+(y) = \operatorname{cl}\left(\Phi^+(y)\right) \quad \text{and} \quad \operatorname{cl} \Phi^{++}(y) = \operatorname{cl}\left(\Phi^{++}(y)\right),$$

the closure of $\Phi^+(y)$ and $\Phi^{++}(y)$ respectively, for every $y \in C$.

Lemma 4.3. *Let C be a nonempty and convex subset of a real topological vector space. Let* $\Phi : C \times C \rightrightarrows \mathbb{R}$ *be a set-valued mapping, and assume that the following conditions hold:*

1. $\Phi(x, x) \subset \mathbb{R}_+$, *for every* $x \in C$;
2. Φ *is convexly quasi-convex in its second variable on C.*

Then the set-valued mappings $\operatorname{cl} \Phi^{++} : C \rightrightarrows C$ *and* $\operatorname{cl} \Phi^+ : C \rightrightarrows C$ *are KKM mappings.*

Proof. It suffices to prove that the set-valued mapping $\Phi^{++} : C \rightrightarrows C$ is a KKM mapping. Let $\{y_1, \ldots, y_n\} \subset C$ and $\{\lambda_1, \ldots, \lambda_n\} \subset \mathbb{R}_+$ be such that $\sum_{i=1}^{n} \lambda_i = 1$. Put $\tilde{y} = \sum_{i=1}^{n} \lambda_i y_i$. By assumption (2), for $\{z_1, \ldots, z_n\}$ with $z_i \in \Phi(\tilde{y}, y_i)$ for every $i = 1, \ldots, n$, there exists $z \in \Phi(\tilde{y}, \tilde{y})$ such that

$$z \leq \max\{z_i : i = 1, \ldots, n\}.$$

We have $z \geq 0$ since $\Phi(\tilde{y}, \tilde{y}) \subset \mathbb{R}_+$ by assumption (1). It follows that there exists $i_0 \in \{1, \ldots, n\}$ such that $\Phi(\tilde{y}, y_{i_0}) \cap \mathbb{R}_-^* = \emptyset$, which implies that $\Phi(\tilde{y}, y_{i_0}) \subset \mathbb{R}_+$. Otherwise, all the z_i can be taken in $\mathbb{R}_-^*$, and therefore $z \in \mathbb{R}_-^*$, which is impossible. We conclude that

$$\sum_{i=1}^{n} \lambda_i y_i = \tilde{y} \in \Phi^{++}(y_{i_0}) \subset \bigcup_{i=1}^{n} \Phi^{++}(y_i),$$

which proves that Φ^{++} is a KKM mapping. $\qquad\square$

The following result generalizes both [7, Theorem 3.1] obtained for set-valued equilibrium problems when the self-segment-dense set D is equal to C, and [8, Theorem 3.1] for single-valued equilibrium problems.

Theorem 4.5. *Let C be a nonempty, closed, and convex subset of a real topological vector space. Let* $\Phi : C \times C \rightrightarrows \mathbb{R}$ *be a set-valued mapping, and assume that the following conditions hold:*

1. $\Phi(x, x) \subset \mathbb{R}_+$, *for every* $x \in C$;
2. Φ *is convexly quasi-convex in its second variable on C;*
3. *there exist a compact set K of C and a point* $y_0 \in K$ *such that* $\Phi(x, y_0) \cap \mathbb{R}_-^* \neq \emptyset$, *for every* $x \in C \setminus K$;
4. Φ *is l-upper semicontinuous in its first variable on K.*

Then the set of solutions of the set-valued equilibrium problem (Ssvep) is a nonempty and compact set.

Proof. Assumption (1) yields $\Phi^{++}(y)$ is nonempty, for every $y \in C$. We observe that $\operatorname{cl} \Phi^{++}(y)$ is closed for every $y \in C$, and $\operatorname{cl} \Phi^{++}(y_0)$ is compact since it lies in K by assumption (3).

The set-valued mapping cl $\Phi^{++} : C \rightrightarrows C$ is a KKM mapping by Lemma 4.3. Then, by using Ky Fan lemma, we have

$$\bigcap_{y \in C} \text{cl} \, \Phi^{++}(y) \neq \emptyset.$$

Since the subset $\Phi^{++}(y_0)$ is contained in the compact K, then

$$\bigcap_{y \in C} \Phi^{++}(y) = \bigcap_{y \in C} \left(\Phi^{++}(y) \cap K \right),$$

and

$$\bigcap_{y \in C} \text{cl} \, \Phi^{++}(y) = \bigcap_{y \in C} \left(\text{cl} \, \Phi^{++}(y) \cap K \right).$$

We remark that for all $y \in C$, $\Phi^{++}(y)$ is the upper inverse set $\Phi^+([0, +\infty[, y)$ of $[0, +\infty[$ by the set-valued mapping $\Phi(., y)$ which is l-upper semicontinuous on K. Then, by Proposition 4.5, we have cl $\Phi^{++}(y) \cap K = \Phi^{++}(y) \cap K$. Therefore

$$\bigcap_{y \in C} \text{cl} \, \Phi^{++}(y) = \bigcap_{y \in C} \left(\text{cl} \, \Phi^{++}(y) \cap K \right) = \bigcap_{y \in C} \left(\Phi^{++}(y) \cap K \right) = \bigcap_{y \in C} \Phi^{++}(y).$$

It follows that the set of solutions of the strong set-valued equilibrium problem (Ssvep) is nonempty, and compact since it is closed and contained in the compact set K. $\qquad \square$

Now, we turn to weak set-valued equilibrium problems. First, we obtain the following result which also generalizes [8, Theorem 3.1] for single-valued equilibrium problems by using u-upper semicontinuity which is derived from upper semicontinuity of set-valued mappings rather than l-upper semicontinuity in Theorem 4.5 which is derived from lower semicontinuity.

Theorem 4.6. *Let C be a nonempty, closed, and convex subset of a real topological vector space. Let $\Phi : C \times C \rightrightarrows \mathbb{R}$ be a set-valued mapping, and assume that the following conditions hold:*

1. *$\Phi(x, x) \subset \mathbb{R}_+$, for every $x \in C$;*
2. *Φ is convexly quasi-convex in its second variable on C;*
3. *there exist a compact set K of C and a point $y_0 \in K$ such that $\Phi(x, y_0) \subset \mathbb{R}^*_-$, for every $x \in C \setminus K$;*
4. *Φ is u-upper semicontinuous in its first variable on K.*

Then the set of solutions of the set-valued equilibrium problem (Wsvep) is a nonempty and compact set.

Proof. Assumption (1) yields that $\Phi^+(y)$ is nonempty, for every $y \in C$. We observe that cl $\Phi^+(y)$ is closed for every $y \in C$, and cl $\Phi^+(y_0)$ is compact since it lies in K, by assumption (3).

The set-valued mapping cl $\Phi^+ : C \rightrightarrows C$ is a KKM mapping by Lemma 4.3. Then, by the Ky Fan lemma, we have

$$\bigcap_{y \in C} \text{cl} \, \Phi^+(y) \neq \emptyset.$$

Since the subset $\Phi^+(y_0)$ is contained in the compact K, then

$$\bigcap_{y \in C} \Phi^+(y) = \bigcap_{y \in C} \left(\Phi^+(y) \cap K \right),$$

and

$$\bigcap_{y \in C} \text{cl} \, \Phi^+(y) = \bigcap_{y \in C} \left(\text{cl} \, \Phi^+(y) \cap K \right).$$

We remark that for all $y \in C$, $\Phi^+(y)$ is the lower inverse set $\Phi^-([0, +\infty[, y)$ of $[0, +\infty[$ by the set-valued mapping $\Phi(., y)$ which is u-upper semicontinuous on K. Then, by Proposition 4.7, we have cl $\Phi^+(y) \cap K = \Phi^+(y) \cap K$. Therefore

$$\bigcap_{y \in C} \text{cl} \, \Phi^+(y) = \bigcap_{y \in C} \left(\text{cl} \, \Phi^+(y) \cap K \right) = \bigcap_{y \in C} \left(\Phi^+(y) \cap K \right) = \bigcap_{y \in C} \Phi^+(y).$$

It follows that the set of solutions of the set-valued equilibrium problem (Wsvep) is nonempty and compact, since it is closed and contained in the compact set K. $\square$

In many applications, the set-valued Φ is concave in its second variable. We give here the following result for concavely quasi-convex set-valued mappings.

Lemma 4.4. *Let C be a nonempty convex subset of a real topological vector space. Let $\Phi : C \times C \rightrightarrows \mathbb{R}$ be a set-valued mapping, and assume that the following conditions hold:*

1. $\Phi(x, x) \cap \mathbb{R}_+ \neq \emptyset$, *for every $x \in C$;*
2. Φ *is concavely quasi-convex in its second variable on C.*

Then, the set-valued mapping cl $\Phi^+ : C \rightrightarrows C$ *is a KKM mapping.*

Proof. Let $\{y_1, \ldots, y_n\} \subset C$ and $\{\lambda_1, \ldots, \lambda_n\} \subset \mathbb{R}_+$ be such that $\sum_{i=1}^n \lambda_i = 1$. Put $\tilde{y} = \sum_{i=1}^n \lambda_i y_i$. By assumption (2), for $z \in \Phi(\tilde{y}, \tilde{y})$, there exist $\{z_1, \ldots, z_n\}$ with $z_i \in \Phi(\tilde{y}, y_i)$ for every $i = 1, \ldots, n$, such that

$$z \leq \max \{z_i : i = 1, \ldots, n\}.$$

It follows that there exists $i_0 \in \{1, \ldots, n\}$ such that $\Phi(\tilde{y}, y_{i_0}) \cap \mathbb{R}_+ \neq \emptyset$. Otherwise, all the z_i are in $\mathbb{R}_-^*$, and therefore $z \in \mathbb{R}_-^*$. Since $z \in \Phi(\tilde{y}, \tilde{y})$, then

$\Phi(\tilde{y}, \tilde{y}) \subset \mathbb{R}^*_-$, which yields a contradiction since $\Phi(\tilde{y}, \tilde{y}) \cap \mathbb{R}_+ \neq \emptyset$ by assumption (1). We conclude that

$$\sum_{i=1}^{n} \lambda_i y_i = \tilde{y} \in \Phi^+(y_{i_0}) \subset \bigcup_{i=1}^{n} \Phi^+(y_i),$$

which proves that $\mathrm{cl}\,\Phi^+$ is a KKM mapping. $\qquad\qquad\qquad\square$

The following result generalizes both [7, Theorem 3.2] obtained for set-valued equilibrium problems when the self-segment-dense set D is equal to C, and [7, Theorem 3.1] for single-valued equilibrium problems. Here, we remark that the conclusion is the same as in Theorem 4.6 for convexly quasi-convex set-valued mappings, but with weaker first condition.

Theorem 4.7. *Let C be a nonempty, closed, and convex subset of a real topological vector space. Let $\Phi : C \times C \rightrightarrows \mathbb{R}$ be a set-valued mapping, and assume that the following conditions hold:*

1. $\Phi(x, x) \cap \mathbb{R}_+ \neq \emptyset$, *for every* $x \in C$;
2. Φ *is concavely quasi-convex in its second variable on* C;
3. *there exist a compact set K of C and a point $y_0 \in K$ such that $\Phi(x, y_0) \subset \mathbb{R}^*_-$, for every* $x \in C \setminus K$;
4. Φ *is u-upper semicontinuous in its first variable on* K.

Then, the set of solutions of the set-valued equilibrium problem (Wsvep) *is a nonempty and compact set.*

Proof. By using Lemma 4.4 instead of Lemma 4.3, the proof follows step by step that of Theorem 4.6. $\qquad\qquad\qquad\square$

4.2.4 Application to Browder Variational Inclusions

Browder variational inclusions appear as a generalization of Browder-Hartman-Stampacchia variational inequalities and have many applications, including applications to nonlinear elliptic boundary value problems and the surjectivity of set-valued mappings.

Let C be a nonempty, closed, and convex subset of a real normed vector space X. A set-valued operator $F : C \rightrightarrows X^*$ is said to be coercive on C if there exists $y_0 \in C$ such that

$$\lim_{\substack{\|x\| \to +\infty \\ x \in C}} \frac{\inf_{x^* \in F(x)} \langle x^*, x - y_0 \rangle}{\|x\|} = +\infty.$$

We observe that if F is coercive on C, then there exists $R > 0$ such that $y_0 \in K_R$ and $\langle x^*, y_0 - x \rangle \subset \mathbb{R}^*_-$, for every $x \in C \setminus K_R$ and every $x^* \in F(x)$, where $K_R = \{x \in C : \|x\| \leq R\}$. Clearly, K_R is weakly compact whenever X is reflexive. The set K_R (which may not be unique) is called a set of coerciveness. In what follows, we will need a compact set of coerciveness. Unfortunately, closed balls in X are not compact except if X is finite dimensional space.

In the sequel, for $x \in X$ and a subset A of X^*, we set

$$\langle A, x \rangle = \left\{ \langle x^*, x \rangle : x^* \in A \right\}.$$

Problems of the form: "find $x \in C$ such that $\langle A, x \rangle \subset \mathbb{R}_+$ or $\langle A, x \rangle \cap \mathbb{R}_+ \neq \emptyset$" are called Browder variational inclusions.

We note that the condition of either X is a Banach space or the set-valued operator F has convex values on the set of coerciveness is required.

In the next result, we do not need the weak* compactness of the values of the set-valued operator. We say that a subset S of X^* *attains its pairwise upper bounds* on a subset A if for every $z \in A$, the set $\{\langle x^*, z \rangle : x^* \in S\}$ has a maximum in $\mathbb{R}$. We observe that if a subset S of X^* is weak* compact, then the set $\{\langle x^*, z \rangle : x^* \in S\}$ is compact, and therefore it attains its minimum and a maximum, for every $z \in X$.

By using our notions of semicontinuity and convexity of real set-valued mappings, we obtain the following existence result. Here, Theorem 4.7 will be used because the constructed real set-valued bifunction in the proof is concave in its second variable.

Theorem 4.8. *Let X be a real normed vector space, C a nonempty, closed, and convex subset of X. Suppose that $F : C \rightrightarrows X^*$ has the following conditions:*

1. *there exist a compact subset K of C and $y_0 \in K$ such that $\langle F(x), y_0 - x \rangle \subset \mathbb{R}_-^*$, for every $x \in C \setminus K$;*
2. *F is upper semicontinuous on K;*
3. *for every $x \in K$, $F(x)$ is norm bounded and attains its pairwise upper bounds on $C - x$.*

Then there exists $\overline{x} \in K$ such that $\langle F(\overline{x}), y - \overline{x} \rangle \cap \mathbb{R}_+ \neq \emptyset$, for every $y \in C$.

Proof. Define the set-valued mapping $\Phi : C \times C \rightrightarrows \mathbb{R}$ by

$$\Phi(x, y) := \langle F(x), y - x \rangle.$$

We show that hypotheses of Theorem 4.7 are satisfied. We remark that Φ is concave in its second variable, and then it is concavely quasi-convex in its second variable. Except the last condition, all the other conditions hold easily from our assumptions.

To prove that Φ is u-upper semicontinuous in its first variable on K, fix $y \in C$, and let $x \in K$ and $\lambda \in \mathbb{R}$ be such that $\Phi(x, y) \subset \,]-\infty, \lambda[$. It follows that $\langle F(x), y - x \rangle \subset \,]-\infty, \lambda[$. Set $\lambda_x := \max(\langle F(x), y - x \rangle) < \lambda$, $\delta := \frac{\lambda - \lambda_x}{2}$ and

$$\delta_1 := \min \left\{ \frac{\delta}{3(\|x\| + 1)}, \frac{\delta}{3(\|y\| + 1)} \right\},$$

where $\|.\|$ denotes the norm of X. Set $O := \bigcup_{x^* \in F(x)} B_{X^*}(x^*, \delta_1)$, where $B_{X^*}(x^*, \delta_1) = \{z \in X^* : \|z - x^*\|_* < \delta_1\}$, and $\|.\|_*$ denotes the norm of X^*. We observe that $F(x)$ is contained in the open set O, and by the upper semicontinuity of F on K, let $\eta > 0$ be such that $F(w) \subset O$ for every $w \in B_X(x, \eta) \cap C$, where $B_X(x, \eta) = \{w \in X : \|w - x\| < \eta\}$. Since $F(x)$ is norm bounded, put $\|F(x)\|_* := \sup\{\|x^*\|_* : x^* \in F(x)\}$ which is in $\mathbb{R}$. Finally, we set

$$\eta_1 := \min\left\{\frac{\delta}{3\,(\|F(x)\|_* + 1)}, \eta, 1\right\},$$

and $U = B_X(x, \eta_1) \cap C$ which is an open subset of C containing x.

We show that $\Phi(z, y) \subset \,]-\infty, \lambda[$, for every $z \in U$. To do this, let $z \in U$ and $z^* \in F(z)$. Let $x_0^* \in F(x)$ be such that $z^* \in B_{X^*}(x_0^*, \delta_1)$. We have

$$
\begin{aligned}
\left|\langle z^*, y - z\rangle - \langle x_0^*, y - x\rangle\right| &= \left|\langle x_0^* - z^*, z\rangle + \langle x_0^*, x - z\rangle - \langle x_0^* - z^*, y\rangle\right| \\
&\leq \|x_0^* - z^*\|_* \|z\| + \|x_0^*\|_* \|x - z\| + \|x_0^* - z^*\|_* \|y\| \\
&< \frac{\delta\,(\|x\| + \eta_1)}{3\,(\|x\| + 1)} + \frac{\delta\|x_0^*\|_*}{3\,(\|F(x)\|_* + 1)} + \frac{\delta\|y\|}{3\,(\|y\| + 1)} \\
&< \frac{\delta}{3} + \frac{\delta}{3} + \frac{\delta}{3} = \delta.
\end{aligned}
$$

It follows that $\langle z^*, y - z\rangle < \langle x_0^*, y - x\rangle + \delta \leq \lambda_x + \delta = \frac{\lambda + \lambda_x}{2} < \lambda$. Since z is arbitrary in U and z^* is arbitrary in $F(z)$, then $\Phi(z, y) \subset \,]-\infty, \lambda[$, for every $z \in U$. This means that Φ is u-upper semicontinuous in its first variable on K. $\qquad\square$

Next, we obtain the following results on the existence of solutions of Browder variational inclusions under assumptions of demicontinuity.

Recall that an open half-space in a real Hausdorff topological vector space E is a subset of the form

$$\{u \in E : \varphi(u) < r\}$$

for some continuous linear functional φ on E, not identically zero, and for some real number r.

Let X be a Hausdorff topological space and E a real Hausdorff topological vector space. Recall that a set-valued operator $F : X \rightrightarrows E$ is said to be *upper demicontinuous at* $x \in X$ if for every open half-space H containing $F(x)$, there exists a neighborhood U of x such that $F(x') \subset H$ for all $x' \in U$. Next, F is said to be upper demicontinuous on X if it is upper demicontinuous at every point of X. We say that F is upper demicontinuous on a subset S of X if it is upper demicontinuous at every point of S.

Proposition 4.10. *Let X be a real normed vector space, C be a nonempty, closed, and convex subset of X, and $S \subset C$. Suppose that $F : C \rightrightarrows X^*$ has the following conditions:*

1. *F is upper semicontinuous on S to X^* endowed with the weak* topology;*
2. *F has weak* compact values on S.*

Then F is upper demicontinuous on S to X^* endowed with the weak* topology.

Proof. Let $x \in K$ and consider an open half-space H in X^* of the form

$$\left\{ u \in X^* : \varphi(u) < r \right\}$$

such that $F(x) \subset H$, where φ is a weak* continuous linear functional on X^*, not identically zero, and $r \in \mathbb{R}$. Then, $\varphi(F(x))$ is compact and $\varphi(F(x)) \subset$ $]-\infty, r[$. Set $r_x := \max(\varphi(F(x))) < r$, $\delta := \frac{r-r_x}{2}$ and $\delta_1 := \frac{\delta}{\|\varphi\|}$. Note that $\|\varphi\| \in \mathbb{R}^*$ since φ is also continuous with respect to the strong topology, and not identically zero. Finally, put $O := \bigcup_{x^* \in F(x)} B_{X^*}(x^*, \delta_1)$, where $B_{X^*}(x^*, \delta_1) = \{z \in X^* : \|z - x^*\|_* < \delta_1\}$, and $\|.\|_*$ denotes the norm of X^*. We observe that $F(x)$ is contained in the open set O, and by the upper semicontinuity of F on K, let U be an open subset of C such that $F(z) \subset O$, for every $z \in U$.

We show that $F(z) \subset H$, for every $z \in U$. To do this, let $z \in U$ and $z^* \in F(z)$. Let $x_0^* \in F(x)$ be such that $z^* \in B_{X^*}(x_0^*, \delta_1)$. We have

$$\left| \varphi(z^*) - \varphi(x_0^*) \right| \leq \|\varphi\| \|z^* - x_0^*\| < \|\varphi\| \delta_1 = \|\varphi\| \frac{\delta}{\|\varphi\|} = \delta.$$

It follows that $\varphi(z^*) < \varphi(x_0^*) + \delta \leq r_x + \delta = \frac{r+r_x}{2} < r$. Since z is arbitrary in U and z^* is arbitrary in $F(z)$, then $F(z) \subset H$, for every $z \in U$. This means that F is upper demicontinuous on K. $\qquad\square$

Now, by using the notion of demicontinuous set-valued operators, we obtain the following result on the existence of solutions of Browder variational inclusions.

Theorem 4.9. *Let X be a real normed vector space, C a nonempty, closed, and convex subset of X. Suppose that $F : C \rightrightarrows X^*$ has the following conditions:*

1. *there exist a compact subset K of C and $y_0 \in C$ such that $\langle F(x), y - x \rangle \subset \mathbb{R}_-^*$, for every $x \in C \setminus K$;*
2. *F is upper demicontinuous on K to X^* endowed with the weak* topology.*

Then, there exists $\overline{x} \in K$ such that $\langle F(\overline{x}), y - \overline{x} \rangle \cap \mathbb{R}_+ \neq \emptyset$, for every $y \in C$.

Proof. Define the set-valued mapping $\Phi : C \times C \rightrightarrows \mathbb{R}$ by

$$\Phi(x, y) := \langle F(x), y - x \rangle.$$

It remains to prove that Φ is u-upper semicontinuous in its first variable on K. Fix $y \in C$, and let $x \in K$ and $\lambda \in \mathbb{R}$ be such that $\Phi(x, y) \subset]-\infty, \lambda[$. That is, $\langle F(x), y - x \rangle \subset]-\infty, \lambda[$. Consider φ defined on X^* by $\varphi(u) := \langle u, y - x \rangle$, for very $u \in X^*$. Then φ is not identically zero linear functional on X^* and it is weak* continuous. It follows that $F(x)$ is in the open half-space

$$H = \left\{ u \in X^* : \varphi(u) < \lambda \right\}$$

in X^*. Since F is upper demicontinuous on K, let U be an open neighborhood of x such that $F(x') \subset H$, for every $x' \in U$. It follows that $\Phi(x', y) \subset \,]-\infty, \lambda[$ for every $x' \in U$, which proves that Φ is u-upper semicontinuous in its first variable on K. $\qquad\square$

4.3 EQUILIBRIUM PROBLEMS GIVEN BY THE SUM OF TWO FUNCTIONS

An interesting special case of the equilibrium problem is, where the bifunction is given in the form $f(x, y) = g(x, y) + h(x, y)$ with $g, h : A \times A \to \mathbb{R}$. It was investigated already in [42], where the authors obtained existence results by imposing their assumptions separately on g and h. As stressed in [42], if $g = 0$, the result becomes a variant of Ky Fan's theorem [74], whereas for $h = 0$ it becomes a variant of the Browder-Minty theorem for variational inequalities (see, for instance, [45]).

4.3.1 The Vector-Valued Case

In this subsection we present the results obtained by Kassay and Miholca in [103] related to weak vector equilibrium problems, in the special case when the (vector-valued) bifunction is given by the sum of two other bifunctions.

Let X be a real topological vector space and $A \subset X$. Consider another real topological vector space Y, partially ordered by a proper convex cone $C \subset Y$ with nonempty interior. Let $g, h : A \times A \to Y$ and consider the problem of finding an element $x \in A$, such that:

$$g(x, y) + h(x, y) \notin -intC \quad \text{for all } y \in A. \qquad \text{(SWVEP)}$$

Throughout this section, if not otherwise stated, $A, B \subset X$ are nonempty convex sets (B being typically a compact subset of A, but not always). Let us first recall the following concept. If $B \subset A$, then $core_A B$, the core of B relative to A, is defined through

$$a \in core_A B \iff (a \in B \text{ and } B \cap (a, y] \neq \emptyset \text{ for all } y \in A \backslash B),$$

where $(a, y] = \{\lambda a + (1 - \lambda)y : \lambda \in [0, 1)\}$. Note that $core_A A = A$.

The following simple property will be useful in the sequel.

Lemma 4.5. *For all $x, y \in Y$ we have:*

$$x \in C, \ y \notin -intC \Rightarrow x + y \notin -intC.$$

The convexity concept for scalar functions has been extended in a natural way for vector-valued functions, according to the partial order introduced by the cone C.

Definition 4.3. A function $F : X \to Y$ is called C-convex, iff for each $x, y \in A$ and $\lambda \in [0, 1]$,

$$\lambda F(x) + (1 - \lambda)F(y) - F(\lambda x + (1 - \lambda)y) \in C.$$

F is said to be C-concave iff $-F$ is C-convex.

Next we present some monotonicity conditions for vector-valued bifunctions. In order to do this, let us first recall several specific monotonicity concepts for scalar bifunctions considered within the literature in the recent years. Most of these notions were inspired by similar (generalized) monotonicity concepts defined for operators acting from a topological vector space to its dual space.

Definition 4.4. The bifunction $f : A \times A \to \mathbb{R}$ is said to be

(i) *monotone* iff $f(x, y) + f(y, x) \leq 0$ for all $x, y \in A$;
(ii) *properly quasi-monotone* iff for arbitrary integer $n \geq 1$, all $x_1, \cdots, x_n \in A$ and all $\lambda_1, \cdots, \lambda_n \geq 0$ such that $\sum_{i=1}^{n} \lambda_i = 1$ it holds that

$$\min_{1 \leq i \leq n} f\left(x_i, \sum_{j=1}^{n} \lambda_j x_j\right) \leq 0.$$

Proper quasi-monotonicity was introduced by Zhou and Chen in [176] under the name of 0-*diagonal quasi-concavity*. Aiming to obtain existence results for (scalar) equilibrium problems, the authors of [93] introduced the following (slightly stronger) variant of proper quasi-monotonicity (called by themselves *property P4"*):

Definition 4.5. (cf. [93]) A bifunction $f : A \times A \to \mathbb{R}$ is said to be *essentially quasi-monotone* iff for arbitrary integer $n \geq 1$, for every $x_1, \cdots, x_n \in A$ and $\lambda_1, \cdots, \lambda_n \geq 0$ such that $\sum_{i=1}^{n} \lambda_i = 1$, it holds that

$$\sum_{i=1}^{n} \lambda_i f\left(x_i, \sum_{j=1}^{n} \lambda_j x_j\right) \leq 0.$$

The concept of essential quasi-monotonicity has been extended to vector-valued bifunctions in [103] as follows:

Definition 4.6. A bifunction $f : A \times A \to Y$ is said to be C-*essentially quasi-monotone* iff for arbitrary integer $n \geq 1$, for all $x_1, ... x_n \in A$ and all $\lambda_1, ... \lambda_n \geq 0$ such that $\sum_{i=1}^{n} \lambda_i = 1$ it holds that

$$\sum_{i=1}^{n} \lambda_i f\left(x_i, \sum_{j=1}^{n} \lambda_j x_j\right) \notin int C.$$

The next simple property provides sufficient conditions for C-essential quasi-monotonicity.

Proposition 4.11. *Suppose that $f : A \times A \to Y$ is C-monotone and C-convex in the second argument. Then f is C-essentially quasi-monotone.*

Proof. Take $x_1, \dots x_n \in A$ and $\lambda_1, \dots \lambda_n \geq 0$ such that $\sum_{i=1}^{n} \lambda_i = 1$ and set $z := \sum_{j=1}^{n} \lambda_j x_j$. Then

$$\sum_{i=1}^{n} \lambda_i f(x_i, z) \leq_C \sum_{i=1}^{n} \sum_{j=1}^{n} \lambda_i \lambda_j f(x_i, x_j)$$

$$= \frac{1}{2} \sum_{i,j=1}^{n} \lambda_i \lambda_j (f(x_i, x_j) + f(x_j, x_i)) \leq_C 0. \qquad \square$$

The next example shows that a C-essentially quasi-monotone bifunction is not necessarily C-monotone, even if it is C-convex in the second argument.

Example 4.8. Let $f : [0, 1] \times [0, 1] \to \mathbb{R}^2$ given by $f = (f_1, f_2)$, where $f_1(x, y) = |x - y|$, $f_2(x, y) = 0$ for every $x, y \in [0, 1]$. It is easy to see that f is $\mathbb{R}_+^2$-essentially quasi-monotone, $\mathbb{R}_+^2$-convex in the second argument, but not $\mathbb{R}_+^2$-monotone, since $f(1, 0) + f(0, 1) = (2, 0) \notin -\mathbb{R}_+^2$.

To start, let us first prove the following three lemmas. All of them serve as tools for the proofs of the main results. Moreover, the first one can also be seen as an existence result for a special vector equilibrium problem, therefore it seems interesting on its own.

Lemma 4.6. *Suppose that B is a compact subset of X, let $g : B \times B \to Y$ and $h : B \times B \to Y$ be given bifunctions satisfying:*

(i) *g is C-essentially quasi-monotone and C-lower semicontinuous in the second argument;*

(ii) *h is C-upper semicontinuous in the first argument and C-convex in the second argument; $h(x, x) \in C$ for all $x \in B$.*

Then there exists $\overline{x} \in B$ such that

$$h(\overline{x}, y) - g(y, \overline{x}) \notin -intC,$$

for all $y \in B$.

Proof. Let, for each fixed $y \in B$,

$$S(y) := \{x \in B : h(x, y) - g(y, x) \notin -intC\}. \tag{4.27}$$

Let us show that $\bigcap_{y \in B} S(y) \neq \emptyset$. Indeed, let $\{y_1, y_2, \dots, y_n\} \subset B$ and set $I := \{1, 2, \dots, n\}$. Take arbitrary $z \in conv\{y_i : i \in I\}$. Then $z = \sum_{i \in I} \lambda_i y_i$ with $\lambda_i \geq 0$

and $\sum_{i \in I} \lambda_i = 1$. Assume, by contradiction, that

$$h(z, y_i) - g(y_i, z) \in -intC,$$

for all $i \in I$. From this we have

$$\sum_{i \in I} \lambda_i h(z, y_i) - \sum_{i \in I} \lambda_i g(y_i, z) \in -intC. \tag{4.28}$$

Since g is C-essentially quasi-monotone it follows that

$$\sum_{i \in I} \lambda_i g(y_i, \sum_{i \in I} \lambda_i y_i) \notin intC. \tag{4.29}$$

On the other hand, since $h(x, x) \in C$ for all $x \in B$, and h is C-convex in the second argument,

$$\sum_{i \in I} \lambda_i h(z, y_i) \in C. \tag{4.30}$$

Therefore, by Lemma 4.5, (4.29) and (4.30) it follows that

$$\sum_{i \in I} \lambda_i h(z, y_i) - \sum_{i \in I} \lambda_i g(y_i, z) \notin -intC, \tag{4.31}$$

which contradicts (4.28). Hence we obtain

$$conv\{y_i : i \in I\} \subset \bigcup_{i \in I} S(y_i).$$

Now, since h is C-upper semicontinuous in the first argument, and g is C-lower semicontinuous in the second argument, it follows that the function F defined by $F(x) = h(x, y) - g(y, x)$ is C-upper semicontinuous. By Lemma 4.1 (iii), the sets $S(y)$ are closed for every $y \in B$, and since B is compact, they are compact too. Hence, by the KKM theorem (Chapter 3, Theorem 3.2), $\cap_{y \in B} S(y) \neq \emptyset$. Therefore, there exists at least one $\overline{x} \in B$ such that

$$h(\overline{x}, y) - g(y, \overline{x}) \notin -intC,$$

for all $y \in B$. $\qquad\square$

The next lemma makes the connection between the special equilibrium problem considered in Lemma 4.6 and the equilibrium problem we are interested in.

Lemma 4.7. *Let $g : B \times B \to Y$ and $h : B \times B \to Y$ be given bifunctions satisfying:*

(i) *g is C-convex in the second argument, $g(x, x) \in C$ for all $x \in B$, and for all $x, y \in B$ the function $t \in [0, 1] \to g(ty + (1 - t)x, y)$ is C-upper semicontinuous at 0;*

(ii) *h is C-convex in the second argument; $h(x, x) = 0$ for all $x \in B$.*

If there exists $\overline{x} \in B$ such that $h(\overline{x}, y) - g(y, \overline{x}) \notin -intC$ for all $y \in B$, then $h(\overline{x}, y) + g(\overline{x}, y) \notin -intC$ for all $y \in B$.

Proof. Let $y \in B$ be arbitrary and let $x_\lambda := \lambda y + (1 - \lambda)\overline{x}$, $0 < \lambda \leq 1$. Then $x_\lambda \in B$. By the hypothesis we obtain

$$(1 - \lambda)h(\overline{x}, x_\lambda) - (1 - \lambda)g(x_\lambda, \overline{x}) \notin -intC. \tag{4.32}$$

Since g is C-convex in the second argument and $g(x, x) \in C$ for all $x \in B$, then for all $0 < \lambda \leq 1$,

$$\lambda g(x_\lambda, y) + (1 - \lambda)g(x_\lambda, \overline{x}) \in C. \tag{4.33}$$

By Lemma 4.5, (4.32) and (4.33) we have

$$(1 - \lambda)h(\overline{x}, x_\lambda) + \lambda g(x_\lambda, y) \notin -intC. \tag{4.34}$$

Since h is C-convex in the second argument and $h(x, x) = 0$ for all $x \in B$, then

$$\lambda h(\overline{x}, y) + (1 - \lambda)h(\overline{x}, \overline{x}) - h(\overline{x}, x_\lambda) = \lambda h(\overline{x}, y) - h(\overline{x}, x_\lambda) \in C.$$

Thus

$$(1 - \lambda)\lambda h(\overline{x}, y) - (1 - \lambda)h(\overline{x}, x_\lambda) \in C. \tag{4.35}$$

From (4.34) and (4.35) and using Lemma 4.5, we have

$$(1 - \lambda)\lambda h(\overline{x}, y) + \lambda g(x_\lambda, y) \notin -intC.$$

Dividing the last relation by $\lambda > 0$ we obtain

$$(1 - \lambda)h(\overline{x}, y) + g(x_\lambda, y) \notin -intC, \tag{4.36}$$

for all $0 < \lambda \leq 1$. We will prove that (4.36) implies

$$h(\overline{x}, y) + g(\overline{x}, y) \notin -intC.$$

Suppose by contradiction that

$$h(\overline{x}, y) + g(\overline{x}, y) \in -intC.$$

Hence there exists $k \in intC$ such that

$$h(\overline{x}, y) + g(\overline{x}, y) + k \in -intC. \tag{4.37}$$

Since the set $\frac{k}{2} - intC$ is open and $0 \in \frac{k}{2} - intC$, there exists $\mu > 0$ such that

$$-\lambda h(\overline{x}, y) \in \frac{k}{2} - intC, \tag{4.38}$$

for all $0 \leq \lambda \leq \mu$. Since for all $x, y \in B$ the function $t \in [0, 1] \to g(ty + (1-t)x, y)$ is C-upper semicontinuous at 0, it follows that there exists $\delta > 0$ such that

$$g(x_\lambda, y) \in g(\overline{x}, y) + \frac{k}{2} - intC, \tag{4.39}$$

for all $0 \leq \lambda \leq \delta$. Let us take $\eta = \min\{\mu, \delta\}$. By (4.37), (4.38), and (4.39) we obtain that

$$g(x_\lambda, y) + (1-\lambda)h(\overline{x}, y) \in -intC,$$

for all $0 \leq \lambda \leq \eta$, which contradicts (4.36). Therefore,

$$h(\overline{x}, y) + g(\overline{x}, y) \notin -intC. \qquad \square$$

Finally, the technical result below serves for exploiting the coercivity condition we are going to assume in Theorem 5.5 below (assumption (iii)).

Lemma 4.8. *Let $B \subset A$. Assume that $F : A \to Y$ is C-convex, $x_0 \in core_A B$, $F(x_0) \in -C$, and $F(y) \notin -intC$ for all $y \in B$. Then $F(y) \notin -intC$ for all $y \in A$.*

Proof. Assume that there exists a $y \in A$ such that $f(y) \in -intC$ and set for each $\lambda \in [0, 1]$ $x_\lambda := \lambda y + (1-\lambda)x_0$. By C-convexity

$$F(x_\lambda) \leq_C \lambda F(y) + (1-\lambda)F(x_0) \in -intC - C \subset -intC, \quad \forall \lambda \in (0, 1]. \tag{4.40}$$

On the other hand, since $x_0 \in core_A B$, there exists a sufficiently small $\lambda > 0$ for which $x_\lambda \in B$, and this contradicts (4.40). $\qquad \square$

Remark 4.1. As the next example shows, the assumption $F(x_0) \in -C$ within Lemma 4.8 cannot be weakened to $F(x_0) \notin intC$.

Example 4.9. Let $X = A := \mathbb{R}$, $B := [-1, 1]$, $Y := \mathbb{R}^2$, $C := \mathbb{R}_+^2$, $F(x) = (x+1, x-1)$, and $x_0 = 0$. Then F is obviously $\mathbb{R}_+^2$-convex (furthermore, both components are affine functions), $x_0 \in core_A B$, $F(x_0) = (1, -1) \notin intC$ and $F(y) \notin -intC$ for each $y \in B$. However, for instance, for $y = -2$ we get $F(-2) = (-1, -3) \in -intC$.

Now we are in a position to state our main result. Note that the assumption of compactness upon the domain in Lemma 4.6 was essential for its proof. However, this condition appears rather demanding when dealing with equilibrium problems since it cannot be guaranteed in many applications. To overcome this difficulty, it is common to assume different kinds of *coercivity conditions*. We take over the coercivity condition originated in the scalar case from [42].

Theorem 4.10. *Suppose that $g : A \times A \to Y$ and $h : A \times A \to Y$ satisfy:*

(i) *g is C-essentially quasi-monotone, C-convex and C-lower semicontinuous in the second argument; $g(x,x) \in C \cap (-C)$ for all $x \in A$, and for all $x, y \in A$ the function $t \in [0,1] \to g(ty + (1-t)x, y)$ is C-upper semicontinuous at 0;*

(ii) *h is C-upper semicontinuous in the first argument and C-convex in the second argument; $h(x,x) = 0$ for all $x \in A$;*

(iii) *There exists a nonempty compact convex subset C of A such that for every $x \in C \setminus core_A C$ there exists an $a \in core_A C$ such that*

$$g(x,a) + h(x,a) \in -C.$$

Then there exists $\overline{x} \in C$ such that

$$g(\overline{x}, y) + h(\overline{x}, y) \notin -intC,$$

for all $y \in A$.

Proof. By Lemma 4.6, it follows that there exists at least one $\overline{x} \in C$ such that

$$h(\overline{x}, y) - g(y, \overline{x}) \notin -intC,$$

for all $y \in C$. By Lemma 4.7, we obtain that

$$h(\overline{x}, y) + g(\overline{x}, y) \notin -intC,$$

for all $y \in C$. Set $F(\cdot) = h(\overline{x}, \cdot) + g(\overline{x}, \cdot)$. It is obvious that F is C-convex and

$$F(y) \notin -intC,$$

for all $y \in C$. If $\overline{x} \in core_A C$, then set $x_0 := \overline{x}$. If $\overline{x} \in C \setminus core_A C$, then set $x_0 := a$, where a is as in assumption (iii). In both cases $x_0 \in core_A C$, and $F(x_0) \in -C$. Hence, by Lemma 4.8, it follows that

$$F(y) \notin -intC,$$

for all $y \in A$. Thus, there exists $\overline{x} \in C$ such that

$$g(\overline{x}, y) + h(\overline{x}, y) \notin -intC,$$

for all $y \in A$. □

The next result due to Kazmi [105] is a particular case of Theorem 4.10. X and Y are the same as before, $A \subset X$ is a nonempty closed convex set and $C \subset Y$ is a proper pointed closed convex cone with nonempty interior.

Corollary 4.5. ([105], Theorem 7) *Suppose that $g : A \times A \to Y$ and $h : A \times A \to Y$ satisfy:*

(i) g is C-monotone, C-convex, and continuous in the second argument; $g(x, x) = 0$ for all $x \in A$, and for all $x, y \in A$ the function $t \in [0, 1] \to g(ty + (1 - t)x, y)$ is continuous at 0;

(ii) h is continuous in the first argument and C-convex in the second argument; $h(x, x) = 0$ for all $x \in A$;

(iii) There exists a nonempty compact convex subset C of A such that for every $x \in C \setminus core_A C$ there exists an $a \in core_A C$ such that

$$g(x, a) + h(x, a) \in -C.$$

Then there exists $\overline{x} \in C$ such that

$$g(\overline{x}, y) + h(\overline{x}, y) \notin -intC,$$

for all $y \in A$.

Proof. The continuity assumptions obviously imply C-lower (upper) semicontinuity, while the essential quasi-monotonicity of g follows by Proposition 4.11. □

Remark 4.2. Theorem 4.10 improves from several points of view the above result of Kazmi. With respect to the monotonicity, notice that the bifunction f defined in Example 4.8 satisfies all requirements demanded upon g in item (i) of Theorem 4.10, but since it is not $\mathbb{R}^2_+$-monotone, it doesn't satisfy item (i) of Corollary 4.5. Another improvement, related to the continuity assumptions, can be identified within the next example, obtained by a slight modification of Example 9.27 in [25].

Example 4.10. Let $A := \{(x, y) \in \mathbb{R}^2 : x > 0\} \cup \{(0, 0)\}$ and consider the function $F : A \to \mathbb{R}$ given by

$$F(x, y) = \begin{cases} \frac{y^2}{x}, & x > 0 \\ 0, & x = 0. \end{cases}$$

It is obvious that F is convex and lower semicontinuous, but not continuous at $(0, 0)$. Indeed, take any sequence $\{x_n\}_{n \in \mathbb{N}}$ with $x_n > 0$ and $x_n \to 0$ whenever $n \to \infty$. Then $F(x_n^2, x_n) = 1$ for each n, but $F(0, 0) = 0$, i.e., F is not continuous at $(0, 0)$. Now let $Y := \mathbb{R}$ and $C := [0, \infty)$, and consider the bifunction $g : A \times A \to \mathbb{R}$ given by $g(a, b) := F(b) - F(a)$, where $a = (x, y)$, $b = (u, v) \in A$. Then g satisfies all assumptions of Theorem 4.10 (i), but not item (i) of Corollary 4.5, due to the lack of continuity.

Thanks to the improvements made for Theorem 7 of Kazmi [105], the next result of Blum and Oettli [42] becomes a particular case of Theorem 4.10.

Corollary 4.6. ([42], Theorem 1) *Let X be a real topological vector space, $A \subset X$ a nonempty closed convex set, $g : A \times A \to \mathbb{R}$ and $h : A \times A \to \mathbb{R}$ satisfying:*

(i) *g is monotone (Definition 4.4 (i)), convex, and lower semicontinuous in the second argument; $g(x, x) = 0$ for all $x \in A$, and for all $x, y \in A$ the function $t \in [0, 1] \to g(ty + (1 - t)x, y)$ is upper semicontinuous at 0;*

(ii) *h is upper semicontinuous in the first argument and convex in the second argument; $h(x, x) = 0$ for all $x \in A$;*

(iii) *There exists a nonempty compact convex subset C of A such that for every $x \in C \setminus core_A C$ there exists an $a \in core_A C$ such that*

$$g(x, a) + h(x, a) \leq 0.$$

Then there exists $\overline{x} \in C$ such that

$$g(\overline{x}, y) + h(\overline{x}, y) \geq 0,$$

for all $y \in A$.

Proof. Set $Y := \mathbb{R}$ and $C := [0, \infty)$ and apply Theorem 4.10. □

Next we prove a corollary of Theorem 4.10 in which no monotonicity assumptions are made on the bifunction g; the lack of this requirement is substituted by assuming C-concavity of g in its first argument. In this way, the algebraic conditions upon g become symmetric. Apparently, this provides us a new result even in the particular case of scalar functions (i.e., where $Y := \mathbb{R}$ and $C := [0, \infty)$).

Corollary 4.7. *Suppose that $g : A \times A \to Y$ and $h : A \times A \to Y$ satisfy:*

(i) *g is C-concave in the first argument, C-convex and C-lower semicontinuous in the second argument; $g(x, x) \in C \cap (-C)$ for all $x \in A$, and for all $x, y \in A$ the function $t \in [0, 1] \to g(ty + (1 - t)x, y)$ is C-upper semicontinuous at 0;*

(ii) *h is C-upper semicontinuous in the first argument and C-convex in the second argument; $h(x, x) = 0$ for all $x \in A$;*

(iii) *There exists a nonempty compact convex subset C of A such that for every $x \in C \setminus core_A C$ there exists an $a \in core_A C$ such that*

$$g(x, a) + h(x, a) \in -C.$$

Then there exists $\overline{x} \in C$ such that

$$g(\overline{x}, y) + h(\overline{x}, y) \notin -intC,$$

for all $y \in A$.

Proof. Let $n \geq 1$, $x_1, ..., x_n \in A$, $\lambda_1, ..., \lambda_n \geq 0$ with $\sum_{i=1}^{n} \lambda_i = 1$ be arbitrary and set $z := \sum_{i=1}^{n} \lambda_i x_i$. Then by concavity of g with respect to its first variable, we have

$$\sum_{i=1}^{n} \lambda_i g(x_i, z) - g\left(\sum_{i=1}^{n} \lambda_i x_i, z\right) \in -C.$$

Since

$$g(\sum_{i=1}^{n} \lambda_i x_i, z) = g(z, z) \in -C,$$

it follows by summing up these relations that

$$\sum_{i=1}^{n} \lambda_i g(x_i, z) \in -C,$$

implying that

$$\sum_{i=1}^{n} \lambda_i g(x_i, z) \notin intC,$$

which means that g is C-essentially quasi-monotone, and such the statement follows by Theorem 4.10. □

Let us remark that the assumptions of Corollary 4.7 do not imply the monotonicity of g even in the simplest case when $X = Y = \mathbb{R}$ and $C = \mathbb{R}_+$. The next example shows an instance when all assumptions of Corollary 4.7 hold, but g is not monotone.

Example 4.11. Let $F : \mathbb{R} \to \mathbb{R}$ be a convex and lower bounded function and consider the numbers a and b such that $0 < b < a < 2b$. Set

$$g(x, y) = ax(y - x) + b(y - x)^2, \quad h(x, y) = F(y) - F(x) \text{ and}$$
$$f(x, y) = g(x, y) + h(x, y).$$

It is obvious that $g(x, x) = 0$ and the function g is concave in the first, convex in the second argument; moreover, it is (globally) continuous. The concavity of g follows by $b < a$. The same properties are valid for h. Moreover, the lower boundedness of F assures that $\lim_{|x| \to +\infty}[F(x) + (a - b)x^2] = +\infty$, and from this we conclude that $\lim_{|x| \to +\infty} f(x, 0) = -\infty$, showing that the coercivity assumption (iii) of Corollary 4.7 holds with $a = 0$. Thus, all hypotheses of this corollary hold. On the other hand, g is not monotone, since

$$g(x, y) + g(y, x) = (2b - a)(y - x)^2 > 0, \quad \forall x \neq y.$$

We conclude that Corollary 4.7 can be applied for the bifunctions given in Example 4.11, but it is not the case either for Corollary 4.5, or Corollary 4.6.

In what follows we provide several sufficient conditions for the coercivity required in assumption (iii) of Theorem 4.10 (or Corollary 4.7) when X is a reflexive Banach space endowed with the weak topology. It is well-known that in this setting every closed, convex, and bounded set (in particular closed balls) is (weakly) compact. Hence, all conditions which we formulate below are vacuously satisfied when the (closed and convex) set $A \subset X$ is bounded. Thus, in the sequel we shall suppose that A is closed, convex and unbounded. Let $a \in A$ be a fixed element, $g, h : A \times A \to Y$ be given bifunctions. Let us start with the following:

(C) there exists $\rho > 0$ such that for all $x \in A$: $\|x - a\| = \rho$ one has $g(x, a) + h(x, a) \in -C$.

Proposition 4.12. *Under condition (C), assumption (iii) in Theorem 4.10 is satisfied.*

Proof. Let $B := \{x \in A : \|x - a\| \leq \rho\}$. Then B is weakly compact and $a \in core_A B$. Moreover, $x \in B \setminus core_A B$ iff $\|x - a\| = \rho$. Thus $g(x, a) + h(x, a) \in -C$, hence (iii) is fulfilled. $\square$

Next we give mild sufficient conditions separately on g and h for (C). Consider the following assumptions.

(G) (upper boundedness of $g(\cdot, a)$ on a closed ball): there exist $M \in Y$ and $r > 0$ such that

$$M - g(x, a) \in C, \text{ whenever } x \in A, \ \|x - a\| \leq r,$$

and

(H) there exists an element $u \in -intC$ such that for all $t > 0$ there is an $R > 0$ satisfying

$$\forall x \in A : \|x - a\| \geq R : tu\|x - a\| - h(x, a) \in C.$$

Remark 4.3. (H) is obviously fulfilled when $Y := \mathbb{R}$, $C := [0, \infty)$ and

$$\frac{h(x, a)}{\|x - a\|} \to -\infty \text{ whenever } \|x - a\| \to \infty, \ x \in A.$$

(Condition (c) in [42].) Indeed, take $u = -1$ and arbitrary $t > 0$. Since

$$\frac{h(x, a)}{\|x - a\|} \to -\infty \text{ whenever } \|x - a\| \to \infty,$$

we can find $R > 0$ such that for all $x \in A$:

$$\|x - a\| \geq R, \ \frac{h(x, a)}{\|x - a\|} \leq -t,$$

proving the assertion.

Next we need the following technical lemma concerning the function g.

Lemma 4.9. *Suppose that g satisfies (G) and $g(\cdot, a)$ is C-concave with $g(a, a) \in C$. Then*

$$\frac{M}{r} - \frac{g(x,a)}{\|x-a\|} \in C, \quad \forall x \in A, \ \|x-a\| \geq r,$$

where the vector M and the number r are defined in (G).

Proof. Let $x \in A$ such that $\|x - a\| \geq r$. Set

$$y := \frac{r}{\|x-a\|} x + \left(1 - \frac{r}{\|x-a\|}\right) a.$$

Since A is convex, it follows that $y \in A$ and $\|y - a\| = r$. Therefore,

$$M - g(y,a) \in C. \tag{4.41}$$

Since $g(\cdot, a)$ is C-concave,

$$g(y,a) - \frac{r}{\|x-a\|} g(x,a) - \left(1 - \frac{r}{\|x-a\|}\right) g(a,a) \in C. \tag{4.42}$$

Summing up (4.41) and (4.42) we obtain that

$$M - \frac{r}{\|x-a\|} g(x,a) - \left(1 - \frac{r}{\|x-a\|}\right) g(a,a) \in C.$$

This implies by

$$\left(1 - \frac{r}{\|x-a\|}\right) g(a,a) \in C$$

that

$$M - \frac{r}{\|x-a\|} g(x,a) \in C,$$

which proves the assertion. $\qquad\qquad\qquad\qquad\qquad\qquad\qquad\qquad\square$

Now we are able to provide sufficient conditions, separately on g and on h, for the coercivity assumption (iii) in Theorem 4.10.

Proposition 4.13. *Assume that*

(i) *g satisfies (G) and $g(\cdot, a)$ is C-concave with $g(a,a) \in C$;*
(ii) *h satisfies (H).*

Then condition (iii) of Theorem 4.10 is fulfilled.

Proof. Let $v := M/r$, with M and r provided by (G) and take $u \in -\text{int}C$ given by (H). It is easy to see that there exists a sufficiently large $t > 0$ such that

$$v + tu \in -\text{int}C. \tag{4.43}$$

Take $R > 0$ according to (H) and let $x \in A$ such that $\|x - a\| \geq \max\{R, r\}$. By Lemma 4.9

$$v - \frac{g(x, a)}{\|x - a\|} \in C,$$

which, together with (4.43) implies that

$$\frac{g(x, a)}{\|x - a\|} + tu \in -intC. \tag{4.44}$$

On the other hand, by (H),

$$tu - \frac{h(x, a)}{\|x - a\|} \in C,$$

which, together with (4.44) implies that

$$\frac{g(x, a)}{\|x - a\|} + \frac{h(x, a)}{\|x - a\|} \in -intC.$$

This implies that $g(x, a) + h(x, a) \in -intC$, i.e., condition (C) is satisfied. Hence, the statement follows by Proposition 4.12. $\qquad\square$

The next result, of Weierstrass type, might have some interest on its own: gives sufficient conditions for lower (upper) boundedness of a C-lower (C-upper) semicontinuous function.

Lemma 4.10. *Let C be a compact subset of X and $F : C \to Y$.*

(i) *if F is C-lower semicontinuous on C, then it is lower bounded, i.e., there exists a vector $m \in Y$ such that $F(x) - m \in intC$ for all $x \in C$;*

(ii) *if F is C-upper semicontinuous on C, then it is upper bounded, i.e., there exists a vector $M \in Y$ such that $M - F(x) \in intC$ for all $x \in C$.*

Proof. It is enough to prove item (i), (ii) follows by a similar argument. Supposing the contrary, for each $v \in Y$ there exists $x_v \in C$ such that $F(x_v) - v \notin intC$. Consider for each $v \in Y$ the level sets

$$L_v := \{x \in C : F(x) - v \notin intC\}.$$

By Lemma 4.1 item (iii), it follows that the nonempty set L_v is closed for every $v \in Y$. Since C is compact, L_v is compact too. Let $v \in -intC$ be arbitrary. Then

$$u \in Y \text{ with } u - v \in C \Rightarrow L_v \subset L_u. \tag{4.45}$$

Indeed, let $x \in L_v$, i.e., $F(x) - v \notin intC$. By Lemma 4.5, it follows that $u - F(x) \notin -intC$, i.e., $x \in L_u$.

Now take for every $n \in \mathbb{N}$ a vector $x_n \in C$ such that $x_n \in L_{nv}$. By compactness, there exists a subsequence $\{x_{n_k}\}$ of $\{x_n\}$ converging to the element $x \in C$.

Let us show that $x \in L_{tv}$ for every $t > 0$. To do this, take any $k \in \mathbb{N}$ such that $n_k > t$. Then by (4.45),

$$x_{n_k} \in L_{n_k v} \subset L_{tv}.$$

Since L_{tv} is a compact set, it follows that $x \in L_{tv}$, i.e.,

$$F(x) - tv \notin intC. \tag{4.46}$$

On the other hand, since $v \in -intC$, there exists a sufficiently large $\tau > 0$ such that

$$F(x) - \tau v \in intC,$$

contradicting (4.46). $\qquad\qquad\qquad\qquad\qquad\qquad\qquad\qquad\qquad\qquad\qquad\square$

Summarizing, we have the following existence result in reflexive Banach spaces. The basic assumptions upon the set A, the space Y, and the cone C remain the same.

Theorem 4.11. *Suppose that X is a reflexive Banach space. Let $g : A \times A \to Y$ and $h : A \times A \to Y$ satisfying the following properties:*

- **(i)** *g is C-concave and weakly C-upper semicontinuous in the first argument; C-convex and weakly C-lower semicontinuous in the second argument; $g(x, x) \in C \cap (-C)$ for all $x \in A$;*
- **(ii)** *h is weakly C-upper semicontinuous in the first argument; C-convex in the second argument; $h(x, x) = 0$, for all $x \in A$ and (H) holds.*

Then there exists $\overline{x} \in A$ such that

$$g(\overline{x}, y) + h(\overline{x}, y) \notin -intC, \quad \forall y \in A.$$

Proof. We shall verify the assumptions of Corollary 4.7 in the reflexive Banach space setting, endowed with the weak topology. Conditions (i) and (ii) are trivially satisfied, thus we only have to verify (iii). To do this, we shall make use of Proposition 4.13. Let us prove that g satisfies condition (G). Take any $a \in A$ and a sufficiently large $r > 0$ such that the set $C := \{x \in A : \|x - a\| \leq r\}$ is nonempty. This set is also weakly compact and $g(\cdot, a)$ being weakly C-upper semicontinuous, by Lemma 4.10 (ii) there exists a vector $M \in Y$ such that $M - g(x, a) \in intC$ for all $x \in C$, i.e., (G) holds. This completes the proof. $\quad\square$

In the scalar case, i.e., when $Y := \mathbb{R}$ and $C := [0, \infty]$, we obtain a simplified form of Theorem 4.11.

Corollary 4.8. *Let $g : A \times A \to \mathbb{R}$ and $h : A \times A \to \mathbb{R}$ satisfying the following properties:*

- **(i)** *g is concave and upper semicontinuous in the first argument, convex and lower semicontinuous in the second argument, and $g(x, x) = 0$ for all $x \in A$;*

(ii) *h is weakly upper semicontinuous in the first argument, convex in the second argument, $h(x,x) = 0$ for all $x \in A$, and*

$$\frac{h(x,a)}{\|x-a\|} \to -\infty \text{ whenever } \|x-a\| \to \infty, \quad x \in A.$$

Then there exists $\overline{x} \in A$ such that

$$g(\overline{x}, y) + h(\overline{x}, y) \geq 0, \quad \forall y \in A. \tag{4.47}$$

Proof. Since X is reflexive, each concave and upper semicontinuous function is weakly upper semicontinuous, and similarly, each convex and lower semicontinuous function is weakly lower semicontinuous. By Remark 4.3, condition (H) holds. Thus, the assertion follows by Theorem 4.11. □

Example 4.12. Let X be a reflexive Banach space and suppose that $F : X \to \mathbb{R} \cup \{+\infty\}$ is a proper, convex and lower semicontinuous function with $\operatorname{dom} F$ unbounded. It is well-known from convex analysis that F has a global minimum point whenever it satisfies the following coercivity condition

$$\lim_{\|x\| \to +\infty} \frac{F(x)}{\|x\|} \to +\infty.$$

This fact can be easily reobtain by Corollary 4.8. Indeed, take $g \equiv 0$, $A := \operatorname{dom} F$ and $h(x,y) := F(y) - F(x)$. Since F is convex and lower semicontinuous, it is weakly lower semicontinuous as well, thus h is weakly upper semicontinuous in the first argument. Therefore, assumption (ii) of Corollary 4.8 is satisfied. It is obvious that the solution $\overline{x} \in A$ of (4.47) is a global minimum point of F.

4.3.2 The Set-Valued Case

In order to unify and extend some results on vector and set-valued equilibrium problems when the considered bifunction appears as a sum of two other bifunctions, Kassay, Miholca, and Vinh [104] introduce the vector quasi-equilibrium problem for the sum of two set-valued mappings (for short, VQEP) as follows: let X, Y be real topological vector spaces, K a nonempty convex subset of X, C a proper convex cone in Y with $\operatorname{int} C \neq \emptyset$. For $A : K \rightrightarrows K$ a set-valued mapping with nonempty values and $G, H : K \times K \rightrightarrows Y$ set-valued bifunctions with nonempty values,

(VQEP) find $\bar{x} \in A(\bar{x})$ such that

$$G(\bar{x}, y) + H(\bar{x}, y) \subset Y \setminus (-\operatorname{int} C) \text{ for all } y \in A(\bar{x}).$$

In this subsection we present some results from [104]. We start with recalling the necessary definitions.

Let X be a topological space and Y a nonempty set. The mapping $T : X \rightrightarrows Y$ is said to have open lower sections if the inverse mapping T^{-1} defined by

$$T^{-1}(y) = \{x \in X : y \in T(x)\}$$

is open-valued, i.e., for all $y \in Y$, $T^{-1}(y)$ is open in X.

Definition 4.7. Let X be a topological space and Y a topological vector space. A mapping $T : X \rightrightarrows Y$ is called a Browder-Fan mapping iff the following conditions are satisfied:

1. for each $x \in X$, $T(x)$ is nonempty and convex;
2. T has open lower sections.

Recall the following technical result.

Lemma 4.11. (Yannelis and Prabhakar [173]) *Let X, Y be topological vector spaces and $T : X \rightrightarrows Y$ be a set-valued mapping with open lower sections. Define the set-valued mapping $\operatorname{conv}T : X \rightrightarrows Y$ by $\operatorname{conv}T(x) = conv(T(x))$ for all $x \in X$. Then $\operatorname{conv}T$ has also open lower sections.*

The following result is known as the Browder-Fan fixed point theorem.

Lemma 4.12. ([173], Theorem 3.3) *Let K be a nonempty compact convex subset of a topological vector space and $T : K \rightrightarrows K$ a Browder-Fan mapping. Then T admits a fixed point.*

In the results below, Browder-Fan mappings having closed fixed point set play a special role. Below we give such an example. Denote by $\mathcal{F}(T)$ the set of fixed points of the mapping T.

Example 4.13. Let $X = \mathbb{R}$, $K = [0, 1]$. Let $T : [0, 1] \rightrightarrows [0, 1]$ be a mapping defined by

$$T(x) = \left[\frac{1}{2}, 1\right] \text{ for all } x \in K.$$

Then $T(x)$ is nonempty convex subset of K and

$$T^{-1}(y) = \begin{cases} \emptyset & \text{if } y \in [0, \frac{1}{2}), \\ K & \text{if } y \in [\frac{1}{2}, 1] \end{cases}$$

is open in K. Therefore, T is a Browder-Fan mapping. Moreover, the set $\mathcal{F}(T) = \left[\frac{1}{2}, 1\right]$ is closed in K.

Next, recall an important result concerning the existence of maximal elements.

Lemma 4.13. ([173], Theorem 5.1) *Let K be a nonempty compact convex subset of a topological vector space and $F :\rightrightarrows K$ a set-valued mapping satisfying the following conditions:*

1. *For all $x \in K$, $x \notin F(x)$ and $F(x)$ is convex;*
2. *F has open lower sections.*

Then there exists $\bar{x} \in K$ such that $F(\bar{x}) = \emptyset$.

We now recall some concepts of generalized convexity of set-valued mappings.

Definition 4.8. Let K be a nonempty convex subset of a vector space X, C a proper convex cone of a vector space Y and $F : K \rightrightarrows Y$ a set-valued mapping with nonempty values.

1. F is said to be upper C-convex iff for any pair $x, y \in K$, $\alpha \in [0, 1]$, we have

$$\alpha F(x) + (1 - \alpha)F(y) \subset F(\alpha x + (1 - \alpha)y) + C. \qquad (4.48)$$

2. F is said to be lower C-convex iff for any pair $x, y \in K$, $\alpha \in [0, 1]$, we have

$$F(\alpha x + (1 - \alpha)y) \subset \alpha F(x) + (1 - \alpha)F(y) - C. \qquad (4.49)$$

Note that in case of single-valued functions, where $\subset$ reduces to $\in$, the concepts given by (4.48) and (4.49) become the same: both reduce to the well-known C-convexity for vector functions (see Definition 4.3). However, these concepts are different in case of set-valued functions. We illustrate this by the following example.

Example 4.14. Let $X = Y = \mathbb{R}$, $K = [0, 1]$ and $C := \mathbb{R}_+ = [0, +\infty)$.
1. Let $F : [0, 1] \rightrightarrows \mathbb{R}$ be a mapping defined by

$$F(x) = \begin{cases} [0, x], & x \neq \frac{1}{2} \\ [0, 1], & x = \frac{1}{2}. \end{cases}$$

Since the right-hand side of (4.48) is always $[0, +\infty)$, it is clear that this mapping satisfies (4.48). On the other hand, by taking $x = \frac{1}{5}$, $y = \frac{4}{5}$ and $\alpha = \frac{1}{2}$ in (4.49), one obtains $[0, 1]$ for the left and $(-\infty, \frac{1}{2}]$ for the right-hand side, hence, (4.49) is false.
2. Let $F : [0, 1] \rightrightarrows \mathbb{R}$ given by

$$F(x) = \begin{cases} [0, x], & x \neq \frac{1}{2} \\ [\frac{1}{4}, \frac{1}{2}], & x = \frac{1}{2}. \end{cases}$$

It is easy to see that for any $x, y, \alpha \in [0, 1]$ one has $F(\alpha x + (1 - \alpha)y) \subset [0, \alpha x + (1 - \alpha)y]$. Moreover, $\alpha F(x) + (1 - \alpha)F(y) - C = (-\infty, \alpha x + (1 - \alpha)y]$ and such, (4.49) holds. On the other hand, for $x = \frac{1}{5}$, $y = \frac{4}{5}$ and $\alpha = \frac{1}{2}$, we obtain that $\alpha F(x) + (1 - \alpha)F(y) = [0, \frac{1}{2}]$, while $F(\alpha x + (1 - \alpha)y) + C = F(\frac{1}{2}) + C = [\frac{1}{4}, +\infty)$, hence (4.48) doesn't hold.

Now, we recall the following characterizations of semicontinuity properties of set-valued mappings (see Chapter 1). Let $F : X \rightrightarrows Y$ be a set-valued mapping between two topological spaces X and Y. The domain of F is defined to be the set $dom F = \{x \in X : F(x) \neq \emptyset\}$.

The mapping F is upper semicontinuous (shortly, usc) at $x_0 \in dom F$ if for any open set V of Y with $F(x_0) \subset V$, there exists a neighborhood U of x_0 such that $F(x) \subset V$ for all $x \in U$.

The mapping F is lower semicontinuous (shortly, lsc) at $x_0 \in dom F$ if for any open set V of Y with $F(x_0) \cap V \neq \emptyset$, there exists a neighborhood U of x_0 such that $F(x) \cap V \neq \emptyset$ for all $x \in U$.

The mapping F is continuous at $x_0 \in dom F$ if it is both usc and lsc at x_0. The mapping F is continuous (resp., usc, lsc) if $dom F = X$ and if F is continuous (resp., usc, lsc) at each point $x \in X$.

If Y is a partially ordered topological vector space, then the above definitions of the semicontinuity can be weakened. More precisely, we have the following definitions.

Definition 4.9. Let X be a topological space, Y a topological vector space with a proper convex cone C. Let $F : X \rightrightarrows Y$. We say that

1. F is C-upper semicontinuous (shortly, C-usc) at $x_0 \in dom F$ iff for any open set V of Y with $F(x_0) \subset V$ there exists a neighborhood U of x_0 such that

$$F(x) \subset V + C \quad \text{for each } x \in dom F \cap U.$$

2. F is C-lower semicontinuous (shortly, C-lsc) at $x_0 \in dom F$ iff for any open set V of Y with $F(x_0) \cap V \neq \emptyset$ there exists a neighborhood U of x_0 such that

$$F(x) \cap [V + C] \neq \emptyset \quad \text{for each } x \in dom F \cap U.$$

3. F is C-usc (resp., C-lsc) iff $dom F = X$ and F is C-usc (resp., C-lsc) at each point of $dom F$.

The next result will be useful in the sequel.

Lemma 4.14. ([80], Lemma 2) *Let X and Y be real topological vector spaces and K be a nonempty subset of X. Let C be a proper convex cone in Y with $int C \neq \emptyset$. If $F : K \rightrightarrows Y$ is C-lower semicontinuous on K, then the set $B = \{x \in K : F(x) \subset Y \setminus int C\}$ is closed in K.*

The extension of monotonicity for set-valued bifunctions has been considered in a natural way.

Definition 4.10. Let X, Y be vector spaces, K a nonempty convex subset of X, and C a proper convex cone in Y. A set-valued mapping $F : K \times K \rightrightarrows Y$ is said to be C-monotone iff for any $x, y \in K$

$$F(x, y) + F(y, x) \subset -C.$$

The concept of *C-essential quasi-monotonicity* (see Definition 4.6) can also be extended in a natural way for set-valued bifunctions.

Definition 4.11. Let X be a vector space, Y a topological vector space, K a nonempty convex subset of X, and C a proper convex cone in Y with $intC \neq \emptyset$. The bifunction $F : K \times K \rightrightarrows Y$ with nonempty values is said to be *generalized C-essentially quasi-monotone* iff for an arbitrary integer $n \geq 1$, for all $x_1, x_2, ..., x_n \in K$ and all $\lambda_1, \lambda_2, ..., \lambda_n \geq 0$ such that $\sum_{i=1}^{n} \lambda_i = 1$ it holds that

$$\sum_{i=1}^{n} \lambda_i F(x_i, \sum_{j=1}^{n} \lambda_j x_j) \cap intC = \emptyset.$$

The next two statements provide sufficient conditions for generalized C-essential quasi-monotonicity.

Lemma 4.15. *Let X, Y be topological vector spaces, K a nonempty convex subset of X, C a proper convex cone in Y with $intC \neq \emptyset$, and $F : K \times K \rightrightarrows Y$ a bifunction with nonempty values. Suppose that*

1. $F(x, x) \subset C$ *for all $x \in K$;*
2. *F is C-monotone and upper C-convex in its second argument.*

Then F is generalized C-essentially quasi-monotone.

Proof. Take $x_1, x_2, ..., x_n \in K$ and $\lambda_1, \lambda_2, ..., \lambda_n \geq 0$ such that $\sum_{i=1}^{n} \lambda_i = 1$. Set $z := \sum_{j=1}^{n} \lambda_j x_j$. Then by the assumptions, we have

$$\sum_{i=1}^{n} \lambda_i F(x_i, z) \subset -C - \sum_{i=1}^{n} \lambda_i F(z, x_i) \subset -C - F(z, z) - C \subset -C.$$

Moreover, we have $intC \cap (-C) = \emptyset$. Hence

$$\sum_{i=1}^{n} \lambda_i F(x_i, z) \cap intC = \emptyset.$$

The proof is complete. □

The following result is a generalization of Proposition 4.11.

Lemma 4.16. *Let X, Y be topological vector spaces, K a nonempty convex subset of X, and C be a proper convex cone in Y with $intC \neq \emptyset$, $F : K \times K \rightrightarrows Y$ a bifunction with nonempty values. Suppose that F is C-monotone and lower C-convex in its second argument. Then F is generalized C-essentially quasi-monotone.*

Proof. Take $x_1, x_2, ..., x_n \in K$ and $\lambda_1, \lambda_2, ..., \lambda_n \geq 0$ such that $\sum_{i=1}^{n} \lambda_i = 1$. Set $z := \sum_{j=1}^{n} \lambda_j x_j$. Then by the assumptions, we have

$$\sum_{i=1}^{n} \lambda_i F(x_i, z) \subset \sum_{i,j=1}^{n} \lambda_i \lambda_j F(x_i, x_j) - C$$

$$= \frac{1}{2} \sum_{i,j=1}^{n} \lambda_i \lambda_j (F(x_i, x_j) + F(x_j, x_i)) - C.$$

Hence

$$\sum_{i=1}^{n} \lambda_i F(x_i, z) \subset -C.$$

The proof is complete. $\qquad\qquad\qquad\qquad\qquad\qquad\qquad\qquad\qquad\square$

The following example shows that a generalized C-essentially quasi-monotone bifunction is not necessary C-monotone, even if it is upper C-convex in its second argument.

Example 4.15. Let $X = \mathbb{R}$, $K = [0, 1]$, $Y = \mathbb{R}^2$ and $C = \mathbb{R}_+^2$. Let $F : [0, 1] \times [0, 1] \rightrightarrows \mathbb{R}^2$ given by

$$F(x, y) = [(0, 0), (|x - y|, 0)] \text{ for every } x, y \in [0, 1],$$

where $[(0, 0), (|x - y|, 0)]$ denotes the line segment joining $(0, 0)$ and $(|x - y|, 0)$. It is easy to see that F is generalized $\mathbb{R}_+^2$-essentially quasi-monotone, upper $\mathbb{R}_+^2$-convex in its second argument, but not $\mathbb{R}_+^2$-monotone, since $F(1, 0) + F(0, 1) = [(0, 0), (2, 0)] \not\subset -\mathbb{R}_+^2$.

Finally, we need the following result.

Lemma 4.17. ([80], Lemma 6) *Let X, Y be real topological vector spaces, K and D nonempty convex subsets of X with $D \subset K$, C a proper convex cone in Y with $\text{int} C \neq \emptyset$, and $F : K \rightrightarrows Y$ a set-valued mapping with nonempty values. Assume that*

1. *$F : K \rightrightarrows Y$ is upper C-convex;*
2. *$x_0 \in \text{core}_K D$; $F(x_0) \not\subset Y \setminus (-C)$;*
3. *$F(y) \subset Y \setminus (-\text{int} C)$ for all $y \in D$.*

Then $F(y) \subset Y \setminus (-\text{int} C)$ for all $y \in K$.

Next, using the result on the existence of maximal elements (Lemma 4.13), we give some new existence theorems which improve, extend and unify the main results of Blum and Oettli [42], Fu [80] and Kassay and Miholca [103].

To start, we first need two lemmas, which serve as tools for the proof of the main result.

Lemma 4.18. *Let X, Y be real topological vector spaces and D a nonempty compact convex subset of X. Let C be a proper convex cone in Y with $intC \neq \emptyset$. Let $G, H : D \times D \rightrightarrows Y$ be set-valued mappings with nonempty values and $A : D \rightrightarrows D$ a Browder-Fan mapping such that*

$$\mathcal{F}(A) = \{x \in D : x \in A(x)\}$$

is closed in D. Assume that

1. $H(x, x) \subset C$ *for all $x \in D$;*
2. G *is generalized C-essentially quasi-monotone;*
3. G *is C-lower semicontinuous in its second argument;*
4. H *is $-C$-lower semicontinuous in its first argument and upper C-convex in its second argument.*

Then there exists a point $\bar{x} \in D$ such that

$$\bar{x} \in A(\bar{x}) \text{ and } G(y, \bar{x}) - H(\bar{x}, y) \subset Y \setminus intC, \tag{4.50}$$

for all $y \in A(\bar{x})$.

Proof. For $x \in D$, we define

$$P(x) = \{y \in D : G(y, x) - H(x, y) \not\subset Y \setminus intC\}.$$

Consider the set-valued mapping S from D to itself defined by

$$S(x) = \begin{cases} \text{conv} P(x) \cap A(x) & \text{if } x \in \mathcal{F}(A), \\ A(x) & \text{if } x \in D \setminus \mathcal{F}(A), \end{cases}$$

where the set-valued mapping $\text{conv} P : D \rightrightarrows D$ is defined by $\text{conv} P(x) = conv(P(x))$. It is easy to see that for any $x \in D$, $S(x)$ is convex and

$$S^{-1}(y) = [(\text{conv} P)^{-1}(y) \cap A^{-1}(y)] \cup [A^{-1}(y) \cap (D \setminus \mathcal{F}(A))].$$

From the assumptions, for any $y \in D$, $A^{-1}(y)$ and $D \setminus \mathcal{F}(A))$ are open in D. Moreover, we have

$$P^{-1}(y) = \{x \in D : G(y, x) - H(x, y) \not\subset Y \setminus intC\}.$$

For any fixed y, since $G(y, x) - H(x, y)$ is C-lower semicontinuous in x, then by Lemma 4.14,

$$L = \{x \in D : G(y, x) - H(x, y) \subset Y \setminus intC\}$$

is closed in D. Therefore

$$P^{-1}(y) = D \setminus L$$

is open in D. Hence $(\operatorname{conv} P)^{-1}(y)$ is open in D by Lemma 4.11, so we have $S^{-1}(y)$ is also open in D.

Further, we claim that for all $x \in D$, $x \notin S(x)$. Indeed, suppose to the contrary that there exists a point $z \in D$ such that $z \in S(z)$. If $z \in D \setminus \mathcal{F}(A)$ then $z \in A(z)$ which is a contradiction. So $z \in \mathcal{F}(A)$ and we have $z \in S(z) = \operatorname{conv} P(z) \cap A(z)$. We deduce that there exist $\{y_1, y_2, ..., y_n\} \subset P(z)$ such that $z = \sum_{i=1}^{n} \lambda_i y_i$, $\lambda_i \geq 0$, $\sum_{i=1}^{n} \lambda_i = 1$. By the definition of P we can see that

$$G(y_i, z) - H(z, y_i) \not\subset Y \setminus \operatorname{int} C \text{ for all } i = 1, 2, ..., n.$$

Then, there exist $a_i \in G(y_i, z)$, $b_i \in H(z, y_i)$ such that $a_i - b_i \in \operatorname{int} C$. Thus,

$$\sum_{i=1}^{n} \lambda_i (a_i - b_i) \in \operatorname{int} C. \tag{4.51}$$

By the assumption (2), G is generalized C-essentially quasi-monotone, therefore we have

$$\sum_{i=1}^{n} \lambda_i G(y_i, z) \cap \operatorname{int} C = \emptyset. \tag{4.52}$$

Since $H(x, y)$ is upper C-convex in y, we get

$$\sum_{i=1}^{n} \lambda_i H(z, y_i) \subset H(z, z) + C \subset C + C = C,$$

and therefore

$$-\sum_{i=1}^{n} \lambda_i H(z, y_i) \subset -C. \tag{4.53}$$

By (4.52), (4.53) it follows that

$$\sum_{i=1}^{n} \lambda_i (a_i - b_i) \notin \operatorname{int} C, \tag{4.54}$$

which contradicts (4.51). Applying Lemma 4.13, we conclude that there exists a point $\bar{x} \in D$ with $S(\bar{x}) = \emptyset$. If $\bar{x} \in D \setminus \mathcal{F}(A))$, then $S(\bar{x}) = A(\bar{x}) = \emptyset$, contradicting the fact that A has nonempty values. Therefore, $\bar{x} \in \mathcal{F}(A)$ and $\operatorname{conv} P(\bar{x}) \cap A(\bar{x}) = \emptyset$. This clearly implies that $P(\bar{x}) \cap A(\bar{x}) = \emptyset$, hence, for all $y \in A(\bar{x})$ one has $y \notin P(\bar{x})$, i.e.,

$$\bar{x} \in A(\bar{x}) \text{ and } G(y, \bar{x}) - H(\bar{x}, y) \subset Y \setminus \operatorname{int} C,$$

for all $y \in A(\bar{x})$. Thus, the result holds and the proof is complete. $\qquad \square$

Remark 4.4. Observe that Lemma 4.18 fails to hold if the closedness assumption on the set $\mathcal{F}(A)$ is violated.

This remark is illustrated by the following example.

Example 4.16. Let $X = \mathbb{R}$, $D = [0, 1]$, $Y = \mathbb{R}^2$ and $C = \mathbb{R}^2_+$.

1. Let $G : D \times D \rightrightarrows \mathbb{R}^2$ given by $G(x, y) = \{(|x - y|, 0)\}$ for every $x, y \in D$. By Example 1 in [103], F is upper $\mathbb{R}^2_+$-convex in its second argument, generalized $\mathbb{R}^2_+$-essentially quasi-monotone but not C-monotone.
2. Let $H : D \times D \rightrightarrows \mathbb{R}^2$ given by $H(x, y) = \{(0, x - y)\}$ for every $x, y \in D$.
3. Let $A : D \rightrightarrows D$ be the mapping defined by

$$
A(x) = \begin{cases}
0 & \text{if } x = 1, \\
[0, 1] & \text{if } x \in (0, 1), \\
1 & \text{if } x = 0.
\end{cases}
$$

Then $A(x)$ is a nonempty convex subset of D and $A^{-1}(y)$ is open in D for all $x, y \in D$. Therefore, A is a Browder-Fan mapping. Moreover, the set $\mathcal{F}(A) = (0, 1)$ is open in D.

It is easy to see that each of conditions (1), (2), (3), (4) of Lemma 4.18 is satisfied. However, (4.50) has no solution. Indeed, if $\bar{x}$ is a solution of (4.50) then $\bar{x} \in (0, 1)$ and

$$
G(y, \bar{x}) - H(\bar{x}, y) \subset Y \setminus intC,
$$
$$
\Longleftrightarrow (|\bar{x} - y|, y - \bar{x}) \notin intC,
$$

for all $y \in A(\bar{x}) = [0, 1]$, which is impossible.

The next lemma makes the connection between the special equilibrium problem considered in Lemma 4.18 and the equilibrium problem we are interested in.

Lemma 4.19. *Let X, Y be real topological vector spaces and D a nonempty closed convex subset of X. Let C be a proper convex cone in Y with $intC \neq \emptyset$. Let $G, H : D \times D \rightrightarrows Y$ be set-valued mappings with nonempty values and $A : D \rightrightarrows D$ a set-valued mapping with nonempty convex values. Assume that*

1. $G(x, x) \subset C$ *and* $0 \in H(x, x)$ *for all* $x \in D$;
2. *for all* $x, y \in D$, *the mapping* $g : [0, 1] \rightrightarrows Y$ *defined by*

$$
g(t) := G(ty + (1 - t)x, y)
$$

is $-C$-lower semicontinuous at $t = 0$;
3. *G, H are upper C-convex in their second argument.*

If there exists a point $\bar{x} \in D$ such that

$$\bar{x} \in A(\bar{x}) \text{ and } G(y, \bar{x}) - H(\bar{x}, y) \subset Y \setminus intC \text{ for all } y \in A(\bar{x})$$

then

$$\bar{x} \in A(\bar{x}) \text{ and } G(\bar{x}, y) + H(\bar{x}, y) \subset Y \setminus (-intC) \text{ for all } y \in A(\bar{x}).$$

Proof. Let $\bar{x} \in D$ be such that

$$\bar{x} \in A(\bar{x}) \text{ and } G(y, \bar{x}) - H(\bar{x}, y) \subset Y \setminus intC \text{ for all } y \in A(\bar{x}).$$

We set $x_t := ty + (1-t)\bar{x}, t \in [0, 1]$. It is clear that $x_t \in A(\bar{x})$ for all $t \in [0, 1]$ and therefore, we have

$$\bar{x} \in A(\bar{x}) \text{ and } G(x_t, \bar{x}) - H(\bar{x}, x_t) \subset Y \setminus intC. \qquad (4.55)$$

By the assumption (1) and the upper C-convexity of $G(x, .)$ and $H(x, .)$, we have

$$tG(x_t, y) + (1-t)G(x_t, \bar{x}) \subset G(x_t, x_t) + C \subset C + C = C, \qquad (4.56)$$
$$tH(\bar{x}, y) \subset tH(\bar{x}, y) + (1-t)H(\bar{x}, \bar{x}) \subset H(\bar{x}, x_t) + C. \qquad (4.57)$$

By (4.56) and (4.57), we obtain

$$tG(x_t, y) + t(1-t)H(\bar{x}, y) \subset -(1-t)G(x_t, \bar{x}) + (1-t)H(\bar{x}, x_t) + C. \qquad (4.58)$$

We claim that

$$G(x_t, y) + (1-t)H(\bar{x}, y) \subset Y \setminus (-intC) \; \forall t \in (0, 1]. \qquad (4.59)$$

Indeed, if (4.59) is false, then there exist some $t \in (0, 1]$ and some $a \in G(x_t, y), b \in H(\bar{x}, y)$ such that

$$a + (1-t)b \in -intC. \qquad (4.60)$$

By (4.58), there exist $z \in G(x_t, \bar{x}), w \in H(\bar{x}, x_t)$ and $\bar{c} \in C$ such that

$$t[a + (1-t)b] = -(1-t)(z-w) + \bar{c}.$$

By (4.60), we have

$$(1-t)(z-w) = -t[a + (1-t)b] + \bar{c} \in intC + \bar{c} \subset intC.$$

Hence, $z - w \in intC$, which contradicts (4.55). Let $h(t) = G(x_t, y) + (1-t)H(\bar{x}, y), t \in [0, 1]$. Suppose that $h(0) \not\subset Y \setminus (-intC)$, then there is a point $v \in h(0)$ such that $v \in -intC$. By the assumption (2), $h(t)$ is $-C$-lsc at $t = 0$, then there is a $\delta \in (0, 1)$ such that for all $t \in [0, \delta]$, $h(t) \cap (-intC - C) = h(t) \cap (-intC) \neq \emptyset$. This contradicts (4.59). Thus we obtain $h(0) \subset Y \setminus (-intC)$, that is,

$$G(\bar{x}, y) + H(\bar{x}, y) \subset Y \setminus (-intC) \ \forall y \in A(\bar{x}).$$

This completes the proof of the lemma. □

We are now in a position to prove our main result.

Theorem 4.12. *Let X, Y be real topological vector spaces, K a nonempty closed convex subset of X, and D a nonempty compact convex subset of K. Let C be a proper convex cone in Y with $intC \neq \emptyset$. Let $G, H : K \times K \rightrightarrows Y$ be set-valued bifunctions with nonempty values and $A : D \rightrightarrows K$ a Browder-Fan mapping such that $B(x) := A(x) \cap D \neq \emptyset$ for all $x \in D$ and*

$$\mathcal{F}(A) = \{x \in D : x \in A(x)\}$$

is closed in D. Assume that

1. $G(x, x) \subset C$, $G(x, x) \cap (-C) \neq \emptyset$ and $0 \in H(x, x) \subset C$ for all $x \in K$;
2. G is generalized C-essentially quasi-monotone;
3. For all $x, y \in K$, the mapping $g : [0, 1] \rightrightarrows Y$ defined by

$$g(t) := G(ty + (1 - t)x, y)$$

   is $-C$-lower semicontinuous at $t = 0$;
4. G is upper C-convex and C-lower semicontinuous in its second argument;
5. H is $-C$-lower semicontinuous in its first argument and upper C-convex in its second argument;
6. Suppose that for any $x \in B(x) \setminus core_{A(x)} B(x)$, one can find a point $a \in core_{A(x)} B(x)$ such that

$$G(x, a) + H(x, a) \not\subset Y \setminus (-C).$$

Then there exists a point $\bar{x} \in B(\bar{x})$ such that

$$G(\bar{x}, y) + H(\bar{x}, y) \subset Y \setminus (-intC),$$

for all $y \in A(\bar{x})$.

Proof. The set-valued mapping $B : D \rightrightarrows D$ satisfies $B^{-1}(y) = A^{-1}(y)$ for all $y \in D$ and $\mathcal{F}(B) = \mathcal{F}(A)$. Therefore, B is also a Browder-Fan mapping and its fixed point set is nonempty and closed in D. By Lemma 4.18, there exists $\bar{x} \in B(\bar{x})$ such that

$$G(y, \bar{x}) - H(\bar{x}, y) \subset Y \setminus intC,$$

for all $y \in B(\bar{x})$. Applying Lemma 4.19, we get

$$\bar{x} \in B(\bar{x}) \text{ and } G(\bar{x}, y) + H(\bar{x}, y) \subset Y \setminus (-intC), \qquad (4.61)$$

for all $y \in B(\bar{x})$. Further, we define the set-valued mapping $\Phi : K \rightrightarrows Y$ by

$$\Phi(y) = G(\bar{x}, y) + H(\bar{x}, y), \quad y \in K.$$

Assumptions (4) and (5) show that Φ is upper C-convex and it follows from (4.61) that

$$\Phi(y) \subset Y \setminus (-intC) \text{ for all } y \in B(\bar{x}).$$

If $\bar{x} \in core_{A(\bar{x})} B(\bar{x})$ then we set $x_0 = \bar{x}$, otherwise, since $\bar{x} \in B(\bar{x})$ we set $x_0 = a$, where a is from the assumption (6). Then we always have $\Phi(x_0) \not\subset Y \setminus (-C)$. Using Lemma 4.17 with $B(\bar{x})$ instead of D and $A(\bar{x})$ instead of K (observe that $A(\bar{x})$ is nonempty and convex, $B(\bar{x}) \subset A(\bar{x})$ is nonempty), we conclude that

$$\Phi(y) \subset Y \setminus (-intC) \text{ for all } y \in A(\bar{x}).$$

It follows that

$$G(\bar{x}, y) + H(\bar{x}, y) \subset Y \setminus (-intC) \text{ for all } y \in A(\bar{x}).$$

This completes the proof. $\qquad\qquad\qquad\qquad\qquad\qquad\qquad\qquad\quad\square$

4.4 EXISTENCE OF SOLUTIONS OF QUASI-EQUILIBRIUM PROBLEMS

This section deals with quasi-equilibrium problems in the setting of real Banach spaces. By a fixed point theory approach, we obtain existence results under mild conditions of continuity improving some old existing results in this area. By a selection theory approach, we make use of the Michael selection theorem to overcome the separability of the Banach spaces and generalize some results obtained recently in the literature. Finally, we deal with the existence of approximate solutions for quasi-equilibrium problems and by arguments mixing both selection theory and fixed point theory, we obtain some results for quasi-equilibrium problems involving sub-lower semicontinuous set-valued mappings.

Although the equilibrium problem subsumes several kinds of problems, there are many problems described by variational inequalities involving constraints that depend on the solution itself. In this direction, we refer to *quasi-variational inequalities*, considered early in the literature in connection with stochastic impulse control problems, where the constraint set is subject to modifications. For more recent existence results for quasi-variational inequalities with applications to Nash equilibria of generalized games, we refer to [60,81].

In the spirit to describe in a more again general framework most of problems arising in nonlinear analysis, it has been considered and adopted recently in the literature the notion of *quasi-equilibrium problem*, which appears as an equilibrium problem in which the constraint set is subject to modifications. The quasi-equilibrium problem is a unified formulation which encompasses many relevant problems such as quasi-variational inequalities, mixed quasi-variational like inequalities and all the special cases of the equilibrium problem. See also the seminal paper [130], where this formulation has been first used as a pure mathematical object. The first existence results have been established and applied to different optimization problems including Nash equilibrium problems under constraints and quasi-variational inequalities for monotone operators.

Many problems related to the term *equilibrium* and arising from different areas of sciences can be mathematically modeled as special cases of the unified formulation called the equilibrium problem. Also, the equilibrium problem subsumes many mathematical special cases which are in relation to the term equilibrium such as Nash equilibrium problems and economic equilibrium problems. Then one can naturally guess that this is the reason for which the term equilibrium problem has been chosen to name this unified formulation. The last decades have witnessed an exceptional growth in theoretical advances on the equilibrium problem and its applications in concrete cases. Maybe, the simplicity of this formulation is the principal reason which has allowed all these advancements. We point out that the equilibrium problem has never been introduced in order to deal directly with other problems which are not described by the old existing concepts. Furthermore, if we assume that a problem is directly modeled as an equilibrium problem by using an inequality involving a bifunction, then nothing can impose that this inequality is a variational inequality. Unfortunately, this is not the task for which the concept of the equilibrium problem has been introduced, but to describe various existing concepts in a common way in order to deeply study them altogether.

Let us point out that there are some other unified mathematical formulations encompassing different special cases of the equilibrium problem which have been also considered in the literature. We especially think about the general conditions considered in [124] as a structure giving rise to what is called there "equilibrium problems of a certain type." These general conditions express what is called "the common laws," and it is shown that many equilibrium problems arising from different areas of sciences fulfill the common laws. Similar to the equilibrium problem considered in this paper, the equilibrium problems of this above type subsumes many problems of nonlinear analysis as particular cases. This is an important different point of view, which has also allowed to obtain different results on concrete cases, and especially on the traffic equilibrium problem.

In this section, we deal with existence of solutions and approximate solutions of the quasi-equilibrium problem. After presenting the necessary background, we first develop an approach based on fixed point theory to solve quasi-equilibrium problems under mild conditions of semicontinuity and hemicontinuity. In this approach, we are interested in solving the equilibrium problem defined on the images of a given set-valued mapping. Then we seek a fixed point to a related set-valued mapping defined in the sequel and called "the selection set-valued mapping." An example of a bifunction and an application to variational inequalities have been also given in order to highlight our techniques developed in this section. Next, we follow a selection theory approach and make use of the Michael selection theorem for paracompact Hausdorff topological spaces. We obtain existence results in the settings of real Banach spaces instead of separable real Banach spaces considered recently in the literature with the Michael selection theorem version for perfectly normal spaces, which is more restrictive in our purpose. The final part of this section is devoted to the existence of approximate solutions of the quasi-equilibrium problem. For this purpose, we develop a connection between the involved set-valued mapping and the bifunction. We also make use of the notion of sub-lower semicontinuous set-valued mappings, introduced in relationship with the notion of approximate continuous selection, to carry out existence of approximate solutions of the quasi-equilibrium problem. This approach combines arguments and techniques from fixed point theory and selection theory and has been already considered for lower semicontinuous set-valued mappings.

We first recall the equilibrium problem and notations we are going to consider in this section. Let C be a nonempty subset of a Hausdorff topological space E and $\Phi : C \times C \longrightarrow \mathbb{R}$ be a bifunction, called equilibrium bifunction iff $\Phi(x, x) = 0$, for every $x \in C$. We recall that the *equilibrium problem* is a problem of the form

$$\text{find } x^* \in C \text{ such that } \Phi\left(x^*, y\right) \geq 0 \quad \text{for all } y \in C, \qquad \text{(EP)}$$

where the set C is called the constraint set.

A *quasi-equilibrium problem* is a problem of the form:

$$\text{find } x^* \in A\left(x^*\right) \text{ such that } \Phi\left(x^*, y\right) \geq 0 \quad \text{for all } y \in A\left(x^*\right), \qquad \text{(QEP)}$$

where $A : C \rightrightarrows C$ is a set-valued mapping on C. In order words, a quasi-equilibrium problem is an equilibrium problem in which the constraint set is subject to modifications depending on the considered point.

If X is a real topological Hausdorff vector space, then there is the notion of hemicontinuity for real-valued functions defined on X which is the semicontinuity on line segments. A function $f : X \longrightarrow \mathbb{R}$ is said to be *lower hemicontinuous* at x iff for every $\epsilon > 0$ and every $z \in X$, there exists $t_z \in [0, 1]$ such that

$$f(tz + (1 - t)x) \geq f(x) - \epsilon \quad \text{for all } t \in \left[0, t_z\right].$$

The function f is said to be *upper hemicontinuous* at x iff $-f$ is lower hemicontinuous at x. It is said to be *hemicontinuous* at x iff it is lower and upper hemicontinuous at x. A function f is said to be lower (resp., upper) hemicontinuous on a subset S of X iff it is lower (resp., upper) hemicontinuous at every point of S. It is said to be hemicontinuous on S iff it is lower and upper hemicontinuous on S.

We now recall some notions of convexity for real-valued functions defined on a real topological Hausdorff vector space X. A function $f : X \longrightarrow \mathbb{R}$ is said to be

1. *quasi-convex* on X iff, for every $x_1, x_2 \in X$,

$$f(\lambda x_1 + (1 - \lambda) x_2) \leq \max \{ f(x_1), f(x_2) \} \quad \text{for all } \lambda \in [0, 1];$$

2. *semistrictly quasi-convex* on X iff, for every $x_1, x_2 \in C$ such that $f(x_1) \neq f(x_2)$, we have

$$f(\lambda x_1 + (1 - \lambda) x_2) < \max \{ f(x_1), f(x_2) \} \quad \text{for all } \lambda \in]0, 1[;$$

3. *explicitly quasi-convex* on X iff it is quasi-convex and semistrictly quasi-convex.

Note that there is not any inclusion relationship between the class of semistrictly quasi-convex functions and that of quasi-convex functions. However, if f is a lower semicontinuous and semistrictly quasi-convex function, then f is explicitly quasi-convex; see [112].

There are several notions relative to monotonicity of bifunctions that play an important role in the results related to existence of solutions of equilibrium problem. Recall that a bifunction $\Phi : X \times X \longrightarrow \mathbb{R}$ is said to be *pseudo-monotone* on X iff

$$\Phi(x, y) \geq 0 \Longrightarrow \Phi(y, x) \leq 0, \quad \text{for all } x, y \in X.$$

Clearly, if Φ is pseudo-monotone on C, then for every $x \in C$, $\Phi(x, x) = 0$ if and only if $\Phi(x, x) \geq 0$.

The graph of a set-valued mapping $F : X \rightrightarrows Y$ is the set

$$\text{grph}(F) := \{ (x, y) \in X \times Y : y \in F(x) \}.$$

If $X = Y$, we denote by $\text{fix}(F)$ the fixed points set of F. That is,

$$\text{fix}(F) := \{ x \in X : x \in F(x) \}.$$

For a set-valued mapping $F : X \rightrightarrows Y$ and $B \subset Y$, the set-valued mapping $F \cap B$ is defined by $(F \cap B)(x) = F(x) \cap B$, for every $x \in X$.

Recall that a single-valued mapping $f : X \rightarrow Y$ is said to be a selection of a set-valued mapping $F : X \rightrightarrows Y$ iff $f(x) \in F(x)$, for every $x \in X$.

4.4.1 A Fixed Point Theory Approach

In what follows, we deal with the existence of solutions of quasi-equilibrium problems by following a fixed point theory approach.

The following result is the real topological Hausdorff vector space version of some generalizations of the Ky Fan minimax inequality theorem recently obtained in [6,11].

Theorem 4.13. *Let C be a nonempty, closed, and convex subset of a real topological Hausdorff vector space E. Let $\Phi : C \times C \longrightarrow \mathbb{R}$ be a bifunction and suppose the following assumptions hold:*

1. *$\Phi(x, x) \geq 0$, for every $x \in C$;*
2. *Φ is quasi-convex in its second variable on C;*
3. *there exist a compact subset K of C and $y_0 \in K$ such that*

$$\Phi(x, y_0) < 0 \quad \text{for all } x \in C \setminus K;$$

4. *Φ is upper semicontinuous in its first variable on K.*

Then the equilibrium problem (EP) has a solution.

In the presence of pseudo-monotonicity and explicit quasi-convexity, the upper semicontinuity of the bifunction f in its first variable can be weakened to upper hemicontinuity.

Theorem 4.14. *Let C be a nonempty, closed, and convex subset of a real topological Hausdorff vector space E. Let $\Phi : C \times C \longrightarrow \mathbb{R}$ be an equilibrium bifunction and suppose the following assumptions hold:*

1. *Φ is pseudo-monotone on C;*
2. *Φ is explicitly quasi-convex in its second variable on C;*
3. *there exists a compact subset K of C and $y_0 \in K$ such that*

$$\Phi(x, y_0) < 0 \quad \text{for all } x \in C \setminus K;$$

4. *Φ is upper hemicontinuous in its first variable on K;*
5. *Φ is lower semicontinuous in its second variable on K.*

Then the equilibrium problem (EP) has a solution.

Although the fundamental role of the equilibrium problem is to unify different abstract and practice problems in a common way in order to study them, we provide here the following example of an equilibrium bifunction defined on a real Banach space. This example is constructed to emphasize the importance of Theorem 4.13, where the involved bifunction is not upper semicontinuous in its first variable on the whole space. Note that the compact set K used here, and in Theorem 4.13 and Theorem 4.14, is called in the literature the *set of coerciveness*.

Example 4.17. Let $(E, \|.\|)$ be a real Banach space and take K a compact subset of X such that $0 \in K \subset B(0, 1)$. Define $\Phi : E \times E \rightrightarrows \mathbb{R}$ by

$$\Phi(x, y) = \begin{cases} \dfrac{\|y\|^2 - \|x\|^2}{2} & \text{if } \|x\| = 2, \\ \|y\|^2 - \|x\|^2 & \text{otherwise.} \end{cases}$$

All hypotheses of Theorem 4.13 are satisfied with $y_0 = 0$. To show that Φ is not upper semicontinuous in its first variable on the whole space E, let $y \in E$ be such that $\|y\| > 2$. Let $(x_n)_n$ be a sequence in E converging to $x \in E$ such that $\|x\| = 2$ and $\|x_n\| \neq 2$, for every n. Then

$$\limsup_{n \to +\infty} \Phi(x_n, y) = \|y\|^2 - 4 > \frac{\|y\|^2 - 4}{2} = \Phi(2, y).$$

It follows that ϕ is not upper semicontinuous in its first variable at any $x \in E$ such that $\|x\| = 2$.

Now, we give an application of our techniques on equilibrium problems developed above and especially Theorem 4.14, to the special case of nonlinear variational inequalities. In this example, the operator L is not necessarily hemicontinuous on the whole space.

Consider the special case of a *nonlinear variational inequality* of the form

$$\text{find } x^* \in C \text{ such that } \langle Lx^*, y - x^* \rangle \geq 0 \quad \text{for all } y \in C, \tag{VI}$$

where C is a nonempty convex subset of a real Banach space $(E, \|.\|)$, E^* the dual of E, $L : C \to E^*$ is an operator and $\langle , \rangle$ denotes the duality pairing between E^* and E.

We observe that $x^* \in C$ is a solution of the variational inequality problem (VI) if and only if x^* is a solution of the equilibrium problem (EP) with the bifunction $\Phi_L : C \times C \to \mathbb{R}$ defined by

$$\Phi_L(x, y) = \langle Lx, y - x \rangle.$$

The bifunction Φ_L is linear and continuous in its second variable on C endowed with the weak topology. However, the upper semicontinuity of Φ_L in its first variable is too strong in many applications since L can be chosen only hemicontinuous in the following sense. The operator L is said to be hemicontinuous at a point $x \in C$ iff the restriction of L on any segment containing x and contained in C is continuous at x. We will say that L is hemicontinuous on a subset S of C iff it is hemicontinuous at every point of S. Clearly, Φ_L is hemicontinuous in its first variable on a subset S contained in C whenever L is hemicontinuous on S.

We recall that the operator L is said to be pseudo-monotone on C iff whenever $x, y \in C$, we have

$$\langle Lx, y - x \rangle \geq 0 \Longrightarrow \langle Ly, y - x \rangle \leq 0,$$

which is equivalent to the pseudo-monotonicity of the bifunction Φ_L.

Finally, a notion of coerciveness for operators exists in the literature, which generalizes that for bilinear forms on Hilbert spaces. The operator L is said to be coercive on C iff there exists $y_0 \in C$ such that

$$\lim_{\substack{\|x\| \to +\infty \\ x \in C}} \frac{\langle Lx, x - y_0 \rangle}{\|x\|} = +\infty.$$

We observe that if L is coercive on C, then there exists $R > 0$ such that $y_0 \in \overline{B}(0, R)$ and

$$\langle Lx, y_0 - x \rangle < 0 \quad \text{for all } x \in C \setminus \overline{B}(0, R)$$

where $\overline{B}(0, R) = \{x \in E : \|x\| \leq R\}$ is the closed ball around 0 with radius R. We denote $K_R = \overline{B}(0, R)$ and call (y_0, K_R) an *adapted couple of coerciveness* of L (which may not be unique).

Proposition 4.14. *Let E be a real reflexive Banach space, C a nonempty, closed, and convex subset of E, and $L : C \to E^*$ an operator. Assume that*

1. *L is pseudo-monotone on C;*
2. *L is coercive on C and let (y_0, K_R) be an adapted couple of coerciveness of L;*
3. *L is hemicontinuous on K_R.*

Then the variational inequality problem (VI) has a solution.

Proof. Consider the space E endowed with the weak topology and take Φ_L the bifunction defined above. Since K_R is weakly compact, then the result holds by applying Theorem 4.14. □

Now, we continue developing our techniques on equilibrium problems and we are interested in the Minty lemma for equilibrium problems which deals in particular with properties such as compactness and convexity of the sets of solutions of equilibrium problems. We will see in particular that the set of solutions in Proposition 4.14 is nonempty, weakly compact and convex since K_R is weakly compact and convex.

In the sequel, for $y \in C$, we define the following sets:

$$\Phi^+(y) = \{x \in C : \Phi(x, y) \geq 0\} \quad \text{and} \quad \Phi^-(y) = \{x \in C : \Phi(y, x) \leq 0\}.$$

Then $x^* \in C$ is a solution of the equilibrium problem (EP) if and only if

$$x^* \in \bigcap_{y \in C} \Phi^+(y).$$

Under assumptions of Theorem 4.14, we obtain that the set of solutions $\text{Sol}(\Phi, C)$ of the equilibrium problem (EP) is nonempty and

$$\text{Sol}(\Phi, C) = \bigcap_{y \in C} \Phi^+(y) \subset \bigcap_{y \in C} \text{cl}\left(\Phi^+(y)\right) \subset K$$

and there exists equality under assumptions of Theorem 4.13. We remark that the set $\bigcap_{y \in C} \text{cl}\left(\Phi^+(y)\right)$ is nonempty and compact. Also, by the pseudo-monotonicity of Φ on C, we have

$$\Phi^+(y) \subset \Phi^-(y) \quad \text{for all } y \in C,$$

and by the explicit quasi-convexity of Φ in its second variable on C and the hemicontinuity in the first variable on K, we prove that

$$\bigcap_{y \in C} \Phi^-(y) \cap K \subset \bigcap_{y \in C} \Phi^+(y).$$

The quasi-convexity of Φ in its second variable on C yields that the set $\Phi^-(y)$ is convex, for every $y \in C$.

The next result is the Minty lemma for the equilibrium problem (EP).

Theorem 4.15. *Suppose the assumptions of Theorem 4.13 or Theorem 4.14 hold. Then the set of solutions $\text{Sol}(\Phi, C)$ of the equilibrium problem (EP) is a nonempty set. If in addition,*

1. *K is convex;*
2. *Φ is pseudo-monotone on C;*
3. *Φ is semistrictly quasi-convex in its second variable on C,*

then, $\text{Sol}(\Phi, C)$ is nonempty, compact and convex.

Proof. It follows from the above remarks that

$$\text{Sol}(\Phi, C) = \left(\bigcap_{y \in C} \Phi^-(y)\right) \cap K.$$

This completes the proof. $\qquad\square$

Now, we are in a position to formulate our existence results for the quasi-equilibrium problem (QEP).

We first observe that a point $x^* \in C$ is a solution of the quasi-equilibrium problem (QEP) if and only if x^* is a fixed point of the set-valued mapping $S : C \rightrightarrows C$ defined by

$$S(x) = \{z \in A(x) : \Phi(z, y) \geq 0 \quad \text{for all } y \in A(z)\}$$

and called in the literature, the selection set-valued mapping.

Theorem 4.16. *Let C be a nonempty subset of a real Banach space E, and $A : C \rightrightarrows C$ a set-valued mapping with nonempty, closed, and convex values. Let $\Phi : C \times C \longrightarrow \mathbb{R}$ be a bifunction and suppose that for every $x \in C$, there exist a nonempty compact and convex subset K_x of $A(x)$ and $y_x \in K_x$ such that $\Phi_{|A(x)}$ satisfies all the conditions in Theorem 4.15 with K_x the set of coerciveness. Then the selection set-valued mapping S has nonempty, compact, and convex values.*

Proof. It suffices to apply Theorem 4.15 to $\Phi_{|A(x)}$, for every $x \in C$. $\qquad\square$

Now, we formulate an existence result for quasi-equilibrium problems by applying the Kakutani fixed point theorem.

Theorem 4.17. *Under the assumptions of Theorem 4.16, we suppose further that there exists a nonempty, closed, and convex subset C_0 of C such that*

1. *$S(C_0)$ is a relatively compact subset of C_0;*
2. *$grph\left(S_{|C_0}\right)$ is closed in $C_0 \times C_0$.*

Then the quasi-equilibrium problem (QEP) has a solution.

Proof. Set $K = \overline{\text{conv}}\,(\text{cl}\,(S(C_0)))$ the closed convex hull of $S(C_0)$. Then K is a nonempty, compact and convex subset of C_0, $S(K) \subset K$, $grph\left(S_{|K}\right)$ is closed in $K \times K$ and $S_{|K}$ has nonempty, closed, and convex values. It follows that $S_{|K}$ is a Kakutani mapping, that is, $S_{|K}$ is upper semicontinuous and has nonempty, compact and convex values. Thus, by the Kakutani fixed point theorem, $S_{|K}$ has a fixed point $x^* \in K$ which is a solution to the quasi-equilibrium problem (QEP). $\qquad\square$

We note that the conditions in Theorem 4.17 involve the selection set-valued mapping itself which is not in the initial data of the quasi-equilibrium problem (QEP). Now, we provide assumptions only on the involved data of the quasi-equilibrium problem (QEP) such that the conditions in Theorem 4.17 are satisfied.

Theorem 4.18. *Suppose that the assumptions of Theorem 4.16 hold and assume further that for $C_0 := \overline{\text{conv}}\left(\bigcup_{x \in C} K_x\right)$ the following conditions hold:*

1. *C_0 is a compact subset of C;*
2. *$(A \cap C_0)_{|C_0}$ is upper semicontinuous;*
3. *$\Phi_{|C_0}$ is upper semicontinuous on $C_0 \times C_0$;*
4. *for every converging sequence $(x_n)_n$ in C_0 to x and for every $y \in A(x)$, there exists a sequence $(y_n)_n$ converging to y and such that $y_n \in A(x_n) \cap C_0$, for every n.*

Then the equilibrium problem (QEP) has a solution.

Proof. The set C_0 is nonempty compact and convex subset of C. Since for every $x \in C$, $S(x) \subset K_x$, then, $S(C_0)$ is contained in C_0. In order to apply Theorem 4.17, it remains to prove that $grph\left(S_{|C_0}\right)$ is closed in $C_0 \times C_0$. For this purpose, take a sequence $(x_n, z_n)_n$ in $C_0 \times C_0$ converging in $C_0 \times C_0$ to (x, z) such that $z_n \in S(x_n)$, for every n. We prove that $z \in S(x)$. We have $z_n \in A(x_n)$ for every n, and

$$\Phi(z_n, y) \geq 0 \quad \text{for all } y \in A(x_n).$$

Since A has closed values, then, by the upper semicontinuity of $(A \cap C_0)_{|C_0}$, we have $z \in A(x)$. Now, let $y \in A(x)$ and let $(y_n)_n$ be a converging sequence in C_0 to y such that $y_n \in A(x_n) \cap C_0$, for every n. Then by the upper semicontinuity of $\Phi_{|C_0}$, we have

$$\Phi(z, y) \geq \limsup_{n \to +\infty} \Phi(z_n, y_n) \geq 0.$$

As y is arbitrary in $A(x)$, we conclude that $z \in S(x)$, which completes the proof. $\qquad\square$

4.4.2 A Selection Theory Approach

We are now concerned with the existence of solutions of quasi-equilibrium problems by following a selection theory approach. This direction has already been considered in [60] in the settings of finite dimensional spaces and developed in [51] for separable Banach spaces.

One of the most known and important result in the selection theory area is the Michael selection theorem which states that every lower semicontinuous set-valued mapping from a paracompact Hausdorff topological space X to the nonempty, closed, and convex subsets of a Banach space has a continuous selection. Motivated by the problem of extending continuous functions defined on closed subsets, Michael obtained in his pioneering paper [126] characterizations of various kinds of topological properties such as paracompactness, normality, collectionwise normality, and perfect normality by means of existence of continuous selections of lower semicontinuous set-valued mappings with values in Banach spaces. Every metric space is both paracompact and perfectly normal, and both these two properties are stronger than collectionwise normality.

In our study, the quasi-equilibrium problem (QEP) is considered in a real Banach space, and instead of the Michael selection theorem for perfectly normal spaces considered in the above mentioned papers, we use here the Michael selection theorem for paracompact Hausdorff topological spaces which is also the more suitable theorem in many analysis studies. The perfectly normal version is more restrictive since it requires separable Banach spaces and imposes that the involved set-valued mapping must have values in the family of convex subsets containing the inside points of their closures.

Beside the existence of continuous selections of lower semicontinuous set-valued mappings, there is the notion of selectionable set-valued mappings which will be important in our purpose. This notion is also interesting since it will prevent us to repeat the proof of some known facts in the selection theory.

Let X and Y be two Hausdorff topological spaces. A set-valued mapping $F : X \rightrightarrows Y$ is said to be *locally selectionable* at a point $x_0 \in X$ iff for every $y_0 \in F(x_0)$ there exist an open neighborhood U_{x_0} of x_0 and a continuous function $f_{x_0} : U_{x_0} \to Y$ such that $f_{x_0}(x_0) = y_0$ and

$$f_{x_0}(x) \in F(x) \quad \text{for all } x \in U_{x_0}.$$

The set-valued mapping F is said to be locally selectionable on X, iff it is locally selectionable at every point of X.

We point out that very locally selectionable set-valued mapping on a paracompact Hausdorff topological space with nonempty convex values in a topological Hausdorff vector space has a continuous selection; see [21, Proposition 10.2].

Theorem 4.19. *Let C be a nonempty subset of a real Banach space E, $A : C \rightrightarrows C$ a set-valued mapping, and $\Phi : C \times C \longrightarrow \mathbb{R}$ a bifunction. Suppose further that there exist a nonempty, closed, and convex subset C_0 of C and a compact subset K of C_0 such that the following conditions hold:*

1. *$A_{|C_0}$ is lower semicontinuous on C_0 and has nonempty, closed, and convex values in K;*
2. *$fix\left(A_{|C_0}\right)$ is nonempty closed subset, and $\Phi(x,x) = 0$, for every $x \in fix\left(A_{|C_0}\right)$;*
3. *the restriction of Φ on $fix\left(A_{|C_0}\right) \times C$ is quasi-convex in its second variable;*
4. *the restriction of Φ on $fix\left(A_{|C_0}\right) \times C$ is upper semicontinuous.*

Then the equilibrium problem (QEP) *has a solution.*

Proof. Define the set-valued mapping $F : fix\left(A_{|C_0}\right) \rightrightarrows C$ by

$$F(x) := \{y \in C : \Phi(x,y) < 0\}.$$

We observe that F has convex values, and by the upper semicontinuity of the restriction of Φ on $fix\left(A_{|C_0}\right) \times C$, the graph of F is open in $fix\left(A_{|C_0}\right) \times C$.

Now, consider the set-valued mapping $G = K \cap F : fix\left(A_{|C_0}\right) \rightrightarrows C$ defined by

$$G(x) := A(x) \cap F(x).$$

The restriction of A on $fix\left(A_{|C_0}\right)$ being a lower semicontinuous set-valued mapping from the paracompact Hausdorff topological space $fix\left(A_{|C_0}\right)$ to the real Banach space E with nonempty, closed, and convex values, then, by the Michael selection theorem, for every $x_0 \in fix\left(A_{|C_0}\right)$ and for every $y_0 \in A(x_0)$, there exists a continuous selection f_{x_0} of $A_{|fix(A_{|C_0})}$ such that $f_{x_0}(x_0) = y_0$; see [21, Corollary 11.1]. This means that $A_{|fix(A_{|C_0})}$ is locally selectionable set-valued mapping at every point of $fix\left(A_{|C_0}\right)$. Since F has an open graph in $fix\left(A_{|C_0}\right) \times C$, it follows by [21, Proposition 10.4] that if $x_0 \in fix\left(A_{|C_0}\right)$ such that $G(x_0) \neq \emptyset$, then G is locally selectionable set-valued mapping at x_0.

We claim that there exists $x_0 \in \operatorname{fix}\left(A_{|C_0}\right)$ such that $G(x_0) = \emptyset$ which proves that x_0 is a solution of the quasi-equilibrium problem (QEP). Assume by contradiction that $G(x_0) \neq \emptyset$, for every $x \in \operatorname{fix}\left(A_{|C_0}\right)$. It follows that G is locally selectionable set-valued mapping with nonempty convex values from the paracompact Hausdorff topological space $\operatorname{fix}\left(A_{|C_0}\right)$ to the real Banach space E. Then G has a continuous selection g. Define the set-valued mapping $H : C_0 \rightrightarrows E$ by

$$H(x) := \begin{cases} \{g(x)\} & \text{iff} \quad x \in \operatorname{fix}\left(A_{|C_0}\right), \\ A(x) & \text{iff} \quad x \notin \operatorname{fix}\left(A_{|C_0}\right). \end{cases}$$

The set-valued mapping H is lower semicontinuous on C_0. Indeed, let $x_0 \in C_0$ and V be an open subset of E such that $H(x_0) \cap V \neq \emptyset$. If $x_0 \notin \operatorname{fix}\left(A_{|C_0}\right)$, by the lower semicontinuity of A, let U be an open neighborhood of x_0 such that

$$U \cap \operatorname{fix}\left(A_{|C_0}\right) = \emptyset \quad \text{and} \quad A(x) \cap V \neq \emptyset \quad \text{for all } x \in U.$$

Then $H(x) \cap V \neq \emptyset$, for every $x \in U$. Otherwise, suppose that $x_0 \in \operatorname{fix}\left(A_{|C_0}\right)$. Then by continuity of g on $\operatorname{fix}\left(A_{|C_0}\right)$, let U_1 be an open neighborhood of x_0 in C_0 such that

$$g(x) \in V \quad \text{for all } x \in U_1 \cap \operatorname{fix}\left(A_{|C_0}\right).$$

On the other hand, by lower semicontinuity of A on C_0, let U_2 be an open neighborhood of x_0 in C_0 such that

$$A(x) \cap V \neq \emptyset \quad \text{for all } x \in U_2.$$

Clearly, $H(x) \cap V \neq \emptyset$, for every $x \in U_1 \cap U_2$. Hence, H is lower semicontinuous at x_0. Now, by applying the Michael selection theorem, the set-valued mapping H has a continuous selection f. Since $H(C_0) \subset A(C_0) \subset K$, then $f : C_0 \to C_0$ is a compact mapping. By the Schauder fixed point theorem, it follows that f has a fixed point, hence there exists $x \in C_0$ such that $x = f(x) \in A(x)$. Therefore, $x \in \operatorname{fix}\left(A_{|C_0}\right)$ which implies that $x \in G(x) \subset F(x)$. Then $\Phi(x, x) < 0$ which yields a contradiction and completes the proof. $\square$

Remark 4.5. We point out that the condition of the restriction of Φ on $\operatorname{fix}\left(A_{|C_0}\right) \times C$ being quasi-convex in its second variable can be replaced by the weaker condition: The set

$$F(x) := \{y \in C : \Phi(x, y) < 0\}$$

is convex, for every $x \in \operatorname{fix}\left(A_{|C_0}\right)$.

We now give conditions on the initial data for which the conditions in Theorem 4.19 are satisfied. By a similar statement involving the Michael selection theorem and the Schauder fixed point theorem, as in the proof of the theorem above, we give here the following sufficient conditions under which the fixed points set of the set-valued mapping A is nonempty and closed. Note that every set-valued mapping with closed graph has closed values. The converse is true under additional conditions such as the upper semicontinuity.

Proposition 4.15. *Let C be a nonempty subset of a real Banach space E and $A : C \rightrightarrows C$ a set-valued mapping. Suppose further that there exist a nonempty, closed, and convex subset C_0 of C and a compact subset K of C_0 such that the following conditions hold:*

1. *$A_{|C_0} : C_0 \rightrightarrows C$ is lower semicontinuous;*
2. *$A_{|C_0} : C_0 \rightrightarrows C$ has nonempty, closed, and convex values in K;*
3. *the graph of $A_{|C_0}$ is closed in $C_0 \times C$.*

Then $\mathrm{fix}\left(A_{|C_0}\right)$ is nonempty, closed, and compact set.

4.4.3 Approximate Solutions of Quasi-Equilibrium Problems

Like approximate selections, approximate solutions are well-known and important tools, which have already been used in quasi-variational inequality studies and in many other areas of nonlinear analysis.

In the sequel, for $\epsilon > 0$ and a set-valued mapping $F : X \rightrightarrows Y$, we denote by $F_\epsilon : X \rightrightarrows Y$ the set-valued mapping defined by

$$F_\epsilon(x) := B\left(F(x), \epsilon\right).$$

For $\epsilon > 0$, we call in what follows an ϵ-solution of the quasi-equilibrium problem (QEP), any $x_\epsilon \in \mathrm{cl}\left(\mathrm{fix}\left(A_\epsilon \cap C\right)\right)$ such that

$$\Phi(x_\epsilon, y) \geq 0 \quad \text{for all } y \in A_\epsilon(x_\epsilon) \cap C,$$

where the closure is taken with respect to the subset C. An approximate solution of the quasi-equilibrium problem (QEP) is any ϵ-solution of the quasi-equilibrium problem (QEP), for any $\epsilon > 0$.

We remark that the set-valued mapping A_ϵ has open values. Then the techniques developed previously fail to be applied to A_ϵ.

Now, we present the notion of sub-lower semicontinuity in the realm of topological vector spaces. This notion is weaker than that of lower semicontinuity and fits very well with the notion of approximate continuous selections. However, the notion of sub-lower semicontinuity seems to be more adapted to our purpose.

Let X be a Hausdorff topological space and Y be a normed vector space. A set-valued mapping $F : X \rightrightarrows Y$ is said to be sub-lower semicontinuous at $x \in X$ iff for every $\epsilon > 0$, there exist $z_x \in F(x)$ and a neighborhood U_x of x such that

$$z_x \in F_\epsilon\left(x'\right) \quad \text{for all } x' \in U_x.$$

The set-valued mapping F is said to be sub-lower semicontinuous on X iff it is sub-lower semicontinuous at every point of X.

The following result provides a localization of the continuous selection of a sub-lower semicontinuous set-valued mapping.

Lemma 4.20. *Let X be a paracompact Hausdorff topological space, Y be a normed vector space, S be a convex subset of Y, $F : X \rightrightarrows Y$ be a set-valued mapping, and $\epsilon > 0$. Suppose that for every $x \in X$, there exist $z_x \in F(x)$ and an open neighborhood U_x of x such that*

$$z_x \in F_\epsilon \left(x' \right) \cap S \quad \text{for all } x' \in U_x.$$

Then there exists a continuous selection $f : X \to S$ of F_ϵ.

Proof. For every $x \in X$, let U_x be an open neighborhood of x and $z_x \in F(x)$ such that $z_x \in F_\epsilon \left(x' \right) \cap S$, for every $x' \in U_x$. Let $(O_i)_{i \in I}$ be an open refinement of the open cover $(U_x)_{x \in X}$ of the paracompact Hausdorff topological space X and let $(p_i)_{i \in I}$ be a partition of unity subordinated to $(O_i)_{i \in I}$. For every $i \in I$, take $x_i \in X$ such that $O_i \subset U_{x_i}$ and define the function $f : X \to Y$ by

$$f(x) = \sum_{i \in I} p_i(x) z_{x_i}$$

which is continuous since it is locally a finite sum of continuous functions. For every $i \in I$ such that $p_i(x) \neq 0$, we have $x \in U_{x_i}$ and then, $z_{x_i} \in F_\epsilon(x)$. By the convexity of $F(x)$, $F_\epsilon(x)$ is also convex, and then, $f(x) \in F_\epsilon(x)$. Also, since S is convex and $z_{x_i} \in S$ for every $i \in I$, then $f(x) \in S$, for every $x \in X$.   □

An adaptation of the proof of the above lemma to our purpose yields the following important tool for the existence of approximate solutions of quasi-equilibrium problems. This result is presented for sub-lower semicontinuous and can be compared to [81, Lemma 2.1] and [51, Theorem 2.3].

Lemma 4.21. *Let X be a paracompact Hausdorff topological space, Y a normed vector space, S a convex subset of Y, $F : X \rightrightarrows Y$ a set-valued mapping with nonempty convex values in S, $\Psi : X \times S \to \mathbb{R}$ a bifunction, $\epsilon > 0$, and $\alpha \in \mathbb{R}$. We define*

$$B_{\Psi,\alpha}(x) = \{ y \in S : \Psi(x, y) < \alpha \}$$

and suppose that for every $x \in X$, the following conditions hold:

1. *the set $F_\epsilon(x) \cap B_{\Psi,\alpha}(x)$ is nonempty and convex;*
2. *there exist $z_x \in F(x)$ and an open neighborhood U_x of x such that*

$$z_x \in F_\epsilon \left(x' \right) \cap B_{\Psi,\alpha} \left(x' \right) \quad \text{for all } x' \in U_x.$$

Then there exists a continuous selection $f_\epsilon : X \to S$ of F_ϵ such that $\Psi(x, f_\epsilon(x)) < \alpha$, for every $x \in X$.

Proof. For every $x \in X$, let $z_x \in F(x)$ and take U_x defined by condition (2). By proceeding as in Lemma 4.20, the convexity of $F_\epsilon(x) \cap B_{\Psi,\alpha}(x)$ for every $x \in X$, yields a continuous selection $f_\epsilon : X \to S$ of the set-valued mapping $H_\epsilon : X \rightrightarrows Y$ defined by

$$H_\epsilon(x) = F_\epsilon(x) \cap B_{\Psi,\alpha}(x).$$

Thus, $f_\epsilon(x) \in F_\epsilon(x)$ and $\Psi(x, f_\epsilon(x)) < \alpha$, for every $x \in X$. $\square$

Remark 4.6. While the convexity of $B_{\Psi,\alpha}(x)$ in the above lemma requires conditions only on Ψ and it is satisfied if Ψ is quasi-convex in its second variable on X, the other conditions seem to be more complicated and require connections between Ψ and F.

We give in what follows the following result, which provides sufficient conditions involving Ψ and F in order to satisfy condition (1) and condition (2) of the above lemma.

Proposition 4.16. *Let X be a paracompact Hausdorff topological space, Y a normed vector space, S a convex subset of Y, $F : X \rightrightarrows Y$ a set-valued mapping with nonempty convex values in S, $\Psi : X \times S \to \mathbb{R}$ a bifunction, $\epsilon > 0$, and $\alpha \in \mathbb{R}$.*

1. *If Ψ is quasi-convex in its second variable on X, then for every $x \in X$, $B_{\Psi,\alpha}(x)$ is convex.*
2. *If $\inf\limits_{y \in F_\epsilon(x)} \Psi(x, y) < \alpha$ for some $x \in X$, then $F_\epsilon(x) \cap B_{\Psi,\alpha}(x) \neq \emptyset$.*
3. *If one of the following two conditions holds:*
   (a) *F is lower semicontinuous on X, Ψ is upper semicontinuous in its first variable on X and $F(x) \cap B_{\Psi,\alpha}(x) \neq \emptyset$, for every $x \in X$;*
   (b) *F is sub-lower semicontinuous on X, Ψ is upper semicontinuous in its first variable on X and $F(x) \subset B_{\Psi,\alpha}(x)$, for every $x \in X$,*
   then condition (2) of Lemma 4.21 is satisfied.

Proof. We verify only the last condition, the other conditions being obvious or already discussed. Let $x \in X$.

In the case where condition (3a) is satisfied, the set-valued mapping F is lower semicontinuous. Let $z_x \in F(x) \cap B_{\Psi,\alpha}(x)$ and by lower semicontinuity of F, let U_x^1 be an open neighborhood of x such that $F(x') \cap B(z_x, \epsilon) \neq \emptyset$, for every $x' \in U_x^1$. By upper semicontinuity of Ψ in its first variable, let U_x^2 be an open neighborhood of x such that $z_x \in B_{\Psi,\alpha}(x')$, for every $x' \in U_x^2$. Clearly, for every $x' \in U_x = U_x^1 \cap U_x^2$, $z_x \in F_\epsilon(x') \cap B_{\Psi,\alpha}(x')$.

In the case where condition (3b) is satisfied, the set-valued mapping F is sub-lower semicontinuous. Let $z_x \in F(x)$ and U_1^x be as in the definition of sub-lower semicontinuity. Since $z_x \in B_{\Psi,\alpha}(x)$, we choose, by upper semicontinuity of Ψ in its first variable, an open neighborhood U_x^2 of x such that $z_x \in B_{\Psi,\alpha}(x')$, for every $x' \in U_x^2$. As above, the result comes by taking $U_x = U_x^1 \cap U_x^2$. $\square$

In [51], the nonemptiness of the fixed points set of A_ϵ, which is crucial for the existence of approximate solutions of the quasi-equilibrium problem (QEP), has been obtained by applying the Fan-Browder fixed point theorem since the lower semicontinuity of A implies that the set-valued mapping A_ϵ has open fibers. This fact can be showed as follows. For every $y \in C$, we have

$$A_\epsilon^{-1}(y) = \{x \in C : y \in B(A(x), \epsilon)\}$$
$$= \{x \in C : A(x) \cap B(y, \epsilon) \neq \emptyset\}$$
$$= A^{-1}(B(y, \epsilon)).$$

We remark that this fact has been used only to prove existence of fixed points of A_ϵ. The existence of a fixed point of any selection of A_ϵ will suffice to overcome the strong condition of the openness of the fibers of A_ϵ.

Now, we present an existence result of approximate solutions of the quasi-equilibrium problem (QEP) in the case of sub-lower semicontinuous set-valued mappings.

Theorem 4.20. *Let C be a nonempty, closed, and convex subset of a real Banach space E, $A : C \rightrightarrows C$ a set-valued mapping, and $\Phi : C \times C \to \mathbb{R}$ a bifunction. Suppose further that the following conditions hold:*

1. *A is sub-lower semicontinuous on C;*
2. *there exists a compact subset K of C such that A has nonempty convex values in K.*

Then for every $\epsilon > 0$, the set-valued mapping $A_\epsilon : C \rightrightarrows C$ has a nonempty fixed points set.
If in addition,

1. *Φ is quasi-convex in its second variable;*
2. *Φ is upper semicontinuous in its first variable on C;*
3. *there exists $\epsilon_0 > 0$ such that $\Phi(x, x) \geq 0$, for every $x \in B(A(x), \epsilon_0) \cap C$;*
4. *for every $0 < \epsilon < \epsilon_0$,*
   (a) *the function defined on $cl(fix(A_\epsilon \cap C))$ by*

   $$x \mapsto \inf_{y \in A_\epsilon(x) \cap C} \Phi(x, y)$$

   attains its supremum γ_ϵ on $cl(fix(A_\epsilon \cap C))$ and this supremum is finite;
   (b) *$A(x) \subset B_{\Phi, \gamma_\epsilon + \frac{1}{n}}(x)$, for every $x \in C$ and $n \in \mathbb{N}^*$.*

Then for every $0 < \epsilon < \epsilon_0$, the quasi-equilibrium problem (QEP) has an ϵ-solution.

Proof. Let $\epsilon > 0$. The set-valued mapping A_ϵ has a nonempty fixed points set. Indeed, put $K_0 = \overline{conv}(K)$ which is a nonempty compact and convex subset of C, and $A(C) \subset K_0$. The set-valued mapping $A : C \rightrightarrows E$ being sub-lower semicontinuous and has nonempty convex values in the convex subset K_0, then, by Lemma 4.20, let $f_\epsilon : C \to K_0$ be a continuous selection of A_ϵ. By the Schauder fixed point theorem, f_ϵ has a fixed point x_ϵ^* which is necessarily in K_0. Thus, $\mathrm{cl}\,(\mathrm{fix}\,(A_\epsilon \cap C))$ is nonempty. Note that $\mathrm{cl}\,(\mathrm{fix}\,(A_\epsilon \cap C))$ is contained in K_0 and then, it is compact.

Now, for $0 < \epsilon < \epsilon_0$, let $x_\epsilon \in \mathrm{cl}\,(\mathrm{fix}\,(A_\epsilon \cap C))$ such that

$$\sup_{x \in \mathrm{cl}(\mathrm{fix}(A_\epsilon \cap C))} \inf_{y \in A_\epsilon(x) \cap C} \Phi(x, y) = \inf_{y \in A_\epsilon(x_\epsilon) \cap C} \Phi(x_\epsilon, y) = \gamma_\epsilon.$$

Put $\alpha_{\epsilon,n} = \gamma_\epsilon + \frac{1}{n}$, for $n \in \mathbb{N}^*$.

By taking $X = S = K_0$ and $Y = E$, it results by Lemma 4.21 applied to A and Φ that there exists a continuous selection $f_\epsilon : K_0 \to K_0$ of A_ϵ such that

$$\Phi(x, f_\epsilon(x)) < \alpha_{\epsilon,n} \quad \text{for all } x \in K_0.$$

Again by the Schauder fixed point theorem, let $\overline{x}_\epsilon \in K_0$ be a fixed point of f_ϵ. It follows that $\overline{x}_\epsilon = f_\epsilon(\overline{x}_\epsilon) \in A_\epsilon(\overline{x}_\epsilon) \cap K_0 \subset B(A(x_\epsilon), \epsilon_0) \cap C$. It results that

$$0 \leq \Phi(\overline{x}_\epsilon, \overline{x}_\epsilon) = \Phi(\overline{x}_\epsilon, f_\epsilon(\overline{x}_\epsilon)) < \alpha_{\epsilon,n} = \gamma_\epsilon + \frac{1}{n}.$$

By letting n go to $+\infty$, we obtain that $\inf_{y \in A_\epsilon(x_\epsilon) \cap C} \Phi(x_\epsilon, y) = \gamma_\epsilon \geq 0$. It follows that we have $x_\epsilon \in \mathrm{cl}\,(\mathrm{fix}\,(A_\epsilon \cap C))$ and

$$\Phi(x_\epsilon, y) \geq 0 \quad \text{for all } y \in A_\epsilon(x_\epsilon) \cap C,$$

which states that the quasi-equilibrium problem (QEP) has an ϵ-solution and completes the proof. $\qquad\square$

Remark 4.7. We point out that the function $x \mapsto \inf_{y \in A_\epsilon(x) \cap C} \Phi(x, y)$ defined on the set $\mathrm{cl}\,(\mathrm{fix}\,(A_\epsilon \cap C))$ is supposed to have a finite supremum. It is well known that the Berge maximum theorem is an important tool usually used to deal with such properties when the set-valued A is lower semicontinuous. Unfortunately, and even if A is lower semicontinuous and the above function is proper, nothing can guarantee that its supremum is finite if no additional conditions on Φ and on the values of A are assumed.

Conclusions

The equilibrium problem, and by consequent, the quasi-equilibrium problem studied in this section have been introduced mainly to describe in a unified way various problems arising in nonlinear analysis and in mathematics in general. The family of problems that can be expressed as an equilibrium problem is growing as far as the other related areas are being developed. Recently, it has been proved that quasi-hemivariational inequalities, which constitute an important variational formulation for several classes of mechanical problems, can be also expressed as an equilibrium problem. On the other hand, one of the interests of such a unified formulation is that many techniques and methods developed for solving a special case may be adapted, with suitable modification, to the other special cases. Motivated by these facts, it has been proved in some recent works that the techniques on weakening semicontinuity and hemicontinuity to the set of coerciveness developed to the equilibrium problem can be applied to various special cases such as quasi-hemivariational inequalities and can be used with other techniques such as the Ekeland variational principle. These techniques have been also highlighted here by an example and an application to nonlinear variational inequalities.

In this direction, we have been concerned here with the quasi-equilibrium problem, which constitutes a relevant mathematical formulation including the equilibrium problem and other concepts such as quasi-variational inequalities. We remark that in the approach based on fixed point theory developed in this section, our techniques on weakening semicontinuity and hemicontinuity are applied easily and directly to the quasi-equilibrium problem. And because of our conviction of always looking for optimal conditions when dealing with such problems, we have also considered the approach based on selection theory. In such a way, we have been able to obtain results improving some recent properties in the literature. We have been also interested in approximate solutions of the quasi-equilibrium problem and highlighted the necessary background for their existence by using the notion of sub-lower semicontinuous set-valued mappings. This study is motivated by the importance of approximate solutions in general in many areas of mathematics, but also by some recent works on approximate solutions of the quasi-equilibrium problem and its special cases.

The techniques developed in the two approaches based on fixed point theory and on selection theory, as well as those developed for approximate solutions, are given under general settings. In such a way, they can be easily applied to several particular cases.

Finally, we point out that this subject is under perpetual advancement, and it may be also interesting to look for weakened conditions on convexity when dealing with existence of solutions and approximate solutions of the quasi-equilibrium problem. The convergence of the sequence of approximate solutions of the quasi-equilibrium problem is also a challenge which has to be considered in the future.

Chapter 5

Well-Posedness for the Equilibrium Problems

Contents

We are servants rather than masters in mathematics.
Charles Hermite (1822–1901)

Chapter points

- Two kinds of well-posedness for scalar equilibrium problems are introduced and the relationship between them is discussed.
- A parametric form of the equilibrium problem is studied together with a new well-posedness concept, which unifies the two different notions of well-posedness introduced before.
- Well-posedness for the strong vector equilibrium problem is discussed.

In optimization problems it often happens that we are not able to find an exact minimizer/maximizer of the objective function (even if it exists). Fortunately, in many practical situations (real-life problems) it is satisfactory to find an approximate minimizer/maximizer "close" in some sense to the exact solution. For this purpose, different algorithms constructing convergent sequences to the minimizers/maximizers have been elaborated and studied along the years. An important

Equilibrium Problems and Applications. https://doi.org/10.1016/B978-0-12-811029-4.00013-4

issue when defining the concept of *well-posedness* is to require *stability under small perturbations*. Roughly speaking, this means that if for some point the value of the function is "close" to its minimal/maximal value (supposing its existence), the point itself should be "close" to the minimizer/maximizer. This requirement leads to the first notion of well-posedness provided by Tykhonov [167] in 1966.

Since this concept has shown to be very useful in optimization, similar notions have been defined for other related problems of interest, like *saddle point problems* and *variational inequalities*. As already mentioned, these problems constitute outstanding particular cases of the (scalar and vector) equilibrium problems. Therefore, the following question arises naturally: how can be assigned a proper definition of well-posedness to (EP) (and (SVEP), respectively – introduced within the last chapters), which extend the above (existing) concepts? Answer to this question has been provided, among others, by Bianchi, Kassay, and Pini [34] and [33], where different kinds of well-posedness both for scalar and vector equilibrium problems have been given and the relationship between them has been explored.

In this chapter we collect some concepts and results from [34] and [33] concerning well-posedness for scalar and the strong vector equilibrium problems. Section 5.1 provides a short background concerning well-posedness for the three relevant particular cases of (EP) (optimization, saddle point problems and variational inequalities). The scalar equilibrium problem is explored in section 5.2. We define in subsection 5.2.1 a concept of well-posedness for (EP) arising in a natural way from Tykhonov well-posedness for optimization problems. We call this concept T_{opt}-well-posedness and we show that both concepts of well-posedness, i.e., for optimization and saddle point problems can be obtained as its particular cases.

5.1 WELL-POSEDNESS IN OPTIMIZATION AND VARIATIONAL INEQUALITIES

At the beginning, well-posedness was considered in connection with optimization problems. Let us recall the first concept which was introduced by A.N. Tykhonov in [167] (see also [68]). Let D be a metric space. For a subset $A \subset D$ we shall denote by $\text{diam}(A) \in [0, +\infty]$ the *diameter* of the set A, i.e., $\sup\{d(a, b) : a, b \in A\}$.

For a scalar optimization problem

$$\min h(a), \qquad a \in D \tag{5.1}$$

where $h : D \to \mathbb{R}$, a sequence $\{a_n\}_n \subseteq D$ is said to be *minimizing* when $h(a_n) \to \inf_D h$ as $n \to \infty$.

Definition 5.1. The optimization problem (5.1) is called *Tykhonov well-posed* if

(i) there exists a unique solution $\bar{a} \in D$ of (5.1);
(ii) every minimizing sequence converges to $\bar{a}$.

In case of maximization problems, the definition of Tykhonov well-posedness is modified using maximizing sequences in a straightforward way. Roughly speaking, the above concept means that points with values close to the value of the problem must be close to the (unique) solution. This property might be very useful when constructing algorithms aimed at solving the problem of interest.

Corresponding notions of well-posedness have been defined for other two particular cases of (EP), namely *saddle point problems* and *variational inequalities*. Let us first recall the saddle point problem. Given two metric spaces X and Y, and $F : X \times Y \to \mathbb{R}$, the saddle point problem is to find a couple $(\bar{x}, \bar{y}) \in X \times Y$ such that

$$F(x, \bar{y}) \leq F(\bar{x}, \bar{y}) \leq F(\bar{x}, y), \qquad \forall x \in X, y \in Y.$$

By defining the bifunction $\omega : X \times Y \to \mathbb{R}$ given by

$$\omega(x, y) = \sup_x F(x, y) - \inf_y F(x, y),$$

the saddle point problem can be reduced to the following optimization problem:

$$\min \omega(x, y) = \min(\sup_x F(x, y) - \inf_y F(x, y)).$$

Since $\omega(x, y) \geq 0$ for every $(x, y) \in X \times Y$, this is equivalent to find $(\bar{x}, \bar{y}) \in X \times Y$ such that $\omega(\bar{x}, \bar{y}) = 0$.

In this way, the following definition follows naturally.

Definition 5.2. (see [52]) The saddle point problem is Tykhonov well-posed if

(i) there exists a unique saddle point $(\bar{x}, \bar{y}) \in X \times Y$;
(ii) every sequence (x_n, y_n) minimizing for ω converges to $(\bar{x}, \bar{y})$.

In case of variational inequalities the idea is similar. Suppose D is a Banach space. Under the assumptions of convexity and Gâteaux differentiability of the objective function h of (5.1), it was proved in [68] that Tykhonov well-posedness is equivalent to the condition

$$\mathrm{diam}(\{a \in D : \langle \nabla h(a), b - a \rangle \geq -\varepsilon \|a - b\|, \forall b \in D\}) \to 0, \qquad \varepsilon \downarrow 0.$$

This equivalence leads naturally to the definition of well-posedness for a general variational inequality: find $a \in D$ such that

$$\langle A(a), b - a \rangle \geq 0 \quad \forall b \in D, \tag{5.2}$$

where the map $A : D \to D^*$ is not necessarily a gradient map.

Definition 5.3. (see [68]) The variational inequality (5.2) is called well-posed if there exists at least one solution, and

$$\text{diam}(\{a \in D : \langle A(a), b - a \rangle \geq -\varepsilon\|a - b\|, \forall b \in D\}) \to 0, \qquad \varepsilon \downarrow 0.$$

As stressed before, optimization, saddle point, and variational inequality problems constitute relevant particular cases of (EP). This fact leads naturally to the questions of assigning a proper definition of well-posedness to (EP), which extends the above concepts. It is also interesting to see which results can be achieved, and how can they be related to the earlier results concerning the mentioned particular cases. This will be the topic of the next sections.

5.2 WELL-POSED SCALAR EQUILIBRIUM PROBLEMS

Starting from Definitions 5.1 (Tykhonov well-posedness for optimization problems) and 5.3 (well-posedness for variational inequalities) we provide in this section natural extensions of well-posedness to a scalar equilibrium problem. Although the latter is a unified representation for both problems (i.e., optimization and variational inequality), the concepts we obtain are different. Furthermore, as shown below, there is no relationship between the two concepts in general (in the sense that no one implies the other). However, under additional assumptions, well-posedness coming from variational inequalities implies the one coming from optimization.

5.2.1 Well-Posedness for the Equilibrium Problems Coming From Optimization

Unless otherwise stated, in what follows (D, d) is a complete metric space and $f : D \times D \to \mathbb{R}$ a given function such that $f(a, a) = 0$ for every $a \in D$. In order to start our analysis, we consider a well-known minimax formulation of (EP). This needs to consider the gap function $g : D \to [-\infty, +\infty)$ defined by

$$g(a) = \inf_{b \in D} f(a, b). \tag{5.3}$$

Particular properties of the function g are the nonpositivity on the set D, and the fact that $g(a^*) = 0$ if and only if a^* is a solution of (EP). Therefore, the following result holds:

Lemma 5.1. *The equilibrium problem has solutions if and only if*

$$\max_{a \in D} g(a) = 0.$$

By the previous formulation of (EP) and Definition 5.1 one can provide a natural definition of Tykhonov well-posedness for equilibrium problems via the function g.

Definition 5.4. (cf. [34]) The equilibrium problem (EP) is T_{opt}-well-posed if

(i) there exists a unique solution $\bar{a} \in D$ of (EP);

(ii) for every sequence $\{a_n\} \subset D$ such that $g(a_n) \to 0$, one has $a_n \to \bar{a}$.

The sequence $\{a_n\}$ in (ii) is still called *maximizing* for g.

The definition given above entails, as particular cases, the notions of well-posedness for optimization and saddle point problems, as proved in the following proposition.

Proposition 5.1. (cf. [34])

(i) *If $f(a, b) = h(b) - h(a)$, then (EP) is T_{opt}-well-posed (in the sense of Definition 5.4) if and only if $\min_{b \in D} h(b)$ is Tykhonov well-posed (in the sense of Definition 5.1).*

(ii) *If $F : X \times Y \to \mathbb{R}$, $D = X \times Y$, $a = (x, y)$ and $b = (u, v)$, define $f : D \times D \to \mathbb{R}$ as $f(a, b) = F(x, v) - F(u, y)$. Then (EP) is T_{opt}-well-posed if and only if the saddle point problem engendered by F is well-posed (in the sense of Definition 5.2).*

Next we give an example of (EP) that is T_{opt}-well-posed.

Example 5.1. Let $f : \mathbb{R} \times \mathbb{R} \to \mathbb{R}$ given by $f(a, b) = -|b - a|a^2 e^{-a}$. The equilibrium problem associated is well-posed; indeed:

(i) $f(\bar{a}, b) \geq 0$ for every $b \in \mathbb{R}$ if and only if $\bar{a} = 0$;

(ii) $g(a) = \inf_{b \in \mathbb{R}} f(a, b) = -\sup_{b \in \mathbb{R}} |b - a|a^2 e^{-a} = \begin{cases} 0, & a = 0 \\ -\infty, & a \neq 0 \end{cases}$

Take a_n such that $g(a_n) \to 0$; from (ii), this means that $a_n = 0$ for n large enough.

In what follows we investigate and characterize T_{opt}-well-posedness from another point of view, involving the notion of some approximate solutions of (EP). To do this, let $\varepsilon > 0$ be given and let us introduce the set

$$\varepsilon - \text{argmin}(EP) = \{a \in D : f(a, b) \geq -\varepsilon, \forall b \in D\}.$$

The family of sets $\{\varepsilon - \text{argmin}(EP)\}_\varepsilon$ is ascending, i.e., if $\varepsilon_1 < \varepsilon_2$, then

$$\varepsilon_1 - \text{argmin}(EP) \subseteq \varepsilon_2 - \text{argmin}(EP).$$

Moreover, the set of solutions of (EP) is the intersection of the sets $\{\varepsilon - \text{argmin}(EP) : \varepsilon > 0\}$.

The next result generalizes Theorem I.11 in [68] on one hand and provides an alternative characterization for T_{opt}-well-posedness, on the other hand.

Theorem 5.1. (cf. [34]) *If (EP) is T_{opt}-well-posed, then*

$$diam(\varepsilon - argmin(EP)) \to 0, \qquad \varepsilon \downarrow 0. \tag{5.4}$$

Moreover, the converse is true if $a \mapsto f(a, b)$ is upper semicontinuous for every $b \in D$, and $\varepsilon - \operatorname{argmin}(EP)$ is nonempty for every $\varepsilon > 0$.

Proof. By contradiction, assume that

$$\operatorname{diam}(\varepsilon - \operatorname{argmin}(EP)) \nrightarrow 0.$$

Then there exist $\alpha > 0$ and $\varepsilon_n \downarrow 0$ such that

$$\operatorname{diam}(\varepsilon_n - \operatorname{argmin}(EP)) \geq 2\alpha, \qquad \forall n \in \mathbb{N}.$$

Take $a_n, a_n' \in D$ such that $a_n, a_n' \in \varepsilon_n - \operatorname{argmin}(EP)$, and $d(a_n, a_n') \geq \alpha$, for every $n \in \mathbb{N}$. From the inequalities

$$f(a_n, b) \geq -\varepsilon_n, \quad f(a_n', b) \geq -\varepsilon_n, \quad \forall n \in \mathbb{N}, \quad \forall b \in D,$$

we get that, for every $n \in \mathbb{N}$,

$$\inf_{b \in D} f(a_n, b) \geq -\varepsilon_n, \quad \inf_{b \in D} f(a_n', b) \geq -\varepsilon_n,$$

i.e.,

$$0 \geq g(a_n) \geq -\varepsilon_n, \quad 0 \geq g(a_n') \geq -\varepsilon_n.$$

The inequalities above imply that $g(a_n) \to 0$ and $g(a_n') \to 0$ if $n \to \infty$, and, by the assumptions, both sequences $\{a_n\}$ and $\{a_n'\}$ converge to the unique solution $\bar{a}$ of (EP), a contradiction.

Conversely, let us first show that every maximizing sequence is convergent, or, equivalently, is a Cauchy sequence. Let $\{a_n\}$ be a maximizing sequence. By contradiction, assume that there exist $\{a_{n_k}\}$ and $\{a_{m_k}\}$, both subsequences of $\{a_n\}$, such that $d(a_{n_k}, a_{m_k}) > \alpha$, for some $\alpha > 0$ and for every $k \in \mathbb{N}$. From (5.4), we can take ε such that

$$\operatorname{diam}(\varepsilon - \operatorname{argmin}(EP)) < \alpha.$$

Since both $\{a_{n_k}\}$ and $\{a_{m_k}\}$ are maximizing sequences, there exists $k_\varepsilon \in \mathbb{N}$ such that for $k \geq k_\varepsilon$ we have that

$$a_{n_k}, a_{m_k} \in \varepsilon - \operatorname{argmin}(EP),$$

therefore $d(a_{n_k}, a_{m_k}) < \alpha$, a contradiction. This shows that $\{a_n\}$ is convergent. Take any maximizing sequence $\{a_n\}$, denote by $\bar{a}$ its limit, and fix any $b \in D$. Then, by upper semicontinuity,

$$f(\bar{a}, b) \geq \limsup_{n \to \infty} f(a_n, b) \geq \limsup_{n \to \infty} g(a_n) = 0.$$

Since $b \in D$ was arbitrary, we conclude that $\bar{a}$ is a solution of (EP). The uniqueness follows immediately from (5.4). $\qquad\square$

For the sake of completeness we report the proof of the following proposition that is the scalar version of Proposition 6.3 in Chapter 6, and that entails the nonemptiness of $\varepsilon - \text{argmin(EP)}$. We recall that the function $f : D \times D \to \mathbb{R}$ satisfies the "triangular inequality" (TI) if

$$f(a, b) \leq f(a, c) + f(c, b),$$

for all $a, b, c \in D$.

Proposition 5.2. *Suppose that the function f satisfies (TI). If there exists $\hat{b} \in D$ such that the function $a \mapsto f(a, \hat{b})$ is upper bounded, then $\varepsilon - \text{argmin(EP)} \neq \emptyset$ for every $\varepsilon > 0$.*

Proof. By the upper boundedness $a \mapsto f(a, \hat{b})$, for every $\varepsilon > 0$ there exists $a_0 \in D$ such that

$$f(a_0, \hat{b}) - f(a, \hat{b}) + \varepsilon > 0, \qquad \forall a \in D.$$

This inequality, together with (TI), gives

$$-\varepsilon < f(a_0, \hat{b}) - f(a, \hat{b}) \leq f(a_0, a), \qquad \forall a \in D,$$

i.e., $a_0 \in \varepsilon - \text{argmin(EP)}$. $\qquad\qquad\square$

In the sequel we need the following concept. The function $c : [0, +\infty) \to [0, +\infty)$ is said to be *forcing* provided it is increasing, $c(0) = 0$, and $t > 0$ implies $c(t) > 0$ (see, for instance, [119]).

Definition 5.5. A function $f : D \times D \to \mathbb{R}$ is said to be *forcing pseudo-monotone* if there exists a forcing function c such that

$$f(a, b) \geq 0 \Longrightarrow f(b, a) \leq -c(d(a, b)), \forall a, b \in D.$$

The next result provides sufficient conditions for T_{opt}-well-posedness (see [34]).

Proposition 5.3. *Assume that f is a forcing pseudo-monotone function and that (EP) has at least one solution. Then (EP) is T_{opt}-well-posed.*

Proof. The uniqueness of the solution follows easily from the assumption of forcing pseudo-monotonicity. Denote by $\bar{a}$ the solution of (EP). Let $\{a_n\}$ be a maximizing sequence for g. We have

$$g(a_n) \leq f(a_n, \bar{a}) \leq -c(d(a_n, \bar{a})) \leq 0.$$

Since $g(a_n) \uparrow 0$, we conclude that $d(a_n, \bar{a}) \to 0$, thereby showing that $a_n \to \bar{a}$. $\qquad\square$

5.2.2 Well-Posedness for the Equilibrium Problems Coming From Variational Inequalities

In Definition 5.3 we provided the concept of well-posedness for a (general) variational inequality, where the key role has been played by the set of ε-approximate solutions, i.e., the set $\{a \in D : \langle A(a), b - a \rangle \geq -\varepsilon \|a - b\|, \forall b \in D\}$. Inspired by this, we can define an alternative notion of well-posedness for (EP) originates from the framework of variational inequalities. To do this, let us consider the set of ε-approximate equilibrium points given by

$$E(\varepsilon) = \{a \in D : f(a, b) \geq -\varepsilon d(a, b), \forall b \in D\},$$

and introduce the following

Definition 5.6. The equilibrium problem (EP) is T_{vi}-well-posed if

  (i) there exists at least one solution $\bar{a} \in D$ of (EP);
  (ii) $\operatorname{diam}(E(\varepsilon)) \to 0, \varepsilon \downarrow 0$.

  Observe that condition (ii) trivially implies the uniqueness of the solution. In the following, we give sufficient conditions for T_{vi}-well-posedness.

Theorem 5.2. *Assume that f is forcing pseudo-monotone and that the solution set of (EP) is nonempty. If at least one of the following conditions holds:*

  (i) *the forcing function c is coercive, that is, $\lim_{t \to \infty} \frac{c(t)}{t} = +\infty$, or*
  (ii) *D is a Banach space and f is concave in its first variable,*

then (EP) is T_{vi}-well-posed.

Proof. Let $\bar{a}$ be any solution. Suppose that assumption (i) holds. We first show that $E(\varepsilon)$ is bounded for any $\varepsilon > 0$. Indeed, fix $\varepsilon > 0$ arbitrarily and take any $a \in E(\varepsilon)$; this implies that $f(a, \bar{a}) \geq -\varepsilon d(a, \bar{a})$. Since $\bar{a}$ is a solution, we know that $f(\bar{a}, a) \geq 0$, and, from the forcing pseudo-monotonicity, $f(a, \bar{a}) \leq -c(d(a, \bar{a}))$. Therefore, for every $a \in E(\varepsilon)$,

$$-\varepsilon d(a, \bar{a}) \leq -c(d(a, \bar{a})),$$

which implies for every $a \in E(\varepsilon) \setminus \{\bar{a}\}$ that

$$\frac{c(d(a, \bar{a}))}{d(a, \bar{a})} \leq \varepsilon. \tag{5.5}$$

This, together with the coercivity of c shows that $E(\varepsilon)$ is bounded.

Now let us show that $\operatorname{diam}(E(\varepsilon)) \to 0$. Supposing the contrary, there exists $\alpha > 0$, $\varepsilon_n \downarrow 0$ and $a_n \in E(\varepsilon_n)$ such that $d(a_n, \bar{a}) \geq \alpha$. Therefore, since c is a forcing function, by (5.5) we obtain

$$0 < c(\alpha) \leq c(d(a_n, \bar{a})) \leq \varepsilon_n d(a_n, \bar{a}) \leq \varepsilon_n \operatorname{diam}(E(\varepsilon_n)) \leq \varepsilon_n \operatorname{diam}(E(R)),$$

where $R > 0$ is an upper bound of the sequence $\{\varepsilon_n\}_{n\in\mathbb{N}}$. Since $E(R)$ is bounded, this relation leads to a contradiction if we let $n \to \infty$, thus proving the assertion.

Suppose now that (ii) holds, and set $d(a, b) = ||a - b||$. By contradiction, if $\text{diam}(E(\varepsilon)) \nrightarrow 0$ as $\varepsilon \downarrow 0$, then (as in the first part) there exists $\alpha > 0$, $\varepsilon_n \downarrow 0$ and $a_n \in E(\varepsilon_n)$ such that $||a_n - \bar{a}|| \geq \alpha$. Let

$$M := \sup\{f(a, \bar{a}), a \in D, ||a - \bar{a}|| \geq \alpha\}. \tag{5.6}$$

From the forcing pseudo-monotonicity of f, we easily get that $M < 0$. Indeed, since $\bar{a}$ is a solution, we obtain for every $a \in D$ with $||a - \bar{a}|| \geq \alpha$ that

$$f(a, \bar{a}) \leq -c(||a - \bar{a}||) \leq -c(\alpha)$$

showing that $M \leq -c(\alpha) < 0$. Since $a_n \in E(\varepsilon_n)$, $f(a_n, \bar{a}) \geq -\varepsilon_n||a_n - \bar{a}||$, for every n. Taking into account the assumption of concavity of $f(\cdot, b)$ and (5.6), the following chain of inequalities holds:

$$-\varepsilon_n\alpha \leq \frac{\alpha}{||a_n - \bar{a}||}f(a_n, \bar{a})$$

$$= \frac{\alpha}{||a_n - \bar{a}||}f(a_n, \bar{a}) + \left(1 - \frac{\alpha}{||a_n - \bar{a}||}\right)f(\bar{a}, \bar{a})$$

$$\leq f\left(\frac{\alpha}{||a_n - \bar{a}||}a_n + (1 - \frac{\alpha}{||a_n - \bar{a}||})\bar{a}, \bar{a}\right)$$

$$\leq M.$$

This is a contradiction, since $M < 0$ and $\varepsilon_n \downarrow 0$. $\qquad\square$

The next result gives alternative sufficient conditions for T_{vi}-well-posedness.

Theorem 5.3. *Assume that f is upper semicontinuous in its first variable and $E(\varepsilon)$ is compact for some $\varepsilon > 0$. If (EP) has a unique solution, then*

$$\text{diam}(E(\varepsilon)) \to 0, \varepsilon \downarrow 0.$$

Proof. Let $\bar{a}$ be the solution of (EP). By contradiction, suppose that $\text{diam}(E(\varepsilon)) \nrightarrow 0$ if $\varepsilon \downarrow 0$. Then, there exists $\alpha > 0$, $\varepsilon_n \downarrow 0$ and $a_n \in E(\varepsilon_n)$ such that $d(a_n, \bar{a}) \geq \alpha$. From the assumptions, there exists $n_0 \in \mathbb{N}$ such that $E(\varepsilon_n)$ is compact for every $n \geq n_0$. Since $a_n \in E(\varepsilon_n) \subseteq E(\varepsilon_{n_0})$, taking, if necessary, a subsequence, we get that $a_n \to a^* \neq \bar{a}$, as $d(\bar{a}, a^*) \geq \alpha$. Let us show that a^* is a solution of (EP), a contradiction. Indeed, fix $b \in D$; from $f(a_n, b) \geq -\varepsilon_n d(a_n, b)$ and the boundedness of $\{a_n\}$, there exists $M_b > 0$ such that

$$f(a_n, b) \geq -\varepsilon_n M_b, \quad \forall n \geq n_0.$$

In particular,

$$\limsup f(a_n, b) \geq 0.$$

From the upper semicontinuity of $f(\cdot, b)$ we get that a^* is a solution. $\qquad\square$

In case D is a finite dimensional space, a similar proof as before provides the following statement:

Corollary 5.1. *Let $D = \mathbb{R}^n$. Assume that f is upper semicontinuous in its first variable and $E(\varepsilon)$ bounded for some $\varepsilon > 0$. If (EP) has a unique solution, then*

$$diam(E(\varepsilon)) \to 0, \varepsilon \downarrow 0.$$

5.2.3 Relationship Between the Two Kinds of Well-Posedness

Once we introduced two kinds of well-posedness for (EP), it is natural to ask whether and under which conditions there is a relationship between these notions. It is not difficult to check that, in general, the two concepts are different, in the sense that there is no relationship between them. To see this, let us first observe that the problem given in Example 5.1 is T_{opt}-well-posed but not T_{vi}-well-posed, since $E(\varepsilon)$ is unbounded for every $\varepsilon > 0$. On the other hand, the following example provides an (EP) that is T_{vi}-well-posed but not T_{opt}-well-posed.

Example 5.2. Let $f : \mathbb{R} \times \mathbb{R} \to \mathbb{R}$ given by

$$f(a, b) := \begin{cases} -\frac{|a|b^2}{(a^2+1)(b^2+1)}, & \text{if } a \neq b, \\ 0, & \text{if } a = b. \end{cases}$$

It is clear that the only solution of (EP) is $\bar{a} = 0$. Also,

$$g(a) = \inf_{b \in \mathbb{R}} f(a, b) = \inf_{b \in \mathbb{R} \setminus \{a\}} -\frac{|a|b^2}{(a^2+1)(b^2+1)}$$

$$= - \sup_{b \in \mathbb{R} \setminus \{a\}} \frac{|a|b^2}{(a^2+1)(b^2+1)} = -\frac{|a|}{a^2+1}.$$

Take the sequence $a_n = n$. Since $\lim_{n \to +\infty} g(n) = 0$, we have that (EP) is not T_{opt}-well-posed. On the other hand, it is easy to see that

$$E(\epsilon) = \{a \in \mathbb{R} : f(a, b) \geq -\epsilon|b - a|, \forall b \in \mathbb{R}\} = \{0\}$$

for every $\epsilon > 0$. Indeed, fix $\epsilon > 0$. Then $0 \in E(\epsilon)$ is trivial, and suppose that for some $a \neq 0$ one has $a \in E(\epsilon)$. The latter implies that

$$-\frac{|a|b^2}{(a^2+1)(b^2+1)} \geq -\epsilon|b - a|, \quad \forall b \in \mathbb{R} \setminus \{a\}.$$

Letting $b \to a$ in this relation, we obtain

$$0 > -\frac{|a|^3}{(a^2+1)^2} \geq 0,$$

a contradiction. Thus, $diam(E(\epsilon)) = 0$ and such, this (EP) is T_{vi}-well-posed.

Despite on the negative fact underlined above, it is desirable to find a relationship between the two well-posedness notions. To this end, we should find a link between the sets $\varepsilon - argmin(EP)$ and $E(\varepsilon)$. The next result provides an inclusion that turns out to be useful for our aim. An analogous property holds for optimization problems (see [68], Ch. 2, Sec. 4). First of all, we need the following lemma, that was proved in Theorem 2 in [32] in the vector-valued case. We say that f satisfies *the triangle inequality* (TI), if

$$f(a, b) \leq f(a, c) + f(b, c), \quad \forall a, b, c \in D.$$

Lemma 5.2. *Let $a_0 \in \varepsilon - argmin(EP)$. Assume that f satisfies condition (TI) and it is lower bounded and lower semicontinuous with respect to its second variable. Let $\lambda > 0$. Then there exists $\bar{a} \in D$ such that*

  (i) $f(\bar{a}, a_0) \geq 0$;
 (ii) $d(\bar{a}, a_0) \leq \lambda$;
(iii) $f(\bar{a}, a) + (\varepsilon/\lambda)d(\bar{a}, a) > 0, \forall a \neq \bar{a}$.

In the sequel, for every $A \subseteq D$, we denote by $^{\varepsilon}A$ the set

$$^{\varepsilon}A = \{a' \in D : d(a', A) \leq \varepsilon\},$$

where

$$d(a', A) = \inf\{d(a', a) : a \in A\}.$$

Theorem 5.4. *Assume that f satisfies condition (TI) and is lower bounded and lower semicontinuous with respect to its second variable. Then for every $\varepsilon > 0$ one has*

$$\varepsilon^2 - argmin(EP) \subseteq {}^{\varepsilon}E(\varepsilon).$$

Proof. Let $a \in \varepsilon^2 - argmin(EP)$. From Lemma 5.2, taking $\lambda = \varepsilon$, there exists $\bar{a} \in D$ such that $f(\bar{a}, b) \geq -\varepsilon d(\bar{a}, b)$, for every $b \in D$, i.e., $\bar{a} \in E(\varepsilon)$. From (ii) in Lemma 5.2, $d(\bar{a}, a) \leq \varepsilon$. In particular, $d(E(\varepsilon), a) \leq \varepsilon$. Since a is arbitrary in $\varepsilon^2 - argmin(EP)$, the proof is complete. $\qquad\square$

Combining Theorem 5.1, Proposition 5.2, and Theorem 5.4, a first relation between T_{opt}-well-posedness and T_{vi}-well-posedness can be derived.

Corollary 5.2. *Assume that f satisfies the following assumptions:*

  (i) *(TI) holds;*
 (ii) *f is lower bounded and lower semicontinuous with respect to its second variable;*
(iii) *f is upper semicontinuous with respect to its first variable;*
(iv) *there exists $\hat{b}$ such that $f(\cdot, \hat{b})$ is upper bounded.*

Then

$$T_{vi}\text{-well-posedness} \quad \Longrightarrow \quad T_{opt}\text{-well-posedness}.$$

5.2.4 Hadamard Well-Posedness

In this subsection we investigate the question whether a unified approach can be given the two (different) well-posedness concepts introduced in the previous subsections. To this aim we deal with a parametric form of an equilibrium problem and a related well-posedness, which it turns to be a common extension of both T_{opt}- and T_{vi}-well-posedness. Let $f : D \times D \times \mathcal{U} \to \mathbb{R}$, where $\mathcal{U} \subset E$, and D, E are metric spaces. For a given $p \in \mathcal{U}$ consider the following equilibrium problem $(EP)_p$: find $\bar{a} \in D$ such that

$$f(\bar{a}, b, p) \geq 0, \qquad \forall b \in D.$$

Denote by $F(p)$ the solutions of $(EP)_p$.

Assuming existence and uniqueness of the solution of $(EP)_{p_0}$, with $p_0 \in \mathcal{U}$, we are interested in the investigation of continuous dependence of the solutions with respect to the data of the problem, i.e., the so-called Hadamard well-posedness.

Definition 5.7. (see, for a comparison, [172]) $(EP)_p$ is said to be Hadamard well-posed at $p_0 \in \mathcal{U}$ if

(i) $F(p_0) = \{\bar{a}\}$,
(ii) for any $p_n \to p_0$, and any $a_n \in F(p_n)$, $\{a_n\}$ converges to $\bar{a}$.

If $E = [0, +\infty)$ and $f_0 : D \times D \to \mathbb{R}$ with $f_0(a, a) = 0$ for every $a \in D$, consider the following expressions for the function f:

(i) $f(a, b, p) = f_0(a, b) + p$,
(ii) $f(a, b, p) = f_0(a, b) + p\, d(a, b)$.

In the first case, $F(p) = p - \operatorname{argmin}(EP)$, while in the second one, $F(p) = E(p)$, where (EP) is defined by f_0. This observation suggests that within the above framework Hadamard well-posedness reduces to T_{opt}-well-posedness in case (i), and to T_{vi}-well-posedness in case (ii), if we take $p_0 = 0$. Indeed, assume that the representation (i) holds and suppose that $(EP)_p$ is Hadamard well-posed at 0. Let $\{a_n\}$ be a sequence in D such that

$$g_0(a_n) = \inf_{b \in D} f_0(a_n, b) \to 0.$$

Choose $p_n = -g_0(a_n) + 1/n > 0$ $(n \geq 1)$. Clearly $p_n \to 0$. Since by the trivial inequality $g_0(a_n) \geq -p_n$ for every $n \geq 1$ we obtain that $a_n \in F(p_n)$, thus $a_n \to \bar{a}$, the unique solution of (EP). Hence (EP) is T_{opt}-well-posed.

Before proving the assertion concerning T_{vi}-well-posedness, let us observe that the Hadamard well-posedness (in the general case) implies that $\operatorname{diam}(F(p)) \to 0$ as $p \to p_0$. Indeed, assume, by contradiction, that $\operatorname{diam}(F(p_n)) \geq 2\alpha > 0$ for a suitable sequence $p_n \to p_0$. Consider two sequences $\{a_n\}$ and $\{b_n\}$ in $F(p_n)$ such that $d(a_n, b_n) \geq \alpha$. From the Hadamard well-posedness and the triangular inequality, we get

$$\alpha \le d(a_n, b_n) \le d(a_n, \bar{a}) + d(b_n, \bar{a}) \to 0 \qquad n \to \infty,$$

a contradiction.

Now supposing that the representation (ii) holds, we obtain by the Hadamard well-posedness that $\mathrm{diam} E(p) \to 0$ as $p \to 0$, therefore (EP) is T_{vi}-well-posed.

Returning to problem $(EP)_p$, it is interesting to remark that, in general, $\mathrm{diam}(F(p)) \to 0$ as $p \to p_0$ does not imply that this problem is Hadamard well-posed, as the following example shows:

Example 5.3. Let $D = E := \mathbb{R}, \mathcal{U} := [0, 1] \subset \mathbb{R}$ and $h : D \times \mathcal{U} \to \mathbb{R}$ given by

$$h(a, p) = \begin{cases} (a - 1)^2 & \text{if } p = 0, \\ 0 & \text{if } p \neq 0 \text{ and } 0 < a < p, \\ 1 & \text{if } p \neq 0 \text{ and } a \le 0 \text{ or } a \ge p. \end{cases}$$

Define the function $f : D \times D \times \mathcal{U} \to \mathbb{R}$ by $f(a, b, p) := h(b, p) - h(a, p)$. Then (for $p_0 := 0$), we get $F(0) = \{1\}$ and $F(p) = (0, p)$ for $p > 0$. It is clear that the associated $(EP)_p$ is not Hadamard well-posed.

It is not surprising that the equilibrium problem in the example above fails to be Hadamard well-posed, since $h(\cdot, p)$ and $h(\cdot, 0)$ have no relationships at all; indeed, in this case, the set $F(p)$ $(p > 0)$ is far from $F(0) = \{1\}$. To give positive results of Hadamard well-posedness, a reasonable approach requires some continuity assumptions on the function f.

Proposition 5.4. *Assume that D is compact and $F(p_0) = \{\bar{a}\}$. If $f(\cdot, b, \cdot)$ is upper semicontinuous at (a, p_0) for every $a, b \in D$, then $(EP)_p$ is Hadamard well-posed at p_0.*

Proof. By contradiction, assume that there exists $\{p_n\}$ such that $p_n \top 0$ and $a_n \in F(p_n)$ such that $d(a_n, \bar{a}) > \alpha > 0$ for some subsequence. Since D is compact, without loss of generality, we can suppose that $a_n \to a^*$. By upper semicontinuity, a^* is in $F(p_0)$. Since $a^* \neq \bar{a}$ we get a contradiction. $\square$

By means of the representations given after Definition 5.7, the above result provides the following sufficient condition for both T_{opt}- and T_{vi}-well-posedness (compare also with Theorem 5.1 and Theorem 5.3).

Corollary 5.3. *Let D be a compact subset of a complete metric space, and let $f_0 : D \times D \to \mathbb{R}$ with $f_0(a, a) = 0$ for every $a \in D$, such that $f_0(\cdot, b)$ is upper semicontinuous for every $b \in D$. If the (EP) associated to f_0 has a unique solution, then this problem is both T_{opt}- and T_{vi}-well-posed.*

Proof. Let $E = [0, +\infty)$ and define the function $f : D \times D \times E \to \mathbb{R}$ according to (i) or (ii) described after Definition 5.7. In both cases $f(\cdot, b, \cdot)$ is upper semicontinuous at $(a, 0)$ for every $a, b \in D$. Then, by Proposition 5.4, $(EP)_p$ is Hadamard well-posed at $p_0 = 0$ and taking into account the observations after Definition 5.7 it follows that the (EP) associated to f_0 is both T_{opt}- and T_{vi}-well-posed. □

5.3 WELL-POSED VECTOR EQUILIBRIUM PROBLEMS

In the previous section we dealt with two specific well-posedness notions concerning scalar equilibrium problems (EP). This idea will be exploited to introduce suitable well-posedness concepts for the (strong) vector equilibrium problem (SVEP). Let us first fix our framework and recall the problem to be tackled.

Let X and Y be topological vector spaces with countable local bases, and K be a closed convex cone in Y with nonempty interior. Given $f : D \times D \to Y$, with $D \subseteq X$ and $f(x, x) = 0$, for all $x \in D$, we recall that the strong vector equilibrium problem, denoted by (SVEP), consists in finding an element $\overline{x} \in D$ such that

$$f(\overline{x}, y) \notin -K_0, \qquad \forall y \in D, \qquad \text{(SVEP)}$$

where K_0 denotes the set $K_0 = K \setminus \{0\}$. We denote by S the solution set and we will suppose in the sequel that S is nonempty.

It is well known that vector equilibrium problems are natural extensions of several problems of practical interest like vector optimization and vector variational inequality problems. Several authors introduced and studied different well-posedness concepts regarding vector optimization problems and vector variational inequalities (see, for instance, [26], [127], [128], [59] and the references therein). Our purpose is to assign reasonable definitions of well-posedness to (SVEP) that recover some previous existing concepts given in [26], [127], [128]. To this aim, in the next sections we present two kinds of well-posedness related to (SVEP), both inspired from the corresponding notions defined for vector optimization problems. The idea for the first originates from the papers of Miglierina and Molho [127], and Miglierina, Molho, and Rocca [128] respectively, which will be called *M-well-posedness*, and for the other from the paper of Bednarczuk [26], called therefore *B-well-posedness*.

5.3.1 M-Well-Posedness of Vector Equilibrium Problems

In this subsection we will discuss the first notion of well-posedness assigned to (SVEP). Recall that the scalar equilibrium problem (EP) is a particular instance of (SVEP) with $Y = \mathbb{R}$ and $K = [0, +\infty)$. According to Lemma 5.1 (EP) admits solutions if and only if $\max_{a \in D} g(a) = 0$, where $g : D \to [-\infty, +\infty)$ is the gap function defined in (5.3).

We start our analysis following a similar approach as in Section 5.2. To this aim, we introduce the set-valued map $\phi : D \to 2^Y$ given by

$$\phi(x) = \min_K(f(x, D)) \qquad (5.7)$$

(see also [16]), where for any $A \subseteq Y$, the (possibly empty) set of minimal elements is defined as follows:

$$\min_K(A) = \{a' \in A : (A - a') \cap (-K_0) = \emptyset\}.$$

The map ϕ generalizes the definition of the function g; in particular, the solutions can be characterized in terms of ϕ since $\overline{x} \in S$ if and only if $0 \in \phi(\overline{x})$. Through the map ϕ, we can define maximizing sequences and approximate solutions, that, as it is well-known, are key concepts in the investigation of well-posedness.

In the next proposition some properties of ϕ are pointed out; in particular, assuming that the solution set is nonempty, we obtain that $\text{dom}(\phi) \neq \emptyset$.

Proposition 5.5. *The map ϕ satisfies the relations:*

(i) $\phi(x) \cap K_0 = \emptyset$, *for all $x \in D$;*
(ii) $\overline{x} \in S \Longleftrightarrow 0 \in \phi(\overline{x})$;
(iii) $\overline{x} \in S \Longleftrightarrow \phi(\overline{x}) \cap K \neq \emptyset$.

Proof. (i) Assume that for some $x' \in D$, $\phi(x') \cap K_0 \neq \emptyset$. Then there exists $y' \in K_0$ such that $y' \in \min_K f(x', D)$, that is equivalent to say that $(f(x', D) - y') \cap (-K_0) = \emptyset$. Since $0 \in f(x', D)$, we get that $-y' \cap (-K_0) = \emptyset$, a contradiction.

(ii) indeed, taking into account that $0 \in f(x, D)$ for every $x \in D$,

$$\overline{x} \in S \Longleftrightarrow f(\overline{x}, y) \notin (-K_0), \forall y \in D \Longleftrightarrow f(\overline{x}, D) \cap (-K) = \{0\};$$

this is equivalent to say that $0 \in \min_K f(\overline{x}, D) = \phi(\overline{x})$.

(iii) trivial, by (i) and (ii). $\qquad\qquad\qquad\square$

The first notion of well-posedness associated to (SVEP) generalizes the definition of T_{opt}-well-posedness for (EP) discussed in Section 5.2. Therefore, the idea leading to this concept goes through the property related to *maximizing sequences*.

In the sequel, we shall denote by $\mathcal{V}_X(0)$ a neighborhood base of the origin in the topological vector space X. The same notation will be used for other spaces.

Definition 5.8. A sequence $\{x_n\} \subset D$ is said to be a *maximizing sequence for ϕ* if for every $V_Y \in \mathcal{V}_Y(0)$, there exists $n_0 \in \mathbb{N}$ such that

$$\phi(x_n) \cap V_Y \neq \emptyset, \qquad \forall n \geq n_0.$$

Definition 5.8 is related to Definition 4.1 in [127] in case of vector optimization, where A_n is a singleton. Indeed, the following proposition holds:

Proposition 5.6. *If $f(x, y) = F(y) - F(x)$, then $\{x_n\}$ is maximizing if and only if*

$$F(x_n) \overset{H}{\to} \min_K F(D),$$

i.e., $\{x_n\}$ is a minimizing sequence for the vector optimization problem, according to [127].

Proof. Since Y is a topological vector space, we can always choose a base of radial, balanced neighborhoods $\mathcal{V}_Y(0)$ of 0 (see [3]). In particular, if $z \in V_Y$, then $-z \in V_Y$.

$\implies$ Fix V_Y; from Definition 5.8, there exists $n_0 \in \mathbb{N}$ such that, for $n \geq n_0$,

$$\phi(x_n) \cap V_Y = (\min_K F(D) - F(x_n)) \cap V_Y \neq \emptyset,$$

that is, there exists $y \in \min_K F(D)$ such that $F(x_n) \in y + V_Y$, if $n \geq n_0$.

$\impliedby$ Take an arbitrary V_Y; for $n \geq n_0$, $F(x_n) \in \min_K F(D) + V_Y$, that is there exists $y \in \min_K F(D)$ such that $y - F(x_n) \in V_Y$, thereby proving that $\phi(x_n) \cap V_Y \neq \emptyset$. $\qquad\square$

The next definition reproduces, in the vector setting, the classical notion of Tykhonov well-posedness given in metric spaces (see, for instance, [128], Definition 3.7), and it generalizes the definition of T_{opt}-well-posedness given in [34].

Concluding this subsection, we are now in the position to introduce the first notion of well-posedness for vector equilibrium problems, the so-called M-well-posedness, which later will be explored and compared with another related concept.

Definition 5.9. We say that the vector equilibrium problem (SVEP) is *M-well-posed* if

(i) there exists at least one solution, i.e., $S \neq \emptyset$;
(ii) for every maximizing sequence, and for every $V_X \in \mathcal{V}_X(0)$, there exists n_0 such that $x_n \in S + V_X$, for every $n \geq n_0$.

5.3.2 B-Well-Posedness of Vector Equilibrium Problems

Another notion of well-posedness can be given in terms of regularity of a suitable approximate solution map. This approach, proposed by Ewa Bednarczuk in [26] for vector optimization problems, has been already exploited by several authors (see, for instance, [127], [128], and the references therein).

In [34] the authors introduced and compared different notions of approximate solutions in the scalar case. One of these is given via the notion of

$\varepsilon - \text{argmin}(\text{EP})$ points, i.e., the set of points $x \in D$ such that $f(x, y) \geq -\varepsilon$, for every $y \in D$.

In the sequel, we extend the definition of $\varepsilon - \text{argmin}(\text{EP})$ to the vector-valued case.

Definition 5.10. (see [33]) Given $\varepsilon \in K$, the set

$$S(\varepsilon) = \{x \in D : \phi(x) \cap (K - \varepsilon) \neq \emptyset\}$$

is called the *ε-approximate solution set* of (SVEP).

Notice that $S(0) = S$, by (iii) in Proposition 5.5.

Remark 5.1. The definition above is also related to the notion of ε-minimal solutions

$$Q(\varepsilon) = \bigcup_{y \in \min_K F(D)} \{x \in D : F(x) \in y + \varepsilon - K\},$$

introduced in [26] (see also [127]). Indeed, in case of vector optimization problems, where $f(x, y) = F(y) - F(x)$, one trivially shows that $S(\varepsilon) = Q(\varepsilon)$: for every $x \in D$, $\phi(x) = \min_K F(D) - F(x)$, and

$$x \in S(\varepsilon) \iff \exists y \in \min_K F(D) : y - F(x) \in K - \varepsilon$$

$$\iff \exists y \in \min_K F(D) : F(x) \in y + \varepsilon - K$$

$$\iff x \in \bigcup_{y \in \min_K F(D)} \{x' \in D : F(x') \in y + \varepsilon - K\}$$

$$\iff x \in Q(\varepsilon).$$

Now we introduce the second concept of well-posedness for vector equilibrium problems. The next definition assumes some continuity of the map $S(\cdot)$, namely its upper Hausdorff continuity. Let us recall that a map $T : Z \to 2^W$, with Z, W topological spaces, is said to be *upper semicontinuous* at z_0 if for every neighborhood U of $T(z_0)$, there exists a neighborhood V of z_0 such that

$$T(z) \subseteq U, \qquad \forall z \in V$$

(see [23]). In case W is also a vector space, the notion above can be weakened by requiring that the arbitrary neighborhood of $T(z_0)$ is of the form $T(z_0) + V_W$, where $V_W \in \mathcal{V}_W(0)$. In this case we say that the map is *upper Hausdorff continuous*.

Definition 5.11. We say that the vector equilibrium problem (SVEP) is *B-well-posed* if

(i) there exists at least one solution, i.e., $S \neq \emptyset$;
(ii) the map $S(\cdot) : K \to 2^X$ is upper Hausdorff continuous at $\varepsilon = 0$, i.e., for every $V_X \in \mathcal{V}_X(0)$ there exists $V_Y \in \mathcal{V}_Y(0)$ such that $S(\varepsilon) \subset S + V_X$ for every $\varepsilon \in V_Y \cap K$.

We would like to point out that the stronger assumption of upper semicontinuity of $S(\cdot)$ appears to be too restrictive, because, in this case, well-behaving problems would not be B-well-posed (see Example 3.1 in [127]).

5.3.3 Relationship Between M- and B-Well-Posedness

This subsection is devoted to the comparison between the two concepts of well-posedness introduced above for vector equilibrium problems.

It turns out that B-well-posedness always implies M-well-posedness, but the converse is not true in general. However, we find a suitable condition under which the converse also holds.

The next proposition extends a similar result in [127].

Proposition 5.7. *Any B-well-posed vector equilibrium problem is M-well-posed.*

Proof. By contradiction, suppose that there exists a maximizing sequence $\{x_n^*\}$ and a neighborhood $V_X^* \in \mathcal{V}_X(0)$ such that

$$x_n^* \notin S + V_X^* \text{ for infinitely many } n\text{'-s.} \tag{5.8}$$

Let $\varepsilon_n \in \int K$ such that $\varepsilon_n \to 0$. Then, for every $n \in \mathbb{N}$, there exists $V_n \in \mathcal{V}_Y(0)$ such that $V_n \subseteq K - \varepsilon_n$. Since $\{x_n^*\}$ is maximizing, for every $n \in \mathbb{N}$ there exists $m_n \in \mathbb{N}$ such that, if $m \geq m_n$,

$$\phi(x_m^*) \cap V_n \neq \emptyset;$$

in particular, $\phi(x_m^*) \cap (K - \varepsilon_n) \neq \emptyset$, i.e., $x_m^* \in S(\varepsilon_n)$, for all $m \geq m_n$. From the B-well-posedness assumption, there exists $n^* \in \mathbb{N}$ such that, for $n \geq n^*$,

$$S(\varepsilon_n) \subseteq S + V_X^*,$$

a contradiction. □

The converse does not hold, even in the particular case of vector optimization, unless some assumptions are added. Indeed, in [127], an example is provided showing that M-well-posedness does not imply B-well-posedness.

Here we reproduce an example given in [33] for those vector equilibrium problems, that cannot be reduced to an optimization problem. This also shows that B-well-posedness is stronger than M-well-posedness.

Example 5.4. Let $K = \mathbb{R}_+^2$ and $f : [0, +\infty) \times [0, +\infty) \to \mathbb{R}^2$ be given by the following rule:

- For $x = 0$ put $f(x, y) = (0, 0)$, $\forall y \geq 0$.
- For $x > 0$ let

$$f(x, y) = \begin{cases} (y - x, 0), & 0 \leq y < 2x \\ (x, -\frac{4x}{y^2}), & y \geq 2x. \end{cases}$$

Obviously $f(x, x) = (0, 0)$ for every $x \geq 0$. It is easy to check that the solution set of the associated vector (SVEP) is $S = \{0\}$. Let us first show that (SVEP) is M-well-posed. To do this, we shall evaluate the set-valued mapping ϕ. We have

$$\phi(x) = \begin{cases} \{(0, 0)\}, & x = 0 \\ \{(-x, 0), (x, -\frac{1}{x})\}, & x > 0. \end{cases}$$

Let $\{x_n\}$ be an arbitrary maximizing sequence. Then, by definition, we have that $\{x_n\} \to 0$ as $n \to +\infty$, which shows that our (SVEP) is M-well-posed.

Now let us prove that (SVEP) is not B-well-posed. Take for this the neighborhood V_X^* of 0 such that $V_X^* \cup D = [0, 1/2)$, and the sequences $\varepsilon_n = (0, \frac{1}{n})$, $x_n = n$ for every $n \geq 1$. Then obviously $x_n \in S(\varepsilon_n)$, but $x_n \notin S + V_X^* = V_X^*$ for every $n \geq 1$, showing that (SVEP) is not B-well-posed.

Now let us give a sufficient condition that enables us to prove the converse implication.

Proposition 5.8. *Assume that the vector equilibrium problem is M-well-posed and for every neighborhood of the origin V_Y there exists a neighborhood of the origin $\tilde{V}_Y$ such that*

$$\phi(D \setminus cl(S)) \cap (K + \tilde{V}_Y) \subseteq V_Y. \tag{5.9}$$

Then, the problem is B-well-posed.

Proof. Suppose, by contradiction, that there exist a neighborhood V_X^* of the origin, a sequence $\{\varepsilon_n\} \subset K$, $\varepsilon_n \to 0$ and $x_n \in S(\varepsilon_n)$ such that

$$x_n \notin S + V_X^*, \quad \forall n \in \mathbb{N};$$

besides, this implies that $x_n \notin cl(S)$. If $\{x_n\}$ is a maximizing sequence, the contradiction is trivial by M-well-posedness. Otherwise, there exist a neighborhood V_Y^* of the origin of Y and a subsequence $\{x_{n_k}\}$ of $\{x_n\}$ such that

$$\phi(x_{n_k}) \cap V_Y^* = \emptyset, \quad \forall k \in \mathbb{N}.$$

Since $x_{n_k} \in S(\varepsilon_{n_k})$, we know that

$$\phi(x_{n_k}) \cap (K - \varepsilon_{n_k}) \neq \emptyset.$$

Let $\tilde{V}_Y^*$ be the neighborhood related to V_Y^* in (5.9). Then, for k large enough, $-\varepsilon_{n_k} \in \tilde{V}_Y^*$. Take $\overline{y}_{n_k} \in \phi(x_{n_k}) \cap (K - \varepsilon_{n_k})$. We have that $\overline{y}_{n_k} \in K + \tilde{V}_Y^*$, which, together with (5.9), leads to the contradiction $\overline{y}_{n_k} \in V_Y^*$. This completes the proof. □

5.3.4 Convexity and Well-Posedness

It is well known that both the assumptions of convexity and monotonicity together with their generalizations are strictly related to many results concerning equilibrium problems. In this section we discuss the role of these conditions in order to single out classes of well-posed vector equilibrium problems.

The following result provides a sufficient condition for M-well-posedness in the framework of concave vector functions. Let us recall that a function $h : D \subseteq X \to Y$, with D convex is said to be K-concave if

$$\lambda h(x) + (1 - \lambda)h(y) \in h(\lambda x + (1 - \lambda)y) - K,$$

for every $x, y \in D$, and for every $\lambda \in [0, 1]$.

Theorem 5.5. *Let X be finite dimensional ($X = \mathbb{R}^n$), $D \subseteq X$ be a closed convex set, and $f : D \times D \to Y$ such that*

(i) *the solution set S of (SVEP) is nonempty and bounded;*
(ii) *the map $\phi : D \to 2^Y$ is upper Hausdorff continuous with closed values;*
(iii) *$f(x, z) \neq 0$ whenever $x \in S$ and $z \in D \setminus S$;*
(iv) *f is continuous and K-concave with respect to its first variable;*
(v) *for every maximizing sequence $\{x_n\} \subset D$ and every $z \in D$, the sequence $\{f(x_n, z)\}$ is bounded in Y.*

Then the problem (SVEP) is M-well-posed.

Proof. Suppose by contradiction that there exist a maximizing sequence $\{x_n\}$ and $\varepsilon > 0$ such that

$$x_n \notin S + \varepsilon B, \tag{5.10}$$

for infinitely many n's, where B denotes the unit open ball in X. Since every subsequence of a maximizing sequence is still maximizing, we may assume for simplicity that relation (5.10) holds for every n. Let us distinguish the following two situations:

1. The sequence $\{x_n\}$ is bounded, hence it has a convergent subsequence $\{x_{n_k}\}$ with limit $x^* \in D$. Assume that $x^* \notin S$, that is $0 \notin \phi(x^*)$. The set $\phi(x^*)$ is closed, nonempty, and does not contain 0; in particular, there exists V_Y such that

$$\left(\phi(x^*) + V_Y\right) \cap V_Y = \emptyset. \tag{5.11}$$

Since $\{x_n\}$ is maximizing, one can choose a sequence $y_n \in \phi(x_n)$ with $y_n \to 0$. By the upper Hausdorff continuity of ϕ at x^*, we have that, definitely,

$$\phi(x_n) \subset \phi(x^*) + V_Y,$$

but this contradicts (5.11).

2. The sequence $\{x_n\}$ is unbounded. Since S is bounded, we obtain that $S + \varepsilon B$ is bounded, thus the set $cl(S + \varepsilon B)$ is compact. Consider the compact set $Q = bd(S + \varepsilon B) = cl(S + \varepsilon B) \setminus \int(S + \varepsilon B)$. For any $x \in S$ we have $x + \varepsilon B \subseteq S + \varepsilon B$, therefore $S \subseteq \int(S + \varepsilon B)$, showing that $S \cap Q = \emptyset$. By the hypothesis, $\{x_n\}$ admits a subsequence (denoted for convenience also by $\{x_n\}$) converging in norm to $+\infty$. Let us suppose (without loss of generality) that $x_n \notin cl(S + \varepsilon B)$ for every n. Fix an arbitrary $\bar{x} \in S$ and for any n, let $x_n' = \lambda_n \bar{x} + (1 - \lambda_n)x_n \in Q$ where

$$\lambda_n := \sup\{\lambda \in [0, 1] : \lambda \bar{x} + (1 - \lambda)x_n \notin S + \varepsilon B\}.$$

It is easy to check that $\lambda_n \to 1$. Indeed, if not, there exists some $\delta < 1$ such that $\lambda_n \leq \delta$ for infinitely many n's. Thus we may write

$$(1 - \lambda_n)x_n = x_n' - \lambda_n \bar{x},$$

from which

$$\|x_n\| \leq \frac{1}{1 - \lambda_n}\|x_n'\| + \frac{\lambda_n}{1 - \lambda_n}\|\bar{x}\| \leq \frac{1}{1 - \delta}(\|x_n'\| + \|\bar{x}\|),$$

for infinitely many n's. But this contradicts the fact that $\|x_n\| \to +\infty$.

The set Q being compact, we can extract from the sequence $\{\lambda_n \bar{x} + (1 - \lambda_n)x_n\}$ a subsequence $\{\lambda_{n_k}\bar{x} + (1 - \lambda_{n_k})x_{n_k}\}$ converging to $x' \in Q$. Then by concavity we obtain for every $z \in D$ and every $k \in \mathbb{N}$:

$$\lambda_{n_k} f(\bar{x}, z) + (1 - \lambda_{n_k})f(x_{n_k}, z) \in f(\lambda_{n_k}\bar{x} + (1 - \lambda_{n_k})x_{n_k}, z) - K. \quad (5.12)$$

Taking the limit of this relation, by the continuity of f and (v) we obtain

$$f(\bar{x}, z) \in f(x', z) - K \quad \forall z \in D.$$

Taking $z = x'$, we get

$$f(\bar{x}, x') \in -K.$$

Since $\bar{x} \in S$, from (iii) the latter implies that $x' \in S$ which contradicts $x' \in Q$.
$\square$

A sufficient condition for M-well-posedness of the vector equilibrium problem can be given more directly in terms of properties of the function f, replacing the assumption (ii) in Theorem 5.5 with a kind of pseudo-monotonicity of f, that reduces to the usual pseudo-monotonicity in the scalar case. Working with this condition ((ii) in Theorem 5.6 below) might have advantages and disadvantages as well. Among its disadvantages we mention that in case of vector optimization and a pointed cone, it leads to the uniqueness of the minimum.

However, beside the fact that it is more explicit than condition (ii) of Theorem 5.5, one may observe that it is weaker than the concept of *strict pseudo-monotonicity* used in [27], and such, it does not imply that the set S should be a singleton (as strict pseudo-monotonicity does).

Theorem 5.6. *Let X be finite dimensional $(X = \mathbb{R}^n)$, $D \subseteq X$ be a closed convex set, and $f : D \times D \to Y$ such that*

   (i) *the solution set S of (SVEP) is nonempty and bounded;*
  (ii) *for every $x, z \in D$ such that $f(x, z) \notin K$ we have $f(z, x) \in -K$;*
 (iii) *$f(x, z) \neq 0$ whenever $x \in S$ and $z \in D \setminus S$;*
 (iv) *f is continuous and K-concave with respect to its first variable;*
  (v) *For every maximizing sequence $\{x_n\} \subset D$ and every $z \in D$, the sequence $\{f(x_n, z)\}$ is bounded in Y.*

   Then the problem (SVEP) is M-well-posed.

Proof. The proof goes as in Theorem 5.5, with a change only in the part 1 (case of bounded sequence): indeed, arguing as in Theorem 5.5, since $\{x_{n_k}\}$ is maximizing, one can choose a sequence $y_{n_k} \in \phi(x_{n_k})$, with $y_{n_k} \to 0$. By the definition of ϕ we obtain

$$[f(x_{n_k}, D) - y_{n_k}] \cap (-K) = \{0\},$$

or, in other words,

$$f(x_{n_k}, z) - y_{n_k} \notin -K_0, \quad \forall z \in D.$$

Let $\bar{x} \in S$ be arbitrary. Put $z = \bar{x}$. By taking the limit in the last relation we obtain by the continuity of f that

$$f(x^*, \bar{x}) \notin -int(K).$$

This implies by (ii) that $f(\bar{x}, x^*) \in -K$, and since $\bar{x} \in S$ we obtain $f(\bar{x}, x^*) = 0$. This contradicts (iii) since by (5.10) $x^* \notin S$. $\qquad\square$

Chapter 6

Variational Principles and Variational Analysis for the Equilibrium Problems

Contents

The butterfly counts not months but moments, and has time enough.
Rabindranath Tagore (1861–1941)

Chapter points

- Ekeland's variational principle is established for scalar and vector equilibrium problems.
- The variational principle is extended to finite and countable systems of equilibrium problems.
- Existence of solutions for different kinds of equilibrium problems are obtained via approximate solutions provided by the Ekeland's variational principle.
- Results on regularity properties of the diagonal subdifferential operator associated to an equilibrium problem are obtained.

6.1 THE EKELAND'S VARIATIONAL PRINCIPLE FOR THE EQUILIBRIUM PROBLEMS

The Ekeland's variational principle (see, Appendix A) has been widely used in nonlinear analysis since it entails the existence of approximate solutions

Equilibrium Problems and Applications. https://doi.org/10.1016/B978-0-12-811029-4.00014-6

of a minimization problem for lower semicontinuous functions on a complete metric space. Since minimization problems are particular cases of equilibrium problems, one is interested in extending Ekeland's theorem to the setting of an equilibrium problem. By providing approximate solutions, it opens the possibility to obtain new existence results for (EP) in the nonconvex setting. In the next two subsections we deal with Ekeland's principle for equilibrium problems: we discuss the scalar case in Subsection 6.1.1, while the vector case in Subsection 6.1.2.

6.1.1 The Scalar Case

In what follows we find a suitable set of conditions on the functions that do not involve convexity and lead to an Ekeland's variational principle for equilibrium and system of equilibrium problems. Via the existence of approximate solutions, we are able to show the existence of equilibria on general closed sets. The results developed in this subsection have been obtained by Bianchi, Kassay, and Pini [31] in a finite dimensional setting.

Theorem 6.1. *Let A be a closed set of a real Banach space and $f : A \times A \to \mathbb{R}$. Assume that the following conditions are satisfied:*

(a) $f(x, \cdot)$ *is lower bounded and lower semicontinuous, for every $x \in A$;*
(b) $f(t, t) = 0$, *for every $t \in A$;*
(c) $f(z, x) \le f(z, y) + f(y, x)$, *for every $x, y, z \in A$.*

Then, for every $\varepsilon > 0$ and for every $x_0 \in A$, there exists $\bar{x} \in A$ such that

$$
\begin{cases}
f(x_0, \bar{x}) + \varepsilon \|x_0 - \bar{x}\| \le 0 \\
f(\bar{x}, x) + \varepsilon \|\bar{x} - x\| > 0, \quad \forall x \in A, \quad x \ne \bar{x}.
\end{cases}
\tag{6.1}
$$

Proof. Without loss of generality, we can restrict the proof to the case $\varepsilon = 1$. Denote by $\mathcal{F}(x)$ the set

$$
\mathcal{F}(x) := \{y \in A : f(x, y) + \|y - x\| \le 0\}.
$$

By (a), $\mathcal{F}(x)$ is closed, for every $x \in A$; by (b), $x \in \mathcal{F}(x)$, hence $\mathcal{F}(x)$ is nonempty for every $x \in A$. Assume $y \in \mathcal{F}(x)$, i.e., $f(x, y) + \|y - x\| \le 0$, and let $z \in \mathcal{F}(y)$ (i.e., $f(y, z) + \|y - z\| \le 0$). Adding both sides of the inequalities, we get, by (c),

$$
0 \ge f(x, y) + \|y - x\| + f(y, z) + \|y - z\| \ge f(x, z) + \|z - x\|,
$$

that is, $z \in \mathcal{F}(x)$. Therefore $y \in \mathcal{F}(x)$ implies $\mathcal{F}(y) \subseteq \mathcal{F}(x)$.
    Define

$$
v(x) := \inf_{z \in \mathcal{F}(x)} f(x, z).
$$

For every $z \in \mathcal{F}(x)$,

$$\|x - z\| \le -f(x, z) \le \sup_{z \in \mathcal{F}(x)} (-f(x, z)) = - \inf_{z \in \mathcal{F}(x)} f(x, z) = -v(x)$$

that is,

$$\|x - z\| \le -v(x), \qquad \forall z \in \mathcal{F}(x).$$

In particular, if $x_1, x_2 \in \mathcal{F}(x)$,

$$\|x_1 - x_2\| \le \|x - x_1\| + \|x - x_2\| \le -v(x) - v(x) = -2v(x),$$

implying that

$$\mathrm{diam}(\mathcal{F}(x)) \le -2v(x), \qquad \forall x \in A.$$

Fix $x_0 \in A$; $x_1 \in \mathcal{F}(x_0)$ exists such that

$$f(x_0, x_1) \le v(x_0) + 2^{-1}.$$

Denote by x_2 any point in $\mathcal{F}(x_1)$ such that

$$f(x_1, x_2) \le v(x_1) + 2^{-2}.$$

Proceeding in this way, we define a sequence $\{x_n\}$ of points of A such that $x_{n+1} \in \mathcal{F}(x_n)$ and

$$f(x_n, x_{n+1}) \le v(x_n) + 2^{-(n+1)}.$$

Notice that

$$\begin{aligned}
v(x_{n+1}) &= \inf_{y \in \mathcal{F}(x_{n+1})} f(x_{n+1}, y) \ge \inf_{y \in \mathcal{F}(x_n)} f(x_{n+1}, y) \\
&\ge \inf_{y \in \mathcal{F}(x_n)} (f(x_n, y) - f(x_n, x_{n+1})) \left(\inf_{y \in \mathcal{F}(x_n)} f(x_n, y) \right) - f(x_n, x_{n+1}) \\
&= v(x_n) - f(x_n, x_{n+1}).
\end{aligned}$$

Therefore,

$$v(x_{n+1}) \ge v(x_n) - f(x_n, x_{n+1}),$$

and

$$-v(x_n) \le -f(x_n, x_{n+1}) + 2^{-(n+1)} \le (v(x_{n+1}) - v(x_n)) + 2^{-(n+1)},$$

that entails

$$0 \le v(x_{n+1}) + 2^{-(n+1)}.$$

It follows that

$$\mathrm{diam}(\mathcal{F}(x_n)) \le -2v(x_n) \le 2 \cdot 2^{-n} \to 0, \qquad n \to \infty.$$

The sets $\{\mathcal{F}(x_n)\}$ being closed and $\mathcal{F}(x_{n+1}) \subseteq \mathcal{F}(x_n)$, we have that

$$\bigcap_n \mathcal{F}(x_n) = \{\bar{x}\}.$$

Since $\bar{x} \in \mathcal{F}(x_0)$, then

$$f(x_0, \bar{x}) + \|\bar{x} - x_0\| \leq 0.$$

Moreover, $\bar{x}$ belongs to all $\mathcal{F}(x_n)$, and, since $\mathcal{F}(\bar{x}) \subseteq \mathcal{F}(x_n)$, for every n, we get that

$$\mathcal{F}(\bar{x}) = \{\bar{x}\}.$$

It follows that $x \notin \mathcal{F}(\bar{x})$ whenever $x \neq \bar{x}$, implying that

$$f(\bar{x}, x) + \|x - \bar{x}\| > 0.$$

This completes the proof. $\qquad\qquad\qquad\qquad\qquad\qquad\qquad\qquad$ □

Remark 6.1. It is easy to see that any function $f(x, y) = g(y) - g(x)$ trivially satisfies (c) (actually with equality). One might wonder whether a bifunction f satisfying all the assumptions of Theorem 6.1 should be of the form $g(y) - g(x)$, and such reducing the result above to the classical Ekeland's principle. It is not the case, as the example below shows: let the function $f : \mathbb{R}^2 \to \mathbb{R}$ be defined by

$$f(x, y) = \begin{cases} e^{-\|x-y\|} + 1 + g(y) - g(x) & x \neq y \\ 0 & x = y \end{cases},$$

where g is a lower bounded and lower semicontinuous function. Then all the assumptions of Theorem 6.1 are satisfied, but clearly f cannot be represented in the above mentioned form.

Next we shall extend the result above for a system of equilibrium problems. Let m be a positive integer, and $I = \{1, 2, ..., m\}$. Consider the functions $f_i : A \times A_i \to \mathbb{R}$, $i \in I$ where $A = \prod_{i \in I} A_i$, and $A_i \subseteq X_i$ is a closed subset of the real Banach space X_i. By a system of equilibrium problems we understand the problem of finding $\bar{x} = (\bar{x}_1, ..., \bar{x}_m) \in A$ such that

$$f_i(\bar{x}, y_i) \geq 0 \quad \forall i \in I, \forall y_i \in A_i. \qquad\qquad\qquad \text{(SEP)}$$

An element of the set $A^i = \prod_{j \neq i} A_j$ will be represented by x^i; therefore, $x \in A$ can be written as $x = (x^i, x_i) \in A^i \times A_i$. If $x \in \prod X_i$, the symbol $|||x|||$ will denote the Tchebiseff norm of x, i.e., $|||x||| = \max_i \|x_i\|_i$ and we shall consider the Banach space $\prod X_i$ endowed with this norm.

Theorem 6.2. *Assume that*

(a) $f_i(x, \cdot) : A_i \to \mathbb{R}$ *is lower bounded and lower semicontinuous for every* $i \in I$;

(b) $f_i(x, x_i) = 0$ *for every* $i \in I$ *and every* $x = (x_1, ..., x_m) \in A$;

(c) $f_i(z, x_i) \le f_i(z, y_i) + f_i(y, x_i)$, *for every* $x, y, z \in A$, *where* $y = (y^i, y_i)$, *and for every* $i \in I$.

Then for every $\varepsilon > 0$ *and for every* $x^0 = (x_1^0, ..., x_m^0) \in A$ *there exists* $\bar{x} = (\bar{x}_1, ..., \bar{x}_m) \in A$ *such that for each* $i \in I$ *one has*

$$f_i(x^0, \bar{x}_i) + \varepsilon \|x_i^0 - \bar{x}_i\|_i \le 0 \qquad (6.2)$$

and

$$f_i(\bar{x}, x_i) + \varepsilon \|\bar{x}_i - x_i\|_i > 0, \quad \forall x_i \in D_i, \ x_i \ne \bar{x}_i. \qquad (6.3)$$

Proof. As before, we restrict the proof to the case $\varepsilon = 1$. Let $i \in I$ be arbitrarily fixed. Denote for every $x \in A$

$$\mathcal{F}_i(x) := \{y_i \in A_i : f_i(x, y_i) + \|x_i - y_i\|_i \le 0\}.$$

These sets are closed and nonempty (for every $x = (x_1, ..., x_m) \in A$ we have $x_i \in \mathcal{F}_i(x)$). Define for each $x \in A$

$$v_i(x) := \inf_{z_i \in \mathcal{F}_i(x)} f_i(x, z_i).$$

In a similar way as in the proof of Theorem 6.1 one can show that $\operatorname{diam}(\mathcal{F}_i(x)) \le -2v_i(x)$ for every $x \in A$ and $i \in I$.

Fix now $x^0 \in A$ and select for each $i \in I$ an element $x_i^1 \in \mathcal{F}_i(x^0)$ such that

$$f_i(x^0, x_i^1) \le v_i(x^0) + 2^{-1}.$$

Put $x^1 := (x_1^1, ..., x_m^1) \in A$ and select for each $i \in I$ an element $x_i^2 \in \mathcal{F}_i(x^1)$ such that

$$f_i(x^1, x_i^2) \le v_i(x^1) + 2^{-2}.$$

Put $x^2 := (x_1^2, ..., x_m^2) \in A$. Continuing this process we define a sequence $\{x^n\}$ in A such that $x_i^{n+1} \in \mathcal{F}_i(x^n)$ for each $i \in I$ and $n \in N$ and

$$f_i(x^n, x_i^{n+1}) \le v_i(x^n) + 2^{-(n+1)}.$$

Using a same argument as in the proof of Theorem 6.1 one can show that

$$\operatorname{diam}(\mathcal{F}_i(x^n)) \le -2v_i(x^n) \le 2 \cdot 2^{-n} \to 0, \quad n \to \infty,$$

for each $i \in I$.

Now define for each $x \in A$ the sets

$$\mathcal{F}(x) := \mathcal{F}_1(x) \times \ldots \times \mathcal{F}_m(x) \subseteq A.$$

The sets $\mathcal{F}(x)$ are closed and using (c) it is immediate to check that for each $y \in \mathcal{F}(x)$ it follows that $\mathcal{F}(y) \subseteq \mathcal{F}(x)$. Therefore, we also have $\mathcal{F}(x^{n+1}) \subseteq \mathcal{F}(x^n)$ for each $n = 0, 1, \ldots$. On the other hand, for each $y, z \in \mathcal{F}(x^n)$ we have

$$|||y - z||| = \max_{i \in I} \|y_i - z_i\|_i \leq \max_{i \in I} \operatorname{diam}\mathcal{F}_i(x^n)) \to 0,$$

thus, $\operatorname{diam}(\mathcal{F}(x^n)) \to 0$ as $n \to \infty$. In conclusion we have

$$\cap_{n=0}^{\infty}\mathcal{F}(x^n) = \{\bar{x}\}, \ \bar{x} \in A.$$

Since $\bar{x} \in \mathcal{F}(x^0)$, i.e., $\bar{x}_i \in \mathcal{F}_i(x^0) \ (i \in I)$ we obtain

$$f_i(x^0, \bar{x}_i) + \|x_i^0 - \bar{x}_i\|_i \leq 0, \quad \forall i \in I,$$

and so, (6.2) holds. Moreover, $\bar{x} \in \mathcal{F}(x^n)$ implies $\mathcal{F}(\bar{x}) \subseteq \mathcal{F}(x^n)$ for all $n = 0, 1, \ldots$, therefore,

$$\mathcal{F}(\bar{x}) = \{\bar{x}\}$$

implying

$$\mathcal{F}_i(\bar{x}) = \{\bar{x}_i\} \quad \forall i \in I.$$

Now for every $x_i \in A_i$ with $x_i \neq \bar{x}_i$ we have by the previous relation that $x_i \notin \mathcal{F}_i(\bar{x})$ and so

$$f_i(\bar{x}, x_i) + \|\bar{x}_i - x_i\|_i > 0.$$

Thus (6.3) holds too, and this completes the proof. $\qquad\square$

As shown by the literature, the existence results of equilibrium problems usually require some convexity (or generalized convexity) assumptions on at least one of the variables of the function involved. Next, using Theorems 6.1 and 6.2, we show the nonemptiness of the solution set of (EP) and (SEP), without any convexity requirement. To this purpose, we recall the definition of approximate equilibrium point, for both cases (see [97] and [31]). We start our analysis with (EP).

Definition 6.1. Given $f : A \times A \to \mathbb{R}$, and $\varepsilon > 0$, $\bar{x} \in A$ is said to be an ε-equilibrium point of f if

$$f(\bar{x}, y) \geq -\varepsilon\|\bar{x} - y\|, \qquad \forall y \in A. \tag{6.4}$$

The ε-equilibrium point is strict, if in (6.1) the inequality is strict for all $y \neq \bar{x}$.

Notice that the second relation of (6.1) gives the existence of a strict ε-equilibrium point, for every $\varepsilon > 0$. Moreover, by (b) and (c) of Theorem 6.1 it follows by the first relation of (6.1) that

$$f(\bar{x}, x_0) \geq \varepsilon \|\bar{x} - x_0\|,$$

"localizing", in a certain sense, the position of the $\bar{x}$.

Theorem 6.1 leads to a set of conditions that are sufficient for the nonemptiness of the solution set of (EP).

Proposition 6.1. *Let A be a compact (not necessarily convex) subset of a real Banach space, and $f : A \times A \to \mathbb{R}$ be a function satisfying the assumptions:*

(a) $f(x, \cdot)$ *is lower bounded and lower semicontinuous, for every $x \in A$;*
(b) $f(t, t) = 0$, *for every $t \in A$;*
(c) $f(z, x) \leq f(z, y) + f(y, x)$, *for every $x, y, z \in A$;*
(d) $f(\cdot, y)$ *is upper semicontinuous, for every $y \in A$.*

Then, the set of solutions of (EP) is nonempty.

Proof. For each $n \in \mathbb{N}$, let $x_n \in A$ a $1/n$-equilibrium point (such point exists by Theorem 6.1), i.e.,

$$f(x_n, y) \geq -\frac{1}{n}\|x_n - y\|, \qquad \forall y \in A.$$

Since A is compact, we can choose a subsequence $\{x_{n_k}\}$ of $\{x_n\}$ such that $x_{n_k} \to \bar{x}$ as $n \to \infty$. Then, by (d),

$$f(\bar{x}, y) \geq \limsup_{k \to \infty} \left(f(x_{n_k}, y) + \frac{1}{n_k}\|x_{n_k} - y\| \right), \qquad \forall y \in A,$$

thereby proving that $\bar{x}$ is a solution of (EP). $\qquad\square$

Let us now consider the following definition of ε-equilibrium point for systems of equilibrium problems. As before, the index set I consists on the finite set $\{1, 2, ..., m\}$.

Definition 6.2. Let A_i, $i \in I$ be subsets of certain real Banach spaces and put $A = \prod_{i \in I} A_i$. Given $f_i : A \times A_i \to \mathbb{R}$, $i \in I$ and $\varepsilon > 0$, the point $\bar{x} \in A$ is said to be an ε-equilibrium point of $\{f_1, f_2, ..., f_m\}$ if

$$f_i(\bar{x}, y_i) \geq -\varepsilon \|\bar{x}_i - y_i\|_i, \qquad \forall y_i \in A_i, \quad \forall i \in I.$$

The following result is an extension of Proposition 6.1, and it can be proved in a similar way.

Proposition 6.2. *Assume that, for every $i \in I$, A_i is compact and $f_i : A \times A_i \to \mathbb{R}$ is a function satisfying the assumptions:*

(a) $f_i(x, \cdot)$ is lower bounded and lower semicontinuous, for every $x \in A$;
(b) $f_i(x, x_i) = 0$, for every $x = (x^i, x_i) \in A$;
(c) $f_i(z, x_i) \leq f_i(z, y_i) + f_i(y, x_i)$, for every $x, y, z \in A$, where $y = (y^i, y_i)$;
(d) $f_i(\cdot, y_i)$ is upper semicontinuous, for every $y_i \in A_i$.

Then, the set of solutions of (SEP) is nonempty.

The study of the existence of solutions of the equilibrium problems on unbounded domains usually involves the same sufficient assumptions as for bounded domains together with a coercivity condition. Bianchi and Pini [38] found coercivity conditions as weak as possible, exploiting the generalized monotonicity properties of the function f defining the equilibrium problem.

Let A be a closed subset of the Euclidean space X and $f : A \times A \to \mathbb{R}$ be a given function.

Consider the following coercivity condition (see [38]):

$$\exists r > 0 : \quad \forall x \in A \setminus K_r, \ \exists y \in A, \ \|y\| < \|x\| : \ f(x, y) \leq 0, \qquad (6.5)$$

where $K_r := \{x \in A : \|x\| \leq r\}$.

We now show that within the framework of Proposition 6.1 condition (6.5) guarantees the existence of solutions of (EP) without supposing compactness of A.

Theorem 6.3. *Suppose that*

(a) $f(x, \cdot)$ is lower bounded and lower semicontinuous, for every $x \in A$;
(b) $f(t, t) = 0$, for every $t \in A$;
(c) $f(z, x) \leq f(z, y) + f(y, x)$, for every $x, y, z \in A$;
(d) $f(\cdot, y)$ is upper semicontinuous, for every $y \in A$.

If (6.5) holds, then (EP) admits a solution.

Proof. We may suppose without loss of generality that K_r is nonempty. For each $x \in A$ consider the nonempty set

$$S(x) := \{y \in A : \|y\| \leq \|x\| : f(x, y) \leq 0\}.$$

Observe that for every $x, y \in A$, $y \in S(x)$ implies $S(y) \subseteq S(x)$. Indeed, for $z \in S(y)$ we have $\|z\| \leq \|y\| \leq \|x\|$ and by (c) $f(x, z) \leq f(x, y) + f(y, z) \leq 0$. On the other hand, since X is an Euclidean space, $K_{\|x\|}$ is compact, hence by (a) we obtain that $S(x) \subseteq K_{\|x\|}$ is a compact set for every $x \in A$. Furthermore, by Proposition 6.1, there exists an element $x_r \in K_r$ such that

$$f(x_r, y) \geq 0, \quad \forall y \in K_r. \qquad (6.6)$$

Suppose that there exists $x \in A$ with $f(x_r, x) < 0$ and put

$$a := \min_{y \in S(x)} \|y\|$$

(the minimum is taken since $S(x)$ is nonempty, compact and the norm is continuous). We distinguish two cases.

Case 1: $a \leq r$. Let $y_0 \in S(x)$ such that $\|y_0\| = a \leq r$. Then we have $f(x, y_0) \leq 0$. Since $f(x_r, x) < 0$, it follows by (c) that

$$f(x_r, y_0) \leq f(x_r, x) + f(x, y_0) < 0,$$

contradicting (6.6).

Case 2: $a > r$. Let again $y_0 \in S(x)$ such that $\|y_0\| = a > r$. Then, by (6.5) we can choose an element $y_1 \in A$ with $\|y_1\| < \|y_0\| = a$ such that $f(y_0, y_1) \leq 0$. Thus, $y_1 \in S(y_0) \subseteq S(x)$ contradicting

$$\|y_1\| < a = \min_{y \in S(x)} \|y\|.$$

Therefore, there is no $x \in A$ such that $f(x_r, x) < 0$, i.e., x_r is a solution of (EP) (on A). This completes the proof. $\qquad\square$

Next we consider (SEP) for noncompact setting. Let us consider the following coercivity condition:

$$\exists r > 0 : \quad \forall x \in A \text{ such that } \|x_i\|_i > r \text{ for some } i \in I,$$
$$\exists y_i \in A_i, \; \|y_i\|_i < \|x_i\|_i \text{ and } f_i(x, y_i) \leq 0. \tag{6.7}$$

We conclude this subsection with the following result which guarantees the existence of solutions for (SEP).

Theorem 6.4. *Suppose that, for every $i \in I$,*

(a) *$f_i(x, \cdot)$ is lower bounded and lower semicontinuous, for every $x \in A$;*
(b) *$f_i(x, x_i) = 0$, for every $x = (x^i, x_i) \in A$;*
(c) *$f_i(z, x_i) \leq f_i(z, y_i) + f_i(y, x_i)$, for every $x, y, z \in A$, where $y = (y^i, y_i)$;*
(d) *$f_i(\cdot, y_i)$ is upper semicontinuous, for every $y_i \in A_i$.*

If (6.7) holds, then (SEP) admits a solution.

Proof. For each $x \in AD$ and every $i \in I$ consider the set

$$S_i(x) := \{y_i \in A_i, \; \|y_i\|_i \leq \|x_i\|_i, \; f_i(x, y_i) \leq 0\}.$$

Observe that, by (c), for every x and $y = (y^i, y_i) \in A$, $y_i \in S_i(x)$ implies $S_i(y) \subseteq S_i(x)$. On the other hand, since the set $\{y_i \in A_i : \|y_i\|_i \leq r\} = K_i(r)$ is a compact subset of A_i, by (a) we obtain that $S_i(x)$ is a nonempty compact set for every $x \in A$. Furthermore, by Proposition 6.2, there exists an element $x_r \in \prod_i K_i(r)$ (observe, we may suppose that $K_i(r) \neq \emptyset$ for all $i \in I$) such that

$$f_i(x_r, y_i) \geq 0, \quad \forall y_i \in K_i(r), \quad \forall i \in I. \tag{6.8}$$

Suppose that x_r is not a solution of (SEP). In this case, there exists $j \in I$ and $z_j \in A_j$ with $f_j(x_r, z_j) < 0$. Let $z^j \in A^j$ be arbitrary and put $z = (z^j, z_j) \in A$. Define

$$a_j := \min_{y_j \in S_j(z)} \|y_j\|_j.$$

We distinguish two cases.

Case 1: $a_j \le r$. Let $\bar{y}_j(z) \in S_j(z)$ such that $\|\bar{y}_j(z)\|_j = a_j \le r$. Then we have $f_j(z, \bar{y}_j(z)) \le 0$. Since $f_j(x_r, z_j) < 0$, it follows by (c) that

$$f_j(x_r, \bar{y}_j(z)) \le f(x_r, z_j) + f(z, \bar{y}_j(z)) < 0,$$

contradicting (6.8).

Case 2: $a_j > r$. Let again $\bar{y}_j(z) \in S_j(z)$ such that $\|\bar{y}_j(z)\|_j = a_j > r$. Let $\bar{y}^j \in A^j$ be arbitrary and put $\bar{y}(z) = (\bar{y}^j, \bar{y}_j(z)) \in A$. Then, by (6.7) we can choose an element $y_j \in A_j$ with $\|y_j\|_j < \|\bar{y}_j(z)\|_j = a_j$ such that $f_j(\bar{y}(z), y_j) \le 0$. Clearly, $y_j \in S_j(\bar{y}(z)) \subseteq S_j(z)$, a contradiction since $\bar{y}_j(z)$ has minimal norm in $S_j(z)$. This completes the proof. $\qquad\square$

6.1.2 The Vector Case

The aim of this subsection is to provide a vector version of Ekeland's theorem related to equilibrium problems. We deal with bifunctions defined on complete metric spaces and with values in locally convex spaces ordered by closed convex cones. To prove this principle, a weak notion of continuity of a vector-valued function is considered, and some of its properties are presented. Via the vector Ekeland's principle, existence results for vector equilibria are proved in both compact and noncompact domains. The results developed in this subsection have been obtained by Bianchi, Kassay, and Pini [32].

Let $f : X \to Y$, where (X, d) is a complete metric space and (Y, K) is a locally convex space ordered by the nontrivial closed convex cone K as follows:

$$x \le_K y \iff y - x \in K.$$

In the vector-valued case there are several possible extensions of the notion of lower semicontinuity for scalar functions.

Let us recall the following definitions given by Borwein, Penot, and Théra in [43]. The vector-valued function f is said to be lower semicontinuous at $x_0 \in X$ if for each neighborhood $\mathcal{V}$ of $f(x_0)$ there exists a neighborhood $\mathcal{U}$ of x_0 such that $f(\mathcal{U}) \subset \mathcal{V} + K$.

The concept of quasi lower semicontinuity weakens the definition given above. The function f is said to be quasi lower semicontinuous (cf. [76]) at $x_0 \in X$ if for each $b \in Y$ such that $b \notin f(x_0) + K$ there exists a neighborhood $\mathcal{U}$

of x_0 in X such that $b \notin f(x) + K$, for each $x \in \mathcal{U}$. A function f is quasi lower semicontinuous on X if it is quasi lower semicontinuous at each point of X.

For the sake of completeness we recall the following result (see, for instance, [76]):

Lemma 6.1. *The function f is quasi lower semicontinuous on X if and only if its lower level sets are closed, i.e., for every $b \in Y$, $L(f, b) = \{x \in X, \ f(x) \in b - K\}$ is closed.*

In general, the quasi lower semicontinuity is not preserved by summation without any additional requirements (see [76], Remark 23). However, it can be proved that if $f, g : X \to \mathbb{R}^n$ are quasi lower semicontinuous and lower bounded (i.e., $f(x) \in b + K$, for some b), then $f + g$ is still quasi lower semicontinuous. One can wonder whether the sum of a quasi lower semicontinuous function f and a lower semicontinuous function g is still a quasi lower semicontinuous function. A positive answer is given in [76], Lemma 24, where the additional assumption of monotone bounds property (MBP) is required on the space (Y, K). Actually, if Y has not the MBP, the answer is negative, even in case of a continuous function g as the following example shows.

Example 6.1. Let $Y := \mathbb{R}^2$ and $K := \{(x, 0) : x \geq 0\}$. Then (Y, K) has no MBP, see [76]. Let $f, g : \mathbb{R} \to \mathbb{R}^2$ defined by $f(t) := (0, 0)$ if $t = 0$ and $(-1, -t)$ otherwise, and $g(t) := (0, t)$ for all t. The function f is quasi lower semicontinuous, while g is continuous, but the sum $f + g$ is clearly not quasi lower semicontinuous at $t = 0$: take, for instance, $b := (-\frac{1}{2}, 0)$.

Taking into account the remarks above, it is interesting to single out classes of functions that can be added to quasi lower semicontinuous functions without destroying this property. In this direction, the next result provides a positive answer on one hand, and will be useful for our purposes on the other hand.

Lemma 6.2. *If $f : X \to Y$ is quasi lower semicontinuous, $g : X \to \mathbb{R}$ is lower semicontinuous, and $e \in K$, then the function $f + ge : X \to Y$ is quasi lower semicontinuous.*

Proof. If $e = 0_Y$ there is nothing to prove. Assume $e \neq 0_Y$, and fix $\bar{x} \in X$. Suppose $\bar{u} := b - g(\bar{x})e - f(\bar{x}) \notin K$. Then the complementary set K^C of K being open, is a neighborhood of $\bar{u}$, or, in other words, the set $K^C - \bar{u}$ is a neighborhood of the origin of Y. As any neighborhood of the origin is an absorbing set (see, for instance, W. Rudin [157], p. 24), there exists $\varepsilon > 0$ such that $\varepsilon e \in K^C - \bar{u}$, that is

$$b - g(\bar{x})e - f(\bar{x}) + \varepsilon e \notin K.$$

Since f is quasi lower semicontinuous, there exists a neighborhood $\mathcal{U}$ of $\bar{x}$ such that

$$b - g(\bar{x})e - f(x) + \varepsilon e \notin K, \quad \forall x \in \mathcal{U}.$$

By the lower semicontinuity of g, there exists a neighborhood $\mathcal{V}$ of $\bar{x}$ such that

$$g(\bar{x}) - \varepsilon < g(x), \quad \forall x \in \mathcal{V}.$$

This implies that for all $x \in \mathcal{V}$ there exists a suitable $k_x \in K$ such that $g(\bar{x})e - \varepsilon e - g(x)e = -k_x$. Therefore, for every $x \in \mathcal{U} \cap \mathcal{V}$, we have

$$b + k_x - g(x)e - f(x) \notin K,$$

implying that $b - g(x)e - f(x) \notin K$. $\qquad\qquad\square$

Denote by K^* the dual cone of the cone K in the topological dual space Y^* (see Section 2.2 in Chapter 2). Let us fix a point $e \in K \setminus (-K)$, and consider a functional $e^* \in K^*$ such that $e^*(e) = 1$. The following result provides a vector-valued version of the Ekeland's principle related to the equilibrium problem.

Theorem 6.5. *Let (X, d) be a complete metric space. Assume that the function $f : X \times X \to Y$ satisfies the following assumptions:*

(i) $f(t, t) = 0_Y$ *for all $t \in X$;*
(ii) $y \to e^*(f(x, y))$ *is lower bounded for all $x \in X$;*
(iii) $f(z, y) + f(y, x) \in f(z, x) + K$ *for any $x, y, z \in X$;*
(iv) $y \to f(x, y)$ *is quasi lower semicontinuous for all $x \in X$.*

Then for every $\varepsilon > 0$ and for every $x_0 \in X$ there exists $\bar{x} \in X$ such that

(a) $f(x_0, \bar{x}) + \varepsilon d(x_0, \bar{x})e \in -K$;
(b) $f(\bar{x}, x) + \varepsilon d(\bar{x}, x)e \notin -K, \forall x \in X$ *with $x \neq \bar{x}$.*

Proof. Without loss of generality, we can restrict the proof to the case $\varepsilon = 1$. For each $x \in X$ consider the set

$$F(x) = \{y \in X, \; f(x, y) + d(x, y)e \in -K\}.$$

By (i) and (iv) $F(x)$ is nonempty and closed for every $x \in X$ (see Lemma 6.1 and 6.2). Assume $y \in F(x)$, i.e.,

$$f(x, y) + d(x, y)e \in -K,$$

and let $z \in F(y)$, i.e.,

$$f(y, z) + d(y, z)e \in -K.$$

Adding both sides of the inclusions above, and taking into account that $-K$ is a convex cone, we get

$$f(x, y) + f(y, z) + (d(x, y) + d(y, z))e \in -K.$$

By (iii) and by the triangle inequality of the distance, we easily get that $z \in F(x)$, therefore $y \in F(x)$ implies $F(y) \subseteq F(x)$.

Let us define the real-valued function $v(x) = \inf_{z \in F(x)} e^*(f(x, z))$. If $z \in F(x)$, then $d(x, z)e = -f(x, z) - k$, for a suitable $k \in K$. Evaluating e^* of both sides, we obtain that $d(x, z) \leq -e^*(f(x, z))$. Arguing as in Theorem 6.1, we get the following chain of inequalities:

$$d(x, z) \leq -e^*(f(x, z))$$
$$\leq - \inf_{z \in F(x)} e^*(f(x, z))$$
$$= -v(x);$$

in particular, for every $x_1, x_2 \in F(x)$,

$$d(x_1, x_2) \leq d(x_1, x) + d(x, x_2) \leq -2v(x),$$

showing that $\mathrm{diam}(F(x)) \leq -2v(x)$.

Starting from $x_0 \in X$, a sequence $\{x_n\}$ of points of X can be defined such that $x_{n+1} \in F(x_n)$ and $e^*(f(x_n, x_{n+1})) \leq v(x_n) + 2^{-(n+1)}$. Notice that, from (iii), it follows that $e^*(f(z, y)) + e^*(f(y, x)) \geq e^*(f(z, x))$; in particular,

$$v(x_{n+1}) \geq \inf_{y \in F(x_n)} e^*(f(x_{n+1}, y))$$
$$\geq (\inf_{y \in F(x_n)} e^*(f(x_n, y))) - e^*(f(x_n, x_{n+1}))$$
$$= v(x_n) - e^*(f(x_n, x_{n+1})).$$

Therefore, like in Theorem 6.1, we obtain that

$$-v(x_n) \leq -e^*(f(x_n, x_{n+1})) + 2^{-(n+1)} \leq v(x_{n+1}) - v(x_n) + 2^{-(n+1)},$$

that entails

$$\mathrm{diam}(F(x_n)) \leq -2v(x_n) \leq 2 \cdot 2^{-n}.$$

This implies that

$$\mathrm{diam}(F(x_n)) \to 0, \qquad n \to \infty.$$

Since the sets $F(x_n)$ are closed and $F(x_{n+1}) \subseteq F(x_n)$, we obtain from this that the intersection of the sets $F(x_n)$ is a singleton $\{\bar{x}\}$ and $F(\bar{x}) = \{\bar{x}\}$. Since $\bar{x} \in F(x_0)$, we get (a). Moreover, if $x \neq \bar{x}$ then $x \notin F(\bar{x})$, and we get (b). This concludes the proof. $\qquad \square$

Remark 6.2. Let us point out that condition (ii) of Theorem 6.5 is clearly weaker than the assumption of lower boundedness of $f(x, \cdot)$. Indeed, if a function $g : X \to Y$ is lower bounded, then there exists $b \in Y$ such that for every $x \in X$, $g(x) \in b + K$. In particular, $e^*(g(x)) \geq e^*(b)$, that is $e^*(g)$ is lower bounded. On the other hand, let us consider the function $g : \mathbb{R} \to \mathbb{R}^2$ defined by $g(t) = (-t, t)$. If $\mathbb{R}^2$ is ordered by the cone $\mathbb{R}^2_+$, then it is easy to see that g is not lower bounded. But if we take $e^* = (1, 1)$, the real-valued function $e^*(g(t)) = 0$ is constant, therefore is obviously (lower) bounded.

By Theorem 6.5 one can easily deduce the following variant of Ekeland's principle for vector equilibrium problems.

Theorem 6.6. *Suppose that the assumptions of Theorem 6.5 hold. Let $\varepsilon > 0$ and $\lambda > 0$ be given and let $x_0 \in X$ such that*

$$f(x_0, y) + \varepsilon e \notin -K, \quad \forall y \in X. \tag{6.9}$$

Then there exists $\bar{x} \in X$ such that:

(a′) $f(\bar{x}, x_0) \in K$;
(b′) $d(\bar{x}, x_0) \le \lambda$;
(c′) $f(\bar{x}, x) + (\varepsilon/\lambda)d(\bar{x}, x)e \notin -K, \forall x \in X, x \ne \bar{x}$.

Proof. Let $\bar{x} \in X$ be the element provided by Theorem 6.5 with ε/λ instead of ε. Then we obtain (c′) by property (b) of Theorem 6.5. Also, by property (a) we have

$$f(x_0, \bar{x}) + \frac{\varepsilon}{\lambda}d(x_0, \bar{x})e \in -K. \tag{6.10}$$

By assumption (i) and (iii) it follows that $f(x, y) + f(y, x) \in K$; in particular, $f(x_0, \bar{x}) = -f(\bar{x}, x_0) + k_0$ ($k_0 \in K$) and this, together with (6.10) implies (a′). Moreover, condition (a) of Theorem 6.5 gives

$$f(x_0, \bar{x}) + \frac{\varepsilon}{\lambda}d(x_0, \bar{x})e = -k_1, \quad k_1 \in K. \tag{6.11}$$

Taking into account (6.9), from (6.11) we get

$$\begin{aligned} f(x_0, \bar{x}) + \varepsilon e &= -\frac{\varepsilon}{\lambda}d(x_0, \bar{x})e + \varepsilon e - k_1 \\ &= -\frac{\varepsilon}{\lambda}(d(x_0, \bar{x}) - \lambda)e - k_1 \notin -K; \end{aligned} \tag{6.12}$$

this implies that $d(x_0, \bar{x}) - \lambda \le 0$, i.e., $d(x_0, \bar{x}) \le \lambda$. This completes the proof. $\square$

Remark 6.3. If we assume that the cone K is pointed (i.e., $K \cap (-K) = \{0\}$), then we can weaken condition (6.9) as follows:

$$f(x_0, y) + \epsilon e \notin -K \setminus \{0\}, \quad \forall y \in X. \tag{6.13}$$

Indeed, from (6.13), in (6.12) we can argue that

$$-\frac{\epsilon}{\lambda}(d(x_0, \bar{x}) - \lambda)e - k_1 \notin -K \setminus \{0\}.$$

If $d(x_0, \bar{x}) - \lambda > 0$, then we get that the left-hand side is in $-K$, and so it must be 0, but this contradicts the pointedness of K. Within this setting we could also recover Theorem 8 in [75], where we put $f(x, y) := g(y) - g(x)$.

In the following proposition we show that a suitable assumption on the function f, which seemingly is quite natural, guarantees the existence of an element $x_0 \in X$ satisfying (6.9).

Proposition 6.3. *Suppose that assumption (iii) of Theorem 6.5 holds and*

(v) *there exists an element $\hat{y} \in X$ such that the function $x \mapsto e^*(f(x, \hat{y}))$ is upper bounded.*

Then there exists an element $x_0 \in X$ satisfying (6.9).

Proof. By (v) we have that $\sup_{z \in X} e^*(f(z, \hat{y})) < \infty$. Let $\varepsilon > 0$ be arbitrary and consider an element $x_0 \in X$ such that

$$e^*(f(x_0, \hat{y})) > \sup_{z \in X} e^*(f(z, \hat{y})) - \varepsilon.$$

This implies that

$$e^*(f(x_0, \hat{y})) - e^*(f(z, \hat{y})) + \varepsilon > 0, \quad \forall z \in X,$$

and this, together with (iii), gives that

$$e^*(f(x_0, z)) + \varepsilon > 0, \quad \forall z \in X. \tag{6.14}$$

Let us show that the inequality above implies (6.9). Indeed, assume by contradiction that there exists $\bar{y}$ and $k_0 \in K$ such that

$$f(x_0, \bar{y}) = -\varepsilon e - k_0.$$

Applying e^* to both sides, we get

$$e^*(f(x_0, \bar{y})) = -\varepsilon - e^*(k_0) \leq -\varepsilon,$$

that contradicts (6.14). $\qquad \square$

One might wonder whether the results of Theorem 6.5 can be obtained by a direct application of Theorem 2.1 in [31] (the scalar Ekeland's principle) to the real function $e^*(f)$. Next we show that this is not the case. In the same time we compare the assumptions of Theorem 6.5 and Theorem 2.1 in [31].

Let us consider the following assumptions:

(i*) $e^*(f(t, t)) = 0$;

(ii*) $y \to e^*(f(x, y))$ is lower bounded for every $x \in X$;

(iii*) $e^*(f(z, x)) \leq e^*(f(z, y)) + e^*(f(y, x))$;

(iv*) $y \to e^*(f(x, y))$ is lower semicontinuous for every $x \in X$.

From Theorem 2.1 in [31] they imply that for every $\epsilon > 0$ and for every $x_0 \in X$ there exists $\bar{x} \in X$ such that

$(\mathbf{a}^*)$ $e^*(f(x_0, \bar{x})) + \varepsilon d(x_0, \bar{x}) \leq 0$;

$(\mathbf{b}^*)$ $e^*(f(\bar{x}, x)) + \varepsilon d(\bar{x}, x) > 0$ for every $x \neq \bar{x}$.

Notice that (i^*) is trivially weaker than (i) in Theorem 6.5. To show that (iii^*) is weaker than the corresponding (iii), let us provide an example. Consider the function $f : \mathbb{R}^2 \to \mathbb{R}$ defined by

$$f(x, y) = \begin{cases} e^{|x-y|} + 1 + g(x) - g(y) & x \neq y \\ 0 & x = y \end{cases},$$

where g is any real-valued function. Assume that $Y = \mathbb{R}^2$ and $K = \mathbb{R}^2_+$. Take $v = (-1, 2)$ and $e^* = (1, 1)$, and define $F : \mathbb{R}^2 \to \mathbb{R}^2$ as $F(x, y) = f(x, y)v$. The function $e^*(F) = f$ satisfies (iii^*) (see [31], Remark 2.1). On the other hand, F does not satisfy (iii), since

$$F(x, y) + F(y, z) - F(x, z) \in K \iff (f(x, y) + f(y, z) - f(x, z))v \in K,$$

and the second inclusion in never satisfied unless $f(x, y) + f(y, z) - f(x, z) = 0$.

Condition (iv^*) is not comparable with (iv). Indeed, take, for instance, the function $f : [0, 1] \times [0, 1] \to \mathbb{R}^2$, defined as $f(x, y) = F(y) - F(x)$, where

$$F(t) = \begin{cases} (-1, 1/|t|) & t \neq 0 \\ (0, 0) & t = 0. \end{cases}$$

The function F is quasi lower semicontinuous if the cone K is the Paretian cone; the same is true for the function $f(x, \cdot)$, for every $x \in [0, 1]$. Take $e^* = (1, 0)$. Then $e^*(f(0, y)) = -1$ if $y \neq 0$, while $e^*(f(0, 0)) = 0$. Therefore the function $e^*(f(x, \cdot))$ is no longer lower semicontinuous.

The converse can be easily showed. Indeed, let us consider the space $Y = \mathbb{R}^2$ ordered by the Paretian cone, and the function $f : \mathbb{R} \to \mathbb{R}^2$ defined as follows: $f(0) = (0, 0)$, $f(t) = (-1, 0)$ if $t \neq 0$. This function is not quasi lower semicontinuous. Take $e^* = (0, 1)$. The function $e^*(f) : \mathbb{R} \to \mathbb{R}$ is constant, and equal to 0. In particular, it is continuous.

It is noteworthy that $(\mathbf{a}^*)$ and $(\mathbf{b}^*)$ entail some interesting results for the vector Ekeland's principle applied to the function f. Since $e^* \in K^*$, by trivial thoughts we know that

$$e^*(k) \leq 0 \Longrightarrow k \notin \text{int}(K), \qquad e^*(k) > 0 \Longrightarrow k \notin -K.$$

Therefore, $(\mathbf{a}^*)$ and $(\mathbf{b}^*)$ give

$(\mathbf{a}'')$ $f(x_0, \bar{x}) + \varepsilon d(x_0, \bar{x})e \notin \text{int}(K)$;

$(\mathbf{b}'')$ $f(\bar{x}, x) + \varepsilon d(\bar{x}, x)e \notin -K, \forall x \neq \bar{x}$.

While condition (b") coincides with the corresponding (b), condition (a") is clearly weaker than (a).

As in the subsection above, now we turn to show the nonemptiness of the solution set of a (this time) weak vector equilibrium problem without any convexity requirements on the set X and the function f, going through the existence of approximate solutions. For this purpose we use Theorem 6.5.

Let (X, d) be a complete metric space, Y a locally convex space ordered by the closed, convex cone K such that $\text{int}(K) \neq \emptyset$, and let $f : X \times X \to Y$ be a given function. Recall that by a weak vector equilibrium problem (see Chapter 4) we understand the problem of finding $\bar{x} \in X$ such that

$$f(\bar{x}, y) \notin -\text{int}(K), \qquad \forall y \in X \qquad \text{(WVEP)}$$

A point $\bar{x}$ satisfying (WVEP) is called a vector equilibrium point. At the same time, we will consider a perturbation of (WVEP) in a fixed direction e. We define an ε-weak vector equilibrium point in the direction e as a point $\bar{x}_\varepsilon \in X$ such that

$$f(\bar{x}_\varepsilon, y) + \varepsilon d(\bar{x}_\varepsilon, y)e \notin -K, \qquad \forall y \in X, \ y \neq \bar{x}_\varepsilon. \qquad \text{(WVEP}_\varepsilon)$$

First we deal with the case of a compact domain X.

Theorem 6.7. *Let (X, d) be a compact complete metric space. Assume that the function $f : X \times X \to Y$ satisfies the following assumptions:*

(i) $f(t, t) = 0_Y$ *for all $t \in X$;*
(ii) $y \to e^*(f(x, y))$ *is lower bounded for all $x \in X$;*
(iii) $f(z, y) + f(y, x) \in f(z, x) + K$ *for any $x, y, z \in X$;*
(iv) $y \to f(x, y)$ *is quasi lower semicontinuous for all $x \in X$;*
(v) $f(\cdot, y)$ *is upper semicontinuous for every $y \in X$, i.e., for every $x_0 \in X$ and every neighborhood $\mathcal{V}$ of $f(x_0, y)$ there exists a neighborhood $\mathcal{U}$ of x_0 such that $f(x, y) \in \mathcal{V} - K$ for all $x \in \mathcal{U}$.*

Then, the set of solutions of (WVEP) is nonempty.

Proof. Taking $\varepsilon = 1/n$, from Theorem 6.5 (b) we find a sequence $\{x_n\}$ where x_n is a $1/n$-weak vector equilibrium point in the direction e, i.e.,

$$f(x_n, y) + \frac{1}{n}d(x_n, y)e \notin -K, \qquad \forall y \neq x_n.$$

By the compactness of X, we can assume that $\{x_n\}$ (or a suitable subsequence) converges to $\bar{x} \in X$. Suppose that $f(\bar{x}, \bar{y}) \in -\text{int}(K)$ for a suitable $\bar{y} \in X$. Take a neighborhood $\mathcal{V}$ of $f(\bar{x}, \bar{y})$ such that $\mathcal{V} \subset -\text{int}(K)$. By assumption (v) there exists a number N such that $f(x_n, \bar{y}) \in \mathcal{V} - K$, for $n \geq N$. Moreover, if n is big enough, $\frac{1}{n}d(x_n, \bar{y})e + \mathcal{V} \subseteq -\text{int}(K)$, thereby

$$f(x_n, \bar{y}) + \frac{1}{n}d(x_n, \bar{y})e \in \mathcal{V} - K + \frac{1}{n}d(x_n, \bar{y})e \subseteq -\text{int}(K),$$

a contradiction. $\qquad\qquad\qquad\qquad\qquad\qquad\qquad\qquad\qquad\qquad\qquad\qquad \square$

Remark 6.4. We can obtain an existence result for (WVEP) through a scalarization approach, under assumptions that are comparable with those of Theorem 6.7. Indeed, let us consider the assumptions (i*)–(iv*), and the following

(v*) $e^*(f(\cdot, y))$ upper semicontinuous for every $y \in X$.

Notice that (v) of Theorem 6.7 implies (v*) (see, for instance, [30]). By Proposition 3.2 in [31] we get that there exists $\bar{x} \in X$ such that

$$e^*(f(\bar{x}, y)) \geq 0, \qquad \forall y \in X.$$

This implies, in particular, that $\bar{x}$ is a solution of (WVEP).

In order to obtain an existence result for (WVEP) in noncompact setting we need to restrict our analysis from a general complete metric space. In the sequel we suppose that the following three assumptions are satisfied:

(A1) The complete metric space (X, d) admits a topology τ (possibly different from the initial topology induced by d) such that the closed balls are compact with respect to τ;

(A2) For every $y \in X$, the distance $x \to d(x, y)$ is lower semicontinuous with respect to τ;

(A3) For every $x \in X$, the level set $L(x) := \{y \in X : f(x, y) \in -K\}$ is closed with respect to τ.

Due to symmetry, it is obvious that (A2) implies: for every $x \in X$, the distance $y \to d(x, y)$ is lower semicontinuous with respect to τ.

Condition (A1) turns out to be a binding condition on the space X if both the metric d and the topology τ are induced by a norm; as a matter of fact, in this case X must be finite dimensional. However, these three conditions are enough general to cover other important cases, as, for instance, infinite dimensional normed spaces.

Example 6.2. Let X be a real reflexive Banach space (the metric d is induced by the norm of X). Then (A1) and (A2) are satisfied if τ is the weak topology on X. Indeed, by the Alaoglu's Theorem (see [3], Theorem 6.25) every closed, bounded and convex subset of X (such as closed balls) is weakly compact. Moreover, the norm being convex and continuous, it is also weakly lower semicontinuous (see [3], Theorem 6.26). Finally, if

(i) $y \to f(x, y)$ is quasi lower semicontinuous (with respect to the norm topology of X) for all $x \in X$;

(ii) for every $x \in X$ the set $L(x)$ is convex,

then (A3) is also satisfied. Indeed, by (i) $L(x)$ is closed (with respect to the norm) by Lemma 6.1, and, by (ii), is convex. Therefore, it is also weakly closed. It is well known that condition (ii) is satisfied in particular if the function $y \to f(x, y)$ is quasi-convex for every $x \in X$ (see, for instance, [30]).

In what follows we always assume that (A1)–(A3) hold. If not stated otherwise, all topological conditions (such as compactness, boundedness, (quasi) lower/upper semicontinuity, etc.) will be considered with respect to the metric d.

The study of the existence of solutions of the equilibrium problems on noncompact domains usually involves the same sufficient assumptions as for compact domains together with a coercivity condition (see [38]). Let us consider the following coercivity condition that extends a similar one in [38], but is here adapted to a metric space and to a vector-valued function. Fix a point $x_0 \in X$. The condition requires that there exists a compact set $C \subseteq X$ such that

$$\forall x \in X \setminus C, \exists y \in X, d(y, x_0) < d(x, x_0): f(x, y) \in -K. \qquad (C_1(x_0))$$

We now show that within the framework of Theorem 6.7, condition $(C_1(x_0))$ guarantees the existence of solutions of (WVEP) without supposing compactness of X.

Theorem 6.8. *Assume that the function* $f : X \times X \to Y$ *satisfies the following assumptions:*

(i) $f(t, t) = 0_Y$ *for all* $t \in X$;
(ii) $y \to e^*(f(x, y))$ *is lower bounded for all* $x \in X$;
(iii) $f(z, y) + f(y, x) \in f(z, x) + K$ *for any* $x, y, z \in X$;
(iv) $y \to f(x, y)$ *is quasi lower semicontinuous* $\forall x \in X$;
(v) $f(\cdot, y)$ *is upper semicontinuous for every* $y \in X$;
(vi) f *satisfies condition* $(C_1(x_0))$ *for a suitable* $x_0 \in X$.

Then, the set of solutions of (WVEP) is nonempty.

Proof. For each $x \in X$ consider the nonempty set

$$S(x) := \{y \in X : d(y, x_0) \leq d(x, x_0) : f(x, y) \in -K\}.$$

Observe that for every $x, y \in X$, $y \in S(x)$ implies $S(y) \subseteq S(x)$. Indeed, for $z \in S(y)$ we have $d(z, x_0) \leq d(y, x_0) \leq d(x, x_0)$ and, by (iii), $f(x, z) \in -K$. On the other hand, since the closed ball $\{y \in X : d(y, x_0) \leq d(x, x_0)\}$ is τ-compact by (A1), we obtain by (A3) that $S(x)$ is a τ-compact set for every $x \in X$. Furthermore, by Theorem 6.7, there exists an element $x_C \in C$ such that

$$f(x_C, y) \notin -\text{int}(K), \quad \forall y \in C. \qquad (6.15)$$

By contradiction, suppose that there exists $\bar{x} \in X$ with $f(x_C, \bar{x}) \in -\text{int}(K)$ and put

$$a := \min_{y \in S(\bar{x})} d(y, x_0)$$

(the minimum is achieved since $S(x)$ is nonempty, τ-compact and the distance is τ-lower semicontinuous by (A2)).

We first show that $S(\bar{x}) \cap C = \emptyset$. Indeed, let $y \in S(\bar{x}) \cap C$. Then $f(\bar{x}, y) \in -K$. Since $f(x_C, \bar{x}) \in -\text{int}(K)$, it follows by (iii) that

$$f(x_C, \bar{x}) + f(\bar{x}, y) \in f(x_C, y) + K,$$

so that $f(x_C, y) \in -\text{int}(K)$, contradicting (6.15) since $y \in C$.

Now choose an element $y_0 \in S(\bar{x})$ such that $d(y_0, x_0) = a$. Since $y_0 \notin C$, by $(C_1(x_0))$ we can choose an element $y_1 \in X$ with $d(y_1, x_0) < d(y_0, x_0) = a$ such that $f(y_0, y_1) \in -K$. Thus, $y_1 \in S(y_0) \subseteq S(\bar{x})$ contradicting

$$d(y_1, x_0) < a = \min_{y \in S(\bar{x})} d(y, x_0).$$

Therefore, there is no $x \in X$ such that $f(x_C, x) \in -\text{int}(K)$, i.e., x_C is a solution of (WVEP) (on X). This completes the proof. $\qquad\square$

6.1.3 The Case of Countable Systems

We are concerned in what follows with a version of Ekeland's variational principle for countable systems of equilibrium problems defined on complete metric spaces. This result is applied to establish the existence of solutions for nonconvex countable systems of equilibrium problems. The results developed in this subsection have been obtained by Alleche and Rădulescu [5].

Consider the following equilibrium problem:

$$f(x^*, y) \geq 0 \quad \text{for all} \quad y \in A, \tag{EP}$$

where A is a given set and $f : A \times A \longrightarrow \mathbb{R}$ is a bifunction. Then f is an *equilibrium bifunction* if $f(x, x) = 0$ for every $x \in E$.

We start with the following preliminary result, which guarantees the existence of solutions to equilibrium problems in the weakly compact case.

Proposition 6.4. *Let A be a nonempty weakly compact subset of a real Banach space E and $f : A \times A \to \mathbb{R}$ be a bifunction. Assume that the following conditions hold:*

1. $f(x, x) = 0$, *for every $x \in A$;*
2. $f(z, x) \leq f(z, y) + f(y, x)$, *for every $x, y, z \in A$;*
3. f *is lower bounded and lower semicontinuous in its second variable;*
4. f *is weakly sequentially upper semicontinuous in its first variable.*

Then the equilibrium problem (EP) *has a solution.*

Proof. By the Ekeland variational principle for equilibrium problems (see Theorem A.3 in Appendix A), for every $n \in \mathbb{N}^*$, there exists $x_n \in A$ a $\frac{1}{n}$-solution of the equilibrium problem (EP). Therefore

$$f(x_n, y) \geq -\frac{1}{n}\|x_n - y\| \quad \forall y \in A.$$

Since A is weakly compact, the sequence $(x_n)_n$ has a weakly converging subsequence $(x_{n_k})_k$ to some $x^* \in A$. Since f is weakly sequentially upper semicontinuous in its first variable on A, we have for all $y \in A$

$$f(x^*, y) \geq \limsup_{k \to +\infty} f(x_{n_k}, y) \geq \limsup_{k \to +\infty} \left(-\frac{1}{n_k} \|x_{n_k} - y\| \right) = 0.$$

This means that x^* is a solution to the equilibrium problem (EP). $\qquad\square$

The following result guarantees the existence of solutions to equilibrium problems in the nonweakly compact case. Instead of the Euclidean space $\mathbb{R}^n$, this generalization makes more clear in the setting of infinite dimensional spaces, the conditions imposed on both A and the subset of coerciveness. This generalization is also obtained under weakened conditions of semicontinuity of the bifunction involved.

Theorem 6.9. *Let A be a nonempty weakly closed subset of a real reflexive Banach space E and $f : A \times A \to \mathbb{R}$ be a bifunction, and suppose the following conditions hold:*

1. $f(x, x) = 0$, *for every $x \in A$;*
2. $f(z, x) \leq f(z, y) + f(y, x)$, *for every $x, y, z \in A$;*
3. *there exists a nonempty weakly compact subset K of A such that*

$$\forall x \in A \setminus K, \quad \exists y \in A, \quad \|y\| < \|x\|, \quad f(x, y) \leq 0;$$

4. f *is weakly sequentially lower semicontinuous in its second variable on K;*
5. *the restriction of f on $K \times K$ is lower bounded in its second variable;*
6. *the restriction of f on $K \times K$ is weakly sequentially upper semicontinuous in its first variable.*

Then the equilibrium problem (EP) has a solution.

Proof. For every $x \in A$, define the subset

$$L(x) = \{ y \in A \mid \|y\| \leq \|x\|, f(x, y) \leq 0 \},$$

and put $S(x)) = cl_A(L(x))$, where the closure is taken with respect to the weak topology of A. We have the following properties:

1. *The subset $S(x)$ is nonempty, for every $x \in A$.* This holds easily from the fact that $x \in L(x)$.
2. *The subset $S(x)$ is weakly compact, for every $x \in A$.* Indeed, for every $x \in A$, the subset $L(x)$ is contained in the weakly compact subset $K_{\|x\|}$ and then, $S(x)$ is weakly compact.
3. *For every $x, y \in A$, if $y \in S(x)$, then $S(y) \subset S(x)$.* Indeed, since $L(y)$ is bounded, then for every $z \in S(y)$, there exists a sequence $(z_n)_n$ in $L(y)$ weakly converging to z. It follows that $\|z_n\| \leq \|y\| \leq \|x\|$ and $f(x, z_n) \leq f(x, y) + f(y, z_n) \leq 0$, for every n. It follows that the sequence $(z_n)_n$ lies in $L(x)$ and then, $z \in S(x)$.

On the other hand, the restriction of f on $K \times K$ satisfies all the conditions of Proposition 6.4 and therefore, there exists $x^* \in K$ such that

$$f(x^*, y) \geq 0 \quad \text{for all } y \in K.$$

Suppose that x^* is not a solution of the equilibrium problem (EP) and let $x \in A$ such that $f(x^*, x) < 0$. Since $S(x)$ is nonempty weakly compact subset, then the norm, which is weakly lower semicontinuous, attains its lower bound on $S(x)$. Let $y_x \in S(x)$ be such that

$$\|y_x\| = \min_{y \in S(x)} \|y\|$$

and since $L(x)$ is bounded, let $(y_n)_n$ be a weakly converging sequence in $L(x)$ to y_x.

We distinguish the following two cases.

Case 1. Assume that $y_x \in K$. Since $f(x^*, x) < 0$, choose $\varepsilon > 0$ such that $f(x^*, x) \leq -\varepsilon$. Since $f(x, y_n) \leq 0$, for every n, then

$$f(x^*, y_n) \leq f(x^*, x) + f(x, y_n) \leq -\varepsilon.$$

The bifunction f being weakly sequentially lower semicontinuous in its second variable on K, we obtain

$$f(x^*, y_x) \leq \liminf_{n \to +\infty} f(x^*, y_n) \leq -\varepsilon < 0$$

which yields a contradiction.

Case 2. Assume that $y_x \notin K$. Then, there exists $y_1 \in A$, $\|y_1\| < \|y_x\|$ and $f(y_x, y_1) \leq 0$. Thus,

$$y_1 \in S(y_x) \subset S(x) \quad \text{and} \quad \|y_1\| < \|y_x\| = \min_{y \in S(x)} \|y\|$$

which is impossible.

The proof is complete. $\qquad\qquad\qquad\qquad\qquad\qquad\qquad\qquad\qquad$ $\square$

Inspired by the study of systems of variational inequalities, countable and noncountable systems of equilibrium problems have been introduced and investigated in the literature, see, for instance, [57]. Instead of finite systems of equilibrium problems as studied in [31] by means of the Ekeland variational principle, we now consider countable systems of equilibrium problems, which are usually defined in the following manner.

Let I be a countable index set which could be identified sometimes to the set $\{i \mid i \in \mathbb{N}\}$. By a system of equilibrium problems we understand the problem of finding $x^* = (x_i^*)_{i \in I} \in A$ such that

$$f_i(x^*, y_i) \geq 0 \quad \text{for all } i \in I \quad \text{and all } y_i \in A_i, \qquad \text{(SEP)}$$

where $f_i : A \times A_i \to \mathbb{R}$, $A = \prod_{i \in I} A_i$ with A_i some given set.

In the sequel, we suppose that A_i is a closed subset of a metric space (X_i, d_i), for every $i \in I$. An element of the set $A^i = \prod_{\substack{j \in I \\ j \neq i}} A_j$ will be represented by x^i; therefore, $x \in A$ can be written as $x = (x^i, x_i) \in A^i \times A_i$. The space $X = \prod_{i \in I} X_i$ will be endowed by the product topology. Without loss of generality, we may assume that d_i is bounded by 1, for every $i \in I$. The distance d on X defined by

$$d(x, y) = \sum_{i \in I} \frac{1}{2^i} d_i(x_i, y_i) \quad \text{for every} \quad x = (x_i)_{i \in I}, y = (y_i)_{i \in I} \in X$$

is a complete metric compatible with the topology of X. Thus, the space (X, d) is a complete metric space.

The following result is the Ekeland variational principle for countable systems of equilibrium problems defined on complete metric spaces. It generalizes Theorem A.3 stated for finite systems of equilibrium problems under the setting of the Euclidean space $\mathbb{R}^n$.

Theorem 6.10. *Let A_i be a nonempty closed subset of a complete metric space (X_i, d_i), for every $i \in I$, and assume that the following conditions hold:*

1. $f_i(x, x_i) = 0$, *for every $i \in I$ and every $x = (x^i, x_i) \in A$;*
2. $f_i(z, x_i) \leq f_i(z, y_i) + f_i(y, x_i)$, *for every $i \in I$, every x_i, $y_i \in A_i$, and every $y, z \in A$ such that $y = (y^i, y_i)$;*
3. f_i *is lower bounded and lower semicontinuous in its second variable, for every $i \in I$.*

Then, for every $\varepsilon > 0$ and for every $x^0 = (x_i^0)_{i \in I} \in A$, there exists $x^* = (x_i^*)_{i \in I} \in A$ such that for each $i \in I$, we have

$$\begin{cases} f_i(x^0, x_i^*) + \varepsilon d_i(x_i^0, x_i^*) \leq 0, \\ f_i(x^*, x_i) + \varepsilon d_i(x_i^* - x_i) > 0, \quad \forall x_i \in A_i, \quad x_i \neq x_i^*. \end{cases}$$

Proof. By replacing f by $\frac{1}{\varepsilon} f$, we may assume without loss of generality that $\varepsilon = 1$. Let $i \in I$ be arbitrary fixed, and for every $x = (x_i)_{i \in I} \in A$, we set

$$F_i(x) = \{y_i \in A_i \mid f_i(x, y_i) + d_i(x_i, y_i) \leq 0\}.$$

Clearly, these subsets are closed and nonempty since $x_i \in F_i(x)$, for every $i \in I$. In addition, if $y_i \in F_i(x)$, for some $x \in A$, $y_i \in A_i$ and $i \in I$, then $F_i(y) \subset F_i(x)$, for every $y = (y^i, y_i) \in A$. Indeed, suppose these conditions hold and let $z = (z_i)_{i \in I} \in F_i(y)$. Then, we have

$$f_i(x, y_i) + d_i(x_i, y_i) \leq 0 \quad \text{and} \quad f_i(y, z_i) + d_i(y_i, z_i) \leq 0.$$

It follows by addition that

$$f_i(x, z_i) + d_i(x_i, z_i) \le f_i(x, y_i) + f_i(y, z_i) + d_i(x_i, y_i) + d_i(y_i, z_i) \le 0$$

and then, $z \in F_i(x)$.

For every $x \in A$, define now

$$v_i(x) = \inf_{z_i \in F_i(x)} f_i(x, z_i)$$

which is finite since f_i is lower bounded in its second variable, for every $i \in I$.

For every $z_i \in F_i(x)$, we have

$$d(x_i, z_i) \le -f_i(x, z_i) \le - \inf_{z_i \in F_i(x)} f_i(x, z_i) = -v_i(x).$$

It follows that $\delta(F_i(x)) \le -2v_i(x)$, for every $i \in I$ and every $x \in A$, where $\delta(S)$ stands for the diameter of the set S.

Fix now $x^0 = (x_i^0)_{i \in I} \in A$ and choose for each $i \in I$ an element $x_i^1 \in F_i(x^0)$ such that

$$f_i(x^0, x_i^1) \le v_i(x^0) + 2^{-1}.$$

Put $x^1 = (x_i^1)_{i \in I} \in A$ and for each $i \in I$ an element $x_i^2 \in F_i(x^0)$ such that

$$f_i(x^1, x_i^2) \le v_i(x^1) + 2^{-2}.$$

Put $x^2 = (x_i^2)_{i \in I} \in A$. Proceeding by induction, we construct a sequence $(x^n)_n$ in A such that $x_i^{n+1} \in F_i(x^n)$ and

$$f_i(x^n, x_i^{n+1}) \le v_i(x^n) + 2^{-(n+1)}, \quad \text{for every} \quad i \in I \quad \text{and every} \quad n \in \mathbb{N}.$$

Note that

$$
\begin{aligned}
v_i(x^{n+1}) &= \inf_{z_i \in F_i(x^{n+1})} f_i(x^{n+1}, z_i) \\
&\ge \inf_{z_i \in F_i(x^n)} f_i(x^{n+1}, z_i) \\
&\ge \inf_{z_i \in F_i(x^n)} \left(f_i(x^n, z_i) - f_i(x^n, x_i^{n+1}) \right) \\
&= \inf_{z_i \in F_i(x^n)} f_i(x^n, z_i) - f_i(x^n, x_i^{n+1}) \\
&= v_i(x^n) - f_i(x^n, x_i^{n+1})
\end{aligned}
$$

which yields

$$v_i\left(x^{n+1}\right) \geq v_i\left(x^n\right) - f_i\left(x^n, x_i^{n+1}\right)$$
$$\geq v_i\left(x^n\right) - \left(v_i\left(x^n\right) + 2^{-(n+1)}\right).$$

It follows that $v_i\left(x^{n+1}\right) \geq -2^{-(n+1)}$ and then,

$$\delta\left(F_i\left(x^n\right)\right) \leq -2v_i\left(x^n\right) \leq 2 \times 2^{-n}.$$

The sequence $(F_i\left(x^n\right))_n$ being a decreasing sequence of closed subsets of the complete metric space (E_i, d_i) with diameter tending to zero, then for every $i \in I$, there exists $x_i^* \in A_i$ such that

$$\bigcap_{n \in \mathbb{N}} \delta\left(F_i\left(x^n\right)\right) = \left\{x_i^*\right\}.$$

Put $x^* = \left(x_i^*\right)_{i \in I} \in A$. For every $i \in I$, since $x_i^* \in F_i\left(x^0\right)$, then

$$f_i\left(x^0, x_i^*\right) + d_i\left(x_i^0, x_i^*\right) \leq 0.$$

On the other hand, since $x_i^* \in F_i\left(x^n\right)$, then $F_i\left(x^*\right) \subset F_i\left(x^n\right)$, for every n and then $F_i\left(x^*\right) = \left\{x_i^*\right\}$, for every $i \in I$.

Now, if $x_i \in A_i$ is such that $x_i \neq x_i^*$, then $x_i \notin F_i\left(x^*\right)$. It follows that

$$f_i\left(x^*, x_i\right) + d_i\left(x_i^*, x_i\right) > 0$$

which completes the proof. $\qquad\square$

When X_i is replaced by a real Banach space E_i, for every $i \in I$, we denote by $\|.\|_i$ the norm of E_i and by d_i its associate distance. As before, we may assume without loss of generality that each d_i is a bounded metric on E_i, for every $i \in I$. The distance d defined on $E = \prod_{i \in I} E_i$ as above makes E a real complete metric topological vector space. Note that the distance d cannot be induced by a norm since I is infinite. In this case weak sequential compactness and weak compactness need not coincide on E.

In the sequel, E will be endowed with the product of the weak topologies of E_i denoted by σ.

The following result guarantees the existence of solutions to countable systems of equilibrium problems in the weakly compact case. It is also a generalization of Proposition 6.4.

Proposition 6.5. *Let A_i be a nonempty weakly closed subset of a real Banach space E_i and $f_i : A \times A_i \to \mathbb{R}$, for every $i \in I$. Assume the following conditions hold:*

1. $f_i(x, x_i) = 0$, for every $i \in I$ and every $x = (x^i, x_i) \in A$;
2. $f_i(z, x_i) \le f_i(z, y_i) + f_i(y, x_i)$, for every $i \in I$, every $x_i, y_i \in A_i$, and every $y, z \in A$ such that $y = (y^i, y_i)$;
3. f_i is lower bounded and lower semicontinuous in its second variable, for every $i \in I$;
4. f_i is sequentially upper semicontinuous in its first variable with respect to the topology σ, for every $i \in I$;
5. A is sequentially compact subset of E with respect to the topology σ.

Then, the system of equilibrium problems (SEP) has a solution.

Proof. By Theorem 6.10, for every $n \in \mathbb{N}^*$, let $x^n = (x_i^n)_{i \in I} \in A$ be a $\frac{1}{n}$-solution of the system of equilibrium problems (SEP). Therefore

$$f_i(x^n, y_i) \ge -\frac{1}{n}\|x_i^n - y_i\|_i \quad \forall y_i \in A_i.$$

Since A is sequentially compact subset of E with respect to the topology σ, then the sequence $(x^n)_n$ has a converging subsequence $(x^{n_k})_k$ to some $x^* = (x_i^*)_{i \in I} \in A$ with respect to the topology σ. It follows that the subsequence $(x_i^{n_k})_k$ is weakly converging to $x_i^* \in A_i$, for every $i \in I$. Since f_i is sequentially upper semicontinuous in its first variable on A with respect to the topology σ, for every $i \in I$, we have

$$f_i(x^*, y_i) \ge \limsup_{k \to +\infty} f_i(x^{n_k}, y_i)$$

$$\ge \limsup_{k \to +\infty} \left(-\frac{1}{n_k}\|x_i^{n_k} - y_i\|\right) = 0 \quad \forall i \in I, \quad \forall y_i \in A.$$

This means that x^* is a solution to the system of equilibrium problems (SEP). □

The following result establishes a sufficient condition for the existence of solutions to countable systems of equilibrium problems in the nonweakly compact case.

Theorem 6.11. *Let A_i be a nonempty weakly closed subset of a real reflexive Banach space E_i and $f_i : A \times A_i \to \mathbb{R}$, for every $i \in I$. Assume that the following conditions hold:*

1. $f_i(x, x_i) = 0$, for every $i \in I$ and every $x = (x^i, x_i) \in A$;
2. $f_i(z, x_i) \le f_i(z, y_i) + f_i(y, x_i)$, for every $i \in I$, every $x_i, y_i \in A_i$, and every $y, z \in A$ such that $y = (y^i, y_i)$;
3. there exists a nonempty closed subset K_i of A_i for every $i \in I$, such that

$$\text{for every} \quad x = (x^i, x_j) \in A \quad \text{with} \quad x_j \notin K_j, \quad \text{for some} \quad j \in I,$$

$$\text{there exists} \quad y_j \in A_j \quad \text{such that} \quad \|y_j\| < \|x_j\| \quad \text{and} \quad f_j(x, y_j) \le 0;$$

4. f_i is weakly sequentially lower semicontinuous in its second variable on K_i, for every $i \in I$;

5. the restriction of f_i on $\left(\prod_{i \in I} K_i \right) \times K_i$ is lower bounded in its second variable, for every $i \in I$;

6. the restriction of f_i on $\left(\prod_{i \in I} K_i \right) \times K_i$ is sequentially upper semicontinuous in its first variable with respect to the topology σ, for every $i \in I$;

7. The subset $\prod_{i \in I} K_i$ is sequentially compact subset of E with respect to the topology σ.

Then, the system of equilibrium problems (SEP) has a solution.

Proof. For every $x = \left(x^i, x_i \right) \in A$ and every $i \in I$, define the subset

$$L_i (x) = \{ y_i \in A_i \mid \| y_i \| \leq \| x_i \|, \, f_i (x, y_i) \leq 0 \},$$

and put $S_i (x)) = cl_{A_i} (L_i (x))$, where the closure is taken with respect to the weak topology of A_i. By the same argument as in the proof of Theorem 6.9, we have the following properties:

1. The subset $S_i (x)$ is nonempty, for every $x \in A$ and every $i \in I$.
2. The subset $S_i (x))$ is weakly compact, for every $x \in A$ and every $i \in I$.
3. For every $i \in I$ and every $x = \left(x^i, x_i \right), \, y = \left(y^i, y_i \right) \in A$, if $y_i \in S_i (x)$, then $S_i (y) \subset S_i (x)$.

On the other hand, the restrictions of f_i on $\left(\prod_{i \in I} K_i \right) \times K_i$, for every $i \in I$ respectively, satisfy all the conditions of Proposition 6.5 and therefore, there exists $x^* = \left(x_1^*, \dots, x_m^* \right) \in \prod_{i \in I} K_i$ such that

$$f_i \left(x^*, y_i \right) \geq 0 \quad \text{for all} \quad i \in I \quad \text{and all} \quad y_i \in K_i.$$

Suppose that x^* is not a solution of the equilibrium problem (SEP) and let $x_j \in A_j$ be such that $f_j \left(x^*, x_j \right) < 0$, for some $j \in I$. Let $x^j \in A^j$ be arbitrary and put $x = \left(x^j, x_j \right) \in A$. Since $S_j (x)$ is nonempty weakly compact subset, then the norm attains its lower bound on $S_j (x)$. Let $y (x)_j \in S_j (x)$ be such that

$$\| y (x)_j \| = \min_{y_j \in S_j (x)} \| y_j \|$$

and since $L_j (x)$ is bounded, let $(y_n)_n$ be a weakly converging sequence in $L_j (x)$ to $y (x)_j$.

We distinguish the following two distinct situations.

Case 1. Assume that $y (x)_j \in K_j$. Since $f_j \left(x^*, x_j \right) < 0$, choose $\varepsilon > 0$ such that $f_j \left(x^*, x_j \right) \leq -\varepsilon$. Since $f_j (x, y_n) \leq 0$, for every n, then

$$f_j \left(x^*, y_n \right) \leq f_j \left(x^*, x_j \right) + f_j (x, y_n) \leq -\varepsilon.$$

The bifunction f_j being weakly sequentially lower semicontinuous in its second variable on K_j, we obtain

$$f_j\left(x^*, y(x)_j\right) \leq \liminf_{n \to +\infty} f_j\left(x^*, y_n\right) \leq -\varepsilon < 0$$

which yields a contradiction.

Case 2. Assume that $y(x)_j \notin K_j$. Let $y^j \in A^j$ be arbitrary and put $y_x = \left(y^j, y(x)_j\right) \in A$. Then, there exists $y_j \in A_j$, $\|y_j\| < \|y(x)_j\|$ and $f_j\left(y_x, y_j\right) \leq 0$. Thus,

$$y_j \in S_j\left(y_x\right) \subset S_j(x) \quad \text{and} \quad \|y_j\| < \|y(x)_j\| = \min_{y_j \in S_j(x)} \|y_j\|$$

which is impossible.

The proof is complete. $\qquad\qquad\qquad\qquad\qquad\qquad\qquad\qquad\qquad\quad\square$

6.2 METRIC REGULARITY, LINEAR OPENNESS AND AUBIN PROPERTY

The aim of this section is to study some regularity properties of the so-called *diagonal subdifferential operator* associated to the equilibrium problem. Ekeland's variational principle will play an important role in proving these properties. The regularity of the diagonal subdifferential operator will provide sensitivity results on parametric equilibrium problems, which will be discussed in the next chapter.

Let E_1, E_2 be metric spaces, and $T : E_1 \rightrightarrows E_2$ be a set-valued mapping. Recall that in Chapter 1 we denoted by $\text{gph}(T)$ the graph of T defined as

$$\text{gph}(T) := \{(x, y) \in E_1 \times E_2 : y \in T(x)\}.$$

Consider the inverse mapping $T^{-1} : E_2 \rightrightarrows E_1$ defined by $T^{-1}(y) := \{x \in E_1 : y \in T(x)\}$. Note that $T^{-1}(y)$ corresponds to the lower inverse of the singleton $B := \{y\}$ as defined in Chapter 1. The open ball centered at $\bar{x}$ with radius r, will be denoted by $B(\bar{x}, r)$ and its closure with $\bar{B}(\bar{x}, r)$. For any subsets A, B of a metric space E consider the excess functional

$$e(A, B) := \sup_{a \in A} d(a, B) = \sup_{a \in A} \inf_{b \in B} d(a, b),$$

under the convention $e(\emptyset, B) := 0$, and $e(A, \emptyset) := +\infty$, for $A \neq \emptyset$.

In the following we recall some notions related to metric regularity of mappings (see, for instance, [67] and [90]). The set-valued mapping T

(i) is *globally metrically regular* if there exists a positive k such that, for all $x \in E_1$, $y \in E_2$

$$d(x, T^{-1}(y)) \leq k d(y, T(x)); \qquad\qquad (6.16)$$

(ii) is *metrically regular* around $(\bar{x}, \bar{y}) \in \mathrm{gph}(T)$ if there is a positive constant k along with a neighborhood $\mathcal{U}$ of $\bar{x}$ and a neighborhood $\mathcal{V}$ of $\bar{y}$ such that (6.16) holds for all $x \in \mathcal{U}$ and $y \in \mathcal{V}$;

(iii) satisfies the *Aubin property* around $(\bar{x}, \bar{y})$ if there exist a positive k, and neighborhoods $\mathcal{U}$ of $\bar{x}$ and $\mathcal{V}$ of $\bar{y}$ such that

$$e(T(x) \cap \mathcal{V}, T(x')) \le kd(x, x'), \quad \forall x, x' \in \mathcal{U}.$$

Furthermore, we recall also some of the at-point properties: the set-valued mapping T is said to be

(iv) *metrically subregular* at $(\bar{x}, \bar{y}) \in \mathrm{gph}(T)$ if there is a positive constant k along with a neighborhood $\mathcal{U}$ of $\bar{x}$ such that

$$d(x, T^{-1}(\bar{y})) \le kd(\bar{y}, T(x)), \quad \forall x \in \mathcal{U}; \tag{6.17}$$

(v) *strongly metrically subregular* at $(\bar{x}, \bar{y}) \in \mathrm{gph}(T)$ if there is a positive constant k along with a neighborhood $\mathcal{U}$ of $\bar{x}$ such that

$$d(x, \bar{x}) \le kd(\bar{y}, T(x)), \quad \forall x \in \mathcal{U}; \tag{6.18}$$

(vi) *calm* at $(\bar{x}, \bar{y}) \in \mathrm{gph}(T)$ if there exist a positive k, and neighborhoods $\mathcal{U} = \mathcal{U}(\bar{x})$, $\mathcal{V} = \mathcal{V}(\bar{y})$ such that

$$e(T(x) \cap \mathcal{V}, T(\bar{x})) \le kd(x, \bar{x}), \quad \forall x \in \mathcal{U}.$$

Note that the global metric regularity of T is equivalent to the openness at linear rate k, i.e., for every $(x, y) \in \mathrm{gph}(T)$,

$$B(y, r) \subseteq T(B(x, kr)), \quad \forall r > 0.$$

In addition, the metric subregularity of T at $(\bar{x}, \bar{y})$ is equivalent to the calmness of T^{-1} at $(\bar{y}, \bar{x})$ (see, for instance, Proposition 2.7 in [18]); in particular, if T is strongly metrically subregular at $(\bar{x}, \bar{y})$, then $T^{-1}(\bar{y}) \cap \mathcal{U} = \{\bar{x}\}$.

The results of this section have been established by Bianchi, Kassay, and Pini in [37].

6.2.1 The Diagonal Subdifferential Operator Associated to an Equilibrium Bifunction

In the sequel we will denote by X a Banach space with X^* its dual space, and by K a nonempty, closed, and convex subset of X. Given a bifunction $f : K \times K \to \mathbb{R}$ such that $f(x, x) = 0$ for all $x \in K$, let us denote by $A^f : X \rightrightarrows X^*$ the following operator (see, for instance, [87]):

$$A^f(x) := \begin{cases} \{x^* \in X^* : f(x, y) \ge \langle x^*, y - x \rangle, \forall y \in K\}, & x \in K \\ \emptyset, & x \in X \setminus K. \end{cases}$$

Let us consider the bifunction $\widehat{f} : K \times X \to \mathbb{R} \cup \{+\infty\}$ obtained by extending in a standard way the bifunction f as follows:

$$\widehat{f}(x, y) := \begin{cases} f(x, y) & y \in K \\ +\infty & y \notin K. \end{cases} \qquad (6.19)$$

Thus, $A^f(x) = \partial \widehat{f}(x, \cdot)(x)$, where ∂ denotes the subdifferential operator usually considered in the convex analysis setting. For this reason, by abuse of language, we refer to the set-valued map A^f as a *diagonal subdifferential operator* of f. In particular, A^f has closed and convex values.

Observe that the equilibrium problem (EP) and the operator A^f are strongly related: $\bar{x} \in K$ is a solution of (EP) if and only if $0 \in A^f(\bar{x})$.

The bifunction f is said to be *cyclically monotone* if

$$\sum_{i=1}^{n} f(x_i, x_{i+1}) \leq 0, \quad \forall n \in \mathbb{N}, \ \forall x_1, \ldots, x_n, x_{n+1} \in K, \ x_{n+1} = x_1.$$

In particular, any cyclically monotone bifunction is *monotone*, i.e., $f(x, y) + f(y, x) \leq 0$, for all $x, y \in K$.

Recall that f satisfies the *triangle inequality* on $K \times K$ if

$$f(x, y) \leq f(x, z) + f(z, y), \qquad \forall x, y, z \in K. \qquad (6.20)$$

6.2.2 Metric Regularity of the Diagonal Subdifferential Operator

The results of this subsection deal with the metric regularity of A^f around a point of its graph. Let us first recall a well-known result concerning the subdifferential of the sum of two convex functions.

Lemma 6.3. (Moreau-Rockafellar) *Let $f, g : X \to \mathbb{R} \cup \{+\infty\}$ be two proper, lower semicontinuous and convex functions such that $\operatorname{int} \operatorname{dom} f \cap \operatorname{dom} g \neq \emptyset$. Then, for all $x \in X$, $\partial(f + g)(x) = \partial f(x) + \partial g(x)$.*

Let $f : K \times K \to \mathbb{R}$ be a bifunction such that $(\bar{x}, \bar{x}^*) \in \operatorname{gph}(A^f)$, and consider the following two properties:

(a) A^f is metrically regular around $(\bar{x}, \bar{x}^*)$, with neighborhoods $\mathcal{U} = B(\bar{x}, r)$ and $\mathcal{V} = B(\bar{x}^*, r')$, and $k > 0$;
(b) there exist $c > 0$ and $\mathcal{U}' = B(\bar{x}, \rho)$, $\mathcal{V}' = B(\bar{x}^*, \rho')$ such that $(A^f)^{-1}(x^*) \neq \emptyset$ for all $x^* \in \mathcal{V}'$, and

$$\inf_{\tilde{x} \in (A^f)^{-1}(x^*)} (f(\tilde{x}, x) - \langle x^*, x - \tilde{x} \rangle) \geq c \cdot d^2(x, (A^f)^{-1}(x^*)), \qquad (6.21)$$

for every $x \in \mathcal{U}' \cap K$, $x^* \in \mathcal{V}'$.

We start with the following results, which provide the link between properties (a) and (b):

Theorem 6.12. *Let f satisfy (a), and the following conditions:*

(i) $f(x, \cdot)$ *is convex and lsc, for every $x \in K$;*

(ii) f *satisfies the triangle inequality (6.20).*

Then f satisfies (b) with $c < 1/4k$, and $\rho = r/2$, and $\rho' = \min\{r', r/2k\}$.
Conversely, if f satisfies (b), and is α-monotone, for some $\alpha > -c$, i.e.,

$$f(x, y) + f(y, x) \le -\alpha \|x - y\|^2, \quad \forall x, y \in K,$$

then (a) holds, with $k = \frac{1}{c+\alpha}$, and $r = \rho$, $r' = \rho'$.

Proof. (a) implies (b): Note that, under the assumption of metric regularity at $(\bar{x}, \bar{x}^*)$, it follows that $(A^F)^{-1}(x^*) \ne \emptyset$ for every $x^* \in V$. In order to prove (6.21), we argue by contradiction.

Suppose that there exists $z \in \mathcal{U}' \cap K$ and $z^* \in V'$ and $\tilde{z} \in (A^F)^{-1}(z^*)$ such that

$$F(\tilde{z}, z) + \langle z^*, \tilde{z} - z \rangle < c\, d^2(z, (A^F)^{-1}(z^*)). \tag{6.22}$$

Observe that $\tilde{z}$ is a global minimizer of the lsc convex function

$$h(\cdot) := \widehat{F}(\tilde{z}, \cdot) + \langle z^*, \tilde{z} - \cdot \rangle.$$

Indeed, $h(\tilde{z}) = 0$, and

$$z^* \in A^F(\tilde{z}) \Leftrightarrow h(x) \ge 0, \quad \forall x \in X.$$

Since, from (6.22), $h(z) < c\, d^2(z, (A^F)^{-1}(z^*))$, we get that $d^2(z, (A^F)^{-1}(z^*)) > 0$.

By applying The Ekeland's Variational Principle (Theorem A.1 in Appendix A) to the function h with

$$\varepsilon := c\, d^2(z, (A^F)^{-1}(z^*)) > 0, \quad \lambda := \frac{1}{2} d(z, (A^F)^{-1}(z^*)) > 0,$$

we get the existence of $u \in K$ with $\|u - z\| \le \frac{1}{2} d(z, (A^F)^{-1}(z^*))$ such that

$$h(x) \ge h(u) - 2c\, d(z, (A^F)^{-1}(z^*)) \|x - u\|, \quad \forall x \in X.$$

Hence, u is a global minimizer of the convex function

$$h(\cdot) + 2c\, d(z, (A^F)^{-1}(z^*)) \| \cdot - u \|$$
$$= \widehat{F}(\tilde{z}, \cdot) + \langle z^*, \tilde{z} - \cdot \rangle + 2c\, d(z, (A^F)^{-1}(z^*)) \| \cdot - u \|;$$

thus,

$$0 \in \partial \left(\widehat{F}(\tilde{z}, \cdot) + \langle z^*, \tilde{z} - \cdot \rangle + 2c\, d(z, (A^F)^{-1}(z^*)) \| \cdot - u \| \right)(u).$$

Since dom $\widehat{F}(\tilde{z}, \cdot)=K$, and dom $(\langle z^*, \tilde{z} - \cdot\rangle +2c\,d(z, (A^F)^{-1}(z^*))\| \cdot -u\|)=X$, by Lemma 6.3,

$$0 \in \partial \widehat{F}(\tilde{z}, \cdot)(u) - z^* + 2c\,d(z, (A^F)^{-1}(z^*))\bar{B}(0, 1). \tag{6.23}$$

Observe that

$$\partial \widehat{F}(\tilde{z}, \cdot)(u) \subset A^F(u). \tag{6.24}$$

Indeed, fix any $u^* \in \partial \widehat{F}(\tilde{z}, \cdot)(u)$. Then $\widehat{F}(\tilde{z}, y) - \widehat{F}(\tilde{z}, u) \geq \langle u^*, y - u\rangle$, for all $y \in X$; in particular, $F(\tilde{z}, y) - F(\tilde{z}, u) \geq \langle u^*, y - u\rangle$ holds for every $y \in K$. By the triangle inequality (6.20) we have

$$F(u, y) \geq F(\tilde{z}, y) - F(\tilde{z}, u),$$

which means that $F(u, y) \geq \langle u^*, y - u\rangle$, i.e., $u^* \in A^F(u)$.

Therefore, from (6.23), there exists an element $x^* \in A^F(u)$ with

$$\|x^* - z^*\| \leq 2c\,d(z, (A^F)^{-1}(z^*)).$$

Additionally, since

$$d(z, (A^F)^{-1}(z^*)) \leq \|z - u\| + d(u, (A^F)^{-1}(z^*))$$
$$\leq \frac{1}{2}d(z, (A^F)^{-1}(z^*)) + d(u, (A^F)^{-1}(z^*)),$$

one has

$$0 < d(z, (A^F)^{-1}(z^*)) \leq 2d(u, (A^F)^{-1}(z^*));$$

hence,

$$d(z^*, A^F(u)) \leq \|x^* - z^*\| \leq 4c\,d(u, (A^F)^{-1}(z^*)). \tag{6.25}$$

Note that

$$\|u - \bar{x}\| \leq \|u - z\| + \|z - \bar{x}\|$$
$$\leq \frac{1}{2}d(z, (A^F)^{-1}(z^*)) + \frac{r}{2}$$
$$\leq \frac{1}{2}(\|z - \bar{x}\| + d(\bar{x}, (A^F)^{-1}(z^*))) + \frac{r}{2} \tag{6.26}$$
$$< \frac{3r}{4} + \frac{k}{2}d(z^*, A^F(\bar{x}))$$
$$\leq r.$$

Hence, $u \in B(\bar{x}, r)$, and we obtain, by (6.25):

$$d(z^*, A^F(u)) \leq 4c\,d(u, (A^F)^{-1}(z^*)) \leq 4ck\,d(z^*, A^F(u)) < d(z^*, A^F(u)),$$

a contradiction.

(b) implies (a): Without loss of generality, we will assume $\alpha < 0$, since α'-monotonicity implies α-monotonicity, for every $\alpha' > \alpha$. Take any $x \in \mathcal{U}$ and $x^* \in \mathcal{V}$.

If either $d(x, (A^F)^{-1}(x^*)) = 0$ or $A^F(x) = \emptyset$, there is nothing to prove. Hence suppose that $(x, x^*) \in (\mathcal{U} \cap K) \times \mathcal{V}$ such that $d(x, (A^F)^{-1}(x^*)) = \tau > 0$. Fix any $\varepsilon > 0$, and take $x_\varepsilon \in (A^F)^{-1}(x^*)$ such that

$$\|x - x_\varepsilon\| < \tau + \varepsilon.$$

From the assumptions, (6.21) implies that

$$F(x_\varepsilon, x) \geq \langle x^*, x - x_\varepsilon \rangle + c \cdot d^2(x, (A^F)^{-1}(x^*)) = \langle x^*, x - x_\varepsilon \rangle + c \cdot \tau^2. \quad (6.27)$$

Let $z^* \in A^F(x)$; then,

$$F(x, x_\varepsilon) \geq \langle z^*, x_\varepsilon - x \rangle. \quad (6.28)$$

Adding (6.27) and (6.28), from (ii) we get

$$c \cdot \tau^2 + \langle x^* - z^*, x - x_\varepsilon \rangle \leq F(x_\varepsilon, x) + F(x, x_\varepsilon) \leq -\alpha \|x - x_\varepsilon\|^2,$$

implying that

$$c \cdot \tau^2 \leq \langle z^* - x^*, x - x_\varepsilon \rangle - \alpha \|x - x_\varepsilon\|^2 < \|z^* - x^*\| \cdot (\tau + \varepsilon) - \alpha(\tau + \varepsilon)^2.$$

Taking the infimum with respect to $z^* \in A^F(x)$, and letting $\varepsilon \to 0$, we have that

$$(c + \alpha)\tau \leq d(x^*, A^F(x)).$$

This implies that (a) holds if $k = \frac{1}{c+\alpha}$. $\qquad\qquad \square$

The next example shows that the triangle inequality is an *essential* assumption in Theorem 6.12. Indeed, let $K = [-1, 1] \subset \mathbb{R}$ and consider $f : [-1, 1] \times [-1, 1] \to \mathbb{R}$ given by $f(x, y) = x(y - x)$. Then it is easy to show that

$$A^f(x) := \begin{cases} (-\infty, -1], & x = -1 \\ x, & x \in (-1, 1) \\ [1, +\infty), & x = 1. \end{cases}$$

Also,

$$(A^f)^{-1}(y) := \begin{cases} -1, & y \in (-\infty, -1] \\ y, & y \in (-1, 1) \\ 1, & y \in [1, +\infty). \end{cases}$$

Now take $\bar{x} = 0$. Then $\bar{x}^* = A^f(0) = 0$ and A^f is metrically regular around $(0, 0)$ with $\mathcal{U} = \mathcal{V} = B(0, 1)$ and $k = 1$. It is obvious that f satisfies the assumption (i) in Theorem 6.12, but not (ii) (the triangle inequality). Indeed, by taking $x = 0$, $y = 1$, $z = -1$ in (6.20) one obtains $0 \leq -2$, a contradiction. Now let us show that there is no $c > 0$ such that (b) is satisfied. An easy calculation shows that $\rho = \rho' = 1/2$, hence one obtains $\mathcal{U}' = \mathcal{V}' = B(0, 1/2)$. Thus, $\tilde{x} = x^*$ in (b) and the left-hand side of this relation vanishes, while for the right-hand side we obtain $c|x - x^*|^2$. This clearly shows that (b) cannot be satisfied for all $x, x^* \in (-1/2, 1/2)$.

6.2.3   Metric Subregularity of the Diagonal Subdifferential Operator

The results of this subsection relate the (strong) metric subregularity of A^f with the behavior of the bifunction f.

Let $f : K \times K \to \mathbb{R}$ be a bifunction such that $(\bar{x}, \bar{x}^*) \in \text{gph}(A^f)$. Let us consider the following two properties:

(a') A^f is metrically subregular at $(\bar{x}, \bar{x}^*)$, with neighborhood $\mathcal{U} = B(\bar{x}, r)$, and $k > 0$;
(b') there exists $\mathcal{U}' = B(\bar{x}, \rho)$ and $c > 0$ such that

$$f(\bar{x}, x) \geq \langle \bar{x}^*, x - \bar{x} \rangle + c\, d^2(x, (A^f)^{-1}(\bar{x}^*)) \quad \forall x \in \mathcal{U}' \cap K.$$

Theorem 6.13. *Let f satisfy (a'), and*

(i) *$f(\bar{x}, \cdot)$ is convex and lower semicontinuous;*
(ii) *f satisfies the triangle inequality (6.20) with $x = \bar{x}$.*

Then, (b') holds with $c < 1/4k$, and $\rho = \frac{2r}{3}$.

Conversely, if f satisfies (b'), and is cyclically monotone, then (a') holds, with $k = \frac{1}{c}$, and $r = \rho$.

Proof. (a') implies (b'): We can follow the same line of the proof of Theorem 6.12, by taking $\tilde{z} = \bar{x}$, $z^* = \bar{x}^*$, and noting that (6.26) becomes

$$\|u - \bar{x}\| \leq \|u - z\| + \|z - \bar{x}\| \leq \frac{1}{2}d(z, (A^f)^{-1}(\bar{x}^*)) + \|z - \bar{x}\|$$
$$\leq \frac{3}{2}\|z - \bar{x}\| < r.$$

(b') implies (a'): Fix $x \in \mathcal{U}$. If $A^f(x) = \emptyset$ there is nothing to show. Otherwise, take any $x^* \in A^f(x)$. Fix $\epsilon > 0$, and denote by x_ϵ a point in $(A^f)^{-1}(\bar{x}^*)$ such that

$$\|x - x_\epsilon\| \leq d(x, (A^f)^{-1}(\bar{x}^*)) + \epsilon. \tag{6.29}$$

By the definition of diagonal subdifferential we have that

$$f(x, x_\epsilon) \geq \langle x^*, x_\epsilon - x \rangle, \qquad f(x_\epsilon, \bar{x}) \geq \langle \bar{x}^*, \bar{x} - x_\epsilon \rangle.$$

From the inequality (6.29), (b') and the cyclic monotonicity, we have that

$$\|x^* - \bar{x}^*\|(d(x, (A^f)^{-1}(\bar{x}^*)) + \epsilon)$$
$$\geq \|x^* - \bar{x}^*\| \cdot \|x - x_\epsilon\|$$
$$\geq \langle x^*, x - x_\epsilon \rangle - \langle \bar{x}^*, x - \bar{x} \rangle - \langle \bar{x}^*, \bar{x} - x_\epsilon \rangle$$
$$\geq -f(x, x_\epsilon) - \langle \bar{x}^*, x - \bar{x} \rangle - f(x_\epsilon, \bar{x})$$
$$\geq -f(x, x_\epsilon) - f(x_\epsilon, \bar{x}) - f(\bar{x}, x) + c\,d^2(x, (A^f)^{-1}(\bar{x}^*))$$
$$\geq c\,d^2(x, (A^f)^{-1}(\bar{x}^*)).$$

By taking $\epsilon \to 0$, we get

$$c\,d^2(x, (A^f)^{-1}(\bar{x}^*)) \leq \|x^* - \bar{x}^*\| d(x, (A^f)^{-1}(\bar{x}^*)).$$

If $d(x, (A^f)^{-1}(\bar{x}^*)) = 0$, there is nothing to prove. Otherwise, we have

$$d(x, (A^f)^{-1}(\bar{x}^*)) \leq \frac{1}{c}\|x^* - \bar{x}^*\|, \quad \forall x^* \in A^f(x).$$

The assertion follows by taking the infimum with respect to $x^* \in A^f(x)$. $\quad\square$

In the following result we present two characterizations of the strong metric subregularity of the map A^f.

Let us take $(\bar{x}, \bar{x}^*) \in \text{gph}(A^f)$, and let us consider the following properties:

(a'') A^f is strongly metrically subregular at $(\bar{x}, \bar{x}^*)$ with neighborhood $\mathcal{U} = B(\bar{x}, r)$, and $k > 0$;

(b'') there exists $\mathcal{U}' = B(\bar{x}, \rho)$, and $c > 0$, such that

$$f(\bar{x}, x) \geq \langle \bar{x}^*, x - \bar{x} \rangle + c\|x - \bar{x}\|^2, \quad \forall x \in \mathcal{U}' \cap K;$$

(c'') there exists a neighborhood $\mathcal{U}'' = B(\bar{x}, \tau)$, along with a positive constant β such that

$$\langle x^* - \bar{x}^*, x - \bar{x} \rangle \geq \beta\|x - \bar{x}\|^2, \quad \forall (x, x^*) \in \text{gph}(A^f), x \in \mathcal{U}''.$$

Then the next theorem holds:

Theorem 6.14. *Let $f : K \times K \to \mathbb{R}$, and $(\bar{x}, \bar{x}^*) \in \text{gph}(A^f)$. If f satisfies (a''), and the following conditions*

(i) $f(\bar{x}, \cdot)$ *is convex and lower semicontinuous;*
(ii) f *satisfies the triangle inequality (6.20) for $x = \bar{x}$,*
then (b'') holds, with $c = 1/4k$ and $\rho = r/3$.

If (b") holds, and f satisfies the condition

$$f(x, \bar{x}) + f(\bar{x}, x) \leq -\alpha \|x - \bar{x}\|^2, \quad x \in \mathcal{U}' \cap K, \tag{6.30}$$

for some $\alpha > -c$, then f satisfies (c") with $\beta = \alpha + c$ and $\tau = \rho$.
(c") always implies (a") with $r = \tau$, and $k = 1/\beta$.

Proof. (a") $\Rightarrow$ (b"): A^f is, in particular, metrically subregular at $(\bar{x}, \bar{x}^*)$ and Theorem 6.13 implies inequality (b') in $B(\bar{x}, 2r/3)$ and $c < 1/4k$. Note that (a") and (b') both hold in $B(\bar{x}, 2r/3) \cap K$. If $(A^f)^{-1}(\bar{x}^*) = \{\bar{x}\}$, it trivially follows, with $\rho = 2r/3$, and $c < 1/4k$. Otherwise, take $z \in (A^f)^{-1}(\bar{x}^*)$, $z \neq \bar{x}$. In particular, $z \in K$. By the assumption of strong metric subregularity, $z \notin B(\bar{x}, 2r/3) \cap K$ (see the comments after (vi) in the Preliminaries), and $\|x - z\| \geq \|x - \bar{x}\|$ for any $x \in B(\bar{x}, r/3) \cap K$. Thus, $d(x, (A^f)^{-1}(\bar{x}^*)) = \|x - \bar{x}\|$ for any $x \in B(\bar{x}, r/3) \cap K$, and (b") holds for the neighborhood $\mathcal{U}' = B(\bar{x}, r/3) \cap K$, and $c < 1/4k$.

(b") $\Rightarrow$ (c"): Take $(x, x^*) \in \text{gph}(A^f)$, $x \in \mathcal{U}' \cap K$, then

$$f(x, \bar{x}) \geq \langle x^*, \bar{x} - x \rangle$$
$$f(\bar{x}, x) \geq \langle \bar{x}^*, x - \bar{x} \rangle + c\|x - \bar{x}\|^2.$$

Thus, from (6.30),

$$\langle x^*, x - \bar{x} \rangle - \langle \bar{x}^*, x - \bar{x} \rangle \geq -f(x, \bar{x}) - f(\bar{x}, x) + c\|x - \bar{x}\|^2 \geq (c + \alpha)\|x - \bar{x}\|^2,$$

and thus (c") holds with $\mathcal{U}'' = \mathcal{U}'$ and $\beta = c + \alpha$.

(c") $\Rightarrow$ (a"): For every $(x, x^*) \in \text{gph}(A^f)$, $x \in \mathcal{U}'' \setminus \{\bar{x}\}$,

$$\|x^* - \bar{x}^*\| \|x - \bar{x}\| \geq \langle x^* - \bar{x}^*, x - \bar{x} \rangle \geq \beta \|x - \bar{x}\|^2.$$

Therefore, $\|x - \bar{x}\| \leq \frac{1}{\beta} \|x^* - \bar{x}^*\|$, for every $x^* \in A^f(x)$, then

$$\|x - \bar{x}\| \leq \frac{1}{\beta} d(\bar{x}^*, A^f(x)), \quad \forall x \in \mathcal{U}'',$$

hence (a") holds for $k = 1/\beta$ and $\mathcal{U} = \mathcal{U}''$. $\qquad\square$

Chapter 7

Applications to Sensitivity of Parametric Equilibrium Problems

Contents

I can observe the game theory is applied very much in economics. Generally, it would be wise to get into the mathematics as much as seems reasonable because the economists who use more mathematics are somehow more respected than those who use less. That's the trend.

John Forbes Nash, Jr. (1928–2015)

Chapter points

- The results presented here include sensitivity analysis of parametric equilibrium problems and variational inclusions.
- Hölder continuity, calmness, and Aubin property of the solution map are derived using regularity properties of the diagonal subdifferential operator discussed in Chapter 6.
- It is developed a natural relationship between the Aubin property and the inverse of the sum of set-valued mappings.
- There are highlighted properties of set-valued pseudo-Lipschitzian mappings in order to deal with the Lipschitzian property of the inverse of the sum of two set-valued mappings.

Equilibrium Problems and Applications. https://doi.org/10.1016/B978-0-12-811029-4.00015-8

187

We shall apply the results of Chapter 6 to obtain sensitivity results concerning parametric equilibrium problems.

Let P be a metric space and K be a nonempty set. Given a parametric bifunction $F : K \times K \times P \to \mathbb{R}$, we consider the set-valued map $S : P \rightrightarrows K$ defined by

$$S(p) := \{x \in K : F(x, y, p) \geq 0, \ \forall y \in K\},$$

i.e., for any $p \in P$, $S(p)$ represents the *solution set* of the *parametric equilibrium problem*: find $\bar{x} \in K$ such that $F(\bar{x}, y, p) \geq 0, \forall y \in K$.

Given an initial value of the parameter, say $\bar{p}$, and a corresponding solution $\bar{x} \in K$, i.e., $\bar{x} \in S(\bar{p})$, it is important from both theoretical and numerical points of view to find out information on the set $S(p)$ for p close to $\bar{p}$. In other words we are interested to know the behavior of the solution set $S(p)$ when p lies in a neighborhood of $\bar{p}$. This is related to the *calmness* of the solution map at $(\bar{p}, \bar{x})$ as we will see in the sequel. Moreover, information about the distance between $S(p)$ and $S(p')$ when p and p' are arbitrary parameters in a neighborhood of $\bar{p}$ are also interesting to obtain, and this is related to the *Aubin property* of the mapping S around $(\bar{p}, \bar{x})$, which will be discussed also in this chapter. Nowadays the relationship between the Aubin property and *metric regularity* of a map on one hand, and calmness and *metric subregularity* on the other hand, are well known facts (see, for instance, [67] and the references therein).

Our aim is to provide both global and local stability results related to the solution map of a parametric equilibrium problem; in particular, sufficient conditions for Hölder continuity, as well as for Aubin property, and calmness of the solution map are provided. These results are obtained by means of regularity properties of the *diagonal subdifferential operator* associated to the equilibrium bifunction, discussed in Chapter 6.

The results of this chapter have been obtained by Bianchi, Kassay, and Pini [37], and Alleche and Rădulescu [9].

7.1 PRELIMINARIES ON GENERALIZED EQUATIONS

In the sequel we will denote by X a Banach space, with X^* its dual space, and by K a nonempty, closed, and convex subset of X. Given a set of parameters P, in what follows we will consider a parametric bifunction $F : K \times K \times P \to \mathbb{R}$, satisfying the conditions:

A.1 $F(x, x, p) = 0$, for every $x \in K$, $p \in P$;

A.2 $F(x, \cdot, p)$ is convex and lower semicontinuous, for every $x \in K$, $p \in P$.

As in Chapter 6, we will denote by $\widehat{F}$ the standard extension of F to $K \times X \times P$ (see (6.19)).

For every $p \in P$, let us denote by $A_p^F : X \rightrightarrows X^*$ the diagonal subdifferential operator for the marginal bifunction $F(\cdot, \cdot, p)$, i.e.,

$$A_p^F(x) := \begin{cases} \{x^* \in X^* : F(x, y, p) \geq \langle x^*, y - x \rangle, \quad \forall y \in K\}, & x \in K \\ \emptyset, & x \in X \setminus K. \end{cases}$$

Then the problem (EP_p, K) can be equivalently formulated in terms of an inclusion involving the operator A_p^F as follows: $\bar{x}$ is a solution of (EP_p, K) if and only if $0 \in A_p^F(\bar{x})$, namely, $\bar{x} \in (A_p^F)^{-1}(0)$. Our aim is to provide regularity result for the solution map like Hölder continuity, calmness, and Aubin property. To this purpose, we briefly recall some basic facts about parametric generalized equations.

Let X, P be metric spaces, and Y be a linear metric space. For any set-valued map $H : X \times P \rightrightarrows Y$, we denote by $S : P \rightrightarrows X$ the solution map of the inclusion $0 \in H(x, p)$, i.e.,

$$S(p) := \{x \in X : 0 \in H(x, p)\} = (H(\cdot, p))^{-1}(0).$$

In the following, we will assume that the solution map is defined on the whole P.

In order to deal with a set-valued map H depending on more than one variable, we give the partial notions of metric regularity, Aubin property, and calmness (see, for instance, [69]). Recall from Chapter 6 that, for any subsets A, B of a metric space, the excess functional is defined as

$$e(A, B) := \sup_{a \in A} d(a, B) = \sup_{a \in A} \inf_{b \in B} d(a, b),$$

under the convention $e(\emptyset, B) := 0$, and $e(A, \emptyset) := +\infty$, for $A \neq \emptyset$.

Definition 7.1. Let $H : X \times P \rightrightarrows Y$, and consider $(\bar{x}, \bar{p}, 0) \in \mathrm{gph}(H)$. Denote by $\mathcal{U}$, $\mathcal{V}$, $\mathcal{W}$, neighborhoods of $\bar{x}$, $\bar{p}$, 0, respectively, and by H_p the marginal map such that $H_p(x) = H(x, p)$, for every $x \in X$ and $p \in P$.

(i) H is said to be metrically regular with respect to x, uniformly with respect to p, around $(\bar{x}, \bar{p}, 0)$ if there exist $k > 0$ and $\mathcal{U}$, $\mathcal{V}$, $\mathcal{W}$ such that

$$d(x, H_p^{-1}(y)) \leq k d(y, H_p(x)), \qquad \forall (x, p, y) \in \mathcal{U} \times \mathcal{V} \times \mathcal{W}; \quad (7.1)$$

(ii) H is said to have the Aubin property with respect to x, uniformly with respect to p, around $(\bar{x}, \bar{p}, 0)$ if there exist $k > 0$ and $\mathcal{U}$, $\mathcal{V}$, $\mathcal{W}$ such that

$$e(H_p(x) \cap \mathcal{W}, H_p(x')) \leq k d(x, x'), \qquad \forall x, x' \in \mathcal{U}, \ p \in \mathcal{V}; \quad (7.2)$$

(iii) H is said to be calm with respect to x, uniformly with respect to p, at $(\bar{x}, \bar{p}, 0)$ if there exist $k > 0$ and $\mathcal{U}$, $\mathcal{V}$, $\mathcal{W}$ such that

$$e(H_p(x) \cap \mathcal{W}, H_p(\bar{x})) \leq k d(x, \bar{x}), \qquad \forall x \in \mathcal{U}, \ p \in \mathcal{V}. \quad (7.3)$$

Similar definitions can be given with respect to p, uniformly with respect to x, by considering the marginal map H_x. Likewise the metric regularity of a map at a point $(\bar{x}, \bar{y})$ is equivalent to the Aubin property of the inverse map at $(\bar{y}, \bar{x})$, similar results can be proved for the partial notions given above.

In the next propositions we recall some sufficient conditions on H entailing suitable sensitivity properties of the solution map.

Proposition 7.1. ([36]) *Suppose that the set-valued map $H : X \times P \rightrightarrows Y$ satisfies the following conditions:*

(i) *there exists $k, \gamma > 0$ such that $e(H(x, p), H(x, p')) \leq kd_P^\gamma(p, p')$, for every $x \in X$, for every $p, p' \in P$;*

(ii) *$H(\cdot, p)$ is globally metrically regular with constant k', uniformly with respect to $p \in P$.*

Then $e(S(p), S(p')) \leq kk'd_P^\gamma(p, p')$, for all $p, p' \in P$.

Proposition 7.2. ([69]) *Let $H : X \times P \rightrightarrows Y$, and consider $(\bar{x}, \bar{p}, 0) \in \text{gph}(H)$. Suppose that the following conditions are satisfied:*

(i) *H has the Aubin property with respect to p, uniformly with respect to x, around $(\bar{x}, \bar{p}, 0)$, with constant k';*

(ii) *H is metrically regular with respect to x, uniformly with respect to p, around $(\bar{x}, \bar{p}, 0)$, with constant k.*

Then S has the Aubin property around $(\bar{p}, \bar{x})$ with constant kk'.

A pointwise version of the propositions above can be proved (see, for instance, Th. 3.1 in [18]):

Proposition 7.3. *Let $\bar{p} \in P$ and $\bar{x} \in X$ be fixed such that $\bar{x} \in S(\bar{p})$. Suppose that $\mathcal{U}(\bar{p})$, $\mathcal{U}(\bar{x})$ and $\mathcal{V}$ are neighborhoods of $\bar{p}$, $\bar{x}$ and 0 in P, X, and Y respectively, satisfying*

(i) *$H(x, \cdot)$ is calm with respect to p uniformly with respect to x at $(\bar{x}, \bar{p}, 0)$, with constant k, and neighborhoods $\mathcal{U}(\bar{p})$, $\mathcal{V}$, for all $x \in \mathcal{U}(\bar{x})$;*

(ii) *$H(\cdot, \bar{p})$ is metrically subregular at $(\bar{x}, 0)$ with constant k', and neighborhood $\mathcal{U}(\bar{x})$.*

Then the map $S : P \rightrightarrows X$ is calm at $(\bar{p}, \bar{x})$ with constant kk', and neighborhoods $\mathcal{U}(\bar{p})$ and $\mathcal{U}(\bar{x})$, i.e.,

$$e(S(p) \cap \mathcal{U}(\bar{x}), S(\bar{p})) \leq kk'd_P(p, \bar{p}), \qquad \forall p \in \mathcal{U}(\bar{p}). \tag{7.4}$$

7.2 HÖLDER CONTINUITY OF THE SOLUTION MAP

In this section we find out conditions on F in order to apply Proposition 7.1 to the set-valued map H, where $H(x, p) = A_p^F(x)$. We focus, first, on condition (i).

Proposition 7.4. *Consider $F : K \times K \times P \to \mathbb{R}$ satisfying assumptions A.1–A.2 and, in addition,*

A.3 *There exist positive k, γ such that*

$$|F(x, y, p) - F(x, y, p')| \le kd^\gamma(p, p')\|x - y\|, \quad \forall x, y \in K, \ p, p' \in P.$$

Then $e(A_p^F(x), A_{p'}^F(x)) \le kd^\gamma(p, p')$, for every $x \in K$, $p, p' \in P$.

Proof. If $A_p^F(x) = \emptyset$ there is nothing to prove. Otherwise, let $x^* \in A_p^F(x)$; then, from the assumptions,

$$F(x, y, p') \ge F(x, y, p) - kd^\gamma(p, p')\|x - y\|$$
$$\ge \langle x^*, y - x \rangle - kd^\gamma(p, p')\|x - y\|;$$

in particular,

$$F(x, y, p') + kd^\gamma(p, p')\|x - y\| \ge \langle x^*, y - x \rangle, \quad \forall y \in K,$$

i.e., $x^* \in \partial(\widehat{F}(x, \cdot, p') + kd^\gamma(p, p')\|x - \cdot\|)(x)$. From Lemma 6.3, we get that $x^* \in A_{p'}^F(x) + \overline{B}(0, kd^\gamma(p, p'))$, i.e., $e(A_p^F(x), A_{p'}^F(x)) \le kd^\gamma(p, p')$. $\square$

A particular case where the assumptions of Proposition 7.4 are satisfied is provided by

$$F(x, y, p) := h(x, y) + \langle g(p), y - x \rangle,$$

where $h(x, x) = 0$, $h(x, \cdot)$ is convex and lower semicontinuous for every $x \in K$, and $g : P \to X^*$ is Hölder continuous of order γ and constant k.

In the next example we provide a class of parametric bifunctions satisfying assumption (i) in Proposition 7.1:

Example 7.1. Take $F : \mathbb{R}^n \times \mathbb{R}^n \times \mathbb{R}^m \to \mathbb{R}$, such that $F \in C^2$ and

$$\left| \frac{\partial^2}{\partial p_i \partial y_j} F(x, \cdot, \cdot)(x, p) \right| \le k, \quad \forall i = 1, \dots, m, \ j = 1, \dots, n,$$

for every $x \in \mathbb{R}^n$, $p \in \mathbb{R}^m$. In this case, $A_p^F(x) = \{\nabla F(x, \cdot, p)(x)\}$, and

$$\|\nabla F(x, \cdot, p)(x) - \nabla F(x, \cdot, p')(x)\|$$
$$\le nm \sup_{i,j} \left| \frac{\partial^2}{\partial p_i \partial y_j} F(x, \cdot, \cdot)(x, p) \right| \cdot \|p - p'\| \le k\|p - p'\|.$$

Conditions leading to (ii) in Proposition 7.1 can be provided via suitable monotonicity assumptions on the diagonal subdifferential operator A^F. Let us first state the following result (for a similar result of local type, see [129], Lemma 3.3). In the rest of this subsection we suppose that the Banach space X is reflexive.

Lemma 7.1. *Let* $T : X \rightrightarrows X^*$ *be a maximal monotone operator satisfying for some positive* α *the monotonicity condition:*

$$\langle v - v', x - x' \rangle \geq \alpha \|x - x'\|^2, \qquad \forall x, x' \in \mathrm{dom}(T), \forall v \in T(x), v' \in T(x').$$
$$(7.5)$$

Then T *is surjective, and globally metrically regular with constant* $1/\alpha$.

Proof. Under the assumptions, the operator T is weakly coercive (i.e., $\inf_{x^* \in T(x)} \|x^*\| \to +\infty$ as $\|x\| \to +\infty$), therefore it is surjective (see Theorem 2.17 in [89]). T is also trivially one-to-one, that is, $T(x) \cap T(x') = \emptyset$ if $x \neq x'$. This entails that T^{-1} is defined and single-valued on the whole X^*.

Let us now show that T is globally metrically regular with constant $1/\alpha$. Let $(x_0, v_0) \in \mathrm{gph}(T)$ and r be a positive real number. Take any $v \in B(v_0, r)$; then, by the one-to-one property of T, there exists a unique $x \in X$ such that $v \in T(x)$. By (7.5) we argue that

$$\|v - v_0\| \geq \alpha \|x - x_0\|.$$

In particular, $x \in B(x_0, r/\alpha)$, thereby proving that T is open at linear rate $1/\alpha$. Since this is equivalent to the global metric regularity, the proof is complete. $\square$

Taking into account the previous results, we can prove the mentioned Hölder continuity of the solution map:

Theorem 7.1. *Let* $F : K \times K \times P \to \mathbb{R}$ *be a parametric bifunction satisfying conditions A.1–A.3. Suppose, in addition, that*

A.4 A_p^F *is maximal monotone for every* $p \in P$, *and satisfies* (7.5), *for some positive* α, *uniformly with respect to* $p \in P$.

Then the solution map S *is single-valued and Hölder continuous with constant* k/α, *i.e.,*

$$\|S(p) - S(p')\| \leq \frac{k}{\alpha} d_P^\gamma(p, p'), \qquad \forall p, p' \in P.$$

Proof. Fix any $p \in P$. Then, by Lemma 7.1, the mapping $H(\cdot, p) = A_p^F$ is globally metrically regular with constant $1/\alpha$, uniformly, with respect to $p \in P$. Moreover, by Proposition 7.4, $e(A_p^F(x), A_{p'}^F(x)) \leq k d_P^\gamma(p, p')$, for every $x \in X$, and every $p, p' \in P$. Then the assertion follows by Proposition 7.1, by noting that, from the assumption A.4, one gets the single-valuedness of the solution map. $\square$

Remark 7.1. In Anh-Khanh-Tam [13], Theorem 3.3, the authors provided conditions on F entailing the Hölder continuity of the solution of the equilibrium problem with respect to the parameter. In the example below, that will be given without parameters for simplicity, we show that Theorem 3.3 in [13] does not include our Theorem 7.1.

Let $X = \mathbb{R}$, $K = [0, +\infty)$ and consider the bifunction $F : K \times K \to \mathbb{R}$ given by

$$F(x, y) := \begin{cases} y^2 - x^2, & y > \frac{x}{2} \\ -\frac{3x^2}{4}, & 0 \le y \le \frac{x}{2}. \end{cases}$$

We show that all the requirements needed in our case are satisfied, but conditions (i)–(ii) of Theorem 3.3 in [13] fail. A.1 is trivial. Observe that $F(x, \cdot)$ is convex and lower semicontinuous for every $x \in K$, i.e., A.2 holds. For A.4 observe that, for every $x \in K$,

$$\partial \widehat{F}(x, \cdot)(x) = \begin{cases} 2x, & x > 0 \\ \{t \in \mathbb{R} : t \le 0\}, & x = 0, \end{cases}$$

which means that A_p^F is maximal monotone and α-strongly monotone with $\alpha = 2$.

On the other hand, let $x = 2$, and observe that $F(2, \cdot)$ is not $h.\beta$-strongly convexlike for every $h, \beta > 0$ (see Definition 2.2 in [65]). Indeed, taking $y_1 = \frac{1}{4}$, $y_2 = \frac{3}{4}$ and $t = \frac{1}{2}$, there is no $z \in K$ such that

$$F(2, z) \le \frac{1}{2} F(2, y_1) + \frac{1}{2} F(2, y_2) - \frac{h}{4} \frac{1}{2^\beta} = -3 - \frac{h}{4} \frac{1}{2^\beta} < -3,$$

as -3 is the minimal value of $F(2, \cdot)$ on K. Thus, assumption (i) in Theorem 3.3 [13] does not hold. Moreover, F is not even monotone; in fact, $F(1, 3) + F(3, 1) > 0$, which shows that assumption (ii) in Theorem 3.3 [13] does not hold either.

In the next result, which also asserts the Hölder continuity of the solution map, all the assumptions will be given directly on F.

Corollary 7.1. *Let $F : K \times K \times P \to \mathbb{R}$ be a parametric bifunction satisfying conditions A.1–A.3. Suppose, in addition, that*

A.4' *$F(\cdot, \cdot, p)$ is α-monotone, uniformly with respect to $p \in P$, for some positive α (see Theorem 6.12);*

A.5 *$F(\cdot, y, p)$ is upper hemicontinuous on K (i.e., upper semicontinuous on line segments in K), for every $y \in K$, $p \in P$.*

Then the solution map S is single-valued and Hölder continuous with constant k/α, i.e.,

$$\|S(p) - S(p')\| \le \frac{k}{\alpha} d_P^\gamma(p, p'), \quad \forall p, p' \in P.$$

Proof. Fix any $p \in P$. By Proposition 3.1 in [87], the map $A_p^F = H(\cdot, p)$ is maximal monotone. It is sufficient to prove that A.4' implies that A_p^F satisfies (7.5). Indeed, take (x, v) and (x', v') in $\mathrm{gph}(A_p^F)$. We have that

$$F(x, x', p) \geq \langle v, x' - x \rangle, \qquad F(x', x, p) \geq \langle v', x - x' \rangle$$

and, by adding up both left and right-hand side, the α-strong monotonicity of A_p^F follows. □

Remark 7.2. As observed by one of the referees, variants providing Lipschitz continuity of the solution map can be achieved as follows. If instead of A3 we suppose the condition:

A.3'

$$\sup_{x \neq y \in K} \frac{|F(x, y, p) - F(x, y, p')|}{\|y - x\|} \text{ is finite on } P \times P,$$

then we can equip the set P with the metric

$$\rho(p, p') = \sup_{x \neq y \in K} \frac{|F(x, y, p) - F(x, y, p')|}{\|y - x\|}.$$

Without loss of generality one may assume that $F(\cdot, \cdot, p) \neq F(\cdot, \cdot, p')$ for $p \neq p'$ because otherwise one could replace P by the equivalence classes with respect to the relation $p \sim p' \Leftrightarrow F(\cdot, \cdot, p) = F(\cdot, \cdot, p')$. Then, using the same arguments as in Proposition 7.4, the bound

$$e(A_p^F(x), A_{p'}^F(x)) \leq \rho(p, p')$$

follows. This gives alternative results, similar to Theorem 7.1 and Corollary 7.1, concerning the Lipschitz continuity of the solution map.

7.3 CALMNESS AND AUBIN PROPERTY OF THE SOLUTION MAP

In the next two propositions we provide conditions on F in order to apply Propositions 7.2 and 7.1 to the set-valued map H, where $H(x, p) = A_p^F(x)$.

Proposition 7.5. Let $F : K \times K \times P \to \mathbb{R}$ be a parametric bifunction. Take $\bar{p} \in P$ and $\bar{x} \in K$ such that $\bar{x} \in S(\bar{p})$; set $\mathcal{U} = B(\bar{x}, r) \cap K$, and denote by $\mathcal{W}(\bar{p})$ a neighborhood of $\bar{p}$. Suppose that the bifunction F satisfies assumption A.1, and the following additional conditions:

A.2' $F(x, \cdot, \bar{p})$ is convex and lower semicontinuous for every $x \in \mathcal{U}$;
A.3' there exists a positive k such that

$$|F(x, y, p) - F(x, y, \bar{p})| \leq kd(p, \bar{p})\|x - y\|,$$
$$\forall x \in \mathcal{U}, y \in K, p \in \mathcal{W}(\bar{p});$$

A.6 $F(\bar{x}, x, \bar{p}) \geq c\, d^2(x, S(\bar{p}))$, *for every* $x \in \mathcal{U}$ *and for some positive c;*
A.7 $F(\cdot, \cdot, \bar{p})$ *is cyclically monotone.*

Then the solution map $S : P \rightrightarrows X$ *is calm at* $(\bar{p}, \bar{x})$.

Proof. From assumptions A.1, A.2' and A.3', following the same steps as in Proposition 7.4 we can argue that the operator $(x, p) \mapsto A_p^F(x)$ is calm with respect to p, uniformly with respect to x at $(\bar{x}, \bar{p}, 0)$. Furthermore, from Theorem 6.13, we get that A_p^F is metrically subregular at $(\bar{x}, 0)$, with constant $k = 1/c$. The assertion follows from Proposition 7.3. $\qquad\square$

Remark 7.3. Note that, if $F(\bar{x}, \cdot, \bar{p})$ is strongly convex, then (b") holds with $\bar{x}^* = 0$; in this case, since $S(\bar{p}) \cap \mathcal{U} = \{\bar{x}\}$ (A.2), A.6 can be simplified as follows:

A.6' $F(\bar{x}, x, \bar{p}) \geq c \, \|x - \bar{x}\|^2$.

Proposition 7.6. *Let* $F : K \times K \times P \to \mathbb{R}$ *be a parametric bifunction. Take* $\bar{p} \in P$ *and* $\bar{x} \in K$ *such that* $\bar{x} \in S(\bar{p})$; *set* $\mathcal{U} = B(\bar{x}, r) \cap K$, *and denote by* $\mathcal{W}, \mathcal{V}$ *neighborhoods of* $\bar{p}$, 0, *respectively. Suppose that* F *satisfies assumptions A.1–A.2, and the following additional conditions:*

A.3" *there exists a positive k such that*

$$|F(x, y, p) - F(x, y, p')| \leq kd(p, p')\|x - y\|,$$

$$\forall x \in \mathcal{U}, y \in K, p, p' \in \mathcal{W};$$

A.6" $(A_p^F)^{-1}(x^*) \neq \emptyset$, *for all* $x^* \in \mathcal{V}$, *and there exists* $c > 0$ *such that*

$$\inf_{\tilde{x} \in (A_p^F)^{-1}(\hat{x})} (F(\tilde{x}, x, p) - \langle x^*, x - \tilde{x} \rangle) \geq c\, d^2(x, (A_p^F)^{-1}(x^*)),$$

$$\forall x \in \mathcal{U}, x^* \in \mathcal{V}, p \in \mathcal{W};$$

A.8 $F(\cdot, \cdot, p)$ *is* α-*monotone, uniformly with respect to* $p \in \mathcal{W}$, *for some* $\alpha > -c$.

Then the solution map $S : P \rightrightarrows X$ *has the Aubin property around* $(\bar{p}, \bar{x})$.

Proof. From assumptions A.1–A.2 and A.3", following the same steps as in Proposition 7.4 we get that $(x, p) \mapsto A_p^F(x)$ is Aubin with respect to p, uniformly with respect to x around $(\bar{x}, \bar{p}, 0)$. Furthermore, from A.6", arguing as in second part of Theorem 6.12, we can show that $(x, p) \mapsto A_p^F(x)$ is metrically regular with respect to x, uniformly with respect to p, around $(\bar{x}, \bar{p}, 0)$. The assertion follows from Proposition 7.2. $\qquad\square$

7.4 APPLICATIONS TO SENSITIVITY OF PARAMETRIC EQUILIBRIUM PROBLEMS AND VARIATIONAL SYSTEMS

Studies about the inverse of the sum of set-valued mappings have drawn in last years the attention of many authors and constitute today an important and active research field. A basic motivation of such studies is related to the existence of solutions of variational inclusions. Recall that a *variational inclusion* (or a *generalized equation*) is a problem of the form

$$\text{find } x \in X \text{ such that } y \in A(x), \qquad \text{(VI)}$$

where A is a set-valued mapping acting between two Banach spaces X and Y, and $y \in Y$ is a given point. In many cases, the point y could be of the form $f(x)$ where f is a single-valued function from X to Y or of the form $f(p, x)$ with p a parameter leading to an important class of variational inclusions called *parameterized generalized equations*.

This problem serves as a general framework for describing in a unified manner various problems arising in nonlinear analysis and in other areas in mathematics including optimization problems and variational inequality problems.

In the simple case of a single-valued mapping A, problem (VI) reduces to a simply functional equation, and it is then related to the surjectivity of the involved single-valued mapping. From the same point of view, in the case of set-valued mappings, the problem is also related to the surjectivity of the involved set-valued mapping in the analogue sense. The pioneering work in this direction is the Banach[1] open mapping theorem which guarantees that a continuous mapping acting between Banach spaces is open if and only if it is surjective.

Among various advancements in this area, there are also the famous work by Lyusternik [121] for nonlinear Fréchet differentiable functions and that of Graves [85] for nonlinear operators acting between Banach spaces. It should be emphasized that no differentiability assumption is made in the theorem of Graves. Also, many investigations about the solution mappings by means of classical differentiability or by the concepts of generalized differentiation have been carried out and several results for variational inclusions have been obtained. This direction has given rise to the rich theory of implicit functions for parameterized generalized equations.

Another point of view having roots in the Milyutin's covering mapping theorem which, in turn, goes back to the theorem of Graves, is what is known in the literature under the name of the *openness with linear rate* or the *covering property*, see [64]. This approach makes use of a constant like that appearing in the Banach open mapping theorem for studying the regularity properties of the inverse of set-valued mappings and it has produced many results with applications to different kinds of variational inclusions in the infinite dimensional settings. We also refer to the notion of *locally covering maps* and its applications to studying the distance to the set of coincidence points of set-valued mappings. Many deep and important results are obtained and applied to different areas of mathematics, including stability and continuous dependence, system of differential inclusions, implicit function theorems, functional equations, and existence of double fixed points.

In this section, we investigate the necessary conditions to deal with the Lipschitzian property of the inverse of the sum of two set-valued mappings. As the inverse of the inverse of a set-valued mapping is the set-valued mapping itself, and since the inverse of a Lipschitzian set-valued mapping need not be Lipschitzian, we wonder why always consider set-valued Lipschitzian mappings if we want to obtain that the inverse of their sum is Lipschitzian. This leads to say that nothing can prevent a set-valued non-Lipschitzian mapping to have an inverse set-valued mapping which is Lipschitzian. However, going back to the Banach open mapping theorem, we understand that this question has roots in the fact that the inverse of a surjective linear and continuous mapping acting between Banach spaces has some regularity properties, and by linearity, the mapping itself is Lipschitzian. Of course, the situation is different when dealing with set-valued mappings. Motivated by this question, we investigate here the property of being set-valued pseudo-Lipschitzian in order to study the Lipschitzian property of the inverse of the sum of two set-valued mappings.

Our analysis is structured as follows. We first provide the necessary background to deal with set-valued mappings in the settings of metric spaces, and introduce some notions defined from the properties of set-valued pseudo-Lipschitzian mappings. Next, we obtain results on the behavior of fixed points sets of set-valued pseudo-contraction mappings. We make use of our results on the behavior of fixed point sets of set-valued pseudo-contraction mappings to deal with the inverse of the sum of set-valued non necessarily Lipschitzian mappings. Under weakened conditions of the Lipschitzian property but with additional conditions on the existence of fixed points, we obtain that the inverse of the sum of two set-valued mappings is Lipschitzian. Finally, we make use of the proximal convergence to develop techniques and obtain results on the sensitivity analysis of variational inclusions.

7.4.1 Pompeiu-Hausdorff Metric and Pseudo-Lipschitz Set-Valued Mappings

Let (X, d) be a metric space. Given $x \in X$ and $r > 0$, we denote by $B(x, r)$ (resp., $\overline{B}(x, r)$) the open (resp., closed) ball around x with radius r.

Let A be a nonempty subset of X. The distance from a point $x \in X$ is defined by $d(x, A) := \inf_{y \in A} d(x, y)$, and, as usual, $d(x, \emptyset) = +\infty$. The open ball around A with radius r is denoted by $B(A, r) := \bigcup_{u \in A} B(u, r)$.

For two subsets A and B of X, the *excess* of A over B (with respect to d) is denoted by $e(A, B)$ and is defined by $e(A, B) := \sup_{x \in A} d(x, B)$. In particular, we adopt the conventions $e(\emptyset, B) := 0$ and $e(A, \emptyset) := +\infty$ if $A \neq \emptyset$.

The distance between A and B (with respect to d) is denoted by Haus (A, B) and is defined by

$$\text{Haus}(A, B) := \max\{e(A, B), e(B, A)\}.$$

Restricted to the closed subsets, Haus is an (extended real-valued) metric called the *Pompeiu-Hausdorff metric*.[2,3]

Let (X, d_X) and (Y, d_Y) be two metric spaces. In the sequel, a set-valued mapping T from X to Y will be denoted by $T : X \rightrightarrows Y$. The domain of T is the set $\text{dom}(T) := \{x \in X \mid T(x) \neq \emptyset\}$, and its graph is given by $\text{grph}(T) := \{(x, y) \in X \times Y \mid y \in T(x)\}$. If the graph of T is closed, then T has closed values. The converse holds under additional conditions, in particular if T is upper semicontinuous.

Recall that a set-valued mapping $T : X \rightrightarrows Y$ is said to be *upper semicontinuous* at a point $x_0 \in X$ if for every open subset V of Y such that $T(x_0) \subset V$, there exists an open neighborhood U of x_0 such that $T(x) \subset V$, for every $x \in U$. The set-valued mapping T is said to be upper semicontinuous if it is upper semicontinuous at every point of X.

For a subset A of X, we denote by $T(A) := \cup_{x \in A} T(x)$, the image of A by T. For a subset B of Y, the inverse image of B by T is $T^{-1}(B) := \{x \in X \mid B \cap T(x) \neq \emptyset\}$, while $T^{-1}(y)$ stands for $T^{-1}(\{y\})$, if $y \in Y$. A set-valued mapping $T : X \rightrightarrows Y$ is upper semicontinuous if and only if $T^{-1}(B)$ is closed, for every closed subset B of Y.

In the sequel, the fixed points set of a set-valued mapping $T : X \rightrightarrows X$ will be denoted by $\text{Fix}(T)$, that is, $\text{Fix}(T) := \{x \in X \mid x \in T(x)\}$.

The Lipschitz continuity (with respect to the Pompeiu-Hausdorff metric) is one of the most popular properties of set-valued mappings. A set-valued mapping $T : X \rightrightarrows Y$ is said to be L-*Lipschitzian* on $M \subset \text{dom}(T)$ if it has closed values on M and there exists $L \geq 0$ such that

$$\text{Haus}(T(x_1), T(x_2)) \leq L d_X(x_1, x_2) \quad \forall x_1, x_2 \in M.$$

If $X = Y$ and $L \in [0, 1)$, then T is called L-*contraction* on M.

To deal with the properties of the inverse of the sum of two set-valued mappings, it has been proved in [35, Lemma 2] the following result for set-valued Lipschitzian mappings. If $T : X \rightrightarrows Y$ is L-Lipschitzian on M, then for every two nonempty subsets A and B of M,

$$e(T(A), T(B)) \leq L e(A, B).$$

This property being not adapted to our techniques, we develop here some analogue properties related to pseudo-Lipschitzian set-valued mappings.

Recall that a set-valued mapping $T : X \rightrightarrows Y$ is said to be pseudo-Lipschitzian around $(x, y) \in \text{grph}(T)$ if there exist a constant $L \geq 0$ and neighborhoods $M_x \subset \text{dom}(T)$ of x and M_y of y such that

$$e\left(T(x_1) \cap M_y, T(x_2)\right) \leq L d_X(x_1, x_2) \quad \forall x_1, x_2 \in M_x.$$

The notion of being pseudo-Lipschitzian around (x, y) is called the *Aubin property* when M_x and M_y are closed balls around x and y, respectively. It is well-known that the Aubin property of the set-valued mapping T turns out to be equivalent to the metric regularity of the set-valued mapping T^{-1}.

We extend the above definition to any two nonempty subsets $M_x \subset \text{dom}(T)$ and $M_y \subset Y$, and we say that T is *L-pseudo-Lipschitzian on M_x with respect to M_y*. When $X = Y$, $M_x = M_y = M$ and $L \in [0, 1)$, the set-valued mapping T is called *L-pseudo-contraction with respect to M*.

Let $M \subset \text{dom}(T)$ and N be two nonempty subsets of X, and S a nonempty subset of Y. We say that T is *fully L-pseudo-Lipschitzian on M for N with respect to S* if for any two nonempty subsets A and B of M, we have

$$e(T(A) \cap S, T(B)) \le Le(A \cap N, B).$$

It follows immediately from the definition that any set-valued fully L-pseudo-Lipschitzian on M for N with respect to S is L-pseudo-Lipschitzian on M with respect to S. It is also fully L-pseudo-Lipschitzian on M for N' with respect to S, for any subset N' containing N.

Conversely, any set-valued L-Lipschitzian mapping $T : X \rightrightarrows Y$ on a subset M is fully L-pseudo-Lipschitzian on M for N with respect to any subset of Y, for any subset N of X containing M.

More generally, we have the following result for set-valued pseudo-Lipschitzian mappings which can be compared to [35, Lemma 2].

Proposition 7.7. *Let $T : X \rightrightarrows Y$ be a set-valued L-pseudo-Lipschitzian on M with respect to S. Then, for any nonempty subsets A and B of M, we have*

$$e(T(A) \cap S, T(B)) \le Le(A, B).$$

In particular, T is fully L-pseudo-Lipschitzian on M for N with respect to S, for any subset N containing M.

Proof. Let A and B be nonempty and contained in M. To avoid any confusion, put $A' = \{x \in A \mid T(x) \cap S \ne \emptyset\}$. Then,

$$
\begin{aligned}
e(T(A) \cap S, T(B)) &= \sup_{u \in T(A) \cap S} d_Y(u, T(B)) \\
&= \sup_{x_1 \in A'} \sup_{u \in T(x_1) \cap S} \inf_{x_2 \in B} d_Y(u, T(x_2)) \\
&\le \sup_{x_1 \in A'} \inf_{x_2 \in B} \sup_{u \in T(x_1) \cap S} d_Y(u, T(x_2)) \\
&= \sup_{x_1 \in A'} \inf_{x_2 \in B} e(T(x_1) \cap S, T(x_2)) \\
&\le L \sup_{x_1 \in A'} \inf_{x_2 \in B} d_X(x_1, x_2) \\
&\le L \sup_{x_1 \in A} d_X(x_1, B) = Le(A, B).
\end{aligned}
$$

Since $e(A, B) = e(A \cap N, B)$ whenever N contains M, then the set-valued mapping T is fully L-pseudo-Lipschitzian on M for N with respect to S. $\square$

Although the notion of being fully pseudo-Lipschitzian seems to fit very well with the other existing notions such as those of being Lipschitzian and pseudo-Lipschitzian, it may be interesting to look for conditions involving it for a subset N which does not necessarily contain M.

Proposition 7.8. *Let $T : X \rightrightarrows Y$ be a set-valued L-pseudo-Lipschitzian on M with respect to S, and let N be a subset of X such that $T(x) \cap S = \emptyset$, whenever $x \in M \setminus N$. Then, T is fully L-pseudo-Lipschitzian on M for N with respect to S.*

Proof. Let A and B be nonempty and contained in M. We remark that $T(A) \cap S = T(A \cap N) \cap S$. The proof then follows step by step that of Proposition 7.7. $\square$

The following example provides us with a set-valued non-Lipschitzian mapping which is fully pseudo-Lipschitzian mapping, where M is not contained in N. We can also choose N in such a way that neither M is contained in N nor N is contained in M.

Example 7.2. Let $T : \mathbb{R}^2 \rightrightarrows \mathbb{R}^2$ be the set-valued mapping defined by

$$T((x, y)) = \begin{cases} \{2x\} \times ([0, 2|x|] \cup [3, +\infty[) & \text{if} \quad \|(x, y)\| < 1, \\ \{2x\} \times]0, x^2] & \text{if} \quad \|(x, y)\| \geq 1. \end{cases}$$

Let $M = S = B((0,0), 1)$ and $N = \left\{(x, y) \in M \mid |x| < \frac{1}{2}\right\}$. In this example, we have $N \subset M$. Clearly, the set-valued mapping T is not Lipschitzian on $\mathbb{R}^2$. However, T is $2\sqrt{2}$-pseudo-Lipschitzian on M with respect to S. We remark that for any $x \in M \setminus N$, $T(x) \cap S = \emptyset$. Then, we conclude by Proposition 7.8 that T is fully $2\sqrt{2}$-pseudo-Lipschitzian on M for N with respect to S.

If we take $N' = N \cup N_1$ where $N_1 \setminus M \neq \emptyset$, then T is still fully $2\sqrt{2}$-pseudo-Lipschitzian on M for N' with respect to S. In this case, neither M is contained in N' nor N' is contained in M.

Finally, recall that if (Y, d) is a linear metric space, the distance d is said to be *shift-invariant metric* if

$$d(y + z, y' + z) = d(y, y') \quad \text{for all } y, y', z \in X.$$

Let A and B be two subsets of a linear metric space (Y, d) with shift-invariant metric d, and $a, b, b' \in Y$. It is shown in [35] that

$$e(A + a, B + a) \leq e(A, B) \quad \text{and} \quad e(A + b, A + b') \leq d(b, b').$$

7.4.2   Fixed Points Sets of Set-Valued Pseudo-Contraction Mappings

Existence of fixed points is a subject which is not limited to set-valued contraction or pseudo-contraction mappings, and in this spirit, we do not make use here of classical conditions assuring existence of fixed points for set-valued mappings. More precisely, we assume that the fixed points sets of the involved set-valued mappings are nonempty and linked in such a way that a result on the behaviors of their fixed points sets is derived. Furthermore, instead of conditions on the distance between the images of the set-valued mappings as considered in some recent papers, we impose conditions only on those for the fixed points.

We do not follow here classical procedures usually employed when dealing with the behaviors of fixed points sets of set-valued mappings. Instead, we make use of the following more precise version of the lemma on existence of fixed points of set-valued pseudo-contraction mappings, which is also called the Dontchev-Hager fixed point theorem; see [28]. This version is enhanced in the sense that not only the completeness is assumed only on the closed ball, but more particularly, only the values of the restriction of the set-valued mapping on the closed ball are assumed to be nonempty and closed. The proof follows, step by step, the arguments used in [66], which are based on techniques having roots in the Banach contraction principle. A proof using arguments based on a weak variant of the Ekeland variational principle has also been carried out in [28].

Lemma 7.2. *Let (X, d) be a metric space. Let $\bar{x} \in X$ and $\alpha > 0$ be such that $\overline{B}(\bar{x}, \alpha)$ is a complete metric subspace. Let $\lambda \in [0, 1)$ and $T : X \rightrightarrows X$ be a set-valued mapping with nonempty closed values on $\overline{B}(\bar{x}, \alpha)$ such that*

1. $d(\bar{x}, T(\bar{x})) < (1 - \lambda)\alpha$ *and*
2. $e\left(T(x) \cap \overline{B}(\bar{x}, \alpha), T(x')\right) \leq \lambda d(x, x') \; \forall x, x' \in \overline{B}(\bar{x}, \alpha).$

Then, T has a fixed point in $\overline{B}(\bar{x}, \alpha)$.

Now, we derive the following result on the behavior of fixed points sets of set-valued mappings. It is worthwhile noticing that one of the general results obtained in this direction is [19, Theorem 4.1]. However, our conditions seem to be somewhat different. In any case, and at the current stage of advancement, it is not easy to see if it is possible to derive our result from it, see Remark 7.4 below for explanation.

Theorem 7.2. *Let (X, d) be a metric space. Let $x_0 \in X$ and $r > 0$ be such that $\overline{B}(x_0, r)$ is a complete metric subspace. Let $\lambda \in (0, 1)$ and $0 < \beta < (1 - \lambda)r$ and let $T, S : X \rightrightarrows X$ be two set-valued mappings such that*

1. T *is λ-pseudo-contraction with respect to $B(x_0, r)$ and has nonempty closed values on $B(x_0, r)$;*
2. S *has nonempty fixed points set and for every $x \in Fix(S)$,*

$$d(x, x_0) < \beta \quad and \quad d(x, T(x)) < \lambda\beta.$$

Then, T has a nonempty fixed points set and

$$e(Fix\,(S)\,, Fix\,(T)) \leq \frac{1}{1-\lambda} \sup_{x \in B(x_0,r)} e\,(S\,(x)\,, T\,(x))\,.$$

Proof. Fix $\varepsilon > 0$ and put

$$\alpha = \min\left\{\frac{1}{1-\lambda} \sup_{x \in B(x_0,r)} e\,(S\,(x)\,, T\,(x)) + \varepsilon, \ \frac{\lambda\beta}{1-\lambda}\right\}.$$

Let $\bar{x} \in Fix\,(S)$ be an arbitrary element.

Claim 1: We prove that $\overline{B}\,(\bar{x}, \alpha) \subset B\,(x_0, r)$. To do this, let $x \in \overline{B}\,(\bar{x}, \alpha)$. Then, from assumption (2), we have

$$d\,(x, x_0) \leq d\,(x, \bar{x}) + d\,(\bar{x}, x_0)$$

$$< \alpha + \beta \leq \frac{1}{1-\lambda}\lambda\beta + \beta < \lambda r + (1-\lambda)\,r = r.$$

Claim 2: We have $d\,(\bar{x}, T\,(\bar{x})) < (1-\lambda)\,\alpha$. Indeed, since $\bar{x} \in Fix\,(S)$, then by assumption (2), $d\,(\bar{x}, T\,(\bar{x})) < \lambda\beta$. Also,

$$d\,(\bar{x}, T\,(\bar{x})) \leq e\,(S\,(\bar{x})\,, T\,(\bar{x})) \leq \sup_{x \in B(x_0,r)} e\,(S\,(x)\,, T\,(x))\,,$$

and, since $d\,(\bar{x}, T\,(\bar{x}))$ is finite, then

$$d\,(\bar{x}, T\,(\bar{x})) < \sup_{x \in B(x_0,r)} e\,(S\,(x)\,, T\,(x)) + (1-\lambda)\,\varepsilon.$$

Thus, $d\,(\bar{x}, T\,(\bar{x})) < (1-\lambda)\,\alpha$.

It results by Claim 1 and assumption (1) that T has nonempty closed values on $\overline{B}\,(\bar{x}, \alpha)$ and for every $x, x' \in \overline{B}\,(\bar{x}, \alpha)$,

$$e\left(T\,(x) \cap \overline{B}\,(\bar{x}, \alpha)\,, T\,(x')\right) \leq e\left(T\,(x) \cap B\,(x_0, r)\,, T\,(x')\right) \leq \lambda d\,(x, x')\,.$$

Now, all hypotheses of Lemma 7.2 are satisfied for T on $\overline{B}\,(\bar{x}, \alpha)$ and then, T has a fixed point $x^* \in \overline{B}\,(\bar{x}, \alpha)$. It follows that

$$d\,(\bar{x}, Fix\,(T)) \leq d\left(\bar{x}, x^*\right) \leq \alpha \leq \frac{1}{1-\lambda} \sup_{x \in B(x_0,r)} e\,(S\,(x)\,, T\,(x)) + \varepsilon.$$

This inequality being valid for any $\bar{x} \in Fix\,(S)$, we obtain

$$e\,(Fix\,(S)\,, Fix\,(T)) \leq \frac{1}{1-\lambda} \sup_{x \in B(x_0,r)} e\,(S\,(x)\,, T\,(x)) + \varepsilon.$$

Letting ε go to zero, we complete the proof. $\qquad\qquad\square$

Remark 7.4. In [19, Theorem 4.1], the authors consider the set of coincidence points of two set-valued mappings Φ and Ψ which is exactly the fixed points set of Φ whenever Ψ is the embedding set-valued mapping Emb_X of X defined by $Emb_X(x) = \{x\}$, for every $x \in X$. Then, according to our notations, we take $\Phi = T$, $\tilde{\Phi} = S$ and $\Psi = \tilde{\Psi} = Emb_X$. In our assumptions, T is λ-pseudo-contraction with respect to $B(x_0, r)$ which is weaker than the property of being pseudo-Lipschitzian with Lipschitz constant λ considered in [19]. But to overcome this fact, we know that it is pseudo-Lipschitzian with Lipschitz constant $\lambda + \varepsilon$, for every $\varepsilon > 0$. According to the notations of [19], we take $x_0^* = y_0^*$ any point in Fix(S) which plays the role of x_0 and y_0 in [19], respectively. But we can not take our x_0 because $d(x_0, T(x_0))$ is not known under our assumptions. Also, we take $R_1 = R_2 = \tilde{R} = \lambda r$, $\beta = \lambda + \varepsilon$ and $\alpha = 1$. As a conclusion, for any $r_1 > 0$ and $r_2 > 0$ verifying condition (3.11) of [19, p. 821], we obtain

$$e\left(\text{Fix}(S) \cap B\left(x_0^*, r_1\right), \text{Fix}(T)\right) \leq \frac{1}{1 - \lambda - \varepsilon} \sup_{x \in B(x_0^*, r_1)} e(S(x), T(x)).$$

It is not clear how to choose, for every $\varepsilon > 0$, r_1 (which depends on ε) in such a way that Fix$(S) \subset B\left(x_0^*, r_1\right) \subset B(x_0, r)$, since the upper bound in the second term of the inequality is taken on $B\left(x_0^*, r_1\right)$. Furthermore, neither X nor the graph of T are assumed to be complete in Theorem 7.2. This condition is required in [19, Theorem 4.1].

Now, we derive the following useful property.

Corollary 7.2. *Let (X, d) be a metric space. Let $x_0 \in X$ and $r > 0$ be such that $\overline{B}(x_0, r)$ is a complete metric subspace. Let $\lambda \in (0, 1)$ and $0 < \beta < (1 - \lambda)r$ and let $T, S : X \rightrightarrows X$ be two set-valued mappings such that*

1. *S and T are λ-pseudo-contractions with respect to $B(x_0, r)$ and have nonempty closed values on $B(x_0, r)$;*
2. *S has nonempty fixed points set and for every $x \in Fix(S)$,*

$$d(x, x_0) < \beta \quad and \quad d(x, T(x)) < \lambda\beta;$$

3. *T has nonempty fixed points set and for every $x \in Fix(T)$,*

$$d(x, x_0) < \beta \quad and \quad d(x, S(x)) < \lambda\beta.$$

Then,

$$Haus(Fix(S), Fix(T)) \leq \frac{1}{1 - \lambda} \sup_{x \in B(x_0, r)} Haus(S(x), T(x)).$$

Remark 7.5. It is worthwhile emphasizing the importance of the above result which allows to replace the excess by the Pompeiu-Hausdorff metric in the conclusion of Theorem 7.2. Even if all the fixed points sets of the involved set-valued mappings are in $B(x_0, r)$, there does not seem to be any result in the literature dealing with set-valued pseudo-contraction mappings which provides such a conclusion; see, for comparison, the recent generalization given in [2] of Lim's lemma.

In the following example, we give two set-valued mappings satisfying the conditions of Theorem 7.2 with respect to each other. Though some conditions are relaxed, this example provides us a situation where the Pompeiu-Hausdorff metric can be used in the conclusion of Theorem 7.2.

Example 7.3. According to Theorem 7.2, let $X = \mathbb{R}^2$, $x_0 = (0, 0)$, $r = 1$ and $\lambda = \frac{1}{\sqrt{2}}$.

Let $T : \mathbb{R}^2 \rightrightarrows \mathbb{R}^2$ be the set-valued mapping defined by

$$T((x, y)) = \begin{cases} \left\{\frac{x}{2}\right\} \times \left(\left[0, \frac{|x|}{2}\right] \cup [3, +\infty[\right) & \text{if} \quad \|(x, y)\| < 1, \\ \{2x\} \times \left]0, x^2\right] & \text{if} \quad \|(x, y)\| \geq 1. \end{cases}$$

Thus, T has nonempty closed values on $B(x_0, r)$ and the images of points of $B(x_0, r)$ are not necessarily included in $B(x_0, r)$. And since, for every (x_1, y_1) and (x_2, y_2) in $B(x_0, r)$, we have

$$e(T((x_1, y_1)) \cap B(x_0, r), T((x_2, y_2))) \leq \frac{1}{\sqrt{2}} |x_1 - x_2|,$$

then, T is λ-pseudo-contraction with respect to $B(x_0, r)$. We note that T is not Lipschitzian on $\mathbb{R}^2$ and $\text{Fix}(T) = \{(0, 0)\}$.

Now, take any $\alpha \in \left]0, 2\sqrt{\frac{\lambda}{5}}\left(1 - \sqrt{\lambda}\right)\right[$ and define $S : \mathbb{R}^2 \rightrightarrows \mathbb{R}^2$ by

$$S((x, y)) = \begin{cases} \left\{\frac{x+\alpha}{2}\right\} \times \left(\left[0, \frac{|x|}{2}\right] \cup [3, +\infty[\right) & \text{if} \quad \|(x, y)\| < 1, \\ \{2x\} \times \left]0, x^3\right] & \text{if} \quad \|(x, y)\| \geq 1. \end{cases}$$

The set-valued mapping S has nonempty closed values on $B(x_0, r)$ and the images of points of $B(x_0, r)$ are not necessarily included in $B(x_0, r)$. Also, it is λ-pseudo-contraction with respect to $B(x_0, r)$ and $\text{Fix}(S) = \{\alpha\} \times \left[0, \frac{\alpha}{2}\right]$. Finally, S is not Lipschitz on $\mathbb{R}^2$.

We set $\beta = \left(1 - \sqrt{\lambda}\right) < (1 - \lambda)r$ and we verify the other conditions of Theorem 7.2.

1. For the unique fixed point $(0, 0)$ of T, we have

$$d((0, 0), S((0, 0))) = \frac{\alpha}{2}$$

$$\leq \sqrt{\frac{\lambda}{5}}\left(1 - \sqrt{\lambda}\right) < \lambda\left(1 - \sqrt{\lambda}\right) = \lambda\beta.$$

2. For any $(\alpha, \gamma) \in \text{Fix}(S)$, we have

$$d\left((\alpha, \gamma), (0, 0)\right) \leq \sqrt{\alpha^2 + \frac{\alpha^2}{4}} = \frac{\sqrt{5}}{2}\alpha = \sqrt{\lambda}\left(1 - \sqrt{\lambda}\right) < \beta$$

and

$$d\left((\alpha, \gamma), T\left((\alpha, \gamma)\right)\right) \leq d\left((\alpha, \gamma), \left(\frac{\alpha}{2}, \frac{\alpha}{2}\right)\right) = \sqrt{\frac{\alpha^2}{4} + \left(\gamma - \frac{\alpha}{2}\right)^2}$$

$$\leq \frac{\alpha}{\sqrt{2}} < \sqrt{2}\sqrt{\frac{\lambda}{5}}\left(1 - \sqrt{\lambda}\right) < \lambda\left(1 - \sqrt{\lambda}\right) = \lambda\beta.$$

Proposition 7.9. *Under assumptions of Theorem 7.2, we have*

$$e(\text{Fix}(S) \cap B, \text{Fix}(T)) \leq \frac{1}{1 - \lambda} \sup_{x \in B(x_0, r)} e(S(x) \cap B, T(x)),$$

for every subset B of X such that $B \cap \text{Fix}(S) \neq \emptyset$.

Proof. It suffices to replace S in Theorem 7.2 by the set-valued mapping $S \cap B$ defined on X by $(S \cap B)(x) = S(x) \cap B$. ☐

7.4.3 Inverse of the Sum of Two Set-Valued Mappings

As in Theorem 7.2 of the last section, the two set-valued mappings involved in the following results, will be connected between them by some additional conditions related to the existence of fixed points. We formulate this connection in the following definition which can be compared to the notion of sum-stable maps used in [69, Definition 4.2].

Let $F, G : X \rightrightarrows Y$ be two set-valued mappings, $x_0 \in X$, $y_0 \in Y$, $B \subset Y$, $\alpha > 0$ and $\beta > 0$. We say that F is (α, β)-*compatible with respect to G on B for x_0 and y_0* if the following conditions hold:

(FP1) for every $y \in B$, there exists $x_y \in X$ such that $\left(y - G\left(x_y\right)\right) \cap \left(F\left(x_y\right) - y_0\right) \neq \emptyset$;

(FP2) if x is such that $(y - G(x)) \cap (F(x) - y_0) \neq \emptyset$ for some $y \in B$, then $d_X(x, x_0) < \beta$ and $d_X\left(x, F^{-1}\left(y' + y_0 - G(x)\right)\right) < \alpha\beta$, for every $y' \in B$ with $y' \neq y$.

Example 7.4. Set $X = Y = \mathbb{R}^2$ and $x_0 = y_0 = (0, 0) \in \mathbb{R}^2$. Choose $\lambda = \frac{1}{\sqrt{2}}$, $\beta = \left(1 - \sqrt{\lambda}\right)$ and $\delta = 2\sqrt{\frac{\lambda}{5}}\left(1 - \sqrt{\lambda}\right)$. Put $B = B(y_0, \delta)$ and define, for every $z \in B$, the set-valued mapping $T_z : \mathbb{R}^2 \rightrightarrows \mathbb{R}^2$ by

$$T_z((x, y)) = \begin{cases} \left\{\frac{x + \|z\|}{2}\right\} \times \left(\left[0, \frac{|x|}{2}\right] \cup [3, +\infty[\right) & \text{if } \|(x, y)\| < 1, \\ \{2x\} \times \left]0, x^3\right] & \text{if } \|(x, y)\| \geq 1. \end{cases}$$

As in Example 7.3, the set-valued mapping T_z is not Lipschitzian but λ-pseudo-contraction with respect to $B(x_0, 1)$, has nonempty closed values on $B(x_0, 1)$ and $\text{Fix}(T_z) = \{\|z\|\} \times \left[0, \frac{\|z\|}{2}\right]$, for every $z \in B$.

For $z \in B$ and $(\alpha, \gamma) \in \text{Fix}(T_z)$, we have

$$d((\alpha, \gamma), x_0) < \beta \quad \text{and} \quad d\left((\alpha, \gamma), T_{z'}((\alpha, \gamma))\right) < \lambda\beta,$$

for every $z' \in B$ such that $z \neq z'$.

Now, if F and G are two set-valued mappings defined on $\mathbb{R}^2$ to $\mathbb{R}^2$ in such a way that for any $z \in B$ and $(x, y) \in \mathbb{R}^2$, we have

$$T_z((x, y)) = F^{-1}(y - G((x, y))),$$

then F is (λ, β)-compatible with respect to G on B for x_0 and y_0

We now formulate the following inverse set-valued mapping result for the sum of two set-valued mappings similar to [35, Theorem 3], where the condition of being Lipschitzian is replaced by some local conditions such as the condition of being pseudo-Lipschitzian.

From now on, the metric of the linear metric space Y will be always assumed to be shift-invariant and (-1)-homogeneous. A metric d_Y on a linear space Y is called α-homogeneous, $\alpha \in \mathbb{R}$, if $d_Y(\alpha x, \alpha y) = |\alpha| d_Y(x, y)$, for every $x, y \in Y$. Every metric associated to a norm is α-homogeneous, for every $\alpha \in \mathbb{R}$. Thus, the metric d_Y is (-1)-homogeneous if $d_Y(-x, -y) = d_Y(x, y)$, for every $x, y \in Y$.

Theorem 7.3. *Let (X, d_X) be a metric space, (Y, d_Y) be a linear metric space, $r > 0$, $x_0 \in X$, and $y_0 \in Y$ be such that $\overline{B}(x_0, r)$ is a complete metric subspace. Let $F, G : X \rightrightarrows Y$ be two set-valued mappings satisfying the following assumptions*

1. *G has nonempty closed values on $B(x_0, r)$, $G(x_0)$ is a bounded set with diameter d_0, and there exist $\alpha > 0$, $\delta > 0$ and a nonempty subset N of Y such that $G(B(x_0, r)) \subset \overline{B}(G(x_0), \alpha r)$, and G is α-pseudo-Lipschitzian on $B(x_0, r)$ with respect to $B(G(x_0), \delta) + y_0 - N$;*
2. *$B(x_0, r) \subset \text{dom}(F)$, $B(y_0, \delta + \alpha r + d_0) \subset F(B(x_0, r))$, F is upper semi-continuous, and there exists $K > 0$ such that $\alpha K < 1$ and F^{-1} is fully K-pseudo-Lipschitzian on $B(y_0, \delta + \alpha r + d_0)$ for N with respect to $B(x_0, r)$;*
3. *there exists $\beta > 0$ such that $\beta < (1 - \alpha K)r$, and F is (α, β)-compatible with respect to G on $B(G(x_0), \delta)$ for x_0 and y_0.*

Then, $(F + G)^{-1}$ is $\frac{K}{1 - \alpha K}$-Lipschitzian on $B(G(x_0) + y_0, \delta)$.

Proof. Let $y \in B(G(x_0), \delta)$ be fixed, and consider the set-valued mapping $T_y : X \rightrightarrows X$ defined by

$$T_y(x) := F^{-1}(y + y_0 - G(x)) = \{t \in X \mid \exists z \in G(x), y + y_0 - z \in F(t)\}.$$

Clearly, Fix $(T_y) = (F + G)^{-1}(y + y_0)$, and it follows by condition (3) that there exist $x_y \in X$, $y_G \in G(x_y)$, and $y_F \in F(x_y)$ such that

$$y - y_G = y_F - y_0.$$

Therefore, $y = y_F + y_G - y_0 \in (F + G)(x_y) - y_0$, hence $x_y \in (F + G)^{-1}(y + y_0)$. This proves in particular that

$$B(G(x_0) + y_0, \delta) \subset \text{dom}(F + G)^{-1}.$$

To verify hypotheses of Theorem 7.2 to any couple of set-valued mappings T_y with $y \in B(G(x_0), \delta)$, we state first the following fact:

$$y + y_0 - G(x) \subset B(y_0, \delta + \alpha r + d_0) \quad \forall x \in B(x_0, r).$$

Indeed, let $x \in B(x_0, r)$ and $z \in G(x)$. Since d_Y is a shift-invariant metric, it suffices to verify that $d_Y(y, z) < \delta + d_0 + \alpha r$. Let $y_{x_0} \in G(x_0)$ be such that $d_Y(y, y_{x_0}) < \delta$ and put $\varepsilon = \delta - d_Y(y, y_{x_0}) > 0$. Let $u_{\varepsilon,z} \in G(x_0)$ be such that $d_Y(u_{\varepsilon,z}, z) < \alpha r + \frac{\varepsilon}{2}$. Then, we obtain

$$d_Y(y, z) \le d_Y(y, y_{x_0}) + d_Y(y_{x_0}, u_{\varepsilon,z}) + d_Y(u_{\varepsilon,z}, z)$$
$$< d_Y(y, y_{x_0}) + d_0 + \alpha r + \frac{\varepsilon}{2}$$
$$= \delta - \varepsilon + d_0 + \alpha r + \frac{\varepsilon}{2} < \delta + d_0 + \alpha r.$$

The set-valued mapping T_y has nonempty closed values on $B(x_0, r)$. Indeed, let $x \in B(x_0, r)$. For every $z \in G(x)$, $y + y_0 - z \in B(y_0, \delta + \alpha r + d_0)$, and then $F^{-1}(y + y_0 - z) \ne \emptyset$. Thus, $T_y(x) \ne \emptyset$, for every $x \in B(x_0, r)$. Moreover, by the upper semicontinuity of F and since $y + y_0 - G(x)$ is closed, then $T_y(x) = F^{-1}(y + y_0 - G(x))$ is closed, for every $x \in B(x_0, r)$.

The set-valued mapping T_y is αK-pseudo-contraction with respect to $B(x_0, r)$. Indeed, for $x_1, x_2 \in B(x_0, r)$, we know from above that $y + y_0 - G(x_1)$ and $y + y_0 - G(x_2)$ are contained in $B(y_0, \delta + \alpha r + d_0)$. Then,

$$d_X(T_y(x_1) \cap B(x_0, r), T_y(x_2))$$
$$= e\left(F^{-1}(y + y_0 - G(x_1)) \cap B(x_0, r), F^{-1}(y + y_0 - G(x_2))\right)$$
$$\le Ke((y + y_0 - G(x_1)) \cap N, y + y_0 - G(x_2)).$$

Since d_Y is shift-invariant and (-1)-homogeneous, then

$$Ke((y + y_0 - G(x_1)) \cap N, y + y_0 - G(x_2))$$
$$= Ke((G(x_1)) \cap (y + y_0 - N), G(x_2)) \le \alpha K d_X(x_1, x_2).$$

To verify the condition (2) of Theorem 7.2, take $y, y' \in B(G(x_0), \delta)$, $y \neq y'$ and suppose $x \in \text{Fix}(T_y)$. Then, by condition (3), $d_X(x, x_0) < \beta$ and

$$d_X\left(x, F^{-1}\left(y' + y_0 - G(x)\right)\right) < \alpha\beta.$$

It follows that $d_X(x, x_0) < \beta$ and $d_X(x, T_y(x)) < \alpha\beta$ which are required.

It remains now to verify that the set-valued mapping $(F + G)^{-1}$ is $\frac{K}{1-\alpha K}$-Lipschitzian on $B(G(x_0) + y_0, \delta)$. Notice that $\text{Fix}(T_y) \subset B(x_0, r)$, for all $y \in B(G(x_0), \delta)$.

For $z, z' \in B(G(x_0) + y_0, \delta)$, let $z = y + y_0$ and $z' = y' + y_0$ with $y, y' \in (G(x_0), \delta)$. We have

$$e\left((F + G)^{-1}(z), (F + G)^{-1}(z')\right) = e\left(\text{Fix}(T_y), \text{Fix}(T_{y'})\right)$$

and

$$e\left(\text{Fix}(T_y), \text{Fix}(T_{y'})\right) = e\left(\text{Fix}(T_y) \cap B(x_0, r), \text{Fix}(T_{y'})\right)$$
$$\leq \frac{1}{1 - \alpha K} \sup_{x \in B(x_0, r)} e\left(T_y(x) \cap B(x_0, r), T_{y'}(x)\right).$$

On the other hand, for every $x \in B(x_0, r)$, we have

$$e\left(T_y(x) \cap B(x_0, r), T_{y'}(x)\right)$$
$$= e\left(F^{-1}(y + y_0 - G(x)) \cap B(x_0, r), F^{-1}(y' + y_0 - G(x))\right)$$
$$\leq Ke\left((y + y_0 - G(x)) \cap N, y' + y_0 - G(x)\right)$$
$$\leq Ke\left(y + y_0 - G(x), y' + y_0 - G(x)\right) \leq Kd_Y(y, y').$$

We conclude that

$$e\left((F + G)^{-1}(z), (F + G)^{-1}(z')\right) \leq \frac{K}{1 - \alpha K} d_Y(y, y') = \frac{K}{1 - \alpha K} d_Y(z, z')$$

which, by interchanging z and z', completes the proof. $\qquad \square$

Remark 7.6. We remark that in condition (1) of the above theorem, the condition of G being α-pseudo-Lipschitzian on $B(x_0, r)$ with respect to

$$B(G(x_0), \delta) + y_0 - B(y_0, \delta + \alpha r + d_0)$$

can be replaced by the weaker condition of G being α-pseudo-Lipschitzian on $B(x_0, r)$ with respect to $y + y_0 - B(y_0, \delta + \alpha r + d_0)$, for every $y \in B(G(x_0), \delta)$.

Now, we obtain a result similar to the classical result due to Graves on the inverse of continuous functions acting between Banach spaces. We first state the following property.

Theorem 7.4. *Suppose that hypotheses of Theorem 7.3 are satisfied such that*

$$\overline{B}\,(y_0, \delta + \alpha r + d_0) \subset F(\overline{B}\,(x_0, r)),$$

F^{-1} *is fully K-pseudo-Lipschitzian on* $\overline{B}\,(y_0, \delta + \alpha r + d_0)$ *for N with respect to* $B\,(x_0, r)$*, and $B\,(G\,(x_0), \delta)$ is replaced by* $\bigcup_{u \in G(x_0)} \overline{B}\,(u, \delta)$ *in the corresponding conditions. Then the set-valued mapping* $(F + G)^{-1}$ *is* $\frac{K}{1 - \alpha K}$*-Lipschitzian on* $\bigcup_{u \in G(x_0)} \overline{B}\,(u + y_0, \delta)$.

Proof. The proof follows step by step the proof of Theorem 7.3 where instead of taking $y \in B\,(G\,(x_0), \delta)$, we take $y \in \bigcup_{u \in G(x_0)} \overline{B}\,(u, \delta)$. The unique fact which merits to be established is that for every $y \in \bigcup_{u \in G(x_0)} \overline{B}\,(u, \delta)$,

$$y + y_0 - G\,(x) \subset B\,(y_0, \delta + \alpha r + d_0) \quad \forall x \in B\,(x_0, r).$$

Let $y \in \bigcup_{u \in G(x_0)} \overline{B}\,(u, \delta)$ and take $u_y \in G\,(x_0)$ such that $y \in \overline{B}\,(u_y, \delta)$. Let $x \in B\,(x_0, r)$ and $z \in G\,(x)$. Since d_Y is a shift-invariant metric, it suffices to verify that $d_Y\,(y, z) \leq \delta + d_0 + \alpha r$. Since $d_X\,(y, u_y) \leq \delta$, let $(\varrho_n)_n$ be an increasing sequence of positive numbers such that $\lim_{n \to +\infty} \varrho_n = 1$ and $\varepsilon_n = \delta - \varrho_n d_X\,(y, u_y) > 0$, for every n. Now, for every n, let $y_{n,z} \in G\,(x_0)$ be such that $d_Y\,(y_{n,z}, z) < \alpha r + \frac{\varepsilon_n}{2}$. Then, we obtain

$$d_Y\,(y, z) \leq d_Y\,(y, u_y) + d_Y\,(u_y, y_{n,z}) + d_Y\,(y_{n,z}, z)$$
$$< d_Y\,(y, u_y) + d_0 + \alpha r + \frac{\varepsilon_n}{2},$$

and since $\lim_{n \to +\infty} \varepsilon_n = \delta - d_Y\,(y, u_y)$, we have

$$d_Y\,(y, z) \leq d_Y\,(y, u_y) + d_0 + \alpha r + \frac{\delta - d_Y\,(y, u_y)}{2}$$
$$= \frac{\delta + d_Y\,(y, u_y)}{2} + d_0 + \alpha r \leq \delta + d_0 + \alpha r$$

which completes the proof. $\qquad\qquad\square$

Remark 7.7. Theorem 7.3 and Theorem 7.4 provide us with the conclusion that the set-valued mapping $(F + G)^{-1}$ is Lipschitzian. In [19, Lemma 4.3], the authors obtain that the inverse of the considered set-valued mapping is pseudo-Lipschitzian, which is a property weaker than that of being Lipschitzian. It should be emphasized that this result has been used to derive sufficient conditions for the existence of double fixed points of set-valued mappings which, in particular, has applications to the problem of regularity of the composition of set-valued mappings, see [91].

Recall that the Banach open mapping theorem guarantees that a linear continuous mapping A from a Banach space X to a Banach space Y is surjective if and only if it is an open mapping. In particular, if A is surjective linear and continuous, then there exists $K > 0$ such that

$$B_Y(0, 1) \subset A(B_X(0, K)).$$

Corollary 7.3. *Let* $(X, \|.\|_X)$ *and* $(Y, \|.\|_Y)$ *be two Banach spaces. Denote by* $A : X \to Y$ *a surjective, linear, and continuous mapping and let K be the constant arising from the Banach open mapping theorem. Let $r > 0$ and $x_0 \in X$. Let* $g : X \to Y$ *be a single-valued mapping and suppose that the following conditions are satisfied:*

1. *there exist $\alpha > 0$ and a subset N of Y containing $A(x_0)$ such that $\alpha K < 1$, $g(B(x_0, r)) \subset \overline{B}(g(x_0), \alpha r)$, and g is α-pseudo-Lipschitzian on $B(x_0, r)$ with respect to $B\left(g(x_0), \frac{1-\alpha K}{K}r\right) + A(x_0) - N$;*
2. A^{-1} *is fully K-pseudo-Lipschitzian on $\overline{B}\left(A(x_0), \frac{1-\alpha K}{K}r + \alpha r\right)$ for N with respect to the set $B(x_0, r)$;*
3. *there exists $\beta > 0$ such that $\beta < (1 - \alpha K)r$, and A is (α, β)-compatible with respect to g on $B\left(g(x_0), \frac{1-\alpha K}{K}r\right)$ for x_0 and y_0.*

Then, $(A + G)^{-1}$ *is* $\frac{K}{1-\alpha K}$*-Lipschitzian on* $\overline{B}\left(A(x_0) + g(x_0), \frac{1-\alpha K}{K}r\right)$.

Proof. Let $F = A$ and $G = g$. From the Banach open mapping theorem,

$$\overline{B}\left(A(x_0), \frac{r}{K}\right) \subset A(\overline{B}(x_0, r)) = F(\overline{B}(x_0, r)).$$

We complete the proof by applying Theorem 7.4 with $\delta = \frac{1-\alpha K}{K}r$, $y_0 = A(x_0)$ and $d_0 = 0$. $\qquad\square$

We now give some remarks about the conditions on the mapping A that have been involved in the proof of Corollary 7.3. The continuity of A implies, by the Banach open mapping theorem, the openness of A. However, the linearity of A is not used in the proof. Instead of that, we need that A^{-1} is fully pseudo-Lipschitzian.

On the other hand, the openness of A can be involved without the linearity of A. In the literature and especially, in Convex Analysis without linearity, generalizations of some implicit function theorems and other questions of Optimization have been obtained without linearity, see [136]. See also [156] where a notion denoted by *PL* weaker than that of the linearity has been recently defined and a generalization of the Banach open mapping theorem has been derived. It is shown in particular, that every surjective continuous mapping acting between Banach spaces and satisfying the conditions of the notion *PL* is open.

7.4.4 Sensitivity Analysis of Variational Inclusions

In what follows, based on proximal convergence, we make use of the results developed previously and develop techniques related to the existence of solutions of variational inclusions.

Let (P, d_P) be a metric space which is called the set of parameters, and let $A : P \times X \rightrightarrows Y$ be a set-valued mapping, where (X, d_X) is metric space and (Y, d_Y) a linear metric space. For a fixed value of the parameter $p \in P$, we consider the parameterized generalized equation:

$$\text{find } x \in \text{dom}(A(p, .)) \text{ such that } 0 \in A(p, x), \qquad \text{(PGE)}$$

where its set of solutions is denoted by $S_A(p)$ which defines a set-valued mapping.

The regularity properties of the solution mapping $p \mapsto S_A(p)$ are related to the theory of implicit functions and its applications for variational inclusions.

We define a measure of the sensitivity of the solutions with respect to small changes in the problem's data in order to apply it to the problem of existence of solutions of variational inclusions. For any $p_0 \in P$, we define the full condition number of A at p_0 with respect to a subset W of X as the extended real-valued number by

$$c_f^*(A \mid p_0, W) = \limsup_{\substack{Z, Z' \to \{p_0\} \\ Z \neq Z', Z \neq \emptyset}} \frac{e\left(S_A(Z) \cap W, S_A(Z')\right)}{e(Z, Z')},$$

where the convergence is taken in the sense of the upper proximal convergence. A net $(Z_\gamma)_\gamma$ is upper proximal convergent to Z if $\lim_\gamma e(Z_\gamma, Z) = 0$. Therefore

$$c_f^*(A \mid p_0, W)$$
$$= \inf_{\varepsilon > 0} \sup \left\{ \frac{e\left(S_A(Z) \cap W, S_A(Z')\right)}{e(Z, Z')} \mid Z, Z' \subset B(p_0, \varepsilon), Z \neq Z', Z \neq \emptyset \right\}.$$

The extended real number $K(A, \delta | p_0, W)$ is defined by

$$K(A, \delta \mid p_0, W)$$
$$= \sup \left\{ \frac{e\left(S_A(Z) \cap W, S_A(Z')\right)}{e(Z, Z')} \mid Z, Z' \subset B(p_0, \delta), Z \neq Z', Z \neq \emptyset \right\}.$$

Then the function $\delta \mapsto K(A, \delta \mid p_0, W)$ is decreasing and for every $p_0 \in P$, we have $\lim_{\delta \to 0} K(A, \delta \mid p_0, W) = c^*(A \mid p_0, W)$.

Proposition 7.10. *If $K(A, \delta \mid p_0, W) < +\infty$, then one of the following alternatives holds:*

1. *there exists a neighborhood $V(p_0)$ of p_0 such that $S_A(p) = \emptyset$, for every $p \in U(p_0)$;*
2. *there exists a neighborhood $V(p_0)$ of p_0 such that $S_A(p) \neq \emptyset$, for every $p \in U(p_0)$.*

In particular, if $0 < K(A, \delta \mid p_0, W) < +\infty$, then there exists a neighborhood $V(p_0)$ of p_0 such that the solutions set of the parameterized generalized equation (PGE) is nonempty, for every $p \in V(p_0)$.

In the sequel we focus on the special case where $P = Y$. We study the parameterized generalized equation associated to $A : Y \times X \rightrightarrows Y$ defined by using a set-valued mapping $F : X \rightrightarrows Y$ as follows:

$$A(p, x) = \begin{cases} F(x) - p & \text{if } x \in B(x_0, r), \\ \emptyset & \text{otherwise.} \end{cases}$$

We remark that $S_A(Z) = F^{-1}(Z)$, for every subset Z of P and it results that in this framework, the full condition number given above takes the more explicit form

$$c_f^*(A \mid p_0, W) = \limsup_{\substack{Z, Z' \to \{p_0\} \\ Z \neq Z', Z \neq \emptyset}} \frac{e\left(F^{-1}(Z) \cap W, F^{-1}(Z')\right)}{e(Z, Z')}.$$

In this setting, we will write $c_f^*(F \mid p_0, W)$ and $K(F, \delta \mid p_0, B(x_0, r))$ instead of $c_f^*(A \mid p_0, W)$ and $K(A, \delta \mid p_0, B(x_0, r))$, respectively.

Now, we obtain the following result on the existence of solutions of parameterized generalized equations.

Theorem 7.5. *Let $r > 0$, $x_0 \in X$, and $p_0 \in Y$ be such that $\overline{B}(x_0, r)$ is a complete metric subspace. Let $G : X \rightrightarrows Y$ be a set-valued mapping. Suppose that*

$$0 < c^*(F \mid p_0, B(x_0, r)) < +\infty$$

and choose $\overline{\delta}$ such that $K\left(F, \overline{\delta} \mid p_0, B(x_0, r)\right) < +\infty$. Suppose further that the following conditions are satisfied

1. *G has nonempty closed values on $B(x_0, r)$, $G(x_0)$ is a bounded set with diameter $d_0 < \overline{\delta}$, and there exist a subset N containing $B\left(p_0, \overline{\delta}\right)$ and*

$$0 < \alpha < \min\left\{\frac{\overline{\delta} - d_0}{r}, \frac{1}{K\left(F, \overline{\delta} \mid p_0, B(x_0, r)\right)}\right\}$$

such that $G(B(x_0, r)) \subset \overline{B(G(x_0), \alpha r)}$, and G is α-pseudo-Lipschitzian on $B(x_0, r)$ with respect to $B\left(G(x_0), \overline{\delta} - \alpha r - d_0\right) + p_0 - N$;
2. *$B(x_0, r) \subset dom(F)$, $B\left(p_0, \overline{\delta}\right) \subset F(B(x_0, r))$ and F is upper semicontinuous;*

3. *there exists $\beta > 0$ such that $\beta < \left(1 - \alpha K \left(F, \overline{\delta} \mid p_0, B(x_0, r)\right)\right) r$, and F is (α, β)-compatible with respect to G on $B\left(G(x_0), \overline{\delta} - \alpha r - d_0\right)$ for x_0 and p_0.*

Then, $c^*(F + G \mid p_0 + y, B(x_0, r)) \leq \dfrac{K(F,\overline{\delta}|p_0, B(x_0,r))}{1-\alpha K(F,\overline{\delta}|p_0, B(x_0,r))} < +\infty$, for every $y \in G(x_0)$.

Proof. Put $\delta = \overline{\delta} - \alpha r - d_0 > 0$. We have $\alpha K\left(F, \overline{\delta} \mid p_0, B(x_0, r)\right) < 1$. Also, for every subset Z, Z' of $B\left(p_0, \overline{\delta}\right)$, we have

$$e\left(F^{-1}(Z) \cap B(x_0, r), F^{-1}(Z')\right) \leq K\left(F, \overline{\delta} \mid p_0, B(x_0, r)\right) e(Z, Z')$$

and then, F^{-1} is fully $K\left(F, \overline{\delta} \mid p_0, B(x_0, r)\right)$-pseudo-Lipschitzian on $B\left(p_0, \overline{\delta}\right)$ for N with respect to $B(x_0, r)$.

By Theorem 7.3, it follows that the set-valued mapping $(F + G)^{-1}$ is $\dfrac{K(F,\overline{\delta}|p_0, B(x_0,r))}{1-\alpha K(F,\overline{\delta}|p_0, B(x_0,r))}$-Lipschitzian on $B(G(x_0) + p_0, \delta)$. Then, for every $y \in G(x_0)$, we have

$$
\begin{aligned}
&c^*(F + G \mid y + p_0, B(x_0, r)) \\
&= \limsup_{\substack{Z, Z' \to \{y+p_0\} \\ Z \neq Z', Z \neq \emptyset}} \frac{e\left((F + G)^{-1}(Z) \cap B(x_0, r), (F + G)^{-1}(Z')\right)}{e(Z, Z')} \\
&\leq \sup_{\substack{Z, Z' \subset B(y+p_0, \delta), \\ Z \neq Z', Z \neq \emptyset}} \frac{e\left((F + G)^{-1}(Z), (F + G)^{-1}(Z')\right)}{e(Z, Z')} \\
&\leq \frac{K\left(F, \overline{\delta} \mid p_0, B(x_0, r)\right)}{1 - \alpha K\left(F, \overline{\delta} \mid p_0, B(x_0, r)\right)} < +\infty,
\end{aligned}
$$

which completes the proof. $\qquad\square$

NOTES

1. Stefan Banach (1892–1945), Polish mathematician and one of the world's most important and influential 20th-century mathematicians. He founded modern functional analysis and helped develop the theory of topological vector spaces. Banach was a member of the Lwów School of Mathematics. His major work was the 1932 book, *Théorie des Opérations Linéaires*, the first monograph on the general theory of functional analysis. Banach himself introduced the concept of *complete normed linear spaces*, which are now known as *Banach spaces*. He also proved several fundamental theorems in the field, and his applications of theory inspired much of the work in functional analysis for the next few decades.

2. Dimitrie Pompeiu (1873–1954), Romanian mathematician. In 1905, he obtained a Ph.D. degree in mathematics in Paris with a thesis written under the direction of Henri Poincaré. He is known for a challenging conjecture in integral geometry, now widely known as the *Pompeiu problem*. Pompeiu constructed a nonconstant, everywhere differentiable functions, with derivative vanishing on a dense set. Such derivatives are now called *Pompeiu derivatives*.

3. Felix Hausdorff (1868–1942), renowned German mathematician with pioneering contributions in analysis. He introduced several fundamental concepts, such as Hausdorff spaces, Hausdorff dimension, Hausdorff metric, Hausdorff density, Hausdorff maximal principle, Hausdorff measure, Hausdorff moment problem, or Hausdorff paradox.

Chapter 8

Applications to Nash Equilibrium

Contents

Look up at the stars and not down at your feet.

Stephen Hawking (1942–2018)

Chapter points

- The result of this approach is to produce a rigorous mathematical analysis for models at the interplay between Nash equilibria and mathematical physics.
- The arguments combine refined analytic tools, variational analysis, fixed point theory, and iterative methods.
- Applications include periodic problems with variational or nonvariational structure as well as problems driven by singular operators.

8.1 INTRODUCTION

Many problems describing models in the real world can be reduced to fixed point problems of the type

$$u = N(u),$$

where N is a nonlinear operator.

Equilibrium Problems and Applications. https://doi.org/10.1016/B978-0-12-811029-4.00016-X

In many cases, the problem has a variational structure, namely it is equivalent to finding the critical points of the associated "energy" functional E, that is $E'(u) = 0$. Thus, the fixed points of the operator N appear as critical points of the functional E. The critical points could be minima, maxima or saddle points, conferring to the fixed points a variational property. Thus, it makes sense to ask whether a fixed point of N is a minimum, or a maximum or a saddle point of E. Problems of this type become more interesting in the case of a system

$$\begin{cases} u = N_1(u, v) \\ v = N_2(u, v), \end{cases} \tag{8.1}$$

which does not have a variational form, but each of its component equations has a variational structure. More precisely, there exist functionals E_1 and E_2 such that the system (8.1) is equivalent to

$$\begin{cases} E_{11}(u, v) = 0 \\ E_{22}(u, v) = 0, \end{cases}$$

where $E_{11}(u, v)$ is the partial derivative of E_1 with respect to u, and $E_{22}(u, v)$ is the partial derivative of E_2 with respect to v.

A nontrivial problem is to see how the fixed points (u, v) of the operator $N = (N_1, N_2)$ are connected to the variational properties of the two functionals. One possible situation, which fits to physical principles, is that a fixed point (u^*, v^*) of N is a Nash-type equilibrium of the functionals E_1, E_2, that is,

$$E_1(u^*, v^*) = \min_u E_1(u, v^*)$$
$$E_2(u^*, v^*) = \min_v E_2(u^*, v).$$

(Note that the relations above correspond to a symmetric form of (2.11) in Chapter 2, for the particular case of $n = 2$, in the sense that "min" is taken instead of "max".)

In the next section, we will focus on this problem in relationship with the Nash equilibrium for Perov contractions. An iterative scheme for finding a Nash-type equilibrium is introduced and its convergence is studied. The result is illustrated with an application to periodic solutions for a second-order differential system, which describes the oscillations of two pendulums.

We first establish a minimum property for classical contractions in the abstract setting of Hilbert space. We start with the case of contractions on the whole space.

Theorem 8.1. *Let X be a Hilbert space and $N : X \to X$ be a contraction with the unique fixed point u^*. Assume that there exists a C^1-functional E bounded from below such that*

$$E'(u) = u - N(u) \quad \text{for all } u \in X. \tag{8.2}$$

Then u^* minimizes the functional E, that is,

$$E\left(u^*\right) = \inf_X E.$$

Proof. By the Bishop-Phelps theorem (Theorem A.4 in Appendix A), there is a sequence (u_n) with

$$E\left(u_n\right) \to \inf_X E \quad \text{and} \quad E'\left(u_n\right) \to 0. \tag{8.3}$$

Let $v_n := E'\left(u_n\right) = u_n - N\left(u_n\right)$. We have $v_n \to 0$ and

$$\left|u_{n+p} - u_n\right| \le \left|N\left(u_{n+p}\right) - N\left(u_n\right)\right| + \left|v_{n+p} - v_n\right|$$
$$\le a\left|u_{n+p} - u_n\right| + \left|v_{n+p} - v_n\right|.$$

Here, $a \in [0, 1)$ is the contraction constant of N. Hence

$$\left|u_{n+p} - u_n\right| \le \frac{1}{1 - a}\left|v_{n+p} - v_n\right|.$$

Since (v_n) is a convergent sequence, this implies that (u_n) is Cauchy, too. It follows that $u_n \to \overline{u}$ for some $\overline{u}$. Now relation (8.3) yields

$$E\left(\overline{u}\right) = \inf_X E \quad \text{and} \quad E'\left(\overline{u}\right) = 0.$$

Relation $E'\left(\overline{u}\right) = 0$ shows that $\overline{u}$ is a fixed point of N, and since N has a unique fixed point, $\overline{u} = u^*$.

An analogue result holds for contractions on a ball $\overline{B}_R = \{u \in X : |u| \le R\}$ of the Hilbert space X. $\qquad\square$

Theorem 8.2. *Let X be a Hilbert space and $N : \overline{B}_R \to X$ be a contraction satisfying the Leray-Schauder condition*

$$u \ne \lambda N\left(u\right) \quad \text{for } |u| = R \text{ and } \lambda \in (0, 1). \tag{8.4}$$

Let u^* denote the unique fixed point of N (guaranteed by the nonlinear alternative). Assume that there exists a C^1-functional E bounded from below on $\overline{B}_R$ such that

$$E'\left(u\right) = u - N\left(u\right) \quad \text{for all } u \in \overline{B}_R.$$

Then u^* minimizes the functional E on $\overline{B}_R$, that is,

$$E\left(u^*\right) = \inf_{\overline{B}_R} E.$$

Proof. As a consequence of Schechter's critical point theorem in a ball (Theorem A.5 in Appendix A), there is a sequence (u_n) of elements from $\overline{B}_R$, with

$$E(u_n) \to \inf_{\overline{B}_R} E \quad \text{and}$$

$$\text{either} \quad E'(u_n) \to 0, \quad \text{or}$$

$$E'(u_n) - \frac{(E'(u_n), u_n)}{R^2} u_n \to 0, \quad |u_n| = R, \quad (E'(u_n), u_n) \leq 0.$$

In the first case, when $E'(u_n) \to 0$, we repeat the argument developed in the proof of Theorem 8.1.

In the second case, since $(E'(u_n), u_n) = R^2 - (N(u_n), u_n)$ and N is bounded as a contraction, we may pass to a subsequence in order to assume the convergence

$$\mu_n := -\frac{(E'(u_n), u_n)}{R^2} \to \mu \geq 0.$$

Furthermore, if $v_n := E'(u_n) + \mu_n u_n$, then

$$(1 + \mu) u_n = v_n + N(u_n) + z_n$$

with $z_n = (\mu - \mu_n) u_n$. Therefore $z_n \to 0$. Next, we observe that

$$(1 + \mu) |u_{n+p} - u_n| \leq |v_{n+p} - v_n| + a |u_{n+p} - u_n| + |z_{n+p} - z_n|$$

and so

$$|u_{n+p} - u_n| \leq \frac{1}{1 + \mu - a} \left(|v_{n+p} - v_n| + |z_{n+p} - z_n| \right).$$

This implies that (u_n) is Cauchy. Let $\overline{u}$ be its limit. Then

$$E(\overline{u}) = \inf_{\overline{B}_R} E \quad \text{and} \quad E'(\overline{u}) + \mu \overline{u} = 0,$$

where $|\overline{u}| = R$ and $\mu \geq 0$. We claim that the case $\mu > 0$ is not possible. Indeed, if we assume that $\mu > 0$, then from $\overline{u} - N(\overline{u}) + \mu \overline{u} = 0$ we would have $\overline{u} = \frac{1}{1+\mu} N(\overline{u})$ which has been excluded by the Leray-Schauder condition (8.4). Hence $\mu = 0$, $E'(\overline{u}) = 0$, that is, $\overline{u} = N(\overline{u})$. Again the uniqueness of the fixed point guarantees $\overline{u} = u^*$. $\quad\square$

We recall that a sequence (u_n) with $(E(u_n))$ converging and $E'(u_n) \to 0$ is called a *Palais-Smale sequence*, while the property of a functional of existing a convergent subsequence for each Palais-Smale sequence, is named the *Palais-Smale condition*. Thus, Theorem 8.1 asserts that if E' is represented by (8.2), then E satisfies even more than the Palais-Smale condition, in the sense that the Palais-Smale sequences are entirely (not only some of their subsequences) convergent.

We point out that if in Theorem 8.2, the operator N is assumed to be more general condensing, then the minimizing sequence (u_n) has a subsequence converging to the absolute minimum of E on $\overline{B}_R$. Indeed, if (u_n) satisfies $E'(u_n) \to 0$, then using a measure α of noncompactness with respect to whom N is condensing, we find

$$\alpha\left(\{u_n\}\right) = \alpha\left(\left\{E'(u_n) + N(u_n)\right\}\right) \qquad (8.5)$$
$$\leq \alpha\left(\left\{E'(u_n)\right\}\right) + \alpha\left(\{N(u_n)\}\right)$$
$$= \alpha\left(\{N(u_n)\}\right).$$

If $\{u_n\}$ is not relatively compact, that is, $\alpha\left(\{u_n\}\right) > 0$, then by the condensing property, $\alpha\left(\{N(u_n)\}\right) < \alpha\left(\{u_n\}\right)$, which in view of (8.5) yields the contradiction $\alpha\left(\{u_n\}\right) < \alpha\left(\{u_n\}\right)$. Hence $\{u_n\}$ is relatively compact, as desired.

If we focus on critical points of a functional E, and not on the fixed points of an operator N, then we can state the following more general result.

Theorem 8.3. *Let X be a Banach space with norm $|.|$ and E be a C^1-functional bounded from below with E' strongly monotone, that is*

$$\left(E'(u) - E'(v), u - v\right) \geq a\,|u - v|^2 \ \text{for all } u, v \in X,$$

and some $a > 0$. Then there exists $u^* \in X$ with

$$E\left(u^*\right) = \inf_X E \quad \text{and} \quad E'\left(u^*\right) = 0.$$

Proof. As in the proof of Theorem 8.1, let (u_n) be such that

$$E(u_n) \to \inf_X E \quad \text{and} \quad E'(u_n) \to 0.$$

Denote $v_n := E'(u_n)$. We have $v_n \to 0$ in X', and

$$a\,|u_{n+p} - u_n|^2 \leq \left(E'\left(u_{n+p}\right) - E'(u_n), u_{n+p} - u_n\right)$$
$$= \left(v_{n+p} - v_n, u_{n+p} - u_n\right) \leq \left|v_{n+p} - v_n\right|\left|u_{n+p} - u_n\right|.$$

It follows that

$$\left|u_{n+p} - u_n\right| \leq \frac{1}{a}\left|v_{n+p} - v_n\right|$$

and the assertion follows as above. $\qquad\square$

Similarly, we have the following generalization of Theorem 8.2.

Theorem 8.4. *Let X be a Hilbert space and E be a C^1 functional such that E' is strongly monotone on $\overline{B}_R$ and*

$$E'(u) + \mu u \neq 0 \ \text{for } |u| = R \text{ and } \mu > 0.$$

Then there exists u^* with

$$E\left(u^*\right) = \inf_{\overline{B}_R} E \quad and \quad E'\left(u^*\right) = 0.$$

Proof. With the notations from the proof of Theorem 8.2, we have

$$
\begin{aligned}
& a\left|u_{n+p} - u_n\right|^2 \\
& \leq \left(E'\left(u_{n+p}\right) - E'\left(u_n\right), u_{n+p} - u_n\right) \\
& = \left(v_{n+p} - v_n, u_{n+p} - u_n\right) - \mu\left(u_{n+p} - u_n, u_{n+p} - u_n\right) \\
& \quad + \left(\mu - \mu_{n+p}\right)\left(u_{n+p}, u_{n+p} - u_n\right) - \left(\mu - \mu_n\right)\left(u_n, u_{n+p} - u_n\right).
\end{aligned}
$$

Hence

$$(a + \mu)\left|u_{n+p} - u_n\right| \leq \left|v_{n+p} - v_n\right| + R\left(\left|\mu - \mu_{n+p}\right| + \left|\mu - \mu_n\right|\right),$$

which implies that (u_n) is a Cauchy sequence. □

8.2 NASH EQUILIBRIUM FOR PEROV CONTRACTIONS

Let $(X_i, |.|_i)$, $i = 1, 2$, be Hilbert spaces identified to their dual spaces and let $X = X_1 \times X_2$. Consider the system

$$
\begin{cases}
u = N_1(u, v) \\
v = N_2(u, v)
\end{cases}
$$

where $(u, v) \in X$. Assume that each equation of the system has a variational form, that is, there exist continuous functionals $E_1, E_2 : X \to \mathbb{R}$ such that $E_1(., v)$ is Fréchet differentiable for every $v \in X_2$, $E_2(u, .)$ is Fréchet differentiable for every $u \in X_1$, and

$$
\begin{aligned}
E_{11}(u, v) &= u - N_1(u, v) \quad\quad (8.6) \\
E_{22}(u, v) &= v - N_2(u, v).
\end{aligned}
$$

As in the previous section, $E_{11}(., v)$, $E_{22}(u, .)$ denote the Fréchet derivatives of $E_1(., v)$ and $E_2(u, .)$, respectively.

We say that the operator $N : X \to X$, $N(u, v) = (N_1(u, v), N_2(u, v))$ is a *Perov contraction* if there exists a matrix $M = \left[m_{ij}\right] \in \mathcal{M}_{2,2}(\mathbb{R}_+)$ such that M^n tends to the zero matrix 0, and the following matricial Lipschitz condition is satisfied

$$
\begin{bmatrix}
|N_1(u, v) - N_1(\overline{u}, \overline{v})|_1 \\
|N_2(u, v) - N_2(\overline{u}, \overline{v})|_2
\end{bmatrix}
\leq M
\begin{bmatrix}
|u - \overline{u}|_1 \\
|v - \overline{v}|_2
\end{bmatrix}
\quad\quad (8.7)
$$

for every $u, \overline{u} \in X_1$ and $v, \overline{v} \in X_2$.

Notice that the property $M^n \to 0$ is equivalent to $\rho(M) < 1$, where $\rho(M)$ is the spectral radius of matrix M, and also to the fact that $I - M$ is non-singular and all the elements of the matrix $(I - M)^{-1}$ are nonnegative (see Precup [143], [144]).

Theorem 8.5. *Assume that the above conditions are satisfied. In addition, we assume that $E_1(., v)$ and $E_2(u, .)$ are bounded from below for every $u \in X_1$, $v \in X_2$, and that there exist positive numbers R and a such that one of the following conditions holds:*

$$\text{either } E_1(u, v) \geq \inf_{X_1} E_1(., v) + a \text{ for } |u|_1 \geq R \text{ and all } v \in X_2,$$
$$\text{or } E_2(u, v) \geq \inf_{X_2} E_2(u, .) + a \text{ for } |v|_2 \geq R \text{ and all } u \in X_1. \tag{8.8}$$

Then the unique fixed point (u^*, v^*) of N (guaranteed by Perov's fixed point theorem) is a Nash-type equilibrium of the pair of functionals (E_1, E_2), that is,

$$E_1(u^*, v^*) = \inf_{X_1} E_1(., v^*)$$
$$E_2(u^*, v^*) = \inf_{X_2} E_2(u^*, .).$$

Proof. Assume that relation (8.8) holds for E_2. We shall construct recursively two sequences (u_n), (v_n), based on the Bishop-Phelps theorem. Let v_0 be any element of X_2. At any step n $(n \geq 1)$ we may find a $u_n \in X_1$ and a $v_n \in X_2$ such that

$$E_1(u_n, v_{n-1}) \leq \inf_{X_1} E_1(., v_{n-1}) + \frac{1}{n}, \quad |E_{11}(u_n, v_{n-1})|_1 \leq \frac{1}{n} \tag{8.9}$$

and

$$E_2(u_n, v_n) \leq \inf_{X_2} E_2(u_n, .) + \frac{1}{n}, \quad |E_{22}(u_n, v_n)|_2 \leq \frac{1}{n}. \tag{8.10}$$

For $\frac{1}{n} < a$, from (8.8) and (8.10) we have $|v_n|_2 < R$. Hence the sequence (v_n) is bounded. Let $\alpha_n := E_{11}(u_n, v_{n-1})$ and $\beta_n := E_{22}(u_n, v_n)$. Clearly $\alpha_n, \beta_n \to 0$. Also

$$u_n - N_1(u_n, v_{n-1}) = \alpha_n$$
$$v_n - N_2(u_n, v_n) = \beta_n.$$

It follows that

$$|u_{n+p} - u_n|_1 \leq |N_1(u_{n+p}, v_{n+p-1}) - N_1(u_n, v_{n-1})|_1 + |\alpha_{n+p} - \alpha_n|_1$$
$$\leq m_{11}|u_{n+p} - u_n|_1 + m_{12}|v_{n+p-1} - v_{n-1}|_2 + |\alpha_{n+p} - \alpha_n|_1$$

$$\leq m_{11} |u_{n+p} - u_n|_1 + m_{12} |v_{n+p} - v_n|_2 + |\alpha_{n+p} - \alpha_n|_1$$
$$+ m_{12} \left(|v_{n+p-1} - v_{n-1}|_2 - |v_{n+p} - v_n|_2 \right).$$

Denote $a_{n,p} = |u_{n+p} - u_n|_1$, $b_{n,p} = |v_{n+p} - v_n|_2$, $c_{n,p} = |\alpha_{n+p} - \alpha_n|_1$, $d_{n,p} = |\beta_{n+p} - \beta_n|_2$. Then

$$a_{n,p} \leq m_{11} a_{n,p} + m_{12} b_{n,p} + c_{n,p} + m_{12} \left(b_{n-1,p} - b_{n,p} \right). \tag{8.11}$$

Similarly, we deduce that

$$b_{n,p} \leq m_{21} a_{n,p} + m_{22} b_{n,p} + d_{n,p}.$$

Hence

$$\begin{bmatrix} a_{n,p} \\ b_{n,p} \end{bmatrix} \leq M \begin{bmatrix} a_{n,p} \\ b_{n,p} \end{bmatrix} + \begin{bmatrix} c_{n,p} + m_{12} \left(b_{n-1,p} - b_{n,p} \right) \\ d_{n,p} \end{bmatrix}.$$

Consequently, since $I - M$ is invertible and its inverse contains only nonnegative elements, we may write

$$\begin{bmatrix} a_{n,p} \\ b_{n,p} \end{bmatrix} \leq (I - M)^{-1} \begin{bmatrix} c_{n,p} + m_{12} \left(b_{n-1,p} - b_{n,p} \right) \\ d_{n,p} \end{bmatrix}.$$

Let $(I - M)^{-1} = [\gamma_{ij}]$. Then

$$a_{n,p} \leq \gamma_{11} \left(c_{n,p} + m_{12} \left(b_{n-1,p} - b_{n,p} \right) \right) + \gamma_{12} d_{n,p} \tag{8.12}$$
$$b_{n,p} \leq \gamma_{21} \left(c_{n,p} + m_{12} \left(b_{n-1,p} - b_{n,p} \right) \right) + \gamma_{22} d_{n,p}.$$

From the second inequality, we deduce that

$$b_{n,p} \leq \frac{\gamma_{21} m_{12}}{1 + \gamma_{21} m_{12}} b_{n-1,p} + \frac{\gamma_{21} c_{n,p} + \gamma_{22} d_{n,p}}{1 + \gamma_{21} m_{12}}. \tag{8.13}$$

We observe that $(b_{n,p})$ is bounded uniformly with respect to p. Lemma 8.1 shows that $b_{n,p} \to 0$ uniformly for $p \in \mathbb{N}$, and hence (v_n) is a Cauchy sequence. Next, the first inequality in (8.12) implies that (u_n) is also Cauchy. Let u^*, v^* be the limits of (u_n), (v_n), respectively. The conclusion now follows if we pass to the limit in (8.9) and (8.10).

In case that E_1 satisfies (8.8), we interchange E_1, E_2 in the construction of the two sequences, more exactly we obtain

$$E_2 (u_{n-1}, v_n) \leq \inf_{X_2} E_2 (u_{n-1}, .) + \frac{1}{n}, \quad |E_{22} (u_{n-1}, v_n)|_2 \leq \frac{1}{n} \tag{8.14}$$

and

$$E_1(u_n, v_n) \leq \inf_{X_1} E_1(., v_n) + \frac{1}{n}, \quad |E_{11}(u_n, v_n)|_1 \leq \frac{1}{n}. \qquad (8.15)$$

This completes the proof. $\qquad\qquad\qquad\qquad\qquad\qquad\qquad\qquad\qquad\qquad$ □

The following elementary result is frequently used to argue the convergence of the iterative schemas.

Lemma 8.1. *Let* $(x_{n,p})$, $(y_{n,p})$ *be two sequences of real numbers depending on a parameter p, such that*

$$(x_{n,p}) \text{ is bounded uniformly with respect to } p,$$

and

$$0 \leq x_{n,p} \leq \lambda x_{n-1,p} + y_{n,p} \text{ for all } n, p \text{ and some } \lambda \in [0, 1). \qquad (8.16)$$

If $y_{n,p} \to 0$ *uniformly with respect to p, then* $x_{n,p} \to 0$ *uniformly with respect to p too.*

Proof. Let $\varepsilon > 0$ be any number. Since $y_{n,p} \to 0$ uniformly with respect to p, there exists n_1 (not depending on p) such that $y_{n,p} \leq \varepsilon$ for all $n \geq n_1$. From $x_{n,p} \leq \lambda x_{n-1,p} + \varepsilon$ $(n \geq n_1)$, we deduce that

$$x_{n,p} \leq \lambda^{n-n_1} x_{n_1} + \varepsilon \left(\lambda + \lambda^2 + ... + \lambda^{n-n_1} \right) \leq \lambda^{n-n_1} c + \varepsilon \frac{\lambda}{1-\lambda},$$

where c is a bound for $x_{n,p}$. This yields $x_{n,p} \to 0$, uniformly in p. $\qquad$ □

Remark 8.1. If instead of condition (8.8) we assume that there exist convergent subsequences (u_{n_j}), (v_{n_j}) of the sequences (u_n), (v_n) given by (8.9) and (8.10), then the conclusion of Theorem 8.5 remains true. To prove this, we first show that the sequence $(b_{n_j-1,1})$ defined by $b_{n_j-1,1} = |v_{n_j} - v_{n_j-1}|_2$ is bounded. Indeed, from (8.13), we obtain that

$$b_{n_j-1,1} \leq \lambda b_{n_j-2,1} + (1 - \lambda)^2 \quad (j \geq j_1).$$

This yields

$$b_{n_j-1,1} \leq \lambda^{n_j-n_{j-1}} b_{n_{j-1}-1,1} + 1 - \lambda \quad (j \geq j_2),$$

whence

$$b_{n_j-1,1} - 1 \leq \lambda \left(b_{n_{j-1}-1,1} - 1 \right) \quad (j \geq j_2). \qquad (8.17)$$

Denote $z_j = b_{n_j-1,1}$. Notice that the case $z_j > 1$ for all $j \geq j_2$ is not possible. Since otherwise $0 \leq z_j - 1 \leq \lambda^{j-j_2} (z_{j_2} - 1)$, whence $z_j \to 1$. However, by (8.16), this would imply the contradiction $1 \leq 1 - \lambda$. Therefore, there exists

$j_3 \geq j_2$ with $z_{j_3} \leq 1$. Then (8.17) implies that $z_j \leq 1$ for all $j \geq j_3$, hence (z_j) is bounded, as claimed.

Next, from Lemma 8.1, applied for $p = 1$ and $x_{j,1} := b_{n_j-1,1}$, we find that $b_{n_j-1,1} \to 0$ as $j \to \infty$. Hence the sequence (v_{n_j-1}) is convergent to the limit v^* of (v_{n_j}). The conclusion follows if we let $j \to \infty$ in (8.9), (8.10) with $n = n_j$.

An analogue result holds for Perov contractions on the Cartesian product $\overline{B}_{R_1} \times \overline{B}_{R_2}$ of two balls of X_1 and X_2.

Theorem 8.6. *Let $N : \overline{B}_{R_1} \times \overline{B}_{R_2} \to X$, $N = (N_1, N_2)$ be a Perov generalized contraction, that is, relation (8.7) is satisfied for $u, \overline{u} \in \overline{B}_{R_1}$ and $v, \overline{v} \in \overline{B}_{R_2}$. Assume that for every $\lambda \in (0, 1)$,*

$$u \neq \lambda N_1(u, v) \quad \text{if} \quad |u|_1 = R_1, \ v \in \overline{B}_{R_2},$$

$$v \neq \lambda N_2(u, v) \quad \text{if} \quad |v|_2 = R_2, \ u \in \overline{B}_{R_1}.$$

In addition, we assume that the representation (8.6) holds on $\overline{B}_{R_1} \times \overline{B}_{R_2}$ for two continuous functionals $E_1, E_2 : X \to \mathbb{R}$ such that $E_1(., v)$ is Fréchet differentiable for every $v \in X_2$, $E_2(u, .)$ is Fréchet differentiable for every $u \in X_1$, and that $E_1(., v)$, $E_2(u, .)$ are bounded from below on $\overline{B}_{R_1}$ and $\overline{B}_{R_2}$ respectively, for every $u \in \overline{B}_{R_1}$, $v \in \overline{B}_{R_2}$. Then the unique fixed point $(u^*, v^*) \in \overline{B}_{R_1} \times \overline{B}_{R_2}$ of N (guaranteed by the nonlinear alternative for Perov contractions, see Precup [143]) is a Nash-type equilibrium in $\overline{B}_{R_1} \times \overline{B}_{R_2}$ of the pair of functionals (E_1, E_2), that is,

$$E_1(u^*, v^*) = \inf_{\overline{B}_{R_1}} E_1(., v^*)$$

$$E_2(u^*, v^*) = \inf_{\overline{B}_{R_2}} E_2(u^*, .).$$

The proof combines arguments from the proofs of Theorems 8.2 and 8.5.

8.2.1 Application: Oscillations of Two Pendulums

Consider the following periodic problem

$$
\begin{aligned}
u''(t) &= \nabla_x F(t, u(t), v(t)) \quad \text{a.e. on } (0, T) \\
v''(t) &= \nabla_y G(t, u(t), v(t)) \quad \text{a.e. on } (0, T) \\
u(0) - u(T) &= u'(0) - u'(T) = 0 \\
v(0) - v(T) &= v'(0) - v'(T) = 0,
\end{aligned}
\tag{8.18}
$$

where $F, G : (0, T) \times \mathbb{R}^{k_1} \times \mathbb{R}^{k_2} \to \mathbb{R}$.

All functions of the type $H : (0, T) \times \mathbb{R}^n \to \mathbb{R}^m$, $H = H(t, x)$ $(n, m \geq 1)$, including $F, G, \nabla_x F$, and $\nabla_y G$, will be assumed to be L^1-Carathéodory, namely $H(., x)$ is measurable for each $x \in \mathbb{R}^n$, $H(t, .)$ is continuous for a.e. $t \in (0, T)$, and such that for each $R > 0$, there exists $b_R \in L^1(0, T; \mathbb{R}_+)$ with $|H(t, x)| \leq b_R(t)$ for a.e. $t \in (0, T)$ and all $x \in \mathbb{R}^n$, $|x| \leq R$.

In our case, the system does not have a variational structure, but it splits into two subsystems having each one a variational form.

A pair $(u, v) \in H^1_p(0, T; \mathbb{R}^{k_1}) \times H^1_p(0, T; \mathbb{R}^{k_2})$ is a solution of problem (8.18) if and only if

$$E_{11}(u, v) = 0, \quad E_{22}(u, v) = 0,$$

where $E_1, E_2 : H^1_p(0, T; \mathbb{R}^{k_1}) \times H^1_p(0, T; \mathbb{R}^{k_2}) \to \mathbb{R}$,

$$E_1(u, v) = \int_0^T \left(\frac{1}{2} |u'|^2 + F(t, u(t), v(t)) \right) dt$$

$$E_2(u, v) = \int_0^T \left(\frac{1}{2} |v'|^2 + G(t, u(t), v(t)) \right) dt.$$

(8.19)

Here, $H^1_p(0, T; \mathbb{R}^k)$ is the space of functions of the form

$$u(t) = \int_0^t v(s)ds + c,$$

with $u(0) = u(T)$, $c \in \mathbb{R}^k$, and $v \in L^2(0, T; \mathbb{R}^k)$.

We define a scalar product in $H^1_p(0, T; \mathbb{R}^{k_i})$ ($i = 1, 2$) by

$$(u, v)_i = \int_0^T \left[(u'(t), v'(t)) + m_i^2 (u(t), v(t)) \right] dt,$$

where $m_i \neq 0$. The corresponding norm is

$$|u|_i = \left(\int_0^T \left(|u'(t)|^2 + m_i^2 |u(t)|^2 \right) dt \right)^{1/2}.$$

We identify the dual $\left(H^1_p(0, T; \mathbb{R}^{k_i}) \right)'$ to $H^1_p(0, T; \mathbb{R}^{k_i})$ via the mapping J_i defined by

$$\left(H^1_p\left(0, T; \mathbb{R}^{k_i}\right) \right)' \ni h \mapsto J_i h = u,$$

the unique weak solution of the problem

$$-u'' + m_i^2 u = h \quad \text{a.e. on } (0, T)$$
$$u(0) - u(T) = u'(0) - u'(T) = 0.$$

Then

$$E_{11}(u, v) = u - J_1\left(m_1^2 u - \nabla_x F(., u, v) \right),$$

$$E_{22}(u, v) = v - J_2\left(m_2^2 v - \nabla_y G(., u, v)\right).$$

Hence

$$N_1(u, v) = J_1\left(m_1^2 u - \nabla_x F(., u, v)\right), \quad N_2(u, v) = J_2\left(m_2^2 v - \nabla_y G(., u, v)\right).$$

In what follows, we use the obvious inequality

$$|u|_{L^2} \le \frac{1}{m_i}|u|_i \quad \left(u \in H_p^1\left(0, T; \mathbb{R}^{k_i}\right)\right) \tag{8.20}$$

and the estimation of the norm of J_i, as linear operator from $L^2\left(0, T; \mathbb{R}^{k_i}\right)$ to $H_p^1\left(0, T; \mathbb{R}^{k_i}\right)$. To obtain this, we start with the definition of the operator J_i, which gives

$$|J_i h|_i^2 = (J_i h, J_i h)_i = (h, J_i h)_{L^2} \le |h|_{L^2}|J_i h|_{L^2} \le \frac{1}{m_i}|h|_{L^2}|J_i h|_i.$$

Hence

$$|J_i h|_i \le \frac{1}{m_i}|h|_{L^2} \quad \left(h \in L^2\left(0, T; \mathbb{R}^{k_i}\right)\right). \tag{8.21}$$

We say that a function $H : (0, T) \times \mathbb{R}^k \to R$ is of *coercive type* if the functional $E : H_p^1\left(0, T; \mathbb{R}^k\right) \to \mathbb{R}$,

$$E(u) = \int_0^T \left(\frac{1}{2}|u'(t)|^2 + H(t, u(t))\right) dt \tag{8.22}$$

is coercive, that is, $E(u) \to +\infty$ as $|u| \to \infty$. Here we have denoted

$$|u| = \left(\int_0^T \left(|u'(t)|^2 + |u(t)|^2\right) dt\right)^{1/2}.$$

Lemma 8.2. *Assume that for some $\gamma \in \mathbb{R} \setminus \{0\}$, $\nabla\left(H - \gamma^2|x|^2\right)$ is bounded by an L^1-function for all $x \in \mathbb{R}^k$ and the average of $H(t, x) - \gamma^2|x|^2$ with respect to t is bounded from below, more exactly:*

$$\left|\nabla\left(H(t, x) - \gamma^2|x|^2\right)\right| \le a(t)$$

for a.e. $t \in (0, T)$, all $x \in \mathbb{R}^k$, some $a \in L^1(0, T; \mathbb{R}_+)$, and

$$\int_0^T H(t, x)\, dt - T\gamma^2|x|^2 \ge C > -\infty$$

for all $x \in \mathbb{R}^k$ and some constant C. Then the functional (8.22) is coercive.

Proof. Denote $H_\gamma (t, x) = H (t, x) - \gamma^2 |x|^2$. For $u \in H^1_p (0, T; \mathbb{R}^k)$, we have $u = \overline{u} + \widehat{u}$ where $\overline{u} = \int_0^T u (t) \, dt$ and $\widehat{u} = u - \overline{u}$. Then

$$E (u) = \int_0^T \left(\frac{1}{2} |u' (t)|^2 + \gamma^2 |u (t)|^2 \right) dt + \int_0^T H_\gamma (t, \overline{u}) \, dt$$

$$+ \int_0^T \left[H_\gamma (t, u (t)) - H_\gamma (t, \overline{u}) \right] dt$$

$$\geq \min \left\{ 1, 2\gamma^2 \right\} |u|^2 + C + \int_0^T \int_0^1 \left(\nabla H_\gamma (t, \overline{u} + s\widehat{u} (t)), \widehat{u} (t) \right) ds \, dt$$

$$\geq \min \left\{ 1, 2\gamma^2 \right\} |u|^2 + C - |a|_{L^1} |\widehat{u}|_\infty .$$

Since $|\widehat{u}|_\infty \leq c |\widehat{u}| \leq c |u|$, we deduce that

$$E (u) \geq \min \left\{ 1, 2\gamma^2 \right\} |u|^2 + C - c |a|_{L^1} |u| \to \infty \text{ as } |u| \to \infty.$$

The proof is now complete. $\qquad\qquad\qquad\qquad\qquad\qquad\qquad\qquad\qquad\qquad\qquad\square$

Notice that if H is of coercive type, then the functional (8.22) is bounded from below. Indeed, the coercivity property implies that there exists a positive number R such that $E (u) \geq 0$ if $|u| > R$. Since the injection of $H^1_p (0, T; \mathbb{R}^k)$ into $C (0, T; \mathbb{R}^k)$ is continuous, there exists $c > 0$ such that $|u|_\infty \leq c |u|$ for every $u \in H^1_p (0, T; \mathbb{R}^k)$. Then, for $|u| \leq R$, $|u|_\infty \leq cR$ and since H is L^1-Carathéodory, $H (t, u (t)) \geq -b (t)$ for a.e. $t \in (0, T)$. As a result, for $|u| \leq R$, one has $E (u) \geq - |b|_{L^1}$. Hence $E (u) \geq - |b|_{L^1}$ for all $u \in H^1_p (0, T; \mathbb{R}^k)$ as we claimed.

Our hypotheses are as follows:

(H1) for each $R > 0$, there exist $\sigma_1, \sigma_2 \in L^1 (0, T; \mathbb{R}_+)$ and $\gamma \neq 0$ such that

$$F (t, x, y) \geq \gamma^2 |x|^2 - \sigma_1 (t) |x| - \sigma_2 (t)$$

for a.e. $t \in (0, T)$, all $x \in \mathbb{R}^{k_1}$ and $y \in \mathbb{R}^{k_2}$ with $|y| \leq R$;

(H2) there exist $g, g_1 : (0, T) \times \mathbb{R}^{k_2} \to \mathbb{R}$ of coercive type with

$$g (t, y) \leq G (t, x, y) \leq g_1 (t, y) \qquad\qquad (8.23)$$

for all $x \in \mathbb{R}^{k_1}$, $y \in \mathbb{R}^{k_2}$, and a.e. $t \in (0, T)$;

(H3) there exist $m_{ij} \in \mathbb{R}_+$ $(i, j = 1, 2)$ with

$$\left| m_1^2 (x - \overline{x}) - \nabla_x (F (t, x, y) - F (t, \overline{x}, \overline{y})) \right| \leq m_{11} |x - \overline{x}| + m_{12} |y - \overline{y}|$$

$$\left| m_2^2 (y - \overline{y}) - \nabla_y (G (t, x, y) - G (t, \overline{x}, \overline{y})) \right| \leq m_{21} |x - \overline{x}| + m_{22} |y - \overline{y}|$$

$$\qquad\qquad (8.24)$$

for all $x, \bar{x} \in \mathbb{R}^{k_1}$, $y, \bar{y} \in \mathbb{R}^{k_2}$ and a.e. $t \in (0, T)$, such that the spectral radius of the matrix

$$M = \begin{bmatrix} \dfrac{m_{11}}{m_1^2} & \dfrac{m_{12}}{m_1 m_2} \\[2mm] \dfrac{m_{21}}{m_1 m_2} & \dfrac{m_{22}}{m_2^2} \end{bmatrix} \tag{8.25}$$

is strictly less than one.

Theorem 8.7. *Under hypotheses (H1)–(H3), problem (8.18) has a unique solution*

$$(u, v) \in H_p^1\left(0, 1; \mathbb{R}^{k_1}\right) \times H_p^1\left(0, 1; \mathbb{R}^{k_2}\right),$$

which is a Nash-type equilibrium of the pair of energy functionals (E_1, E_2) given by (8.19).

Proof. From (H1) we have that $E_1(., v)$ is bounded from below for each $v \in H_p^1\left(0, 1; \mathbb{R}^{k_2}\right)$. Indeed, if $R = |v|_\infty$, then

$$E_1(u, v) \geq \int_0^T \left(\frac{1}{2} |u'(t)|^2 + \gamma^2 |u(t)|^2 - \sigma_1(t) |u(t)| - \sigma_2(t) \right) dt$$

$$\geq C_1 |u|_1^2 - C_2 |u|_1 - C_3$$

whence the desired conclusion.

Next, using the first inequality in (8.23), we have

$$E_2(u, v) \geq \phi(v) := \int_0^T \left(\frac{1}{2} |v'(t)|^2 + g(t, v(t)) \right) dt.$$

Since g is of coercive type, ϕ is bounded from below. Thus, $E_2(u, .)$ is bounded from below even uniformly with respect to u.

Furthermore, if we denote

$$\phi_1(v) = \int_0^T \left(\frac{1}{2} |v'(t)|^2 + g_1(t, v(t)) \right) dt,$$

we fix any number $a > 0$, we use (8.23) and the coercivity of ϕ, then we may find a number $R > 0$ such that

$$\inf E_2(u, .) + a \leq \inf \phi_1 + a \leq \phi(v)$$

for $|v|_2 \geq R$. Since $E_2(u, v) \geq \phi(v)$, this shows that condition (8.8) is satisfied by E_2.

Finally, using (8.20), (8.21) and (8.24) we obtain

$$
\begin{aligned}
|N_1(u, v) - N_1(\bar{u}, \bar{v})|_1 &= \left| J_1\left(m_1^2(u - \bar{u}) - \nabla_x\left(F(., u, v) - F(., \bar{u}, \bar{v}) \right) \right) \right|_1 \\
&\leq \frac{1}{m_1} \left| m_1^2(u - \bar{u}) - \nabla_x\left(F(., u, v) - F(., \bar{u}, \bar{v}) \right) \right|_{L^2} \\
&\leq \frac{m_{11}}{m_1} |u - \bar{u}|_{L^2} + \frac{m_{12}}{m_1} |v - \bar{v}|_{L^2} \\
&\leq \frac{m_{11}}{m_1^2} |u - \bar{u}|_1 + \frac{m_{12}}{m_1 m_2} |v - \bar{v}|_2.
\end{aligned}
$$

A similar inequality holds for N_2 and so condition (8.7) is satisfied with the matrix M given by (8.25). Therefore all the hypotheses of Theorem 8.5 are fulfilled. $\qquad\square$

Example 8.1. Consider the system of two scalar equations

$$
\begin{aligned}
u'' &= 2\gamma_1^2 u + a(t)\sin u(t) + b(t)\cos u(t)\cos v(t) + c(t) \\
v'' &= 2\gamma_2^2 v + A(t)\sin u(t)\cos v(t) + B(t)\cos v(t),
\end{aligned}
\tag{8.26}
$$

where $\gamma_1, \gamma_2 \neq 0$ and $a, b, A, B \in L^\infty(0, T)$, $c \in L^1(0, T)$. In this case,

$$
\begin{aligned}
F(t, x, y) &= \gamma_1^2 x^2 - a(t)\cos x + b(t)\sin x\cos y + c(t)x \\
G(t, x, y) &= \gamma_2^2 y^2 + A(t)\sin x\sin y + B(t)\sin y
\end{aligned}
$$

and we let $m_i = \gamma_i\sqrt{2}$ $(i = 1, 2)$. If the spectral radius of the matrix

$$
M = \begin{bmatrix}
\frac{1}{2\gamma_1^2}(|a|_\infty + |b|_\infty) & \frac{|b|_\infty}{2\gamma_1\gamma_2} \\
\frac{|A|_\infty}{2\gamma_1\gamma_2} & \frac{1}{2\gamma_2^2}(|A|_\infty + |B|_\infty)
\end{bmatrix}
$$

is strictly less than one, then the system (8.26) has a unique T-periodic solution, which is a Nash type equilibrium of the pair of energy functionals of the system.

8.3 NASH EQUILIBRIUM FOR SYSTEMS OF VARIATIONAL INEQUALITIES

In this section, the solutions of some systems of variational inequalities are obtained as Nash-type equilibria of the corresponding systems of Szulkin functionals. This is achieved by an iterative scheme based on Ekeland's variational principle, whose convergence is proved via the vector technique involving inverse-positive matrices. An application to periodic solutions for a system of two second order ordinary differential equations with singular ϕ-Laplace operators is included. In this section we follow the results developed by Precup [146, 147].

Consider the following system of variational inequalities: find $(x, y) \in X \times Y$ such that

$$
\begin{cases}
\langle \mathcal{F}'_x (x, y), u - x \rangle + \varphi (u) - \varphi (x) \geq 0 \\
\langle \mathcal{G}'_y (x, y), v - y \rangle + \psi (v) - \psi (y) \geq 0
\end{cases}
\quad \text{for all } (u, v) \in X \times Y, \quad (8.27)
$$

where X, Y are Banach spaces with norms $|.|_X$, $|.|_Y$ and $\mathcal{F}'_x$, $\mathcal{G}'_y$ are the Fréchet derivatives of $\mathcal{F}$ and $\mathcal{G}$ in the first and second variable, respectively.

We first assume that the following condition is fulfilled:

(H₀) $\mathcal{F}, \mathcal{G} : X \times Y \to \mathbb{R}$ are of class C^1 with respect to the first and the second variable, respectively, and $\varphi : X \to (-\infty, +\infty]$, $\psi : Y \to (-\infty, +\infty]$ are proper, lower semicontinuous and convex functionals.

Then a couple of elements $(x, y) \in D(\varphi) \times D(\psi)$ is a solution of the system if x is a critical point in Szulkin's sense of the functional $\mathcal{F}(., y) + \varphi$ and y is a critical point in Szulkin's sense of the functional $\mathcal{G}(x, .) + \psi$. We are interested in such a solution which is a *Nash-type equilibrium* of the pair of functionals (E_1, E_2), where $E_1, E_2 : X \times Y \to (-\infty, +\infty]$,

$$
E_1 := \mathcal{F} + \varphi, \quad E_2 = \mathcal{G} + \psi,
$$

that is

$$
E_1 (x, y) = \min_{u \in X} E_1 (u, y), \quad E_2 (x, y) = \min_{v \in Y} E_2 (x, v).
$$

From a physical point of view, a Nash-type equilibrium (x, y) for two interconnected mechanisms whose energies are E_1, E_2, is such that the motion of each mechanism is conformed to the minimum energy principle by taking into account the motion of the other.

To obtain such a solution of the system (8.27), an iterative scheme is introduced, a Palais-Smale type condition is defined, and the convergence of the iterative procedure is proved via a vector technique based on inverse-positive matrices. In such a way, the abstract part of this section represents a vectorization of the direct variational principle for Szulkin-type functionals [165].

The main abstract result of this section is illustrated with an application to the study of the periodic problem for a system of equations involving the singular ϕ-Laplace operator:

$$
\begin{cases}
(\phi_1 (x'))' = \nabla_x F_1 (t, x, y) \\
(\phi_2 (y'))' = \nabla_y F_2 (t, x, y).
\end{cases}
\quad (8.28)
$$

We point out that this system is composed by two equations having a variational form each, but without a variational structure in its whole. Another feature of the analysis we will develop is that we work in the Lebesgue space L^2 instead of the standard space of continuous functions.

A function $H : (0, T) \times \mathbb{R}^n \to \mathbb{R}^m$, $H = H(t, x)$ ($n, m \geq 1$) is said to be L^1-*Carathéodory*, if it satisfies the *Carathéodory conditions*, that is, $H(., x)$ is measurable for each $x \in \mathbb{R}^n$ and $H(t, .)$ is continuous for a.e. $t \in (0, T)$; and for each $r > 0$, there is $b_r \in L^1(0, T; \mathbb{R}_+)$ such that $|H(t, x)| \leq b_r(t)$ for a.e. $t \in (0, T)$ and all $x \in \overline{B}_r(\mathbb{R}^n)$.

The function H is said to be (p, q)-*Carathéodory* $(1 \leq p, q < \infty)$ if it satisfies the Carathéodory conditions and $|H(t, x)| \leq a|x|^{p/q} + b(t)$ for all $x \in \mathbb{R}^n$, a.e. $t \in (0, T)$ and some $a \in \mathbb{R}_+$, $b \in L^q(0, T; \mathbb{R}_+)$.

The superposition operator $x \mapsto H(., x(.))$ is well-defined and continuous from $C([0, T]; \mathbb{R}^n)$ to $L^1(0, T; \mathbb{R}^m)$, provided that H is L^1-Carathéodory. The superposition operator is from $L^p(0, T; \mathbb{R}^n)$ to $L^q(0, T; \mathbb{R}^m)$ if H is (p, q)-Carathéodory.

A square matrix of real numbers is said to be *inverse-positive* if it is nonsingular and all the elements of its inverse are nonnegative. A class of such kind of matrices is given by the matrices of the form $I - A$, where I is the unit matrix, the elements of A are nonnegative, and the spectral radius of A is strictly less than one. However, there are matrices A with not all elements nonnegative and spectral radius bigger than one, such that $I - A$ is inverse-positive. An example is the matrix $A = \begin{bmatrix} -2 & a \\ 0 & -1 \end{bmatrix}$, where $a > 0$. Also note that a matrix of the form $\begin{bmatrix} a & -b \\ -c & d \end{bmatrix}$, with $a, b, c, d \geq 0$ is inverse-positive if and only if its determinant is positive, that is, $ad - bc > 0$.

Let us now assume the following hypothesis.

(H$_1$) The functionals $E_1(., y)$ and $E_2(x, .)$ are bounded from below for every $x \in D(\varphi)$ and $y \in D(\psi)$.

Theorem 8.8. *Assume that conditions* (H_0), (H_1) *hold. Then for every* $y_0 \in D(\psi)$, *there exist sequences* (x_n) *and* (y_n) *such that* $x_n \in D(\varphi)$, $y_n \in D(\psi)$,

$$E_1(x_n, y_{n-1}) \leq \inf_X E_1(., y_{n-1}) + \frac{1}{n}, \tag{8.29}$$

$$\langle \mathcal{F}'_x(x_n, y_{n-1}), u - x_n \rangle + \varphi(u) - \varphi(x_n) \geq -\frac{1}{n}|u - x_n|_X, \tag{8.30}$$

$$\text{for every } u \in D(\varphi),$$

$$E_2(x_n, y_n) \leq \inf_Y E_2(x_n, .) + \frac{1}{n}, \tag{8.31}$$

$$\langle \mathcal{G}'_y(x_n, y_n), v - y_n \rangle + \psi(v) - \psi(y_n) \geq -\frac{1}{n}|v - y_n|_Y, \tag{8.32}$$

$$\text{for every } v \in D(\psi).$$

Proof. For $n = 1$, we first obtain x_1 by applying Theorem A.6 to the functional $E_1(., y_0)$. Then y_1 is obtained similarly for the functional $E_2(x_1, .)$. Furthermore, at any step n, we obtain x_n and then y_n by applying Theorem A.6 to $E_1(., y_{n-1})$ and $E_2(x_n, .)$, respectively. $\qquad\square$

We now require a stronger continuity property for $\mathcal{F}, \mathcal{G}$:

(H$_0^*$) Condition (H$_0$) is satisfied and $\mathcal{F}, \mathcal{G}, \mathcal{F}_x', \mathcal{G}_y'$ are continuous on $X \times Y$.

We also define the following Palais-Smale compactness condition for the pair of functionals (E_1, E_2).

(PS*) If $(x_n)_{n\geq 1}$, $(y_n)_{n\geq 0}$ are any sequences such that the conditions (8.29)–(8.32) are satisfied, then (x_n), (y_n) possess convergent subsequences (x_{n_j}), (y_{n_j}) with the additional property

$$y_{n_j} - y_{n_j-1} \to 0 \quad \text{as } j \to \infty. \tag{8.33}$$

Theorem 8.9. *Assume that the conditions (H$_0^*$) and (PS*) are satisfied. Then the system (8.27) has at least one solution which is a Nash-type equilibrium of the pair of functionals (E_1, E_2).*

Proof. By Theorem 8.8, if y_0 is any fixed element of $D(\psi)$, then there are sequences $(x_n)_{n\geq 1}$ and $(y_n)_{n\geq 0}$ satisfying the conditions (8.29)–(8.32). The (PS*) condition guarantees the existence of the convergent subsequences (x_{n_j}), (y_{n_j}) with the additional property (8.33). Let x, y be the limits of the corresponding subsequences. Then

$$x_{n_j} \to x, \quad y_{n_j} \to y \quad \text{and} \quad y_{n_j-1} \to y \quad \text{as } j \to \infty.$$

The conclusion now follows from the inequalities (8.29)–(8.32) written for $n = n_j$, if we pass to the limit with $j \to \infty$ by taking into account (H$_0^*$). $\qquad\square$

The next result gives us a sufficient condition for (PS*) to hold, namely

(H$_2$) There exist constants $m_{ij} \in \mathbb{R}_+$ $(i, j = 1, 2)$ with

$$m_{11}m_{22} - m_{12}m_{21} > 0, \tag{8.34}$$

and exponents $\beta, \gamma > 1$ such that

$$\left\langle \mathcal{F}_x'(x, y) - \mathcal{F}_x'(u, v), x - u \right\rangle \geq m_{11}|x - u|_X^\beta - m_{12}|x - u|_X |y - v|_Y^{\gamma-1}$$

$$\left\langle \mathcal{G}_y'(x, y) - \mathcal{G}_y'(u, v), y - v \right\rangle \geq -m_{21}|x - u|_X^{\beta-1} |y - v|_Y + m_{22}|y - v|_Y^\gamma$$

for all $x, u \in X$; $y, v \in Y$.

Theorem 8.10. *Assume that (H$_0$), (H$_1$), and (H$_2$) hold. If (y_n) is bounded, then the sequences (x_n), (y_n) given by (8.30), (8.32) are convergent.*

Proof. From (8.30) we obtain

$$\langle \mathcal{F}'_x \left(x_{n+p}, y_{n+p-1} \right) - \mathcal{F}'_x \left(x_n, y_{n-1} \right), x_n - x_{n+p} \rangle$$

$$\geq -\left(\frac{1}{n} + \frac{1}{n+p} \right) |x_{n+p} - x_n|_X.$$

Since

$$\langle \mathcal{F}'_x \left(x_{n+p}, y_{n+p-1} \right) - \mathcal{F}'_x \left(x_n, y_{n-1} \right), x_n - x_{n+p} \rangle$$

$$\leq -m_{11} |x_{n+p} - x_n|_X^{\beta} + m_{12} |x_{n+p} - x_n|_X |y_{n+p-1} - y_{n-1}|_Y^{\gamma-1}$$

we deduce

$$m_{11} |x_{n+p} - x_n|_X^{\beta-1} - m_{12} |y_{n+p-1} - y_{n-1}|_Y^{\gamma-1} \leq \frac{2}{n}.$$

Similarly, from (8.32) we deduce that

$$-m_{21} |x_{n+p} - x_n|_X^{\beta-1} + m_{22} |y_{n+p} - y_n|_Y^{\gamma-1} \leq \frac{2}{n}.$$

Denote $a_{n,p} := |x_{n+p} - x_n|_X^{\beta-1}$, $b_{n,p} := |y_{n+p} - y_n|_Y^{\gamma-1}$. Then

$$m_{11} a_{n,p} - m_{12} b_{n,p} \leq m_{12} \left(b_{n-1,p} - b_{n,p} \right) + \frac{2}{n}, \tag{8.35}$$

$$-m_{21} a_{n,p} + m_{22} b_{n,p} \leq \frac{2}{n}.$$

Therefore

$$M \begin{bmatrix} a_{n,p} \\ b_{n,p} \end{bmatrix} \leq \begin{bmatrix} m_{12} \left(b_{n-1,p} - b_{n,p} \right) + \frac{2}{n} \\ \frac{2}{n} \end{bmatrix}, \tag{8.36}$$

where

$$M = \begin{bmatrix} m_{11} & -m_{12} \\ -m_{21} & m_{22} \end{bmatrix}.$$

From (8.34) it follows that the matrix M is inverse-positive. It follows that we can multiply relation (8.36) by M^{-1} to obtain

$$\begin{bmatrix} a_{n,p} \\ b_{n,p} \end{bmatrix} \leq M^{-1} \begin{bmatrix} m_{12} \left(b_{n-1,p} - b_{n,p} \right) + \frac{2}{n} \\ \frac{2}{n} \end{bmatrix}.$$

If $M^{-1} = [d_{ij}]_{1 \leq i,j \leq 2}$, then

$$a_{n,p} \leq d_{11} \left[m_{12} \left(b_{n-1,p} - b_{n,p} \right) + \frac{2}{n} \right] + d_{12} \frac{2}{n}, \tag{8.37}$$

$$b_{n,p} \le d_{21}\left[m_{12}\left(b_{n-1,p} - b_{n,p}\right) + \frac{2}{n}\right] + d_{22}\frac{2}{n}.$$

The last inequality yields

$$b_{n,p} \le \frac{d_{21}m_{12}}{1 + d_{21}m_{12}}b_{n-1,p} + \frac{d_{21} + d_{22}}{1 + d_{21}m_{12}}\frac{2}{n}.$$

Thus, by Lemma 8.1, we deduce that $b_{n,p} \to 0$ in Y, uniformly with respect to p, hence the sequence (y_n) is Cauchy in Y. Now the first inequality of (8.37) implies that the sequence (x_n) is also Cauchy in X. $\qquad\square$

Remark 8.2. We notice that under the assumption (H$_2$), the system (8.27) has at most one solution. Indeed, if (x, y) and $(\overline{x}, \overline{y})$ are two solutions of (8.27), then

$$\left\langle \mathcal{F}'_x\left(x, y\right), \overline{x} - x\right\rangle + \varphi\left(\overline{x}\right) - \varphi\left(x\right) \ge 0$$
$$\left\langle \mathcal{F}'_x\left(\overline{x}, \overline{y}\right), x - \overline{x}\right\rangle + \varphi\left(\overline{y}\right) - \varphi\left(\overline{y}\right) \ge 0$$

whence

$$\left\langle \mathcal{F}'_x\left(x, y\right) - \mathcal{F}'_x\left(\overline{x}, \overline{y}\right), \overline{x} - x\right\rangle \ge 0.$$

It follows that

$$m_{11}\left|x - \overline{x}\right|_X^{\beta - 1} - m_{12}\left|y - \overline{y}\right|_Y^{\gamma - 1} \le 0.$$

Similarly we have

$$-m_{21}\left|x - \overline{x}\right|_X^{\beta - 1} + m_{22}\left|y - \overline{y}\right|_Y^{\gamma - 1} \le 0.$$

These two inequalities yield

$$M\begin{bmatrix} |x - \overline{x}|_X^{\beta - 1} \\ |y - \overline{y}|_Y^{\gamma - 1} \end{bmatrix} \le \begin{bmatrix} 0 \\ 0 \end{bmatrix},$$

whence

$$\begin{bmatrix} |x - \overline{x}|_X^{\beta - 1} \\ |y - \overline{y}|_Y^{\gamma - 1} \end{bmatrix} \le M^{-1}\begin{bmatrix} 0 \\ 0 \end{bmatrix}.$$

Consequently, $|x - \overline{x}|_X^{\beta - 1} = |y - \overline{y}|_Y^{\gamma - 1} = 0$. It follows that $(x, y) = (\overline{x}, \overline{y})$.

The next condition will guarantee the boundedness of the sequence (y_n).

(**H$_3$**) There exist $a, R > 0$ such that

$$E_2\left(x, y\right) \ge \inf_{D(\psi)} E_2\left(x, .\right) + a \quad \text{for } x \in D\left(\varphi\right), \ y \in D\left(\psi\right), \ |y|_Y \ge R.$$

$$(8.38)$$

Theorem 8.11. *If the conditions* $\left(H_0^*\right)$, (H_1), (H_2), *and* (H_3) *hold, then the system (8.27) has a unique solution* (x, y) *which is a Nash-type equilibrium of the pair of functionals* (E_1, E_2).

Proof. For $\frac{1}{n} < a$, from (8.31) and (8.38), we have $|y_n|_Y < R$. Hence the sequence (y_n) is bounded and the conclusion follows from Theorems 8.9, 8.10 and Remark 8.2. □

8.3.1 Application to Periodic Solutions of Second-Order Systems

To illustrate the theory let us consider the periodic problem

$$\left(\phi_1\left(x'\right)\right)' = \nabla_x F_1\left(t, x, y\right) \qquad (8.39)$$
$$\left(\phi_2\left(y'\right)\right)' = \nabla_y F_2\left(t, x, y\right)$$
$$x\left(0\right) - x\left(T\right) = x'\left(0\right) - x'\left(T\right) = 0$$
$$y\left(0\right) - y\left(T\right) = y'\left(0\right) - y'\left(T\right) = 0$$

where $F_1, F_2 : (0, T) \times \mathbb{R}^{k_1} \times \mathbb{R}^{k_2} \to \mathbb{R}$.

We look for solutions (x, y) with $x \in C^1\left([0, T], \mathbb{R}^{k_1}\right)$, $y \in C^1\left([0, T], \mathbb{R}^{k_2}\right)$, such that $|x'|_{L^\infty} < r_1$, $|y'|_{L^\infty} < r_2$, $\phi_1\left(x'\right)$ and $\phi_2\left(y'\right)$ are differentiable a.e., and (8.39) is satisfied a.e. on $(0, T)$.

We shall assume that F_1, F_2 are $(2, 1)$-Carathéodory and $\nabla_x F_1$ and $\nabla_y F_2$ are $(2, 2)$-Carathéodory functions. As concerns the functions ϕ_i, $i = 1, 2$, we shall assume the following condition:

(h$_\phi$) $\phi_i : B_{r_i}\left(\mathbb{R}^{k_i}\right) \to \mathbb{R}^{k_i}$ is a homeomorphism such that $\phi_i\left(0\right) = 0$, $\phi_i = \nabla \Phi_i$ with $\Phi_i : \overline{B}_{r_i}\left(\mathbb{R}^{k_i}\right) \to \mathbb{R}$ of class C^1 on $B_{r_i}\left(\mathbb{R}^{k_i}\right)$, continuous and strictly convex on $\overline{B}_{r_i}\left(\mathbb{R}^{k_i}\right)$ and with $\Phi_i\left(0\right) = 0$.

The typical example of such a homeomorphism is the following function arising from special relativity, $\phi : B_r\left(\mathbb{R}^k\right) \to \mathbb{R}^k$,

$$\phi\left(z\right) = \frac{z}{\sqrt{r^2 - |z|^2}},$$

for which $\phi\left(z\right) = \nabla \Phi\left(z\right)$, $\Phi\left(z\right) = r - \sqrt{r^2 - |z|^2}$.

Finding solutions of the system (8.39) it suffices to obtain pairs (x, y) of functions such that x, y are critical points in Szulkin's sense of the functionals $E_1\left(., y\right)$ and $E_2\left(x, .\right)$, respectively, where $E_1, E_2 : L^2\left(0, T; \mathbb{R}^{k_1}\right) \times L^2\left(0, T; \mathbb{R}^{k_2}\right) \to (-\infty, +\infty]$,

$$E_1 = \mathcal{F} + \varphi, \quad E_2 = \mathcal{G} + \psi \qquad (8.40)$$

$$\mathcal{F}\left(x, y\right) = \int_0^T F_1\left(t, x\left(t\right), y\left(t\right)\right) dt, \quad \mathcal{G}\left(x, y\right) = \int_0^T F_2\left(t, x\left(t\right), y\left(t\right)\right) dt,$$

$$\varphi(x) = \begin{cases} \int_0^T \Phi_1(x'(t)) \, dt, & \text{if } x \in K_1 \\ +\infty, & \text{otherwise,} \end{cases}$$

$$\psi(y) = \begin{cases} \int_0^T \Phi_2(y'(t)) \, dt, & \text{if } y \in K_2 \\ +\infty, & \text{otherwise,} \end{cases}$$

and

$$K_i := \left\{ z \in W^{1,\infty}\left(0, T; \mathbb{R}^{k_i}\right) : z(0) = z(T) \text{ and } |z'|_\infty \le r_i \right\} \quad (i = 1, 2).$$

Thus

$$D(\varphi) = K_1 \quad \text{and} \quad D(\psi) = K_2.$$

By straightforward computation we obtain that the functionals $\mathcal{F}$, $\mathcal{G}$, φ, and ψ satisfy (H_0^*), where

$$X = L^2\left(0, T; \mathbb{R}^{k_1}\right) \quad \text{and} \quad Y = L^2\left(0, T; \mathbb{R}^{k_2}\right).$$

In what follows, we denote by $|.|_X$, $|.|_Y$ the L^2-norms of $L^2\left(0, T; \mathbb{R}^{k_1}\right)$ and $L^2\left(0, T; \mathbb{R}^{k_2}\right)$, respectively.

In order to guarantee condition (H_2) we require the following condition:

(h_F) There exist constants $m_{ij} \in \mathbb{R}_+$ ($i, j = 1, 2$), with

$$m_{11}m_{22} - m_{12}m_{21} > 0,$$

such that

$$\begin{aligned} &\langle \nabla_x F_1(t, x, y) - \nabla_x F_1(t, u, v), \, x - u \rangle \\ &\ge m_{11} |x - u|^2 - m_{12} |x - u| |y - v|, \\ &\langle \nabla_y F_2(t, x, y) - \nabla_y F_2(t, u, v), \, y - v \rangle \\ &\ge -m_{21} |x - u| |y - v| + m_{22} |y - v|^2 \end{aligned} \tag{8.41}$$

for all $x, u \in \mathbb{R}^{k_1}$; $y, v \in \mathbb{R}^{k_2}$.

Indeed, if $x, u \in L^2\left(0, T; \mathbb{R}^{k_1}\right)$ and $y, v \in L^2\left(0, T; \mathbb{R}^{k_2}\right)$, then

$$\begin{aligned} &\langle \mathcal{F}'_x(x, y) - \mathcal{F}'_x(u, v), x - u \rangle \\ &= \int_0^T \langle \nabla_x F_1(t, x(t), y(t)) - \nabla_x F_1(t, u(t), v(t)), \, x(t) - u(t) \rangle \, dt \end{aligned}$$

$$\geq m_{11} \int_0^T |x(t) - u(t)|^2 dt - m_{12} \int_0^T |x(t) - u(t)| |y(t) - v(t)| dt$$

$$\geq m_{11} |x - u|_X^2 - m_{12} |x - u|_X |y - v|_Y.$$

Hence the first inequality in (H$_2$) is fulfilled with $\beta = \gamma = 2$. The second inequality follows similarly.

In order to satisfy (H$_3$) we assume the following coercivity condition on F_2:

(**h$_c$**) There exist L^1-Carathéodory functions $g, h : (0, T) \times \mathbb{R}^{k_2} \to \mathbb{R}$ such that

$$g(t, y) \leq F_2(t, x, y) \leq h(t, y) \tag{8.42}$$

for a.e. $t \in (0, T)$, all $x \in \mathbb{R}^{k_1}$, $y \in \mathbb{R}^{k_2}$, and

$$\alpha(y) := \int_0^T g(t, y(t)) dt \to \infty \quad \text{as } y \in K_2, |y|_Y \to \infty. \tag{8.43}$$

We first notice that α is bounded from below on K_2. Indeed, from (8.43), there exists $R > 0$ such that

$$\alpha(y) \geq 0 \quad \text{for all } y \in K_2 \text{ with } |y|_Y > R. \tag{8.44}$$

On the other hand, if $|y|_Y \leq R$ and $t_0 \in [0, T]$ is such that $|y(t_0)| = |y|_{L^\infty}$, from

$$|y(t)| \geq |y(t_0)| - |y(t) - y(t_0)| = |y|_{L^\infty} - \left| \int_{t_0}^t y'(s) ds \right| \geq |y|_{L^\infty} - Tr_2$$

we have

$$|y|_{L^\infty} \leq |y(t)| + Tr_2 \quad \text{for all } t \in [0, T],$$

whence, by passing to the L^2-norm, we deduce

$$|y|_{L^\infty} \leq \frac{1}{\sqrt{T}} |y|_Y + Tr_2 \leq \frac{1}{\sqrt{T}} R + Tr_2 =: R_1. \tag{8.45}$$

Since g is L^1-Carathéodory, there exists a function $b_{R_1} \in L^1(0, T; \mathbb{R}_+)$ such that $|g(t, y)| \leq b_{R_1}(t)$ for a.e. $t \in (0, T)$ and $y \in \overline{B}_{R_1}(\mathbb{R}^{k_2})$. Then

$$\alpha(y) \geq -|b_{R_1}|_{L^1} \quad \text{for all } y \in K_2 \text{ with } |y|_Y \leq R. \tag{8.46}$$

Relations (8.44) and (8.46) show that α is bounded from below on K_2 as claimed. Next, let

$$\beta(y) := \int_0^T h(t, y(t)) dt.$$

If we fix any number $a > 0$, we use (8.42) and the coercivity of α we may find $R > 0$ such that

$$\inf_{D(\psi)} \mathcal{G}(x, .) + a \leq \inf_{D(\psi)} \beta + a \leq \alpha(y)$$

for all $y \in D(\psi)$ with $|y|_Y \geq R$. Since $\mathcal{G}(x, y) \geq \alpha(y)$, this proves that condition (H$_2$) is satisfied.

Finally, (H$_1$) will be guaranteed by using the following condition:

(h$_b$) For each $R > 0$, there exists $\sigma_R, \eta_R \in L^1(0, T; \mathbb{R}_+)$ and $\gamma_R > 0$ such that

$$F_1(t, x, y) \geq \gamma_R |x|^2 - \sigma_R(t)|x| - \eta_R(t)$$

for a.e. $t \in (0, T)$, all $x \in \mathbb{R}^{k_1}$ and $y \in \overline{B}_R(\mathbb{R}^{k_2})$.

To check (H$_1$), let $x \in K_1$, $y \in K_2$. According to (8.45) we have

$$|y|_{L^\infty} \leq \frac{1}{\sqrt{T}} |y|_Y + T r_2 =: R.$$

Then

$$\mathcal{F}(x, y) \geq \gamma_R |x|_X^2 - |\sigma_R|_{L^1} |x|_{L^\infty} - |\eta_R|_{L^1}.$$

Furthermore, from the similar inequality to (8.45) for K_1, we obtain

$$\mathcal{F}(x, y) \geq \gamma_R |x|_X^2 - |\sigma_R|_{L^1} \left(\frac{1}{\sqrt{T}} |x|_X + T r_1 \right) - |\eta_R|_{L^1},$$

where the right-hand side is bounded from below as a quadratic function. Thus, both functionals $\mathcal{F}(., y)$, $\mathcal{G}(x, .)$ are bounded from below on K_1 and K_2, respectively. On the other hand, the functionals φ and ψ are bounded from below as follows from their definition and the continuity of Φ_1, Φ_2 on their compact domains. Therefore condition (H$_1$) is satisfied.

As a conclusion we have the following theorem.

Theorem 8.12. *Under hypotheses (h)$_\phi$, (h)$_F$, (h)$_c$, and (h)$_b$, the problem (8.39) has a solution (x, y) which is a Nash-type equilibrium of the pair of energy functionals (E_1, E_2) given by (8.40).*

Example 8.2. Consider the coupled system of two scalar equations

$$\begin{aligned}
(\phi_1(x'))' &= m_1^2 x + a_1(t) \sin y + b_1(t) \cos x \cos y + c_1(t) \\
(\phi_2(y'))' &= m_2^2 y + a_2(t) \sin x + b_2(t) \sin x \cos y + c_2(t)
\end{aligned} \tag{8.47}$$

where ϕ_1, ϕ_2 satisfy (h)$_\phi$; $m_1, m_2 \neq 0$; $a_1, a_2, b_1, b_2 \in L^\infty(0, T)$ and $c_1, c_2 \in L^2(0, T)$. In this case,

$$F_1(t, x, y) = m_1^2 x^2 / 2 + a_1(t) x \sin y + b_1(t) \sin x \cos y + c_1(t) x$$

$$F_2(t, x, y) = m_2^2 y^2/2 + a_2(t) y \sin x + b_2(t) \sin x \sin y + c_2(t) y.$$

If

$$m_i^2 > |b_i|_{L^\infty}, \quad i = 1, 2$$

and

$$\left(m_1^2 - |b_1|_{L^\infty}\right)\left(m_2^2 - |b_2|_{L^\infty}\right) > (|a_1|_{L^\infty} + |b_1|_{L^\infty})(|a_2|_{L^\infty} + |b_2|_{L^\infty}),$$

$$(8.48)$$

then the system (8.47) has a T-periodic solution, which is a Nash type equilibrium of the pair of corresponding energy functionals of the system. Indeed, we have

$$\langle \nabla_x F_1(t, x, y) - \nabla_x F_1(t, u, v), \, x - u \rangle$$
$$= m_1^2(x - u)^2 + a_1(t)(\sin y - \sin v)(x - u)$$
$$\quad + b_1(t)(\cos x \cos y - \cos u \cos v)(x - u)$$
$$\geq m_1^2(x - u)^2 - |a_1|_{L^\infty}|x - u||y - v| - |b_1|_{L^\infty}(x - u)^2$$
$$\quad - |b_1|_{L^\infty}|x - u||y - v|$$
$$\geq \left(m_1^2 - |b_1|_{L^\infty}\right)(x - u)^2 - (|a_1|_{L^\infty} + |b_1|_{L^\infty})|x - u||y - v|.$$

Hence the first inequality in (8.41) holds with

$$m_{11} = m_1^2 - |b_1|_{L^\infty}, \quad m_{12} = |a_1|_{L^\infty} + |b_1|_{L^\infty}.$$

Similarly, the second inequality in (8.41) holds with

$$m_{21} = |a_2|_{L^\infty} + |b_2|_{L^\infty}, \quad m_{22} = m_2^2 - |b_2|_{L^\infty}.$$

Thus, (8.48) is equivalent to (8.34). The condition (h)$_c$ also holds with

$$g(t, y) = m_2^2 y^2/2 - (|a_2(t)| + |c_2(t)|)|y| - |b_2(t)|$$
$$h(t, y) = m_2^2 y^2/2 + (|a_2(t)| + |c_2(t)|)|y| + |b_2(t)|$$

as follows using (8.45). Indeed

$$\int_0^T g(t, y(t)) \, dt \geq \frac{m_1^2}{2}|y|_Y^2 - (|a_2|_{L^1} + |c_2|_{L^1})|y|_{L^\infty} - |b_2|_{L^1}$$

$$\geq \frac{m_1^2 T}{2}|y|_Y^2 - (|a_2|_{L^1} + |c_2|_{L^1})\left(\frac{1}{\sqrt{T}}|y|_Y + Tr_2\right) - |b_2|_{L^1}$$

for every $y \in K_2$. This shows that $\alpha(y) \to \infty$ as $y \in K_2$, $|y|_Y \to \infty$.

8.4 NASH EQUILIBRIUM OF NONVARIATIONAL SYSTEMS

Many systems arising in mathematical modeling require positive solutions as acceptable states of the investigated real processes. Mathematically, finding positive solutions means to work in the positive cone of the space of all possible states. However, a cone is an unbounded set and, in many cases, nonlinear problems have several positive solutions. That is why it is important to localize solutions in bounded subsets of a cone. This problem becomes even more interesting in the case of nonlinear systems that do not have a variational structure, but each of its component equations has, namely there exist real "energy" functionals E_1 and E_2 such that the system is equivalent to the equations

$$\begin{cases} E_{11}(u, v) = 0 \\ E_{22}(u, v) = 0. \end{cases}$$

We recall that $E_{11}(u, v)$ is the partial derivative of E_1 with respect to u, and $E_{22}(u, v)$ is the partial derivative of E_2 with respect to v.

A problem of real interest is to see how the solutions (u, v) of this system are connected with the variational properties of the functionals E_1 and E_2. One possible situation, which fits to physical principles, is that a solution (u, v) is a Nash-type equilibrium of the pair of functionals (E_1, E_2), that is,

$$E_1(u, v) = \min_w E_1(w, v)$$

$$E_2(u, v) = \min_w E_2(u, w).$$

A result in this direction is given in Section 8.2 for the case when $\min_w$ is achieved, either on an entire Banach space and then, or on a ball. Nonsmooth analogues of those results, in the abstract framework of Szulkin functionals, have been developed in Section 8.3.

In this section, we are concerned with the localization of a Nash-type equilibrium in the Cartesian product of two conical sets, more exactly if $u \in K_1$ and $v \in K_2$, where K_i ($i = 1, 2$) is a cone of a Hilbert space X_i with norm $\|\cdot\|_i$, and

$$r_1 \leq l_1(u), \quad \|u\|_1 \leq R_1,$$
$$r_2 \leq l_2(v), \quad \|v\|_2 \leq R_2,$$

for some positive numbers r_i and R_i, $i = 1, 2$. The main feature in this section is that $l_i : K_i \to \mathbb{R}_+$ are two *given functionals*. Usually, l_i are the corresponding norms, while here they are upper semicontinuous concave functionals. For instance, in applications, such a functional $l(u)$ can be $\inf u$. If in addition, due to some embedding result, the norm $\|u\|$ is comparable with $\sup u$ in the sense that $\sup u \leq c \|u\|$ for every nonnegative function u and some constant $c > 0$, then the values of any nonnegative function u satisfying $r \leq l(u)$ and $\|u\| \leq R$ belong to the interval $[r, cR]$, which is very convenient for finding multiple solutions located in disjoint annular conical sets.

In the first part of this section we are concerned with the localization of a critical point of minimum type in a convex conical set as above and we explain how this result can be used in order to obtain finitely or infinitely many solutions. The result can be seen as a variational analogue of some Krasnoselskii's type compression-expansion theorems from fixed point theory. Next, we obtain the vector version of this result for gradient type systems. In particular, this result allows to localize individually the components of a solution. The final part of this section is devoted to the existence and localization of Nash-type equilibria for nonvariational systems. An iterative algorithm is used and its convergence is established assuming a local matricial contraction condition. The main abstract result is illustrated with an application dealing with the periodic problem. The results of this section are due to Precup [148].

8.4.1 A Localization Critical Point Theorem

Let X be a real Hilbert space with inner product $\langle ., . \rangle$ and norm $\|.\|$, which is identified with its dual. Assume that $K \subset X$ is a wedge, and let $l : K \to \mathbb{R}_+$ be a concave upper semicontinuous function with $l(0) = 0$. Let $E \in C^1(X)$ be a functional and let $N : X \to X$ be the operator $N(u) := u - E'(u)$.

For any positive numbers r and R we consider the conical set

$$K_{rR} := \{u \in K : r \le l(u) \text{ and } \|u\| \le R\}.$$

Then K_{rR} is a convex set since l is concave, and it is closed since l is upper semicontinuous.

Assume that $K_{rR} \ne \emptyset$ and

$$N(K_{rR}) \subset K.$$

Lemma 8.3. *Let the following conditions be satisfied:*

$$m := \inf_{u \in K_{rR}} E(u) > -\infty; \tag{8.49}$$

there exists $\varepsilon > 0$ such that $E(u) \ge m + \varepsilon$ for

all $u \in K_{rR}$ which simultaneously satisfy $l(u) = r$ and $\|u\| = R$;
$$\tag{8.50}$$

$$l(N(u)) \ge r \text{ for every } u \in K_{rR}. \tag{8.51}$$

Then there exists a sequence $(u_n) \subset K_{rR}$ such that

$$E(u_n) \le m + \frac{1}{n} \tag{8.52}$$

and

$$\left\| E'(u_n) + \lambda_n u_n \right\| \le \frac{1}{n}, \tag{8.53}$$

where

$$\lambda_n = \begin{cases} -\frac{\langle E'(u_n), u_n \rangle}{R^2} & \text{if } \|u_n\| = R \text{ and } \langle E'(u_n), u_n \rangle < 0 \\ 0 & \text{otherwise.} \end{cases} \qquad (8.54)$$

Proof. By Ekeland's variational principle, there exists a sequence $(u_n) \subset K_{rR}$ such that

$$E(u_n) \leq m + \frac{1}{n}, \qquad (8.55)$$

$$E(u_n) \leq E(v) + \frac{1}{n} \|v - u_n\| \qquad (8.56)$$

for all $v \in K_{rR}$ and $n \geq 1$.

We distinguish the following distinct situations.

Case 1. There is a subsequence of (u_n) (also denoted by (u_n)) such that $r \leq l(u_n)$ and $\|u_n\| < R$ for every n. For a fixed but arbitrary n and $t > 0$, consider the element

$$v = u_n - t E'(u_n).$$

Since $v = (1-t)u_n + tN(u_n)$ and both u_n and $N(u_n)$ belong to K, we deduce that $v \in K$ for every $t \in (0, 1)$. Next, the concavity of l and relation (8.51) yield

$$l(v) \geq (1-t)l(u_n) + tl(N(u_n)) \geq r$$

for all $t \in (0, 1)$. In addition, the continuity of the norm gives $\|v\| \leq R$ for every $t \in (0, 1)$ small enough. It follows that $v \in K_{rR}$ for all sufficiently small $t > 0$. Replacing v in (8.56) we obtain

$$E\left(u_n - t E'(u_n)\right) - E(u_n) \geq -\frac{t}{n} \left\| E'(u_n) \right\|.$$

Dividing by t and letting t go to zero yields

$$-\langle E'(u_n), E'(u_n) \rangle \geq -\frac{1}{n} \left\| E'(u_n) \right\|.$$

Therefore

$$\left\| E'(u_n) \right\| \leq \frac{1}{n}.$$

Thus, in this case, relation (8.53) holds with $\lambda_n = 0$.

Case 2. There is a subsequence of (u_n) (also denoted by (u_n)) such that $\|u_n\| = R$ for every n. Passing eventually to a new subsequence, in view of (8.50) and (8.55), we may assume that $l(u_n) > r$ for every n. Two subcases are possible:

(a) For a subsequence (still denoted by (u_n)), we have $\langle E'(u_n), u_n \rangle > 0$ for every n. Then for any fixed index n, the above choice of v in (8.56) is still possible since

$$\|v\|^2 = \|u_n - tE'(u_n)\|^2 = \|u_n\|^2 + t^2 \|E'(u_n)\|^2 - 2t \langle E'(u_n), u_n \rangle$$
$$= R^2 + t^2 \|E'(u_n)\|^2 - 2t \langle E'(u_n), u_n \rangle \le R^2$$

for $0 < t \le 2 \langle E'(u_n), u_n \rangle / \|E'(u_n)\|^2$.

(b) Assume that $\langle E'(u_n), u_n \rangle \le 0$ for every n. Then for any fixed index n, we use (8.56) with

$$v = u_n - t \left(E'(u_n) + \lambda_n u_n + \epsilon u_n \right),$$

where $t, \epsilon > 0$ and $\lambda_n = - \langle E'(u_n), u_n \rangle / R^2 \ge 0$. Since

$$v = (1 - t) \frac{1 - t - t\lambda_n - t\epsilon}{1 - t} u_n + tN(u_n),$$

we immediately see that $v \in K$ for every $t \in (0, 1)$ small enough that $1 - t - t\lambda_n - t\epsilon > 0$. Also,

$$\langle E'(u_n) + \lambda_n u_n + \epsilon u_n, u_n \rangle = \epsilon R^2 > 0,$$

and as in case (a), we find that $\|v\| \le R$ for sufficiently small $t > 0$. On the other hand, from $l(u_n) > r$, we have $\delta l(u_n) = r$ for some number $\delta \in (0, 1)$. Then, for any $\rho \in [\delta, 1]$, we have

$$l(\rho u_n) = l(\rho u_n + (1 - \rho) 0) \ge \rho l(u_n) + (1 - \rho) l(0)$$
$$= \rho l(u_n) \ge \delta l(u_n) = r.$$

In particular, we may take $\rho = (1 - t - t\lambda_n - t\epsilon) / (1 - t)$ which belongs to $[\delta, 1]$ for sufficiently small t. Consequently,

$$l(v) = l \left((1 - t) \frac{1 - t - t\lambda_n - t\epsilon}{1 - t} u_n + tN(u_n) \right)$$
$$= l((1 - t) \rho u_n + tN(u_n)) \ge (1 - t) l(\rho u_n) + t l(N(u_n)) \ge r.$$

Therefore $v \in K_{rR}$ for every sufficiently small $t > 0$. Replacing v in (8.56) and letting $t \to 0$ yields

$$\langle E'(u_n), -E'(u_n) - \lambda_n u_n - \epsilon u_n \rangle \ge -\frac{1}{n} \|E'(u_n) + \lambda_n u_n + \epsilon u_n\|.$$

Finally, let ϵ tend to zero and use $\langle u_n, E'(u_n) + \lambda_n u_n \rangle = 0$ to deduce

$$\left\| E'(u_n) + \lambda_n u_n \right\| \leq \frac{1}{n},$$

which is relation (8.53). □

Lemma 8.3 yields the following critical point theorem.

Theorem 8.13. *Assume that hypotheses of Lemma 8.3 are satisfied. In addition, assume that there is a number v such that*

$$\langle E'(u), u \rangle \geq v \text{ for every } u \in K_{rR} \text{ with } \|u\| = R, \tag{8.57}$$

$$E'(u) + \lambda u \neq 0 \text{ for all } u \in K_{rR} \text{ with } \|u\| = R \text{ and } \lambda > 0, \tag{8.58}$$

and a Palais-Smale type condition holds, more exactly, any sequence as in the conclusion of Lemma 8.3 has a convergent subsequence. Then there exists $u \in K_{rR}$ such that

$$E(u) = m \text{ and } E'(u) = 0.$$

Proof. The sequence (λ_n) given by (8.54) is bounded as a consequence of (8.57). Hence, passing eventually to a subsequence we may suppose that (λ_n) converges to some number λ. Clearly $\lambda \geq 0$. Next, using the Palais-Smale type condition we may assume that the sequence (u_n) converges to some element $u \in K_{rR}$. Then letting $n \to \infty$ in (8.52) and (8.53) gives $E(u) = m$ and $E'(u) + \lambda u = 0$. From (8.54) we have that the case $\lambda > 0$ is possible only if $\|u\| = R$, which is excluded by assumption (8.58). Therefore $\lambda = 0$ and so $E'(u) = 0$. □

If the functional l is continuous on K_{rR}, then instead of hypothesis (8.51) we can take the weaker boundary condition

$$l(N(u)) \geq r \text{ for every } u \in K_{rR} \text{ with } l(u) = r.$$

Let us now assume that there exists $c > 0$ such that

$$l(u) \leq c \|u\| \tag{8.59}$$

for all $u \in K$. Then from the assumption $K_{rR} \neq \emptyset$, we deduce that $r \leq cR$. Indeed, if $u \in K_{rR}$, then $r \leq l(u) \leq c \|u\| \leq cR$.

Also, if

$$r_1 \leq cR_1, \ r_2 \leq cR_2 \text{ and } cR_1 < r_2,$$

then the sets $K_{r_1 R_1}$ and $K_{r_2 R_2}$ are disjoint. Indeed, if $u \in K_{r_1 R_1}$, then

$$r_1 \leq l(u) \leq c \|u\| \leq cR_1 < r_2.$$

Hence $l(u) < r_2$ which shows that $u \notin K_{r_2 R_2}$. The same conclusion holds if

$$r_1 \le cR_1, \ r_2 \le cR_2 \ \text{and} \ r_1 > cR_2.$$

These remarks allow us to state the following multiplicity results.

Theorem 8.14. *Assume that condition (8.59) holds.*

(i) *If there are finite or infinite sequences of numbers* $(r_j)_{1 \le j \le n}$, $(R_j)_{1 \le j \le n}$ *(for $1 \le n \le +\infty$) with $r_j \le cR_j$ for $1 \le j \le n$ and $cR_j < r_{j+1}$ for $1 \le j < n$, such that the assumptions of Theorem 8.13 are satisfied for each of the sets $K_{r_j R_j}$, then for every j, there exists $u_j \in K_{r_j R_j}$ with*

$$E(u_j) = \inf_{K_{r_j R_j}} E \quad \text{and} \quad E'(u_j) = 0. \tag{8.60}$$

(ii) *If there are infinite sequences of numbers* $(r_j)_{j \ge 1}$, $(R_j)_{j \ge 1}$ *with $cR_{j+1} < r_j \le cR_j$ for all j, such that the assumptions of Theorem 8.13 hold for each of the sets $K_{r_j R_j}$, then for every j, there exists $u_j \in K_{r_j R_j}$ which satisfies (8.60).*

8.4.2 Localization of Nash-Type Equilibria of Nonvariational Systems

We first establish a vector version of the localization critical point theorem. For this purpose, we consider two Hilbert spaces X_1 and X_2 with scalar products $\langle ., . \rangle_i$ and norms $\|.\|_i$ ($i = 1, 2$). Let $K_i \subset X_i$ denote two wedges and let $l_i : K_i \to \mathbb{R}_+$ be upper semicontinuous functionals with $l_i(0) = 0$. We assume that E is a C^1-functional on the product space $X_1 \times X_2$. We have $E'(u, v) = (E'_u(u, v), E'_v(u, v))$, for $u \in X_1$, $v \in X_2$, and we denote by N_1, N_2 the operators

$$N_1(u, v) = u - E'_u(u, v), \quad N_2(u, v) = v - E'_v(u, v). \tag{8.61}$$

In what follows, we are interested to find a solution (u, v) of the system

$$\begin{cases} u = N_1(u, v) \\ v = N_2(u, v), \end{cases} \tag{8.62}$$

or equivalently, a critical point of E, that is,

$$\begin{cases} E'_u(u, v) = 0 \\ E'_v(u, v) = 0, \end{cases}$$

which minimizes E in a set of the form $K_{rR} := (K_1)_{r_1 R_1} \times (K_2)_{r_2 R_2}$, where $r = (r_1, r_2)$, $R = (R_1, R_2)$ and

$$(K_i)_{r_i R_i} = \{w \in K_i : r_i \le l_i(w) \ \text{and} \ \|w\|_i \le R_i\}.$$

Applying the Ekeland variational principle to the functional E and to the closed subset K_{rR} of $X_1 \times X_2$ we obtain the following vector versions of Lemma 8.3 and Theorem 8.13.

Lemma 8.4. *Let the following conditions be satisfied:*

$$m := \inf_{(u,v) \in K_{rR}} E(u,v) > -\infty;$$

there exists $\varepsilon > 0$ such that $E(u,v) \geq m + \varepsilon$ if

$$l_1(u) = r_1 \text{ and } \|u\|_1 = R_1, \text{ or } l_2(v) = r_2 \text{ and } \|v\|_2 = R_2;$$

$$l_1(N_1(u,v)) \geq r_1 \text{ and } l_2(N_2(u,v)) \geq r_2 \text{ for every } (u,v) \in K_{rR}.$$

Then there exists a minimizing sequence $(u_n, v_n) \subset K_{rR}$, i.e., $E(u_n, v_n) \to m$ as $n \to \infty$, such that

$$E(u_n, v_n) \leq m + \frac{1}{n},$$

$$\left\| E'_u(u_n, v_n) + \lambda_n u_n \right\|_1 \leq \frac{1}{n} \quad and \quad \left\| E'_v(u_n, v_n) + \mu_n v_n \right\|_2 \leq \frac{1}{n},$$

where

$$\lambda_n = \begin{cases} -\dfrac{\langle E'_u(u_n, v_n), u_n \rangle_1}{R_1^2} & \text{if } \|u_n\|_1 = R_1 \text{ and } \langle E'_u(u_n, v_n), u_n \rangle_1 < 0 \\ 0 & \text{otherwise}, \end{cases}$$

$$\mu_n = \begin{cases} -\dfrac{\langle E'_v(u_n, v_n), v_n \rangle_1}{R_2^2} & \text{if } \|v_n\|_2 = R_2 \text{ and } \langle E'_v(u_n, v_n), v_n \rangle_2 < 0 \\ 0 & \text{otherwise}. \end{cases}$$

Theorem 8.15. *Assume that the assumptions of Lemma 8.4 are satisfied. In addition, we assume that there exists a real number ν such that*

$$\langle E'_u(u,v), u \rangle_1 \geq \nu \text{ for every } (u,v) \in K_{rR} \text{ with } \|u\|_1 = R_1,$$

$$\langle E'_v(u,v), v \rangle_2 \geq \nu \text{ for every } (u,v) \in K_{rR} \text{ with } \|v\|_2 = R_2,$$

$$E'_u(u,v) + \lambda u \neq 0 \text{ for all } (u,v) \in K_{rR} \text{ with } \|u\|_1 = R_1 \text{ and } \lambda > 0,$$

$$E'_v(u,v) + \lambda v \neq 0 \text{ for all } (u,v) \in K_{rR} \text{ with } \|v\|_2 = R_2 \text{ and } \lambda > 0,$$

and the Palais-Smale type condition holds. Then there exists $(u,v) \in K_{rR}$ such that

$$E(u,v) = m \quad and \quad E'(u,v) = 0.$$

Our main purpose in what follows is to deal with system (8.62) but without assuming the existence of a functional E with property (8.61). Instead, we assume that each equation of the system has a variational structure, that is, there are two C^1 functionals $E_i : X := X_1 \times X_2 \to \mathbb{R}$, such that

$$N_1(u, v) = u - E_{11}(u, v), \quad N_2(u, v) = v - E_{22}(u, v),$$

where by E_{11}, E_{22} we mean the partial derivatives of E_1, E_2 with respect to u and v, respectively.

We look for a point (u, v) in a set of the form $K_{rR} := (K_1)_{r_1 R_1} \times (K_2)_{r_2 R_2}$, which solves problem (8.62) and is a *Nash-type equilibrium in* K_{rR} of the pair of functionals (E_1, E_2), more exactly

$$E_1(u, v) = \min_{w \in (K_1)_{r_1 R_1}} E_1(w, v),$$

$$E_2(u, v) = \min_{w \in (K_2)_{r_2 R_2}} E_2(u, w).$$

We say that the operator $N : X \to X$, $N(u, v) = (N_1(u, v), N_2(u, v))$ is a *Perov contraction on* K_{rR} if there exists a matrix $M = [m_{ij}] \in \mathcal{M}_{2,2}(\mathbb{R}_+)$ such that M^n tends to the zero matrix as $n \to \infty$, and the following matricial Lipschitz condition is satisfied

$$\begin{bmatrix} \|N_1(u, v) - N_1(\overline{u}, \overline{v})\|_1 \\ \|N_2(u, v) - N_2(\overline{u}, \overline{v})\|_2 \end{bmatrix} \leq M \begin{bmatrix} \|u - \overline{u}\|_1 \\ \|v - \overline{v}\|_2 \end{bmatrix} \tag{8.63}$$

for every $u, \overline{u} \in (K_1)_{r_1 R_1}$ and $v, \overline{v} \in (K_2)_{r_2 R_2}$.

Notice that for a square matrix of nonnegative elements, the property $M^n \to 0$ is equivalent to $\rho(M) < 1$, where $\rho(M)$ is the spectral radius of matrix M, and also to the fact that $I - M$ is nonsingular and all the elements of the matrix $(I - M)^{-1}$ are nonnegative (see [144]). In case of square matrices M of order 2, the above property is characterized by the inequality

$$\text{tr}(M) < \min\{2, \ 1 + \det(M)\}.$$

We impose the following hypotheses:

(H1) For each $v \in (K_2)_{r_2 R_2}$, the functional $E_1(., v)$ is bounded from below on $(K_1)_{r_1 R_1}$;
for each $u \in (K_1)_{r_1 R_1}$, the functional $E_2(u, .)$ is bounded from below on $(K_2)_{r_2 R_2}$.

(H2) $l_1(N_1(u, v)) \geq r_1$ for every $(u, v) \in K_{rR}$; $N_1(u, v) \neq (1 + \lambda)u$ for all $(u, v) \in K_{rR}$ with $\|u\|_1 = R_1$ and $\lambda > 0$;
$l_2(N_2(u, v)) \geq r_2$ for every $(u, v) \in K_{rR}$; $N_2(u, v) \neq (1 + \lambda)v$ for all $(u, v) \in K_{rR}$ with $\|v\|_2 = R_2$ and $\lambda > 0$.

(H3) For each $v \in (K_2)_{r_2 R_2}$, there exists $\varepsilon > 0$ such that $E_1(u, v) \geq \inf_{(K_1)_{r_1 R_1}} E_1(., v) + \varepsilon$ whenever u simultaneously satisfies $l_1(u) = r_1$ and $\|u\|_1 = R_1$;

for each $u \in (K_1)_{r_1 R_1}$, there exists $\varepsilon > 0$ such that $E_2(u, v) \geq \inf_{(K_2)_{r_2 R_2}} E_2(u, .) + \varepsilon$ whenever v simultaneously satisfies $l_2(v) = r_2$ and $\|v\|_2 = R_2$.

(H4) N is a Perov contraction on K_{rR}.

Let us underline the local character of the contraction condition (H4). This is essential for multiple Nash-type equilibria when (H4) is required to hold on disjoint bounded sets of the type K_{rR} but not on the entire K. Thus the 'slope' of N has to be 'small' on the sets K_{rR} but can be unlimited large between these sets, which makes possible to fulfill the boundary conditions (H2).

Theorem 8.16. *Assume that conditions* (H1)–(H4) *hold. Then there exists a solution* $(u, v) \in K_{rR}$ *of system (8.62) which is a Nash-type equilibrium on* K_{rR} *of the pair of functionals* (E_1, E_2).

Proof. The main idea is to construct recursively two sequences (u_n), (v_n), based on Lemma 8.3. Let v_0 be any element of $(K_2)_{r_2 R_2}$. At any step n ($n \geq 1$) we may find a $u_n \in (K_1)_{r_1 R_1}$ and a $v_n \in (K_2)_{r_2 R_2}$ such that

$$E_1(u_n, v_{n-1}) \leq \inf_{(K_1)_{r_1 R_1}} E_1(., v_{n-1}) + \frac{1}{n}, \quad \|E_{11}(u_n, v_{n-1}) + \lambda_n u_n\|_1 \leq \frac{1}{n}$$

$$(8.64)$$

and

$$E_2(u_n, v_n) \leq \inf_{(K_2)_{r_2 R_2}} E_2(u_n, .) + \frac{1}{n}, \quad \|E_{22}(u_n, v_n) + \mu_n v_n\|_2 \leq \frac{1}{n}, \quad (8.65)$$

where

$$\lambda_n = \begin{cases} -\dfrac{\langle E_{11}(u_n, v_{n-1}), u_n \rangle_1}{R_1^2} & \text{if } \|u_n\|_1 = R_1 \\ & \text{and } \langle E_{11}(u_n, v_{n-1}), u_n \rangle_1 < 0 \\ 0 & \text{otherwise,} \end{cases}$$

and the expression of μ_n is analogous.

Condition (H4) guarantees that the operators N_i are bounded, so the boundedness of the sequences of real numbers (λ_n) and (μ_n). Therefore, passing to subsequences, we may assume that the sequences (λ_n) and (μ_n) are convergent.

Let

$$\alpha_n := E_{11}(u_n, v_{n-1}) + \lambda_n u_n \quad \text{and} \quad \beta_n := E_{22}(u_n, v_n) + \mu_n v_n.$$

We observe that $\alpha_n, \beta_n \to 0$. Also

$$(1 + \lambda_n) u_n - N_1(u_n, v_{n-1}) = \alpha_n \quad (8.66)$$

$$(1 + \mu_n) v_n - N_2(u_n, v_n) = \beta_n.$$

Since $\lambda_n > 0$, the first equality if (8.66) written for n and $n + p$ yields

$$\|u_{n+p} - u_n\|_1$$
$$\leq (1 + \lambda_n) \|u_{n+p} - u_n\|_1$$
$$= \|(1 + \lambda_n) u_{n+p} - (1 + \lambda_n) u_n\|_1$$
$$= \|(1 + \lambda_{n+p}) u_{n+p} - (1 + \lambda_n) u_n - (\lambda_{n+p} - \lambda_n) u_{n+p}\|_1$$
$$\leq \|N_1(u_{n+p}, v_{n+p-1}) - N_1(u_n, v_{n-1})\|_1 + \|\alpha_{n+p} - \alpha_n\|_1$$
$$+ |\lambda_{n+p} - \lambda_n| \|u_{n+p}\|_1 .$$

Furthermore, using $\|u_{n+p}\|_1 \leq R_1$ and relation (8.63) we deduce that

$$\|u_{n+p} - u_n\|_1$$
$$\leq m_{11} \|u_{n+p} - u_n\|_1 + m_{12} \|v_{n+p-1} - v_{n-1}\|_2 + \|\alpha_{n+p} - \alpha_n\|_1$$
$$+ R_1 |\lambda_{n+p} - \lambda_n|$$
$$= m_{11} \|u_{n+p} - u_n\|_1 + m_{12} \|v_{n+p} - v_n\|_2 + \|\alpha_{n+p} - \alpha_n\|_1$$
$$+ R_1 |\lambda_{n+p} - \lambda_n| + m_{12} \left(\|v_{n+p-1} - v_{n-1}\|_2 - \|v_{n+p} - v_n\|_2 \right) .$$

Denote

$$a_{n,p} = \|u_{n+p} - u_n\|_1 , \quad b_{n,p} = \|v_{n+p} - v_n\|_2 ,$$
$$c_{n,p} = \|\alpha_{n+p} - \alpha_n\|_1 + R_1 |\lambda_{n+p} - \lambda_n| ,$$
$$d_{n,p} = \|\beta_{n+p} - \beta_n\|_2 + R_2 |\mu_{n+p} - \mu_n| .$$

Clearly, $c_{n,p} \to 0$ and $d_{n,p} \to 0$ uniformly with respect to p. It follows that

$$a_{n,p} \leq m_{11} a_{n,p} + m_{12} b_{n,p} + c_{n,p} + m_{12} \left(b_{n-1,p} - b_{n,p} \right) . \tag{8.67}$$

Similarly, from the second equality in (8.66), we find

$$b_{n,p} \leq m_{21} a_{n,p} + m_{22} b_{n,p} + d_{n,p} .$$

Hence

$$\begin{bmatrix} a_{n,p} \\ b_{n,p} \end{bmatrix} \leq M \begin{bmatrix} a_{n,p} \\ b_{n,p} \end{bmatrix} + \begin{bmatrix} c_{n,p} + m_{12} \left(b_{n-1,p} - b_{n,p} \right) \\ d_{n,p} \end{bmatrix} .$$

Consequently, since $I - M$ is invertible and its inverse contains only nonnegative elements, we may write

$$\begin{bmatrix} a_{n,p} \\ b_{n,p} \end{bmatrix} \leq (I - M)^{-1} \begin{bmatrix} c_{n,p} + m_{12} \left(b_{n-1,p} - b_{n,p} \right) \\ d_{n,p} \end{bmatrix} .$$

Let $(I - M)^{-1} = [\gamma_{ij}]$. Then

$$a_{n,p} \leq \gamma_{11} \left(c_{n,p} + m_{12} \left(b_{n-1,p} - b_{n,p}\right)\right) + \gamma_{12} d_{n,p} \qquad (8.68)$$
$$b_{n,p} \leq \gamma_{21} \left(c_{n,p} + m_{12} \left(b_{n-1,p} - b_{n,p}\right)\right) + \gamma_{22} d_{n,p}.$$

From the second inequality, one has

$$b_{n,p} \leq \frac{\gamma_{21} m_{12}}{1 + \gamma_{21} m_{12}} b_{n-1,p} + \frac{\gamma_{21} c_{n,p} + \gamma_{22} d_{n,p}}{1 + \gamma_{21} m_{12}}.$$

Clearly $(b_{n,p})$ is bounded uniformly with respect to p. Next, we apply Lemma 8.1. It follows that $b_{n,p} \to 0$ uniformly for $p \in \mathbb{N}$, and hence (v_n) is a Cauchy sequence. Next, the first inequality in (8.68) implies that (u_n) is also a Cauchy sequence. Let u^*, v^* be the limits of the sequences (u_n), (v_n), respectively. The conclusion of Theorem 8.16 now follows if we pass to the limit in (8.64), (8.65) and we use (H2). $\qquad \square$

8.5 APPLICATIONS TO PERIODIC PROBLEMS

8.5.1 Case of a Single Equation

Consider the following periodic problem:

$$-u''(t) + a^2 u(t) = f(u(t)) \quad \text{on } (0, T) \qquad (8.69)$$
$$u(0) - u(T) = u'(0) - u'(T) = 0$$

where $a \neq 0$ and $f : \mathbb{R} \to \mathbb{R}$ is a continuous function with $f(\mathbb{R}_+) \subset \mathbb{R}_+$.
Let $X := H_p^1(0, T)$ be the space of functions of the form

$$u(t) = \int_0^t v(s)\, ds + C,$$

with $u(0) = u(T)$, $C \in \mathbb{R}$ and $v \in L^2(0, T)$, endowed with the inner product

$$\langle u, v \rangle = \int_0^T \left(u'v' + a^2 u v\right) dt$$

and the corresponding norm

$$\|u\| = \left(\int_0^T \left(u'^2 + a^2 u^2\right) dt\right)^{\frac{1}{2}}.$$

Let K be the positive cone of X, that is, $K = \{u \in H_p^1(0, T) : u \geq 0 \text{ on } [0, T]\}$, and let $l : K \to \mathbb{R}_+$ be given by

$$l(u) = \min_{t \in [0,T]} u(t).$$

The energy functional associated to the problem is $E : H_p^1(0, T) \to \mathbb{R}$,

$$E(u) = \frac{1}{2} \|u\|^2 - \int_0^T F(u(t)) \, dt,$$

where

$$F(\tau) = \int_0^\tau f(s) \, ds.$$

The identification of the dual $\left(H_p^1(0, T)\right)'$ to the space $H_p^1(0, T)$ via the mapping $J : \left(H_p^1(0, T)\right)' \to H_p^1(0, T)$, $J(v) = w$, where w is the weak solution of the problem

$$-w'' + a^2 w = v \quad \text{on } (0, T),$$
$$w(0) - w(T) = w'(0) - w'(T) = 0$$

yields to the representation

$$E'(u) = u - N(u),$$

where

$$N(u) = J(f(u(\cdot))).$$

Note that the condition $f(\mathbb{R}_+) \subset \mathbb{R}_+$ guarantees that $N(K) \subset K$.

Let $c > 0$ be the embedding constant of the inclusion $H_p^1(0, T) \subset C[0, T]$, that is, $\|u\|_{C[0,T]} \leq c \|u\|$ for all $u \in H_p^1(0, T)$.

Note that for $u \equiv 1$, the above inequality gives $1 \leq ac\sqrt{T}$, whence $a^2 \geq 1/(c^2 T)$. Also, if r and R are positive numbers and $a\sqrt{T} r \leq R$, then the set K_{rR} is nonempty. Indeed, any constant $\lambda \in \left[r, R/\left(a\sqrt{T}\right)\right]$ belongs to K_{rR}, since $l(\lambda) = \lambda \geq r$ and $\|\lambda\| = \left(\int_0^T a^2 \lambda^2 ds\right)^{1/2} = a\lambda\sqrt{T} \leq R$.

Theorem 8.17. *Let r, R be positive constants such that $a\sqrt{T} r \leq R$. Assume that f is nondecreasing on the interval $[r, cR]$ and that the following conditions hold:*

$$E(r) < \frac{R^2}{2} - TF(cR), \tag{8.70}$$

and

$$f(r) \geq a^2 r, \quad f(cR) \leq \frac{R}{cT}. \tag{8.71}$$

Then problem (8.69) has a positive solution u with $r \leq u(t) \leq cR$ for all $t \in [0, T]$, which minimizes E in the set K_{rR}.

Proof. **(i)** Check of condition (8.49). Let $u \in K_{rR}$. One has $r \le u(t) \le cR$ for all $t \in [0, T]$. Then, since F is nondecreasing on $\mathbb{R}_+$,

$$E(u) \ge - \int_0^T F(u(s))\,ds \ge -TF(cR) > -\infty.$$

(ii) Check of condition (8.50). Take any u with $l(u) = r$ and $\|u\| = R$. Then

$$E(u) = \frac{R^2}{2} - \int_0^T F(u(s))\,ds \ge \frac{R^2}{2} - TF(cR).$$

Thus our claim holds in view of the strict inequality (8.70) and the obvious inequality $m \le E(r)$ (note that the constant function r belongs to K_{rR}).

(iii) Check of condition (8.51). Let $u \in K_{rR}$. Then

$$l(N(u)) = l(J(f(u))) \ge l(J(f(r))) = f(r)l(J(1))$$
$$= \frac{f(r)}{a^2} \ge r,$$

in virtue of the first inequality in (8.71).

(iv) Check of condition (8.58). Assume that $E'(u) + \lambda u = 0$ for some $u \in K_{rR}$ with $\|u\| = R$ and $\lambda > 0$. Then

$$(1 + \lambda)\left(-u'' + a^2 u\right) = f(u),$$

whence

$$R^2 < (1 + \lambda) R^2 = \langle f(u), u \rangle_{L^2} \le Tf(cR)cR,$$

that is

$$\frac{R}{cT} < f(cR),$$

which contradicts the second inequality in (8.71).

(v) Condition (8.57) being immediate and the required Palais-Smale type condition being a consequence of the compact embedding of $H^1_p(0, T)$ into $C[0, T]$, Theorem 8.13 yields the conclusion. $\qquad\square$

Example 8.3. For each $\lambda > 0$, the equation $-u'' + a^2 u = \lambda \sqrt{u}$ has a T-periodic solution satisfying $u(t) \ge \lambda^2/a^4$ for all $t \in [0, T]$.

Indeed, if we take $r = \lambda^2/a^4$, then the first condition from (8.71) is satisfied with equality. Next, we choose R large enough that (8.70) and the second inequality (8.71) hold, that is,

$$E(r) < \frac{R^2}{2} - \lambda \frac{2}{3} T (cR)^{\frac{3}{2}} \quad \text{and} \quad \lambda \sqrt{cR} \le \frac{R}{cT}.$$

8.5.2 Case of a Variational System

We now consider the periodic problem for the following system:

$$-u''(t) + a_1^2 u(t) = f_1(u(t), v(t)) \quad \text{on } (0, T) \qquad (8.72)$$
$$-v''(t) + a_2^2 v(t) = f_2(u(t), v(t)) \quad \text{on } (0, T)$$

in the case when f_1, f_2 are the partial derivatives of a function $F : \mathbb{R}^2 \to \mathbb{R}$ with respect to the first and the second variable, respectively. We assume that $a_i \neq 0$ and $f_i(\mathbb{R}_+ \times \mathbb{R}_+) \subset \mathbb{R}_+$, for $i = 1, 2$.

Let X_1 denote the space $H_p^1(0, T)$ endowed with the scalar product

$$\langle u, v \rangle_1 = \int_0^T \left(u'v' + a_1^2 uv \right) ds$$

and the induced norm $\|.\|_1$. Assume that X_2 is the same space endowed with the analogue scalar product and norm $\langle ., . \rangle_2$, $\|.\|_2$. Also $K_1 = K_2$ is the cone of nonnegative functions in $H_p^1(0, T)$, and $l_1(w) = l_2(w) = \min_{t \in [0,T]} w(t)$ for $w \in H_p^1(0, T)$, $w \geq 0$.

The system has a variational structure since its T-periodic solutions (u, v) are the critical points of the energy functional on $H_p^1(0, T) \times H_p^1(0, T)$,

$$E(u, v) = \frac{1}{2} \left(\|u\|_1^2 + \|v\|_2^2 \right) - \int_0^T F(u(s), v(s)) ds.$$

For $i = 1, 2$, let $c_i > 0$ be the embedding constant of the inclusion $X_i \subset C[0, T]$, that is, $\|w\|_{C[0,T]} \leq c_i \|w\|_i$ for all $w \in H_p^1(0, T)$.

Theorem 8.18. *Let r_i, R_i be positive constants such that $a_i \sqrt{T} r_i \leq R_i$ ($i = 1, 2$). Assume that for $i = 1, 2$, f_i is nondecreasing in each of the variables on $[r_1, c_1 R_1] \times [r_2, c_2 R_2]$ and that the following conditions hold:*

$$E(r_1, r_2) < \frac{R_i^2}{2} - T F(c_1 R_1, c_2 R_2),$$

and

$$f_i(r_1, r_2) \geq a_i^2 r_i, \quad f_i(c_1 R_1, c_2 R_2) \leq \frac{R_i}{c_i T}.$$

Then system (8.72) has a T-solution (u, v) with $r_1 \leq u(t) \leq c_1 R_1$ and $r_2 \leq v(t) \leq c_2 R_2$ for all $t \in [0, T]$, which minimizes E in the set $K_{rR} := (K_1)_{r_1 R_1} \times (K_2)_{r_2 R_2}$.

Example 8.4. The potential of the system

$$-u'' + a_1^2 u = \alpha_1 \sqrt{u} + \gamma v$$

$$-v'' + a_2^2 v = \alpha_2 \sqrt{v} + \gamma u$$

is

$$F(u, v) = \frac{2}{3} \left(\alpha_1 u^{\frac{3}{2}} + \alpha_2 v^{\frac{3}{2}} \right) + \gamma u v.$$

As for Example 8.3, we have the following result: for every numbers $\alpha_i > 0$, $i = 1, 2$, $T > 0$ and $0 \leq \gamma < \min \left\{ 1 / \left(2 c_i^2 T \right) : i = 1, 2 \right\}$, the system has a T-periodic solution with $u(t) \geq \alpha_1^2 / a_1^4$ and $v(t) \geq \alpha_2^2 / a_2^4$ and all $t \in [0, T]$. For the proof, take $r_i = \alpha_i^2 / a_i^4$ $(i = 1, 2)$ and a sufficiently large $R := R_1 = R_2$.

8.5.3 Case of a Nonvariational System

We now consider the system (8.72) for two arbitrary continuous functions f_1, f_2 and use the notations from the previous section. The energy functionals associated to the equations of the system are $E_i : H_p^1(0, T) \times H_p^1(0, T) \to \mathbb{R}$,

$$E_1(u, v) = \frac{1}{2} \|u\|_1^2 - \int_0^T F_1(u(t), v(t)) \, dt,$$

$$E_2(u, v) = \frac{1}{2} \|v\|_2^2 - \int_0^T F_2(u(t), v(t)) \, dt,$$

where

$$F_1(\tau_1, \tau_2) = \int_0^{\tau_1} f_1(s, \tau_2) \, ds, \quad F_2(\tau_1, \tau_2) = \int_0^{\tau_2} f_2(\tau_1, s) \, ds.$$

The identification of the dual $\left(H_p^1(0, T) \right)'$ to the space $H_p^1(0, T)$ via the mapping $J_i : \left(H_p^1(0, T) \right)' \to H_p^1(0, T)$, $J_i(v) = w$, where w is the weak solution of the problem

$$-w'' + a_i^2 w = v \quad \text{on } (0, T),$$
$$w(0) - w(T) = w'(0) - w'(T) = 0$$

yields to the representations

$$E_{11}(u, v) = u - N_1(u, v), \quad E_{22}(u, v) = v - N_2(u, v),$$

where E_{11}, E_{22} stand for the partial derivatives of E_1, E_2 with respect to u and v, respectively, and

$$N_i(u, v) = J_i(f_i(u(\cdot), v(\cdot))).$$

Let $r = (r_1, r_2)$ and $R = (R_1, R_2)$ be such that

$$0 < a_i \sqrt{T} r_i \leq R_i, \quad i = 1, 2.$$

In what follows, we verify that the hypotheses of Theorem 8.16 are fulfilled.

Check of condition (H1): For every $(u, v) \in K_{rR} = (K_1)_{r_1 R_1} \times (K_2)_{r_2 R_2}$ and $t \in [0, T]$, we have

$$r_1 \leq u(t) \leq \|u\|_{C[0,T]} \leq c_1 \|u\|_1 \leq c_1 R_1,$$

and similarly $r_2 \leq v(t) \leq c_2 R_2$. It follows that

$$|f_i(\tau_1, \tau_2)| \leq \rho_i$$

for every $\tau_1 \in [r_1, c_1 R_1]$, $\tau_2 \in [r_2, c_2 R_2]$ and some $\rho_i \in \mathbb{R}_+$ $(i = 1, 2)$. Then

$$E_1(u, v) \geq -\int_0^T \int_0^{u(t)} |f_1(s, v(t))| \, ds \, dt \geq -\int_0^T \int_0^{c_1 R_1} |f_1(s, v(t))| \, ds \, dt$$
$$\geq -c_1 R_1 T \rho_1 > -\infty,$$

and similarly $E_2(u, v) \geq -c_2 R_2 T \rho_2 > -\infty$. Hence condition (H1) holds.

Next, we assume in addition that for $i \in \{1, 2\}$,

$$f_i(\tau_1, \tau_2) \quad \text{is nonnegative and nondecreasing}$$
$$\text{in both variables } \tau_1 \text{ and } \tau_2 \text{ in } [r_1, c_1 R_1] \times [r_2, c_2 R_2], \tag{8.73}$$

$$f_i(r_1, r_2) \geq a_i^2 r_i, \tag{8.74}$$
$$f_i(c_1 R_1, c_2 R_2) \leq R_i / (T c_i), \tag{8.75}$$

and

$$F_i(c_1 R_1, c_2 R_2) - F_i(r_1, r_2) < \frac{1}{2T} \left(R_i^2 - a_i^2 T r_i^2 \right). \tag{8.76}$$

Check of condition (H2): Let $(u, v) \in K_{rR}$. Then from $u(t) \geq r_1$, $v(t) \geq r_2$ and the monotonicity of f_1, we have

$$f_i(u(t), v(t)) \geq f_i(r_1, r_2).$$

This together with (8.74) implies

$$l_i(N_i(u, v)) \geq l_i(J_i(f_i(r_1, r_2))) = \frac{f_i(r_1, r_2)}{a_i^2} \geq r_i.$$

Thus, the first part of (H2) is verified. For the second part, assume that there exists $(u, v) \in K_{rR}$ with $\|u\|_1 = R_1$ and $\lambda > 0$ such that

$$N_1(u, v) = (1 + \lambda) u.$$

Then

$$(1 + \lambda) \left(-u'' + a_1^2 u \right) = f_1(u, v),$$

which gives

$$R_1^2 < (1+\lambda) R_1^2 = (1+\lambda) \|u\|_1^2 = \langle f_1(u,v), u \rangle_{L^2}$$
$$\leq T f_1(c_1 R_1, c_2 R_2) c_1 R_1,$$

whence

$$f_1(c_1 R_1, c_2 R_2) > R_1 / (T c_1),$$

which contradicts (8.75). An analogue reasoning applies if $N_2(u,v) = (1+\lambda) v$ for some $(u,v) \in K_{rR}$ with $\|v\|_2 = R_2$ and $\lambda > 0$. Therefore (H2) holds.

Check of condition (H3): The constant function r_1 belongs to $(K_1)_{r_1 R_1}$ and for any $v \in (K_2)_{r_2 R_2}$, we have

$$E_1(r_1, v) = \frac{1}{2} a_1^2 T r_1^2 - \int_0^T F_1(r_1, v(t)) dt$$
$$\leq \frac{1}{2} a_1^2 T r_1^2 - T F_1(r_1, r_2).$$

Also, for any $(u,v) \in K_{rR}$ with $l_1(u) = r_1$ and $\|u\|_1 = R_1$, one has

$$E_1(u,v) = \frac{1}{2} R_1^2 - \int_0^T F_1(u(t), v(t)) dt \geq \frac{1}{2} R_1^2 - T F_1(c_1 R_1, c_2 R_2).$$

Therefore the first part of (H3) holds with

$$\varepsilon = \frac{1}{2} R_1^2 - T F_1(c_1 R_1, c_2 R_2) - \left(\frac{1}{2} a_1^2 T r_1^2 - T F_1(r_1, r_2) \right)$$

which is positive in view of assumption (8.76). The second part of (H3) can be checked similarly.

Finally, to guarantee (H4) we need some Lipschitz conditions on f_1 and f_2. We assume the existence of nonnegative constants σ_{ij}, $i, j = 1, 2$, such that

$$|f_i(\tau_1, \tau_2) - f_i(\overline{\tau}_1, \overline{\tau}_2)| \leq \sigma_{i1} |\tau_1 - \overline{\tau}_1| + \sigma_{i2} |\tau_2 - \overline{\tau}_2|, \quad i = 1, 2, \quad (8.77)$$
$$\text{for } \tau_1, \overline{\tau}_1 \in [r_1, c_1 R_1] \text{ and } \tau_2, \overline{\tau}_2 \in [r_2, c_2 R_2],$$

and for the matrix $M = \left[\sigma_{ij} / (a_i a_j) \right]_{1 \leq i, j \leq 2}$ one has

$$M^n \to 0 \text{ as } n \to \infty. \quad (8.78)$$

Check of condition (H4): Notice that for $w \in L^2(0, T)$, from

$$\|J_i(w)\|_i^2 = \langle w, J_i(w) \rangle_{L^2} \leq \|w\|_{L^2} \|J_i(w)\|_{L^2} \leq \frac{1}{a_i} \|w\|_{L^2} \|J_i(w)\|_i,$$

one has

$$\|J_i(w)\|_i \le \frac{1}{a_i} \|w\|_{L^2}, \quad w \in L^2(0,T). \tag{8.79}$$

Then using (8.79) and (8.77) we obtain

$$\begin{aligned}
\|N_1(u,v) - N_1(\bar{u},\bar{v})\|_1 &= \|J_1(f_1(u,v) - f_1(\bar{u},\bar{v}))\|_1 \\
&\le \frac{1}{a_1} \|f_1(u,v) - f_1(\bar{u},\bar{v})\|_{L^2} \\
&\le \frac{\sigma_{11}}{a_1} \|u - \bar{u}\|_{L^2} + \frac{\sigma_{12}}{a_1} \|v - \bar{v}\|_{L^2} \\
&\le \frac{\sigma_{11}}{a_1^2} \|u - \bar{u}\|_1 + \frac{\sigma_{12}}{a_1 a_2} \|v - \bar{v}\|_2.
\end{aligned}$$

Similarly,

$$\|N_2(u,v) - N_2(\bar{u},\bar{v})\|_2 \le \frac{\sigma_{21}}{a_2 a_1} \|u - \bar{u}\|_1 + \frac{\sigma_{22}}{a_2^2} \|v - \bar{v}\|_2.$$

Hence (8.63) holds with $m_{ij} = \sigma_{ij}/a_i a_j$.

Therefore we have the following result.

Theorem 8.19. *Under assumptions (8.73)–(8.76), (8.77) and (8.78), there exists a T-periodic solution $(u,v) \in K_{rR}$ of system (8.72) which is a Nash-type equilibrium on K_{rR} of the pair of energy functionals (E_1, E_2).*

Let us underline the fact that all the assumptions on f_1 and f_2 in the above theorem are given with respect to the bounded region $[r_1, c_1 R_1] \times [r_2, c_2 R_2]$. This makes possible to apply Theorem 8.19 to several disjoint such regions obtaining this way multiple solutions of Nash-type.

Example 8.5. Consider the problem of positive T-periodic solutions for the system

$$\begin{aligned}
-u'' + a_1^2 u &= \alpha_1 \sqrt{u} + \gamma_1 v \\
-v'' + a_2^2 v &= \alpha_2 \sqrt{v} + \gamma_2 u
\end{aligned} \tag{8.80}$$

where α_i, γ_i are nonnegative coefficients with $\gamma_i < a_i^2$ $(i = 1, 2)$.

We try to localize a positive solution (u,v) with $r \le u(t)$ and $r \le v(t)$ for all $t \in [0,T]$. We apply the previous result with $r_1 = r_2 =: r$ and $R_1 = R_2 =: R$.

(a) The positivity and monotonicity of f_1 and f_2 on $\mathbb{R}_+ \times \mathbb{R}_+$ required by (8.73) are obvious.

(b) Condition (8.74): We have

$$f_1(r,r) = \alpha_1 \sqrt{r} + \gamma_1 r.$$

Thus we need

$$\alpha_1 \sqrt{r} + \gamma_1 r \geq a_1^2 r.$$

Under the assumption $\gamma_1 < a_1^2$ this gives

$$r \leq \left(\frac{\alpha_1}{a_1^2 - \gamma_1} \right)^2.$$

Similarly, for f_2,

$$r \leq \left(\frac{\alpha_2}{a_2^2 - \gamma_2} \right)^2.$$

(c) Condition (8.75): We have

$$f_1 (c_1 R, c_2 R) = \alpha_1 \sqrt{c_1 R} + \gamma_1 c_2 R.$$

Hence we need

$$\alpha_1 \sqrt{c_1 R} + \gamma_1 c_2 R \leq \frac{R}{T c_1}.$$

This implies $\gamma_1 < 1/(T c_1 c_2)$ and

$$R \geq \frac{\alpha_1^2 T^2 c_1^3}{(1 - T \gamma_1 c_1 c_2)^2}.$$

Similarly, $\gamma_2 < 1/(T c_1 c_2)$ and

$$R \geq \frac{\alpha_2^2 T^2 c_2^3}{(1 - T \gamma_2 c_1 c_2)^2}.$$

(d) Condition (8.76) for $i = 1$ reads as

$$\frac{2}{3} \alpha_1 (c_1 R)^{\frac{3}{2}} + \gamma_1 c_1 c_2 R^2 - F_1 (r, r) < \frac{1}{2T} \left(R^2 - a_1^2 T r^2 \right)$$

and holds for a sufficiently large R provided that

$$\gamma_1 < \frac{1}{2T c_1 c_2}.$$

Similarly,

$$\gamma_2 < \frac{1}{2T c_1 c_2}.$$

(e) Condition (8.77): For $\tau_1 \in [r, c_1 R]$ and $\tau_2 \in [r, c_2 R]$, one has

$$\frac{\partial f_1(\tau_1, \tau_2)}{\partial \tau_1} = \frac{\alpha_1}{2\sqrt{\tau_1}} \leq \frac{\alpha_1}{2\sqrt{r}}, \quad \frac{\partial f_2(\tau_1, \tau_2)}{\partial \tau_2} \leq \frac{\alpha_2}{2\sqrt{r}}.$$

In addition,

$$\frac{\partial f_1(\tau_1, \tau_2)}{\partial \tau_2} = \gamma_1, \quad \frac{\partial f_2(\tau_1, \tau_2)}{\partial \tau_1} = \gamma_2.$$

Hence (8.77) holds with

$$\sigma_{ii} = \frac{\alpha_i}{2\sqrt{r}} \quad \text{and} \quad \sigma_{ij} = \gamma_i \quad \text{for } i \neq j \ (i, j = 1, 2). \tag{8.81}$$

Consequently we have the following result.

Theorem 8.20. *Assume that*

$$\gamma_i < a_i^2, \quad \gamma_i < \frac{1}{2T c_1 c_2} \quad \text{for } i = 1, 2,$$

and there exists $r > 0$ with

$$r \leq \min\left\{ \left(\frac{\alpha_i}{a_i^2 - \gamma_i} \right)^2 : i = 1, 2 \right\},$$

such that the matrix $M = [\sigma_{ij}/(a_i a_j)]_{1 \leq i, j \leq 2}$ where σ_{ij} are given by (8.81) satisfies (8.78). Then (8.80) has a unique T-periodic solution (u, v) such that $u(t) \geq r$ and $v(t) \geq r$ for every $t \in [0, T]$, which is a Nash-type equilibrium of the pair of corresponding energy functionals.

Proof. The existence follows from Theorem 8.19 and the uniqueness is a consequence of the Perov contraction property of the operator N. ☐

In particular, if $a_1 = a_2 =: a$ (when $c_1 = c_2 =: c$) and $\alpha_1 = \alpha_2 =: \alpha$, the assumptions of Theorem 8.20 reduce to the following ones:

$$\gamma_i < \frac{1}{2T c^2}, \quad r \leq \frac{\alpha^2}{\left(a^2 - \min\{\gamma_1, \gamma_2\}\right)^2}$$

and

$$4\left(a^4 - \gamma_1 \gamma_2\right) r - 4\alpha a^2 \sqrt{r} + \alpha^2 > 0$$

(the condition for M to satisfy (8.78)). We may choose

$$r = \frac{\alpha^2}{\left(a^2 - \min\{\gamma_1, \gamma_2\}\right)^2}$$

if

$$\min\{\gamma_1, \gamma_2\} > 2\sqrt{\gamma_1 \gamma_2} - a^2.$$

Chapter 9

Applications to Mathematical Economics

Contents

> *Learning never exhausts the mind.*
>
> Leonardo da Vinci (1452–1519)

Chapter points

- This chapter is dedicated to show some application of the equilibrium theory to mathematical economics.
- Two models are considered: the Walrasian equilibrium model and the n-pole economy.
- The chapter also discusses Pareto optima for n-person games, in the case when the players are permitted to exchange information and to collaborate.

9.1 A DEBREU-GALE-NIKAÏDO THEOREM

The Debreu-Gale-Nikaïdo theorem, which can be proven by Ky Fan's minimax inequality (Theorem 3.3) is a potential tool to prove the existence of a market equilibrium price. Specifically, we will use it to prove the existence of an equilibrium price within the Walras equilibrium model (see Section 9.2 below).

To state the Debreu-Gale-Nikaïdo theorem we first need the following definition. Let K be a compact topological space, Y be a real normed space and $\varphi : K \rightrightarrows Y$ a given set-valued map. As before, we denote by Y^* the topological dual space of Y. The norm of Y^* will be denoted by $\| \cdot \|_*$. For any fixed $p \in Y^*$, define the support function related to φ by

$$\sigma(\varphi(x), p) := \sup_{y \in \varphi(x)} \langle p, y \rangle, \quad \text{for all } x \in K. \tag{9.1}$$

Equilibrium Problems and Applications. https://doi.org/10.1016/B978-0-12-811029-4.00017-1

Definition 9.1. The set-valued map $\varphi : K \rightrightarrows Y$ is called upper hemicontinuous at $x_0 \in K$ if for all $p \in Y^*$ the support function $x \to \sigma(\varphi(x), p)$ is upper semicontinuous at x_0. The map φ is said to be upper hemicontinuous, if it is upper hemicontinuous at every $x_0 \in K$.

The next result provides a sufficient condition for upper hemicontinuity. If $x_0 \in K$ we denote by $\mathcal{V}(x_0)$ the collection of all neighborhoods of x_0 and by B the open unit ball in Y centered at the origin.

Lemma 9.1. *If the mapping φ is upper semicontinuous (as a set-valued mapping), then it is also upper hemicontinuous.*

Proof. Let $x_0 \in K$ be fixed. By the hypothesis φ is upper semicontinuous at x_0, that is (see Chapter 1), for each open set $V \subset Y$ such that $\varphi(x_0) \subset V$, there exists $N(x_0) \in \mathcal{V}(x_0)$ with

$$\varphi(x) \subset V \quad \text{for all } x \in N(x_0). \tag{9.2}$$

For every $\epsilon > 0$ let $V := \varphi(x_0) + \epsilon B \subset Y$, which is an open set. By (9.2) we conclude that

$$\exists\, N(x_0) \in \mathcal{V}(x_0): \ \varphi(x) \subset \varphi(x_0) + \epsilon B \quad \text{for all } x \in N(x_0). \tag{9.3}$$

Fix arbitrary $\epsilon > 0$ and $p \in Y^*$. Then by (9.3)

$$\sigma(\varphi(x), p) \leq \sigma(\varphi(x_0), p) + \sigma(\epsilon B, p) \quad \text{for all } x \in N(x_0),$$

that is,

$$\sigma(\varphi(x), p) \leq \sigma(\varphi(x_0), p) + \epsilon \|p\|_* \quad \text{for all } x \in N(x_0).$$

Hence the mapping $x \mapsto \sigma(\varphi(x), p)$ is upper semicontinuous at x_0. Since x_0 was arbitrary, it follows that $x \mapsto \sigma(\varphi(x), p)$ is upper semicontinuous. $\square$

In what follows we consider the unit simplex

$$M^n := \left\{ x \in \mathbb{R}^n_+ : \sum_{i=1}^n x_i = 1 \right\}.$$

Theorem 9.1. (Debreu-Gale-Nikaïdo) *Let $C : M^n \rightrightarrows \mathbb{R}^n$ be a set-valued map with nonempty compact values. Suppose that*

(i) *C is upper hemicontinuous;*
(ii) *$\forall\, x \in M^n : C(x) - \mathbb{R}^n_+$ is a convex and closed set;*
(iii) *$\forall\, x \in M^n : \sigma(C(x), x) \geq 0$,*

Then there exists $\bar{x} \in M^n$ such that $C(\bar{x}) \cap \mathbb{R}^n_+ \neq \emptyset$.

Proof. Consider the function

$$\phi : M^n \times M^n \to \mathbb{R}, \quad \phi(x, y) = \sigma(C(x), y).$$

It is easy to check that ϕ satisfies the assumptions of Ky Fan's minimax inequality theorem (Theorem 3.3). Indeed,

1. $\phi(x, x) \geq 0$, $\forall x \in M^n$, by assumption (iii);
2. $\phi(\cdot, y) : M^n \to \mathbb{R}$ is upper semicontinuous by assumption (i);
3. $\phi(x, \cdot) : M^n \to \mathbb{R}$ is convex for all $x \in M^n$, since $y \to \sigma(C(x), y)$ is convex.

Since M^n is convex and compact, we may apply Theorem 3.3, and such there exists $\bar{x} \in M^n$:

$$\phi(\bar{x}, y) \geq 0, \quad \forall y \in M^n,$$

or, equivalently

$$\sigma(C(\bar{x}), y) \geq 0, \quad \forall y \in M^n. \tag{9.4}$$

Taking into account the definition of σ, it can be seen immediately that the latter implies

$$\sigma(C(\bar{x}), y) \geq 0, \quad \forall y \in \mathbb{R}^n_+.$$

We show that this condition is equivalent to

$$\sigma(C(\bar{x}) - \mathbb{R}^n_+, y) \geq 0, \quad \forall y \in \mathbb{R}^n. \tag{9.5}$$

Indeed, let $S := C(\bar{x}) - \mathbb{R}^n_+$. Since $\sigma(-\mathbb{R}^n_+, y) = 0$ for $y \in \mathbb{R}^n_+$ and $\sigma(-\mathbb{R}^n_+, y) = +\infty$ for $y \notin \mathbb{R}^n_+$, we obtain that

$$\sigma(S, y) = \sigma(C(\bar{x}), y) + \sigma(-\mathbb{R}^n_+, y) \geq 0, \forall y \in \mathbb{R}^n.$$

Now S is a closed convex set by (ii). Suppose that $0 \notin S$. Then by the separation theorem $\{0\}$ and S can be strongly separated, that is,

$$\exists y \in \mathbb{R}^n : \sup_{z \in S} \langle z, y \rangle < \inf_{z \in \{0\}} \langle z, y \rangle = 0,$$

which contradicts (9.5). In conclusion $0 \in S = C(\bar{x}) - \mathbb{R}^n_+$, hence $C(\bar{x}) \cap \mathbb{R}^n_+ \neq \emptyset$. The proof is now complete. $\square$

9.2 APPLICATION TO WALRAS EQUILIBRIUM MODEL

Consider an economy with l types of elementary commodities each with a unit of measurement. An elementary commodity is described besides its physical properties also by other characteristics such as its location and/or the date when it will be available and, in case of uncertainty, the event which will take place, etc. A set of commodities is a vector $x \in \mathbb{R}^l$ which describes the quantity x_j of each elementary commodity for $j = 1, ..., l$. Suppose that there are n consumers and the set $M \subset \mathbb{R}^l$ represents the available commodities.

Next, we present the so-called classical Walrasian model. The consumption set for each of the n consumers will be denoted by $L_i \subset \mathbb{R}^l$. This is interpreted as the set of commodities which the ith consumer needs. If $x \in L_i$, then the jth component x_j represents the consumer's demand for the elementary commodity j if $x_j \geq 0$ and $|x_j|$ represents the supply of this elementary commodity if $x_j < 0$.

It is natural to ask whether the consumers can share an available commodity. In order to examine this situation, the concept of *allocation* is needed. An allocation is an element $x \in (\mathbb{R}^l)^n$ consisting on n commodities $x_i \in L_i$ such that the value $\sum_{i=1}^{n} x_i$ is available. The set of all allocations is then defined as

$$K := \left\{ x \in \prod_{i=1}^{n} L_i : \sum_{i=1}^{n} x_i \in M \right\}.$$

Assuming that the set K of allocations is nonempty, our aim is to describe a mechanism which allows each consumer to choose its own allocation. The mechanism does not require each consumer to know the set M of available commodities and the choices of the other consumers, but only require each consumer to know his own particular environment and to have access to common information about the state of the economy. This common information will take the form of a price (or price system). The price is regarded as a linear functional $p \in \mathbb{R}^{l*}$ which associates to each commodity $x \in \mathbb{R}^l$ the value $\langle p, x \rangle \in \mathbb{R}$ expressed in monetary units. Suppose that the elementary commodity i is represented by the unit vector $e^j = (0, ..., 0, 1, 0, ..., 0)$ of the canonical basis of $\mathbb{R}^l$, the components $\langle p, e^j \rangle$ of the price p represent the price of the commodity j.

We denote the price simplex by

$$M^l := \left\{ p \in \mathbb{R}^{l*}_+ : \sum_{j=1}^{l} p_j = 1 \right\}.$$

In the case of the Walrasian mechanism, each consumer is described by the set-valued map $D_i : M^l \times \mathbb{R} \rightrightarrows L_i$ which associates a subset of consumptions $D_i(p, r) \subset L_i$ to each price system $p \in \mathbb{R}^{l*}$ and each income $r \in \mathbb{R}$.

The support function σ_M of the set M of available commodities, already discussed in Section 9.1 and given by

$$\sigma_M(p) := \sup_{y \in M} \langle p, y \rangle, \tag{9.6}$$

is regarded as the collective-income function which is the maximum value of the commodities available for each price p. An essential assumption is given by

$$\exists\, r_i : M^l \to \mathbb{R},\ i = 1, \ldots, n : \sum_{i=1}^{n} r_i(p) = \sigma_M(p), \tag{9.7}$$

which means that the collective income is shared between the n consumers.

The income of each consumer is $r_i(P)$ and he is thus led to choose a consumption $x_i \in Di(p, r_i(P))$. This choice is decentralized; it depends only on the price p and is independent of the choice of other consumers.

The following feasibility problem arises: is there any price $\bar{p}$ such that the sum of the consumptions $\sum_{i=1}^{n} \bar{x}_i \in \sum_{i=1}^{n} D_i(\bar{p}, r_i(\bar{p}))$ is available (belongs to M) or such that the consumptions $\bar{x}_i \in D_i(\bar{p}, r_i(\bar{p}))$ form an allocation?

The next definition is of special importance for our purposes.

Definition 9.2. A price $\bar{p} \in M^l$ is called a Walrasian equilibrium price if it is a solution of the inclusion

$$0 \in \sum_{i=1}^{n} D_i(\bar{p}, r_i(\bar{p})) - M. \tag{9.8}$$

The set-valued map $E : M^l \rightrightarrows \mathbb{R}^l$ given by

$$E(p) := \sum_{i=1}^{n} D_i(p, r_i(p)) - M \tag{9.9}$$

is called the excess-demand correspondence.

It is then obvious that the Walrasian equilibrium prices are the zeros of the excess-demand correspondence.

The demand correspondences should satisfy the *collective Walras law* expressed as follows:

$$\forall\, p \in M^l,\ \forall\, x_i \in D_i(p, r_i) : \left\langle p, \sum_{i=1}^{n} x_i \right\rangle \le \sum_{i=1}^{n} r_i(p), \tag{9.10}$$

that is, the consumers cannot spend more than their total income.

A stronger, decentralized law, called *Walras law* is given below.

Every correspondence D_i satisfies the condition

$$\forall\, p \in M^l,\ \forall\, x \in D_i(p, r) : \langle p, x \rangle \le r. \tag{9.11}$$

Now we are in the position to prove the main result of this section: the existence of a Walrasian equilibrium. The next theorem will be proved via the Debreu-Gale-Nikaïdo theorem.

Theorem 9.2. (see Theorem 10.1 in [20]) *Suppose that the following assumptions are satisfied:*

(i) *the set M is convex and may be written as $M = M_0 - \mathbb{R}_+^l$, where M_0 is compact;*

(ii) *the set-valued maps $D_i : M^l \times \mathbb{R} \rightrightarrows L_i$ are upper hemicontinuous with convex, compact values and satisfy the collective Walras law;*

(iii) *the income functions r_i are continuous.*

Then there exists a Walrasian equilibrium.

Proof. Consider the set-valued map $C : M^l \rightrightarrows \mathbb{R}^l$ given by

$$C(p) := M_0 - \sum_{i=1}^{n} D_i(p, r_i(p)). \tag{9.12}$$

We shall apply for this C the Debreu-Gale-Nikaïdo theorem (Theorem 9.1). To this aim let us verify that all assumptions of Theorem 9.1 are satisfied. It is clear that C has nonempty and compact values, since the sets M_0 and $D_i(p, r_i(p))$ are compact by (i). It is also clear that C is upper hemicontinuous.

By assumptions (i) and (ii), for all $p \in M^l$ the set $C(p) - \mathbb{R}_+^l$ is convex and closed.

Also, for every $p \in M^l$ we have that

$$\sum_{i=1}^{n} r_i(p) = \sigma(M, p) = \sigma(M_0 - \mathbb{R}_+^l, p)$$

$$= \sigma(M_0, p) + \sigma(-\mathbb{R}_+^l, p) = \sigma(M_0, p). \tag{9.13}$$

By the collective Walras law (9.10)

$$-\sum_{i=1}^{n} r_i(p) \le \sum_{i=1}^{n} \langle -p, x_i \rangle, \ \forall \ x_i \in D_i(p, r_i(p)).$$

Passing to supremum over $x_i \in D_i(p, r_i(p))$ we obtain

$$-\sum_{i=1}^{n} r_i(p) \le \sup_{x_i \in D_i(p, r_i(p))} \sum_{i=1}^{n} \langle -p, x_i \rangle. \tag{9.14}$$

Thus

$$\sigma(C(p), p) = \sigma(M_0, p) + \sup_{x_i \in D_i(p, r_i(p))} \sum_{i=1}^{n} \langle -p, x_i \rangle$$

$$\overset{(9.14)}{\geq} \sigma(M_0, p) - \sum_{i=1}^{n} r_i(p)$$

$$\overset{(9.13)}{=} \sigma(M_0, p) - \sigma(M_0, p) = 0.$$

Consequently we may apply the Debreu-Gale-Nikaïdo (Theorem 9.1) and such

$$\exists \, \bar{p} \in M^l : \ C(\bar{p}) \cap \mathbb{R}_+^l \neq \emptyset,$$

or, in other words

$$0 \in C(\bar{p}) - \mathbb{R}_+^l = M_0 - \sum_{i=1}^{n} D_i(\bar{p}, r_i(\bar{p})) - \mathbb{R}_+^l$$

$$= M - \sum_{i=1}^{n} D_i(\bar{p}, r_i(\bar{p}))$$

$$= -E(\bar{p}).$$

Hence $0 \in -E(\bar{p})$, and therefore, $\bar{p}$ is a Walrasian equilibrium price. $\qquad \square$

An important particular case is obtained when $M := w - \mathbb{R}_+^l$ is the set of commodities less than the available commodity $w \in \mathbb{R}_+^l$.

Corollary 9.1. *Suppose that assumptions (ii) and (iii) of Theorem 9.2 hold and*

$$w = \sum_{i=1}^{n} w_i$$

is allocated to the n consumers.

Then there exists a Walrasian equilibrium price $\bar{p}$ and consumptions $\bar{x}_i \in D_i(\bar{p}, \langle \bar{p}, w_i \rangle)$ such that $\sum_{i=1}^{n} \bar{x}_i \leq \sum_{i=1}^{n} w_i$.

9.3 NASH EQUILIBRIA WITHIN n-POLE ECONOMY

In this section we illustrate the concept of a Nash equilibrium point defined in Chapter 2, Subsection 2.2.4 with one of the easiest models in economy, the so-called n-pole economy. In this economy we have n producers with $n \geq 2$ which compete on the market, that is, they produce and sell the same product. We consider the producers as players in an n-person game where the strategy sets are given by $S_i = \mathbb{R}_+$ ($i = 1, 2, ..., n$). The strategy $s \in \mathbb{R}_+$ stands for the production of s units of the product. It is reasonable to assume that the price of the product on the market is determined by demand. More precisely, we assume that there is an affine relationship of the form:

$$p(s_1, \ldots, s_n) = \alpha - \beta \left(\sum_{i=1}^{n} s_i \right) \tag{9.15}$$

where α, β are positive constants. It is easy to see that once the total production increases, the price decreases. Assume that the individual cost functions for each producer are given by

$$c_i(s_i) = \gamma_i s_i + \delta_i, \tag{9.16}$$

where γ_i, δ_i are fixed costs for $i = 1, \ldots, n$. By these data we can easily calculate the gain of each producer (player), which is

$$f_i(s_1, \ldots, s_n) = p(s_1, \ldots, s_n)s_i - c_i(s_i), \quad i = 1, \ldots, n. \tag{9.17}$$

Using relations (9.15) and (9.16) the formula (9.17) can be evaluated as

$$f_i(s_1, \ldots, s_n) = \left(\alpha - \beta \sum_{i=1}^{n} s_i \right) s_i - \gamma_i s_i - \delta_i$$

$$= \beta s_i \left(\frac{\alpha - \gamma_i}{\beta} - \sum_{i=1}^{n} s_i \right) - \delta_i$$

$$= \beta s_i \left(u_i - \sum_{i=1}^{n} s_i \right) - \delta_i, \quad i = 1, \ldots, n, \tag{9.18}$$

where $u_i := \frac{\alpha - \gamma_i}{\beta}$.

Let $U = U_1 \times \ldots \times U_n \subseteq \prod_{i=1}^{n} S_i$ the common feasible strategy set, where $U_i = [0, u_i], i = 1, \ldots, n$.

In what follows, for the sake of simplicity, we will suppose that

$$\begin{cases} \delta_i = 0, \ i = 1, \ldots, n \\ \gamma_i = \gamma > 0, \ i = 1, \ldots, n \\ \beta = 1 \\ u_1 = u_2 = \ldots = u_n = u. \end{cases}$$

Thus, the profit function (9.18) for $s \in U$ is given by

$$f_i(s) = s_i \left(u - \sum_{i=1}^{n} s_i \right), \quad i = 1, \ldots, n.$$

By summing up these relations with respect to i, we can easily determine the maximal total profit, since

$$\sum_{i=1}^{n} f_i(s) = u \sum_{i=1}^{n} s_i - \left(\sum_{i=1}^{n} s_i\right)^2$$

attains its maximum at $\sum_{i=1}^{n} s_i = \frac{u}{2}$, and such, the maximal total profit will be $\frac{u^2}{4}$.

Let us introduce the decision functions

$$g_i : U_1 \times \ldots \times U_{i-1} \times U_{i+1} \times \ldots \times U_n \to U_i, \ i = 1, \ldots, n, \qquad (9.19)$$

and examine the first player's optimal decision function (rule). His decision $g_1(s_2, \ldots, s_n)$ depends on the other players decisions and must be taken in such a way that

$$f_1(g_1(s_2, \ldots, s_n), s_2, \ldots, s_n) = \max_{s_1 \in [0,u]} f_1(s).$$

Thus

$$f_1(g_1(s_2, \ldots, s_n), s_2, \ldots, s_n) = \max_{s_1 \in [0,u]} f_1(s) = \max_{s_1 \in [0,u]} s_1 \left(u - \sum_{i=1}^{n} s_i\right)$$

$$= \max_{s_1 \in [0,u]} (s_1 u - s_1^2 - s_1 \sum_{i=2}^{n} s_i).$$

Since in s_1 we have a polynomial function of degree 2, the maximum of f_1 is attained at $s_1 = \left(u - \sum_{i=2}^{n} s_i\right)/2$, therefore

$$g_1(s_2, \ldots, s_n) = \frac{u - \sum_{i=2}^{n} s_i}{2}.$$

In a similar way we can determine the optimal decisions of the other players.

$$g_k(s_1, \ldots, s_{k-1}, s_{k+1}, \ldots, s_n) = \frac{u - \sum_{\substack{i=1 \\ i \neq k}}^{n} s_i}{2}, \ k = 1, \ldots, n.$$

In what follows, let us calculate the Nash equilibrium point of this game. It can be seen that $\bar{s} = (\bar{s}_1, \ldots, \bar{s}_n)$ is a Nash equilibrium point if and only if

$$\begin{cases} g_1(\bar{s}_2, \ldots, \bar{s}_n) = \bar{s}_1 \\ \vdots \\ g_n(\bar{s}_1, \ldots, \bar{s}_{n-1}) = \bar{s}_n. \end{cases}$$

By using the decision functions the system above can be written as

$$
\begin{cases}
\bar{s}_1 = \frac{u - \sum_{i=2}^n s_i}{2} \\
\vdots \\
\bar{s}_j = \frac{u - \sum_{\substack{i=1 \\ i \ne j}}^n s_i}{2} \\
\vdots \\
\bar{s}_n = \frac{u - \sum_{i=1}^{n-1} s_i}{2}
\end{cases}
\Leftrightarrow
\begin{cases}
2\bar{s}_1 + \bar{s}_2 + \ldots + \bar{s}_n = u \\
\vdots \\
\bar{s}_1 + \ldots 2\bar{s}_j + \ldots + \bar{s}_n = u \\
\vdots \\
\bar{s}_1 + \bar{s}_2 + \ldots + 2\bar{s}_n = u.
\end{cases}
$$

This system has a unique solution, namely

$$
\bar{s} = (\bar{s}_1, \ldots, \bar{s}_n) = \left(\frac{u}{n+1}, \ldots, \frac{u}{n+1} \right),
$$

which is the Nash equilibrium point of the game. This means that each player has the same optimal strategy $\frac{u}{n+1}$, and the same optimal gain

$$
f_i(\bar{s}) = \frac{u}{n+1} \left(u - \frac{nu}{n+1} \right) = \frac{u^2}{(n+1)^2}, \quad i = 1, \ldots, n.
$$

It is worth mentioning that in this case the sum of the gains $\frac{nu^2}{(n+1)^2}$ is less than the maximal total gain $\frac{u^2}{4}$. This means that in case the players cooperate and everyone agrees to choose the same $\frac{u}{2n}$ strategy, then

$$
f_i \left(\frac{u}{2n}, \ldots, \frac{u}{2n} \right) = \frac{u}{2n} \left(u - \frac{u}{2} \right) = \frac{u^2}{4n} > \frac{u^2}{(n+1)^2},
$$

as $n \ge 2$ and in this way the total profit is maximal, since equals $\frac{u^2}{4}$.

9.4 PARETO OPTIMALITY FOR n-PERSON GAMES

Consider two players Alex and Bob and assume that they choose their strategies using their loss functions f_A and f_B from $A \times B$ to $\mathbb{R}$.

We say that a pair $(\bar{x}, \bar{y}) \in A \times B$ is a noncooperative equilibrium if and only if

$$
f_A(\bar{x}, \bar{y}) = \inf_{x \in A} f_A(x, \bar{y}) \quad \text{and} \quad f_B(\bar{x}, \bar{y}) = \inf_{y \in B} f_B(\bar{x}, y).
$$

It follows that a noncooperative equilibrium is an alternative in which any player optimizes his own criterion, assuming that his partner's choice is fixed. This corresponds to a situation with individual stability.

If we assume that the players communicate, exchange information, and co-operate then the notion of noncooperative equilibrium does not provide the only reasonable scheme for solution of a game in strategic form. More precisely, it is possible to find a strategy pair $(x, y) \in A \times B$ such that

$$f_A(x, y) < f_A(\bar{x}, \bar{y}) \quad \text{and} \quad f_B(x, y) < f_B(\bar{x}, \bar{y}).$$

In such a case, the players Alex and Bob have losses strictly less than in the case of noncooperative equilibrium $(\bar{x}, \bar{y})$. Thus, there is a lack of collective stability, in the sense that the two players can each find better strategies for themselves. The corresponding notion of *Pareto optimum* is associated to an allocation for which there are no possible alternative allocations whose realization would cause every player to gain.

Definition 9.3. We say that a strategy pair $(x_*, y_*) \in A \times B$ is Pareto[1] optimal (or Pareto-efficient) if there are no other strategy pairs $(x, y) \in A \times B$ such that $f_A(x, y) < f_A(x_*, y_*)$ and $f_B(x, y) < f_B(x_*, y_*)$.

As in the cases of two-person games, the decision rules in the case of n players are determined by loss functions. More precisely, the behavior of the kth player $(1 \leq k \leq n)$ is defined by a loss function $f^k : E \to \mathbb{R}$, which evaluates the loss $f^k(x)$ inflicted on the kth player by each multistrategy x. Accordingly, we define the multiloss function $f : E \to \mathbb{R}^n$ by

$$f(x) := (f^1(x), \dots, f^n(x)) \quad \text{for all } x \in E.$$

Definition 9.4. We say that a multistrategy $\bar{x} \in E$ is Pareto optimal if there are no other multistrategies $x \in E$ such that

$$f^i(x) < f^i(\bar{x}) \quad \text{for all } i = 1, \dots, n. \tag{9.20}$$

In the case of two-person games we have observed that there may be a number of Pareto optima. Thus, a natural problem that arises is to choose these optima.

Let us attribute a weight $\lambda^k \geq 0$ to the kth player. If the player accept this weighting, they may agree to collaborate and to minimize the weighted function

$$f_\lambda(x) := \sum_{i=1}^{n} \lambda^i f^i(x) \tag{9.21}$$

over the set E.

If the vector $\lambda = (\lambda^1, \dots, \lambda^n)$ is not zero, we observe that any multistrategy $\bar{x} \in E$ which minimizes $f_\lambda(x)$ is a Pareto minimum. Indeed, arguing by contradiction, we find x satisfying inequalities (9.20). Multiplying these relations by $\lambda_i \geq 0$ and summing them, we obtain

$$f_\lambda(x) < f_\lambda(\bar{x}),$$

which is a contradiction.

If n players could be made to agree on a weighting λ, we would no longer have a game problem proper, but a simple optimization problem. However, it is interesting to know the conditions under which Pareto optimum may be obtained by minimizing a function f_λ associated with a weighting λ which is borne in some way by this Pareto optimum. This question has a positive answer in the following property, by applying convexity arguments.

Proposition 9.1. *Suppose that the strategy sets E^i are convex and that the loss functions $f^i : E \to \mathbb{R}$ are convex. Then any Pareto optimum $\overline{x}$ may be associated with a nonzero weight $\lambda \in \mathbb{R}^n$ such that $\overline{x}$ minimizes the function f_λ over E.*

Proof. We first observe that

$$f(E) + \text{int}(\mathbb{R}^n_+) \text{ is a convex set.}$$

It follows that an element $\overline{x} \in E$ is a Pareto minimum if and only if

$$f(\overline{x}) \notin f(E) + \text{int}(\mathbb{R}^n_+).$$

By the separation theorem for convex sets, we deduce that there exists $\lambda \in \mathbb{R}^n$, $\lambda \neq 0$, such that

$$\langle \lambda, f(\overline{x}) \rangle = \inf_{\substack{x \in E \\ u \in \text{int}(\mathbb{R}^n_+)}} (\langle \lambda, f(x) \rangle + \langle \lambda, u \rangle).$$

It follows that λ is positive and that $\overline{x}$ minimizes the function $x \to f_\lambda(x) = \langle \lambda, f(x) \rangle$ over E. $\qquad\square$

We point out that a Pareto minimum also minimizes other functions.

For example, we introduce the *virtual minimum* α, which is defined by its components

$$\alpha^i := \inf_{x \in E} f^i(x).$$

We say that the game is *bounded below* if $\alpha^i > -\infty$ for all $i = 1, \ldots, n$. In this case, we take $\beta^i < \alpha^i$ for all i and set $\beta := (\beta^1, \ldots, \beta^n) \in \mathbb{R}^n$.

Proposition 9.2. *Suppose that the game is bounded below. Then an element $\overline{x} \in E$ is a Pareto minimum if and only if there exists $\lambda \in \text{int}(\mathbb{R}^n_+)$ such that $\overline{x}$ minimizes the function g_λ defined by*

$$g_\lambda(x) := \max_{i=i,\ldots,n} \frac{1}{\lambda^i}(f^i(x) - \beta^i) \tag{9.22}$$

over E.

Proof. **(a)** Assume that $\overline{x} \in E$ minimizes g_λ on E and is not a Pareto minimum. Then there exists $x \in E$ satisfying inequalities (9.20). Subtracting β^i, and multiplying by $\frac{1}{\lambda^i}$ and taking the maximum of the two terms, we obtain the contradiction $g_\lambda(x) < g_\lambda(\overline{x})$.

(b) Let $\overline{x}$ be a Pareto minimum. We take

$$\lambda^i = f^i(\overline{x}) - \beta^i > 0$$

such that $g_\lambda(\overline{x}) = 1$.

Let $x \in E$ be such that $g_\lambda(x) < g_\lambda(\overline{x})$. Then

$$\max_{i=1,\dots,n} \left(\frac{f^i(x) - \beta^i}{f^i(\overline{x}) - \beta^i} \right) < 1,$$

which implies inequalities (9.20). □

We can also define conservative strategies for the players. We set

$$f^{i\sharp}(x^i) := \sup_{\hat{x}^i \in E^{\hat{i}}} f^i(x^i, x^{\hat{i}}).$$

Definition 9.5. We say that $x^{i\sharp} \in E^i$ is a conservative strategy for the ith player if

$$f^{i\sharp}(x^{i\sharp}) = \inf_{x^i \in E^i} \sup_{\hat{x}^i \in E^{\hat{i}}} f^i(x^i, x^{\hat{i}})$$

and we say the number $v_i^\sharp$ defined by

$$v_i^\sharp := \inf_{x^i \in E^i} \sup_{\hat{x}^i \in E^{\hat{i}}} f^i(x^i, x^{\hat{i}})$$

is the conservative value of the game.

We point out that the conservative value $v_i^\sharp$ may be used as a threat, by refusing to accept any multistrategy x such that

$$f^i(x) > v_i^\sharp$$

since by playing a conservative strategy $x^{i\sharp}$ the loss $f^i(x^{i\sharp}, x^i)$ is strictly less than $f^i(x)$.

Suppose that

$$v_i^\sharp > \alpha^i \quad \text{for all } i = 1, \dots, n.$$

This assumption says that the conservative value is strictly greater than the virtual minimum.

Consider the function $g_0 : E \to \mathbb{R}$ defined by

$$g_0(x) = \max_{i=1,\dots,n} \frac{f^i(x) - \alpha^i}{v_i^{\#} - \alpha^i}.$$

Taking $\beta^i = \alpha^i$ and $\lambda^i = v_i^{\#} - \alpha^i$, Proposition 9.2 implies that

if $x_0 \in E$ minimizes g_0 on E, then x_0 is a Pareto minimum.

If $d := \min_{x \in E} g_0(x)$, it follows that x_0 minimizes g_0 on E if and only if

$$f^i(x_0^i) \le (1 - d)v_i^{\#} + d\alpha^i \quad \text{for all } i, \dots, n.$$

This property suggests that such choices of Pareto optima should be viewed as best compromise solutions.

Other methods of selection by optimization involve minimizing functions

$$x \mapsto s\left(\frac{f^1(x) - \alpha^1}{v_1^{\#} - \alpha^1}, \dots, \frac{f^n(x) - \alpha^n}{v_n^{\#} - \alpha^n} \right) \tag{9.23}$$

on E, where the function s satisfies the following increasing property

if $a^i > b^i$ for all i, then $s(a) > s(b)$.

We observe that $\bar{x} \in E$ that minimizes (9.23) is a Pareto minimum. We also note that the function (9.23) remains invariant whenever the loss functions f^i are replaced by functions $a_i f^i + b_i$, where $a_i > 0$.

We say that by replacing the functions f^i by the functions g^i

$$g^i(x) = \frac{f^i(x) - \alpha^i}{v_i^{\#} - \alpha^i},$$

then we have normalized the same game. For the normalized game the virtual minimum is zero and the conservative value is 1.

In a general setting (not only concerning n-person games), a state of affairs is Pareto-optimal if there is no alternative state that would make some people better off without making anyone worse off. Alternatively, a state of affairs x is said to be Pareto-inefficient (or suboptimal) if there is some state of affairs y such that no one strictly prefers x to y and at least one person strictly prefers y to x. We conclude that the concept of Pareto-optimality assumes that anyone would prefer an option that is cheaper, more efficient, or more reliable or that otherwise comparatively improves one's condition.

In his most influential work *Manuale d'economia politica* (1906), Pareto further developed his theory of pure economics and his analysis of ophelimity (power to give satisfaction). He laid the foundation of modern welfare economics with his concept of Pareto optimum, stating that "the optimum allocation of the resources of a society is not attained so long as it is possible to make at least one individual better off in his own estimation while keeping others as well off as before in their own estimation".

NOTE

1. Vilfredo Pareto (1848–1923), Italian engineer and economist, who used the concept in his studies of economic efficiency and income distribution. The concept has been applied in academic fields such as economics, engineering, and the life sciences. He shared with Léon Walras the conviction of the applicability of mathematics to the social sciences.

Chapter 10

Applications to Variational Inequalities and Related Topics

Contents

Mathematics is the art of giving the same name to different things.
Henri Poincaré (1854–1912)

Chapter points

- The results of this chapter are at the interplay between set-valued equilibrium problems, variational inclusions, and fixed point properties of multi-valued mappings.
- The arguments combine abstract topological tools (hemicontinuity and semicontinuity of bifunctions, lower and upper inverse sets) with Ky Fan's lemma and properties of KKM mappings.
- Includes extensions of several classical results in the framework of set-valued analysis.
- The content of this chapter is based on recent original results obtained by Alleche and Rădulescu [6], [7].

10.1 QUASI-HEMIVARIATIONAL INEQUALITIES

Let E be a real Banach space which is continuously embedded in $L^p(\Omega; \mathbb{R}^n)$, for some $1 < p < +\infty$ and $n \geq 1$, where Ω is a bounded domain in $\mathbb{R}^m$, $m \geq 1$. Let i be the canonical injection of E into $L^p(\Omega; \mathbb{R}^n)$.

Equilibrium Problems and Applications. https://doi.org/10.1016/B978-0-12-811029-4.00018-3

In this section, we study the existence of solutions for the following quasi-hemivariational inequality:

find $u \in E$ and $u^* \in A(u)$ such that

$$\langle u^*, v \rangle_E + h(u) J^0(iu; iv) \geq \langle Fu, v \rangle_E \quad \text{for all } v \in E, \qquad (10.1)$$

where $A : E \rightrightarrows E^*$ is a nonlinear set-valued mapping, $F : E \to E^*$ is a nonlinear operator, $J : L^p(\Omega; \mathbb{R}^n) \to \mathbb{R}$ is a locally Lipschitz functional, J^0 denotes the generalized derivative of J in the sense of Clarke and $h : E \to \mathbb{R}$ is a given nonnegative functional.

We point out that if $h = 0$ in problem (10.1) then we obtain the standard case of *variational inequalities*, see Lions[1] and Stampacchia[2] [117] and Kinderlehrer and Stampacchia [107]. The setting corresponding to $h \equiv 1$ in problem (10.1) describes the *hemivariational inequalities*, which were introduced by Panagiotopoulos [137], [138]. These inequality problems appear as a generalization of variational inequalities, but they are much more general than these ones, in the sense that they are not equivalent to minimum problems but give rise to substationarity problems. The general case when h is nonconstant corresponds to *quasi-hemivariational inequalities*, which were first studied by Naniewicz and Panagiotopoulos [134, Section 4.5], in relationship with relevant models in mechanics and engineering. We also refer to the monographs by Motreanu and Panagiotopoulos [132] and Motreanu and Rădulescu [131] for a thorough variational and topological analysis of hemivariational inequalities.

The quasi-hemivariational inequality problem (10.1) has been studied in Costea and Rădulescu [58]. The authors considered the following quasi-hemivariational inequality:

find $u \in C$ and $u^* \in A(u)$ such that

$$\langle u^*, v - u \rangle_E + h(u) J^0(iu; iv - iu) \geq \langle Fu, v - u \rangle_E \quad \text{for all } v \in C, \quad (10.2)$$

where C is a nonempty, closed, and convex subset of E satisfying some additional conditions. Several results on the existence of solutions of the quasi-hemivariational inequality problem (10.2) have been obtained in two cases: (i) when C is a nonempty, convex, and compact subset of E; (ii) when C is a nonempty, convex, closed, and bounded (then weakly compact) subset of a reflexive Banach space. Characterizations and applications for solving the quasi-hemivariational inequality problem (10.1) are derived.

We observe that if C is a linear subspace and in particular, if C is the whole space E, then the quasi-hemivariational inequality problem (10.2) is equivalent to the following quasi-hemivariational inequality:

find $u \in C$ and $u^* \in A(u)$ such that

$$\langle u^*, v \rangle_E + h(u) J^0(iu; iv) \geq \langle Fu, v \rangle_E \quad \text{for all } v \in C,$$

which is exactly the formulation of the quasi-hemivariational inequality problem (10.1) with E replaced by C.

In this section, we follow a direct approach by studying the existence of solutions of the quasi-hemivariational inequality problem (10.2) when C is a nonempty, closed, and convex subset of E. It follows that all the results obtained can be then applied to the quasi-hemivariational inequality problem (10.1).

We first introduce some concepts of continuity of functions and set-valued mappings and obtain some results and characterizations.

Next, we introduce a coercivity condition on a compact or weakly compact subset and use the concept of continuity on a subset for solving the quasi-hemivariational inequality problem (10.2) when C is a nonempty, closed, and convex subset of E.

Finally, we obtain some results on the existence of solutions of equilibrium problems by using the concept of continuity on a subset of equilibrium bifunctions in their first or second variable. Applications for solving quasi-hemivariational inequalities are given.

10.1.1 Some Concepts of Continuity

Let $(X, \| \cdot \|_X)$ be a Banach space.

A function $\phi : X \to \mathbb{R}$ is called *locally Lipschitzian* if for every $u \in X$, there exists a neighborhood U of u and a constant $L_u > 0$ such that

$$|\phi(w) - \phi(v)| \leq L_u \|w - v\|_X \quad \text{for all } u \in U, \text{ for all } v \in U.$$

If $\phi : X \to \mathbb{R}$ is locally Lipschitzian near $u \in X$, then the *generalized directional derivative* of ϕ at u in the direction of $v \in X$, denoted by $\phi^0(u, v)$, is defined by

$$\phi^0(u, v) = \limsup_{\substack{w \to u \\ \lambda \downarrow 0}} \frac{\phi(w + \lambda u) - \phi(w)}{\lambda}.$$

Suppose that $\phi : X \to \mathbb{R}$ is locally Lipschitz near $u \in X$. Then the following properties hold:

1. the function $v \mapsto \phi^0(u, v)$ is finite, positively homogeneous and subadditive;
2. the function $(u, v) \mapsto \phi^0(u, v)$ is upper semicontinuous.

We refer to Clarke [56, Proposition 2.1.1] for proofs and related properties.

Before introducing some concepts of continuity, we recall some general results on convergence of sequences.

Let X be a Hausdorff topological space. Recall that a subset B of X is said to be *sequentially closed* if whenever $(x_n)_n$ is a sequence in B converging to x, then $x \in B$. A space is called *sequential* if every sequentially closed subset is closed. Every metric space and more generally, every Fréchet-Urysohn[3] space is a sequential space. A space X is called *Fréchet-Urysohn space* if whenever x is in the closure of a subset B of X, there exists a sequence in B converging to x.

The weak topology of Banach spaces is not sequential in general. However, bounded subsets of reflexive Banach spaces endowed with the weak topology have the following property: if a point x is in the weak closure of a bounded subset B of a reflexive Banach space, then there exists a sequence in B weakly converging to x (see Denkowski, Migórski, and Papageorgiou [61, Proposition 3.6.23]). Thus, every bounded and weakly sequentially closed subset of a reflexive Banach space is closed.

We say that a subset B has the *Fréchet-Urysohn property* if whenever x is in the closure of B, there exists a sequence in B converging to x. Every subset of a Fréchet-Urysohn space has the Fréchet-Urysohn property.

In the sequel, for a subset B of X, we denote by

$$\text{Exp}(B) = \left\{ x \in X \mid \exists (x_n)_n, \ x_n \in B \text{ such that } x_n \longrightarrow x \right\},$$

the sequential explosion of B. Of course, $\text{Exp}(B)$ is neither closed nor sequentially closed in general.

Let $x \in X$. A function $f : X \to \mathbb{R}$ is called

1. *sequentially upper semicontinuous at x* if for every sequence $(x_n)_n$ in X converging to x, we have

$$f(x) \geq \limsup_{n \to +\infty} f(x_n),$$

where $\displaystyle \limsup_{n \to +\infty} f(x_n) = \inf_n \sup_{k \geq n} f(x_k)$;

2. *sequentially lower semicontinuous at x* if $-f$ is sequentially upper semicontinuous at x, that is, for every sequence $(x_n)_n$ of X converging to x, we have

$$f(x) \leq \liminf_{n \to +\infty} f(x_n),$$

where $\displaystyle \liminf_{n \to +\infty} f(x_n) = \sup_n \inf_{k \geq n} f(x_k)$.

The function f is said to be *sequentially upper* (resp., *sequentially lower*) *semicontinuous* on a subset S of X if it is sequentially upper (resp., sequentially lower) semicontinuous at every point of S.

If sequences are replaced by generalized sequences (nets) in the above definition of sequentially upper (resp., sequentially lower) semicontinuous function, we obtain the notion of upper (resp., lower) semicontinuous function.

The following result shows how easy is to construct sequentially upper (resp., sequentially lower) semicontinuous functions on a subset which are not sequentially upper (resp., sequentially lower) semicontinuous on the whole space.

Proposition 10.1. *Let $f : X \longrightarrow \mathbb{R}$ be a function and let S be a subset of X. If the restriction $f_{|U}$ of f on an open subset U containing S is sequentially upper (resp., sequentially lower) semicontinuous, then any extension of $f_{|U}$ to* *the space X is a sequentially upper (resp., sequentially lower) semicontinuous function on S.*

The following lemma provides us some properties of sequentially upper and sequentially lower semicontinuous functions on a subset.

Proposition 10.2. *Let $f : X \longrightarrow \mathbb{R}$ be a function, S a subset of X, and $a \in \mathbb{R}$.*
1. *If f is sequentially upper semicontinuous on S, then*

$$Exp\left(\{x \in X \mid f(x) \geq a\}\right) \cap S = \{x \in S \mid f(x) \geq a\}.$$

Moreover, the trace on S of upper level sets of f are sequentially closed in S.
2. *If f is sequentially lower semicontinuous at S with respect to C, then*

$$Exp\left(\{x \in X \mid f(x) \leq a\}\right) \cap S = \{x \in S \mid f(x) \leq a\}.$$

Moreover, the trace on S of lower level sets of f are sequentially closed in S.

Proof. The second statement being similar to the first one, we prove only the case of the sequential upper semicontinuity. Let

$$x^* \in \mathrm{Exp}\left(\{x \in X \mid f(x) \geq a\}\right) \cap S.$$

Let $(x_n)_n$ be a sequence in $\mathrm{Exp}\left(\{x \in X \mid f(x) \geq a\}\right)$ converging to x^*. Since $x^* \in S$, then by the sequential upper semicontinuity of f on S, we have

$$f\left(x^*\right) \geq \limsup_{n \to +\infty} f(x_n) \geq a.$$

It follows that $x^* \in \{x \in S \mid f(x) \geq a\}$. The converse holds from the fact that

$$\{x \in S \mid f(x) \geq a\} = \{x \in X \mid f(x) \geq a\} \cap S,$$

which is obvious as well as the sequential closeness in S of the trace on S of upper level sets of f. □

Next, we introduce a generalization of lower semicontinuity of set-valued functions when the space X is a real topological Hausdorff vector space.

We say that a set-valued mapping $T : X \rightrightarrows Y$ is *lower quasi-hemicontinuous* at $x \in X$, if whenever $z \in X$ and $(\lambda_n)_n$ a sequence in $]0, 1[$ such that $\lim_{n \to +\infty} \lambda_n = 0$, there exists a sequence $\left(z_n^*\right)_n$ converging to some element x^* of $T(x)$ such that $z_n^* \in T(x + \lambda_n(z - x))$, for every n.

The set-valued function T will be said lower quasi-hemicontinuous on a subset S of X if T is lower quasi-hemicontinuous at every point of S.

The following result shows that the notion of quasi-hemicontinuity of set-valued mappings is also a generalization of different other notions.

Proposition 10.3. *Let* $T : X \rightrightarrows Y$ *be a set-valued mapping and suppose that one of the following assumptions holds:*

1. T *is lower semicontinuous at* $x \in X$;
2. T *has a continuous selection.*

Then T *is lower quasi-hemicontinuous at* x.

Proof. The second statement is obvious. The first assertion follows from the fact that T is lower semicontinuous at $x \in X$ if and only if for every generalized sequence $(x_\lambda)_{\lambda \in \Lambda}$ converging to x, and for every $x^* \in T(x)$, there exists a generalized sequence $\left(x_\lambda^*\right)_{\lambda \in \Lambda}$ converging to x^* such that $x_\lambda^* \in T(x_\lambda)$, for every $\lambda \in \Lambda$, see Papageorgiou and Kyritsi-Yiallourou [139, Proposition 6.1.4]. $\square$

Although the notion of semicontinuity of set-valued mappings is important for the existence of continuous selections (Michael's selection theorem), it is not essential. This means that under additional conditions, different continuous set-valued mappings with respect to other hyperspace topology may have continuous selections and then, they are lower quasi-hemicontinuous.

As in Proposition 10.1, the following result shows how easy we construct lower quasi-hemicontinuous set-valued mapping on a subset without being lower quasi-hemicontinuous on the whole space.

Proposition 10.4. *Let* $T : X \rightrightarrows Y$ *be a set-valued mapping and let* S *be a subset of* X. *If the restriction* $T_{|U}$ *of* T *on an open and convex subset* U *containing* S *is lower quasi-hemicontinuous, then any extension of* $T_{|U}$ *to the space* X *is a lower quasi-hemicontinuous set-valued mapping on* S.

A set-valued mapping $T : E \rightrightarrows 2^{E^*}$ is said to be *relaxed α-monotone* if there exists a functional $\alpha : E \to \mathbb{R}$ such that for every $u, v \in E$, we have

$$\langle v^* - u^*, v - u \rangle \geq \alpha (v - u) \quad \text{for all } u^* \in T(u), \text{ all } v^* \in T(v).$$

10.1.2 Existence Results for Quasi-Hemivariational Inequalities

For any $v \in C$, we define the following set:

$$\Theta (v) = \left\{ u \in C \mid \inf_{v^* \in A(v)} \langle v^*, v - u \rangle + h(u) J^0 (iu; iv - iu) \right.$$
$$\left. - \langle Fu, v - u \rangle \geq \alpha (v - u) \right\}. \tag{10.3}$$

The following result gives a sufficient condition for the existence of solutions of quasi-hemivariational inequalities.

Theorem 10.1. *Let* C *be a nonempty, closed, and convex subset of the real Banach space* E *which is continuously imbedded in* $L^p (\Omega; \mathbb{R}^n)$. *Suppose that the following assumptions hold:*

1. *there exists a compact subset K of C and $v_0 \in K$ such that the following condition holds: for every $u \in C \setminus K$, there exists $v^* \in A(v_0)$ such that*

$$\langle v^*, v_0 - u \rangle + h(u) J^0(iu; iv_0 - iu) - \langle Fu, v_0 - u \rangle - \alpha(v_0 - u) < 0;$$

2. $\alpha : E \to \mathbb{R}$ *is a functional such that for every $u \in C$,* $\lim\limits_{n \to +\infty} \frac{\alpha(\lambda_n u)}{\lambda_n} = 0$ *whenever $(\lambda_n)_n$ is a sequence in $]0, 1[$ such that* $\lim\limits_{n \to +\infty} \lambda_n = 0$ *and* $\limsup\limits_{n \to +\infty} \alpha(u_n) \geq \alpha(u)$ *whenever $(u_n)_n$ is a sequence in C converging to u;*

3. *A is relaxed α-monotone and lower quasi-hemicontinuous on K with respect to the weak* topology of E^*;*

4. *h is a nonnegative sequentially lower semicontinuous functional on K;*

5. *F is an operator such that for every $v \in C$, $u \mapsto \langle Fu, v - u \rangle$ is sequentially lower semicontinuous on K.*

Then the quasi-hemivariational inequality problem (10.2) has at least one solution.

Proof. By using the relaxed α-monotonicity of A and the subadditivity of the function $v \mapsto J^0(iu; iv)$, we obtain that the set-valued mapping $v \mapsto \Theta(v)$ is a KKM mapping. To do this, let $\{v_1, \ldots, v_n\} \subset C$ and put $u_0 = \sum_{k=1}^n \lambda_k v_k$ where $\lambda_k \in]0, 1[$ for every $k = 1, \ldots n$ and $\sum_{k=1}^n \lambda_k = 1$. Assuming that $u_0 \notin \bigcup_{k=1}^n \Theta(v_k)$, then for every $k = 1, \ldots n$, we have

$$\inf_{v^* \in A(v_k)} \langle v^*, v_k - u_0 \rangle + h(u_0) J^0(iu_0; iv_k - iu_0) - \langle Fu, v_k - u_0 \rangle < \alpha(v_k - u_0).$$

For every $k = 1, \ldots n$, choose $v_k^* \in A(v_k)$ such that

$$\langle v_k^*, v_k - u_0 \rangle + h(u_0) J^0(iu_0; iv_k - iu_0) - \langle Fu, v_k - u_0 \rangle < \alpha(v_k - u_0).$$

Since A is relaxed α-monotone, then for every $u_0^* \in A(u_0)$, we have

$$\langle v_k^*, v_k - u_0 \rangle + h(u_0) J^0(iu_0; iv_k - iu_0) - \langle Fu, v_k - u_0 \rangle$$
$$< \alpha(v_k - u_0)$$
$$\leq \langle v_k^* - u_0^*, v_k - u_0 \rangle.$$

Therefore

$$\langle u_0^*, v_k - u_0 \rangle + h(u_0) J^0(iu_0; iv_k - iu_0) - \langle Fu, v_k - u_0 \rangle < 0$$
$$\text{for all } u_0^* \in A(u_0).$$

Since the function $v \mapsto J^0(iu; iv)$ is subadditive, then for any $u_0^* \in A(u_0)$, we have

$$0 = \langle u_0^*, u_0 - u_0 \rangle + h(u_0) J^0(iu_0; iu_0 - iu_0) - \langle Fu, u_0 - u_0 \rangle$$

$$= \langle u_0^*, \sum_{k=1}^{n} \lambda_k (v_k - u_0) \rangle + h(u_0) J^0 \left(iu_0; \sum_{k=1}^{n} \lambda_k (iv_k - iu_0) \right)$$

$$- \langle Fu, \sum_{k=1}^{n} \lambda_k (v_k - u_0) \rangle$$

$$\leq \sum_{k=1}^{n} \lambda_k \left(\langle u_0^*, v_k - u_0 \rangle + h(u_0) J^0 (iu_0; iv_k - iu_0) - \langle Fu, v_k - u_0 \rangle \right) < 0.$$

This is a contradiction and then the set-valued mapping $v \mapsto \Theta(v)$ is a KKM mapping. Since $\Theta(v_0)$ is contained in K which is compact, then by Ky Fan's lemma, we have

$$\bigcap_{v \in C} \overline{\Theta(v)} \neq \emptyset.$$

We now prove that for every $v \in C$, we have

$$\overline{\Theta(v)} \cap K = \Theta(v) \cap K.$$

To do this, let $v \in C$ and $u \in \overline{\Theta(v)} \cap K$. Let $(u_n)_n$ be a sequence in $\Theta(v)$ converging to u.

Let $v^* \in A(v)$ be arbitrary. We have for all $n \geq 1$

$$\alpha(v - u_n) \leq \langle v^*, v - u_n \rangle + h(u_n) J^0 (iu_n; iv - iu_n) - \langle Fu_n, v - u_n \rangle.$$

Since $u \in K$, then

$$\alpha(v - u)$$
$$\leq \limsup_{n \to +\infty} \alpha(v - u_n)$$
$$\leq \limsup_{n \to +\infty} \left(\langle v^*, v - u_n \rangle + h(u_n) J^0 (iu_n; iv - iu_n) - \langle Fu_n, v - u_n \rangle \right)$$
$$\leq \langle v^*, v - u \rangle + h(u) J^0 (iu; iv - iu) - \langle Fu, v - u \rangle.$$

It follows that $u \in \Theta(v) \cap K$.

Now, by using the fact that $\Theta(v_0)$ is contained in K, we conclude that

$$\bigcap_{v \in C} \overline{\Theta(v)} = \bigcap_{v \in C} \Theta(v),$$

and then,

$$\bigcap_{v \in C} \Theta(v) \neq \emptyset.$$

Finally, let $u_0 \in \bigcap_{v \in C} \Theta(v)$. This means that $u_0 \in K$ and for every $w \in C$, we have

$$\inf_{w^* \in A(w)} \langle w^*, w - u \rangle + h(u) J^0(iu; iw - iu) - \langle Fu, w - u \rangle \geq \alpha(w - u).$$

Let $v \in C$ be arbitrary and define $w_n = u_0 + \lambda_n(v - u_0)$ where $(\lambda_n)_n$ is a sequence in $]0, 1[$ such that $\lim\limits_{n \to +\infty} \lambda_n = 0$. By lower quasi-hemicontinuity of A on K, let $w_n^* \in A(w_n)$ be such that $w_n^* \xrightarrow{w^*} u_0^* \in A(u_0)$. Since the function $v \mapsto J^0(iu; iv)$ is positively homogeneous, we obtain

$$\langle w_n^*, v - u_0 \rangle + h(u_0) J^0(iu_0; iv - iu_0) - \langle Fu_0, v - u_0 \rangle \geq \frac{\alpha(\lambda_n(v - u))}{\lambda_n}.$$

Letting n go to $+\infty$, we obtain that

$$\langle u_0^*, v - u_0 \rangle + h(u_0) J^0(iu_0; iv - iu_0) - \langle Fu_0, v - u_0 \rangle \geq 0$$

which completes the proof. $\qquad\qquad\qquad\qquad\qquad\qquad\qquad\qquad\square$

The following result provides an additional existence property for quasi-hemivariational inequalities.

Theorem 10.2. *Let C be a nonempty, closed, and convex subset of the real reflexive Banach space E which is compactly imbedded in $L^p(\Omega; \mathbb{R}^n)$. Suppose that the following hypotheses are fulfilled:*

1. *there exist a weakly compact subset K of C and $v_0 \in K$ such that the following condition holds: for every $u \in C \setminus K$, there exists $v^* \in A(v_0)$ such that*

$$\langle v^*, v_0 - u \rangle + h(u) J^0(iu; iv_0 - iu) - \langle Fu, v_0 - u \rangle - \alpha(v_0 - u) < 0;$$

2. *$\alpha : E \to \mathbb{R}$ is a functional such that for every $u \in C$, $\lim\limits_{n \to +\infty} \frac{\alpha(\lambda_n u)}{\lambda_n} = 0$ whenever $(\lambda_n)_n$ is a sequence in $]0, 1[$ such that $\lim\limits_{n \to +\infty} \lambda_n = 0$ and $\limsup\limits_{n \to +\infty} \alpha(u_n) \geq \alpha(u)$ whenever $(u_n)_n$ is a sequence in C weakly converging to u;*

3. *A is relaxed α-monotone and lower quasi-hemicontinuous on K with respect to the weak* topology of E^*;*

4. *h is a nonnegative weakly sequentially lower semicontinuous functional on K;*

5. *F is an operator such that for every $v \in C$, $u \mapsto \langle Fu, v - u \rangle$ is weakly sequentially lower semicontinuous on K.*

Then the function $v \mapsto \Theta(v)$ is a KKM mapping and

$$Exp(\Theta(v)) \cap K = \Theta(v) \cap K \quad \text{for all } v \in C.$$

If, in addition, $\Theta(v)$ has the Fréchet-Urysohn property, for every $v \in C$, then the quasi-hemivariational inequality problem (10.2) has at least one solution.

Proof. By the same proof as in Theorem 10.1, we obtain that the set-valued mapping $v \mapsto \Theta(v)$ is a KKM mapping.

Now, let $v \in C$ and $u \in \mathrm{Exp}(\Theta(v)) \cap K$. Let $(u_n)_n$ be a sequence in $\Theta(v)$ weakly converging to u. Since the compact embedding i is compact, it maps weakly convergent sequences into strongly convergent sequences. Let $v^* \in A(v)$ be arbitrary. We have

$$\alpha(v - u_n) \leq \langle v^*, v - u_n \rangle + h(u_n) J^0(iu_n; iv - iu_n) - \langle Fu_n, v - u_n \rangle \quad \text{for all } n.$$

Since $u \in K$, then

$$\alpha(v - u)$$
$$\leq \limsup_{n \to +\infty} \alpha(v - u_n)$$
$$\leq \limsup_{n \to +\infty} \left(\langle v^*, v - u_n \rangle + h(u_n) J^0(iu_n; iv - iu_n) - \langle Fu_n, v - u_n \rangle \right)$$
$$\leq \langle v^*, v - u \rangle + h(u) J^0(iu; iv - iu) - \langle Fu, v - u \rangle.$$

Thus, $u \in \Theta(v) \cap K$.

Suppose now that $\Theta(v)$ has the Fréchet-Urysohn property, for every $v \in C$. Then

$$\mathrm{Exp}(\Theta(v)) = \overline{\Theta(v)} \quad \text{for all } v \in C$$

where the closure is taken with respect to the weak topology. Since the set-valued mapping $v \mapsto \Theta(v)$ is a KKM mapping and since $\Theta(v_0)$ is contained in K which is weakly compact, then by Ky Fan's lemma, we have

$$\bigcap_{v \in C} \mathrm{Exp}(\Theta(v)) \neq \emptyset.$$

By the same arguments as in the proof of Theorem 10.1, we conclude that

$$\bigcap_{v \in C} \mathrm{Exp}(\Theta(v)) = \bigcap_{v \in C} \Theta(v),$$

and then,

$$\bigcap_{v \in C} \Theta(v) \neq \emptyset.$$

With similar arguments as in the proof of Theorem 10.1, we conclude that the quasi-hemivariational problem (10.2) has at least one solution. $\square$

10.2 EQUILIBRIUM PROBLEMS VERSUS QUASI-HEMIVARIATIONAL INEQUALITIES

Equilibrium problems are very general and they include as particular cases, Nash equilibrium problems and convex minimization problems. Relevant applications in physics, optimization, and economics are described by models based on equilibrium problems.

Let C be a nonempty, closed, and convex subset of a real topological Hausdorff vector space X. An *equilibrium problem* in the sense of Blum, Muu, and Oettli [42,133] is a problem of the form:

$$\text{find} \quad u \in C \quad \text{such that} \quad f(u, v) \geq 0 \quad \text{for all } v \in C, \qquad (10.4)$$

where $f : C \times C \to \mathbb{R}$ is a bifunction such that $f(u, u) \geq 0$, for every $u \in C$. Such a bifunction is called an *equilibrium bifunction*.

We present in this section some results about the existence of solutions of equilibrium problems and apply these results for solving quasi-hemivariational inequalities.

In the sequel, we define the following sets: for every $v \in C$, we put

$$f^+(v) = \{u \in C \mid f(u, v) \geq 0\}$$

and

$$f^-(v) = \{u \in C \mid f(v, u) \leq 0\}.$$

A function $f : C \to \mathbb{R}$ is said to be

1. *semistrictly quasi-convex* on C if, for every $u_1, u_2 \in C$ such that $f(u_1) \neq f(u_2)$, we have

$$f(\lambda u_1 + (1 - \lambda) u_2) < \max\{f(u_1), f(u_2)\} \quad \text{for all } \lambda \in \,]0, 1[\,;$$

2. *explicitly quasi-convex* on C if it is quasi-convex and semistrictly quasi-convex.

The following result extends the Ky Fan minimax inequality theorem for sequentially upper semicontinuous bifunctions on their first variable on a subset of a real Banach space.

Theorem 10.3. *Let C be a nonempty, closed, and convex subset of the real Banach space E. Let $f : C \times C \longrightarrow \mathbb{R}$ be an equilibrium bifunction and suppose that the following assumptions hold:*

1. *f is quasi-convex in its second variable on C;*
2. *there exists a compact subset K of C and $v_0 \in K$ such that*

$$f(u, v_0) < 0 \quad \text{for all } u \in C \setminus K;$$

3. *f is sequentially upper semicontinuous in its first variable on K.*

Then the equilibrium problem (10.4) has a solution.

Proof. Since f is an equilibrium bifunction, then $\overline{f^+(v)}$ is nonempty and closed, for every $v \in C$.

By quasi-convexity of f in its second variable, the mapping $v \mapsto f^+(v)$ is a KKM mapping and since $f^+(v_0)$ is contained in the compact subset K, then by Ky Fan's lemma, we have

$$\bigcap_{v \in C} \overline{f^+(v)} \neq \emptyset.$$

On the other hand, we have

$$\bigcap_{v \in C} \overline{f^+(v)} = \bigcap_{y \in C} \left(\overline{f^+(v)} \cap K \right).$$

Since

$$\mathrm{Exp}\left(f^+(v)\right) = \overline{f^+(v)} \quad \text{for all } v \in C,$$

then by Proposition 10.2, we have

$$\overline{f^+(v)} \cap K = f^+(v) \cap K \quad \text{for all } v \in C.$$

Thus,

$$\bigcap_{v \in C} f^+(v) = \bigcap_{v \in C} \overline{f^+(v)} \neq \emptyset$$

which completes the proof. □

The equilibrium problem (10.4) can be also solved when the bifunction f is not upper semicontinuous on its first variable. In this case some additional conditions are needed.

The bifunction $f : C \times C \longrightarrow \mathbb{R}$ is said to be *pseudo-monotone* on C if

$$f(u, v) \geq 0 \Longrightarrow f(v, u) \leq 0, \quad \text{for all } u, v \in C.$$

The following result extends to the abstract setting of a real Banach space E some results of Alleche [4], Bianchi and Schaible [39] on the existence of solutions for pseudo-monotone equilibrium problems.

Theorem 10.4. *Let C be a nonempty, closed, and convex subset of the real Banach space E. Let $f : C \times C \longrightarrow \mathbb{R}$ be an equilibrium bifunction and suppose that the following assumptions hold:*

1. *f is pseudo-monotone on C;*
2. *there exists a compact subset K of C and $v_0 \in K$ such that*

$$f(u, v_0) < 0 \quad \text{for all } u \in C \setminus K;$$

3. *f is upper hemicontinuous in its first variable on K;*

4. f is explicitly quasi-convex in its second variable on C;
5. f is sequentially lower semicontinuous in its second variable on K.

Then the equilibrium problem (10.4) *has a solution.*

Proof. By the same arguments as in the proof of Theorem 10.3, we obtain that

$$\bigcap_{v \in C} \left(\overline{f^+(v)} \cap K \right) = \bigcap_{v \in C} \overline{f^+(v)} \neq \emptyset.$$

Since f is sequentially lower semicontinuous in its second variable on K, then by applying Proposition 10.2, we have

$$\overline{f^-(v)} \cap K = f^-(v) \cap K \quad \text{for all } v \in C.$$

From pseudo-monotonicity, we have $f^+(v) \subset f^-(v)$, for every $v \in C$. It follows that

$$\bigcap_{v \in C} \left(\overline{f^+(v)} \cap K \right) \subset \bigcap_{v \in C} \left(f^-(v) \cap K \right).$$

By using the hemicontinuity of f in its first variable on K and the explicit quasi-convexity, we have

$$\bigcap_{v \in C} \left(f^-(v) \cap K \right) \subset \bigcap_{v \in C} f^+(v).$$

A combination of the above statements yields

$$\bigcap_{y \in C} \overline{f^+(y)} = \bigcap_{y \in C} f^+(y).$$

This completes the proof. $\qquad\qquad\qquad\qquad\qquad\qquad\qquad\qquad$ □

Theorem 10.3 and Theorem 10.4 remain true if the real Banach space E is replaced by a real topological Hausdorff vector space such that the subset C is a Fréchet-Urysohn space.

Now we apply the above theorems to derive results on the existence of solution of quasi-hemivariational inequalities.

Define the equilibrium bifunction $\Psi : C \times C \to \mathbb{R}$ by

$$\Psi(u, v) = \inf_{v^* \in A(v)} \langle v^*, v - u \rangle + h(u) J^0(iu; iv - iu) - \langle Fu, v - u \rangle.$$

Although we are aware of the intrinsic properties of the generalized directional derivative, we do not know if Ψ satisfies any condition of continuity or of convexity in its first or second variable. In other words, even under assumptions of Theorem 10.1 and Theorem 10.2, it is not clear whether Ψ satisfies any condition of Theorem 10.3 or Theorem 10.4.

The following result provides us with a sufficient condition for solving the quasi-hemivariational inequality problem (10.2). Note that the concept of relaxed α-monotonicity is no longer needed.

Theorem 10.5. *Let C be a nonempty, closed, and convex subset of the real Banach space E. Suppose that A is lower quasi-hemicontinuous on K with respect to the weak* topology of E^*. If the equilibrium problem*

$$\text{find } u \in C \text{ such that } \Psi(u, v) \geq 0 \quad \text{for all } v \in C$$

has a solution, then the quasi-hemivariational inequality problem (10.2) has a solution.

Let us point out that by a classical method, we can also define an equilibrium bifunction $\Psi : C \times C \to \mathbb{R}$ as follows:

$$\Psi(u, v) = \sup_{u^* \in A(u)} \langle u^*, v - u \rangle + h(u) J^0(iu; iv - iu) - \langle Fu, v - u \rangle.$$

Clearly, any solution of the quasi-hemivariational inequality problem (10.2) is a solution of the equilibrium problem

$$\text{Find } \quad u \in C \quad \text{such that} \quad \Psi(u, v) \geq 0 \quad \text{for all } v \in C. \tag{10.5}$$

The converse does not hold easily as in Theorem 10.5 and it seems to need additional conditions on the values of the set-valued mapping A.

10.3 BROWDER VARIATIONAL INCLUSIONS

Browder variational inclusions appear in the literature as a generalization of Browder-Hartman-Stampacchia variational inequalities. These inequality problems are presented as a weak type of multi-valued variational inequalities, since they involve set-valued mappings in their definition. Browder variational inclusions have many applications, including applications to the surjectivity of set-valued mappings and to nonlinear elliptic boundary value problems. Browder variational inclusions can be reformulated by means of set-valued equilibrium problems.

Although set-valued equilibrium problems have already been considered in the literature, the authors have focused on the applications to Browder variational inclusions, or to other areas such as fixed point theory and economic equilibrium theory. It should be mentioned here that the results obtained in these papers on set-valued equilibrium problems are very general and need to be improved. When these results are applied to single-valued equilibrium problems, their assumptions become simple conditions of continuity and convexity. On the other hand, single-valued equilibrium problems have known in last decades several important and deep advancements.

Let C be a nonempty subset of a Hausdorff topological space and $f : C \times C \rightrightarrows \mathbb{R}$ a set-valued mapping.

Following Alleche and Rădulescu [7], a *set-valued equilibrium problem* is a problem of the form

$$\text{find } x^* \in C \text{ such that } f\left(x^*, y\right) \subset \mathbb{R}_+ \quad \text{for all } y \in C. \qquad \text{(Ssvep)}$$

We will also consider in this section the following weaker set-valued equilibrium problem

$$\text{find } x^* \in C \text{ such that } f\left(x^*, y\right) \cap \mathbb{R}_+ \neq \emptyset \quad \text{for all } y \in C. \qquad \text{(Wsvep)}$$

Recall that the equilibrium problem is a problem of the form

$$\text{find } x^* \in C \text{ such that } \varphi\left(x^*, y\right) \geq 0 \quad \text{for all } y \in C, \qquad \text{(EP)}$$

where $\varphi : C \times C \to \mathbb{R}$ is a bifunction.

10.3.1 Strong and Weak Set-Valued Equilibrium Problems

The compactness of the domain C in the existence of solutions of equilibrium problems is a rather restrictive condition. We will consider here a condition involving a set of coerciveness.

Theorem 10.6. *Let X be a Hausdorff locally convex topological vector space, C a nonempty, closed, and convex subset of X, and $D \subset C$ a self-segment-dense set in C. Let $f : C \times C \rightrightarrows \mathbb{R}$ be a set-valued mapping, and assume that the following conditions hold:*

1. *for all $x \in D$, $f(x, x) \subset \mathbb{R}_+$;*
2. *for all $x \in D$, $y \mapsto f(x, y)$ is convex on D;*
3. *for all $x \in C$, $y \mapsto f(x, y)$ is lower semicontinuous on $C \setminus D$;*
4. *there exist a compact set K of C and $y_0 \in D$ such that $f(x, y_0) \cap \mathbb{R}_-^* \neq \emptyset$, for all $x \in C \setminus K$;*
5. *for all $y \in D$, $x \mapsto f(x, y)$ is lower semicontinuous on K.*

Then the set-valued equilibrium problem (Ssvep) has a solution.

Proof. We define the set-valued mapping $f^+ : C \rightrightarrows C$ by

$$f^+(y) = \{x \in C \mid f(x, y) \subset \mathbb{R}_+\} \quad \text{for all } y \in C.$$

Clearly, $x_0 \in C$ is a solution of the set-valued equilibrium problem (Ssvep) if and only if $x_0 \in \bigcap_{y \in C} f^+(y)$.

Assumption (1) yields $f^+(y)$ is nonempty, for every $y \in D$. Now, consider the set-valued mapping $\operatorname{cl}\left(f^+\right) : D \rightrightarrows \mathbb{R}$ defined by

$$\operatorname{cl}\left(f^+\right)(y) = \operatorname{cl}\left(f^+(y)\right) \quad \text{for all } y \in D.$$

Clearly, $\mathrm{cl}\left(f^+\right)(y)$ is closed for every $y \in D$, and $\mathrm{cl}\left(f^+\right)(y_0)$ is compact since it lies in K by assumption (4).

We now prove that the set-valued mapping $\mathrm{cl}\left(f^+\right)$ is a KKM mapping. Let $\{y_1, \ldots, y_n\} \subset D$ be a finite subset and $\{\lambda_1, \ldots, \lambda_n\} \subset \mathbb{R}_+$ such that $\sum_{i=1}^n \lambda_i = 1$. We first assume that $\sum_{i=1}^n \lambda_i y_i \in D$. Then, by assumption (1) and assumption (2), we have

$$\sum_{i=1}^n \lambda_i f\left(\sum_{i=1}^n \lambda_i y_i, y_i\right) \subset f\left(\sum_{i=1}^n \lambda_i y_i, \sum_{i=1}^n \lambda_i y_i\right) \subset \mathbb{R}_+.$$

The convexity of $\mathbb{R}_-^*$ yields that there exists $i_0 \in \{1, \ldots, n\}$ such that $f\left(\sum_{i=1}^n \lambda_i y_i, y_{i_0}\right) \subset \mathbb{R}_+$, which implies that

$$\sum_{i=1}^n \lambda_i y_i \in f^+\left(y_{i_0}\right) \subset \bigcup_{i=1}^n f^+\left(y_i\right).$$

Consequently, for every finite subset $\{y_1, \ldots, y_n\} \subset D$ and $\{\lambda_1, \ldots, \lambda_n\} \subset \mathbb{R}_+$ such that $\sum_{i=1}^n \lambda_i = 1$, we have

$$\mathrm{conv}\{y_1, \ldots y_n\} \cap D \subset \bigcup_{i=1}^n f^+\left(y_i\right)$$

and then,

$$\mathrm{cl}\left(\mathrm{conv}\{y_1, \ldots y_n\} \cap D\right) \subset \mathrm{cl}\left(\bigcup_{i=1}^n f^+\left(y_i\right)\right) = \bigcup_{i=1}^n \mathrm{cl}\left(f^+\left(y_i\right)\right).$$

By applying Lemma 1.3, we obtain that

$$\mathrm{conv}\{y_1, \ldots y_n\} \subset \bigcup_{i=1}^n \mathrm{cl}\left(f^+\left(y_i\right)\right)$$

which proves that the set-valued mapping $\mathrm{cl}\left(f^+\right)$ is a KKM mapping.

Next, by Ky Fan's lemma, we have

$$\bigcap_{y \in D} \mathrm{cl}\left(f^+\left(y\right)\right) \neq \emptyset.$$

Since $y_0 \in D$ and $\mathrm{cl}\left(f^+\left(y_0\right)\right)$ is contained in K, then we have

$$\bigcap_{y \in D} \mathrm{cl}\left(f^+\left(y\right)\right) = \left(\bigcap_{y \in D} \mathrm{cl}\left(f^+\left(y\right)\right)\right) \cap K = \bigcap_{y \in D}\left(\mathrm{cl}\left(f^+\left(y\right)\right) \cap K\right).$$

According to our notation, we remark that for every $y \in D$, $f^+(y)$ is the upper inverse set $f^+(\mathbb{R}_+, y)$ of $\mathbb{R}_+$ by the set-valued mapping $f(., y)$ which is lower semicontinuous on K by assumption (5). Then, by applying Proposition 1.5, we obtain that for every $y \in D$,

$$\mathrm{cl}\left(f^+(y)\right) \cap K = f^+(y) \cap K.$$

Since $y_0 \in D$ and $f^+(y_0)$ is contained in K, then we have

$$\bigcap_{y \in D} \left(\mathrm{cl}\left(f^+(y)\right) \cap K\right) = \bigcap_{y \in D} \left(f^+(y) \cap K\right) = \bigcap_{y \in D} f^+(y).$$

It follows that $\bigcap_{y \in D} f^+(y) \neq \emptyset$, hence there exists $x_0 \in C$ such that $f(x_0, y) \subset \mathbb{R}_+$, for every $y \in D$.

It remains now to extend the above statement to the whole C in order to state that x_0 is a solution of the set-valued equilibrium problem (Ssvep). Let $y \in C \setminus D$. Since $D \subset f^+(x_0, \mathbb{R}_+) = \left\{y' \in C \mid f(x_0, y') \subset \mathbb{R}_+\right\}$ and D is dense in C, then $y \in \mathrm{cl}\left(f^+(x_0, \mathbb{R}_+)\right) \cap (C \setminus D)$. According to Proposition 1.5 again, assumption (3) yields that

$$\mathrm{cl}\left(f^+(x_0, \mathbb{R}_+)\right) \cap (C \setminus D) = f^+(x_0, \mathbb{R}_+) \cap (C \setminus D).$$

It follows that $y \in f^+(x_0, \mathbb{R}_+)$ which means that $f^+(x_0, y) \subset \mathbb{R}_+$ and completes the proof. $\qquad\square$

Remark 10.1. We note that f is convex (resp., lower semicontinuous) if and only if $-f$ is convex (resp., lower semicontinuous). Therefore, if we replace f by $-f$ in the above theorem, we obtain the inclusion in $\mathbb{R}_-$.

We now give an example of a set-valued mapping verifying all the conditions of Theorem 10.6 without being lower semicontinuous in its first variable on the whole space.

Example 10.1. Let $X = D = \mathbb{R}$, $K = [-1, +1]$ and $y_0 = 0$. Define the set-valued mapping $f : \mathbb{R} \times \mathbb{R} \rightrightarrows \mathbb{R}$ by

$$f(x, y) = \begin{cases} \left[\frac{y^2 - x^2}{2}, +\infty\right[& \text{if } x = 2, \\ \left[y^2 - x^2, +\infty\right[& \text{otherwise.} \end{cases}$$

Then f is convex in its second variable and that $f(x, x) = \mathbb{R}_+$, for every $x \in X$. Also, for every $x \notin K$, we have $f(x, 0) = -x^2 < 0$ if $x \neq 2$ and $f(x, 0) = -2 < 0$ if $x = 2$.

To show that f is lower semicontinuous in its first variable on K, fix $y \in \mathbb{R}$ and let V be an open subset of $\mathbb{R}$ such that $f(\overline{x}, y) \cap V \neq \emptyset$ where $\overline{x} \in K$. Then $2 - \overline{x} \geq 1$ and furthermore $f(\overline{x}, y) = \left[y^2 - \overline{x}^2, +\infty\right[$. Let

$z \in \left[y^2 - \overline{x}^2, +\infty \right[\cap V$ and $\varepsilon > 0$ be such that $]z - \varepsilon, z + \varepsilon[\subset V$. Choose $0 < \delta < 1$ such that $\left| x^2 - \overline{x}^2 \right| < \varepsilon$ whenever $|x - \overline{x}| < \delta$. Note that $\left| x^2 - \overline{x}^2 \right| = \left| \left(y^2 - x^2 \right) - \left(y^2 - \overline{x}^2 \right) \right|$ and then, $y^2 - x^2 < y^2 - \overline{x}^2 + \varepsilon \leq z + \varepsilon$ whenever $|x - \overline{x}| < \delta$. Thus, $f(x, y) \cap V \neq \emptyset$, for every $x \in]\overline{x} - \delta, \overline{x} + \delta[$.

Now, let us show that f is not lower semicontinuous in its first variable on the whole space $\mathbb{R}$. Take for example $y = 3$ and show that the set-valued mapping $f(\cdot, 3)$ is not lower semicontinuous at the point 2. To do this, consider the open interval $V =]2, 3[$, and since $f(2, 3) = \left[\frac{5}{2}, +\infty \right[$, then $f(2, 3) \cap V \neq \emptyset$. However, if U is an open neighborhood of 2, then $\left] 2, \sqrt{5} \right[\cap U \neq \emptyset$ and for $z \in \left] 2, \sqrt{5} \right[\cap U$, we have $f(z, 3) = \left[9 - z^2, +\infty \right[$. Since $9 - z^2 > 4$, then $f(z, 3) \cap V = \emptyset$.

The weaker set-valued equilibrium problem (Wsvep) is also solvable under the conditions of Theorem 10.6 since it is a particular case and a weaker version of the set-valued equilibrium problem (Ssvep). However, we provide here some other conditions involving concavity and upper semicontinuity to obtain an existence result for the set-valued equilibrium problem (Wsvep).

Theorem 10.7. *Let X be a Hausdorff locally convex topological vector space, C a nonempty, closed, and convex subset of X, and $D \subset C$ a self-segment-dense set in C. Let $f : C \times C \rightrightarrows \mathbb{R}$ be a set-valued mapping, and assume that the following conditions hold:*

1. *for all $x \in D$, $f(x, x) \cap \mathbb{R}_+ \neq \emptyset$;*
2. *for all $x \in D$, $y \mapsto f(x, y)$ is concave on D;*
3. *for all $x \in C$, $y \mapsto f(x, y)$ is upper semicontinuous on $C \setminus D$;*
4. *there exist a compact set K of C and $y_0 \in D$ such that $f(x, y_0) \subset \mathbb{R}_-^*$, for all $x \in C \setminus K$;*
5. *for all $y \in D$, $x \mapsto f(x, y)$ is upper semicontinuous on K.*

Then the set-valued equilibrium problem (Wsvep) *has a solution.*

Proof. We define the following set-valued mapping $f^- : C \rightrightarrows C$ by

$$f^-(y) = \{x \in C \mid f(x, y) \cap \mathbb{R}_+ \neq \emptyset\} \quad \text{for all } y \in C.$$

We observe that $x_0 \in C$ is a solution of the set-valued equilibrium problem (Wsvep) if and only if $x_0 \in \bigcap_{y \in C} f^-(y)$.

Now, consider the set-valued mapping $\mathrm{cl}\left(f^- \right) : D \rightrightarrows \mathbb{R}$ defined by

$$\mathrm{cl}\left(f^- \right)(y) = \mathrm{cl}\left(f^-(y) \right) \quad \text{for all } y \in D.$$

As above, $f^-(y)$ is nonempty for every $y \in D$. Also, $\mathrm{cl}\left(f^- \right)(y)$ is closed for every $y \in D$, and $\mathrm{cl}\left(f^- \right)(y_0)$ is compact since it lies in K.

To prove that the set-valued mapping $\text{cl}\left(f^-\right)$ is a KKM mapping, let $\{y_1, \ldots, y_n\} \subset D$ be a finite subset and $\{\lambda_1, \ldots, \lambda_n\} \subset \mathbb{R}_+$ such that $\sum_{i=1}^{n} \lambda_i = 1$ and $\sum_{i=1}^{n} \lambda_i y_i \in D$. Then, by assumptions (1) and (2), we obtain

$$\sum_{i=1}^{n} \lambda_i f\left(\sum_{i=1}^{n} \lambda_i y_i, y_i\right) \supset f\left(\sum_{i=1}^{n} \lambda_i y_i, \sum_{i=1}^{n} \lambda_i y_i\right) \cap \mathbb{R}_+ \neq \emptyset.$$

The convexity of $\mathbb{R}^*_-$ yields that there exists $i_0 \in \{1, \ldots, n\}$ such that $f\left(\sum_{i=1}^{n} \lambda_i y_i, y_{i_0}\right) \cap \mathbb{R}_+ \neq \emptyset$ which implies that

$$\sum_{i=1}^{n} \lambda_i y_i \in f^-\left(y_{i_0}\right) \subset \bigcup_{i=1}^{n} f^-\left(y_i\right).$$

Consequently, for every finite subset $\{y_1, \ldots, y_n\} \subset D$ and $\{\lambda_1, \ldots, \lambda_n\} \subset \mathbb{R}_-$ such that $\sum_{i=1}^{n} \lambda_i = 1$, we have

$$\text{conv}\,\{y_1, \ldots y_n\} \cap D \subset \bigcup_{i=1}^{n} f^-\left(y_i\right)$$

and then,

$$\text{cl}\,(\text{conv}\,\{y_1, \ldots y_n\} \cap D) \subset \text{cl}\left(\bigcup_{i=1}^{n} f^-\left(y_i\right)\right) = \bigcup_{i=1}^{n} \text{cl}\left(f^-\left(y_i\right)\right).$$

By applying Lemma 1.3, we have

$$\text{conv}\,\{y_1, \ldots y_n\} \subset \bigcup_{i=1}^{n} \text{cl}\left(f^-\left(y_i\right)\right)$$

which proves that the set-valued mapping $\text{cl}\left(f^-\right)$ is a KKM mapping.

By Ky Fan's lemma, we obtain

$$\bigcap_{y \in D} \text{cl}\left(f^-\left(y\right)\right) \neq \emptyset,$$

and since $y_0 \in D$ and $\text{cl}\left(f^-\left(y_0\right)\right) \subset K$, then

$$\bigcap_{y \in D} \text{cl}\left(f^-\left(y\right)\right) = \bigcap_{y \in D} \left(\text{cl}\left(f^-\left(y\right)\right)\right) \cap K = \bigcap_{y \in D} \left(\text{cl}\left(f^-\left(y\right)\right) \cap K\right).$$

According to our notation, we remark that for every $y \in D$, $f^-\left(y\right)$ is the lower inverse set $f^-\left(\mathbb{R}_+, y\right)$ of $\mathbb{R}_+$ by the set-valued mapping $f\left(., y\right)$ which is upper semicontinuous on K by assumption (5). Then, by applying Proposition 1.5, we obtain that for every $y \in D$,

$$\text{cl}\left(f^-(y)\right) \cap K = f^-(y) \cap K.$$

Since $y_0 \in D$ and $f^-(y_0)$ is contained in K, we have

$$\bigcap_{y \in D}\left(\text{cl}\left(f^-(y)\right) \cap K\right) = \bigcap_{y \in D}\left(f^-(y) \cap K\right) = \bigcap_{y \in D} f^-(y).$$

It follows that $\bigcap_{y \in D} f^-(y) \neq \emptyset$, hence there exists $x_0 \in C$ such that $f(x_0, y) \cap \mathbb{R}_+ \neq \emptyset$, for every $y \in D$.

It remains now to extend the above statement to the whole C in order to state that x_0 is a solution of the set-valued equilibrium problem (Wsvep). Let $y \in C \setminus D$. Since $D \subset f^-(x_0, \mathbb{R}_+) = \left\{y' \in C \mid f\left(x_0, y'\right) \cap \mathbb{R}_+ \neq \emptyset\right\}$ and D is dense in C, then $y \in \text{cl}\left(f^-(x_0, \mathbb{R}_+)\right) \cap (C \setminus D)$. According to Proposition 1.5 again, assumption (3) yields that

$$\text{cl}\left(f^-(x_0, \mathbb{R}_+)\right) \cap (C \setminus D) = f^-(x_0, \mathbb{R}_+) \cap (C \setminus D).$$

It follows that $y \in f^-(x_0, \mathbb{R}_+)$ which means that $f^-(x_0, y) \cap \mathbb{R}_+ \neq \emptyset$ and completes the proof. □

Once again, remark that any solution of the set-valued equilibrium problem (Ssvep) or the set-valued equilibrium problem (Wsvep) is a solution of the classical equilibrium problem (EP), where $f : C \times C \rightrightarrows \mathbb{R}$ is defined by $f(x, y) = \{\varphi(x, y)\}$ and φ is a single-valued bifunction. However, when the notions of convexity and concavity in the sense of set-valued mappings are applied to f, we obtain the linearity (on D) of the single-valued mapping φ which is a strong condition for solving equilibrium problems. Also, lower and upper semicontinuity in the sense of set-valued mappings applied to f turn out to be the continuity of φ. In what follows, we provide conditions weaker than linearity and continuity to obtain an existence result for the equilibrium problems (EP).

Theorem 10.8. *Let X be a Hausdorff locally convex topological vector space, C a nonempty, closed, and convex subset of X, and $D \subset C$ a self-segment-dense set in C. Let $\varphi : C \times C \to \mathbb{R}$ be a bifunction, and assume that the following conditions hold:*

1. *for all $x \in D$, $\varphi(x, x) \geq 0$;*
2. *for all $x \in D$, $y \mapsto \varphi(x, y)$ is convex on D;*
3. *for all $x \in C$, $y \mapsto \varphi(x, y)$ is lower semicontinuous on $C \setminus D$;*
4. *there exist a compact set K of C and $y_0 \in D$ such that $\varphi(x, y_0) < 0$, for all $x \in C \setminus K$;*
5. *for all $y \in D$, $x \mapsto \varphi(x, y)$ is lower semicontinuous on K.*

Then the equilibrium problem (EP) has a solution.

Proof. We proceed as above and define the following set-valued mapping $\varphi^+ : C \rightrightarrows C$ by

$$\varphi^+ (y) = \{x \in C \mid \varphi (x, y) \geq 0\}.$$

We observe that $x_0 \in C$ is a solution of the equilibrium problem (EP) if and only if $x_0 \in \bigcap_{y \in C} \varphi^+ (y)$.

We also consider the set-valued mapping $\mathrm{cl} \left(\varphi^+ \right) : D \rightrightarrows \mathbb{R}$ defined by

$$\mathrm{cl} \left(\varphi^+ \right) (y) = \mathrm{cl} \left(\varphi^+ (y) \right) \quad \text{for all } y \in D.$$

We have that $\varphi^+ (y)$ is nonempty, for every $y \in D$. Also, $\mathrm{cl} \left(\varphi^+ \right) (y)$ is closed for every $y \in D$, and $\mathrm{cl} \left(\varphi^+ \right) (y_0)$ is compact.

To prove that $\mathrm{cl} \left(\varphi^+ \right)$ is a KKM mapping, let $\{y_1, \ldots, y_n\} \subset D$ be a finite subset and $\{\lambda_1, \ldots, \lambda_n\} \subset \mathbb{R}_+$ such that $\sum_{i=1}^{n} \lambda_i = 1$ and $\sum_{i=1}^{n} \lambda_i y_i \in D$. We have

$$\max_{i=1,\ldots,n} \varphi \left(\sum_{i=1}^{n} \lambda_i y_i, y_i \right) \geq \varphi \left(\sum_{i=1}^{n} \lambda_i y_i, \sum_{i=1}^{n} \lambda_i y_i \right) \geq 0.$$

Then, there exists $i_0 \in \{1, \ldots, n\}$ such that $\varphi \left(\sum_{i=1}^{n} \lambda_i y_i, y_{i_0} \right) \geq 0$ which implies that

$$\sum_{i=1}^{n} \lambda_i y_i \in \varphi^+ \left(y_{i_0} \right) \subset \bigcup_{i=1}^{n} \varphi^+ (y_i).$$

Consequently, for every finite subset $\{y_1, \ldots, y_n\} \subset D$ and $\{\lambda_1, \ldots, \lambda_n\} \subset \mathbb{R}_-$ such that $\sum_{i=1}^{n} \lambda_i = 1$, we have

$$\mathrm{conv} \{y_1, \ldots y_n\} \cap D \subset \bigcup_{i=1}^{n} \varphi^+ (y_i)$$

and then,

$$\mathrm{cl} \left(\mathrm{conv} \{y_1, \ldots y_n\} \cap D \right) \subset \mathrm{cl} \left(\bigcup_{i=1}^{n} \varphi^+ (y_i) \right) = \bigcup_{i=1}^{n} \mathrm{cl} \left(\varphi^+ (y_i) \right).$$

By applying Lemma 1.3, we obtain that

$$\mathrm{conv} \{y_1, \ldots y_n\} \subset \bigcup_{i=1}^{n} \mathrm{cl} \left(\varphi^+ (y_i) \right)$$

which proves that the set-valued mapping $\mathrm{cl} \left(\varphi^+ \right) : D \rightrightarrows \mathbb{R}$ is a KKM mapping.

By applying Ky Fan's lemma, we have

$$\bigcap_{y \in D} \operatorname{cl}\left(\varphi^+(y)\right) \neq \emptyset.$$

Since $y_0 \in D$ and $\operatorname{cl}\left(\varphi^+(y_0)\right) \subset K$, then

$$\bigcap_{y \in D} \operatorname{cl}\left(\varphi^+(y)\right) = \bigcap_{y \in D}\left(\operatorname{cl}\left(\varphi^+(y)\right)\right) \cap K = \bigcap_{y \in D}\left(\operatorname{cl}\left(\varphi^+(y)\right) \cap K\right).$$

By applying Proposition 1.3, assumption (5) yields that for every $y \in D$,

$$\operatorname{cl}\left(\varphi^+(y)\right) \cap K = \varphi^+(y) \cap K$$

and then,

$$\bigcap_{y \in D}\left(\operatorname{cl}\left(\varphi^+(y)\right) \cap K\right) = \bigcap_{y \in D}\left(\varphi^+(y) \cap K\right) = \bigcap_{y \in D}\varphi^+(y).$$

It follows that $\bigcap_{y \in D}\varphi^+(y) \neq \emptyset$ which means that there exists $x_0 \in C$ such that $\varphi(x_0, y) \geq 0$, for every $y \in D$.

As above, by assumption (3), we can apply Proposition 1.3 to the set $C \setminus K$ and obtain that $\varphi(x_0, y) \geq 0$, for every $y \in C$. That is, x_0 is a solution of the equilibrium problem (EP). $\qquad\square$

We point out that the solutions sets of the equilibrium problems studied in Theorems 10.6, 10.7 and 10.8 are always included in the set of coerciveness K.

10.3.2 Browder Variational Inclusions: Existence of Solutions

Browder variational inclusion problems have been considered in the literature as a generalization of Browder-Hartman-Stampacchia variational inequality problems. These problems are also presented in the literature as a weak type of multi-valued variational inequalities.

Let X be a real normed vector space X. For $x \in X$ and a subset A of X^*, we put $\langle A, x \rangle = \{\langle x^*, x \rangle \mid x^* \in A\}$.

The following result is related with Theorem 4.8.

Theorem 10.9. *Let X be a real normed vector space, C a nonempty, closed, and convex subset of X. Suppose that $F : C \rightrightarrows X^*$ satisfies the following conditions:*

1. *there exist a compact subset K of C and $y_0 \in C$ such that $\langle x^*, y - x \rangle < 0$, for every $x \in C \setminus K$ and every $x^* \in F(x)$;*
2. *F is upper semicontinuous on K;*
3. *F has weak* compact values on K.*

Then there exists $x_0 \in K$ such that $\langle F(x_0), y - x_0 \cap \mathbb{R}_+ \neq \emptyset$, for every $y \in C$.

Proof. Define the set-valued mapping $f : C \times C \rightrightarrows \mathbb{R}$ by

$$f(x, y) = \langle F(x), y - x \rangle.$$

We show that all the conditions of Theorem 10.7 are satisfied with $D = C$.

Condition (1) and condition (3) are obviously satisfied. Condition (4) holds easily from our assumption on the subset K.

To prove condition (2), let $x \in C$, $\{y_1, \ldots, y_n\} \subset C$ a finite subset and $\{\lambda_1, \ldots, \lambda_n\} \subset \mathbb{R}_+$ such that $\sum_{i=1}^{n} \lambda_i = 1$. Take $x^* \in F(x)$, and by linearity, we have

$$\langle x*, \sum_{i=1}^{n} \lambda_i y_i - x \rangle = \sum_{i=1}^{n} \lambda_i \langle x*, y_i - x \rangle \in \sum_{i=1}^{n} \lambda_i \langle F(x), y_i - x \rangle$$

which implies that $\langle F(x), \sum_{i=1}^{n} \lambda_i y_i - x \rangle \subset \sum_{i=1}^{n} \lambda_i \langle F(x), y_i - x \rangle$. It follows that

$$f\left(x, \sum_{i=1}^{n} \lambda_i y_i\right) \subset \sum_{i=1}^{n} \lambda_i f(x, y_i).$$

To prove condition (5), fix $y \in D$, V an open subset of $\mathbb{R}$ and let $x \in f^+(V, y) \cap (C \setminus K)$ where $f^+(V, y) = \{x' \in C \mid \langle F(x'), y - x' \rangle \subset V\}$. First, we claim that there exists $\delta > 0$ such that

$$B_{\mathbb{R}}\left(\langle x^*, y - x \rangle, \delta\right) \subset V \quad \text{for all } x^* \in F(x)$$

where $B_{\mathbb{R}}(\langle x^*, y - x \rangle, \delta) = \{t \in \mathbb{R} \mid |t - \langle x^*, y - x \rangle| < \delta\}$. Indeed, for every $x^* \in F(x)$, let $\varepsilon_{x^*} > 0$ be such that $B_{\mathbb{R}}(\langle x^*, y - x \rangle, 2\varepsilon_{x^*}) \subset V$ and define

$$U_{x^*} = \left\{z^* \in X^* \mid \langle z^*, y - x \rangle \in B_{\mathbb{R}}\left(x^*, y - x\right), \varepsilon_{x^*}\right)\right\}.$$

The family $\{U_{x^*} \mid x^* \in F(x)\}$ being a weak* open cover of $F(x)$ which is weak* compact, let $\{x_1^*, \ldots, x_n^*\} \subset F(x)$ be such that $F(x) \subset \bigcup_{i=1}^{n} U_{x_i^*}$. Put

$$\delta = \min_{i=1, \ldots, n} \varepsilon_{x_i^*}.$$

If $t \in B_{\mathbb{R}}\langle x^*, y - x \rangle, \delta)$ for some $x^* \in F(x)$, then $x^* \in U_{x_i^*}$, for some $i = 1, \ldots, n$. Since

$$|t - \langle x_i^*, y - x \rangle| \leq |t - \langle x^*, y - x \rangle| + |\langle x^*, y - x \rangle - \langle x_i^*, y - x \rangle|$$
$$< \delta + \varepsilon_{x_i^*} \leq 2\varepsilon_{x_i^*},$$

then, $t \in B_{\mathbb{R}}\left(\langle x_i^*, y - x \rangle, 2\varepsilon_{x_i^*}\right) \subset V$.

Let

$$\delta_1 = \min\left\{\frac{\delta}{3(\|x\| + 1)}, \frac{\delta}{3(\|y\| + 1)}\right\}$$

and $O = \bigcup_{x^* \in F(x)} B_{X^*}(x^*, \delta_1)$, where $B_{X^*}(x^*, \delta_1) = \{z \in X^* \mid \|z - x^*\|_* < \delta_1\}$, and $\|.\|$ and $\|.\|_*$ denote respectively the norm of X and X^*. Clearly O is an open set containing $F(x)$, and by the upper semicontinuity of F on K, let $\eta > 0$ be such that $F(w) \subset O$ for every $w \in B_X(x, \eta) \cap C$, where $B_X(x, \eta) = \{w \in X \mid \|w - x\| < \eta\}$. Put

$$\eta_1 = \min\left\{\frac{\delta}{3\,(\|F(x)\|_* + 1)}, \eta, 1\right\}$$

where $\|F(x)\|_* = \max\{\|x^*\|_* \mid x^* \in F(x)\}$. Put $U = B_X(x, \eta_1) \cap C$ which is an open subset of C containing x.

We will show that $f(z, y) \subset V$, for every $z \in U$. To do this, let $z \in U$ and $z^* \in F(z)$. Let $x_0^* \in F(x)$ be such that $F(z^*) \subset B_{X^*}(x_0^*, \delta_1)$. We have

$$
\begin{aligned}
\left|\langle z^*, y - z\rangle - \langle x_0^*, y - x\rangle\right| &= \left|\langle x_0^* - z^*, z\rangle + \langle x_0^*, x - z\rangle - \langle x_0^* - z^*, y\rangle\right| \\
&\leq \|x_0^* - z^*\|_*\|z\| + \|x_0^*\|_*\|x - z\| + \|x_0^* - z^*\|_*\|y\| \\
&< \frac{\delta\,(\|x\| + \eta_1)}{3\,(\|x\| + 1)} + \frac{\delta\|x_0^*\|_*}{3\,(\|F(x)\|_* + 1)} + \frac{\delta\|y\|}{3\,(\|y\| + 1)} \\
&< \frac{\delta}{3} + \frac{\delta}{3} + \frac{\delta}{3} = \delta.
\end{aligned}
$$

It follows that $\langle z^*, y - z\rangle \in B_{\mathbb{R}}\left(\langle x_0^*, y - x\rangle, \delta\right) \subset V$. Since z is arbitrary in U and z^* is arbitrary in $F(z)$, then $f(z, y) \subset V$, for every $z \in U$.

By Theorem 10.7, we conclude that there exists $x_0 \in C$ such that $f(x_0, y) \cap \mathbb{R}_+ \neq \emptyset$, for every $y \in C$. $\square$

When F is a single-valued mapping, we obtain a solution to the Browder-Hartman-Stampacchia variational inequality problems, as stated in the following property.

Corollary 10.1. *Let X be a real normed vector space, C a nonempty, closed, and convex subset of X. Suppose that $f : C \to X^*$ has the following conditions*

1. *there exist a compact subset K of C and $y_0 \in C$ such that $\langle f(x), y - x\rangle < 0$, for every $x \in C \setminus K$;*
2. *F is continuous on K.*

Then there exists $x_0 \in K$ such that $\langle f(x_0), y - x_0\rangle \geq 0$, for every $y \in C$.

10.3.3   Pseudo-Monotone Case

We are now concerned with set-valued equilibrium problems under conditions of pseudo-monotonicity. Concepts such as strict quasi-convexity, hemicontinuity and pseudo-monotonicity for extended real set-valued mappings are introduced and applied to obtain results on the existence of solutions of set-valued equilibrium problems generalizing those in the literature in the pseudo-monotone case. Applications to Browder variational inclusions under weakened conditions are given. In particular, it is shown that the upper semicontinuity from line segments of the involved pseudo-monotone set-valued operator is not needed in the whole space when solving Browder variational inclusions. We follow the results obtained by Alleche and Rădulescu [10].

Let C be a nonempty convex subset of a real topological Hausdorff vector space. A set-valued mapping $F : C \rightrightarrows \mathbb{R}$ is said to be *convex* on C if whenever $\{x_1, \ldots, x_n\} \subset C$ and $\{\lambda_1, \ldots, \lambda_n\} \subset \mathbb{R}_+$ such that $\sum_{i=1}^{n} \lambda_i = 1$, we have

$$\sum_{i=1}^{n} \lambda_i F(x_i) \subset F\left(\sum_{i=1}^{n} \lambda_i x_i\right),$$

where the sum denotes here the usual Minkowski sum of sets. The set-valued mapping $F : C \rightrightarrows \mathbb{R}$ is said to be *concave* on C if whenever $\{x_1, \ldots, x_n\} \subset C$ and $\{\lambda_1, \ldots, \lambda_n\} \subset \mathbb{R}_+$ such that $\sum_{i=1}^{n} \lambda_i = 1$, we have

$$F\left(\sum_{i=1}^{n} \lambda_i x_i\right) \subset \sum_{i=1}^{n} \lambda_i F(x_i).$$

Let $F : C \rightrightarrows \overline{\mathbb{R}}$ be an extended real set-valued mapping. We say that F is *convexly quasi-convex* on C if whenever $\{x_1, \ldots, x_n\} \subset C$ and $\{\lambda_1, \ldots, \lambda_n\} \subset \mathbb{R}_+$ such that $\sum_{i=1}^{n} \lambda_i = 1$, then for every $\{z_1, \ldots, z_n\}$ with $z_i \in F(x_i)$ for every $i = 1, \ldots, n$, there exists $z \in F\left(\sum_{i=1}^{n} \lambda_i x_i\right)$ such that

$$z \leq \max\{z_i \mid i = 1, \ldots, n\}.$$

We observe that the convex quasi-convexity of extended real set-valued mappings generalizes both the convexity of set-valued mappings and the quasi-convexity of extended real single-valued mappings.

We have the following obvious characterization.

Proposition 10.5. *Let C be a nonempty convex subset of a real topological Hausdorff vector space. An extended real set-valued mapping $F : C \rightrightarrows \overline{\mathbb{R}}$ is convexly quasi-convex on C if and only if the set $[F \leq \lambda]$ is convex, for every $\lambda \in \overline{\mathbb{R}}$.*

We say that F is *concavely quasi-convex* on C if whenever $\{x_1, \ldots, x_n\} \subset C$ and $\{\lambda_1, \ldots, \lambda_n\} \subset \mathbb{R}_+$ such that $\sum_{i=1}^{n} \lambda_i = 1$, then for every $z \in F\left(\sum_{i=1}^{n} \lambda_i x_i\right)$, there exist $\{z_1, \ldots, z_n\}$ with $z_i \in F(x_i)$ for every $i = 1, \ldots, n$ such that

$$z \leq \max\{z_i \mid i = 1, \ldots, n\}.$$

The concave quasi-convexity of extended real set-valued mappings generalizes both the concavity of set-valued mappings and the quasi-convexity of extended real single-valued mappings.

We have the following characterization.

Proposition 10.6. *Let C be a nonempty convex subset of a real topological Hausdorff vector space. If an extended real set-valued mapping $F : C \rightrightarrows \overline{\mathbb{R}}$ is concavely quasi-convex on C, then the set $[F \subseteq \lambda]$ is convex, for every $\lambda \in \overline{\mathbb{R}}$.*

Now, we introduce the following notion of semistrict quasi-convexity of extended real set-valued mappings. We say that F is *semistrictly convexly quasi-convex* on C if whenever $x_1, x_2 \in C$ such that $F(x_1) \neq F(x_2)$ and $\lambda \in \,]0, 1[$, then for every $z_1 \in F(x_1)$ and $z_2 \in F(x_2)$, the following hold

1. there exists $z \in F(\lambda x_1 + (1 - \lambda) x_2)$ such that

$$z < \max\{z_1, z_2\};$$

2. whenever $z' \in F(\lambda x_1 + (1 - \lambda) x_2)$, we have

$$\text{if } z' \leq \max\{z_1, z_2\}, \text{ then } z' < \max\{z_1, z_2\}.$$

Every convex extended real set-valued mapping and every semistrictly quasi-convex extended real single-valued mapping is semistrictly convexly quasi-convex extended real set-valued mapping. We point out that there is not any inclusion relationship between the class of semistrictly quasi-convex real single-valued mappings and that of quasi-convex real single-valued mappings. It follows that there is not any inclusion relationship between the class of semistrictly convexly quasi-convex extended real set-valued mappings and that of convexly quasi-convex extended real set-valued mappings.

Example 10.2. Let $C = [-1, 1]$ and $F : C \rightrightarrows \mathbb{R}$ be the set-valued defined by

$$F(x) = \begin{cases} \left[\frac{1}{2}, 1\right] & \text{if } x \neq 0, \\ \left[\frac{3}{2}, 2\right] & \text{if } x = 0. \end{cases}$$

The set-valued F is not convexly quasi-convex since for $x_1 = -1$, $x_2 = 1$ and $\lambda_1 = \lambda_2 = \frac{1}{2}$, we have $\lambda_1 x_1 + \lambda_2 x_2 = 0$. Then clearly, for $z_1 \in F(x_1)$ and $z_2 \in F(x_2)$, we have

$$z > \max\{z_1, z_2\},$$

for every $z \in F(\lambda_1 x_1 + \lambda_2 x_2)$. However, F is semistrictly convexly quasi-convex. Indeed, take $x_1, x_2 \in C$, and in order to apply the definition, we must assume (without loss of generality) that $x_1 = 0$ and $x_2 \neq 0$. Then for $\lambda \in \,]0, 1[$, we have

$$F(\lambda x_1 + (1 - \lambda) x_2) = F((1 - \lambda) x_2) = \left[\frac{1}{2}, 1\right] \text{ and } F(x_1) = \left[\frac{3}{2}, 2\right].$$

Clearly, for every $z_1 \in F(x_1)$, $z_2 \in F(x_2)$ and $z \in F(\lambda x_1 + (1 - \lambda) x_2)$, we have $z < \max\{z_1, z_2\}$.

Remark 10.2. The notion of semistrictly convexly quasi-convex extended real set-valued mapping will be used in Proposition 10.9 and Proposition 10.10 below, where we need only condition (2). Condition (1) has been used in order to make this notion a generalization of the notion of semistrictly quasi-convex extended real single-valued mapping.

In the sequel, an extended real set-valued mappings will be said *explicitly convexly quasi-convex* if it is both convexly quasi-convex and semistrictly convexly quasi-convex.

In the literature, various concepts related to continuity on line segments of single-valued and set-valued mappings defined on real topological Hausdorff vector spaces have been introduced and used in different works. In what follows, we introduce the notions of upper hemicontinuous and quasi-upper hemicontinuous extended real set-valued mappings which generalize both the upper hemicontinuity of extended real single-valued mapping and the lower semicontinuity of set-valued mappings.

Let X be a real topological Hausdorff vector space. For $x, y \in X$, we set $[x, y] = \{\lambda x + (1 - \lambda) y \mid \lambda \in [0, 1]\}$, the line segment starting at x and ending at y. We also set $]x, y[= [x, y] \setminus \{x, y\}$. We say that a set-valued mapping $F : X \rightrightarrows \overline{\mathbb{R}}$ is

1. *upper hemicontinuous* at a point $x \in X$ if whenever $x' \in X$, there exists a sequence $(t_n)_n$ in $]0, 1[$ converging to 0 such that for every $z \in F(x)$, there exists a sequence $(z_n)_n$ with $z_n \in F(t_n x' + (1 - t_n) x)$ for every n, and such that

$$z \geq \limsup_{n \to +\infty} z_n,$$

   where $\limsup\limits_{n \to +\infty} z_n = \inf\limits_n \sup\limits_{k \geq n} z_k$;

2. *quasi-upper hemicontinuous* at a point $x \in X$ if whenever $x' \in X$ there exist a sequence $(t_n)_n$ in $]0, 1[$ converging to 0, a point $z \in F(x)$, and a sequence $(z_n)_n$ with $z_n \in F(t_n x' + (1 - t_n) x)$ for every n such that

$$z \geq \limsup_{n \to +\infty} z_n.$$

The set-valued mapping F is said to be upper hemicontinuous (resp., quasi-upper hemicontinuous) on X if it is upper hemicontinuous (resp., quasi-upper hemicontinuous) at every point of X. It is said to be upper hemicontinuous (resp., quasi-upper hemicontinuous) on a subset $S \subset X$, if it is upper hemicontinuous (resp., quasi-upper hemicontinuous) at every point of S.

Remark 10.3. Note that when $x \neq x'$ in the above definition, then we have $t_n x' + (1 - t_n) x \in]x', x[$, for every n.

Proposition 10.7. *Let X be a real topological Hausdorff vector space, $x \in X$, and $F : X \rightrightarrows \overline{\mathbb{R}}$ a set-valued mapping. Suppose that one of the following assumptions holds:*

1. *F is lower semicontinuous at x;*
2. *F has a selection which is upper hemicontinuous at x.*

Then F is upper hemicontinuous at x.

Proof. The second statement is obvious. The first one comes from the fact that F is lower semicontinuous at $x \in X$ if and only if for every generalized sequence $(x_\lambda)_{\lambda \in \Lambda}$ converging to x, and for every $z \in F(x)$, there exists a generalized sequence $(z_\lambda)_{\lambda \in \Lambda}$ converging to z such that $z_\lambda \in F(x_\lambda)$, for every $\lambda \in \Lambda$. $\qquad \square$

Even if the existence of continuous selections is subject which is not limited to lower semicontinuous set-valued mapping, Michael's selection theorem remains the pioneering work in this direction which guarantees that every lower semicontinuous set-valued mapping with nonempty, closed, and convex values from a paracompact space to a Banach space has a continuous selection.

Proposition 10.8. *Let X be a real topological Hausdorff vector space and $F : X \rightrightarrows \overline{\mathbb{R}}$ a set-valued mapping. Suppose that for every $x \in S$ and $x' \in X$, the restriction of F on $[x', x]$ has an upper hemicontinuous selection. Then F is upper hemicontinuous on S.*

Remark 10.4. We remark that in Proposition 10.8, we are interested in the restriction of F on the line segment $[x', x]$ which is a space that enjoys different important properties. In comparison with Michael's selection theorem, it should be interesting to look for conditions on F in order to obtain such an upper hemicontinuous selection without being necessarily continuous.

In many applications, upper hemicontinuous set-valued mappings is constructed from upper semicontinuous set-valued operators from line segments as in the results of the last section of this paper. We construct here an upper hemicontinuous set-valued mapping which is not lower semicontinuous.

Example 10.3. Let $X = \{(x, y) \in \mathbb{R}^2 \mid y > 0\} \cup \{(0, 0)\} \subset \mathbb{R}^2$ and define the set-valued mapping $F : X \rightrightarrows \mathbb{R}^2$ by

$$F((x, y)) = \begin{cases} \left[\frac{4x^2}{y}, +\infty\right[\times \left[\frac{x^4}{y^2}, +\infty\right[& \text{if } y > 0, \\ \mathbb{R}^2 & \text{if } y = 0. \end{cases}$$

The function $f : X \rightrightarrows \mathbb{R}^2$ defined by

$$f((x, y)) = \begin{cases} \left(\frac{4x^2}{y}, \frac{x^4}{y^2}\right) & \text{if } y > 0, \\ (0, 0) & \text{if } y = 0, \end{cases}$$

is upper hemicontinuous selection of F which is not continuous. Indeed, the hemicontinuity being obvious, we will just prove that f is not continuous at

$(0, 0)$. We have

$$\lim_{\substack{x \to 0 \\ x > 0}} f\left((\sqrt{x}, x)\right) = \lim_{\substack{x \to 0 \\ x > 0}} \left(4\sqrt{x}, 1\right) = (0, 1) \neq (0, 0) = f\left((0, 0)\right).$$

The set-valued mapping F is not lower semicontinuous at $(0, 0)$. Indeed, let $V = B\left((0, 0), 1\right)$ be the open ball around $(0, 0)$ with radius 1. We have $F\left((0, 0)\right) \cap V \neq \emptyset$, but for any open neighborhood U of $(0, 0)$, we can choose a small enough $a > 0$ such that $\left(\sqrt{a}, a\right) \in U$. Now, for every $(x, y) \in F\left((\sqrt{a}, a)\right)$, we have $x \geq 4\sqrt{a}$ and $y \geq 1$. Then $\sqrt{x^2 + y2} \geq 1$. It follows that $(x, y) \notin V$, and then $F\left((\sqrt{a}, a)\right) \cap V = \emptyset$.

Next, we are concerned with the existence of solutions of both strong set-valued equilibrium problems and weak set-valued equilibrium problems in the pseudo-monotone case.

We now recall the notion of KKM mapping and the intersection lemma of Ky Fan [73]. We refer to Chapter 4 for more details.

Let X be a real topological Hausdorff vector space and M a subset of X. A set-valued mapping $F : M \rightrightarrows X$ is said to be a KKM mapping if for every finite subset $\{x_1, \ldots, x_n\}$ of M, we have

$$\text{conv}\{x_1, \ldots x_n\} \subset \bigcup_{i=1}^{n} F(x_i).$$

By Ky Fan's lemma [73], assuming that

1. F is a KKM mapping,
2. $F(x)$ is closed for every $x \in M$, and
3. there exists $x_0 \in M$ such that $F(x_0)$ is compact,

then $\bigcap_{x \in M} F(x) \neq \emptyset$.

We define the following set-valued mappings $f^+, f^{++} : C \rightrightarrows C$ by

$$f^+(y) = \left\{ x \in C \mid f(x, y) \cap \overline{\mathbb{R}}_+ \neq \emptyset \right\} \quad \text{for all } y \in C,$$

and

$$f^{++}(y) = \left\{ x \in C \mid f(x, y) \subset \overline{\mathbb{R}}_+ \right\} \quad \text{for all } y \in C.$$

We remark that $f^{++}(y) \subset f^+(y)$, for every $y \in C$. We also remark that

1. $x_0 \in C$ is a solution of the weak set-valued equilibrium problem (SVEP(W)) if and only if $x_0 \in \bigcap_{y \in C} f^+(y)$, and
2. $x_0 \in C$ is a solution of the strong set-valued equilibrium problem (Ssvep) if and only if $x_0 \in \bigcap_{y \in C} f^{++}(y)$.

Set

$$\mathrm{cl}\, f^+ (y) = \mathrm{cl}\, \left(f^+ (y) \right) \quad \text{and} \quad \mathrm{cl}\, f^{++} (y) = \mathrm{cl}\, \left(f^{++} (y) \right),$$

the closure of $f^+ (y)$ and $f^{++} (y)$, respectively, for every $y \in C$.

Lemma 10.1. *Let C be a nonempty convex subset of a real topological vector space. Let $f : C \times C \rightrightarrows \mathbb{R} \cup \{+\infty\}$ be a set-valued mapping, and assume that the following conditions hold:*

1. $f(x, x) \subset \overline{\mathbb{R}}_+$, *for every $x \in C$;*
2. *f is convexly quasi-convex in its second variable on C.*

Then the set-valued mappings $\mathrm{cl}\, f^{++} : C \rightrightarrows C$ and $\mathrm{cl}\, f^+ : C \rightrightarrows C$ are KKM mappings.

Proof. It suffices to prove that the set-valued mapping $f^{++} : C \rightrightarrows C$ is a KKM mapping. Let $\{y_1, \ldots, y_n\} \subset C$ and $\{\lambda_1, \ldots, \lambda_n\} \subset \mathbb{R}_+$ be such that $\sum_{i=1}^n \lambda_i = 1$. Set $\tilde{y} = \sum_{i=1}^n \lambda_i y_i$. By assumption (2), for $\{z_1, \ldots, z_n\}$ with $z_i \in f(\tilde{y}, y_i)$ for every $i = 1, \ldots, n$, there exists $z \in f(\tilde{y}, \tilde{y})$ such that

$$z \le \max \{z_i \mid i = 1, \ldots, n\}.$$

We have $z \ge 0$ since $f(\tilde{y}, \tilde{y}) \subset \overline{\mathbb{R}}_+$ by assumption (1). It follows that there exists $i_0 \in \{1, \ldots, n\}$ such that $f(\tilde{y}, y_{i_0}) \cap \mathbb{R}^*_- = \emptyset$, which implies that $f(\tilde{y}, y_{i_0}) \subset \overline{\mathbb{R}}_+$. Otherwise, all the z_i can be taken in $\mathbb{R}^*_-$, and therefore $z \in \mathbb{R}^*_-$, which is impossible. We conclude that

$$\sum_{i=1}^n \lambda_i y_i = \tilde{y} \in f^{++} (y_{i_0}) \subset \bigcup_{i=1}^n f^{++} (y_i),$$

which proves that f^{++} is a KKM mapping. $\qquad \square$

First, we deal with strong set-valued equilibrium problems. The following result emphasizes the role of upper hemicontinuity when solving set-valued equilibrium problems.

We define the following set-valued mapping $f^{--} : C \rightrightarrows C$ by

$$f^{--} (y) = \{x \in C \mid f(y, x) \subset \mathbb{R}_-\} \quad \text{for all } y \in C,$$

and we set

$$\mathrm{cl}\, f^{--} (y) = \mathrm{cl}\, \left(f^{--} (y) \right),$$

the closure of $f^{--} (y)$, for every $y \in C$.

Proposition 10.9. *Let C be a nonempty convex subset of a real topological vector space. Let $f : C \times C \rightrightarrows \mathbb{R} \cup \{+\infty\}$ be a set-valued mapping and suppose the following assumptions hold:*

1. $f(x, x) \subset \overline{\mathbb{R}}_+$, *for every* $x \in C$;
2. f *is explicitly convexly quasi-convex in its second variable on* C;
3. f *is upper hemicontinuous in its first variable on a subset* S *of* C.

Then

$$\bigcap_{y \in C} \left(f^{--}(y) \cap S \right) \subset \bigcap_{y \in C} f^{++}(y).$$

Proof. Without loss of generality, we may assume that

$$\bigcap_{y \in C} \left(f^{--}(y) \cap S \right) \neq \emptyset.$$

Take $x \in \bigcap_{y \in C} \left(f^{--}(y) \cap S \right)$ and let $y \in C$ be an arbitrary point. By upper hemicontinuity of f in its first variable on S, let $(t_n)_n$ be a sequence in $]0, 1[$ converging to 0, and for $z \in f(x, y)$, let $(z_n)_n$ be a sequence with $z_n \in f(x_n, y)$ for every n, and such that

$$z \geq \limsup_{n \to +\infty} z_n,$$

where $x_n = t_n y + (1 - t_n) x$. We have in particular that $x \in f^{--}(x_n)$ for every n. Thus, $f(x_n, x) \subset \mathbb{R}_-$, for every n. By convex quasi-convexity of f in its second variable, for $z_n \in f(x_n, y)$ and $w_x^n \in f(x_n, x)$, there exists $w_n \in f(x_n, x_n)$ such that

$$w_n \leq \max \left\{ z_n, w_x^n \right\}.$$

We have $w_n \geq 0$ since $f(x_n, x_n) \subset \overline{\mathbb{R}}_+$. We also have $z_n \geq 0$. Indeed, assume that $z_n < 0$. Then $w_x^n \geq 0$, otherwise $w_n < 0$ which is impossible. This yields that $w_x^n = 0$ and then, $z_n < w_x^n$. Since z_n and w_x^n are arbitrary in $f(x_n, y)$ and $f(x_n, x)$, respectively, then $f(x_n, y) \neq f(x_n, x)$. By semistrict convex quasi-convexity of f in its second variable, we obtain $w_n < \max \left\{ z_n, w_x^n \right\} = w_x^n = 0$, which is impossible. We conclude that

$$z \geq \limsup_{n \to +\infty} z_n \geq 0.$$

Since z is arbitrary in $f(x, y)$, then $x \in f^{++}(y)$. Since y is arbitrary in C, then $x \in \bigcap_{y \in C} f^{++}(y)$, which completes the proof. $\qquad\square$

Next, we obtain a result on the existence of solutions of strong set-valued equilibrium problems.

We say that a bifunction $f : C \times C \rightrightarrows \mathbb{R} \cup \{+\infty\}$ is *strongly pseudo-monotone on* C if for every $x, y \in C$,

$$f(x, y) \subset \overline{\mathbb{R}}_+ \Longrightarrow f(y, x) \subset \mathbb{R}_-.$$

Example 10.4. Define the set-valued mapping $f : \mathbb{R} \times \mathbb{R} \rightrightarrows \mathbb{R}$ by

$$f(x, y) = \begin{cases} [y^2 - x^2, +\infty[& \text{if } |y| > |x|, \\ \{0\} & \text{if } |y| = |x|, \\ ]-\infty, y^2 - x^2] & \text{if } |y| < |x|. \end{cases}$$

Clearly, $f(x, x) = f(-x, -x) = f(x, -x) = f(-x, x) = \{0\}$, for every $x \in \mathbb{R}$. If $f(x, y) \subset \mathbb{R}_+$, then necessarily, we have $|y| \geq |x|$. It follows that $f(y, x)$ is either equal to $\{0\}$ or to $]-\infty, x^2 - y^2]$ which are included in $\mathbb{R}_-$. It follows that f is strongly pseudo-monotone on $\mathbb{R}$.

Theorem 10.10. *Let C be a nonempty, closed, and convex subset of a real topological vector space. Let $f : C \times C \rightrightarrows \mathbb{R} \cup \{+\infty\}$ be a set-valued mapping, and assume that the following conditions hold:*

1. $f(x, x) \subset \overline{\mathbb{R}}_+$, *for every $x \in C$;*
2. *f is strongly pseudo-monotone on C;*
3. *f is explicitly convexly quasi-convex in its second variable on C;*
4. *there exist a compact set K of C and a point $y_0 \in K$ such that $f(x, y_0) \cap \mathbb{R}_-^* \neq \emptyset$, for every $x \in C \setminus K$;*
5. *f is l-lower semicontinuous in its second variable on K;*
6. *f is upper hemicontinuous in its first variable on K.*

Then the set of solutions of the set-valued equilibrium problem (Ssvep) is nonempty compact set. It is also convex whenever f is concavely quasi-convex in its second variable on C and K is convex.

Proof. Assumption (1) yields $f^{++}(y)$ is nonempty, for every $y \in C$. We observe that $\mathrm{cl}\,f^{++}(y)$ is closed for every $y \in C$, and $\mathrm{cl}\,f^{++}(y_0)$ is compact since it lies in K by assumption (4). Also, the set-valued mapping $\mathrm{cl}\,f^{++}$ is a KKM mapping by Lemma 10.1. By the Ky Fan lemma, we have

$$\bigcap_{y \in C} \mathrm{cl}\,f^{++}(y) \neq \emptyset.$$

Since the subset $\mathrm{cl}\,f^{++}(y_0)$ is contained in the compact K, then

$$\bigcap_{y \in C} \mathrm{cl}\,f^{++}(y) = \bigcap_{y \in C} \left(\mathrm{cl}\,f^{++}(y) \cap K \right).$$

By strong pseudo-monotonicity, we have $f^{++}(y) \subset f^{--}(y)$, for every $y \in X$. We remark that for every $y \in C$, $f^{--}(y)$ is the upper inverse set $f^+(y,]-\infty, 0])$ of $]-\infty, 0]$ by the set-valued mapping $f(y, .)$ which is l-lower semicontinuous on K. It follows that $\mathrm{cl}\,f^{--}(y) \cap K = f^{--}(y) \cap K$. Hence

$$\bigcap_{y \in C} \left(\mathrm{cl}\,f^{++}(y) \cap K \right) \subset \bigcap_{y \subset C} \left(\mathrm{cl}\,f^{--}(y) \cap K \right) = \bigcap_{y \in C} \left(f^{--}(y) \cap K \right).$$

By Proposition 10.9, we have

$$\bigcap_{y \in C} \left(f^{--}(y) \cap K \right) \subset \bigcap_{y \in C} f^{++}(y).$$

This yields that

$$\bigcap_{y \in C} \operatorname{cl} f^{++}(y) = \bigcap_{y \in C} f^{++}(y).$$

It follows that the set of solutions of the set-valued equilibrium problem (Ssvep) is the nonempty set $\bigcap_{y \in C} \operatorname{cl} f^{++}(y)$ which is compact since it is closed and contained in the compact set K.

By Proposition 10.6, the concave quasi-convexity of f in its second variable on C yields that the set $f^{--}(y)$ is convex, for every $y \in C$. Since we also have

$$\bigcap_{y \in C} \operatorname{cl} f^{++}(y) = \left(\bigcap_{y \in C} f^{--}(y) \right) \cap K,$$

then the set of solutions of the set-valued equilibrium problem (Ssvep) is convex whenever K is convex. $\qquad\square$

Now, we deal with weak set-valued equilibrium problems. The following result emphasizes the role of quasi-upper hemicontinuity when solving set-valued equilibrium problems.

We define the following set-valued mapping $f^- : C \rightrightarrows C$ by

$$f^-(y) = \{x \in C \mid f(y, x) \cap \mathbb{R}_- \neq \emptyset\} \quad \text{for all } y \in C,$$

and we set

$$\operatorname{cl} f^-(y) = \operatorname{cl} \left(f^-(y) \right),$$

the closure of $f^-(y)$, for every $y \in C$.

Proposition 10.10. *Let C be a nonempty convex subset of a real topological vector space. Let $f : C \times C \rightrightarrows \mathbb{R} \cup \{+\infty\}$ be a set-valued mapping and suppose the following assumptions hold:*

1. $f(x, x) \subset \overline{\mathbb{R}}_+$, *for every $x \in C$;*
2. f *is explicitly convexly quasi-convex in its second variable on C;*
3. f *is quasi-upper hemicontinuous in its first variable on a subset S of C.*

Then

$$\bigcap_{y \in C} \left(f^-(y) \cap S \right) \subset \bigcap_{y \in C} f^+(y).$$

Proof. Pick $x \in \bigcap_{y \in C} \left(f^-(y) \cap S \right)$ and let $y \in C$ be an arbitrary point. By quasi-upper hemicontinuity of f in its first variable on S, let $(t_n)_n$ be a sequence in $]0, 1[$ converging to 0, a point $z \in f(x, y)$, and a sequence $(z_n)_n$ with $z_n \in f(x_n, y)$ for every n, such that

$$z \geq \limsup_{n \to +\infty} z_n,$$

where $x_n = t_n y + (1 - t_n) x$. By convex quasi-convexity of f in its second variable, for $z_n \in f(x_n, y)$ and $w_x^n \in f(x_n, x) \cap \mathbb{R}_-$, there exists $w_n \in f(x_n, x_n)$ such that

$$w_n \leq \max \left\{ z_n, w_x^n \right\}.$$

By using the semistrict convex quasi-convexity of f in its second variable, we obtain that $z_n \geq 0$, and we conclude that

$$z \geq \limsup_{n \to +\infty} z_n \geq 0,$$

which completes the proof. $\qquad\square$

Next, we obtain a result on the existence of solutions of weak set-valued equilibrium problems.

We say that a bifunction $f : C \times C \rightrightarrows \mathbb{R} \cup \{+\infty\}$ is *weakly pseudo-monotone on C* if for every $x, y \in C$,

$$f(x, y) \cap \overline{\mathbb{R}}_+ \neq \emptyset \Longrightarrow f(y, x) \cap \mathbb{R}_- \neq \emptyset.$$

Example 10.5. Define the set-valued mapping $f : \mathbb{R} \times \mathbb{R} \rightrightarrows \mathbb{R}$ by

$$f(x, y) = \begin{cases} [0, +\infty[& \text{if } y \geq x, \\ ]-\infty, x - y] & \text{if } y < x. \end{cases}$$

We remark that $f(x, y) \cap \mathbb{R}_- \neq \emptyset$, for every $x, y \in \mathbb{R}$. Then, f is obviously weakly pseudo-monotone on $\mathbb{R}$. However, f can not be strongly pseudo-monotone on $\mathbb{R}$ since $f(1, 2) = [0, +\infty[\subset \overline{\mathbb{R}}_+$, but $f(2, 1) =]-\infty, 1] \not\subset \mathbb{R}_-$.

We note that for real single-valued mappings, the weak pseudo-monotonicity coincides with the strong pseudo-monotonicity, and it is called, in this case, the pseudo-monotonicity.

Theorem 10.11. *Let C be a nonempty, closed, and convex subset of a real topological vector space. Let $f : C \times C \rightrightarrows \mathbb{R} \cup \{+\infty\}$ be a set-valued mapping, and assume that the following conditions hold:*

1. $f(x, x) \subset \overline{\mathbb{R}}_+$, *for every* $x \in C$;
2. f *is weakly pseudo-monotone on* C;
3. f *is explicitly convexly quasi-convex in its second variable on* C;

4. *there exist a compact set K of C and a point $y_0 \in K$ such that $f(x, y_0) \subset \mathbb{R}_-^*$, for every $x \in C \setminus K$;*
5. *f is u-lower semicontinuous in its second variable on K;*
6. *f is quasi-upper hemicontinuous in its first variable on K.*

Then the set of solutions of the set-valued equilibrium problem (SVEP(W)) is nonempty compact set. It is also convex whenever K is convex.

Proof. As in the proof of Theorem 10.10, $\mathrm{cl} f^+(y)$ is nonempty and closed for every $y \in C$, $\mathrm{cl} f^+(y_0)$ is compact and the set-valued mapping $\mathrm{cl} f^+$ is a KKM mapping. By the Ky Fan lemma and since the subset $\mathrm{cl} f^+(y_0)$ is contained in the compact K, we have

$$\bigcap_{y \in C} \left(\mathrm{cl} f^+(y) \cap K \right) = \bigcap_{y \in C} \mathrm{cl} f^+(y) \neq \emptyset.$$

By weak pseudo-monotonicity, we have $f^+(y) \subset f^-(y)$. Since f is u-lower semicontinuity in its second variable on K, we have $\mathrm{cl} f^-(y) \cap K = f^-(y) \cap K$, for every $y \in X$. It follows that

$$\bigcap_{y \in C} \left(\mathrm{cl} f^+(y) \cap K \right) \subset \bigcap_{y \in C} \left(\mathrm{cl} f^-(y) \cap K \right) = \bigcap_{y \in C} \left(f^-(y) \cap K \right).$$

By Proposition 10.10, we have

$$\bigcap_{y \in C} \left(f^-(y) \cap K \right) \subset \bigcap_{y \in C} f^+(y).$$

This yields that

$$\bigcap_{y \in C} \mathrm{cl} f^+(y) = \bigcap_{y \in C} f^+(y).$$

We deduce that the set of solutions of the set-valued equilibrium problem (SVEP(W)) is the nonempty compact set $\bigcap_{y \in C} \mathrm{cl} f^+(y)$. By Proposition 10.5, we have that the set $f^-(y)$ is convex, for every $y \in C$. Since we also have

$$\bigcap_{y \in C} \mathrm{cl} f^+(y) = \left(\bigcap_{y \in C} f^-(y) \right) \cap K,$$

then the set of solutions of the set-valued equilibrium problem (SVEP(W)) is convex whenever K is convex. $\qquad\square$

We illustrate the previous results with a class of Browder variational inclusions involving pseudo-monotone set-valued operators. Browder variational inclusions, which generalize Browder-Hartman-Stampacchia variational inequalities, have many applications to nonlinear elliptic boundary value problems and the surjectivity of set-valued mappings.

Let C be a nonempty, closed, and convex subset of a real normed vector space X. A set-valued operator $F : C \rightrightarrows X^*$ is said to be coercive on C if there exists $y_0 \in C$ such that

$$\lim_{\substack{\|x\| \to +\infty \\ x \in C}} \inf_{x^* \in F(x)} \langle x^*, x - y_0 \rangle > 0,$$

or if the stronger condition

$$\lim_{\substack{\|x\| \to +\infty \\ x \in C}} \frac{\inf_{x^* \in F(x)} \langle x^*, x - y_0 \rangle}{\|x\|} = +\infty$$

is satisfied. It is not hard to see that under both the two notions of coerciveness of F, there exists $R > 0$ such that $y_0 \in K_R$ and $\inf_{x^* \in F(x)} \langle x^*, y_0 - x \rangle < 0$, for every $x \in C \setminus K_R$, where $K_R = \{x \in C \mid \|x\| \le R\}$. We observe that K_R is weakly compact whenever X is reflexive. The set K_R is called a set of coerciveness, and the couple (y_0, K_R) may not be unique.

Recall that a set-valued operator $F : C \rightrightarrows E^*$ is called pseudo-monotone on C if for every $x, y \in C$

$$\langle x^*, y - x \rangle \ge 0 \Longrightarrow \langle y^*, x - y \rangle \le 0 \quad \text{for all } x^* \in F(x), \text{ for all } y^* \in F(y).$$

In the sequel, for $x \in X$ and a subset A of X^*, we set

$$\langle A, x \rangle = \left\{ \langle x^*, x \rangle \mid x^* \in A \right\}.$$

Problems of the form: "find $x_0 \in C$ such that $\langle A, x_0 \rangle \subset \mathbb{R}_+$" or "find $x_0 \in C$ such that $\langle A, x_0 \rangle \cap \mathbb{R}_+ \ne \emptyset$" are called Browder variational inclusions.

Let X and Y be two real Hausdorff topological vector spaces and C is a nonempty convex subset of X. Recall that $F : C \rightrightarrows Y$ is said to be *upper semicontinuous from line segments in C at $x \in C$* if for every $x' \in C$, the restriction of F on the line segment $[x', x]$ is upper semicontinuous at x. This means that for every $x' \in C$, there exists an open neighborhood U of x such that $F(z) \subset V$, for every $z \in U \cap [x', x]$. We say that F is upper semicontinuous from line segments in C on a subset S of C if it is upper semicontinuous from line segments in C at every point of S.

Theorem 10.12. *Let C be a nonempty, closed, and convex subset of a real Banach space X, and $F : C \rightrightarrows X^*$ a set-valued operator. Suppose that the following conditions hold:*

1. *F is pseudo-monotone on C;*
2. *there exist a weakly compact subset K of C and $y_0 \in K$ such that*
   $$\sup_{z^* \in F(x)} \langle z^*, y_0 - x \rangle < 0, \text{ for every } x \in C \setminus K;$$
3. *F upper semicontinuous from line segments in C on K to X^* endowed with the weak* topology;*

4. *F has weak* compact values on C;*
5. *For every $x \in K$ and $x' \in C$, $F\left([x', x]\right)$ is norm bounded.*

Then there exists $x_0 \in K$ such that $\langle F(x_0), y - x_0 \rangle \cap \mathbb{R}_+ \neq \emptyset$, for every $y \in C$.

Proof. First, we define the following extended real single-valued mapping $f : C \times C \rightrightarrows \mathbb{R} \cup \{+\infty\}$ by

$$f(x, y) = \sup_{z^* \in F(x)} \langle z^*, y - x \rangle,$$

which also, it can be seen as an extended real set-valued mapping. Now, we verify for f and X endowed with the weak topology, the assumptions of Theorem 10.10 or Theorem 10.11, where the five first conditions are the same in this case.

We have $f(x, x) = 0 \in \mathbb{R}_+$, for every $x \in C$. For $z \in C$ fixed, the function $z^* \mapsto \langle z^*, y - z \rangle$ is weak* continuous on X^* and therefore, by Weierstrass theorem, it attains its maximum on weak* compact sets. Thus, for every $x \in C$, there exists $x^* \in F(x)$ such that

$$f(x, y) = \langle x^*, y - x \rangle,$$

which provides easily that f is pseudo-monotone on C.

For every $x \in C$ and $x^* \in F(x)$, the function $y \to \langle x^*, y - x \rangle$ is linear and weakly continuous. Then f being the superior envelope of a family of convex and weakly lower semicontinuous functions, it is then convex and weakly lower semicontinuous in its second variable on C.

It remains to prove that f is upper hemicontinuous in its first variable on K. We note that the strong topology and the weak topology coincide on line segments of X. Let $y \in C$ be fixed, $x \in K$ and $x' \in C$. Take a sequence $(x_n)_n$ in $[x', x]$ converging to x. Take $x^* \in F(x)$ such that $f(x, y) = \langle x^*, y - x \rangle$, and $x_n^* \in F(x_n)$ such that $f(x_n, y) = \langle x_n^*, y - x_n \rangle$, for every n.

Suppose first that there exists $a \in \mathbb{R}$ such that $f(x_n, y) \geq a$, for every n. We claim that the sequence $(x_n^*)_n$ has a weak* cluster point $\tilde{x}^* \in F(x)$. Indeed, suppose the contrary holds. Then the weak* compactness of $F(x)$ yields the existence of a weak* open set V containing $F(x)$ and $n_0 \in \mathbb{N}$ such that $x_n^* \notin V$, for every $n \geq n_0$. The upper semicontinuity of F from line segments in C at x yields the existence of an open neighborhood U of x such that $F(z) \subset V$, for every $z \in U \cap [x', x]$. Since $(x_n)_n$ is converging to x, let $n_1 \in \mathbb{N}$ be such that $x_n \in U$, for every $n \geq n_1$. Then $x_n^* \in F(x_n) \subset V$, for every $n \geq n_1$. A contradiction.

Let now $(x_{n_\lambda}^*)_{\lambda \in \Lambda}$ be a subnet of $(x_n^*)_n$ converging to $\tilde{x}^*$ in the weak* topology of X^*. The subnet $(x_{n_\lambda})_{\lambda \in \Lambda}$ also converges to x, and therefore, for $\varepsilon > 0$, let $\lambda_0 \in \Lambda$ be such that for every $\lambda \geq \lambda_0$, we have

$$\|x - x_{n_\lambda}\| \leq \frac{\varepsilon}{2\left(\|F\left([x', x]\right)\| + 1\right)},$$

where $\| F\left([x', x]\right)\| = \sup\limits_{z^* \in F([x',x])} \| z^*\|$. Let also $\lambda_1 \in \Lambda$ be such that

$$\| \tilde{x}^* - x_{n_\lambda}^*\| \leq \frac{\varepsilon}{2\left(\| y - x\| + 1\right)}.$$

Let $\tilde{\lambda} \in \Lambda$ be such that $\tilde{\lambda} \geq \lambda_0$ and $\tilde{\lambda} \geq \lambda_1$. It results that for every $\lambda \geq \tilde{\lambda}$, we have

$$\left|\langle \tilde{x}^*, y - x\rangle - \langle x_{n_\lambda}^*, y - x_{n_\lambda}\rangle\right| = \left|\langle \tilde{x}^* - x_{n_\lambda}^*, y - x\rangle + \langle x_{n_\lambda}^*, x_{n_\lambda} - x\rangle\right|$$
$$\leq \| \tilde{x}^* - x_{n_\lambda}^*\| \| y - x\| + \| x_{n_\lambda}^*\| \| x - x_{n_\lambda}\|$$
$$\leq \frac{\varepsilon}{2} + \frac{\varepsilon}{2} = \varepsilon.$$

We conclude that

$$f(x, y) \geq \langle \tilde{x}^*, y - x\rangle = \lim_\lambda \langle x_{n_\lambda}^*, y - x_{n_\lambda}\rangle = \lim_\lambda f(x_\lambda, y) \geq a.$$

Now, we claim that $f(x, y) \geq \limsup\limits_{n \to +\infty} f(x_n, y)$. Suppose the contrary holds and let $\lambda > 0$ be such that

$$f(x, y) + \lambda < \limsup\limits_{n \to +\infty} f(x_n, y).$$

Put $a = f(x, y) + \lambda$ which is then in $\mathbb{R}$ (but this also holds from the fact that $F(x)$ is weak* compact). Now if a subsequence $\left(x_{n_k}\right)_k$ of $(x_n)_n$ is such that $f\left(x_{n_k}, y\right) \geq a$ for every k, then by the above statement, we obtain

$$f(x, y) \geq a > f(x, y),$$

which is impossible. Then there exists $n_0 \in \mathbb{N}$ such that $f(x_n, y) < a$, for every $n \geq n_0$. It results that

$$\limsup\limits_{\substack{n \geq n_0 \\ n \to +\infty}} f(x_n, y) \leq a < \limsup\limits_{n \to +\infty} f(x_n, y),$$

which yields a contradiction since $\limsup\limits_{\substack{n \geq n_0 \\ n \to +\infty}} f(x_n, y) = \limsup\limits_{n \to +\infty} f(x_n, y)$. We conclude that $f(x, y) \geq \limsup\limits_{n \to +\infty} f(x_n, y)$, which completes the proof. $\square$

Remark 10.5. We remark that in the proof of Theorem 10.12 above, if we assume the mild condition of F has *weak* compact values only on K* instead of all C, we can still prove that

$$f(x, y) \geq a.$$

Indeed, for $\delta > 0$, let $x_n^* \in F(x_n)$ be such that $\langle x_n^*, y - x_n \rangle > a - \delta$, for every n. Using similar arguments, we state that the sequence $(x_n^*)_n$ has a subnet $(x_{n_\lambda}^*)_{\lambda \in \Lambda}$ converging to some $\tilde{x}^* \in F(x)$ in the weak* topology of X^*. We also obtain that

$$f(x, y) \geq \langle \tilde{x}^*, y - x \rangle = \lim_\lambda \langle x_{n_\lambda}^*, y - x_{n_\lambda} \rangle \geq a - \delta.$$

By letting δ go to zero, we conclude that $f(x, y) \geq a$.

We note that all the other statements of Theorem 10.12 remain true under this mild condition except the pseudo-monotonicity of F. In this case, we can assume the following condition:

$$\sup_{z^* \in F(x)} \langle z^*, y - x \rangle \geq 0 \Longrightarrow \sup_{z^* \in F(y)} \langle z^*, x - y \rangle \leq 0 \quad \text{for all } x, y \in C,$$

instead of the pseudo-monotonicity of F.

In order to make further discussion in this subject about the existence of solutions of Browder variational inclusions, recall that an open half-space in a real Hausdorff topological vector space E is a subset of the form

$$\{u \in E \mid \varphi(u) < r\}$$

for some continuous linear functional φ on E, not identically zero, and for some real number r.

Let X be a Hausdorff topological space and E a real Hausdorff topological vector space. A set-valued operator $F : C \rightrightarrows Y$ is said to be *upper demicontinuous at* $x \in X$ if for every open half-space H containing $F(x)$, there exists a neighborhood U of x such that $F(z) \subset H$ for every $z \in U$. It said to be upper demicontinuous on X if it is upper demicontinuous at every point of X.

We say that a set-valued operator $A : X \rightrightarrows Y$ is *upper demicontinuous from line segments in X at* $x \in C$ if for every $x' \in C$ and every open half-space H containing $F(x)$, there exists a neighborhood U of x such that $F(z) \subset H$ for every $z \in U \cap [x', x]$. We say that F is upper demicontinuous from line segments in X on a subset S of C if it is upper demicontinuous from line segments in X at every point of S.

Proposition 10.11. *Let X be a real normed vector space, C a nonempty convex subset of X, and $S \subset C$. If $F : C \rightrightarrows X^*$ is upper semicontinuous from line segments in X on S to X^* endowed with the weak* topology, then F is upper demicontinuous from line segments in X on S to X^* endowed with the weak* topology.*

Proof. Let $x \in K$ and consider an open half-space H in X^* of the form

$$\{u \in X^* \mid \varphi(u) < r\}$$

such that $F(x) \subset H$, where φ is a weak* continuous linear functional on X^*, not identically zero, and $r \in \mathbb{R}$. Then $\varphi(F(x)) \subset \,]-\infty, r[$. Put $O = \varphi^{-1}(]-\infty, r[)$, which is a weak* open subset containing $F(x)$. By the upper semicontinuity of F from line segments in X on S to X^* endowed with the weak* topology, for every $x' \in C$, there exists a neighborhood U of x such that $F(z) \subset O$, for every $z \in U \cap [x', x]$. That is, $F(z) \subset H$, for every $z \in U \cap [x', x]$. $\qquad\square$

It is not clear at the stage of development whether upper semicontinuity from line segments in C in Theorem 10.12 can be weakened to upper demicontinuity or to upper demicontinuity from line segments in C.

10.4 FIXED POINT THEORY

In this section we are interested to obtain a version of the Kakutani, Schauder, and Brouwer fixed point theorems. For this purpose, we develop some results on the continuity of the distance function and the marginal function.

Recall that if X is a real normed vector space, $x \in X$, and A is a nonempty subset of X, then

$$\text{dist}(x, A) = \inf_{z \in A} \|x - z\|$$

is called the distance between x and A, where $\|.\|$ is the norm of X. Obviously, the (real-valued) distance function $x \mapsto \text{dist}(x, A)$ is nonexpansive, and therefore continue. It is also convex whenever A is convex, see Aubin and Frankowska [23].

The situation is more complicated when A depends on x as the image of x by a set-valued mapping.

First, we establish the following result on the distance function generalizing the second item in Papageorgiou and Kyritsi-Yiallourou [139, Theorem 6.1.15].

Proposition 10.12. *Let X be a Hausdorff topological space, S a subset of X, (Y, d) a metric space, and $F : X \rightrightarrows Y$ a set-valued mapping with nonempty values. If F is upper semicontinuous on S, then for every $y \in Y$, the function $x \mapsto \text{dist}(y, F(x))$ is lower semicontinuous on S.*

Proof. Fix $y \in Y$ and let $a \in \mathbb{R}$. By Proposition 1.3, we have to prove that

$$\text{cl}(\{x \in X \mid \text{dist}(y, F(x)) \le a\}) \cap S = \{x \in S \mid \text{dist}(y, F(x)) \le a\}.$$

Let $\overline{x} \in \text{cl}(\{x \in X \mid \text{dist}(y, F(x)) \le a\}) \cap S$.

Take a net $(x_\alpha)_{\alpha \in \Lambda}$ in the set $\{x \in X \mid \text{dist}(y, F(x)) \le a\}$ converging to $\overline{x}$. Let $\varepsilon > 0$ be arbitrary, and put

$$V = \{y' \in Y \mid \text{dist}(y', F(\overline{x})) < \varepsilon\},$$

which is an open subset containing $F(\overline{x})$. By the upper semicontinuity of F at $\overline{x}$, there exists $\alpha_0 \in \Lambda$ such that $F(x_\alpha) \subset V$, for every $\alpha \ge \alpha_0$. For every $\alpha \ge \alpha_0$ and every $z \in F(x_\alpha)$, we remark that

$$\text{dist}(y, F(\overline{x})) \le d(y, z) + \text{dist}(z, F(\overline{x})) < d(y, z) + \varepsilon$$

and then, dist $(y, F(\overline{x})) \leq$ dist $(y, F(x_\alpha)) + \varepsilon \leq a + \varepsilon$. Since $\varepsilon > 0$ is arbitrary, then dist $(y, F(\overline{x})) \leq a$. $\qquad\square$

In the sequel, we need to establish the following generalization of the Berge maximum theorem which is useful in many applications, see Papageorgiou and Kyritsi-Yiallourou [139, Theorem 6.1.18].

Let X and Y be Hausdorff topological spaces, $F : X \rightrightarrows Y$ a set-valued mapping, and $\psi : X \times Y \to \overline{\mathbb{R}}$ a function. The marginal (or value) extended real-valued function $g : X \to \overline{\mathbb{R}}$ is defined by

$$g(x) = \sup_{y \in F(x)} \psi(x, y).$$

Theorem 10.13. *Let* X *and* Y *be two Hausdorff topological spaces,* S *a nonempty subset of* X, $F : X \rightrightarrows Y$ *a set-valued mapping, and* $\psi : X \times Y \to \overline{\mathbb{R}}$ *a function.*

1. *If* ψ *is lower semicontinuous on* $S \times Y$ *and* F *is lower semicontinuous on* S, *then the marginal function* $g : X \to \overline{\mathbb{R}}$ *is lower semicontinuous on* S.
2. *If* ψ *is upper semicontinuous on* $S \times Y$ *and there exists an open subset* U *containing* S *such that the function* $y \mapsto \psi(x, y)$ *is upper semicontinuous on* Y *for every* $x \in U$, *and* F *is upper semicontinuous on* S *and has nonempty compact values on* U, *then the marginal function* $g : X \to \overline{\mathbb{R}}$ *is upper semicontinuous on* S.

Proof. Let $a \in \mathbb{R}$. By Proposition 1.3, we have to prove that

$$\text{int}(\{x \in X \mid g(x) > a\}) \cap S = \{x \in S \mid g(x) > a\}.$$

Let $\overline{x} \in \{x \in S \mid g(x) > a\}$. Then by the definition of the marginal function g, let $\overline{y} \in F(\overline{x})$ such that $\psi(\overline{x}, \overline{y}) > a$. The function ψ being lower semicontinuous on $S \times Y$, then by Proposition 1.3, let $W_1 \times V$ be an open neighborhood of $(\overline{x}, \overline{y})$ such that

$$\psi(x, y) > a \quad \text{for all } x \in W_1, \text{ for all } y \in V.$$

Since F is lower semicontinuous on S and $\overline{x} \in F^-(V) \cap S$, then by Proposition 1.5, let W_2 be an open neighborhood of $\overline{x}$ such that $W_2 \subset F^-(V)$. Taking $W = W_1 \cap W_2$, we have $F(x) \cap V \neq \emptyset$, for every $x \in W$. Fix $y_x \in F(x) \cap V$, for every $x \in W$. Then $\psi(x, y_x) > a$ which implies that $g(x) > a$. It follows that $\overline{x} \in W \subset \{x \in X \mid g(x) > a\}$. This concludes the proof of the first statement of the theorem.

Let $a \in \mathbb{R}$. By Proposition 1.3, we have to prove that

$$\text{cl}(\{x \in X \mid g(x) \geq a\}) \cap S = \{x \in S \mid g(x) \geq a\}.$$

Let $\overline{x} \in \text{cl}(\{x \in X \mid g(x) \geq a\}) \cap S$ and take a net $(x_\alpha)_{\alpha \in \Lambda}$ in the set $\{x \in X \mid g(x) \geq a\}$ converging to $\overline{x}$. Since $\overline{x} \in S \subset U$, we may assume without loss of generality that $(x_\alpha)_{\alpha \in \Lambda}$ is in U. For every $\alpha \in \Lambda$, the function $y \mapsto \psi(x_\alpha, y)$ is upper semicontinuous on Y and therefore, by Weierstrass theorem, it attains its maximum on the compact set $F(x_\alpha)$. Let $y_\alpha \in F(x_\alpha)$ be such that $g(x_\alpha) = \psi(x_\alpha, y_\alpha)$, for every $\alpha \in \Lambda$.

The net $(y_\alpha)_{\alpha \in \Lambda}$ has a cluster point in $F(\overline{x})$. Indeed, suppose the contrary holds. Then the compactness of $F(\overline{x})$ yields the existence of an open set V containing $F(\overline{x})$ and $\alpha_0 \in \Lambda$ such that $y_\alpha \notin V$, for every $\alpha \geq \alpha_0$. The upper semicontinuity of F at $\overline{x}$ yields the existence of an open neighborhood W of $\overline{x}$ such that $F(x) \subset V$, for every $x \in W$. Since $(x_\alpha)_{\alpha \in \Lambda}$ is converging to $\overline{x}$, let $\alpha_1 \in \Lambda$ be such that $x_\alpha \in W$, for every $\alpha \geq \alpha_1$. Then $y_\alpha \in V$, for every $\alpha \geq \max\{\alpha_0, \alpha_1\}$. A contradiction.

Now, take $\overline{y} \in F(\overline{x})$ and $(y_\alpha)_{\alpha \in \Gamma}$ a subnet of $(y_\alpha)_{\alpha \in \Lambda}$ converging to $\overline{y}$. The subnet $(x_\alpha, y_\alpha)_{\alpha \in \Gamma}$ converges to $(\overline{x}, \overline{y}) \in S \times Y$ and satisfies $\psi(x_\alpha, y_\alpha) \geq a$, for every $\alpha \in \Gamma$. Since ψ is upper semicontinuous on $S \times Y$, then, we conclude by Proposition 1.3 that $\psi(\overline{x}, \overline{y}) \geq a$. It follows that $g(\overline{x}) \geq \psi(\overline{x}, \overline{y}) \geq a$ which completes the proof. $\qquad\qquad\square$

We formulate the following version of the Kakutani fixed point theorem.

Theorem 10.14. *Let X be a real normed vector space, C a nonempty, closed, and convex subset of X, and $D \subset C$ a self-segment-dense set in C. Suppose that $F : C \rightrightarrows X$ has the following conditions*

1. *F has nonempty convex values on C;*
2. *there exist a compact subset K of C and $y_0 \in D$ such that*

$$\text{dist}(y_0, F(x)) < \text{dist}(x, F(x)), \text{ for every } x \in C \setminus K;$$

3. *F is continuous on K and has closed values on K;*
4. *$F(x) \cap K \neq \emptyset$, for every $x \in K$.*

Then F has a fixed point.

Proof. We define the set-valued mapping $f : C \times C \to \mathbb{R}$ by

$$f(x, y) = \text{dist}(y, F(x)) - \text{dist}(x, F(x)) + [0, +\infty[.$$

Note that

$$f(x, y) = \left[\text{dist}(y, F(x)) - \text{dist}(x, F(x)), +\infty\right[.$$

We are now going to verify the conditions of Theorem 10.6. Condition (1) is verified since $f(x, x) = [0, +\infty[= \mathbb{R}_+$. Also, the convexity of $y \mapsto \text{dist}(y, F(x))$ on C yields easily the convexity of f in its second variable on C, for every $x \in C$. To verify condition (3), fix $x \in C$ and $y \in C$, and let V be an open subset of $\mathbb{R}$ such that $f(x, y) \subset V$. Let $\varepsilon > 0$ such that $\left[\text{dist}(y, F(x)) - \text{dist}(x, F(x)) - \varepsilon, +\infty\right[\subset V$. By lower semicontinuity of $y \mapsto \text{dist}(y, F(x)) - \text{dist}(x, F(x))$, let U be an open neighborhood of y such that

$$\text{dist}(y', F(x)) - \text{dist}(x, F(x)) \geq \text{dist}(y, F(x)) - \text{dist}(x, F(x)) - \varepsilon$$
$$\text{for all } y' \in U.$$

This means that $f(x, y') \subset V$, for every $y' \in U$, and then in particular, condition (3) is satisfied.

Condition (4) is obvious. To verify condition (5), fix $y \in C$ and let V be an open subset of C. Put $f^+(V, y) = \{x \in C \mid f(x, y) \subset V\}$ and let $x \in f^+(V, y) \cap K$. By Proposition 1.5, it suffices to show that $x \in \text{int}(f^+(V, y)) \cap K$. We have $f(x, y) \subset V$. As above, let $\varepsilon > 0$ such that $[\text{dist}(y, F(x)) - \text{dist}(x, F(x)) - \varepsilon, +\infty[\subset V$. The function $x \mapsto \text{dist}(y, F(x)) - \text{dist}(x, F(x))$ is lower semicontinuous on K. Indeed, by Proposition 10.12, the function $x \mapsto \text{dist}(y, F(x))$ is lower semicontinuous on K. Now, taking $\psi : C \times X \to \mathbb{R}$ defined by $\psi(x, y) = -\|y - x\|$, we have

$$g(x) = \sup_{y \in F(x)} \psi(x, y)$$
$$= \sup_{y \in F(x)} (-\|y - x\|) = - \inf_{y \in F(x)} (\|y - x\|) = -\text{dist}(x, F(x)).$$

It follows by Theorem 10.13 that the function $x \mapsto -\text{dist}(x, F(x))$ is lower semicontinuous on K.

Let U be an open neighborhood of x such that

$$\text{dist}(y, F(x')) - \text{dist}(x', F(x')) \geq \text{dist}(y, F(x)) - \text{dist}(x, F(x)) - \varepsilon$$
$$\text{for all } x' \in U.$$

This means that $f(x', y) \subset V$, for every $x' \in U$.

We conclude, by applying Theorem 10.6, that there exists $x_0 \in C$ such that $f(x_0, y) \subset \mathbb{R}_+$, for every $y \in C$. Then $\text{dist}(y, F(x_0)) - \text{dist}(x_0, F(x_0)) \geq 0$, for every $y \in C$. Note that $x_0 \in K$ and by taking $y \in F(x_0) \cap K$, we have $\text{dist}(x_0, F(x_0)) \leq 0$ which provide necessarily that $x_0 \in F(x_0)$. $\square$

In what follows, by applying Theorem 10.7, we derive the following version of the Schauder fixed point theorem and, in particular, of the Brouwer fixed point theorem.

Theorem 10.15. *Let X be a real normed vector space, C a nonempty, closed, and convex subset of X and $D \subset C$ a self-segment-dense set in C. Suppose that $f : C \to C$ has the following conditions*

1. *there exist a compact subset K of C and* $y_0 \in D$ *such that*

$$\| y_0 - f(x) \| < \| x - f(x) \|, \quad \text{for every } x \in C \setminus K;$$

2. *f is continuous on K.*

Then f has a fixed point.

Proof. Consider the bifunction $f : C \times C \to \mathbb{R}$ defined by

$$f(x, y) = \| y - f(x) \| - \| x - f(x) \| +]-\infty, 0]$$

Note that

$$f(x, y) =]-\infty, \| y - f(x) \| - \| x - f(x) \|].$$

We are now going to verify the conditions of Theorem 10.7. Condition (1) is verified since $f(x, x) =]-\infty, 0]$ and then, $0 \in f(x, x) \cap \mathbb{R}_+$, for every $x \in C$. Also, the convexity of $y \mapsto \| y - f(x) \|$ on C yields easily the concavity of f in its second variable on C, for every $x \in C$.

Now, fix $x \in C$ and $y \in C$, and let V be an open subset of $\mathbb{R}$ such that $f(x, y) \subset V$. Let $\varepsilon > 0$ such that

$$]-\infty, \| y - f(x) \| - \| x - f(x) \| + \varepsilon] \subset V.$$

By continuity of $y \mapsto \| y - f(x) \| - \| x - f(x) \|$, let U be an open neighborhood of y such that

$$\| y' - f(x) \| - \| x - f(x) \| \le \| y - f(x) \| - \| x - f(x) \| + \varepsilon \quad \text{for all } y' \in U.$$

This means that $f(x, y') \subset V$, for every $y' \in U$, and then in particular, condition (3) is satisfied.

Condition (4) is obvious. To verify condition (5), fix $y \in C$ and let V be an open subset of C. Put $f^+(V, y) = \{ x \in C \mid f(x, y) \subset V \}$ and let $x \in f^+(V, y) \cap K$. By Proposition 1.5, it suffices to show that $x \in \operatorname{int}(f^+(V, y)) \cap K$. We have $f(x, y) \subset V$. As above, let $\varepsilon > 0$ such that $]-\infty, \| y - f(x) \| - \| x - f(x) \| + \varepsilon] \subset V$ and by continuity of $x \mapsto \| y - f(x) \| - \| x - f(x) \|$, let U be an open neighborhood of x such that

$$\| y - f(x') \| - \| x' - f(x') \| \le \| y - f(x) \| - \| x - f(x) \| + \varepsilon \quad \text{for all } x' \in U.$$

This means that $f(x', y) \subset V$, for every $x' \in U$.

We conclude, by applying Theorem 10.7, that there exists $x_0 \in C$ such that $f(x_0, y) \cap \mathbb{R}_+ \ne \emptyset$, for every $y \in C$. Taking $y = f(x_0)$, we have $]-\infty, -\| x_0 - f(x_0) \|] \cap \mathbb{R}_+ \ne \emptyset$ which provide necessarily that $\| x_0 - f(x_0) \| \le 0$ and then, $f(x_0) = x_0$. $\qquad \square$

In our applications, we have focused our attention on weakening only semi-continuity. We remark that in both Theorem 10.14 and Theorem 10.15, the self-segment-dense set D does not play any role in the proofs and can be replaced merely by C. We refer to László and Viorel [115] for some applications that involve the weakened condition of self-segment-dense subsets to a generalized Debreu-Gale-Nikaido-type theorem and to a Nash equilibrium of noncooperative games. Furthermore, by introducing a suitable set of coerciveness, it is possible to carry out similar applications with weakened conditions of both semicontinuity and convexity.

NOTES

1. Jacques-Louis Lions (1928–2001) was a professor at the famous Collège de France from 1973 until his retirement in 1998. He made several important contributions to the qualitative theory of nonlinear partial differential equations. He received the SIAM's John von Neumann Lecture prize (1986) and the Japan Prize for Applied Mathematics (1991). Jacques-Louis Lions was president of the French Academy of Sciences from 1997 to 1999.
2. Guido Stampacchia (1922–1978) was an Italian mathematician, known for his work on the theory of variational inequalities, the calculus of variations and the theory of elliptic partial differential equations. The Stampacchia Medal, an international prize awarded every three years for contributions to the calculus of variations, has been established in 2003.
3. Maurice Fréchet (1878–1973) was a French mathematician who made major contributions to the topology of points sets and introduced the concept of metric space. Independently of Riesz, he discovered the representation theorem in the space of Lebesgue square integrable functions. Pavel Urysohn (1898–1924) was a Soviet mathematician who is best known for his contributions in dimension theory, and for developing Urysohn's metrization theorem and Urysohn's lemma, which are fundamental results in topology.

Chapter 11

Regularization and Numerical Methods for Equilibrium Problems

Contents

The energy of the mind is the essence of life.

Aristotle (384–322 B.C.)

Chapter points

- A proximal point algorithm based on Bregman functions associated to equilibrium problems is studied and its convergence to a solution is shown.
- We prove that the Tikhonov regularization method can be applied to pseudo-monotone equilibrium problems with strictly pseudo-monotone bifunctions as regularized equilibrium bifunctions, as well as strongly monotone bifunctions.
- We obtain a generalization of Berge's maximum theorem and developed new techniques in the qualitative analysis of quasi-hemivariational inequalities.
- We study the relationship between quasi-hemivariational inequalities and equilibrium problems.
- We apply the Tikhonov regularization method to quasi-hemivariational inequality problems.

Equilibrium Problems and Applications. https://doi.org/10.1016/B978-0-12-811029-4.00019-5

- A subgradient extragradient method for solving equilibrium problems is discussed together with some numerical results.

11.1 THE PROXIMAL POINT METHOD

The proximal point method was presented in [154] as a procedure for finding zeroes of monotone operators in Hilbert spaces. This procedure can be seen as a dynamic regularization of a (possibly ill-conditioned) original problem. The interesting feature of the proximal iteration is that convergence is achieved with bounded regularization parameters, which avoids the ill-conditioning of the iterations. The proximal point method has been an important tool for solving variational inequalities, and we focus on its application for solving the equilibrium problem in reflexive Banach spaces.

The regularization methods for equilibrium problems given in [94] and [96] involve powers of the norm. This poses the question of whether a more general kind of regularization can be used, and still obtain similar convergence results. Moreover, the use of a regularization function with a prescribed domain opens the way for the development of a method which penalizes infeasibility of the iterates. We address this question in the general setting of reflexive Banach spaces. First, we consider a Bregman proximal regularization of the equilibrium problem, and analyze existence and uniqueness of solutions. Second, we introduce a method based on Bregman regularizations, and establish conditions under which: (i) the method is asymptotically convergent, and (ii) all its weak accumulation points solve the original equilibrium problem.

The results of this section have been published in R. Burachik and G. Kassay [46].

11.1.1 Bregman Functions and Their Properties

The notion of Bregman function has its origin in [44] and this name was first used by Censor and Lent in [54]. Bregman functions have been extensively used for convex optimization algorithms in finite dimensional spaces. It has also been used for defining "generalized" versions of the proximal point method for finite dimensional spaces, for Hilbert spaces, and for Banach spaces. A useful tool for comparing the Bregman distance with the distance induced by the norm of the Banach space, leads to the notions of *modulus of convexity* and *total convexity* of f (the latter introduced in [47]).

Throughout the section, if not otherwise specified, X is a reflexive Banach space. Let $\varphi : X \to \mathbb{R} \cup \{+\infty\}$ be a convex, proper and lower semicontinuous function. Denote by $D := \mathrm{dom}\,(\varphi)$ its domain, and its interior by $\mathrm{int}\,D$. Assume from now on that $\mathrm{int}\,D \neq \emptyset$ and that φ is Gâteaux differentiable on $\mathrm{int}\,D$. The *Bregman distance* with respect to φ is the function $D_\varphi : D \times \mathrm{int}\,D \to \mathbb{R}$ defined by:

$$D_\varphi(z, x) := \varphi(z) - \varphi(x) - \langle \nabla\varphi(x), z - x \rangle, \tag{11.1}$$

where $\nabla\varphi(\cdot)$ is the Gâteaux differential of φ defined in int D. The function $D_\varphi(\cdot, \cdot)$ is not a distance in the usual sense of the term (in general, it is not symmetric and does not satisfy the triangular inequality). However, there is a "three point property" which takes the place of this inequality in the proofs.

Proposition 11.1. *Given $x \in D$, $y, z \in int\, D$, the following equality is straightforward*

$$\langle\nabla\varphi(y) - \nabla\varphi(z), z - x\rangle = D_\varphi(x, y) - D_\varphi(x, z) - D_\varphi(z, y). \qquad (11.2)$$

In order to state our assumptions on the function φ, we need to recall the concept of total convexity.

Recall that $\mathbb{R}_+$ denotes the set of nonnegative real numbers and $\mathbb{R}_{++} := \mathbb{R}_+ \setminus \{0\}$. Following [48], we define the *modulus of convexity* of φ, $\nu_\varphi : int\, D \times \mathbb{R}_+ \to \mathbb{R}_+$ by

$$\nu_\varphi(z, t) := \inf\{D_\varphi(x, z) : \|x - z\| = t\}. \qquad (11.3)$$

The function φ is said to be *totally convex* in int D if and only if $\nu_\varphi(z, t) > 0$ for all $z \in int\, D$ and $t > 0$. The result below, which will be useful in the sequel, has been proved in [48].

Proposition 11.2. *Let $z \in int\, D$. The function $\nu_\varphi(z, \cdot)$ is strictly increasing on $\mathbb{R}_{++}$, i.e., if $0 < \alpha < \beta$ then $\nu_\varphi(z, \alpha) < \nu_\varphi(z, \beta)$.*

In finite dimensional spaces total convexity is equivalent to strict convexity. Totally convex functions are always strictly convex, but the reverse implication does not hold in general if the space is infinite dimensional. For instance, in l^p there exist strictly convex functions which are not totally convex (see [48]). Uniformly convex functions are totally convex (see [48]), but in the spaces L^p and l^p with $1 < p < 2$ the function $\varphi(x) = \|x\|_p^p$ is totally convex (see [48]), while it is not uniformly convex. We will see later on that total convexity also turns out to be a key property in our convergence analysis.

Now we are ready to state the following basic assumption on φ.

B_1: The *right* level sets of $D_\varphi(y, \cdot)$:

$$S_{y,\alpha} := \{z \in int\, D : D_\varphi(y, z) \leq \alpha\}$$

are bounded for all $\alpha \geq 0$ and for all $y \in D$.

B_2: (total convexity on bounded subsets) The function φ is *totally convex on bounded subsets*, that is, for any bounded set $C \subset int\, D$, and any $t \in \mathbb{R}_{++}$, it holds that

$$\inf_{z \in C} \nu_\varphi(z, t) > 0. \qquad (11.4)$$

B_3: If $\{x^k\} \subset int\, D$ and $\{y^k\} \subset int\, D$ are bounded sequences such that $\lim_{k \to \infty} \|x^k - y^k\| = 0$, then

$$\lim_{k \to \infty} \left(\nabla\varphi(x^k) - \nabla\varphi(y^k)\right) = 0.$$

Condition B_3 has been widely used in the literature (see, for instance, [50, Theorem 4.7(a)]).

The lemma below was proved in [49, Lemma 2.1.2, page 67].

Lemma 11.1. *Assume that D_φ verifies B_2. Suppose that $\{x^k\} \subset D$ and that the sequence $\{y^k\} \subset int\, D$ is bounded. Assume that*

$$\lim_{k \to \infty} D_\varphi(x^k, y^k) = 0.$$

Then $(x^k - y^k) \to 0$ and hence $\{x^k\}$ is also bounded and all weak accumulation points of $\{y^k\}$ and $\{x^k\}$ must coincide. If, additionally, $\{x^k\} \subset int\, D$ and D_φ verifies B_3, then we have

$$\lim_{k \to \infty} \|\nabla\varphi(x^k) - \nabla\varphi(y^k)\| = 0.$$

Next let us recall the concept of duality map.

Definition 11.1. Consider $\varphi : X \to \mathbb{R}$ defined by

$$\varphi(x) = \frac{1}{2}\|x\|^2.$$

The *duality mapping* $J : X \rightrightarrows X^*$ is the subdifferential $\partial\varphi$ of φ.

The result below related to single-valuedness and continuity of the duality map J can be found, e.g., in [24, Theorem 1.2].

Theorem 11.1. *Let X be a Banach space. If the dual space X^* is strictly convex, then the normalized duality mapping $J : X \to X^*$ is single-valued and demicontinuous (i.e., continuous from the strong topology of X to the weak* topology of X^*). If X^* is uniformly convex, then J is uniformly continuous on every bounded subset of X.*

The next proposition establishes the continuity properties of $\nabla\varphi$ and its proof can be found in [142, Proposition 2.8, page 19].

Proposition 11.3. *The map $\nabla\varphi : int\, D \to X^*$ is demicontinuous in $int\, D$. In other words, it is continuous at any $x \in int\, D$ from the strong topology of X to the weak topology of X^*. In particular, if X^* is strictly convex and $\varphi = (1/2)\|\cdot\|^2$, then the duality mapping $J = \partial\varphi : X \to X^*$ is demicontinuous from X to X^*.*

11.1.2 The Basic Hypotheses for the Equilibrium Problem

In what follows we assume the next three basic properties on the equilibrium problem. Let X be a Banach space, $K \subset X$ a closed and convex set, and $f : K \times K \to \mathbb{R}$ a bifunction such that

(P1) $f(x, x) = 0$ for all $x \in K$.

(P2) $f(\cdot, y) : K \to \mathbb{R}$ is upper hemicontinuous for all $y \in K$, i.e., for all $x, z \in K$

$$\limsup_{t \downarrow 0} f(tz + (1 - t)x, y) \le f(x, y).$$

(P3) $f(x, \cdot) : K \to \mathbb{R}$ is convex and lower semicontinuous for all $x \in K$.

In order to analyze existence and uniqueness of equilibrium problems, we shall consider the following additional assumptions on f.

(P4) $f(x, y) + f(y, x) \le 0$ for all $x, y \in K$.

(P4°) There exists $\theta \ge 0$ such that $f(x, y) + f(y, x) \le \theta \langle \nabla \varphi(x) - \nabla \varphi(y), x - y \rangle$ for all $x, y \in K$.

(P4•) There exists $\theta \ge 0$ such that $f(x, y) + f(y, x) \le \theta \|x - y\|^2$ for all $x, y \in K$.

(P5) For any sequence $\{x^n\} \subset K$ satisfying $\lim_{n \to \infty} \|x^n\| = +\infty$, there exists $u \in K$ and $n_0 \in \mathbb{N}$ such that $f(x^n, u) \le 0$ for all $n \ge n_0$.

Remark 11.1. Condition (P4°) is weaker than the classical monotonicity condition of f (see condition (P4)) since the right-hand side of condition (P4°) is nonnegative. If X^* is strictly convex and $\varphi = (1/2)\| \cdot \|^2$, then condition (P4°) reduces to

$$f(x, y) + f(y, x) \le \theta \langle J(x) - J(y), x - y \rangle.$$

In particular, if X is a Hilbert space, then this condition reduces to the (generalized) monotonicity condition (P4•) in [96]. Indeed, for this particular case $J = I$ where I is the identity operator.

11.1.3   A Bregman Regularization for the Equilibrium Problem

Let $K \subset X$ be a closed and convex set and let $f : K \times K \to \mathbb{R}$ be a bifunction such that conditions (P1), (P2) and (P3) hold. Take φ verifying the following assumption:

H_2: $K \subset \text{int } D$.

Fix $\gamma > 0$ and $\bar{x} \in K \subset \text{int } D$. The regularization of f will be defined as $\tilde{f} : K \times K \to \mathbb{R}$ given by

$$\tilde{f}(x, y) = f(x, y) + \gamma \langle \nabla \varphi(x) - \nabla \varphi(\bar{x}), y - x \rangle. \tag{11.5}$$

Consider a bifunction $g : K \times K \to \mathbb{R}$. Define the *resolvent operator induced by the Bregman function* φ as the set-valued map $\text{Res}_g^\varphi : X \rightrightarrows K$ given by

$$\text{Res}_g^\varphi(x) := \{z \in K \; : \; g(z, y) + \langle \nabla \varphi(z) - \nabla \varphi(x), y - z \rangle \ge 0, \, \forall \, y \in K\}.$$

This definition and (11.5) imply that $\hat{x}$ is a solution of EP($\tilde{f}, K$) if and only if $\hat{x} \in \text{Res}_{\frac{1}{\gamma} f}^\varphi(\bar{x})$.

The next result establishes basic properties of the regularized function $\tilde{f}$.

Proposition 11.4. *Take $\bar{x} \in K$ and suppose that H_2 holds and that f satisfies conditions (P1)–(P3) and (P4°) with $\theta < \gamma$. Then $\tilde{f}$ satisfies conditions (P1), (P2), (P3) and (P4). Moreover, if for every sequence $\{x^n\} \subset K$ such that $\lim_{n\to\infty} \|x^n\| = \infty$, we have*

(P6) $\liminf\limits_{n\to\infty} \left[f(\bar{x}, x^n) + (\gamma - \theta)\langle \nabla\varphi(\bar{x}) - \nabla\varphi(x^n), \bar{x} - x^n \rangle \right] > 0,$

then $\tilde{f}$ satisfies condition (P5).

Proof. It is clear that $\tilde{f}$ satisfies condition (P1). Since $y \mapsto \langle \nabla\varphi(x) - \nabla\varphi(\bar{x}), y - x \rangle$ is convex and continuous, it follows that $\tilde{f}$ satisfies condition (P3). To show that condition (P2) holds for $\tilde{f}$, we will show that the map

$$x \mapsto \langle \nabla\varphi(x) - \nabla\varphi(\bar{x}), y - x \rangle$$

is continuous at every $x \in K$. To this end let $\{x^n\} \subset K$ be a sequence converging strongly to $x \in K$. Then $\langle \nabla\varphi(\bar{x}), x^n \rangle \to \langle \nabla\varphi(\bar{x}), x \rangle$, while $\langle \nabla\varphi(x^n), y - x^n \rangle \to \langle \nabla\varphi(x), y - x \rangle$ follows by Proposition 11.3. Thus $\langle \nabla\varphi(x^n) - \nabla\varphi(\bar{x}), y - x^n \rangle \to \langle \nabla\varphi(x) - \nabla\varphi(\bar{x}), y - x \rangle$ and we are done. We claim now that $\tilde{f}$ satisfies condition (P4). Indeed, by condition (P4°) we get that

$$\tilde{f}(x, y) + \tilde{f}(y, x) = f(x, y) + f(y, x) - \gamma\langle \nabla\varphi(y) - \nabla\varphi(x), y - x \rangle$$
$$\leq (\theta - \gamma)\langle \nabla\varphi(y) - \nabla\varphi(x), y - x \rangle \leq 0.$$

Next we show that $\tilde{f}$ satisfies condition (P5). We have by condition (P4°) and (11.5) that

$$\tilde{f}(x^n, \bar{x}) = f(x^n, \bar{x}) + \gamma\langle \nabla\varphi(x^n) - \nabla\varphi(\bar{x}), \bar{x} - x^n \rangle$$
$$= f(x^n, \bar{x}) - \gamma\langle \nabla\varphi(\bar{x}) - \nabla\varphi(x^n), \bar{x} - x^n \rangle$$
$$\leq -f(\bar{x}, x^n) - (\gamma - \theta)\langle \nabla\varphi(\bar{x}) - \nabla\varphi(x^n), \bar{x} - x^n \rangle$$
$$= -(f(\bar{x}, x^n) + (\gamma - \theta)\langle \nabla\varphi(\bar{x}) - \nabla\varphi(x^n), \bar{x} - x^n \rangle). \qquad (11.6)$$

By assumption there exists n_0 such that the expression between parentheses is nonnegative for all $n \geq n_0$. This implies that condition (P5) holds for $\tilde{f}$. $\qquad \square$

Corollary 11.1. *If f satisfies condition (P4°) with $\theta < \gamma$, and assuming either*

(i) *K is bounded, or*
(ii) *X^* is strictly convex and $\varphi = (1/2)\| \cdot \|^2$,*

then $\tilde{f}$ satisfies condition (P5).

Proof. Using Proposition 5.5 it is enough to check that condition (P6) holds under (i) or (ii). Condition (i) trivially implies condition (P6). Hence it is enough to prove that (ii) implies condition (P6). Note that in this case $\nabla\varphi = J$.

By Theorem 11.1 we also know that J is single-valued and demicontinuous. Take a sequence $\{x^n\}$ in K such that $\|x^n\| \to \infty$ and denote $\Delta_n = \langle J(\bar{x}) - J(x^n), \bar{x} - x^n \rangle$. Our assumptions imply that

$$\Delta_n \geq (\|\bar{x}\| - \|x^n\|)^2 > 0, \quad \text{for } n \text{ large enough.} \tag{11.7}$$

We claim that $\operatorname{dom} \partial f(\bar{x}, \cdot) \cap K \neq \emptyset$. Indeed, the subdifferential of a proper, lower semicontinuous and convex function is maximal monotone in any Banach space (see, e.g., [153]). If we extend the function $f(\bar{x}, \cdot)$ to the whole space X by defining it as $+\infty$ outside K, then we have that $\partial f(\bar{x}, \cdot)$ is maximal monotone. On the other hand, the operator T defined as $T(x) = \emptyset$ for all $x \in X$ is certainly not maximal monotone, because its graph is monotone and strictly contained in the graph of every nontrivial maximal monotone operator. Thus $\operatorname{dom} \partial f(\bar{x}, \cdot)$ should be nonempty. Since $\partial f(\bar{x}, z) = \emptyset$ for every $z \notin K$, it follows that $\operatorname{dom} \partial f(\bar{x}, \cdot) \cap K \neq \emptyset$ must hold. Hence the claim is true and there exists $v \in \partial f(\bar{x}, \hat{x})$ for some $\hat{x} \in K$. Therefore, we can write the subgradient inequality

$$\begin{aligned} f(\bar{x}, x^n) &\geq f(\bar{x}, \hat{x}) + \langle v, x^n - \hat{x} \rangle \\ &= f(\bar{x}, \hat{x}) - \langle v, \hat{x} \rangle + \langle v, x^n \rangle \\ &\geq A - B\|x^n\|, \end{aligned} \tag{11.8}$$

where $A := f(\bar{x}, \hat{x}) - \langle v, \hat{x} \rangle$ and $B := \|v\|$. Altogether, we have

$$\liminf_{n \to \infty} \left[f(\bar{x}, x^n) + (\gamma - \theta)\Delta_n \right]$$
$$\geq \liminf_{n \to \infty} \left[A - B\|x^n\| + (\gamma - \theta)(\|\bar{x}\| - \|x^n\|)^2 \right] = +\infty,$$

and condition (P6) is established. By Proposition 11.4 we conclude that condition (P5) holds in this case. $\qquad \square$

The next result establishes the existence and uniqueness of the solution of $\mathrm{EP}(\tilde{f}, K)$.

Corollary 11.2. *Let all basic assumptions in Proposition 11.4 be valid. Then the following assertions hold:*

(i) *If condition (P6) stated in Proposition 11.4 holds, then $\mathrm{EP}(\tilde{f}, K)$ admits at least one solution.*

(ii) *If φ is strictly convex, then $\mathrm{EP}(\tilde{f}, K)$ admits at most one solution.*

Altogether, if condition (P6) holds and φ is strictly convex, then $\mathrm{EP}(\tilde{f}, K)$ has a unique solution.

Proof. From Proposition 11.4 we have that $\tilde{f}$ satisfies condition (P5). Using now [93, Theorem 4.3] we obtain that $\mathrm{EP}(\tilde{f}, K)$ has a solution. This proves (i). For proving (ii), assume that both x' and x'' solve $\mathrm{EP}(\tilde{f}, K)$. Hence

$$0 \leq \tilde{f}(x', x'') = f(x', x'') + \gamma \langle \nabla\varphi(x') - \nabla\varphi(\bar{x}), x'' - x' \rangle, \tag{11.9}$$

$$0 \le \tilde{f}(x'', x') = f(x'', x') + \gamma \langle \nabla \varphi(x'') - \nabla \varphi(\bar{x}), x' - x'' \rangle. \tag{11.10}$$

Adding (11.9) and (11.10), and using (P4°) we get that

$$
\begin{aligned}
0 &\le f(x', x'') + f(x'', x') - \gamma \langle \nabla \varphi(x'') - \nabla \varphi(x'), x'' - x' \rangle \\
&\le (\theta - \gamma) \langle \nabla \varphi(x'') - \nabla \varphi(x'), x'' - x' \rangle.
\end{aligned}
\tag{11.11}
$$

Since $\theta - \gamma < 0$ and $\nabla \varphi$ is strictly monotone, we obtain from (11.11) that $x' = x''$, as asserted. The last statement is a direct combination of (i) and (ii). $\square$

In the following result, we assume that φ is *coercive*, i.e., $\displaystyle \lim_{\|x\| \to \infty} \frac{\varphi(x)}{\|x\|} = +\infty$.

Corollary 11.3. (see [151, Lemma 1, page 130]) *Let φ be a coercive and Gâteaux differentiable function. If the bifunction $g : K \times K \to \mathbb{R}$ satisfies conditions (P1)–(P4), then $\operatorname{Res}_g^\varphi(\bar{x}) \ne \emptyset$ for every $\bar{x} \in K$.*

Proof. Note that all assumptions of Corollary 11.2 hold. Therefore, it is enough to prove that condition (P6) holds for a coercive φ. Take a sequence $\{x^n\}$ in K such that $\|x^n\| \to \infty$ and denote $\Delta_n := \langle \nabla \varphi(\bar{x}) - \nabla \varphi(x^n), \bar{x} - x^n \rangle$. Using the convexity of φ we can write

$$
\begin{aligned}
\Delta_n &= \langle \nabla \varphi(\bar{x}), \bar{x} - x^n \rangle - \langle \nabla \varphi(x^n), \bar{x} - x^n \rangle \\
&\ge \langle \nabla \varphi(\bar{x}), \bar{x} - x^n \rangle + \left[\varphi(x^n) - \varphi(\bar{x}) \right] \\
&= \|x^n\| \left[\frac{\langle \nabla \varphi(\bar{x}), \bar{x} - x^n \rangle}{\|x^n\|} + \frac{\varphi(x^n)}{\|x^n\|} - \frac{\varphi(\bar{x})}{\|x^n\|} \right].
\end{aligned}
\tag{11.12}
$$

On the other hand, we can write (as in the proof of Corollary 11.1(ii)),

$$f(\bar{x}, x^n) \ge A - B \|x^n\|, \tag{11.13}$$

where A and B are as in the proof of Corollary 11.1(ii). Combining (11.12) and (11.13) and re-arranging the resulting expression we have

$$
\begin{aligned}
&\liminf_{n \to \infty} \left[f(\bar{x}, x^n) + (\gamma - \theta) \Delta_n \right] \\
&\ge \liminf_{n \to \infty} \left[A - B \|x^n\| + (\gamma - \theta) \|x^n\| \left(\frac{\langle \nabla \varphi(\bar{x}), \bar{x} - x^n \rangle}{\|x^n\|} + \frac{\varphi(x^n)}{\|x^n\|} - \frac{\varphi(\bar{x})}{\|x^n\|} \right) \right] \\
&= \liminf_{n \to \infty} \left[A + (\gamma - \theta) \|x^n\| \right. \\
&\qquad \times \left. \left(\frac{\langle \nabla \varphi(\bar{x}), \bar{x} - x^n \rangle}{\|x^n\|} + \frac{\varphi(x^n)}{\|x^n\|} - \frac{\varphi(\bar{x})}{\|x^n\|} - \frac{B}{(\gamma - \theta)} \right) \right].
\end{aligned}
$$

The coercivity assumption implies that the expression between the inner brackets tends to infinity, and hence condition (P6) is established. $\square$

Remark 11.2. The previous corollary proves that condition (P6) is weaker than the coercivity assumption. Moreover, condition (P6) is strictly weaker than coercivity, since there exist Bregman functions which are not coercive but still satisfy (P6). Let $X = \mathbb{R}$, $K \subset (0, +\infty)$ and consider $\varphi(x) = x - \log x + 1$. This function is not coercive since $\lim_{x \to +\infty} \varphi(x)/x < \infty$. However, it is easy to verify from the definition that (P6) holds provided $\gamma - \theta$ is large enough. Indeed, take $t_n \to \infty$. With the notation used in Corollary 11.3 with $\bar{t}$ instead of $\bar{x}$ and t_n instead of x^n, we can write

$$\left[f(\bar{t}, t_n) + (\gamma - \theta)\Delta_n \right]$$
$$\geq A - Bt_n + (\gamma - \theta)\left[(\varphi_2'(\bar{t}) - \varphi_2'(t_n))(\bar{t} - t_n) \right]$$
$$= A - Bt_n + (\gamma - \theta)\frac{(\bar{t} - t_n)^2}{\bar{t}t_n}$$
$$= A + t_n \left[\frac{(\gamma - \theta)}{\bar{t}}(1 - \frac{\bar{t}}{t_n})^2 - B \right].$$

Note now that the expression between parentheses is positive for large enough $\gamma - \theta$ and n, hence condition (P6) holds in this case. How large should be $\gamma - \theta$ depends also on the bifunction f, through the number B (see the proof of Corollary 11.1).

Remark 11.3. Assuming condition (P4) and strict convexity of φ, Lemma 2(i) in [151] proves that EP($\tilde{f}$, K) has at most one solution. Since condition (P4°) is weaker than condition (P4), the uniqueness result in [151, Lemma 2(i)] can be concluded from Corollary 11.2(ii).

Corollary 11.4. *Let all assumptions in Proposition 11.4 be valid. Assume that X^* is strictly convex and $\varphi = (1/2)\| \cdot \|^2$. Then EP($\tilde{f}$, K) has a unique solution.*

Proof. Note that $J = \partial\varphi$ is strictly monotone by Petryshyn's theorem [140]. Hence the claim follows from Corollary 11.2. □

11.1.4 A Bregman Proximal Method for the Equilibrium Problem

Assume from now on that φ is strictly convex, that all the hypotheses of Proposition 11.4 hold, and furthermore that condition (P6) is satisfied.

Take a sequence of regularization parameters $\{\gamma_k\} \subset (\theta, \bar{\gamma}]$, for some $\bar{\gamma} > 0$. Based on the regularized problem (11.5) and the existence and uniqueness of its solution (Corollaries 11.2 and 11.4), we construct the following algorithm for solving EP(f, K). Choose $x_0 \in K$ and construct the sequence $\{x_k\} \subset K$ as follows. Given $x^k \in K$, x^{k+1} is the unique solution of the problem EP(f_k, K), where $f_k : K \times K \to \mathbb{R}$ is given by

$$f_k(x, y) = f(x, y) + \gamma_k \langle \nabla\varphi(x) - \nabla\varphi(x^k), y - x \rangle. \tag{11.14}$$

Theorem 11.2. *Let X be a reflexive Banach space and consider $EP(f, K)$. For all $x_0 \in K$, we have the following.*

(i) *The sequence $\{x^k\}$ generated by the proximal point algorithm is well defined;*

(ii) *If, additionally, B_1 and B_2 hold for D_φ and $S^d(f, K) \neq \emptyset$, then the sequence $\{x^k\}$ is bounded and $\lim_{k \to \infty} \|x^{k+1} - x^k\| = 0$;*

(iii) *under the assumptions of item (ii) and assuming either*
    (iiia) X^* uniformly convex and $\varphi = (1/2)\| \cdot \|^2$, or
    (iiib) D_φ satisfies B_3,
the sequence $\{x^k\}$ is an asymptotically solving sequence for $EP(f, K)$, i.e.,

$$0 \leq \liminf_{k \to \infty} f(x^k, y), \ \forall y \in K. \tag{11.15}$$

(iv) *if additionally $f(\cdot, y)$ is weakly upper semicontinuous for all $y \in K$, then all weak cluster points of $\{x^k\}$ solve $EP(f, K)$.*

Proof. Item (i) is obvious by Corollary 11.2. For item (ii) take an arbitrary $x^* \in S^d(f, K)$. Since x^{k+1} solves $EP(f_k, K)$, one has

$$0 \leq f_k(x^{k+1}, x^*) = f(x^{k+1}, x^*) + \gamma_k \langle \nabla\varphi(x^{k+1}) - \nabla\varphi(x^k), x^* - x^{k+1} \rangle,$$

and since $f(x^{k+1}, x^*) \leq 0$ one gets

$$\langle \nabla\varphi(x^{k+1}) - \nabla\varphi(x^k), x^* - x^{k+1} \rangle \geq 0. \tag{11.16}$$

Now using (11.2) (the "three point identity") for Bregman distances we may write

$$\langle \nabla\varphi(x^{k+1}) - \nabla\varphi(x^k), x^* - x^{k+1} \rangle$$
$$= D_\varphi(x^*, x^k) - D_\varphi(x^{k+1}, x^k) - D_\varphi(x^*, x^{k+1}),$$

which, together with (11.16) leads to

$$D_\varphi(x^{k+1}, x^k) + D_\varphi(x^*, x^{k+1}) \leq D_\varphi(x^*, x^k). \tag{11.17}$$

It follows that the sequence $\{D_\varphi(x^*, x^k)\}$ is decreasing, and being nonnegative, it converges. In particular it is bounded; and by condition B_1 we conclude that the sequence $\{x^k\}$ is also bounded. By (11.17),

$$0 \leq D_\varphi(x^{k+1}, x^k) \leq D_\varphi(x^*, x^k) - D_\varphi(x^*, x^{k+1}) \tag{11.18}$$

and since the rightmost expression in (11.18) converges to 0 we get that

$$\lim_{k \to \infty} D_\varphi(x^{k+1}, x^k) = 0.$$

Now we can apply Lemma 11.1 to the sequences $\{x^k\}$ and $\{x^{k+1}\}$, because the sequence $\{x^k\}$ is bounded and D_φ verifies B_2, to conclude that $\lim_{k\to\infty} \|x^{k+1} - x^k\| = 0$.

For item (iii) under assumption (iiia), observe that X^* being uniformly convex, the normalized duality map J is uniformly continuous on bounded subsets of X (by Theorem 11.1), and therefore,

$$\lim_{k\to\infty} \|Jx^{k+1} - Jx^k\| = 0. \tag{11.19}$$

Now fix any $y \in K$. Since x^{k+1} solves EP(f_k, K), we have

$$0 \le f(x^{k+1}, y) + \gamma_k \langle Jx^{k+1} - Jx^k, y - x^{k+1} \rangle$$
$$\le f(x^{k+1}, y) + \gamma_k \|Jx^{k+1} - Jx^k\| \|y - x^{k+1}\|. \tag{11.20}$$

Since $\{\gamma_k\}$ is bounded by $\bar{\gamma}$ and $\{x^k\}$ is bounded by (ii), we obtain by (11.19) that

$$0 \le \liminf_{k\to\infty} f(x^k, y), \quad \forall y \in K, \tag{11.21}$$

and hence $\{x^k\}$ is an asymptotically solving sequence for EP(f, K).

For item (iii) under assumption (iiib), we have that B_2^* and Lemma 11.1 yield

$$\lim_{k\to\infty} \|\nabla\varphi(x^{k+1}) - \nabla\varphi(x^k)\| = 0. \tag{11.22}$$

Now fix any $y \in K$. Since x^{k+1} solves EP(f_k, K), we have

$$0 \le f(x^{k+1}, y) + \gamma_k \langle \nabla\varphi(x^{k+1}) - \nabla\varphi(x^k), y - x^{k+1} \rangle$$
$$\le f(x^{k+1}, y) + \gamma_k \|\nabla\varphi(x^{k+1}) - \nabla\varphi(x^k)\| \|y - x^{k+1}\|. \tag{11.23}$$

Since $\{\gamma_k\}$ is bounded by $\bar{\gamma}$ and $\{x^k\}$ is bounded by (ii), we obtain by (11.22) that

$$0 \le \liminf_{k\to\infty} f(x^k, y), \quad \forall y \in K, \tag{11.24}$$

and hence $\{x^k\}$ is an asymptotically solving sequence for EP(f, K).

The proof of item (iv) is the same as in [96, Theorem 1(iv)]. We reproduce it here for completeness. By (ii) the sequence $\{x^k\}$ has weak cluster points, all of which belong to the (weakly closed and convex set) K. Let $\hat{x}$ be a weak cluster point of $\{x^k\}$, and let $\{x^{k_j}\}$ be a subsequence weakly converging to $\hat{x}$. Since $f(\cdot, y)$ is weakly upper semicontinuous, we can write

$$f(\hat{x}, y) \ge \limsup_j f(x^{k_j}, y) \ge 0, \quad \forall y \in K,$$

which yields $\hat{x} \in S(f, K)$. $\qquad\qquad\qquad\square$

Proposition 11.5. *Assume that* $\nabla\varphi$ *is weak-to-weak continuous and that the hypotheses of Theorem 11.2 hold. If* $S(f, K) = S^d(f, K)$, *then the sequence* $\{x^k\}$ *converges weakly to a solution of the problem EP(f, K).*

Proof. By Theorem 11.2 it suffices to check that there exists only one weak cluster point of $\{x^k\}$. Let x' and x'' be two weak cluster points of $\{x^k\}$ and consider the subsequences $\{x^{i_k}\}$ and $\{x^{j_k}\}$ converging weakly to x' and x'', respectively. By item (iv) of Theorem 11.2 it follows that both x' and x'' belong to $S(f, K) = S^d(f, K)$. By (11.17) both $D_\varphi(x', x^k)$ and $D_\varphi(x'', x^k)$ are convergent, say to $\sigma \geq 0$ and $\mu \geq 0$. Taking limits on both sides of the relation

$$\langle \nabla\varphi(x^{i_k}) - \nabla\varphi(x^{j_k}), x' - x'' \rangle$$
$$= [D_\varphi(x', x^{j_k}) - D_\varphi(x', x^{i_k})] - [D_\varphi(x'', x^{j_k}) - D_\varphi(x'', x^{i_k})],$$

we obtain:

$$\langle \nabla\varphi(x') - \nabla\varphi(x''), x' - x'' \rangle = [\sigma - \sigma] - [\mu - \mu] = 0,$$

and hence $x' = x''$ by the strict monotonicity of $\nabla\varphi$. $\qquad\square$

The proof of the next result follows directly from the last proposition.

Corollary 11.5. *Suppose that* X *has a weak-to-weak continuous normalized duality mapping* J. *Assume that the hypotheses of Theorem 11.2 with (iiia) hold. If* $S(f, K) = S^d(f, K)$, *then the sequence* $\{x^k\}$ *converges weakly to a solution of the problem EP(f, K).*

11.2 THE TIKHONOV REGULARIZATION METHOD

Let C be a nonempty, closed, and convex subset of a real Banach space E and let $f : C \times C \longrightarrow \mathbb{R}$ be a bifunction satisfying $f(x, x) = 0$, for every $x \in C$. Such a bifunction f is called an *equilibrium bifunction*.

Recall that an *equilibrium problem* in the sense of Blum, Muu, and Oettli (see [42,133]) is a problem of the form:

$$\text{find } x^* \in C \text{ such that } f(x^*, y) \geq 0 \quad \forall y \in C, \tag{EP}$$

where its set of solutions is denoted by $SEP(C, f)$.

Equilibrium problems are in relationship with quasi-hemivariational inequalities. Recall that if E is a real Banach space which is continuously embedded in $L^p(\Omega; \mathbb{R}^n)$, for some $1 < p < +\infty$ and $n \geq 1$, where Ω is a bounded domain in $\mathbb{R}^m$, $m \geq 1$, then a *quasi-hemivariational inequality* is a problem of the form:

$$\text{find } u \in E \text{ and } z \in A(u) \text{ such that}$$
$$\langle z, v \rangle + h(u) J^0(iu; iv) - \langle Fu, v \rangle \geq 0 \quad \forall v \in E,$$

where i is the canonical injection of E into $L^p(\Omega; \mathbb{R}^n)$, $A : E \rightrightarrows E^*$ is a nonlinear multi-valued mapping, $F : E \to E^*$ is a nonlinear operator, $J : L^p(\Omega; \mathbb{R}^n) \to \mathbb{R}$ is a locally Lipschitz functional, and $h : E \to \mathbb{R}$ is a given nonnegative functional.

Consider the following quasi-hemivariational inequality:

$$\text{find } u \in C \text{ and } z \in A(u) \text{ such that}$$

$$\langle z, v - u \rangle + h(u) J^0(iu; iv - iu) - \langle Fu, v - u \rangle \geq 0 \quad \forall v \in C, \qquad \text{(QHVI)}$$

where its set of solutions is denoted by $\text{SQHVI}(C, A)$. Note that in the special case when C is the whole space E, the above two formulations of quasi-hemivariational inequalities are one and the same.

Regularization methods, which are widely used in convex optimization and variational inequalities, have been also considered for equilibrium problems. The *proximal point method* and the *Tikhonov regularization method* are fundamental regularization techniques for handling ill-posed problems.

In this section, we first deal with the Tikhonov regularization method for *pseudo-monotone equilibrium problems*. Under weakened conditions of upper semicontinuity of bifunctions in their first variable on a subset and of convexity, we prove that strictly pseudo-monotone bifunctions can be also used as regularization bifunctions as well as strongly monotone bifunctions. We extend Berge's maximum theorem and develop some results in the qualitative analysis of quasi-hemivariational inequalities to establish the relationship between quasi-hemivariational inequality problems and equilibrium problems. We also give examples and apply the Tikhonov regularization method to quasi-hemivariational inequalities.

11.2.1 Auxiliary Results

Let X be Hausdorff topological space, $x \in X$ and $f : X \longrightarrow \mathbb{R}$ be a function. Recall that f is said to be

1. *upper semicontinuous* at x if for every $\epsilon > 0$, there exists an open neighborhood U of x such that

$$f(y) \leq f(x) + \epsilon \quad \forall y \in U;$$

2. *lower semicontinuous* at x if for every $\epsilon > 0$, there exists an open neighborhood U of x such that

$$f(y) \geq f(x) - \epsilon \quad \forall y \in U.$$

If X is a metric space (or more generally, a Fréchet-Urysohn space), then f is upper (resp., lower) semicontinuous at $x \in X$ if and only if for every sequence $(x_n)_n$ in X converging to x, we have

$$f(x) \geq \limsup_{n \to +\infty} f(x_n) \quad (\text{resp.,} \ f(x) \leq \liminf_{n \to +\infty} f(x_n)),$$

where $\limsup\limits_{n \to +\infty} f(x_n) = \inf\limits_{n} \sup\limits_{k \geq n} f(x_k)$ and $\liminf\limits_{n \to +\infty} f(x_n) = \sup\limits_{n} \inf\limits_{k \geq n} f(x_k)$.

Proposition 11.6. *Let* $f : X \longrightarrow \mathbb{R}$ *be a function and let* S *be a subset of* X. *If the restriction* $f_{|U}$ *of* f *on an open subset* U *containing* S *is upper (resp., lower) semicontinuous on* S, *then any extension of* $f_{|U}$ *to the whole space* X *is upper (resp., lower) semicontinuous on* S.

The following result provides us with some properties of upper (resp., lower) semicontinuous functions.

Proposition 11.7. *Let* $f : X \longrightarrow \mathbb{R}$ *be a function,* S *a subset of* X, *and* $a \in \mathbb{R}$.

1. *f is upper semicontinuous on S if and only if*

$$\overline{\{x \in X \mid f(x) \geq a\}} \cap S = \{x \in S \mid f(x) \geq a\}.$$

In particular, if f is upper semicontinuous on S, then the trace on S of any upper level set of f is closed in S.

2. *f is lower semicontinuous at S if and only if*

$$\overline{\{x \in X \mid f(x) \leq a\}} \cap S = \{x \in S \mid f(x) \leq a\}.$$

In particular, if f is lower semicontinuous on S, then the trace on S of any lower level set of f is closed in S.

Proof. The second statement being similar to the first one, we prove only the case of upper semicontinuity. Let

$$x^* \in \overline{\{x \in X \mid f(x) \geq a\}} \cap S.$$

Clearly, $x^* \in S$. To prove that $f(x^*) \geq a$, we argue by contradiction and assume that $f(x^*) < a$. Take $\epsilon > 0$ such that $f(x^*) + \epsilon < a$. By upper semicontinuity of f at x^*, let U be an open neighborhood of x^* such that $f(y) \leq f(x^*) + \epsilon$, for every $y \in U$. It follows that

$$U \cap \{x \in X \mid f(x) \geq a\} = \emptyset,$$

which is a contradiction.

Conversely, let $x^* \in S$, $\epsilon > 0$ and put $a = f(x^*) + \epsilon$. We have $f(x^*) < a$ and then

$$x^* \notin \overline{\{x \in X \mid f(x) \geq a\}}.$$

Let U be an open neighborhood of x^* such that $\{x \in X \mid f(x) \geq a\} \cap U = \emptyset$. It follows that

$$f(y) < a = f(x^*) + \epsilon \quad \forall y \in U.$$

Finally, we have

$$\{x \in X \mid f(x) \geq a\} \cap S = \{x \in S \mid f(x) \geq a\},$$

which yields that the trace on S of any upper level set of f is closed in S. □

In the sequel, for $y \in C$, we define the following sets:

$$f^+(y) = \{x \in C \mid f(x, y) \geq 0\} \quad \text{and} \quad f^-(y) = \{x \in C \mid f(y, x) \leq 0\}.$$

Clearly, $x^* \in C$ is a solution of the equilibrium problem (EP) if and only if $x^* \in \bigcap_{y \in C} f^+(y)$.

The following result is a generalization of the Ky Fan's minimax inequality theorem.

Theorem 11.3. *Let $f : C \times C \longrightarrow \mathbb{R}$ be an equilibrium bifunction and suppose the following assumptions hold:*

1. *f is quasi-convex in its second variable on C;*
2. *there exists a compact subset K of C and $y_0 \in K$ such that*

$$f(x, y_0) < 0 \quad \forall x \in C \setminus K;$$

3. *f is upper semicontinuous in its first variable on K.*

Then, the equilibrium problem (EP) has a solution and its set of solutions $SEP(C, f)$ is a nonempty compact set.

Proof. Since f is an equilibrium bifunction, then $\overline{f^+(y)}$ is nonempty and closed, for every $y \in C$.

By quasi-convexity of f in its second variable, the mapping $y \mapsto f^+(y)$ is a KKM mapping and since $f^+(y_0)$ is contained in the compact subset K, then by Ky Fan's lemma, we have

$$\bigcap_{y \in C} \overline{f^+(y)} \neq \emptyset.$$

On the other hand, we have

$$\bigcap_{v \in C} \overline{f^+(y)} = \bigcap_{y \in C} \left(\overline{f^+(y)} \cap K \right).$$

By Proposition 11.7, we have

$$\overline{f^+(y)} \cap K = f^+(y) \cap K \quad \forall y \in C.$$

Thus,

$$\bigcap_{y \in C} f^+(y) = \bigcap_{y \in C} \overline{f^+(y)} \neq \emptyset.$$

The compactness of the set of solutions is obvious. □

The Minty lemma for equilibrium problems deals in particular with properties such as compactness and convexity of the set of solutions of equilibrium problems. For more properties of the set of solutions of equilibrium problems, we need some additional concepts of monotonicity for bifunctions.

A bifunction $f : C \times C \longrightarrow \mathbb{R}$ is called

1. *strongly monotone* on C with modulus β if

$$f(x, y) + f(y, x) \leq -\beta \|x - y\|^2, \quad \forall x, y \in C;$$

2. *monotone* on C if

$$f(x, y) + f(y, x) \leq 0, \quad \forall x, y \in C;$$

3. *strictly pseudo-monotone* on C if

$$f(x, y) \geq 0 \Longrightarrow f(y, x) < 0, \quad \forall x, y \in C, x \neq y;$$

4. *pseudo-monotone* on C if

$$f(x, y) \geq 0 \Longrightarrow f(y, x) \leq 0, \quad \forall x, y \in C.$$

Every strongly monotone bifunction is both monotone and strictly pseudo-monotone and every strictly pseudo-monotone bifunction f is pseudo-monotone provided it is an equilibrium bifunction, that is, $f(x, x) = 0, \forall x \in C$.

The following result deals with equilibrium problems defined on non necessarily convex sets and its proof is elementary. We call such a problem, a *nonconvex equilibrium problem*.

Proposition 11.8. *Let $f : C \times C \longrightarrow \mathbb{R}$ be a strictly pseudo-monotone bifunction. Then for every subset A of C, the following nonconvex equilibrium problem*

$$\text{find } x^* \in A \text{ such that } f(x^*, y) \geq 0 \quad \forall y \in A$$

has at most one solution.

We also need the following notions about convexity of functions. A function $f : C \longrightarrow \mathbb{R}$ is said to be

1. *semistrictly quasi-convex* on C if, for every $x_1, x_2 \in C$ such that $f(x_1) \neq f(x_2)$, we have

$$f(\lambda x_1 + (1 - \lambda) x_2) < \max\{f(x_1), f(x_2)\} \quad \forall \lambda \in {]0, 1[};$$

2. *explicitly quasi-convex* on C if it is quasi-convex and semistrictly quasi-convex.

Note that there is not any inclusion relationship between the class of semistrictly quasi-convex functions and that of quasi-convex functions. However, if f is a lower semicontinuous and semistrictly quasi-convex function, then f is explicitly quasi-convex.

The following results provide some additional properties of the set of solutions of equilibrium problems.

Theorem 11.4. *Under assumptions of Theorem 11.3 and suppose the following conditions hold:*

1. f *is pseudo-monotone*;
2. f *is explicitly quasi-convex in its second variable on C.*

Then the equilibrium problem (EP) *has a solution and its set of solutions SEP* (C, f) *is nonempty compact set. If in addition, K is convex, then SEP* (C, f) *is convex.*

Proof. The first part of this theorem being proved above, we prove the second part. By pseudo-monotonicity, we have $f^+ (y) \subset f^- (y)$, for every $y \in C$. Since $\bigcap_{y \in C} f^+ (y) \subset K$, then

$$\bigcap_{y \in C} f^+ (y) \subset \left(\bigcap_{y \in C} f^- (y) \right) \cap K.$$

Now, by explicit quasi-convexity, we obtain

$$\left(\bigcap_{y \in C} f^- (y) \right) \cap K \subset \bigcap_{y \in C} f^+ (y).$$

It follows that

$$\bigcap_{y \in C} f^+ (y) = \left(\bigcap_{y \in C} f^- (y) \right) \cap K.$$

By quasi-convexity, the set $f^- (y)$ is convex, for every y. Thus, the set of solutions SEP (C, θ) is convex whenever K is convex. □

Note that Theorem 11.4 also holds if we replace upper semicontinuity of f in the first variable by upper hemicontinuity in the first variable and lower semicontinuity in the second variable. Recall that upper hemicontinuity is upper semicontinuity on line segments.

11.3 THE TIKHONOV REGULARIZATION METHOD FOR EQUILIBRIUM PROBLEMS

The *Tikhonov regularization method* (or *ridge regression* in statistics) is a powerful tool in convex optimization to handle discrete or continuous ill-posed problems. In the framework of monotone variational inequalities, the basic idea of this method is to perturb the problem with a strongly monotone operator depending on a regularization parameter to the monotone cost operator to obtain a strongly monotone variational inequality. The optimal regularization parameter is usually unknown and usually in practical problems it is determined by various methods, such as the discrepancy principle, cross-validation, L-curve method, Bayesian interpretation, restricted maximum likelihood, and unbiased predictive risk estimator. The resulting regularized inequality problem has a unique solution that depends on the regularization parameter. Next, passing to the limit as the parameter goes to a suitable value, the unique solution of the regularized problem tends to a solution of the original problem. We point out that if the cost operator is pseudo-monotone rather than monotone, then the monotonicity of the regularized problem may fail.

We define a regularized equilibrium problem for the equilibrium problem (EP). Let $\theta : C \times C \longrightarrow \mathbb{R}$ be an equilibrium bifunction that we call the *regularization equilibrium bifunction*. Then, for every $\epsilon > 0$, we define the equilibrium bifunction $f_\epsilon : C \times C \longrightarrow \mathbb{R}$ by

$$f_\epsilon (x, y) = f (x, y) + \epsilon \theta (x, y)$$

and we associate with the equilibrium problem (EP), the regularized equilibrium problem defined as follows:

$$\text{find } x_\epsilon^* \in C \text{ such that } f_\epsilon \left(x_\epsilon^*, y \right) \geq 0 \quad \forall y \in C, \tag{REP}$$

where its set of solutions is denoted by SREP (C, f_ϵ).

Note that when f or θ is pseudo-monotone, the regularized equilibrium bifunction f_ϵ does not inherit any monotonicity property from f and θ in general. Also, while the sum of two convex function is convex, this fact does not remain true for quasi-convex functions. The sum of two quasi-convex functions need not be quasi-convex even if one of the functions involved is linear.

In the following result, we avoid the lower semicontinuity of f and θ in their second variable on C, the convexity of f and θ is weakened to the quasi-convexity of the regularized bifunction, and the upper semicontinuity of f and θ in their first variable is weakened to the set of uniform coerciveness. We also point out that we do not need the quasi-convexity of f or θ in their second variable.

Theorem 11.5. *Let $(\epsilon_n)_n$ be a sequence of positive numbers such that $\lim\limits_{n \to +\infty} \epsilon_n = 0$ and suppose the following conditions hold:*

1. *f and θ are pseudo-monotone on C;*
2. *$f + \epsilon_n \theta$ is quasi-convex in the second variable on C, for every n;*
3. *there exist a compact subset K of C and $y_0 \in C$ such that $f (x, y_0) < 0$, for every $x \in C \setminus K$;*
4. *f and θ are upper semicontinuous in the first variable on K.*

Then any cluster point $x^* \in C$ of a sequence $(x_n)_n$ with $x_n \in SREP\left(C, f_{\epsilon_n}\right) \cap K$ for every n, is a solution to the nonconvex equilibrium problem:

$$\text{find } x^* \in SEP\left(C, f\right) \text{ such that } \theta\left(x^*, y\right) \geq 0 \quad \forall y \in SEP\left(C, f\right). \quad \text{(NC-EP)}$$

Assume in addition that the following hypotheses hold:

1. θ *is strictly pseudo-monotone on C;*
2. *there exists $A \subset K$ such that $\theta\left(x, y_0\right) < 0$, for every $x \in C \setminus A$.*

Then the regularized equilibrium problem (REP) *is solvable, for every n, and any sequence $(x_n)_n$ with $x_n \in SREP\left(C, f_{\epsilon_n}\right)$ for every n, converges to the unique solution of the nonconvex equilibrium problem* (NC-EP).

Proof. Let $(x_n)_n$ be a sequence with $x_n \in SREP\left(C, f_{\epsilon_n}\right) \cap K$ for every n, and admitting $x^* \in C$ as a cluster point. We have $x^* \in K$ and without loss of generality, we may assume that $(x_n)_n$ converges to x^*.

First we will prove that $x^* \in SEP\left(C, f\right)$ and therefore $SEP\left(C, f\right)$ is not empty. We know that for every n,

$$f\left(x_n, y\right) + \epsilon_n \theta\left(x_n, y\right) \geq 0 \quad \forall y \in C.$$

By upper semicontinuity of f and θ in their first variable on K and the properties of the upper limits, we have

$$f\left(x^*, y\right) \geq \limsup_{n \to +\infty} f\left(x_n, y\right) + \limsup_{n \to +\infty} \epsilon_n \theta\left(x_n, y\right)$$
$$\geq \limsup_{n \to +\infty} \left(f\left(x_n, y\right) + \epsilon_n \theta\left(x_n, y\right)\right) \geq 0 \quad \forall y \in C.$$

It results that $x^* \in SEP\left(C, f\right)$. Now, let $z \in SEP\left(C, f\right)$. By pseudo-monotonicity of f, we have $f\left(x_n, z\right) \leq 0$, for every n. Then

$$\epsilon_n \theta\left(x_n, z\right) \geq -f\left(x_n, z\right) \geq 0 \quad \forall n,$$

which implies that $\theta\left(x_n, z\right) \geq 0$. Letting n go to $+\infty$, we obtain by upper semicontinuity of θ in its first variable on K that $\theta\left(x^*, z\right) \geq 0$. Thus,

$$\theta\left(x^*, z\right) \geq 0 \quad \forall z \in SEP\left(C, f\right)$$

which completes the proof of the first part.

To prove the second part of the theorem, note that for every n,

$$f\left(x_n, y_0\right) + \epsilon_n \theta\left(x_n, y_0\right) < 0 \quad \forall x \in C \setminus K.$$

By Theorem 11.3, the regularized equilibrium problem $\left(REP\left(C, f_{\epsilon_n}\right)\right)$ is solvable and its set of solutions $SREP\left(C, f_{\epsilon_n}\right)$ is contained in K. Let $(x_n)_n$ be a sequence such that $x_n \in SREP\left(C, f_{\epsilon_n}\right)$, for every n. Then the sequence $(x_n)_n$ has a cluster point $x^* \in K$ and by the first part of the theorem, x^* is a solution to the ·

nonconvex equilibrium problem (NC-EP). Since θ is strictly pseudo-monotone, then by Proposition 11.8, the above nonconvex equilibrium problem (NC-EP) has a unique solution. It follows that every subsequence of the sequence $(x_n)_n$ admits this unique solution of the nonconvex equilibrium problem (NC-EP) as a cluster point. Thus, the sequence $(x_n)_n$ converges to the unique solution of the nonconvex equilibrium problem (NC-EP). $\qquad\square$

Remark 11.4. 1. Note that in the case of a finite dimensional real Banach space E, if θ is strongly monotone on C, and θ and f are convex and lower semicontinuous in the second variable on C, then the sequence $(f + \epsilon_n\theta)_n$ is uniformly coercive whenever f has a set of coerciveness. This means that even if we consider a strongly monotone bifunction θ as a regularization bifunction, Theorem 11.5 can also be seen as a generalization of [62, Theorem 2.9] since the upper semicontinuity on the first variable is weakened. We choose in this case θ such that both θ and f are upper semicontinuous in their first variable on the subset of the uniform coerciveness.

2. We point out that Theorem 11.5 provides us with a tool to use the Tikhonov regularization method in the case of equilibrium problems involving nonupper semicontinuous bifunctions on their first variable.

3. Finally, even if strongly monotone bifunctions seem to be more widely used in the Tikhonov regularization method, our Theorem 11.5 presents a generalization in several directions of [62, Theorem 2.9] and provides us with a largest family of bifunctions to use in the Tikhonov regularization method.

11.3.1 Examples of Suitable Bifunctions

We first construct in what follows two bifunctions f and θ satisfying all the conditions of Theorem 11.5 without being upper semicontinuous in their first variable on the whole space C. The bifunction f is pseudo-monotone nonstrictly pseudo-monotone and θ is strictly pseudo-monotone nonstrongly monotone on C.

Example 11.1. Let $E = C = \mathbb{R}$, $K = [-1, +1]$ and $y_0 = 0$.

(I) First consider the bifunction $f : C \times C \longrightarrow \mathbb{R}$ defined by

$$f(x, y) = \begin{cases} (x+2)(y-x) & \text{if } x \in]-\infty, -2[, \\ (x+1)(y-x) & \text{if } x \in [-2, -1[, \\ \max(x, 0)(y-x) & \text{otherwise.} \end{cases}$$

1. Clearly, $f(x, x) = 0$, for every $x \in C$ and $f(x, 0) < 0$, for every $x \notin [-1, +1]$.

2. To verify that f is pseudo-monotone on C, let $x, y \in C$ such that $f(x, y) \geq 0$.

(a) If $x \in]-\infty, -2[$, then $f(x, y) = (x + 2)(y - x)$. It follows that $y - x \leq 0$ and then, $y < -2$. Thus $f(y, x) = (y + 2)(x - y) \leq 0$.

(b) If $x \in [-2, -1[$, then $y - x \leq 0$ and then, $y < -1$. If $y \in [-2, -1[$, then $f(y, x) = (y + 1)(x - y) \leq 0$, and if $y \in]-\infty, -2[$, then $f(y, x) = (y + 2)(x - y) \leq 0$.

(c) If $x \geq -1$, then $y \geq x$. It follows that $y \geq -1$ and then $f(y, x) = \max(y, 0)(x - y) \leq 0$.

3. Clearly, f is convex in its second variable on C and upper semicontinuous in its first variable on $[-1, +1]$.

4. To see that f is not upper semicontinuous in its first variable on C, consider $y > -2$ and take a sequence $(x_n)_n$ in $]-\infty, -2[$ converging to -2. We have

$$f(-2, y) = -(y + 2) < 0 = \limsup_{n \to +\infty} (x_n + 2)(y + 2)$$

$$= \limsup_{n \to +\infty} f(x_n, y).$$

5. Note that in addition, f is not lower semicontinuous in its first variable on C. To see this fact, consider $y < -2$ and take a sequence $(x_n)_n$ in $]-\infty, -2[$ converging to -2. We have

$$f(-2, y) = -(y + 2) > 0 = \liminf_{n \to +\infty} (x_n + 2)(y + 2)$$

$$= \liminf_{n \to +\infty} f(x_n, y).$$

6. Finally, let us point out that f is not strictly pseudo-monotone on C since $f(x, y) = f(y, x) = 0$ whenever $x, y \in [-1, 0]$.

(II) Now, consider the bifunction $\theta : C \times C \longrightarrow \mathbb{R}$ is defined by

$$\theta(x, y) = \begin{cases} \frac{y^4 - x^4}{65} & \text{if } x = 2, \\ y^4 - x^4 & \text{otherwise.} \end{cases}$$

1. Clearly $\theta(x, x) = 0$, for every $x \in C$ and $\theta(x, 0) < 0$, for every $x \notin K = [-1, +1]$. It is also easy to see that θ is strictly pseudo-monotone and not strongly monotone on C.

2. To see that θ is convex in its second variable, let $x \in C$ be fixed.

   (a) if $x = 2$, then $\theta(2, y) = \frac{y^4 - 16}{65}$, for every $y \in C$. The function $y \mapsto \frac{y^4 - 16}{65}$ is convex on C.

   (b) if $x \neq 2$, then $\theta(x, y) = y^4 - x^4$, for every $y \in C$. The function $y \mapsto y^4 - x^4$ is convex on C.

3. To see that θ is upper semicontinuous in its first variable on $[-1, +1]$, let $y \in C$ be fixed and denote by $f : C \longrightarrow \mathbb{R}$ the function defined by

$$f(x) = \theta(x, y).$$

The restriction $f_{|U}$ of f on the open set $U =]-\infty, 2[$ containing $[-1, +1]$ is defined by $f_{|U}(x) = y^4 - x^4$ which is continuous on U and then by Proposition 11.6, f is upper semicontinuous on $[-1, +1]$.

4. Finally, the bifunction θ is not upper semicontinuous in its first variable on C. Indeed, consider $y = 3$ for example. Let $(x_n)_n$ be a converging sequence to 2 such that $x_n \neq 2$, for every n. We have

$$\theta(2, 3) = 1 < 65 = \limsup_{n \to +\infty} \theta(x_n, 3).$$

Convexity and generalized convexity are important fields in many areas of mathematics and more particularly, in Optimization since convex and concave functions entail several useful properties. Moreover, quasi-convexity and, by analogy, quasi-concavity, reveal properties of special interest in Economics Theory.

As observed, the sum of two quasi-convex functions need not be quasi-convex even if one of the functions involved is linear. This means that the sum of two non necessarily quasi-convex functions may be quasi-convex. Also, any quasi-convex function could be split into a sum of two functions and it seems that in general, nothing can justify that these functions must be quasi-convex. In other words, this subject is very rich and for this reason, studies about convexity and generalized convexity abound in the literature. Characterizations by means of various notions including the notion of differentiability and different sufficient conditions to obtain quasi-convexity as well as other stronger notions such as convexity, strict convexity, and strict quasi-convexity are deeply developed and many examples are constructed by several authors.

However, we recall here the following basic properties which will inspire us in the construction of our next examples:

1. If f is a quasi-convex function, then for every $\alpha \geq 0$, αf is quasi-convex.
2. Every monotone function of one real variable is quasi-convex.
3. The sum of two monotone functions of one real variable with the same sense of monotonicity is monotone, and therefore quasi-convex.

Now, we modify the bifunction θ of Example 11.1 in such a way that all its above properties are conserved but it is quasi-convex nonconvex bifunction in the second variable. Note that it could be more easy to construct further examples if we relax the condition on the semicontinuity of the bifunctions to the whole space rather than only on the set of coerciveness.

Example 11.2. Let $E = C = \mathbb{R}$, $K = [-1, +1]$ and $y_0 = 0$.
The bifunction $\theta : C \times C \longrightarrow \mathbb{R}$ is now defined by

$$\theta(x, y) = \begin{cases} \dfrac{y^4 - x^4}{65} & \text{if} \quad (x, y) \in \{2\} \times]-\infty, 3], \\ y^4 - x^4 & \text{otherwise.} \end{cases}$$

1. To see that θ is quasi-convex in its second variable, treat only the case of $x = 2$. In this case, we have

$$\theta\,(2, y) = \begin{cases} \frac{y^4 - 16}{65} & \text{if } y \in \,]-\infty, 3]\,, \\ y^4 - 16 & \text{otherwise.} \end{cases}$$

We have that $\theta\,(2, 3) \le \theta\,(2, y)$, for every $y \in\,]3, +\infty[$. A combination with the other properties of the bifunction θ yields easily that the function $y \mapsto \theta\,(2, y)$ is quasi-convex on C.

2. To see that the function $y \mapsto \theta\,(2, y)$ is not convex, choose $y_1 = 3$ and $y_2 = 4$ for example. Take the point

$$y = \frac{1}{2} y_1 + \left(1 - \frac{1}{2}\right) y_2 = \frac{7}{2}$$

in the line segment between y_1 and y_2. We have

$$\theta\,(2, y) = \theta\left(2, \frac{7}{2}\right) = \frac{7^4}{16} - 16.$$

In the other hand, we have

$$\frac{1}{2}\theta\,(2, y_1) + \left(1 - \frac{1}{2}\right)\theta\,(2, y_2) = \frac{1}{2} + \frac{1}{2}\left(4^4 - 16\right) = \frac{241}{2} < \theta\,(2, y).$$

Now, we show that the regularized bifunction constructed from f and θ as in Theorem 11.5 is quasi-convex in its second variable.

Example 11.3. Let ϵ be a positive number and consider the regularized bifunction $f_\epsilon = f + \epsilon\theta$ as in Theorem 11.5. Then, the bifunction f_ϵ is defined on $C \times C$ by

$$f_\epsilon\,(x, y) = \begin{cases} (x + 2)\,(y - x) + \epsilon\left(y^4 - x^4\right) & \text{if } x \in\,]-\infty, -2[\,, \\ (x + 1)\,(y - x) + \epsilon\left(y^4 - x^4\right) & \text{if } x \in [-2, -1[\,, \\ \max\,(x, 0)\,(y - x) + \epsilon\frac{y^4 - x^4}{65} & \text{if } (x, y) \in \{2\} \times\,]-\infty, 3]\,, \\ \max\,(x, 0)\,(y - x) + \epsilon\left(y^4 - x^4\right) & \text{otherwise.} \end{cases}$$

As above, only the quasi-convexity of the function $y \mapsto f_\epsilon\,(2, y)$ is important to verify, the other cases come readily from the definition. In this case, we have

$$f_\epsilon\,(2, y) = \begin{cases} 2\,(y - 2) + \epsilon\frac{y^4 - 16}{65} & \text{if } y \in\,]-\infty, 3]\,, \\ 2\,(y - 2) + \epsilon\left(y^4 - 16\right) & \text{otherwise.} \end{cases}$$

By the same argument as above, remark that $f_\epsilon\,(2, 3) \le f_\epsilon\,(2, y)$, for every $y \in\,]3, +\infty[$, and this completes the proof.

11.3.2 Applications to Quasi-Hemivariational Inequalities

We now intend to point out the relationship between equilibrium problems and quasi-hemivariational inequalities. We develop results in the qualitative analysis of quasi-hemivariational inequalities and give a generalization to Berge's maximum theorem in order to apply the Tikhonov regularization for quasi-hemivariational inequalities.

Recall that a function $\phi : E \to \mathbb{R}$ is called *locally Lipschitzian* if for every $u \in E$, there exists a neighborhood U of u and a constant $L_u > 0$ such that

$$|\phi(w) - \phi(v)| \le L_u \|w - v\|_X \quad \forall w \in U, \forall v \in U.$$

If $\phi : E \to \mathbb{R}$ is locally Lipschitzian near $u \in E$, then the *Clarke generalized directional derivative* of ϕ at u in the direction of $v \in E$, denoted by $\phi^0(u, v)$, is defined by

$$\phi^0(u, v) = \limsup_{\substack{w \to u \\ \lambda \downarrow 0}} \frac{\phi(w + \lambda v) - \phi(w)}{\lambda}.$$

We will use the following properties of locally Lipschitz functionals. Suppose that $\phi : E \to \mathbb{R}$ is locally Lipschitzian near $u \in E$. Then,

1. the function $v \mapsto \phi^0(u, v)$ is finite, positively homogeneous, and subadditive;
2. the function $(u, v) \mapsto \phi^0(u, v)$ is upper semicontinuous.

Remark 11.5. To avoid any confusion in the definition of semicontinuity on subsets, the functions h and F, and the multi-valued mapping A will be considered from C rather than from E.

We observe that any solution of the quasi-hemivariational inequality (QHVI) is a solution of the equilibrium problem (EP) where the equilibrium bifunction $\Phi : C \times C \to \mathbb{R}$ is defined by

$$\Phi(u, v) = \sup_{z \in A(u)} \langle z, v - u \rangle + h(u) J^0(iu; iv - iu) - \langle Fu, v - u \rangle \quad \forall u, v \in C.$$

The converse needs some additional conditions on the multi-valued mapping A and holds by a classical approach.

Theorem 11.6. *If A has nonempty, convex and weak* compact values, then any solution of the equilibrium problem (EP) is a solution of the quasi-hemivariational inequality problem (QHVI).*

Proof. Let $u^* \in C$ be such that $\Phi(u^*, v) \ge 0$, for every $v \in C$, and assume that there does not exist $z \in A(u^*)$ satisfying

$$\langle z, v - u^* \rangle + h(u^*) J^0(iu^*; iv - iu^*) - \langle Fu^*, v - u^* \rangle \ge 0 \quad \forall v \in C.$$

Clearly, for every $z \in A(u^*)$, there exist $v_z \in C$ and $\epsilon_z > 0$ such that

$$\langle z, v_z - u^* \rangle + h(u^*) J^0(iu^*; iv_z - iu^*) - \langle Fu^*, v_z - u^* \rangle < -\epsilon_z.$$

Since, for every $v \in C$, the mapping defined on E^* by

$$z \mapsto \langle z, v - u^* \rangle + h(u^*) J^0(iu^*; iv - iu^*) - \langle Fu^*, v - u^* \rangle$$

is weak* continue, then for every $z \in A(u^*)$, we choose a weak* open subset O_z of E^* such that

$$\langle z', v_z - u^* \rangle + h(u^*) J^0(iu^*; iv_z - iu^*) - \langle Fu^*, v_z - u^* \rangle < -\epsilon_z \quad \forall z' \in O_z.$$

For every $z \in A(u^*)$, we have $z \in O_z$ and then, $\{O_z \mid z \in A(u^*)\}$ is a weak* open cover of $A(u^*)$. Since $A(u^*)$ is weak* compact, there exist $z_j \in C$, $j = 1, \ldots, n$ such that $\{O_{z_j} \mid j = 1, \ldots, n\}$ is a finite subcover of $A(u^*)$. Put $v_j = v_{z_j}$, $j = 1, \ldots, n$ and $\epsilon = \min\{\epsilon_{z_j} \mid j = 1, \ldots, n\}$. Clearly for all $z \in A(u^*)$, we have

$$\min_{j=1,\ldots,n} \left(\langle z, v_j - u^* \rangle + h(u^*) J^0(iu^*; iv_j - iu^*) - \langle Fu^*, v_j - u^* \rangle \right) < -\epsilon.$$

The Clarke generalized directional derivative being finite, then for every $j = 1, \ldots, n$, the functions

$$z \mapsto \langle z, v_j - u^* \rangle + h(u^*) J^0(iu^*; iv_j - iu^*) - \langle Fu^*, v_j - u^* \rangle,$$

defined on the convex set $A(u^*)$, are concave and proper with domain containing $A(u^*)$, and therefore there exist $\mu_j \geq 0$, $j = 1, \ldots, n$, with $\sum_{j=1}^n = 1$ such that for all $z \in A(u^*)$

$$\sum_{j=1}^n \mu_j \left(\langle z, v_j - u^* \rangle + h(u^*) J^0(iu^*; iv_j - iu^*) - \langle Fu^*, v_j - u^* \rangle \right) < -\epsilon.$$

Set $v^* = \sum_{j=1}^n \mu_j v_j$. Then $v^* \in C$ and by the positive homogeneity and the subadditivity of the Clarke generalized directional derivative in its second variable, we have

$$\langle z, v^* - u^* \rangle + h(u^*) J^0(iu^*; iv^* - iu^*) - \langle Fu^*, v^* - u^* \rangle < -\epsilon \quad \forall z \in A(u^*),$$

which implies that $\Phi(u^*, v^*) < 0$, a contradiction. $\qquad\square$

We turn now into studying the properties inherited by the equilibrium bifunctions defined from quasi-hemivariational inequalities.

Theorem 11.7. *The bifunction Φ is lower semicontinuous and convex in its second variable on C.*

Proof. From the positive homogeneity and the subadditivity of the Clarke generalized directional derivative in its second variable, the function

$$v \mapsto \langle z, v - u \rangle + h(u) J^0(iu; iv - iu) - \langle Fu, v - u \rangle$$

is convex, for every $u \in C$ and every $z \in A(u^*)$. It is also lower semicontinuous since the Clarke generalized directional derivative is lower semicontinuous. The bifunction Φ being the superior envelope of a family of convex and lower semicontinuous functions, it is then convex and lower semicontinuous in its second variable on C. □

The properties inherited by Φ in its first variable are more complicated and need additional conditions on the functions and multi-valued mappings involved in the quasi-hemivariational inequalities.

Recall that a multi-valued mapping T from a topological space X with values in the set of subsets of a topological space Y is called *upper semicontinuous* at a point $x \in X$ if whenever V an open subset containing $T(x)$, there exist an open neighborhood U of x such that $T(x') \subset V$, for every $x' \in U$. We say that T is upper semicontinuous on a subset S of X if T is upper semicontinuous at every point of S.

The following result is a generalization of the well-known Berge's maximum theorem.

Theorem 11.8. *Let X and Y be two Hausdorff topological spaces, S a nonempty subset of X, U an open subset containing S, $T : X \rightrightarrows Y$ a multi-valued mapping, and $\psi : Y \times X \to \mathbb{R} \cup \{+\infty\}$ a function. Suppose that ψ is upper semicontinuous on $Y \times U$ and T is upper semicontinuous on S with nonempty compact values on U. Then the value function $f : X \to \mathbb{R} \cup \{+\infty\}$ defined by*

$$f(x) = \sup_{y \in T(x)} \psi(y, x)$$

is upper semicontinuous on S.

Proof. By Proposition 11.6, it suffices to prove that the restriction $g = f_{|U}$ of f on U is upper semicontinuous on S. Let $a \in \mathbb{R}$ and by Proposition 11.7, we have to prove that

$$\overline{\{x \in U \mid g(x) \geq a\}} \cap S = \{x \in S \mid g(x) \geq a\},$$

where the closure is taken with respect to U. Let $x^* \in \overline{\{x \in U \mid g(x) \geq a\}} \cap S$ and choose a net $(x_\alpha)_{\alpha \in \Lambda}$ in $\{x \in U \mid g(x) \geq a\}$ converging in U to x^*. Since $x_\alpha \in U$, then the restriction of the function ψ on $Y \times \{x_\alpha\}$ is upper semicontinuous and therefore, by the Weierstrass theorem, it attains its maximum on the compact set $T(x_\alpha)$, for every $\alpha \in \Lambda$. Let $y_\alpha \in T(x_\alpha)$ be such that $g(x_\alpha) = \psi(y_\alpha, x_\alpha)$, for every $\alpha \in \Lambda$.

The net $(y_\alpha)_{\alpha \in \Lambda}$ has a cluster point in $T(x^*)$. Indeed, suppose the contrary holds. Then the compactness of $T(x^*)$ yields the existence of an open set V

containing $T(x^*)$ and $\alpha_0 \in \Lambda$ such that $y_\alpha \notin V$, for every $\alpha \geq \alpha_0$. It follows by upper semicontinuity of T at x^* the existence of an open neighborhood W of x^* such that $T(x) \subset V$, for every $x \in W$. Let $\alpha_1 \in \Lambda$ be such that $x_\alpha \in W$, for every $\alpha \geq \alpha_1$. Thus $y_\alpha \in V$, for every $\alpha \geq \alpha_1$. Contradiction.

Take now $y^* \in T(x)$ and $(y_\alpha)_{\alpha \in \Gamma}$ a subnet of $(y_\alpha)_{\alpha \in \Lambda}$ converging to y^*. The net $((y_\alpha, x_\alpha))_{\alpha \in \Gamma}$ is in $Y \times U$, converging to (y^*, x^*) and satisfies

$$\psi(y_\alpha, x_\alpha) \geq a \quad \forall \alpha \in \Gamma.$$

By upper semicontinuity of ψ on $Y \times U$, it follows that $g(x^*) \geq \psi(y^*, x^*) \geq a$, which completes the proof. $\qquad\square$

We give in what follows a sufficient condition for the upper semicontinuity in its first variable of the equilibrium bifunction Φ.

Corollary 11.6. *Let K be a subset of C, U be an open subset containing K and suppose the following conditions hold:*

1. *the nonlinear multi-valued mapping A is upper semicontinuous on K with respect to the strong topology of E^* and has nonempty compact values on U;*
2. *for every $v \in C$, the mapping $u \in C \mapsto h(u) J^0(iu; iv - iu)$ is upper semicontinuous on U;*
3. *for every $v \in C$, the mapping $u \in C \mapsto \langle F(u), v - u \rangle$ is lower semicontinuous on U.*

Then Φ is upper semicontinuous in its first variable on K.

Proof. Let $v \in C$ be fixed and define the function $\psi : E^* \times C \to \mathbb{R}$ by

$$\psi(z, u) = \langle z, v - u \rangle + h(u) J^0(iu; iv - iu) - \langle Fu, v - u \rangle.$$

The function ψ being a sum of upper semicontinuous functions on $E^* \times U$, it is upper semicontinuous on $E^* \times U$, where E^* is equipped with the strong topology. It follows by Theorem 11.8 that the value function $u \mapsto \Phi(u, v)$ is upper semicontinuous on K. $\qquad\square$

Corollary 11.7. *Let K be a subset of C, U be an open subset containing K and suppose the following conditions hold:*

1. *the nonlinear multi-valued mapping A is upper semicontinuous on K with respect to the weak* topology of E^* and has nonempty weak* compact values on U;*
2. *for every $v \in C$, the mapping*

$$(z, u) \in E^* \times U \mapsto \langle z, v - u \rangle + h(u) J^0(iu; iv - iu) - \langle Fu, v - u \rangle$$

is upper semicontinuous on $E^* \times U$.

Then Φ is upper semicontinuous in its first variable on K.

Recall that a multi-valued mapping $T : C \to 2^{E^*}$ is said to be:

1. *pseudo-monotone* on C if

$$\langle z, u - v \rangle \leq 0 \Longrightarrow \langle t, v - u \rangle \geq 0 \quad \forall u, v \in C, \forall z \in A(u), \forall t \in A(v);$$

2. *strictly pseudo-monotone* if

$$\langle z, u - v \rangle \leq 0 \Longrightarrow \langle t, v - u \rangle > 0 \quad \forall u, v \in C, \forall z \in A(u), \forall t \in A(v).$$

We observe that if T has weak* compact values, then T is pseudo-monotone (resp., strictly pseudo-monotone) if and only if the equilibrium bifunction θ is pseudo-monotone (resp., strictly pseudo-monotone) where $\theta : C \times C \to \mathbb{R}$ is defined by

$$\theta(u, v) = \sup_{z \in T(u)} \langle z, v - u \rangle.$$

This follows from the fact that for every $u, v \in C$, by the weak* compactness of the values of T, there exist $z \in T(u)$ and $t \in T(v)$ such that

$$\theta(u, v) = \langle z, v - u \rangle \quad \text{and} \quad \theta(v, u) = \langle t, u - v \rangle.$$

Now, to apply the Tikhonov regularization for quasi-hemivariational inequalities, first we take a multi-valued function $G : C \to 2^{E^*}$ and $\epsilon > 0$, and define the multi-valued function $A_\epsilon : C \to 2^{E^*}$ by

$$A_\epsilon(x) = A(x) + \epsilon G(x).$$

The regularized quasi-hemivariational inequality has the following form:

Find $u \in C$ and $z \in A_\epsilon(u)$ such that

$$\langle z, v - u \rangle + h(u) J^0(iu; iv - iu) - \langle Fu, v - u \rangle \geq 0 \quad \forall v \in C. \quad \text{(RQHVI)}$$

As previously, we denote its set of solutions by $\text{SRQHVI}(C, A_\epsilon)$.

We say that the quasi-hemivariational inequality (QHVI) is pseudo-monotone on C if the associated equilibrium bifunction Φ is pseudo-monotone on C.

Theorem 11.9. *Let K be a compact subset of C, U an open subset containing K and $(\epsilon_n)_n$ is a sequence of positive numbers such that $\lim_{n \to +\infty} \epsilon_n = 0$. Suppose that the following assumptions hold:*

1. *G is pseudo-monotone on C, upper semicontinuous on K with respect to the strong topology of E^* and has nonempty, convex and compact values on C;*
2. *the quasi-hemivariational inequality (QHVI) is pseudo-monotone on C;*
3. *A is upper semicontinuous on K with respect to the strong topology of E^* and has nonempty, convex and compact values on C;*
4. *for every $v \in C$, the mapping $u \in C \mapsto h(u) J^0(iu; iv - iu)$ is upper semicontinuous on U;*

5. *for every $v \in C$, the mapping $u \in C \mapsto \langle F(u), v - u \rangle$ is lower semicontinuous on U;*

6. *there exists $v_0 \in C$ such that*

$$\langle z, v_0 - u \rangle + h(u) J^0(iu; iv_0 - iu) - \langle Fu, v_0 - u \rangle < 0$$

$$\forall u \in C \setminus K, \forall z \in A(u).$$

Then any cluster point $x^* \in C$ of a sequence $(x_n)_n$ with $x_n \in SRQHVI\left(C, A_{\epsilon_n}\right) \cap K$ for every n, is a solution to the multi-valued variational inequality:

> *Find $u \in SQHVI(C, A)$ and $z \in G(u)$ such that*
> $$\langle z, v - u \rangle \geq 0 \quad \forall v \in SQHVI(C, A).$$

Assume in addition, that the following conditions hold:

1. *G is strictly pseudo-monotone on C;*

2. *there exists $K' \subset K$ such that $\langle z, v_0 - u \rangle < 0$, for every $u \in C \setminus K'$ and every $z \in G(u)$.*

Then the regularized quasi-hemivariational inequality $(RQHVI\left(C, F_{\epsilon_n}\right))$ is solvable, for every n, and any sequence $(x_n)_n$ with $x_n \in SRQHVI\left(C, F_{\epsilon_n}\right)$ for every n, converges to the unique solution of the multi-valued variational inequality problem:

> *Find $u \in SQHVI(C, A)$ and $z \in G(u)$ such that*
> $$\langle z, v - u \rangle \geq 0 \quad \forall v \in SQHVI(C, A).$$

Proof. Note that

$$\sup_{z \in A_\epsilon(x)} \langle z, y - x \rangle = \sup_{z \in A(x)} \langle z, y - x \rangle + \epsilon \sup_{z \in G(x)} \langle z, y - x \rangle \quad \forall x, y \in C.$$

The result holds now easily from the results developed above and by applying Theorem 11.5. $\qquad\square$

Under assumptions of Theorem 11.9, the set of solutions of the quasi-hemivariational inequality (QHVI) is nonempty and compact. It is also convex whenever K is convex.

11.4 A SUBGRADIENT EXTRAGRADIENT METHOD FOR SOLVING EQUILIBRIUM PROBLEMS

The aim of this section is to provide a further numerical method for solving equilibrium problems (EP). Our framework will be a real Hilbert space, denoted H. Let K be a nonempty closed convex subset of H and $f : K \times K \to \mathbb{R}$ a bifunction. Let us recall that (EP) is defined as:

$$\text{find } x \in K \text{ such that } f(x, y) \geq 0 \ \forall y \in K. \tag{11.25}$$

Some iterative methods have been proposed to solve various classes of equilibrium problems. In these papers, the bifunction f is assumed to satisfy the following conditions

(A1) $f(x, x) = 0$ for all $x \in K$;

(A2) f is monotone on K, i.e., $f(x, y) + f(y, x) \le 0$ for all $x, y \in K$;

(A3) $\limsup\limits_{t \to 0^+} f(x + t(z - x), y) \le f(x, y)$ for all $x, y, z \in K$;

(A4) $f(x, \cdot)$ is convex and lower semicontinuous on C.

Under these assumptions, Combettes and Hirstoaga [57] showed that for each $r > 0$ and $x \in H$ the mapping $T_r^f : H \to K$ defined by

$$T_r^f(x) = \left\{ z \in K : f(z, y) + \frac{1}{r}\langle y - z, z - x \rangle \ge 0 \ \forall y \in K \right\} \qquad (11.26)$$

is single-valued. Based on the mapping T_r^f, the algorithm in [57] generates the sequence $\{x^n\}$ by $x^0 \in H$ and,

$$x^{n+1} = T_{r_n}^f x^n \quad \text{for every } n \in \mathbb{N},$$

equivalently, $x^{n+1} \in K$ such that

$$f(x^{n+1}, y) + \frac{1}{r_n}\langle y - x^{n+1}, x^{n+1} - x^n \rangle \ge 0 \text{ for every } y \in K, \qquad (11.27)$$

where $\{r_n\} \subset (0, +\infty)$ satisfies the condition $\liminf\limits_{n \to \infty} r_n > 0$. From computational point of view, it is in general difficult to compute x^{n+1} in (11.27).

The next algorithm was first introduced by Antipin [17] in finite dimensional vector spaces.

$$\begin{cases} x_0 \in K, \\ y^n = \operatorname*{argmin}\limits_{y \in K}\left\{ \lambda f(x^n, y) + \frac{1}{2}\|y - x^n\|^2 \right\}, \\ x^{n+1} = \operatorname*{argmin}\limits_{y \in K}\left\{ \lambda f(y^n, y) + \frac{1}{2}\|y - x^n\|^2 \right\}, \ n \ge 0. \end{cases} \qquad (11.28)$$

The advantage of (11.28) is that two strongly convex programming problems are solved at each iteration, which seems numerically easier than solving the nonlinear inequality (11.27). In 2010, the authors in [150] studied the algorithm (11.28) for pseudo-monotone equilibrium problems in Hilbert spaces. Under mild conditions, they obtained the weak convergence of the sequences generated by (11.28).

Recently, Lyashko and Semenov [120] proposed a Popov type algorithm for pseudo-monotone equilibrium problems. The algorithm in [120] (called two-step proximal algorithm) is summarized as follows: choose $x^0 = y^0 \in C, \epsilon > 0$

and $0 < \lambda < \frac{1}{2(2c_1+c_2)}$, where c_1, c_2 are positive constants (see (B5) in Section 11.3).

Step 1. For x^n and y^n, compute

$$x^{n+1} = \operatorname*{argmin}_{y \in C} \left\{ \lambda f(y^n, y) + \frac{1}{2} \| y - x^n \|^2 \right\}.$$

Step 2. If $\max\{ \|x^{n+1} - x^n\|, \|y^n - x^n\| \} \leq \epsilon$ then stop, else compute

$$y^{n+1} = \operatorname*{argmin}_{y \in C} \left\{ \lambda f(y^n, y) + \frac{1}{2} \| y - x^{n+1} \|^2 \right\}.$$

Step 3. Set $n := n + 1$, and go to Step 1.

The weak convergence of their algorithm is proved under usual assumptions imposed on bifunctions in which they required that for all bounded sequences $\{x^n\}$, $\{y^n\}$ satisfying $\|x^n - y^n\| \to 0$ one has $f(x^n, y^n) \to 0$ (condition (A6)). It is worth mentioning that their condition (A6) is rather strong. On the other hand, in Lyashko and Semenov's algorithm and most other algorithms, it must either solve two strongly convex programming problems or solve one strongly convex programming problem and compute one projection onto the feasible set. Therefore, their computations are expensive if the bifunctions and the feasible sets have complicated structures.

Recently, the authors of [99] improved Lyashko and Semenov's algorithm such that the subprogram in Step 1 has been solved over a halfspace instead of over C, and furthermore, some assumptions on f have been weakened. In the next subsections we present their algorithm and convergence results.

11.4.1 A Projection Algorithm for Equilibrium Problems

As usual, the weak convergence will be denoted by "$\rightharpoonup$" and the strong convergence by "$\to$" in the Hilbert space H. Let K be a nonempty closed convex subset of H and $f : H \times H \to \mathbb{R}$ a bifunction satisfying:

(B1) $f(x, x) = 0$ for all $x \in K$;

(B2) f is pseudo-monotone on K, i.e., $f(x, y) \geq 0 \Longrightarrow f(y, x) \leq 0$ for all $x, y \in K$;

(B3) For any arbitrary sequence $\{z^k\}$ such that $z^k \rightharpoonup z$, if $\limsup\limits_{k \to \infty} f(z^k, y) \geq 0$ for all $y \in K$ then $z \in EP(f)$;

(B4) $f(x, \cdot)$ is convex and lower semicontinuous for every $x \in H$;

(B5) There exist positive numbers c_1 and c_2 such that the triangular inequality

$$f(x, y) + f(y, z) \geq f(x, z) - c_1 \|x - y\|^2 - c_2 \|y - z\|^2 \qquad (11.29)$$

holds for all $x, y, z \in H$;

(B6) For all bounded sequences $\{x^n\}, \{y^n\} \subset C$ such that $\|x^n - y^n\| \to 0$, the inequality

$$\limsup_{n \to \infty} f(x^n, y^n) \geq 0$$

holds;

(B7) $EP(f) \neq \emptyset.$

Next let us make some comments on the assumptions above.

Remark 11.6. The condition (B3) was first introduced by Khatibzadeh and Mohebbi in [106]. It is easy to see that if $f(., y)$ is weakly upper semicontinuous for all $y \in K$ then f satisfies the condition (B3). However, the converse is not true in general.

This remark is illustrated by the following counterexample modified from Remark 2.1 of [106].

Example 11.4. Let $H = l^2$, $K = \{\xi = (\xi_1, \xi_2, ...) \in l^2 : \xi_i \geq 0 \ \forall i = 1, 2, ...\}$ and

$$f(x, y) = (y_1 - x_1) \sum_{i=1}^{\infty} (x_i)^2.$$

Take $x^k = (0, ..., 0, \underset{k}{1}, 0, ...)$, we have $x^k \rightharpoonup x = (0, ..., 0, ...)$ and $x \in EP(f)$. Obviously, there is a $y \in K$ such that

$$\limsup_{k \to \infty} f(x^k, y) > 0 = f(x, y).$$

Then $f(., y)$ is not weakly upper semicontinuous. We now show that f satisfies the condition (B3). If $z^k = (z_1^k, z_2^k, ...) \rightharpoonup z = (z_1, z_2, ...)$ is an arbitrary sequence and $\limsup_{k \to \infty} f(z^k, y) \geq 0$ for all $y \in K$, then we have

$$\limsup_{k \to \infty} (y_1 - z_1^k) \sum_{i=1}^{\infty} (z_i^k)^2 \geq 0.$$

Since $\lim_{k \to \infty} (y_1 - z_1^k) = y_1 - z_1$, we get

$$(y_1 - z_1) \limsup_{k \to \infty} \sum_{i=1}^{\infty} (z_i^k)^2 \geq 0,$$

thus $y_1 \geq z_1$. Hence, $f(z, y) \geq 0$ for all $y \in K$, i.e., f satisfies the condition (B3).

Remark 11.7. Under (B1), assumption (B6') is weaker than the joint weak lower semicontinuity of f on the product $K \times K$, as usually assumed by several authors. Indeed, let $\{x^n\}, \{y^n\}$ be bounded sequences in K with $\|x^n - y^n\| \to 0$. Thus there exists a subsequence $\{x^{n_k}\}$ of $\{x^n\}$ converging weakly to $\bar{x} \in K$. By the assumption, the subsequence $\{y^{n_k}\}$ converges weakly to the same $\bar{x}$. Hence,

$$\limsup_{n \to \infty} f(x^n, y^n) \geq \limsup_{k \to \infty} f(x^{n_k}, y^{n_k}) \geq \liminf_{k \to \infty} f(x^{n_k}, y^{n_k}) \geq f(\bar{x}, \bar{x}) = 0.$$

Remark 11.8. We will hereafter consider two important particular cases of the equilibrium problem, namely the optimization problem and the variational inequality problem in which (B6) is satisfied under mild conditions.

1. Let $f(x, y) = F(y) - F(x)$, where K is a nonempty closed convex subset of H and $F : H \to \mathbb{R}$ is a *uniformly continuous* function on K. Then f satisfies (B6). Indeed, if $\|x^n - y^n\| \to 0$, then by uniform continuity we have $F(x^n) - F(y^n) \to 0$, as $n \to \infty$, hence

$$\limsup_{n \to \infty} f(x^n, y^n) = \lim_{n \to \infty} f(x^n, y^n) = 0.$$

2. In case of variational inequalities, i.e., $f(x, y) := \langle Ax, y - x \rangle$, where $A : K \to H$ is an operator, assumption (B6) is satisfied if A is bounded on bounded sets. Indeed, fix an element $z \in C$. Then

$$f(x^n, y^n) = \langle Ax^n, y^n - x^n \rangle \geq -\|Ax^n\|\|x^n - y^n\|$$
$$\geq -M\|x^n - y^n\|,$$

where M is a positive constant such that $\|Ax^n\| \leq M$. Hence, by the assumption

$$\limsup_{n \to \infty} f(x^n, y^n) \geq -\lim_{n \to \infty} M\|x^n - y^n\| = 0.$$

Remark 11.9. Condition (11.29) was introduced by Mastroeni [123] to prove the convergence of the Auxiliary Principle Method for equilibrium problems. Note that

1. If $f(x, y) = \langle Ax, y - x \rangle$, where $A : K \to H$ is Lipschitz continuous with constant $L > 0$ then f satisfies the inequality (11.29) with constants $c_1 = c_2 = \frac{L}{2}$. Indeed, for each $x, y, z \in K$, we have

$$f(x, y) + f(y, z) - f(x, z) = \langle Ax, y - x \rangle + \langle Ay, z - y \rangle - \langle Ax, z - x \rangle$$
$$= -\langle Ay - Ax, y - z \rangle$$
$$\geq -\|Ax - Ay\|\|y - z\|$$
$$\geq -L\|x - y\|\|y - z\|$$

$$\geq -\frac{L}{2}\|x - y\|^2 - \frac{L}{2}\|y - z\|^2$$
$$= -c_1\|x - y\|^2 - c_2\|y - z\|^2.$$

Thus f satisfies the inequality (11.29).

2. If there exists $\Lambda > 0$ such that

$$|f(v, w) - f(x, w) - f(v, y) + f(x, y)|$$
$$\leq \Lambda\|v - x\|\|w - y\| \quad \forall v, w, x, y \in K, \tag{11.30}$$

then it is easy to see that f also satisfies the inequality (11.29). The inequality (11.30) is called Lipschitz type inequality and has been introduced by Antipin [17]. In the framework of a finite dimensional space, he showed that if f is a differentiable function whose partial derivative with respect to the first variable satisfies the Lipschitz type inequality, then the inequality (11.30) holds. Therefore, the class of these functions also satisfies the inequality (11.29).

In order to describe the announced projection algorithm for solving pseudo-monotone equilibrium problems, recall that the $N_K(x)$ denotes the normal cone of the set K at $x \in K$ (see Chapter 1, Section 1.1), and the subdifferential of a function $g : H \to (-\infty, \infty]$ at $x \in H$ is defined as the set of all subgradients of g at x:

$$\partial g(x) := \{w \in H : g(y) - g(x) \geq \langle w, y - x \rangle \ \forall y \in H\}.$$

Let K be a nonempty closed convex subset of H. As well-known, for every element $x \in H$, there exists a unique nearest point in K, denoted by $P_K x$ such that[1]

$$\|x - P_C x\| = \inf\{\|x - y\| : y \in C\}.$$

P_K is called the metric projection of H onto K. It is well known that P_K can be characterized either by property (a) or by (b) below.[2]

(a) $\langle x - P_C x, y - P_C x \rangle \leq 0$ for all $x \in H$ and $y \in C$;
(b) $\|P_C x - y\|^2 \leq \|x - y\|^2 - \|x - P_C x\|^2$ for all $x \in H$, $y \in C$.

We also need the following auxiliary results.

Lemma 11.2. ([86]) *Let C be a nonempty closed convex subset of a real Hilbert space H and $g : H \to \mathbb{R}$ a lower semicontinuous convex function. Then, x^* is a solution of the following convex problem*

$$\min\{g(x) : x \in C\}$$

if and only if

$$0 \in \partial g(x^*) + N_C(x^*).$$

Lemma 11.3. (Opial [135]) *Let $\{x^n\}$ be a sequence of elements of the Hilbert space H which converges weakly to $x \in H$. Then we have*

$$\liminf_{n \to \infty} \|x^n - x\| < \liminf_{n \to \infty} \|x^n - y\| \quad \forall y \in H \setminus \{x\}.$$

Now the algorithm (called **algorithm (A)** in the sequel) is as follows.

Step 1: Specify $x^0, y^0 \in K$ and $\lambda > 0$;
   Compute

$$x^1 = \operatorname*{argmin}_{y \in K} \left\{ \lambda f(y^0, y) + \frac{1}{2} \|y - x^0\|^2 \right\},$$

$$y^1 = \operatorname*{argmin}_{y \in K} \left\{ \lambda f(y^0, y) + \frac{1}{2} \|y - x^1\|^2 \right\}.$$

Step 2: Given x^n, y^n and y^{n-1} $(n \geq 1)$, let $w^n \in \partial f(y^{n-1}, .)(y^n)$ such that there exists an element $q^n \in N_K(y^n)$ satisfying

$$0 = \lambda w^n + y^n - x^n + q^n, \tag{11.31}$$

and construct the halfspace

$$H_n = \{z \in H : \langle x^n - \lambda w^n - y^n, z - y^n \rangle \leq 0\}.$$

Compute

$$x^{n+1} = \operatorname*{argmin}_{y \in H_n} \left\{ \lambda f(y^n, y) + \frac{1}{2} \|y - x^n\|^2 \right\},$$

$$y^{n+1} = \operatorname*{argmin}_{y \in K} \left\{ \lambda f(y^n, y) + \frac{1}{2} \|y - x^{n+1}\|^2 \right\}.$$

Step 3: If $x^{n+1} = x^n$ and $y^n = y^{n-1}$ then stop. Otherwise, set $n := n + 1$, and return to Step 2.

The existence of $w^n \in \partial f(y^{n-1}, .)(y^n)$ and $q^n \in N_K(y^n)$ satisfying (11.31) is guaranteed by Lemma 11.2. Hence, the algorithm (A) is well-defined.

The following lemmas are helpful to analyze the convergence of algorithm (A).

Lemma 11.4. $C \subseteq H_n$, $\forall n \geq 1$.

Proof. From (11.31), we obtain

$$q^n = x^n - \lambda w^n - y^n \quad \forall n \geq 1,$$

where $w^n \in \partial f(y^{n-1}, .)(y^n)$ and $q^n \in N_K(y^n)$. Moreover, we have

$$N_K(y^n) = \{q \in H : \langle q, y - y^n \rangle \leq 0 \, \forall y \in K\}.$$

Therefore, we infer that

$$\langle x^n - \lambda w^n - y^n, y - y^n \rangle \leq 0 \; \forall y \in K \; \forall n \geq 1.$$

This shows that $K \subseteq H_n \; \forall n \geq 1$. $\square$

Lemma 11.5. *If* $x^{n+1} = x^n$ *and* $y^n = y^{n-1}$ *then* $y^n \in EP(f)$.

Proof. If $x^n = x^{n+1}$ we have

$$0 \in \lambda \partial f(y^n, .)(x^{n+1}) + x^{n+1} - x^n + N_{H_n}(x^{n+1}) = \lambda \partial f(y^n, .)(x^n) + N_{H_n}(x^n),$$

thus there exists $w_1^n \in \partial f(y^n, .)(x^n)$ such that $-\lambda w_1^n \in N_{H_n}(x^n)$, that is, $\langle w_1^n, z - x^n \rangle \geq 0$ for all $z \in H_n$. Hence,

$$\lambda(f(y^n, z) - f(y^n, x^n)) \geq \lambda \langle w_1^n, z - x^n \rangle \geq 0 \; \forall z \in H_n, \tag{11.32}$$

With $z \in H_n$ and $y^n = y^{n-1}$ we get

$$\langle x^n - \lambda w^n - y^n, z - y^n \rangle \leq 0, \tag{11.33}$$

where $w^n \in \partial f(y^n, .)(y^n)$ is the chosen element satisfying (11.31). We deduce that

$$\lambda(f(y^n, z) - f(y^n, y^n)) \geq \lambda \langle w^n, z - y^n \rangle \geq \langle x^n - y^n, z - y^n \rangle.$$

Taking into account that $x^n = x^{n+1} \in H_n$ we obtain

$$\lambda f(y^n, x^n) \geq \lambda \langle w^n, x^n - y^n \rangle \geq \langle x^n - y^n, x^n - y^n \rangle \geq 0. \tag{11.34}$$

Combining (11.32) and (11.34) we have

$$\lambda f(y^n, z) \geq \lambda(f(y^n, z) - f(y^n, x^n)) \geq 0 \; \forall z \in H_n.$$

Since $K \subseteq H_n$, we arrive at

$$f(y^n, z) \geq 0 \; \forall z \in K.$$

This means that $y^n \in EP(f)$. $\square$

Remark 11.10. If $x^{n+1} = y^{n+1} = y^n$ then we also obtain $y^n \in EP(f)$.

Proof. If $x^{n+1} = y^{n+1} = y^n$ then from the fact that y^n is the unique solution to the strongly convex problem

$$\min_{y \in K} \left\{ \lambda f(y^n, y) + \frac{1}{2} \|y - y^n\|^2 \right\},$$

and Lemma 11.2, we deduce that

$$0 = \lambda w^n + y^n - y^n + q,$$

where $w^n \in \partial f(y^n, .)(y^n)$ and $q \in N_K(y^n)$. Since

$$N_K(y^n) = \{q \in H : \langle q, z - y^n \rangle \le 0 \ \forall z \in K\},$$

we obtain

$$\langle -\lambda w^n, z - y^n \rangle \le 0 \ \forall z \in K.$$

Moreover, we have

$$\lambda(f(y^n, z) - f(y^n, y^n)) \ge \lambda \langle w^n, z - y^n \rangle \ge 0 \ \forall z \in K.$$

Taking into account that $f(y^n, y^n) = 0$ we arrive at

$$f(y^n, z) \ge 0 \ \forall z \in K.$$

This means that $y^n \in EP(f)$. $\qquad\qquad\qquad\qquad\qquad\qquad\square$

The next statement plays a crucial role in the proof of the convergence results.

Lemma 11.6. *Let $\{x^n\}$ and $\{y^n\}$ be the sequences generated by algorithm (A) and $z \in EP(f)$. Then*

$$\|x^{n+1} - z\|^2 \le \|x^n - z\|^2 - (1 - 4\lambda c_1)\|x^n - y^n\|^2$$
$$- (1 - 2\lambda c_2)\|x^{n+1} - y^n\|^2 + 4\lambda c_1\|x^n - y^{n-1}\|^2.$$

Proof. From $x^{n+1} = \underset{y \in H_n}{\mathrm{argmin}}\left\{\lambda f(y^n, y) + \dfrac{1}{2}\|y - x^n\|^2\right\}$ and Lemma 11.2, we have

$$0 = \lambda w_1^n + x^{n+1} - x^n + q_1^n,$$

where $w_1^n \in \partial f(y^n, .)(x^{n+1})$ and $q_1^n \in N_{H_n}(x^{n+1})$. From the definition

$$N_{H_n}(x^{n+1}) = \{q \in H : \langle q, y - x^{n+1} \rangle \le 0 \ \forall y \in H_n\},$$

and Lemma 11.4, it follows that

$$\langle x^n - x^{n+1} - \lambda w_1^n, z - x^{n+1} \rangle \le 0.$$

Consequently,

$$\langle x^n - x^{n+1}, z - x^{n+1} \rangle \le \lambda \langle w_1^n, z - x^{n+1} \rangle \le \lambda(f(y^n, z) - f(y^n, x^{n+1})).$$

We have

$$\|x^{n+1} - z\|^2$$
$$= \|x^n - z\|^2 + \|x^{n+1} - x^n\|^2 + 2\langle x^{n+1} - x^n, x^n - z\rangle$$
$$\leq \|x^n - z\|^2 - \|x^{n+1} - x^n\|^2 + 2\langle x^{n+1} - x^n, x^{n+1} - z\rangle$$
$$\leq \|x^n - z\|^2 - \|x^{n+1} - x^n\|^2 + 2\lambda(f(y^n, z) - f(y^n, x^{n+1})) \qquad (11.35)$$
$$= \|x^n - z\|^2 - \|x^{n+1} - x^n\|^2 + 2\lambda[f(y^{n-1}, y^n) - f(y^{n-1}, x^{n+1})]$$
$$\quad + 2\lambda[f(y^{n-1}, x^{n+1}) - f(y^{n-1}, y^n) - f(y^n, x^{n+1})] + 2\lambda f(y^n, z)$$
$$= \|x^n - z\|^2 - \|x^{n+1} - x^n\|^2 + A + B + 2\lambda f(y^n, z),$$

where

$$A = 2\lambda[f(y^{n-1}, y^n) - f(y^{n-1}, x^{n+1})],$$
$$B = 2\lambda[f(y^{n-1}, x^{n+1}) - f(y^{n-1}, y^n) - f(y^n, x^{n+1})].$$

From $x^{n+1} \in H_n$ we obtain $\langle x^n - \lambda w^n - y^n, x^{n+1} - y^n\rangle \leq 0$, where $w^n \in \partial f(y^{n-1}, .)(y^n)$. Using the definition of the subdifferential we arrive at

$$f(y^{n-1}, y) - f(y^{n-1}, y^n) \geq \langle w^n, y - y^n\rangle \quad \forall y \in H.$$

Therefore,

$$2\lambda[f(y^{n-1}, x^{n+1}) - f(y^{n-1}, y^n)] \geq 2\lambda\langle w^n, x^{n+1} - y^n\rangle$$
$$\geq 2\langle x^n - y^n, x^{n+1} - y^n\rangle.$$

It follows that

$$A \leq 2\langle y^n - x^n, x^{n+1} - y^n\rangle$$
$$= \|x^{n+1} - x^n\|^2 - \|x^n - y^n\|^2 - \|x^{n+1} - y^n\|^2.$$

By the assumption (B5), we get

$$B = 2\lambda[f(y^{n-1}, x^{n+1}) - f(y^{n-1}, y^n) - f(y^n, x^{n+1})]$$
$$\leq 2\lambda[c_1\|y^{n-1} - y^n\|^2 + c_2\|y^n - x^{n+1}\|^2].$$

On the other hand, we have

$$\|y^{n-1} - y^n\|^2 = \|y^n - x^n\|^2 + \|x^n - y^{n-1}\|^2 + 2\langle y^n - x^n, x^n - y^{n-1}\rangle$$
$$\leq 2(\|y^n - x^n\|^2 + \|x^n - y^{n-1}\|^2).$$

So, we obtain

$$B \leq 2\lambda[2c_1\|y^n - x^n\|^2 + 2c_1\|x^n - y^{n-1}\|^2 + c_2\|y^n - x^{n+1}\|^2].$$

It implies that

$$\|x^{n+1} - z\|^2 \leq \|x^n - z\|^2 - (1 - 4\lambda c_1)\|x^n - y^n\|^2$$
$$- (1 - 2\lambda c_2)\|x^{n+1} - y^n\|^2$$
$$+ 4\lambda c_1\|x^n - y^{n-1}\|^2 + 2\lambda f(y^n, z). \tag{11.36}$$

It follows from $z \in EP(f)$ and the pseudo-monotonicity of f that $f(y^n, z) \leq 0$. Then the inequality (11.36) implies

$$\|x^{n+1} - z\|^2 \leq \|x^n - z\|^2 - (1 - 4\lambda c_1)\|x^n - y^n\|^2$$
$$- (1 - 2\lambda c_2)\|x^{n+1} - y^n\|^2 + 4\lambda c_1\|x^n - y^{n-1}\|^2. \tag{11.37}$$

The proof is complete. □

We are now in a position to give the convergence of the sequence generated by algorithm (A).

Theorem 11.10. *Let K be a nonempty closed convex subset of H. Let $f : H \times H \to \mathbb{R}$ satisfying (B1)–(B7). Assume further that $\lambda \in \left(0, \frac{1}{2(2c_1 + c_2)}\right)$. Then the sequence $\{x^n\}$ generated by algorithm (A) converges weakly to a solution of the EP (11.25).*

Proof. We split the proof into several steps:

Step 1: We first show the boundedness of the sequence $\{x^n\}$. Let $z \in EP(f)$. The inequality (11.37) can be rewritten as

$$\|x^{n+1} - z\|^2 \leq \|x^n - z\|^2 - (1 - 4\lambda c_1)\|x^n - y^n\|^2$$
$$- (1 - 2\lambda c_2 - 4\lambda c_1)\|x^{n+1} - y^n\|^2$$
$$+ 4\lambda c_1\|x^n - y^{n-1}\|^2 - 4\lambda c_1\|x^{n+1} - y^n\|^2. \tag{11.38}$$

We fix a number $N \in \mathbb{N}$ and consider the inequality (11.38) for all the numbers $N, N + 1, ..., M$, where $M > N$. Adding these inequalities, we obtain

$$\|x^{M+1} - z\|^2 \leq \|x^N - z\|^2 - (1 - 4\lambda c_1) \sum_{n=N}^{M} \|x^n - y^n\|^2$$

$$- (1 - 2\lambda c_2 - 4\lambda c_1) \sum_{n=N}^{M} \|x^{n+1} - y^n\|^2 + 4\lambda c_1\|x^N - y^{N-1}\|^2$$

$$- 4\lambda c_1\|x^{M+1} - y^M\|^2 \tag{11.39}$$

$$\leq \|x^N - z\|^2 + 4\lambda c_1\|x^N - y^{N-1}\|^2. \tag{11.40}$$

The inequality (11.40) leads to the boundedness of $\{x^n\}$. Hence, there exists $\bar{x} \in H$ and a subsequence $\{x^{n_k}\}$ of $\{x^n\}$ such that $x^{n_k} \rightharpoonup \bar{x}$. Moreover, from the inequality (11.39), we obtain the convergence of the series

$$\sum_{n=1}^{\infty} \|x^{n+1} - y^n\|^2 \text{ and } \sum_{n=1}^{\infty} \|x^n - y^n\|^2.$$

Thus, we have

$$\lim_{n \to \infty} \|x^{n+1} - y^n\| = \lim_{n \to \infty} \|x^n - y^n\| = 0. \tag{11.41}$$

Step 2: Let us show that $\bar{x} \in EP(f)$. It follows from (11.41) that $y^{n_k} \rightharpoonup \bar{x} \in K$. We have

$$\|y^n - y^{n+1}\| \le \|y^n - x^{n+1}\| + \|x^{n+1} - y^{n+1}\|. \tag{11.42}$$

Combining (11.41) and (11.42) we deduce that

$$\lim_{n \to \infty} \|y^n - y^{n+1}\| = 0. \tag{11.43}$$

Therefore, we get $y^{n_k+1} \rightharpoonup \bar{x}$.

It follows from

$$y^{n+1} = \operatorname*{argmin}_{y \in K}\left\{ \lambda f(y^n, y) + \frac{1}{2}\|y - x^{n+1}\|^2 \right\}$$

and Lemma 11.2 that there exist $w^{n+1} \in \partial f(y^n, .)(y^{n+1})$ and $q^{n+1} \in N_C(y^{n+1})$ such that

$$0 = \lambda w^{n+1} + y^{n+1} - x^{n+1} + q^{n+1}.$$

From the definition of $N_K(y^{n+1})$, we deduce that

$$\langle x^{n+1} - y^{n+1} - \lambda w^{n+1}, y - y^{n+1} \rangle \le 0 \ \forall y \in K,$$

or

$$\langle x^{n+1} - y^{n+1}, y - y^{n+1} \rangle \le \langle \lambda w^{n+1}, y - y^{n+1} \rangle \ \forall y \in K.$$

On the other hand, since $w^{n+1} \in \partial f(y^n, .)(y^{n+1})$, we get

$$\langle w^{n+1}, y - y^{n+1} \rangle \le f(y^n, y) - f(y^n, y^{n+1}) \ \forall y \in K.$$

Hence, we arrive at

$$\frac{\langle x^{n+1} - y^{n+1}, y - y^{n+1} \rangle}{\lambda} \le f(y^n, y) - f(y^n, y^{n+1}) \ \forall y \in K. \tag{11.44}$$

Since the left-hand side converges to zero, replacing n in (11.44) by n_k we have by (11.43) and the assumption (B6) that

$$0 \leq \limsup_{k \to \infty} f(y^{n_k}, y^{n_k+1})$$

$$= \limsup_{k \to \infty} \left(\frac{\langle x^{n_k+1} - y^{n_k+1}, y - y^{n_k+1} \rangle}{\lambda} + f(y^{n_k}, y^{n_k+1}) \right)$$

$$\leq \limsup_{k \to \infty} f(y^{n_k}, y) \quad \forall y \in K.$$

Now under the condition (B3), we obtain, $\bar{x} \in EP(f)$.

Step 3: We claim that $x^n \rightharpoonup \bar{x}$. On the contrary, assume that there is a subsequence $\{x_{m_k}\}$ such that $x_{m_k} \rightharpoonup \tilde{x}$ as $k \to \infty$ and $\bar{x} \neq \tilde{x}$. Arguing as in Step 2, we also obtain $\tilde{x} \in EP(f)$. It follows from the inequality (11.38) and the condition $0 < \lambda < \frac{1}{2(2c_1+c_2)}$ that

$$\|x^{n+1} - z\|^2 + 4\lambda c_1 \|x^{n+1} - y^n\|^2$$
$$\leq \|x^n - z\|^2 + 4\lambda c_1 \|x^n - y^{n-1}\|^2 \quad \forall z \in EP(f).$$

Thus, for all $z \in EP(f)$, the sequence $\{\|x^n - z\|^2 + 4\lambda c_1 \|x^n - y^{n-1}\|^2\}$ must be convergent. From (11.41) we have

$$\lim_{n \to \infty} \|x^n - z\|^2 \in \mathbb{R} \quad \forall z \in EP(f).$$

By Lemma 11.3 (Opial lemma), we have

$$\lim_{n \to \infty} \|x^n - \bar{x}\|^2 = \lim_{k \to \infty} \|x^{n_k} - \bar{x}\|^2$$

$$= \liminf_{k \to \infty} \|x^{n_k} - \bar{x}\|^2 < \liminf_{k \to \infty} \|x^{n_k} - \tilde{x}\|^2$$

$$= \lim_{k \to \infty} \|x^{n_k} - \tilde{x}\|^2 = \lim_{n \to \infty} \|x^n - \tilde{x}\|^2$$

$$= \lim_{k \to \infty} \|x^{m_k} - \tilde{x}\|^2 = \liminf_{k \to \infty} \|x^{m_k} - \tilde{x}\|^2$$

$$< \liminf_{k \to \infty} \|x^{m_k} - \bar{x}\|^2$$

$$= \lim_{k \to \infty} \|x^{m_k} - \bar{x}\|^2 = \lim_{n \to \infty} \|x^n - \bar{x}\|^2,$$

which is a contradiction. Thus, $\bar{x} = \tilde{x}$ and this completes the proof. $\qquad \square$

Next we show that algorithm (A) is able to provide us more: strong convergence, if we slightly strengthen the assumptions. The further assumption guaranteeing this is the nonemptiness of the interior of $EP(f)$.

Theorem 11.11. *Suppose that beside the assumptions of Theorem 11.10, intEP(f) $\neq \emptyset$ holds. Then the sequence $\{x^n\}$ generated by algorithm (A) converges strongly to a solution of the EP (11.25).*

Proof. Take the sequence $\alpha_n := 4\lambda c_1 \|x^n - y^{n-1}\|^2$. Then from the inequality (11.38) we deduce that

$$\|x^{n+1} - z\|^2 \leq \|x^n - z\|^2 + \alpha_n - \alpha_{n+1} \quad \forall z \in EP(f). \tag{11.45}$$

Now fix an element $u \in intEP(f)$ and choose $r > 0$ such that $\|v - u\| \leq r$ implies $v \in EP(f)$. Then for any $x_{n+1} \neq x_n$ we have

$$\left\| x_{n+1} - \left(u - r \frac{x_{n+1} - x_n}{\|x_{n+1} - x_n\|} \right) \right\|^2$$
$$\leq \left\| x_n - \left(u - r \frac{x_{n+1} - x_n}{\|x_{n+1} - x_n\|} \right) \right\|^2 + \alpha_n - \alpha_{n+1}. \tag{11.46}$$

Simplifying the inequality (11.46), we obtain

$$2r\|x_{n+1} - x_n\| \leq \|x_n - u\|^2 - \|x_{n+1} - u\|^2 + \alpha_n - \alpha_{n+1}. \tag{11.47}$$

Let $M > N$ be arbitrary positive integers. By summing up the inequality (11.47) from N to $M - 1$ we obtain

$$2r\|x_M - x_N\| \leq \|x_N - u\|^2 - \|x_M - u\|^2 + \alpha_N - \alpha_M. \tag{11.48}$$

Taking into account that the sequence $\beta_n := \|x_n - u\|^2 + \alpha_n$ converges, we conclude that the sequence $\{x_n\}$ is Cauchy, therefore, (strongly) convergent.

Since we already showed that each weak cluster point of $\{x_n\}$ is a solution of EP (Step 2 in the proof of Theorem 11.10), the proof is complete. $\qquad \square$

In the following theorem we will show that our method has at least R-linear rate of convergence under a strong pseudo-monotonicity assumption of f. A bifunction $f : H \times H \to \mathbb{R}$ is said to be γ-strongly pseudo-monotone on $K \subset H$ (see [63]) if there exists $\gamma > 0$ such that for any $x, y \in K$

$$f(x, y) \geq 0 \Longrightarrow f(y, x) \leq -\gamma \|x - y\|^2.$$

Theorem 11.12. *Let C be a nonempty closed convex subset of H. Let $f : H \times H \to \mathbb{R}$ be a bifunction satisfying conditions (B1), (B4), (B5), (B7) and be γ-strongly pseudo-monotone on K. Assume that $\lambda \in \left(0, \min\left\{ \frac{1}{16\gamma}; \frac{3}{16c_1}; \frac{1}{4c_1 + 2c_2 + \gamma} \right\} \right)$. Then the sequence $\{x^n\}$ generated by the algorithm (A) converges strongly to the unique solution x^* of the EP (11.25). Moreover, there exist $M > 0$ and $\mu \in (0, 1)$ such that*

$$\|x^{n+1} - x^*\| \leq M\mu^n \quad \forall n \geq 1. \tag{11.49}$$

Proof. The uniqueness follows by the strong pseudo-monotonicity. Using similar arguments as in the proof of Lemma 11.6, it follows from (11.36) that

$$
\begin{aligned}
\|x^{n+1} - x^*\|^2 &\le \|x^n - x^*\|^2 - (1 - 4\lambda c_1)\|x^n - y^n\|^2 \\
&\quad - (1 - 2\lambda c_2)\|x^{n+1} - y^n\|^2 \\
&\quad + 4\lambda c_1 \|x^n - y^{n-1}\|^2 + 2\lambda f(y^n, x^*) \\
&\le \|x^n - x^*\|^2 - (1 - 4\lambda c_1)\|x^n - y^n\|^2 \\
&\quad - (1 - 2\lambda c_2)\|x^{n+1} - y^n\|^2 \\
&\quad + 4\lambda c_1 \|x^n - y^{n-1}\|^2 - 2\gamma\lambda\|y^n - x^*\|^2 \\
&= (1 - 2\gamma\lambda)\|x^n - x^*\|^2 - (1 - 4\lambda c_1 + 2\gamma\lambda)\|x^n - y^n\|^{+2} \\
&\quad - (1 - 2\lambda c_2)\|x^{n+1} - y^n\|^2 + 4\lambda c_1\|x^n - y^{n-1}\|^2 \\
&\quad - 4\gamma\lambda\langle y^n - x^n, x^n - x^*\rangle.
\end{aligned}
$$

Applying the inequality $-4\gamma\lambda\langle y^n - x^n, x^n - x^*\rangle \le 16\gamma^2\lambda^2\|x^n - x^*\|^2 + \frac{1}{4}\|y^n - x^n\|^2$, we obtain

$$
\begin{aligned}
\|x^{n+1} - x^*\|^2 &\le (1 - 2\gamma\lambda + 16\gamma^2\lambda^2)\|x^n - x^*\|^2 \\
&\quad - (\frac{3}{4} - 4\lambda c_1 + 2\gamma\lambda)\|x^n - y^n\|^2 \\
&\quad + 4\lambda c_1\|x^n - y^{n-1}\|^2 - (1 - 2\lambda c_2)\|x^{n+1} - y^n\|^2.
\end{aligned}
$$

Taking into account the fact that $\lambda \le \min\left\{\frac{1}{16\gamma}; \frac{3}{16c_1}\right\}$, we have

$$
\begin{aligned}
\|x^{n+1} - x^*\|^2 &\le (1 - \gamma\lambda)\|x^n - x^*\|^2 + 4\lambda c_1\|x^n - y^{n-1}\|^2 \\
&\quad - (1 - 2\lambda c_2)\|x^{n+1} - y^n\|^2 \\
&= (1 - \gamma\lambda)\left(\|x^n - x^*\|^2 + \frac{4\lambda c_1}{1 - \gamma\lambda}\|x^n - y^{n-1}\|^2\right) \\
&\quad - \frac{4\lambda c_1}{1 - \gamma\lambda}\|x^{n+1} - y^n\|^2 \\
&\quad - \left(1 - 2\lambda c_2 - \frac{4\lambda c_1}{1 - \gamma\lambda}\right)\|x^{n+1} - y^n\|^2. \quad\quad (11.50)
\end{aligned}
$$

From the condition $\lambda < \frac{1}{4c_1 + 2c_2 + \gamma}$, it is easy to see that $1 - 2\lambda c_2 - \frac{4\lambda c_1}{1 - \gamma\lambda} > 0$. Hence

$$
\begin{aligned}
\|x^{n+1} - x^*\|^2 &+ \frac{4\lambda c_1}{1 - \gamma\lambda}\|x^{n+1} - y^n\|^2 \\
&\le (1 - \gamma\lambda)\left(\|x^n - x^*\|^2 + \frac{4\lambda c_1}{1 - \gamma\lambda}\|x^n - y^{n-1}\|^2\right).
\end{aligned}
$$

Let $\mu := 1 - \gamma\lambda \in (0, 1)$, $M := \|x^1 - x^*\|^2 + \frac{4\lambda c_1}{1-\gamma\lambda}\|x^1 - y^0\|^2$. From the last inequality and by induction, we arrive at

$$\|x^{n+1} - x^*\|^2 \le \|x^{n+1} - x^*\|^2 + \frac{4\lambda c_1}{1-\gamma\lambda}\|x^{n+1} - y^n\|^2 \le M\mu^n.$$

This finishes the proof of Theorem 11.12. □

11.4.2 Applications to Variational Inequalities

Recall that if the equilibrium bifunction f is defined by $f(x, y) = \langle Ax, y - x \rangle$ for every $x, y \in K$, with $A : H \to H$, then the equilibrium problem (11.25) reduces to the *variational inequality problem* (VIP):

$$\text{find } x^* \in K \text{ such that } \langle Ax^*, y - x^* \rangle \ge 0 \ \forall y \in K. \qquad (11.51)$$

(See also (2.18) in Chapter 2.)

The set of solutions of the problem (11.51) is denoted by $VI(K, A)$.

In this situation, algorithm (A) reduces to Algorithm 1 of Malitsky and Semenov [122], which is known as a subgradient extragradient type algorithm for monotone variational inequalities. In the sequel we shall refer to it as **algorithm (B)**.

Step 1: Specify $x^0, y^0 \in K$ and $\lambda > 0$;
Compute

$$\begin{cases} x^1 = P_K(x^0 - \lambda A y^0), \\ y^1 = P_K(x^1 - \lambda A y^0). \end{cases}$$

Step 2: Given x^n, y^n and y^{n-1}, construct the halfspace

$$H_n = \{z \in H : \langle x^n - \lambda A y^{n-1} - y^n, z - y^n \rangle \le 0\}.$$

Step 3: Compute

$$\begin{cases} x^{n+1} = P_{H_n}(x^n - \lambda A y^n), \\ y^{n+1} = P_K(x^{n+1} - \lambda A y^n). \end{cases}$$

Step 4: If $x^{n+1} = x^n$ and $y^n = y^{n-1}$ then stop. Otherwise, set $n := n + 1$, and return to Step 2.

To guarantee that f is jointly weakly lower semicontinuous on $H \times H$, the authors in [169] required the weak-to-strong continuity of $A : H \to H$, i.e., A is such that for any sequence $\{x^n\} \subset H$,

$$x^n \rightharpoonup x \implies Ax^n \to Ax. \qquad (11.52)$$

As indicated before, we do not need anymore the joint weak lower semi-continuity of f, but only the weak upper semicontinuity of $f(\cdot, y)$. To this end, we remind the following concept for single-valued operators (called F-hemicontinuity in [125]).

Definition 11.2. Let X be a normed space with X^* its dual space and K a closed convex subset of X. The mapping $A : K \to X^*$ is called F-*hemicontinuous* iff for all $y \in K$, the function $x \mapsto \langle A(x), x - y \rangle$ is weakly lower semicontinuous on K (or equivalently, $x \mapsto \langle A(x), y - x \rangle$ is weakly upper semicontinuous on K).

Clearly, any weak-to-strong continuous mapping is also F-hemicontinuous, but vice-versa not, as the following example shows.

Example 11.5. ([102]) Consider the Hilbert space $l^2 = \{x = (x^i)_{i \in \mathbf{N}} : \sum_{i=1}^{\infty} |x^i|^2 < \infty\}$ and $A : l^2 \to l^2$ be the identity operator. Take an arbitrary sequence $\{x_n\} \subseteq l^2$ converging weakly to $\bar{x}$. Since the function $x \mapsto \|x\|^2$ is continuous and convex, it is weakly lower semicontinuous. Hence,

$$\|\bar{x}\|^2 \le \liminf_{n \to \infty} \|x_n\|^2,$$

which clearly implies

$$\langle \bar{x}, \bar{x} - y \rangle \le \liminf_{n \to \infty} \langle x_n, x_n - y \rangle,$$

for all $y \in l^2$, i.e., A is F-hemicontinuous.

On the other hand, we take $x_n = e_n = (0, 0, ..., 0, 1, 0, ...)$ with 1 in the nth position. It is obvious that $e_n \rightharpoonup 0$, but $\{e_n\}$ does not have any strongly convergent subsequence, as $\|e_n - e_m\| = \sqrt{2}$ for $m \neq n$. Therefore, A is not weak-to-strong continuous.

The next result, establishing weak convergence of algorithm (B) is a consequence of Theorem 11.10.

Corollary 11.8. *Let K be a nonempty closed convex subset of H. Let $A : H \to H$ be a pseudo-monotone, F-hemicontinuous, Lipschitz continuous mapping with constant $L > 0$ such that $VI(C, A) \neq \emptyset$. Let $\{x^n\}$, $\{y^n\}$ be the sequences generated by algorithm (B) with $0 < \lambda < \frac{1}{3L}$. Then the sequences $\{x^n\}$ and $\{y^n\}$ converge weakly to the same point $x^* \in VI(C, A)$.*

Proof. For each pair $x, y \in K$, we define

$$f(x, y) := \langle Ax, y - x \rangle.$$

From the assumptions, it is easy to check that all assumptions of Theorem 11.10 are satisfied. Note that Step 3 of algorithm (B) can be written as

$$
\begin{cases}
x^{n+1} = \underset{y \in H_n}{\operatorname{argmin}} \left\{ \lambda \langle Ay^n, y - y^n \rangle + \frac{1}{2} \|y - x^n\|^2 \right\}, \\
y^{n+1} = \underset{y \in K}{\operatorname{argmin}} \left\{ \lambda \langle Ay^n, y - y^n \rangle + \frac{1}{2} \|y - x^{n+1}\|^2 \right\}.
\end{cases}
$$

It follows that

$$
\begin{cases}
x^{n+1} = \underset{y \in H_n}{\operatorname{argmin}} \left\{ \frac{1}{2} \|y - (x^n - \lambda Ay^n)\|^2 \right\} = P_{H_n}(x^n - \lambda Ay^n), \\
y^{n+1} = \underset{y \in K}{\operatorname{argmin}} \left\{ \frac{1}{2} \|y - (x^{n+1} - \lambda Ay^n)\|^2 \right\} = P_K(x^{n+1} - \lambda Ay^n).
\end{cases}
$$

By Theorem 11.10, the sequences $\{x^n\}$ and $\{y^n\}$ converge weakly to $x^* \in EP(f)$. It means that the sequences $\{x^n\}$ and $\{y^n\}$ converge weakly to $x^* \in VI(C, A)$. Hence, the result is true and the proof is complete. $\qquad \square$

Note that in order to apply Corollary 11.8 one needs to know the Lipschitz constant L. When A is Lipschitz continuous but the Lipschitz constant is unknown, or cannot be calculated easily, we propose the following self-adaptive algorithm (**algorithm (C)**).

Step 1: Take $x^0, y^0 \in K$, $\mu \in (0, \frac{1}{3})$. Set $n = 0$.
Compute

$$
\begin{cases}
x^1 = P_K(x^0 - Ay^0), \\
y^1 = P_K(x^1 - Ay^0).
\end{cases}
$$

Step 2: Given x^n, y^n and y^{n-1} $(n \geq 1)$, define

$$
\lambda_n = \begin{cases}
\mu \frac{\|y^n - y^{n-1}\|}{\|Ay^n - Ay^{n-1}\|} & \text{if } \|Ay^n - Ay^{n-1}\| \neq 0; \\
1 & \text{otherwise,}
\end{cases}
\tag{11.53}
$$

and construct the halfspace

$$
\mathcal{H}_n = \{z \in H : \langle x^n - \lambda_n Ay^{n-1} - y^n, z - y^n \rangle \leq 0\}.
$$

Compute

$$
\begin{cases}
x^{n+1} = P_{\mathcal{H}_n}(x^n - \lambda_n Ay^n), \\
y^{n+1} = P_K(x^{n+1} - \lambda_n Ay^n).
\end{cases}
\tag{11.54}
$$

Step 3: If $x^{n+1} = x^n$ and $y^n = y^{n-1}$ then stop. Otherwise, set $n := n + 1$, and return to Step 2.

Remark 11.11. Since A is Lipschitz continuous with constant L, from (11.53), we have

$$\lambda_n \geq \min\{1; \frac{\mu}{L}\}. \tag{11.55}$$

In what follows, we assume that

(C1) A is pseudo-monotone on H;
(C2) A is F-hemicontinuous, Lipschitz continuous but the Lipschitz constant L is unknown;
(C3) $VI(K, A) \neq \emptyset$.

We are now in a position to give the weak convergence of the sequence generated by algorithm (C).

Theorem 11.13. *Assume that $A : H \to H$ is a mapping satisfying conditions (C1)–(C3). Then the sequences $\{x^k\}$ and $\{y^k\}$ converge weakly to the same element of $VI(K, A)$.*

Proof. The proof is divided into two steps:

Step 1: We show that for each $z \in VI(K, A)$, the following inequality holds:

$$\left\| x^{n+1} - z \right\|^2 \leq \left\| x^n - z \right\|^2 - (1 - 2\mu) \left\| x^{n+1} - y^n \right\|^2$$
$$- (1 - \mu) \left\| x^n - y^n \right\|^2 + \mu \left\| x^n - y^{n-1} \right\|^2. \tag{11.56}$$

Indeed, since $z \in VI(K, A) \subset \mathcal{H}_n$ and $x^{n+1} = P_{\mathcal{H}_n}(x^n - \lambda_n Ay^n)$, the characterization (b) of the metric projection provides

$$\left\| x^{n+1} - z \right\|^2 \leq \left\| x^n - \lambda_n Ay^n - z \right\|^2 - \left\| x^n - \lambda_n Ay^n - x^{n+1} \right\|^2$$
$$= \left\| x^n - z \right\|^2 - \left\| x^n - x^{n+1} \right\|^2 - 2\lambda_n \left\langle Ay^n, x^{n+1} - z \right\rangle. \tag{11.57}$$

It follows from the pseudo-monotonicity of A and $z \in VI(K, A)$ that $\langle Ay^n, y^n - z \rangle \geq 0$. Adding this term to the right-hand side of (11.57) we obtain

$$\left\| x^{n+1} - z \right\|^2 \leq \left\| x^n - z \right\|^2 - \left\| x^n - x^{n+1} \right\|^2 - 2\lambda_n \left\langle Ay^n, x^{n+1} - y^n \right\rangle$$
$$= \left\| x^n - z \right\|^2 - \left\| x^n - y^n \right\|^2 - \left\| x^{n+1} - y^n \right\|^2 - 2\left\langle x^n - y^n, y^n - x^{n+1} \right\rangle$$
$$- 2\lambda_n \left\langle Ay^n, x^{n+1} - y^n \right\rangle$$

$$= \left\| x^n - z \right\|^2 - \left\| x^n - y^n \right\|^2 - \left\| x^{n+1} - y^n \right\|^2$$
$$+ 2\lambda_n \left\langle Ay^{n-1} - Ay^n, x^{n+1} - y^n \right\rangle + 2 \left\langle x^n - \lambda_n Ay^{n-1} - y^n, x^{n+1} - y^n \right\rangle.$$

Since $x^{n+1} \in \mathcal{H}_n$, we have $\left\langle x^n - \lambda_n Ay^{n-1} - y^n, x^{n+1} - y^n \right\rangle \le 0$. The fourth term of the above inequality is estimated as follows.

$$2\lambda_n \left\langle Ay^{n-1} - Ay^n, x^{n+1} - y^n \right\rangle \le 2\mu \left\| y^{n-1} - y^n \right\| \left\| x^{n+1} - y^n \right\|$$
$$\le 2\mu \left(\left\| y^{n-1} - x^n \right\| + \left\| x^n - y^n \right\| \right) \left\| x^{n+1} - y^n \right\|$$
$$\le \mu \left(\left\| y^{n-1} - x^n \right\|^2 + 2 \left\| x^{n+1} - y^n \right\|^2 + \left\| x^n - y^n \right\|^2 \right).$$

Therefore, we get the desired inequality (11.56).

Step 2: We prove that the sequence $\{x^k\}$ converges weakly to $\bar{x} \in VI(K, A)$. First, it follows from (11.56) that

$$\left\| x^{n+1} - z \right\|^2 \le \left\| x^n - z \right\|^2 - (1 - 3\mu) \left\| x^{n+1} - y^n \right\|^2$$
$$- (1 - \mu) \left\| x^n - y^n \right\|^2 + \mu \left\| x^n - y^{n-1} \right\|^2 - \mu \left\| x^{n+1} - y^n \right\|^2.$$
$$(11.58)$$

We fix a number $N \in \mathbb{N}$ and consider the inequality (11.58) for all the numbers $N, N+1, ..., M$, where $M > N$. Adding these inequalities, we obtain

$$\left\| x^{M+1} - z \right\|^2 \le \left\| x^N - z \right\|^2 - (1 - \mu) \sum_{n=N}^{M} \left\| x^n - y^n \right\|^2$$
$$- (1 - 3\mu) \sum_{n=N}^{M} \left\| x^{n+1} - y^n \right\|^2$$
$$+ \mu \left\| x^N - y^{N-1} \right\|^2 - \mu \left\| x^{M+1} - y^M \right\|^2$$
$$\le \left\| x^N - z \right\|^2 + \mu \left\| x^N - y^{N-1} \right\|^2.$$

Thus we obtain the boundedness of the sequences $\{x^n\}$, $\{y^n\}$, and then, as in Step 1 in the proof of Theorem 11.10,

$$\lim_{n \to \infty} \left\| x^{n+1} - y^n \right\| = \lim_{n \to \infty} \left\| x^n - y^n \right\| = 0. \qquad (11.59)$$

Consequently,

$$\lim_{n \to \infty} \left\| y^{n+1} - y^n \right\| = 0. \qquad (11.60)$$

We now choose a subsequence $\{x_{n_k}\}$ of $\{x_n\}$ such that $x_{n_k} \rightharpoonup \bar{x}$. By (11.59), $y^{n_k} \rightharpoonup \bar{x}$ and $\bar{x} \in K$. For all $x \in K$ with allowance for characterization (a) of the metric projection and (11.54), we get

$$\left\langle y^{n_k+1} - x^{n_k+1} + \lambda_{n_k} Ay^{n_k}, y - y^{n_k+1} \right\rangle \geq 0 \quad \forall y \in K.$$

Hence,

$$0 \leq \left\langle y^{n_k+1} - x^{n_k+1} + \lambda_{n_k} Ay^{n_k}, y - y^{n_k+1} \right\rangle = \left\langle y^{n_k+1} - x^{n_k+1}, y - y^{n_k+1} \right\rangle$$
$$+ \lambda_{n_k} \left\langle Ay^{n_k}, y^{n_k} - y^{n_k+1} \right\rangle + \lambda_{n_k} \left\langle Ay^{n_k}, y - y^{n_k} \right\rangle \quad \forall y \in K.$$

Dividing both sides of the last inequality by λ_{n_k} we get

$$0 \leq \frac{\left\langle y^{n_k+1} - x^{n_k+1}, y - y^{n_k+1} \right\rangle}{\lambda_{n_k}} + \left\langle Ay^{n_k}, y^{n_k} - y^{n_k+1} \right\rangle$$
$$+ \left\langle Ay^{n_k}, y - y^{n_k} \right\rangle \quad \forall y \in K.$$

Passing to the limit for k tending to ∞ in the above inequality and using weak lower semicontinuity of the function $x \mapsto \langle Ax, x - y \rangle$ together with (11.55), (11.59) and (11.60) we obtain

$$\langle A\bar{x}, y - \bar{x} \rangle \geq 0 \quad \forall y \in K,$$

i.e., $\bar{x} \in VI(K, A)$.

Now, in view of (11.58) we have

$$\left\| x^{n+1} - z \right\|^2 + \mu \left\| x^{n+1} - y^n \right\|^2 \leq \left\| x^n - z \right\|^2 + \mu \left\| x^n - y^{n-1} \right\|^2. \quad (11.61)$$

Therefore the sequence $\{\|x^n - z\|^2 + \mu \|x^n - y^{n-1}\|^2\}$ is convergent. From (11.59) we have

$$\lim_{n \to \infty} \|x^n - z\|^2 \in \mathbb{R}.$$

We claim that $x^n \rightharpoonup \bar{x}$. On the contrary, assume that there is a subsequence $\{x_{m_k}\}$ such that $x_{m_k} \rightharpoonup \tilde{x}$ as $k \to \infty$ and $\bar{x} \neq \tilde{x}$. Using the same argument as above, we also obtain $\tilde{x} \in VI(K, A)$. Finally, as in Step 3 of Theorem 11.10, we obtain $x_n \rightharpoonup \bar{x}$ by Lemma 11.3 (Opial's lemma). The convergence of $\{y^n\}$ to $\bar{x}$ is guaranteed by (11.59). This finishes the proof of Theorem 11.13. $\qquad \square$

11.4.3 Numerical Results

In this subsection some numerical results will be presented in order to test algorithm (A) and compare it with other similar algorithms within the literature. The MATLAB codes run on a PC (with Intel®Core2™ Quad Processor Q9400 2.66Ghz 4GB Ram) under MATLAB Version 7.11 (R2010b).

TABLE 11.1 The parameters used in Example 11.6

j	$\hat{\alpha}_j$	$\hat{\beta}_j$	$\hat{\gamma}_j$	$\bar{\alpha}_j$	$\bar{\beta}_j$	$\bar{\gamma}_j$
1	0.0400	2.00	0.00	2.0000	1.0000	25.0000
2	0.0350	1.75	0.00	1.7500	1.0000	28.5714
3	0.1250	1.00	0.00	1.0000	1.0000	8.0000
4	0.0116	3.25	0.00	3.2500	1.0000	86.2069
5	0.0500	3.00	0.00	3.0000	1.0000	20.0000
6	0.0500	3.00	0.00	3.0000	1.0000	20.0000

Example 11.6. (Nash-Cournot equilibrium models of electricity markets) In this example, we apply the proposed algorithm to a Cournot-Nash equilibrium model of electricity markets. In this model, it is assumed that there are three electricity companies i $(i = 1, 2, 3)$. Each company i owns several generating units with index set I_i. In this example, suppose that $I_1 = \{1\}$, $I_2 = \{2, 3\}$, $I_3 = \{4, 5, 6\}$. Let x_j be the power generation of unit j $(j = 1, \ldots, 6)$ and assume that the electricity price p can be expressed by:

$$p = 378.4 - 2 \sum_{j=1}^{6} x_j.$$

The cost of a generating unit j is defined as $c_j(x_j) := \max\{\hat{c}_j(x_j), \bar{c}_j(x_j)\}$ with

$$\hat{c}_j(x_j) := \frac{\hat{\alpha}_j}{2} x_j^2 + \hat{\beta}_j x_j + \hat{\gamma}_j$$

and

$$\bar{c}_j(x_j) := \bar{\alpha}_j x_j + \frac{\bar{\beta}_j}{\bar{\beta}_j + 1} \bar{\gamma}_j^{-1/\bar{\beta}_j} (x_j)^{(\bar{\beta}_j+1)/\bar{\beta}_j},$$

where the parameters $\hat{\alpha}_j$, $\hat{\beta}_j$, $\hat{\gamma}_j$, $\bar{\alpha}_j$, $\bar{\beta}_j$ and $\bar{\gamma}_j$ are given in Table 11.1.

Suppose that the profit of the company i is given by

$$f_i(x) := p \sum_{j \in I_i} x_j - \sum_{j \in I_i} c_j(x_j) = \left(378.4 - 2 \sum_{l=1}^{6} x_l \right) \sum_{j \in I_i} x_j - \sum_{j \in I_i} c_j(x_j),$$

where $x = (x_1, \ldots, x_6)^T$ subject to the constraint $x \in C := \left\{ x \in \mathbb{R}^6 : x_j^{\min} \leq x_j \leq x_j^{\max} \right\}$ with $x_j^{\min}$ and $x_j^{\max}$ given in Table 11.2.

We define the equilibrium bifunction f by

$$f(x, y) := \sum_{i=1}^{3} (\varphi_i(x, x) - \varphi_i(x, y)),$$

TABLE 11.2 The parameters used in Example 11.6

j	1	2	3	4	5	6
x_j^{min}	0	0	0	0	0	0
x_j^{max}	80	80	50	55	30	40

where

$$\varphi_i(x, y) := \left[378,4 - 2 \left(\sum_{j \notin I_i} x_j + \sum_{j \in I_i} y_j \right) \right] \sum_{j \in I_i} y_j - \sum_{j \in I_i} c_j(y_j).$$

Then the Nash-Cournot equilibrium models of electricity markets can be reformulated as an equilibrium problem (see [111]):

$$\text{find } x^* \in C \text{ such that } f(x^*, y) \geq 0 \ \forall y \in C. \qquad (EP(f, C))$$

Similar to [149], we rewrite the function f as

$$f(x, y) = \langle (A + B)x + By + a, y - x \rangle + c(y) - c(x), \qquad (11.62)$$

where

$$A := 2 \sum_{i=1}^{3} \bar{q}^i (q^i)^T, \quad B := 2 \sum_{i=1}^{3} q^i (q^i)^T,$$

$$a := -378.4 \sum_{i=1}^{3} q^i, \quad c(x) := \sum_{j=1}^{6} c_j(x_j).$$

Here the vectors $q^i := (q_1^i, \ldots, q_6^i)$ and $\bar{q}^i := (\bar{q}_1^i, \ldots, \bar{q}_6^i)$ are defined by

$$q_j^i = \begin{cases} 1 & \text{if } j \in I_i \\ 0 & \text{if } j \notin I_i \end{cases}$$

and $\bar{q}_j^i = 1 - q_j^i$ for all $i = 1, 2, 3$ and $j = 1, \ldots, 6$. However, the function f defined by (11.62) is not pseudo-monotone. Thanks to Lemma 7 in [149], the problem $EP(f, C)$ is equivalent to the problem $EP(f_1, C)$ where the function f_1 is given by

$$f_1(x, y) = \langle A_1 x + B_1 y + a, y - x \rangle + c(y) - c(x),$$

with $A_1 := A + \frac{3}{2}B$ and $B_1 := \frac{1}{2}B$. It is easy to see that the function f_1 satisfies all assumptions (B1)–(B7). We will apply the algorithm (A) to solve the problem $EP(f_1, C)$. Choose $\lambda = 0.02$, $x^0 = (0, \ldots, 0)^T$ and the stopping criteria $\|x^{n-1} - x^n\| < 10^{-4}$. The results are tabulated in Table 11.3.

TABLE 11.3 The results of algorithm (A) in Example 11.6

Iter.	x_1^n	x_2^n	x_3^n	x_4^n	x_5^n	x_6^n
0	0	0	0	0	0	0
1	7.2329	6.9704	6.9729	6.6977	6.6976	6.6976
2	11.1446	10.4950	10.4936	9.8546	9.8519	9.8519
3	14.8503	13.7060	13.6949	12.6240	12.6166	12.6166
4	17.7731	16.0636	16.0387	14.5041	14.4906	14.4906
5	20.2529	17.9295	17.8874	15.8785	15.8578	15.8578
6	22.3430	19.3752	19.3134	16.8342	16.8056	16.8056
7	24.1385	20.5089	20.4254	17.4901	17.4531	17.4531
8	25.6973	21.3988	21.2920	17.9217	17.8760	17.8760
9	27.0678	22.1005	21.9693	18.1894	18.1347	18.1347
...	...	...	...	...	...	...
3568	46.6551	32.1196	15.0304	23.4718	11.6675	11.6675

TABLE 11.4 The accuracy of the three algorithms in Example 11.6

	Algorithm (A)	Algorithm 1 [149]	Algorithm 2 [149]
$\|x^* - prox_{f_1}(x^*)\|$	0.0026	0.0088	0.0915
No. iter.	3568	4416	6850

The approximate solution obtained after 3568 iterations is

$$x^* = (46.6551 \quad 32.1196 \quad 15.0304 \quad 23.4718 \quad 11.6675 \quad 11.6675)^T.$$

We note that this result is slightly different from the ones obtained by Algorithms 1 and 2 in [149]. To check the accuracy of these algorithms, we will use the quantity $\|x^* - prox_{f_1}(x^*)\|$, where $prox_{f_1}$ is the proximity operator of f_1, i.e.,

$$prox_{f_1} : \mathbb{R}^6 \to \mathbb{R}^6, \ prox_{f_1}(x) := \operatorname{argmin}\left\{\lambda f_1(x, y) + \frac{1}{2}\|y - x\|^2 : y \in C\right\}.$$

It is easy to see that x^* is a solution of problem $EP(f_1, C)$ if and only if $x^* = prox_{f_1}(x^*)$. Hence, the smaller the value of $\|x^* - prox_{f_1}(x^*)\|$ is, the more accurate the algorithm is. Choosing $\lambda = 0.05$, the comparison results are reported in Table 11.4.

From Table 11.4, we observe that in this example, the result obtained by our algorithm is more accurate than by Algorithms 1 and 2 in [149] even the new algorithm requires fewer iterations.

TABLE 11.5 Comparison of the three algorithms in Example 11.7

	EGM		Popov's Alg.		Alg. (A)	
	CPU times (s)	Iter.	CPU times (s)	Iter.	CPU times (s)	Iter.
$p = 30, m = 20$	1.2563	96	1.3752	96	1.1430	97
$p = 30, m = 30$	2.0369	100	1.9203	100	1.3180	102
$p = 50, m = 20$	3.6452	155	3.2950	155	2.6257	157
$p = 50, m = 30$	4.1871	154	3.7750	154	3.0050	156
$p = 50, m = 50$	5.9796	150	5.0016	150	4.1230	152
$p = 50, m = 100$	6.0657	148	5.6674	148	4.2408	151
$p = 50, m = 200$	9.3348	137	8.6526	138	6.1459	141
$p = 50, m = 500$	9.5166	135	8.8857	137	5.8242	142
$p = 100, m = 100$	30.0713	299	29.5453	299	20.7186	303
$p = 100, m = 200$	38.1460	294	37.3275	294	24.8415	299
$p = 100, m = 500$	55.2270	274	52.9948	275	33.5809	281
$p = 100, m = 1000$	70.3557	260	58.5535	263	34.5569	270

Example 11.7. In this example, we compare the performance of the proposed algorithm with the extragradient algorithm given in [150] and with Popov's extragradient algorithm [120]. Let $H = \mathbb{R}^p$ and

$$f : \mathbb{R}^p \times \mathbb{R}^p \to \mathbb{R}, \ f(x, y) = \langle Ax + By, y - x \rangle \ \forall x, y \in \mathbb{R}^p,$$

where A and B are matrices defined by $B = M^T.M + pI$, $A = B + N^T.N + 2pI$; M and N are $p \times p$ matrices; $M(i, j)$ and $N(i, j) \in (0, 1)$ are randomly generated, and I is the identity matrix. The feasible set C is $C := \{x \in \mathbb{R}^p : Dx \leq d\}$, where D is an $m \times p$ matrix and $d = (d_1, \ldots, d_m)^T$ with $D(i, j)$, $d_i \in (0, 1)$ randomly generated for all $i = 1, \ldots, m$, $j = 1, \ldots, p$.

We can see that all assumptions (B1)–(B7) are satisfied and the equilibrium problem (11.25) has a unique solution $x^* = (0, \ldots, 0)^T$. We will apply algorithm (A) (Alg. (A)), the extragradient method described in (11.28) (EGM) and Popov's extragradient algorithm [120] (Popov's Alg.) to solve this problem. To run these three algorithms, we use the same parameter $\lambda = \frac{1}{2(\|A\| + \|B\|) + 4}$, the same starting point x^0, which is randomly generated, and the same stopping criteria $\|x^n - x^*\| < 10^{-3}$.

We have generated some random samples with different choices of m and p. The results are tabulated in Table 11.5.

From Table 11.5, we observe that the time consumed by algorithm (A) is less than that of (EGM) and of Popov's extragradient algorithm, even when the proposed algorithm requires more iterations. It is clearly shown that algorithm (A) performs better than the two known algorithms, especially when the function f

and the feasible set K are more complicated (when m and p are large). This happens because as mentioned in Remark 11.7, at each iteration of algorithm (A), we solve one subprogram over a halfspace (one constraint) instead of the feasible set K (many constraints) as in the considered two algorithms.

It is worth noting that our proposed algorithm computes the value of the bifunction f in the first argument only one time at each iteration, and hence, the new method is very effective when the equilibrium bifunction f is complicated and computationally expensive. We will illustrate this advantage by the following example.

Example 11.8. Consider the problem (11.25) where

$$f : \mathbb{R}^p \times \mathbb{R}^p \to \mathbb{R}, \ f(x, y) = \langle Ax, y - x \rangle \quad (11.63)$$

and $K := \{(x_1, \ldots, x_p) \in \mathbb{R}^p : \sum_{i=1}^{p} x_i = 0\}$. Here A is the proximity operator of the function $g(x) = \|x\|^4$, namely,

$$A : \mathbb{R}^p \to \mathbb{R}^p, \ A(x) := \operatorname{argmin}\left\{\|y\|^4 + \frac{1}{2}\|y - x\|^2 : y \in \mathbb{R}^p\right\} \ \forall x \in \mathbb{R}^p.$$

We note that $A(x)$ does not have a closed form and it can be computed efficiently, for example, by the MATLAB Optimization Toolbox, however, its computation is expensive. It is easy to see that all assumptions (B1)–(B7) are satisfied and the problem (11.25) has a unique solution $x^* = (0, \ldots, 0)^T$. We will apply algorithm (A) (Alg. (A)), the extragradient method (11.28) (EGM) and the subgradient extragradient method (SEM) in [53] to solve this problem. As in Example 11.7, we use the same parameter $\lambda = 0.1$, the stopping criteria $\|x^n - x^*\| < 10^{-4}$ and the same starting point x^0, which is randomly generated.

In our experiments, we test the different choices of x^0 for both cases $p = 100$ and $p = 500$. The comparison results are given in Tables 11.6 and 11.7. As shown in this example, our algorithm has much lower time consumption than the other two, although the number of iterations in all of them is almost the same.

To investigate the effect of the step size λ, we implement the three methods, using different step sizes. The results are reported in Table 11.8. We can see that the number of iterations and computational time depend crucially on the step size.

Next, we compare the performance of algorithm (A) with the modified projection-type method (MPM) (Algorithm 3.2 in [162]). The parameters are chosen as follows.

- In algorithm (A), $\mu = \frac{1}{4}$;
- In MPM, P is the identity matrix, $\theta = 1.5$, $\rho = 0.5$, $\beta = 0.9$, $\alpha = 1$.

TABLE 11.6 Comparison of the three algorithms in Example 11.8: the case $p = 100$

	Ex. 1		Ex. 2		Ex. 3	
	CPU times (s)	Iter.	CPU times (s)	Iter.	CPU times (s)	Iter.
EGM	9.9265	136	9.7181	136	9.5595	134
SEM	8.8113	136	8.5276	136	8.6867	134
Alg. (A)	4.3703	136	3.3658	89	3.5988	133

TABLE 11.7 Comparison of the three algorithms in Example 11.8: the case $p = 500$

	Ex. 1		Ex. 2		Ex. 3	
	CPU times (s)	Iter.	CPU times (s)	Iter.	CPU times (s)	Iter.
EGM	65.1697	171	65.5159	171	68.6349	173
SEM	64.4563	172	66.3343	171	68.5598	173
Alg. (A)	31.8188	172	32.6529	171	33.0386	173

TABLE 11.8 Performance of the three algorithms with different step sizes

	Alg. (A)		SEM		EGM	
	CPU times (s)	Iter.	CPU times (s)	Iter.	CPU times (s)	Iter.
$\lambda = 0.01$	88.1636	1438	180.1058	1439	180.2931	1439
$\lambda = 0.05$	17.8215	289	34.9525	289	35.0651	289
$\lambda = 0.1$	8.3393	144	17.1418	145	16.9643	145
$\lambda = 0.2$	4.9168	79	9.7717	80	9.4802	80
$\lambda = 0.3$	3.0769	54	6.5293	56	6.3676	56

TABLE 11.9 Comparison of algorithm (A) with the Modified projection method in [162]

	MPM		Algorithm (A)	
	CPU times (s)	Iter.	CPU times (s)	Iter.
$n = 3$	2.5911	54	0.5307	38
$n = 10$	11.1413	123	0.5954	38
$n = 50$	16.3885	141	0.6245	38
$n = 100$	41.1386	162	0.9394	39
$n = 200$	79.7956	201	1.5275	40

We apply the two algorithms for solving (11.63) with the same starting point x^0, which is randomly generated and use the same stopping rule $\|x^n - x^*\| < 10^{-4}$. The results are presented in Table 11.9. As we can see from this table, the computational time of MPM is much greater than that of our method. This happens because at each iteration of the modified projection method, to find the largest $\alpha \in \{\alpha_{i-1}, \alpha_{i-1}\beta, \alpha_{i-1}\beta^2, \ldots\}$ satisfying

$$\alpha(x^i - z(\alpha))^T (A(x^i) - A(z^i(\alpha))) \le (1 - \rho)\|x^i - z^i(\alpha)\|^2,$$

we have to compute the value of the mapping A many times. As we noted, this procedure is computationally very expensive.

NOTES

1. This fact has been proved in finite dimensions in Chapter 3, Lemma 3.2.
2. These properties have been proved in Chapter 3, Lemma 3.3.

Appendix A

Ekeland Variational Principle

If people do not believe that mathematics is simple, it is only because they do not realize how complicated life is.

John von Neumann (1903–1957)

The Ekeland[1] variational principle [70] was established in 1974 and is the nonlinear version of the Bishop-Phelps theorem [141]. As pointed out in [71], "the grandfather of it all is the celebrated 1961 theorem of Bishop and Phelps (see [41,141]) that the set of continuous linear functionals on a Banach space E which attain their maximum on a prescribed closed convex bounded subset $X \subset E$ is norm-dense in E^*".

The main feature of Ekeland's variational principle is how to use the norm completeness and a partial ordering to obtain a point where a linear functional achieves its supremum on a closed bounded convex set. For any bounded from below, lower semicontinuous functional f, the Ekeland variational principle provides a minimizing sequence whose elements minimize an appropriate sequence of perturbations of f which converges locally uniformly to f.

Roughly speaking, the Ekeland variational principle states that there exist points which are almost points of minima and where the "gradient" is small. In particular, it is not always possible to minimize a nonnegative continuous function on a complete metric space. A major consequence of the Ekeland variational principle is that even if it is not always possible to minimize a nonnegative C^1 functional f on a Banach space, there is always a minimizing sequence $(u_n)_{n \geq 1}$ such that $f'(u_n) \to 0$ as $n \to \infty$. The Ekeland variational principle is a fundamental tool that is effective in numerous situations, which led to many new results and strengthened a series of known results in various fields of analysis, geometry, the Hamilton-Jacobi theory, extremal problems, the Ljusternik-Schnirelmann theory, etc.

In what follows, we state the original version of the Ekeland variational principle, which is valid in the general framework of complete metric spaces. This property asserts that in mathematical analysis there exist nearly optimal solutions to some optimization problems. Ekeland's variational principle can be used when the lower level set of minimization problems is not compact, so that the Bolzano-Weierstrass theorem cannot be applied.

Theorem A.1. *Let (X, d) be a complete metric space and let $f : X \to \mathbb{R} \cup \{\infty\}$ be a lower semicontinuous, bounded from below functional with $D(f) =$*

$\{u \in X : f(u) < \infty\} \neq \emptyset$. *Then for every $\varepsilon > 0$, $\lambda > 0$, and $u \in X$ such that*

$$f(u) \leq \inf_X f + \varepsilon$$

there exists an element $v \in X$ such that

(a) $f(v) \leq f(u)$;

(b) $d(v, u) \leq \frac{1}{\lambda}$;

(c) $f(w) > f(v) - \varepsilon \lambda d(w, v)$ *for each $w \in X \setminus \{v\}$.*

Proof. It suffices to prove our assertion for $\lambda = 1$. The general case is then obtained by replacing d with an equivalent metric λd. We define the relation on X by:

$$w \leq v \iff f(w) + \varepsilon d(v, w) \leq f(v).$$

We first observe that this relation defines a partial ordering on X. Next, we construct inductively a sequence $\{u_n\} \subset X$ as follows: $u_0 = u$, and assuming that u_n has been defined, we set

$$S_n = \{w \in X : w \leq u_n\}$$

and choose $u_{n+1} \in S_n$ so that

$$f(u_{n+1}) \leq \inf_{S_n} f + \frac{1}{n+1}.$$

Since $u_{n+1} \leq u_n$ then $S_{n+1} \subset S_n$ and by the lower semicontinuity of f, S_n is closed. We now show that $\operatorname{diam} S_n \to 0$. Indeed, if $w \in S_{n+1}$, then $w \leq u_{n+1} \leq u_n$ and consequently,

$$\varepsilon d(w, u_{n+1}) \leq f(u_{n+1}) - f(w) \leq \inf_{S_n} f + \frac{1}{n+1} - \inf_{S_n} f = \frac{1}{n+1}.$$

This estimate implies that

$$\operatorname{diam} S_{n+1} \leq \frac{2}{\varepsilon(n+1)}$$

and our claim follows. The fact that X is complete implies that $\cap_{n \geq 0} S_n = \{v\}$ for some $v \in X$. In particular, $v \in S_0$, that is, $v \leq u_0 = u$ and hence

$$f(v) \leq f(u) - \varepsilon d(u, v) \leq f(u)$$

and moreover,

$$d(u, v) \leq \frac{1}{\varepsilon}(f(u) - f(v)) \leq \frac{1}{\varepsilon}(\inf_X f + \varepsilon - \inf_X f) = 1.$$

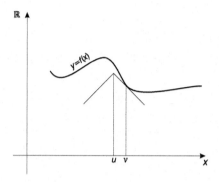

$\mathbb{R}$

$y=f(x)$

$u\ v$

x

FIGURE A.1 Geometric illustration of the Ekeland variational principle

Now, let $w \neq v$. To complete the proof we must show that $w \leq v$ implies $w = v$. If $w \leq v$, then $w \leq u_n$ for each integer $n \geq 0$, that is, $w \in \cap_{n \geq 0} S_n = \{v\}$. So, $w \nleq v$, which is actually (c). $\qquad\square$

In $\mathbb{R}^N$ equipped with the Euclidean metric, properties (a) and (c) in the statement of the Ekeland variational principle are completely intuitive as Fig. A.1 shows. Indeed, assuming that $\lambda = 1$, let us consider a cone lying below the graph of f, with slope $+1$, and vertex projecting onto u. We move up this cone until it first touches the graph of f at some point $(v, f(v))$. Then the point v satisfies both (a) and (c).

In the case when $X = \mathbb{R}^N$ we can give the following simple alternative proof of the Ekeland variational principle, which is due to Hiriart-Urruty [88]. Indeed, consider the perturbed functional

$$g(w) := f(w) + \varepsilon \lambda \|w - u\|, \qquad w \in \mathbb{R}^N.$$

Since f is lower semicontinuous and bounded from below, then g is lower semicontinuous and $\lim_{\|w\| \to \infty} g(w) = +\infty$. Therefore there exists $v \in \mathbb{R}^N$ minimizing g on $\mathbb{R}^N$ such that for all $w \in \mathbb{R}^N$

$$f(v) + \varepsilon \lambda \|v - u\| \leq f(w) + \varepsilon \lambda \|w - u\|. \tag{A.1}$$

By letting $w = u$ we find

$$f(v) + \varepsilon \lambda \|v - u\| \leq f(u)$$

and (a) follows. Now, since $f(u) \leq \inf_{\mathbb{R}^N} f + \varepsilon$, we also deduce that $\|v - u\| \leq 1/\lambda$.

We infer from relation (A.1) that for any w,

$$f(v) \leq f(w) + \varepsilon \lambda \left[\|w - u\| - \|v - u\| \right] \leq f(w) + \varepsilon \lambda \|w - u\|,$$

which is the desired inequality (c).

Taking $\lambda = \dfrac{1}{\sqrt{\varepsilon}}$ in the above theorem we obtain the following property.

Corollary A.1. *Let (X, d) be a complete metric space and let $f : X \to \mathbb{R} \cup \{\infty\}$ be a lower semicontinuous, bounded from below and $D(f) = \{u \in X : f(u) < \infty \} \neq \emptyset$. Then for every $\varepsilon > 0$ and every $u \in X$ such that*

$$f(u) \leq \inf_X f + \varepsilon$$

there exists an element $u_\varepsilon \in X$ such that

(a) $f(u_\varepsilon) \leq f(u)$;
(b) $d(u_\varepsilon, u) \leq \sqrt{\varepsilon}$;
(c) $f(w) > f(u_\varepsilon) - \sqrt{\varepsilon} d(w, u_\varepsilon)$ *for each $w \in X \setminus \{u_\varepsilon\}$.*

Let $(X, \| \cdot \|)$ be a real Banach space, $X^\star$ its topological dual endowed with its natural norm, denoted for simplicity also by $\| \cdot \|$. We denote by $\langle \cdot, \cdot \rangle$ the duality mapping between X and $X^\star$, that is, $\langle x^\star, u \rangle = x^\star(u)$ for every $x^\star \in X^\star$, $u \in X$. Theorem A.1 readily implies the following property, which asserts the existence of *almost critical points*. In other words, the Ekeland variational principle can be viewed as a generalization of the Fermat theorem which establishes that interior extrema points of a smooth functional are necessarily critical points of this functional.

Corollary A.2. *Let X be a Banach space and let $f : X \to \mathbb{R}$ be a lower semicontinuous functional which is bounded from below. Assume that f is Gâteaux differentiable at every point of X. Then for every $\varepsilon > 0$ there exists an element $u_\varepsilon \in X$ such that*

(i) $f(u_\varepsilon) \leq \inf_X f + \varepsilon$;
(ii) $\| f'(u_\varepsilon) \| \leq \varepsilon$.

Letting $\varepsilon = 1/n$, $n \in \mathbb{N}$, Corollary A.2 gives rise to a minimizing sequence for the infimum of a given function which is bounded from below. Note however that such a sequence need not converge to any point. Indeed, let $f : \mathbb{R} \to \mathbb{R}$ be defined by $f(s) = e^{-s}$. Then $\inf_\mathbb{R} f = 0$, and any minimizing sequence fulfilling (a) and (b) from Corollary A.2 tends to $+\infty$.

The following consequence of the Ekeland variational principle has been of particular interest in our arguments. Roughly speaking, this property establishes the existence of *almost critical points* for bounded from below C^1 functionals defined on Banach spaces.

Sullivan [164] observed that the Ekeland variational principle characterizes complete metric spaces in the following sense.

Theorem A.2. *Let (M, d) be a metric space. Then M is complete if and only if the following holds: for every mapping $f : M \to (-\infty, \infty]$, $f \not\equiv \infty$, which is bounded from below, and for every $\varepsilon > 0$, there exists $z_\varepsilon \in M$ such that*

(i) $f(z_\varepsilon) \leq \inf_M f + \varepsilon$;
(ii) $f(x) > f(z_\varepsilon) - \varepsilon d(x, z_\varepsilon)$, *for any $x \in M \setminus \{z_\varepsilon\}$.*

The following extended form of the Ekeland variational principle, called *Ekeland variational principle for equilibrium problems*, has been introduced in [31].

Theorem A.3. *Let A be a nonempty closed subset of a complete metric space (X, d) and $\Phi : A \times A \to \mathbb{R}$ be a bifunction. Assume that the following conditions hold:*

1. $\Phi(x, x) = 0$, *for every $x \in A$;*
2. $\Phi(z, x) \leq \Phi(z, y) + \Phi(y, x)$, *for every $x, y, z \in A$;*
3. Φ *is lower bounded and lower semicontinuous in its second variable.*

Then, for every $\varepsilon > 0$ and for every $x_0 \in A$, there exists $x^* \in A$ such that

$$\begin{cases} \Phi(x_0, x^*) + \varepsilon d(x_0, x^*) \leq 0, \\ \Phi(x^*, x) + \varepsilon d(x^*, x) > 0, & \text{for all } x \in A, \quad x \neq x^*. \end{cases}$$

A.1 BISHOP-PHELPS THEOREM

The statement of the Bishop-Phelps theorem in the setting of complete metric spaces is the following.

Theorem A.4. *Let (X, d) be a complete metric space, $f : X \to \mathbb{R}$ be lower semicontinuous and bounded from below and $\varepsilon > 0$. Then for any $u_0 \in X$, there exists $u \in X$ such that*

$$f(u) \leq f(u_0) - \varepsilon d(u_0, u)$$

and

$$f(u) < f(v) + \varepsilon d(u, v)$$

for every $v \neq u$.

Let $(H, | \cdot |)$ be a Hilbert space which is identified with its dual and let $(., .)$ denote the inner product on H. Let B_R be the closed ball of H of radius R centered at the origin and let ∂B_R denote its boundary.

In relationship with the Bishop-Phelps theorem, we recall here the following Schechter's critical point theorem in a ball, see [159,160].

Theorem A.5. *Let H be a Hilbert space and assume that $f : B_R \to \mathbb{R}$ is a C^1-functional, bounded from below. There exists a sequence $(x_n) \subset B_R$ such that $f(x_n) \to \inf_{B_R} f$ and one of the following two situations holds:*

(a) $f'(x_n) \to 0$ *as $n \to \infty$;*
(b) $|x_n| = R$, $(f'(x_n), x_n) \leq 0$ *for all n and*

$$f'(x_n) - \frac{(f'(x_n), x_n)}{R^2} x_n \to 0 \quad \text{as } n \to \infty.$$

If, in addition, $(f'(x), x) \geq -a > -\infty$ for all $x \in \partial B_R$, f satisfies a Palais-Smale compactness condition guaranteeing that any sequence as above has a convergent subsequence, and the boundary condition

$$f'(x) + \mu x \neq 0 \quad \text{for all } x \in \partial B_R \text{ and } \mu > o$$

holds, then there exists $x \in B_R$ with

$$f(x) = \inf_{B_R} f \quad \text{and} \quad f'(x) = 0.$$

We refer to Precup [145] for a direct proof of Theorem A.5 by using the Bishop-Phelps theorem.

A.2   CASE OF SZULKIN-TYPE FUNCTIONALS

We now state the following consequence of Ekeland's variational principle in the case of Szulkin-type functionals. We refer to Szulkin [165] for proofs and related results.

Theorem A.6. *Let Z be a Banach space with norm $|.|_Z$, $\Xi : Z \to \mathbb{R}$ a C^1-functional and $\eta : Z \to (-\infty, +\infty]$ a proper lower semicontinuous and convex function. If the functional $E := \Xi + \eta$ is bounded from below on $D(\eta)$, then there exists a sequence (z_n) such that*

$$E(z_n) \leq \inf_Z E + \frac{1}{n}$$

and

$$\langle \Xi'(z_n), z' - z_n \rangle + \eta(z') - \eta(z_n) \geq -\frac{1}{n}|z' - z_n|_Z \quad \text{for all } z' \in Z.$$

In addition, any limit point z of the sequence (z_n) is a minimizer and a critical point of E, that is,

$$E(z) = \inf_Z E,$$
$$\langle \Xi'(z), z' - z \rangle + \eta(z') - \eta(z) \geq 0 \quad \text{for all } z' \in Z.$$

The existence of a limit point of the sequence (z_n) in the above theorem is guaranteed if E satisfies a Palais-Smale type compactness condition, namely: if (z_n) is any sequence such that $E(z_n) \to c \in \mathbb{R}$ and

$$\langle \Xi'(z_n), z' - z_n \rangle + \eta(z') - \eta(z_n) \geq -\varepsilon_n |z' - z_n|_Z \quad \text{for all } z' \in Z, \quad \text{(A.2)}$$

where $\varepsilon_n \to 0$, then (z_n) has a convergent subsequence.

We note a sufficient condition for the Palais-Smale type condition to hold:

$$\langle \Xi'(z) - \Xi'(z'), z - z' \rangle \geq \mu \, |z - z'|_Z^\beta \quad \text{for all } z, z' \in Z, \qquad \text{(A.3)}$$

and some $\beta > 1$ and $\mu > 0$. Indeed, if (z_n) satisfies (A.2), then from

$$\langle \Xi'(z_n), z_{n+p} - z_n \rangle + \eta \left(z_{n+p} \right) - \eta \left(z_n \right) \geq -\varepsilon_n \, |z_{n+p} - z_n|_Z$$
$$\langle \Xi'\left(z_{n+p} \right), z_n - z_{n+p} \rangle + \eta \left(z_n \right) - \eta \left(z_{n+p} \right) \geq -\varepsilon_{n+p} \, |z_n - z_{n+p}|_Z$$

we deduce that

$$\langle \Xi'(z_n) - \Xi'\left(z_{n+p} \right), z_{n+p} - z_n \rangle \geq - \left(\varepsilon_n + \varepsilon_{n+p} \right) |z_n - z_{n+p}|_Z \, .$$

Using relation (A.3) we obtain

$$\mu \, |z_n - z_{n+p}|_Z^\beta \leq \left(\varepsilon_n + \varepsilon_{n+p} \right) |z_n - z_{n+p}|_Z \, ,$$

whence

$$|z_n - z_{n+p}|_Z \leq \left(\frac{\varepsilon_n + \varepsilon_{n+p}}{\mu} \right)^{1/(\beta - 1)} .$$

This implies that the sequence (z_n) is Cauchy and so convergent. In particular, condition (A.3) holds if Z is a Hilbert space identified with its dual, $\Xi'(z) = z - T(z)$ and T is a contraction with the Lipschitz constant $m < 1$. In this case, $\mu = 1 - m$ and $\beta = 2$.

NOTE

1. Ivar Ekeland (1944–) is a French mathematician of Norwegian descent. He has written influential monographs and textbooks on nonlinear functional analysis, the calculus of variations, and mathematical economics.

Appendix B

Minimization Problems and Fixed Point Theorems

There is nothing permanent except change.
Heraclitus, pre-Socratic Greek philosopher (c. 535–c. 475 B.C.)

In this appendix, we recall some basic facts concerning the minimization of lower semicontinuous functionals defined on metric spaces. These properties are used to deduce the Caristi fixed point theorem and the Banach contraction principle.

Let K be a subset of a metric space X and assume that $f : X \to \mathbb{R}$ is a given function. We are looking for solutions $x_0 \in K$ of the following minimization problem:

$$f(x_0) = \inf\{f(x) : x \in K\}. \tag{B.1}$$

We start by introducing a related minimization problem. Let $f_K : X \to \mathbb{R} \cup \{+\infty\}$ be the function defined by

$$f_K(x) := \begin{cases} f(x), & \text{if } x \in K \\ +\infty, & \text{if } x \notin K. \end{cases}$$

We observe that any solution of problem (B.1) is a solution of the problem

$$f_K(x_0) = \inf\{f_K(x) : x \in X\} \tag{B.2}$$

and conversely. Thus, we introduce the class of functions f from X to $\mathbb{R} \cup \{+\infty\}$ with the domain

$$\text{Dom } f := \{x \in X;\ f(x) < +\infty\}. \tag{B.3}$$

We observe that $K = \text{Dom}(f_K)$. We say that a function f from X to $\mathbb{R} \cup \{+\infty\}$ is nontrivial if its domain is nonempty.

Definition B.1. Let K be a subset of X. We say that the function $\psi_K : X \to \mathbb{R} \cup \{\infty\}$ defined by

$$\psi_K(x) = \begin{cases} 0, & \text{if } x \in K \\ +\infty, & \text{if } x \notin K \end{cases}$$

is the indicator function of K.

Note that the sum $f + \psi_K$ of a function f and the indicator function of a subset K may be identified with the restriction of f to K. We point out that the minimization problem (B.1) is equivalent to the problem

$$f(x_0) + \psi_K(x_0) = \inf\{f(x) + \psi_K(x);\ x \in K\}. \tag{B.4}$$

This new formulation of the minimization problem will enable us to derive interesting properties of its possible solutions in a convenient way.

We can characterize a function f from X to $\mathbb{R} \cup \{+\infty\}$ by its epigraph, which is a subset of $X \times R$.

Definition B.2. Let f be a function from X to $\mathbb{R} \cup \{+\infty\}$. The subset

$$\mathrm{Epi}\,(f) := \{(x, \lambda) \in X \times \mathbb{R};\ f(x) \leq \lambda\} \tag{B.5}$$

is called the epigraph of f.

We observe that the epigraph of f is nonempty if and only if f is nontrivial. The following property of the epigraph is useful in many circumstances.

Proposition B.1. *Consider a family of functions f_i from X to $\mathbb{R} \cup \{+\infty\}$ and its upper envelope $\sup_{i \in I} f_i$. Then*

$$\mathrm{Epi}\left(\sup_{i \in I} f_i\right) = \bigcap_{i \in I} \mathrm{Ep}\,(f_i).$$

A related notion is introduced in the following definition.

Definition B.3. Let f be a function from X to $\mathbb{R} \cup \{+\infty\}$. The set

$$S(f, \lambda) := \{x \in X;\ f(x) \leq \lambda\}$$

is called a lower section of f.

Let $\alpha := \inf_{x \in X} f(x)$ and let M be the set of solutions of problem (B.1). We observe that M can be written in the form

$$M = \bigcap_{\lambda > \alpha} S(f_K, \lambda).$$

Thus, the set M of solutions inherits the properties of the sections of f which are stable with respect to intersection (for instance, closed, compact, convex, etc.).

Proposition B.2. *Consider a family of functions f_i from X to $\mathbb{R} \cup \{\infty\}$ and its upper envelope $\sup_{i \in I} f_i$. Then*

$$S\left(\sup_{i \in I} f_i, \lambda\right) = \bigcap_{i \in I} S(f_i, \lambda).$$

We recall that a function f from X to $\mathbb{R} \cup \{+\infty\}$ is lower semicontinuous at x_0 if for all $\lambda < f(x_0)$, there exists $\eta > 0$ such that $\lambda \leq f(x)$ for all $x \in B(x_0, \eta)$. A function is upper semicontinuous at x_0 if $-f$ is lower semicontinuous at x_0. By definition we deduce that

$$\liminf_{x \to x_0} f(x) := \sup_{\eta > 0} \inf_{B(x_0, \eta)} f(x).$$

Moreover, a function f from X to $\mathbb{R} \to \{+\infty\}$ is lower semicontinuous at x_0 if and only if

$$f(x_0) \leq \liminf_{x \to x_0} f(x).$$

Proposition B.3. *Let f be a function from X to $\mathbb{R} \cup \{+\infty\}$. The following assertions are equivalent:*

(i) *f is lower semicontinuous;*
(ii) *the epigraph of f is closed;*
(iii) *all sections $S(f, \lambda)$ of f are closed.*

Proof. (i) Let $(x_n, \lambda_n) \in \mathrm{Epi}\,(f)$ be a sequence of elements converging to (x, λ). We show that $(x, \lambda) \in \mathrm{Epi}\,(f)$, hence $f(x) \leq \lambda$. Indeed, by the lower semicontinuity of f we have

$$f(x) \leq \liminf_{n \to \infty} f(x_n) \leq \liminf_{n \to \infty} \lambda_n = \lim_{n \to \infty} \lambda_n = \lambda,$$

since $f(x_n) \leq \lambda$ for all n.

(ii) We suppose that $\mathrm{Epi}\,(f)$ is closed and we show that an arbitrary section $S(f, \lambda)$ is also closed. For this purpose, we consider a sequence $(x_n) \subset S(f, \lambda)$ converging to x. We show that $x \in S(f, \lambda)$, hence $(x, \lambda) \in \mathrm{Epi}\,(f)$. But this is a consequence of the fact that the sequence of elements (x_n, λ) of the epigraph of f, which is closed, converges to (x, λ).

(iii) We suppose that all sections of f are closed. We take $x_0 \in X$ and $\lambda < f(x_0)$. Then (x_0, λ) does not belong to $S(f, \lambda)$, which is a closed set. It follows that there exists $\eta > 0$ such that $B(x_0, \eta) \cap S(f, \lambda) = \emptyset$, that is, $\lambda \leq f(x)$ for all $x \in B(x_0, \eta)$. We conclude that f is lower semicontinuous at x_0. $\square$

We remark that if f is not lower semicontinuous, then we can associate to f the function $\overline{f}$, whose epigraph is the closure of the epigraph of f, namely

$$\mathrm{Epi}\,(\overline{f}) := \overline{\mathrm{Epi}\,(f)}.$$

This is the largest lower semicontinuous function smaller than or equal to f.

Corollary B.1. *A subset K of X is closed if and only if its indicator function is lower semicontinuous.*

Proof. In fact, $\mathrm{Epi}\,(\psi_K) = K \times \mathbb{R}_+$ is closed if and only if K is closed. $\square$

Proposition B.4. *Assume that the functions* f, g, f_i *from* X *to* $\mathbb{R} \cup \{+\infty\}$ *are lower semicontinuous. Then the following properties hold:*

  (i) $f + g$ *is lower semicontinuous;*
  (ii) *if* $\alpha > 0$, *then* αf *is lower semicontinuous;*
  (iii) $\inf(f, g)$ *is lower semicontinuous;*
  (iv) *if* A *is a continuous mapping from* Y *to* X *then* $f \circ A$ *is lower semicontinuous;*
  (v) $\sup_{i \in I} f_i$ *is lower semicontinuous.*

Proposition B.5. *Assume that* K *is a closed subset of* X *and let* f *be a lower semicontinuous function from the metric subspace* K *to* $\mathbb{R}$. *Then the function* f_K *from* X *to* $\mathbb{R} \cup \{+\infty\}$ *is lower semicontinuous.*

Proof. We first observe that the sections $S(f_K, \lambda)$ and $S(f, \lambda)$ are identical. Since $S(f, \lambda)$ is closed in K and since K is closed in X, it follows that $S(f_K, \lambda) = S(f, \lambda)$ is closed in X.   □

In the study of minimization problems, the following class of functions plays an important role.

Definition B.4. A function f from X to $\mathbb{R} \cup \{+\infty\}$ is said to be lower semi-compact (or inf-compact) if all its lower sections are relatively compact.

Theorem B.1. *Assume that a nontrivial function* f *from* X *to* $\mathbb{R} \cup \{+\infty\}$ *is both lower semicontinuous and lower semicompact. Then the set* M *of elements at which* f *attains its minimum is nonempty and compact.*

Proof. Let $\alpha = \inf_{x \in X} f(x) \in \mathbb{R}$ and $\lambda_0 > \alpha$. For all $\lambda \in (\alpha, \lambda_0]$, there exists $x_\lambda \in S(f, \lambda) \subset S(f, \lambda_0)$. Since the set $S(f, \lambda_0)$ is compact, then a subsequence of elements $x_{\lambda'}$ converges to some $x_0 \in S(f, \lambda_0)$. Since f is lower semicontinuous, we deduce that

$$f(x_0) \leq \liminf_{x_{\lambda'} \to x_0} f(x_{\lambda'}) \leq \liminf_{\lambda > \alpha} \lambda = \alpha \leq f(x_0).$$

It follows that $f(x_0) = \alpha$. Moreover, $M = \cap_{\alpha < \lambda \leq \lambda_0} S(f, \lambda)$ being an intersection of compact sets, is compact.   □

Corollary B.2. *Any lower semicontinuous function from a compact subset* $K \subset X$ *to* $\mathbb{R}$ *is bounded below and attains its minimum.*

Proof. We apply Theorem B.1 to the function f_K defined by $f_K(x) = f(x)$ if $x \in K$ and $f_K(x) = +\infty$ if $x \notin K$. We notice that f_K is lower semicontinuous (since K is closed and f is lower semicontinuous) and that f_K is lower semicompact, K being relatively compact. The proof is now complete.   □

Theorem B.1 is a simple and general property for the existence of solutions of an optimization problem. The difficulty essentially arises in the verification of the hypotheses. For instance, if a general vector space E is infinite dimensional, we can supply it with topologies which are not equivalent, contrary to the case of finite dimensional vector spaces. In this case, since compact subsets remain compact when the topology is weaker, supplying E with weaker topologies increases the possibilities of having f lower semicompact. But continuous or lower semicontinuous functions remain continuous or lower semicontinuous respectively whenever the topology of E is stronger, so that strengthening the topology of E is advantageous. Hence, for applying Theorem B.1, we have to construct topologies on E satisfying opposite requirements.

The following existence property does not use compactness, but instead it requires stronger assumptions on the regularity of the function.

Proposition B.6. *Assume that K is a **compact** topological space and that g is a lower semicontinuous function from $X \times K$ to $\mathbb{R} \cup \{+\infty\}$. Then the function $f : X \to \mathbb{R} \cup \{+\infty\}$ defined by $f(x) := \inf_{y \in K} g(x, y)$ is also lower semicontinuous.*

Proof. Fix $\lambda \in \mathbb{R}$ and let $(x_n) \subset S(f, \lambda)$ be a sequence that converges to x_0. We prove that $x_0 \in S(f, \lambda)$. By Corollary B.2, since the mapping $y \mapsto f(x_n, y)$ is lower semicontinuous and K is compact, there exists $y_n \in K$ such that $f(x_n) = g(x_n, y_n)$. It follows that, up to a subsequence, (y_n) converges to $y_0 \in K$. Then the sequence of pairs $(x_n, y_n) \subset S(g, \lambda)$ converges to (x_0, y_0), which belongs to $S(g, \lambda)$ since g is a lower semicontinuous function. Since $f(x_0) \leq f(x_0, y_0) \leq \lambda$, we conclude that $x_0 \in S(f, \lambda)$. $\square$

Proposition B.7. *Consider n lower semicontinuous functions f_i from X to $\mathbb{R} \cup \{+\infty\}$ and suppose that at least one of them is lower semicompact. Define the mapping F from $K := \cap_{i=1}^{m} \mathrm{Dom} f_i$ to $\mathbb{R}^n$ by $F(x) := (f_1(x), ..., f_n(x))$. Then the set $F(K) + \mathbb{R}_+^n$ is closed in $\mathbb{R}^n$.*

Proof. Consider the sequences $(x_n) \subset K$ and $(u_n) \subset \mathbb{R}_+^n$ such that the sequence of elements $y_n := F(x_n) + u_n$ converges to some y of $\mathbb{R}^n$. We show that $y \in F(K) + \mathbb{R}_+^n$.

Let f_{i_0} be the function that is both lower-continuous and lower semicompact. Since $f_{i_0}(x_n) + u_{n i_0}$ converges to y_{i_0}, there exists n_0 such that $|y_{i_0} - f_{i_0}(x_n) - u_{n i_0}| \leq 1$ whenever $n \geq n_0$. Since $f_{i_0}(x_n) \leq y_{i_0} - u_{n i_0} + 1 \leq y_{i_0} + 1$, we deduce that for all $n \geq n_0$ we have $x_n \in S(f_{i_0}, y_{i_0} + 1)$, which is compact. Thus, up to a subsequence, (x_n) converges to an element x_0. Since f_i is lower semicontinuous, we have for all $i = 1, ..., n$

$$f_i(x_0) \leq \liminf_{n \to \infty} f_i(x_n) = \liminf_{n \to \infty}(y_{n_i} - u_{n_i}) \leq \liminf_{n \to \infty} y_{n_i} = y_i.$$

Thus, setting $u_i := y_i - f_i(x_0) \geq 0$, we obtain that $y = F(x_0) + u$, where $x_0 \in K$ and $u \in \mathbb{R}_+^n$. $\square$

B.1 CARISTI AND BANACH FIXED POINT THEOREMS

If $G : X \to 2^X$ then a solution $\overline{x}$ of the inclusion

$$\overline{x} \in G(\overline{x}) \tag{B.6}$$

is called a fixed point of G.

We start with the following fixed point theorem, which is due to Caristi.

Theorem B.2. *Let G be a nontrivial correspondence of a complete metric space X into 2^X. We suppose that there exists a proper, positive, lower semicontinuous function f from X to $\mathbb{R}_+ \cup \{+\infty\}$ such that for all $x \in X$ there exists $y \in G(x)$ such that $f(y) + d(x, y) \le f(x)$. Then G has a fixed point.*
Moreover, if

$$f(y) + d(y, x) \le f(x) \quad \text{for all } x \in X, \text{ all } y \in G(x), \tag{B.7}$$

then there exists $\overline{x} \in X$ such that $G(\overline{x}) = \{\overline{x}\}$.

Proof. By Ekeland's variational principle, there exists $\overline{x} \in X$ such that

$$f(\overline{x}) < f(x) + \varepsilon d(x, \overline{x}) \quad \text{for all } x \ne \overline{x}, \tag{B.8}$$

with $\varepsilon < 1$. Let $\overline{y} \in G(\overline{x})$ be such that $f(\overline{y}) + d(\overline{x}, y) \le f(\overline{x})$. If $\overline{y}$ is not equal to $\overline{x}$, relation (B.8) with $x := \overline{y}$ implies that $d(\overline{x}, \overline{y}) \le \varepsilon d(\overline{x}, \overline{y})$, which is impossible since $\varepsilon < 1$. It follows that $\overline{y} = \overline{x}$.

If the stronger condition (B.7) is fulfilled then all such elements $\overline{y}$ satisfying $\overline{y} \in G(\overline{x})$ are equal to $\overline{x}$, hence $G(\overline{x}) = \{\overline{x}\}$. $\qquad\qquad\square$

In the next result, f is no longer assumed to be lower semicontinuous. However the correspondence G must have a closed graph. The graph of a correspondence G from E to F is defined by

$$\text{Graph } (G) := \{(x, y); \ y \in G(x)\}. \tag{B.9}$$

Theorem B.3. *Let X be a complete metric space. We consider a correspondence G from X to 2^X with a closed graph. Assume that there exists a nontrivial positive function f from X to $\mathbb{R}_+ \cup \{+\infty\}$ satisfying the hypothesis of Theorem B.2. Then G has a fixed point.*

Proof. Fix $x_0 \in \text{Dom } f$ and use a recurrence to calculate a sequence $(x_n) \subset X$ such that

$$x_{n+1} \in G(x_n), \qquad d(x_{n+1}, x_n) \le f(x_n) - f(x_{n+1}). \tag{B.10}$$

This implies that the sequence of positive numbers $f(x_n)$ is decreasing, hence it converges to a real number α. Adding the inequalities (B.10) from $n = p$ to

$n = q - 1$, the triangle inequality implies that

$$d(x_p, x_q) \leq \sum_{n=p}^{q-1} d(x_{n+1}, x_n) \leq f(x_p) - f(x_q).$$

It follows that (x_n) is a Cauchy sequence, so it converges to an element $\overline{x} \in X$. Since the pairs (x_n, x_{n+1}) belong to the graph of G, which is closed, and converge to the pair $(\overline{x}, \overline{x})$ which thus belongs to the graph of G, the limit $\overline{x}$ is a fixed point of G. $\square$

As a corollary we obtain the Banach-Picard fixed point theorem for contractions.

Theorem B.4. *Suppose that X is a complete metric space and that $g : X \to X$ is a contraction, that is, there exists $k \in (0, 1)$ such that $d(g(x), g(y)) \leq kd(x, y)$ for all $x, y \in X$. Then g has a unique fixed point.*

Proof. We associate g with the function f from X to $\mathbb{R}_+$ defined by

$$f(x) := \sum_{n=0}^{\infty} d(g^n(x), g^{n+1}(x)).$$

By hypothesis we have

$$d(g^n(x), g^{n+1}(x)) \leq kd(g^{n-1}(x), g^n(x)) \leq kd(x, g(x)).$$

It follows that f satisfies the condition

$$0 \leq f(x) \leq \frac{1}{1-k} d(x, g(x)) < +\infty.$$

On the other hand, note that

$$f(x) = d(x, g(x)) + \sum_{n=1}^{\infty} d(g^n(x), g^{n+1}(x)) = d(x, g(x)) + f(g(x)).$$

Thus, by Theorem B.3, there exists a fixed point for the contraction g. Moreover, if $\overline{x}$ and $\overline{y}$ are fixed points of g, then the inequality

$$d(\overline{x}, \overline{y}) = d(g(\overline{x}), g(\overline{y})) \leq kd(\overline{x}, \overline{y})$$

implies that $d(\overline{x}, \overline{y}) = 0$ since $k < 1$. We conclude that $\overline{x} = \overline{y}$. $\square$

Appendix C

Nonsmooth Clarke Theory and Generalized Derivatives

The study of mathematics, like the Nile, begins in minuteness but ends in magnificence.

Charles Caleb Colton, English cleric (1780–1832)

In this appendix, we recall the basic elements of the theory of generalized gradients for locally Lipschitz functionals, in the sense of Clarke [56].

Let X be a real Banach space endowed with the norm $\| \cdot \|$. The dual space of X is denoted X^* and is equipped with the dual norm $\| \cdot \|_*$ defined by

$$\|\zeta\|_* = \sup\{\langle \zeta, v \rangle : v \in X, \ \|v\| \leq 1\}.$$

We recall that a functional $f : X \to \mathbb{R}$ is called locally Lipschitz if for every $x \in X$ there exist a neighborhood V of x in X and a constant $K > 0$ such that

$$|f(y) - f(z)| \leq K \|y - z\| \text{ for all } y, z \in V.$$

Definition C.1. The generalized directional derivative of a locally Lipschitz functional $f : X \to \mathbb{R}$ at a point $u \in X$ in the direction $v \in X$, denoted $f^0(u; v)$, is defined by

$$f^0(u; v) = \limsup_{x \to u; \, t \to 0^+} \frac{f(x + tv) - f(x)}{t}.$$

The locally Lipschitz continuity of f at u ensures that $f^0(u; v) \in \mathbb{R}$ for all $v \in X$. The function $f^0(u; \cdot) : X \to \mathbb{R}$ is subadditive, positively homogeneous and satisfies the inequality

$$|f^0(u; v)| \leq K \|v\| \quad \text{for all } v \in X,$$

where $K > 0$ is the Lipschitz constant of f near the point $u \in X$. Moreover, the function $(u, v) \mapsto f^0(u; v)$ is upper semicontinuous.

Definition C.2. The generalized gradient of a locally Lipschitz functional $f : X \to \mathbb{R}$ at a point $u \in X$, denoted $\partial f(u)$, is the subset of X^* defined by

$$\partial f(u) = \{\zeta \in X^* : f^0(u; v) \geq \langle \zeta, v \rangle \text{ for all } v \in X\}.$$

Using the Hahn-Banach theorem, we deduce that $\partial f(u) \neq \emptyset$.

Proposition C.1. *Let* $f : X \to \mathbb{R}$ *be Lipschitz continuous on a neighborhood of a point* $u \in X$. *Then the following properties hold.*

(i) $\partial f(u)$ *is a convex, weak* compact subset of* X^* *and*

$$\|\zeta\|_* \leq K \quad \text{for all } \zeta \in \partial f(u),$$

where $K > 0$ *is the Lipschitz constant of* f *near* u.

(ii) *We have*

$$f^0(u; v) = \max\{\langle \zeta, v \rangle : \zeta \in \partial f(u)\} \quad \text{for all } v \in X.$$

The following result establishes useful properties of the generalized gradient.

Proposition C.2. *Let* $f : X \to \mathbb{R}$ *be a locally Lipschitz functional. Then the following properties hold.*

(i) *For all* $u \in X$, $\varepsilon > 0$ *and* $v \in X$, *there exists* $\delta > 0$ *such that whenever* $w \in \partial f(x)$ *with* $\|x - u\| < \delta$ *we can find* $z \in \partial f(u)$ *satisfying* $|\langle w - z, v \rangle| < \varepsilon$.

(ii) *The function* $\lambda : X \to \mathbb{R}$ *given by*

$$\lambda(x) = \min_{w \in \partial f(x)} \|w\|_*$$

is lower semicontinuous.

Proof. (i) Arguing by contradiction, we assume that there exist $u \in X$, $v \in X$, $\varepsilon_0 > 0$ and sequences $\{x_n\} \subset X$, $\{\xi_n\} \subset X^*$ with $\xi_n \in \partial f(x_n)$ such that

$$\|x_n - u\| < \frac{1}{n}$$

and

$$|\langle \xi_n - w, v \rangle| \geq \varepsilon_0 \quad \text{for all } w \in \partial f(u). \tag{C.1}$$

Since $x_n \to u$ and $\xi_n \in \partial f(x_n)$ we can suppose that $\|\xi_n\|_* \leq K$, where $K > 0$ is the Lipschitz constant around u, and $\xi_n \xrightarrow{*} \xi$ weakly* in X^* as $n \to \infty$.

We claim that

$$\xi \in \partial f(u). \tag{C.2}$$

Indeed, the fact that $\xi_n \in \partial f(x_n)$ implies

$$\langle \xi_n, y \rangle \leq f^0(x_n; y), \quad \text{for all } y \in X.$$

Definition C.1 yields sequences $\lambda_n \to 0^+$, $h_n \to 0$ such that for all $y \in X$

$$\frac{f(x_n + h_n + \lambda_n y) - f(x_n + h_n)}{\lambda_n} \geq f^0(x_n; y) - \frac{1}{n} \geq \langle \xi_n, y \rangle - \frac{1}{n}.$$

Passing to the limit, we obtain

$$f^0(u; y) \geq \limsup_{n \to \infty} \frac{f(x_n + h_n + \lambda_n y) - f(x_n + h_n)}{\lambda_n}$$

$$\geq \limsup_{n \to \infty} \left[\langle \xi_n, y \rangle - \frac{1}{n} \right] = \langle \xi, y \rangle, \text{ for all } y \in X.$$

Definition C.2 shows that relation (C.2) is true.

Letting $n \to \infty$ in (C.1) leads to a contradiction with relation (C.2). This contradiction establishes property (i).

(ii) Applying the Banach-Alaoglu theorem, in the definition of $\lambda(x)$ we deduce that the minimum makes sense.

In order to show that the function λ is lower semicontinuous, let us suppose, on the contrary, that there exists a sequence $\{x_n\}$ such that $x_n \to u$ and

$$\liminf_{n \to \infty} \lambda(x_n) < \lambda(u).$$

We know that there is $w_n \in \partial f(x_n)$ with $\lambda(x_n) = \|w_n\|_*$. Therefore we can choose a subsequence of $\{w_n\}$, denoted again $\{w_n\}$, and an element $z \in \partial f(u)$ such that $w_n \overset{*}{\rightharpoonup} z$ weakly*. Then we obtain

$$\liminf_{n \to \infty} \|w_n\|_* \geq \|z\|_* \geq \lambda(u).$$

This contradiction shows that assertion (ii) is valid. $\qquad\qquad \square$

We conclude with the following mean value theorem due to Lebourg [116].

Theorem C.1. *Given the points x and y in X and a real-valued function f which is Lipschitz continuous on an open set containing the segment*

$$[x, y] = \{(1 - t)x + ty : t \in [0, 1]\},$$

then there exist $u = x + t_0(y - x)$, with $0 < t_0 < 1$, and $x^* \in \partial f(u)$ such that

$$f(y) - f(x) = \langle x^*, y - x \rangle.$$

Proof. Consider the function $\theta : [0, 1] \to \mathbb{R}$ defined by

$$\theta(t) = f(x + t(y - x)) + t[f(x) - f(y)], \text{ for all } t \in [0, 1].$$

The continuity of θ combined with the equalities $\theta(0) = \theta(1) = f(x)$ yields a point $t_0 \in {]0, 1[}$ where θ assumes a local minimum or maximum. A direct verification ensures that $0 \in \partial \theta(t_0)$ and

$$\partial \theta(t_0) \subset \langle \partial f(x + t_0(y - x)), y - x \rangle + [f(x) - f(y)]$$

(see Lebourg [116] or Clarke [56, p. 41]). It follows that there exists $x^* \in \partial f(x + t_0(y - x))$ such that the conclusion of Theorem C.1 holds. $\quad\square$

We refer to the monographs by Clarke [56] and Motreanu and Rădulescu [131] for more details, proofs, and applications of Clarke's generalized gradient theory.

Appendix D

Elements of Szulkin Critical Point Theory

Imagination will often carry us to worlds that never were. But without it we go nowhere.

Carl Sagan[1] (1934–1996)

In Chapter 8 we used elements of critical point theory in the sense of Szulkin [165] in relationship with Nash equilibria of some classes of nonlinear systems. Our aim in this appendix is to recall the basic notions and properties concerning the Szulkin theory for nonsmooth functionals. Throughout this appendix we assume that X is a real Banach space.

Definition D.1. Let $\Phi : X \to \mathbb{R}$ be a continuously differentiable function and let $\Psi : X \to \mathbb{R} \cup \{+\infty\}$ be a proper, convex and lower semicontinuous function. We say that the functional $\Phi + \Psi : X \to \mathbb{R} \cup \{+\infty\}$ satisfies the Palais-Smale condition if every sequence $\{u_n\} \subset X$ with $\Phi(u_n) + \Psi(u_n)$ bounded and for which there exists a sequence $\{\varepsilon_n\} \subset \mathbb{R}^+$ with $\varepsilon_n \downarrow 0$, and such that

$$\Phi'(u_n)(v - u_n) + \Psi(v) - \Psi(u_n) \geq -\varepsilon_n \|v - u_n\| \quad \text{for all } v \in X,$$

contains a (strongly) convergent subsequence in X.

Definition D.2. Let $\Phi : X \to \mathbb{R}$ be a locally Lipschitz functional and let $\Psi : X \to \mathbb{R} \cup \{+\infty\}$ be a proper, convex and lower semicontinuous function. We say that the functional $\Phi + \Psi : X \to \mathbb{R} \cup \{+\infty\}$ satisfies the Palais-Smale condition if every sequence $\{u_n\} \subset X$ with $\Phi(u_n) + \Psi(u_n)$ bounded and for which there exists a sequence $\{\varepsilon_n\} \subset \mathbb{R}^+$, $\varepsilon_n \downarrow 0$, such that

$$\Phi^0(u_n; v - u_n) + \Psi(v) - \Psi(u_n) \geq -\varepsilon_n \|v - u_n\| \quad \text{for all } v \in X,$$

contains a (strongly) convergent subsequence in X.

Lemma D.1. *Let $\chi : X \to \mathbb{R} \cup \{+\infty\}$ be a lower semicontinuous, convex function with $\chi(0) = 0$. If*

$$\chi(x) \geq -\|x\| \quad \text{for all } x \in X,$$

then there exists some $z \in X^*$ such that $\|z\|_* \leq 1$ and

$$\chi(x) \geq \langle z, x \rangle \quad \text{for all } x \in X.$$

Proof. Consider the following convex subsets A and B of $X \times \mathbb{R}$:

$$A = \{(x, t) \in X \times \mathbb{R} : \|x\| < -t\}$$

and

$$B = \{(x, t) \in X \times \mathbb{R} : \chi(x) \leq t\}.$$

Notice that A is an open set and due to the condition $\chi(x) \geq -\|x\|$, we have $A \cap B = \emptyset$. By the separation theorem for convex sets, we deduce the existence of real numbers α and β and of $w \in X^*$ such that $(w, \alpha) \neq (0, 0)$,

$$\langle w, x \rangle - \alpha t \geq \beta \quad \text{for all } (x, t) \in \bar{A}$$

and

$$\langle w, x \rangle - \alpha t \leq \beta \quad \text{for all } (x, t) \in B.$$

We see that $\beta = 0$ since $(0, 0) \in \bar{A} \cap B$.

Set $t = -\|x\|$ in the first inequality above. It follows that

$$\langle w, x \rangle \geq -\alpha \|x\| \quad \text{for all } x \in X,$$

which implies $\alpha > 0$ and $\|w\|_* \leq \alpha$.

Set $z = \alpha^{-1} w$ and $t = \chi(x)$ in the second equality above. We deduce that

$$\langle z, x \rangle \leq \chi(x) \quad \text{for all } x \in X.$$

Since $\|w\|_* \leq \alpha$ we obtain $\|z\|_* \leq 1$. The conclusion is achieved. $\qquad\square$

Next, we are concerned with nonsmooth functionals which can be written as a sum of a locally Lipschitz function and a convex, proper, and lower semi-continuous functional (possibly, taking the value $+\infty$). Namely, we consider functionals $f : X \to \,]-\infty, +\infty]$, which satisfy the following structure hypothesis:

(H_f) $f = \Phi + \Psi$, where $\Phi : X \to \mathbb{R}$ is locally Lipschitz and $\Psi : X \to \,]-\infty, +\infty]$ is convex, proper, lower semicontinuous.

Definition D.3. An element $u \in X$ is said to be a critical point of functional $f : X \to \,]-\infty, +\infty]$ satisfying assumption (H_f) if

$$\Phi^0(u; x - u) + \Psi(x) - \Psi(u) \geq 0 \quad \text{for all } x \in X.$$

If $\Psi = 0$, Definition D.3 introduces the notion of critical point for a locally Lipschitz functional. In particular, if $\Psi = 0$ and Φ is continuously differentiable, we obtain the usual concept of critical point. In the case where Φ is continuously differentiable and Ψ is convex, lower semicontinuous, and proper, Definition D.3 reduces with the notion of critical point in the sense of Szulkin.

An equivalent formulation of Definition D.3 is that $u \in X$ is a critical point of $f : X \to]-\infty, +\infty]$ if and only if

$$0 \in \partial \Phi(u) + \partial \Psi(u),$$

where $\partial \Phi(u)$ denotes the generalized gradient of Φ and $\partial \Psi(u)$ is the subdifferential of Ψ in the sense of convex analysis.

Given a real number c, we denote

$$K_c(f) = \{u \in X : f(u) = c, \ u \text{ is a critical point of } f\}.$$

We say that the number $c \in \mathbb{R}$ is a critical value of the functional $f : X \to]-\infty, +\infty]$ satisfying (H_f) if $K_c(f) \neq \emptyset$.

The following result provides critical points in the sense of Definition D.3.

Proposition D.1. *Let the function f satisfy hypothesis (H_f). Then each local minimum of f is a critical point of f in the sense of Definition D.3.*

Proof. Suppose that u is a local minimum of f and fix $v \in X$. Using the convexity of Ψ we deduce that

$$0 \leq f((1-t)u + tv) - f(u) \leq \Phi(u + t(v-u)) - \Phi(u) + t(\Psi(v) - \Psi(u))$$

for all small $t > 0$.

Dividing by t and letting $t \to 0^+$ we infer that u is a critical point of f in the sense of Definition D.3. $\qquad\square$

The appropriate Palais-Smale condition for the function $f : X \to]-\infty, +\infty]$ in (H_f) at the level $c \in \mathbb{R}$ is stated below.

Definition D.4. The function $f : X \to]-\infty, +\infty]$ satisfying assumption (H_f) is said to verify the Palais-Smale condition at the level $c \in \mathbb{R}$ if any sequence $\{x_n\} \subset X$ such that $f(x_n) \to c$ and

$$\Phi^0(x_n; x - x_n) + \Psi(x) - \Psi(x_n) \geq -\varepsilon_n \|x_n - x\| \quad \text{for all } n \in \mathbb{N}, \ x \in X,$$

where $\varepsilon_n \to 0^+$, has a strongly convergent subsequence.

A direct computation shows that the inequality in Definition D.4 is equivalent with

$$\Phi^0(x_n; x - x_n) + \Psi(x) - \Psi(x_n) \geq \langle z_n, x - x_n \rangle \quad \text{for all } n \in \mathbb{N}, \ x \in X,$$

for some sequence $\{z_n\} \subset X^*$ with $z_n \to 0$.

NOTE

1. Carl Sagan (1934–1996) was an American astronomer, cosmologist, astrophysicist, astrobiologist, and science communicator in astronomy and other natural sciences. Sagan assembled the first physical messages sent into space: the Pioneer plaque and the Voyager Golden Record, universal messages that could potentially be understood by any extraterrestrial intelligence that might find them.

Bibliography

[1] John Forbes, Nash Jr. (1928–2015), Notices Amer. Math. Soc. 63 (5) (2016) 492–504, Camillo De Lellis, coordinating editor.

[2] S. Adly, A.L. Dontchev, M. Théra, On one-sided Lipschitz stability of set-valued contractions, Numer. Funct. Anal. Optim. 35 (2014) 837–850.

[3] C.D. Aliprantis, K.C. Border, Infinite Dimensional Analysis, Springer, 1999.

[4] B. Alleche, On hemicontinuity of bifunctions for solving equilibrium problems, Adv. Nonlinear Anal. 3 (2014) 69–80.

[5] B. Alleche, V.D. Rădulescu, The Ekeland variational principle for equilibrium problems revisited and applications, Nonlinear Anal. Real World Appl. 23 (2015) 17–25.

[6] B. Alleche, V.D. Rădulescu, Equilibrium problems techniques in the qualitative analysis of quasi-hemivariational inequalities, Optimization 64 (2015) 1855–1868.

[7] B. Alleche, V.D. Rădulescu, Set-valued equilibrium problems with applications to Browder variational inclusions and to fixed point theory, Nonlinear Anal. Real World Appl. 28 (2016) 251–268.

[8] B. Alleche, V.D. Rădulescu, Solutions and approximate solutions of quasi-equilibrium problems in Banach spaces, J. Optim. Theory Appl. 170 (2016) 629–649.

[9] B. Alleche, V.D. Rădulescu, Inverse of the sum of set-valued mappings and applications, Numer. Funct. Anal. Optim. 38 (2017) 139–159.

[10] B. Alleche, V.D. Rădulescu, Further on set-valued equilibrium problems in the pseudo-monotone case and applications to Browder variational inclusions, Optim. Lett. (2018), https://doi.org/10.1007/s11590-018-1233-2.

[11] B. Alleche, V.D. Rădulescu, M. Sebaoui, The Tikhonov regularization for equilibrium problems and applications to quasi-hemivariational inequalities, Optim. Lett. 9 (2015) 483–503.

[12] G. Allen, Variational inequalities, complementarity problems, and duality theorems, J. Math. Anal. Appl. 58 (1977) 1–10.

[13] L.Q. Anh, P.Q. Khanh, T.N. Tam, On Hölder continuity of solution maps of parametric primal and dual Ky Fan inequalities, TOP 23 (2015) 151–167.

[14] Q.H. Ansari, A.P. Farajzadeh, S. Schaible, Existence of solutions of strong vector equilibrium problems, Taiwanese J. Math. 16 (2012) 165–178.

[15] Q.H. Ansari, I.V. Konnov, J.-C. Yao, On generalized vector equilibrium problems, Nonlinear Anal. 47 (2001) 543–554.

[16] Q.H. Ansari, I.V. Konnov, J.C. Yao, Characterization of solutions for vector equilibrium problems, J. Optim. Theory Appl. 113 (3) (2002) 435–447.

[17] A.S. Antipin, The convergence of proximal methods to fixed points of extremal mappings and estimates of their rate of convergence, Comput. Math. Math. Phys. 35 (1992) 539–551.

[18] M. Apetrii, M. Durea, M. Strugariu, On subregularity properties of set-valued mappings, Set-Valued Var. Anal. 21 (2013) 93–126.

[19] A.V. Arutyunov, E.R. Avakov, S.E. Zhukovskiy, Stability theorems for estimating the distance to a set of coincidence points, SIAM J. Optim. 25 (2) (2015) 807–828.

[20] J.-P. Aubin, Optima and Equilibria. An Intoduction to Nonlinear Analysis, Grad. Texts in Math., vol. 140, Springer-Verlag, Berlin, Heidelberg, New York, 2003.

[21] J.-P. Aubin, A. Cellina, Differential Inclusion, Set-Valued Maps and Viability Theory, Springer-Verlag, Berlin, 1984.

[22] J.-P. Aubin, I. Ekeland, Applied Nonlinear Analysis, John Wiley, New York, 1984.

[23] J.-P. Aubin, H. Frankowska, Set-Valued Analysis, Systems & Control: Foundations & Applications, Birkhäuser, 1984.

[24] V. Barbu, Nonlinear Differential Equations of Monotone Types in Banach Spaces, Springer, 2010.

[25] H.H. Bauschke, P.L. Combettes, Convex Analysis and Monotone Operator Theory in Hilbert Spaces, Springer, 1999.

[26] E. Bednarczuk, An approach to well-posedness in vector optimization: consequences to stability, Control Cybernet. 23 (1994) 107–122.

[27] E. Bednarczuk, Strong pseudomonotonicity, sharp efficiency and stability for parametric vector equilibria, ESAIM Proc. 17 (2007) 9–18.

[28] G. Beer, A.L. Dontchev, The weak Ekeland variational principle and fixed points, Nonlinear Anal. 102 (2014) 91–96.

[29] A. Bensoussan, J.-L. Lions, Nouvelles méthodes en contrôle impulsionnel, Appl. Math. Optim. 1 (1974/1975) 289–312.

[30] M. Bianchi, N. Hadjisavvas, S. Schaible, Vector equilibrium problems with generalized monotone bifunctions, J. Optim. Theory Appl. 92 (1997) 527–542.

[31] M. Bianchi, G. Kassay, R. Pini, Existence of equilibria via Ekeland's principle, J. Math. Anal. Appl. 305 (2005) 502–512.

[32] M. Bianchi, G. Kassay, R. Pini, Ekeland's principle for vector equilibrium problems, Nonlinear Anal. 66 (2007) 1454–1464.

[33] M. Bianchi, G. Kassay, R. Pini, Well-posedness for vector equilibrium problems, Math. Methods Oper. Res. 70 (2009) 171–182.

[34] M. Bianchi, G. Kassay, R. Pini, Well-posed equilibrium problems, Nonlinear Anal. 72 (2010) 460–468.

[35] M. Bianchi, G. Kassay, R. Pini, An inverse map result and some applications to sensitivity of generalized equations, J. Math. Anal. Appl. 339 (2013) 279–290.

[36] M. Bianchi, G. Kassay, R. Pini, Linear openness of the composition of set-valued maps and applications to variational systems, Set-Valued Var. Anal. 24 (2016) 581–595.

[37] M. Bianchi, G. Kassay, R. Pini, Stability of equilibria via regularity of the subdifferential operators, Set-Valued Var. Anal. 25 (2016) 789–805.

[38] M. Bianchi, R. Pini, Coercivity conditions for equilibrium problems, J. Optim. Theory Appl. 124 (2005) 79–92.

[39] M. Bianchi, S. Schaible, Generalized monotone bifunctions and equilibrium problems, J. Optim. Theory Appl. 90 (1996) 31–43.

[40] G. Bigi, G. Kassay, A. Capata, Existence results for strong vector equilibrium problems and their applications, Optimization 61 (2012) 567–583.

[41] E. Bishop, R.R. Phelps, A proof that all Banach spaces are subreflexive, Bull. Amer. Math. Soc. 67 (1961) 97–98.

[42] E. Blum, W. Oettli, From optimization and variational inequalities to equilibrium problems, Math. Student 63 (1994) 123–145.

[43] J. Borwein, J.P. Penot, M. Théra, Conjugate convex operators, J. Math. Anal. Appl. 102 (1984) 399–414.

[44] L.M. Bregman, The relaxation method of finding the common points of convex sets and its application to the solution of problems in convex programming, USSR Comput. Math. Math. Phys. 7 (1967) 200–217.

[45] F.E. Browder, The fixed point theory of multi-valued mappings in topological vector spaces, Math. Ann. 177 (1968) 283–301.

[46] R. Burachik, G. Kassay, On a generalized proximal point method for solving equilibrium problems in Banach spaces, Nonlinear Anal. 75 (2012) 6456–6464.

[47] D. Butnariu, Y. Censor, S. Reich, Iterative averaging of entropic projections for solving stochastic convex feasibility problems, Comput. Optim. Appl. 8 (1997) 21–39.

[48] D. Butnariu, A.N. Iusem, Local moduli of convexity and their applications to finding almost common points of measurable families of operators, in: Y. Censor, S. Reich (Eds.), Recent Developments in Optimization Theory and Nonlinear Analysis, in: AMS Contemp. Math., 1997, pp. 61–91.

[49] D. Butnariu, A.N. Iusem, Totally Convex Functions for Fixed Point Computation and Infinite Dimensional Optimization, Kluwer, Dordrecht, 2000.

[50] D. Butnariu, G. Kassay, A proximal-projection method for finding zeroes of set-valued operators, SIAM J. Control Optim. 47 (2008) 2096–2136.

[51] M. Castellani, M. Giuli, Approximate solutions of quasiequilibrium problems in Banach spaces, J. Global Optim. 64 (3) (2016) 615–620.

[52] E. Cavazzuti, J. Morgan, Well-Posed Saddle Point Problems, Lect. Notes Pure Appl. Math., vol. 86, 1983, pp. 61–76.

[53] Y. Censor, A. Gibali, S. Reich, The subgradient extragradient method for solving variational inequalities in Hilbert space, J. Optim. Theory Appl. 148 (2011) 318–335.

[54] Y. Censor, A. Lent, An iterative row-action method for interval convex programming, J. Optim. Theory Appl. 34 (1981) 321–353.

[55] S.S. Chang, Y. Zhang, Generalized KKM theorem and variational inequalities, J. Math. Anal. Appl. 159 (1991) 208–223.

[56] F.H. Clarke, Optimization and Nonsmooth Analysis, SIAM edition, Society for Industrial and Applied Mathematics, Philadelphia, 1990.

[57] L.P. Combettes, S.A. Hirstoaga, Equilibrium programming in Hilbert spaces, J. Nonlinear Convex Anal. 6 (2005) 117–136.

[58] N. Costea, V.D. Rădulescu, Inequality problems of quasi-hemivariational type involving set-valued operators and a nonlinear term, J. Global Optim. 52 (2012) 743–756.

[59] G.P. Crespi, A. Guerraggio, M. Rocca, Well posedness in vector optimization problems and vector variational inequalities, J. Optim. Theory Appl. 132 (2007) 213–226.

[60] P. Cubiotti, J.C. Yao, Nash equilibria of generalized games in normed spaces without upper semicontinuity, J. Global Optim. 46 (4) (2010) 509–519.

[61] Z. Denkowski, S. Migórski, N.S. Papageorgiou, An Introduction to Nonlinear Analysis: Theory, Library of Congress, Kluwer Academic, New York, 2003.

[62] B.V. Dinh, L.D. Muu, On penalty and gap function methods for bilevel equilibrium problems, J. Appl. Math. 2011 (2011) 646452.

[63] B.V. Dinh, L.D. Muu, A projection algorithm for solving pseudomonotone equilibrium problems and it's application to a class of bilevel equilibria, Optimization 64 (2015) 559–575.

[64] A.V. Dmitruk, A.A. Milyutin, N.P. Osmolovskii, Ljusternik's theorem and the theory of the extremum, Uspekhi Mat. Nauk 35 (6) (1980) 11–46.

[65] A.L. Dontchev, W.W. Hager, Implicit functions, Lipschitz maps and stability in optimization, Math. Oper. Res. 19 (1994) 753–768.

[66] A.L. Dontchev, W.W. Hager, An inverse mapping theorem for set-valued maps, Proc. Amer. Math. Soc. 121 (2) (1994) 481–489.

[67] A.L. Dontchev, R.T. Rockafellar, Implicit Functions and Solution Mappings, second edition, Springer, 2014.

[68] A.L. Donthchev, T. Zolezzi, Well-Posed Optimization Problems, Lecture Notes in Math., vol. 1543, Springer-Verlag, Berlin, 1993.

[69] M. Durea, R. Strugariu, Openness stability and implicit multifunction theorems: applications to variational systems, Nonlinear Anal. 75 (2012) 1246–1259.

[70] I. Ekeland, On the variational principle, J. Math. Anal. Appl. 47 (1974) 324–353.

[71] I. Ekeland, Nonconvex minimization problems, Bull. Amer. Math. Soc. 1 (1979) 443–474.

[72] K. Fan, Minimax theorems, Proc. Natl. Acad. Sci. USA 39 (1953) 42–47.

[73] K. Fan, A generalization of Tychonoff's fixed point theorem, Math. Ann. 142 (1961) 305–310.

[74] K. Fan, A minimax inequality and its application, in: O. Shisha (Ed.), Inequalities, vol. 3, Academic, New York, 1972, pp. 103–113.

[75] C. Finet, Variational principles in partially ordered Banach spaces, J. Nonlinear Convex Anal. 2 (2001) 167–174.

[76] C. Finet, L. Quarta, C. Troestler, Vector-valued variational principles, Nonlinear Anal. 52 (2003) 197–218.

[77] J.B.G. Frenk, G. Kassay, Introduction to convex and quasiconvex analysis, in: N. Hadjisavvas, S. Komlósi, S. Schaible (Eds.), Handbook of Generalized Convexity and Monotonicity, Springer, Berlin, Heidelberg, New York, 2005, pp. 3–87.

[78] J.B.G. Frenk, G. Kassay, On noncooperative games and minimax theory, in: T.S.H. Driessen, J.B. Timmer, A.B. Khmelnitskaya (Eds.), Proceedings of the 4th Twente Workshop on Cooperative Game Theory Joint with 3rd Dutch-Russian Symposium, Enschede, 2005, pp. 61–69.

[79] J.B.G. Frenk, G. Kassay, J. Kolumbán, On equivalent results in minimax theory, European J. Oper. Res. 157 (2004) 46–58.

[80] J.-Y. Fu, Vector equilibrium problems. Existence theorems and convexity of solution set, J. Global Optim. 31 (2005) 109–119.

[81] P.G. Georgiev, Parametric Borwein-Preiss variational principle and applications, Proc. Amer. Math. Soc. 133 (2005) 3211–3226.

[82] P.G. Georgiev, T. Tanaka, Fan's inequality for set-valued maps, Nonlinear Anal. 47 (2001) 607–618.

[83] F. Giannessi, Vector Variational Inequalities and Vector Equilibria: Mathematical Theories, Kluwer Academic Publishers, Dordrecht, The Netherlands, 2000.

[84] X.H. Gong, Efficiency and Henig efficiency for vector equilibrium problems, J. Optim. Theory Appl. 108 (2001) 139–154.

[85] L.M. Graves, Some mapping theorems, Duke Math. J. 17 (1950) 111–114.

[86] O. Güler, Foundations of Optimization, Springer, 2010.

[87] N. Hadjisavvas, H. Khatibzadeh, Maximal monotonicity of bifunctions, Optimization 59 (2010) 147–160.

[88] J.-B. Hiriart-Urruty, A short proof of the variational principle for approximate solutions of a minimization problem, Amer. Math. Monthly 90 (1983) 206–207.

[89] S. Hu, N.S. Papageorgiou, Handbook of Multivalued Analysis—Volume I: Theory, Kluwer Academic Publishers, 1997.

[90] A.D. Ioffe, Metric regularity and subdifferential calculus, Russian Math. Surveys 55 (2000) 501–558.

[91] A.D. Ioffe, Metric regularity, fixed points and some associated problems of variational analysis, J. Fixed Point Theory Appl. 15 (2014) 67–99.

[92] A.N. Iusem, G. Kassay, W. Sosa, An existence result for equilibrium problems with some surjectivity consequences, J. Convex Anal. 16 (2009) 807–826.

[93] A.N. Iusem, G. Kassay, W. Sosa, On certain conditions for the existence of solutions of equilibrium problems, Math. Program. 116 (2009) 259–273.

[94] A.N. Iusem, M. Nasri, Inexact proximal point methods for equilibrium problems in Banach spaces, Numer. Funct. Anal. Optim. 28 (2007) 1279–1308.

[95] A.N. Iusem, W. Sosa, New existence results for equilibrium problems, Nonlinear Anal. 52 (2003) 621–635.

[96] A.N. Iusem, W. Sosa, On the proximal point method for equilibrium problems in Hilbert spaces, Optimization 59 (2010) 1259–1274.

[97] P. Kas, G. Kassay, Z. Boratas-Sensoy, On generalized equilibrium points, J. Math. Anal. Appl. 296 (2004) 619–633.

[98] G. Kassay, The equilibrium problem and its applications to optimization, minimax problems and Nash equilibria, in: Q.H. Ansari (Ed.), Topics in Nonlinear Analysis and Optimization, Word Education, Delhi, 2012, pp. 203–226.

[99] G. Kassay, T.N. Hai, N.T. Vinh, Coupling Popov's algorithm with subgradient extragradient method for solving equilibrium problems, J. Nonlinear Convex Anal. 19 (2018) 959–986.

[100] G. Kassay, I. Kolumbán, On the Knaster-Kuratowski-Mazurkiewicz and Ky Fan's Theorems, Babes-Bolyai University Cluj, Seminar on Mathematical Analysis, Preprint Nr. 7, 1990, pp. 87–100.

[101] G. Kassay, J. Kolumbán, On a generalized sup-inf problem, J. Optim. Theory Appl. 91 (1996) 651–670.

[102] G. Kassay, M. Miholca, Existence results for variational inequalities with surjectivity consequences related to generalized monotone operators, J. Optim. Theory Appl. 159 (2013) 721–740.

[103] G. Kassay, M. Miholca, On vector equilibrium problems given by sum of two functions, J. Global Optim. 63 (2015) 195–211.

[104] G. Kassay, M. Miholca, N.T. Vinh, Vector quasi-equilibrium problems for the sum of two multivalued mappings, J. Optim. Theory Appl. 169 (2016) 424–442.

[105] K.R. Kazmi, On vector equilibrium problem, Proc. Indian Acad. Sci. Math. Sci. 110 (2000) 213–223.

[106] H. Khatibzadeh, V. Mohebbi, Proximal point algorithm for infinite pseudo-monotone bifunctions, Optimization 65 (2016) 1629–1639.

[107] D. Kinderlehrer, G. Stampacchia, An Introduction to Variational Inequalities, Academic Press, New York, 1980.

[108] M.D. Kirszbraun, Über die Zusammenziehenden und Lipschitzschen Transformationen, Fund. Math. 22 (1934) 7–10.

[109] B. Knaster, C. Kuratowski, S. Mazurkiewicz, Ein beweis des fixpunktsatzes für n-dimensionale simplexe, Fund. Math. 14 (1929) 132–138.

[110] H. Kneser, Sur un theoreme fondamental de la theorie des jeux, C. R. Acad. Sci. Paris 234 (1952) 2418–2420.

[111] I.V. Konnov, Combined Relaxation Methods for Variational Inequalities, Springer, Berlin, 2000.

[112] I.V. Konnov, S. Schaible, Duality for equilibrium problems under generalized monotonicity, J. Optim. Theory Appl. 104 (2000) 395–408.

[113] A. Kristály, C. Varga, Set-valued versions of Ky Fan's inequality with application to variational inclusion theory, J. Math. Anal. Appl. 282 (2003) 8–20.

[114] S. Lásló, A. Viorel, Generalized monotone operators on dense sets, Numer. Funct. Anal. Optim. 36 (7) (2015) 901–929.

[115] S. László, A. Viorel, Densely defined equilibrium problems, J. Optim. Theory Appl. 166 (2015) 52–75.

[116] G. Lebourg, Valeur moyenne pour gradient généralisé, C. R. Acad. Sci. Paris Sér. A-B 281 (19) (1975), Ai, A795–A797.

[117] J.-L. Lions, G. Stampacchia, Variational inequalities, Comm. Pure Appl. Math. 20 (1967) 493–519.

[118] D.T. Luc, Theory of Vector Optimization, Springer-Verlag, Berlin, 1989.

[119] R. Lucchetti, Convexity and Well-Posed Problems, CMS Books Math., Springer, New York, 2006.

[120] S.I. Lyashko, V.V. Semenov, A new two-step proximal algorithm of solving the problem of equilibrium programming, in: B. Goldengorin (Ed.), Optimization and Applications in Control and Data Sciences, in: Springer Optim. Appl., vol. 115, 2016, pp. 315–326.

[121] L.A. Lyusternik, On the conditional extrema of functionals, Sb. Math. 41 (1934) 390–401.

[122] Y.V. Malitsky, V.V. Semenov, An extragradient algorithm for monotone variational inequalities, Cybernet. Systems Anal. 50 (2014) 271–277.

[123] G. Mastroeni, On auxiliary principle for equilibrium problems, in: P. Daniele, F. Giannessi, A. Maugeri (Eds.), Equilibrium Problems and Variational Models, Kluwer Academic, Norwell, 2003, pp. 289–298.

[124] A. Maugeri, Equilibrium problems and variational inequalities, in: Equilibrium Problems: Nonsmooth Optimization and Variational Inequality Methods, in: Nonconvex Optim. Appl., vol. 58, Kluwer Acad. Publ., Dordrecht, 2001, pp. 187–205.

[125] A. Maugeri, F. Raciti, On existence theorems for monotone and nonmonotone variational inequalities, J. Convex Anal. 16 (2009) 899–911.

[126] E. Michael, Continuous selections I, Ann. of Math. 63 (1956) 361–382.

[127] E. Miglierina, E. Molho, Well-posedness and convexity in vector optimization, Math. Methods Oper. Res. 58 (2003) 375–385.

[128] E. Miglierina, E. Molho, M. Rocca, Well-posedness and scalarization in vector optimization, J. Optim. Theory Appl. 126 (2005) 391–409.

[129] B.S. Mordukhovich, T.T.A. Nghia, Local monotonicity and full stability for parametric variational systems, SIAM J. Optim. 26 (2016) 1032–1059.

[130] U. Mosco, Implicit Variational Problems and Quasi-Variational Inequalities, Lecture Notes in Math., vol. 543, Springer, Berlin, 1976, pp. 83–156.

[131] D. Motreanu, V. Rădulescu, Variational and Non-Variational Methods in Nonlinear Analysis and Boundary Value Problems, Nonconvex Optim. Appl., vol. 67, Kluwer Academic Publishers, Dordrecht, 2003.

[132] D. Motreanu, P.D. Panagiotopoulos, Minimax Theorems and Qualitative Properties of the Solutions of Hemivariational Inequalities, Nonconvex Optim. Appl., vol. 29, Kluwer Academic Publishers, Dordrecht, 1999.

[133] L.D. Muu, W. Oettli, Convergence of an adaptive penalty scheme for finding constrained equilibria, Nonlinear Anal. 18 (1992) 1159–1166.

[134] Z. Naniewicz, P.D. Panagiotopoulos, Mathematical Theory of Hemivariational Inequalities and Applications, Marcel Dekker, New York, 1995.

[135] Z. Opial, Weak convergence of the sequence of successive approximations for nonexpansive mappings, Bull. Amer. Math. Soc. 73 (1967) 591–597.

[136] D. Pallaschke, S. Rolewicz, Foundations of Mathematical Optimization: Convex Analysis Without Linearity, Springer Science+Business Media, Dordrecht, 1997.

[137] P.D. Panagiotopoulos, Nonconvex energy functions. Hemivariational inequalities and substationarity principles, Acta Mech. 42 (1983) 160–183.

[138] P.D. Panagiotopoulos, Inequality Problems in Mechanics and Applications: Convex and Nonconvex Energy Functions, Birkhäuser, Boston, 1985.

[139] N.S. Papageorgiou, S. Kyritsi-Yiallourou, Handbook of Applied Analysis, Adv. Mech. Math., vol. 19, Springer, New York, 2009.

[140] W.V. Petryshyn, A characterization of strict convexity of Banach spaces and other uses of duality mappings, J. Funct. Anal. 6 (1970) 282–291.

[141] R. Phelps, Support cones in Banach spaces and their applications, Adv. Math. 13 (1974) 1–19.

[142] R. Phelps, Convex Functions, Monotone Operators, and Differentiability, Lecture Notes in Math., vol. 1364, Springer, 1993.

[143] R. Precup, Methods in Nonlinear Integral Equations, Kluwer Academic Publishers, Dordrecht, 2002.

[144] R. Precup, The role of matrices that are convergent to zero in the study of semilinear operator systems, Math. Comput. Modelling 49 (3–4) (2009) 703–708.

[145] R. Precup, On a bounded critical point theorem of Schechter, Stud. Univ. Babeş-Bolyai Math. 58 (1) (2013) 87–95.

[146] R. Precup, Nash-type equilibria and periodic solutions to nonvariational systems, Adv. Nonlinear Anal. 3 (4) (2014) 197–207.

[147] R. Precup, Nash-type equilibria for systems of Szulkin functionals, Set-Valued Var. Anal. 24 (3) (2016) 471–482.

[148] R. Precup, A critical point theorem in bounded convex sets and localization of Nash-type equilibria of nonvariational systems, J. Math. Anal. Appl. 463 (1) (2018) 412–431.

[149] T.D. Quoc, P.N. Anh, L.D. Muu, Dual extragradient algorithms to equilibrium problems, J. Global Optim. 52 (2012) 139–159.

[150] T.D. Quoc, L.D. Muu, V.H. Nguyen, Extragradient algorithms extended to equilibrium problems, Optimization 57 (2008) 749–776.

[151] S. Reich, S. Sabach, Two strong convergence theorems for Bregman strongly nonexpansive operators in reflexive Banach spaces, Nonlinear Anal. 73 (2010) 122–135.

[152] R.T. Rockafellar, Convex Analysis, Princeton University Press, Princeton, 1970.

[153] R.T. Rockafellar, On the maximal monotonicity of subdifferential mappings, Pacific J. Math. 33 (1970) 209–216.

[154] R.T. Rockafellar, Monotone operators and the proximal point algorithm, SIAM J. Control Optim. 14 (1976) 877–898.

[155] R.T. Rockafellar, R.J.-B. Wets, Variational Analysis, Springer, 1997.

[156] L. Ronglu, Z. Shuhui, C. Swartzc, An open mapping theorem without continuity and linearity, Topology Appl. 175 (2010) 2086–2093.

[157] W. Rudin, Functional Analysis, McGraw-Hill, 1973.

[158] J. Schauder, Der fixpunktsatz in funktionalräumen, Studia Math. 2 (1930) 171–180.

[159] M. Schechter, A bounded mountain pass lemma without the (PS) condition and applications, Trans. Amer. Math. Soc. 331 (2) (1992) 681–703.

[160] M. Schechter, Linking Methods in Critical Point Theory, Birkhäuser Boston, Inc., Boston, MA, 1999.

[161] R. Sethi, J. Weibull, What is… Nash equilibrium? Notices Amer. Math. Soc. 63 (5) (2016) 526–528.

[162] M.V. Solodov, P. Tseng, Modified projection-type methods for monotone variational inequalities, SIAM J. Control Optim. 34 (1996) 1814–1830.

[163] E. Sperner, Ein satz über untermengen einer endlichen menge, Math. Z. 27 (1928) 544–548.

[164] F. Sullivan, A characterization of complete metric spaces, Proc. Amer. Math. Soc. 83 (1981) 345–346.

[165] A. Szulkin, Minimax principles for lower semicontinuous functions and applications to nonlinear boundary value problems, Ann. Inst. H. Poincaré Anal. Non Linéaire 3 (2) (1986) 77–109.

[166] T. Tanaka, Generalized semicontinuity and existence theorems for cone saddle points, Appl. Math. Optim. 36 (1997) 313–322.

[167] A.N. Tykhonov, On the stability of functional optimization problems, USSR Comput. Math. Math. Phys. 6 (4) (1966) 28–33.

[168] J. von Neumann, Zur theorie der gessellschaftsspiele, Math. Ann. 100 (1928) 295–320.

[169] P.T. Vuong, J.J. Strodiot, V.H. Nguyen, On extragradient-viscosity methods for solving equilibrium and fixed point problems in a Hilbert space, Optimization 64 (2015) 429–451.

[170] A. Wald, Generalization of a theorem by von Neumann concerning zero-sum two-person games, Ann. of Math. 46 (2) (1945) 281–286.

[171] A. Wald, Statistical Decision Functions, 2nd edition, Chelsea, New York, 1971.

[172] H. Yang, J. Yu, Unified approaches to well-posedness with some applications, J. Global Optim. 31 (2005) 371–381.

[173] N.C. Yannelis, N.D. Prabhakar, Existence of maximal elements and equilibria in linear topological spaces, J. Math. Econom. 12 (1983) 233–245.

[174] E. Zeidler, Nonlinear Functional Analysis and Its Applications, vol. 4, Springer, New York, 1986.

[175] E. Zeidler, Applied Functional Analysis: Applications to Mathematical Physics, Appl. Math. Sci., vol. 109, Springer, New York, 1995.

[176] J.X. Zhou, G. Chen, Diagonal convexity conditions for problems in convex analysis and quasi-variational inequalities, J. Math. Anal. Appl. 132 (1988) 213–225.

Index

Printed in the United States
By Bookmasters